Publications of the John Gower Society

XII

HISTORIANS ON JOHN GOWER

Publications of the John Gower Society

ISSN 0954-2817

Series Editors
R. F. Yeager (*University of West Florida, emeritus*)
Alastair J. Minnis (*Yale University, emeritus*)

Editorial Board
David R. Carlson (*University of Ottawa*)
Helen Cooper (*University of Cambridge*)
Siân Echard (*University of British Columbia*)
Andy Galloway (*Cornell University*)
Brian W. Gastle (*Western Carolina University*)
Linne Mooney (*University of York*)
Peter Nicholson (*University of Hawaii*)
Derek Pearsall (*Harvard University*)
Russell A. Peck (*University of Rochester*)
Ana Sáez-Hidalgo (*University of Valladolid*)
Nicholas Watson (*Harvard University*)

This series aims to provide a forum for critical studies of the poetry of John Gower and its influence on English and continental literatures during the late Middle Ages and into the present day. Although its main focus is on the single poet, comparative studies which throw new light on Gower, his work and his historical and cultural context are also welcomed.

Proposals or queries should be sent in the first instance to the series editors or to the publisher, at the addresses given below; all submissions will receive prompt and informed consideration.

R. F. Yeager, Professor of English, *emeritus*
University of West Florida
byeager@uwf.edu

Alastair J. Minnis, Douglas Tracy Smith Professor, *emeritus*
Yale University
alastair.minnis@yale.edu

Boydell & Brewer Limited, PO Box 9, Woodbridge, Suffolk, IP12 3DF, UK

Previously published volumes in this series are listed at the end of this volume.

Historians
on John Gower

Edited by
Stephen H. Rigby

with
Siân Echard

D. S. Brewer

© Contributors 2019

All Rights Reserved. Except as permitted under current legislation
no part of this work may be photocopied, stored in a retrieval system,
published, performed in public, adapted, broadcast,
transmitted, recorded or reproduced in any form or by any means,
without the prior permission of the copyright owner

First published 2019
D. S. Brewer, Cambridge
Paperback edition 2023

ISBN 978-1-84384-537-9 hardback
ISBN 978-1-84384-701-4 paperback

D. S. Brewer is an imprint of Boydell & Brewer Ltd
PO Box 9, Woodbridge, Suffolk IP12 3DF, UK
and of Boydell & Brewer Inc.
668 Mt Hope Avenue, Rochester, NY 14620-2731, USA
website: www.boydellandbrewer.co.uk

A CIP catalogue record for this book is available
from the British Library

The publisher has no responsibility for the continued existence or accuracy
of URLs for external or third-party internet websites referred to in this book,
and does not guarantee that any content on such websites is, or will remain,
accurate or appropriate

For Robert F. Yeager

CONTENTS

List of Illustrations	ix
Notes on Editors and Contributors	xii
Acknowledgements	xv
List of Abbreviations	xvi
A Note on the References	xviii
Preface: Gower in Context	xx

PART I: GOWER'S LIFE AND WORKS   1

    Chronology of Gower's Life Records   3
    Martha Carlin

1. Gower's Life   22
   Martha Carlin

2. Gower's Works   121
   Stephen H. Rigby

PART II: GOWER AND LAY SOCIETY   139

3. Nobility and Chivalry   141
   David Green

4. The Peasants and the Great Revolt   167
   Mark Bailey

5. Towns and Trade   191
   James Davis

6. Men of Law   213
   Anthony Musson

CONTENTS

PART III: GOWER AND THE CHURCH — 241

7 The Papacy, Secular Clergy and Lollardy — 243
   David Lepine

8 Monastic Life — 271
   Martin Heale

9 The Friars — 291
   Jens Röhrkasten

PART IV: GOWER AND GENDER — 321

10 Women and Power — 323
    Katherine J. Lewis

11 Masculinity — 351
    Christopher Fletcher

PART V: GOWER AND POLITICS — 379

12 Political Theory — 381
    Stephen H. Rigby

13 Gower, Richard II and Henry IV — 425
    Michael Bennett

PART VI: GOWER AND COSMOGRAPHY — 489

14 Natural Sciences — 491
    Seb Falk

Select Bibliography — 527

Index — 537

LIST OF ILLUSTRATIONS

Gower's Life

Fig. 1.1: John Gower's tomb, chaplet, and effigy, from Richard Gough, *Sepulchral Monuments in Great Britain*, vol. II, part 2 (1796). By courtesy of The Lewis Walpole Library, Yale University.   22

Fig. 1.2: John Gower's seal, from BL, Harley Charter 50 I. 14 (1373); brass of Sir Robert Gower (d. c. 1349), formerly in Brabourne church, Kent. From W. Warwick, 'On Gower, the Kentish Poet, His Character and Works', *Archaeologia Cantiana*, 6 (1866).   26

Fig. 1.3: Plan of the eastern part of St Saviour's church, Southwark (formerly the priory church of St Mary Overy; now Southwark Cathedral), from M. Concanen, Jr, and A. Morgan, *History and Antiquities of the Parish of St Saviour's, Southwark* (1795). By courtesy of the Yale Center for British Art, Yale University.   93

Fig. 1.4: Gower's tomb: detail of effigy.   101

Fig. 1.5: Sketch of the collar of SS from Gower's tomb effigy, from William Thompson, *The History and Antiquities of the Collegiate Church of St Saviour (St Marie Overie), Southwark* (1904). By courtesy of the Yale Center for British Art, Yale University.   101

Fig. 1.6: Engraved portrait of John Gower, by George Vertue (1727). By courtesy of The Lewis Walpole Library, Yale University.   102

Fig. 1.7: Gower's tomb, by George Vertue (1727): detail from Fig. 1.6. By courtesy of The Lewis Walpole Library, Yale University.   102

Fig. 1.8: Engraved portrait of John Gower by John Simco (1792). By courtesy of The Lewis Walpole Library, Yale University.   103

LIST OF ILLUSTRATIONS

Fig. 1.9: Chaplet of Gower's tomb effigy, by Richard Gough (1796): detail of Fig. 1.1. By courtesy of The Lewis Walpole Library, Yale University.   103

Fig. 1.10: Gower's tomb: armorial panel.   104

Fig. 1.11: John Gower's signet, from his acquittance to Sir John Cobham (1382). From W. Warwick, 'On Gower, the Kentish Poet, His Character and Works', *Archaeologia Cantiana*, 6 (1866).   105

Map 1.1: Places in Kent and metropolitan London where John Gower held property, resided for a time, or visited. (Map by courtesy of Nick Higham and Cath D'Alton.)   28

Map 1.2: Places outside Kent and metropolitan London where John Gower held property, resided for a time, or visited. (Map by courtesy of Nick Higham and Cath D'Alton.)   31

Map 1.3: Southwark: the priory of St Mary Overy and surrounding area near London Bridge, *c*. 1520, from *A Map of Tudor London*, British Historic Towns Atlas, in association with The London Topographical Society (2018).   58

Gower, Richard II and Henry IV

Fig 13.1: Heraldry depicted on the first folio of the 'Stafford MS' of Gower's *Confessio Amantis* (EL 26 A 17, Huntington Library, San Marino, CA, USA).   458

> (a), (d) and (e) The three shields on EL 26 A 17, fol. 1r. Huntington Library, San Marino, CA, USA.
>
> (b) Seal of Henry of Lancaster, earl of Derby, 1394 (TNA, PRO, DL 27/310).
>
> (c) Visualisation of arms of Henry of Lancaster, earl of Derby, based on description in *A Roll of Arms of the Reign of Richard II*, ed. Thomas Willement (London, 1834), pp. 4–5.
>
> (f) Depiction of livery of Thomas of Woodstock, duke of Gloucester, as inherited by his grandson, Humphrey Stafford, duke of Buckingham (d. 1460) (*Records of Buckinghamshire, or Papers and Notes on the History, Antiquities, and Architecture of the County*, 3 (1870), p. 261). Photoshopped by Gillian Ward.

Natural Sciences

Fig 14.1: 'Alchandreus', *Benedictum*, 18:15–18. The Bodleian Libraries, The University of Oxford, MS Digby 147, f. 123r.   505

Fig 14.2: Pisces, in John Gower, *Confessio Amantis*. The Morgan Library & Museum. MS M.126, f. 157v. Purchased by J. Pierpont Morgan (1837–1913), 1903. Photograph: The Morgan Library & Museum, New York.   511

Fig 14.3: Pisces, in Michael Scot, *Liber introductorius*. The Bodleian Libraries, The University of Oxford, MS Bodl. 266, f. 109v.   511

The editors, contributors and publishers are grateful to all the institutions and persons listed for permission to reproduce the materials in which they hold copyright. Every effort has been made to trace the copyright holders; apologies are offered for any omission, and the publishers will be pleased to add any necessary acknowledgement in subsequent editions.

NOTES ON EDITORS AND CONTRIBUTORS

Mark Bailey Professor of Late Medieval History, University of East Anglia. His publications include *Medieval Suffolk: An Economic and Social History to 1500* (2007); *The Decline of Serfdom in Late Medieval England* (2014); and 'The Ploughman', in S. H. Rigby and A. J. Minnis, eds, *Historians on Chaucer: The 'General Prologue' to the Canterbury Tales* (2014).

Michael Bennett Emeritus Professor of History at the University of Tasmania. His publications include *Richard II and the Revolution of 1399* (1999); 'Henry of Bolingbroke and the Revolution of 1399' in G. Dodd and D. Biggs, eds, *Henry IV: The Establishment of the Regime 1399–1406* (2003); 'William called Long Will', *The Yearbook of Langland Studies* (2012); and 'John Gower, Squire of Kent, the Peasants' Revolt, and the *Visio Anglie*', *Chaucer Review*, 51 (2018).

Martha Carlin Professor of History at the University of Wisconsin-Milwaukee. Her publications include 'Gower's Southwark', in A. Sáez-Hidalgo, B. Gastle, and R. F. Yeager, eds, *The Routledge Research Companion to John Gower* (2017); 'The Host', in S. H. Rigby and A. J. Minnis, eds, *Historians on Chaucer: The 'General Prologue' to the Canterbury Tales* (2014); *Lost Letters of Medieval Life: English Society, 1200–1250*, with David Crouch (2013); and *Medieval Southwark* (1996).

James Davis Senior Lecturer in Medieval History at Queen's University Belfast. His publications include *Medieval Market Morality: Life, Law and Ethics in the English Marketplace 1200–1500* (2012); and 'Baking for the Common Good: A Reassessment of the Assize of Bread in Medieval England', *Economic History Review*, 57 (2004).

Siân Echard Professor of English at the University of British Columbia. She is co-editor of *The Encyclopedia of Medieval Literature in Britain* (2017). Her publications include *A Companion to Gower* (2004); *Printing the Middle Ages* (2008); and numerous articles and chapters on Gower's Latin, manuscripts, and post-medieval transmission history.

Seb Falk Research Fellow in History of Science, Girton College, University of Cambridge. His publications include 'The Medieval Universe', in I. Johnson, ed., *Geoffrey Chaucer in Context* (2019) and '"I have found written in this book": Learning Astronomy in Medieval Monasteries', *Studies in Church History*, 55 (2019). His study of medieval science, *The Light Ages*, will be published in 2020.

NOTES ON EDITORS AND CONTRIBUTORS

Christopher Fletcher Chargé de recherche (Assistant Research Professor) at the Centre National de la Recherche Scientifique (CNRS) and the University of Lille, France. His publications include *Richard II: Manhood, Youth and Politics, 1377–99* (2008). He also co-edited *Government and Political Life in England and France, c.1300–1500* (2015) and *The Palgrave Handbook of Masculinity and Political Culture in Europe* (2018).

David Green Senior Lecturer in British Studies at Harlaxton College. His publications include *The Hundred Years War: A People's History* (2014); and *Edward the Black Prince: Power in Medieval Europe* (2007).

Martin Heale Reader in Medieval History at the University of Liverpool. His publications include *Monasticism in Late Medieval England, c.1300–1535* (2009); *The Abbots and Priors of Late Medieval and Reformation England* (2016); and 'The Monk' in S. H. Rigby and A. J. Minnis, eds, *Historians on Chaucer: The 'General Prologue' to the Canterbury Tales* (2014).

David Lepine Honorary Research Fellow at the University of Exeter. His publications include 'Cathedrals and Charity', *English Historical Review*, 126 (2011); 'The Parson' in S. H. Rigby and A. J. Minnis, eds, *Historians on Chaucer: The 'General Prologue' to the Canterbury Tales* (2014); and 'Let Them Praise Him in Church: Orthodox Reform at Salisbury Cathedral in the First Half of the Fifteenth Century' in V. Gillespie and K. Ghosh, eds, *After Arundel* (2012).

Katherine J. Lewis Senior Lecturer in History at the University of Huddersfield. Her publications include *The Cult of St Katherine of Alexandria in Late Medieval England* (2000); *Kingship and Masculinity in Late Medieval England* (2013) and 'The Prioress and the Second Nun' in S. H. Rigby and A. J. Minnis, eds, *Historians on Chaucer: The 'General Prologue' to the Canterbury Tales* (2014). She has also co-edited *St Katherine of Alexandria: Texts and Contexts in Western Medieval Europe* (2003); and *A Companion to the Book of Margery Kempe* (2004).

Anthony Musson Head of Research at Historic Royal Palaces. His publications include *Medieval Law in Context* (2001); *Crime, Law and Society in the Later Middle Ages* (2009); and 'The Sergeant of Law', in S. H. Rigby and A. J. Minnis, eds, *Historians on Chaucer: The 'General Prologue' to the Canterbury Tales* (2014).

Stephen Rigby Emeritus Professor of Medieval Social and Economic History, University of Manchester. His publications include *English Society in the Later Middle Ages: Class, Status and Gender* (1995); *Chaucer in Context: Society, Allegory and Gender* (1996); and *Wisdom and Chivalry: Chaucer's Knight's Tale and Medieval Political Theory* (2009). He was also the chief editor of *Historians on Chaucer: The General Prologue to the Canterbury Tales* (2014).

Jens Röhrkasten Lecturer in Medieval History, University of Birmingham. His publications include: *The Mendicant Houses of Medieval London 1221–1539* (2004); 'Zu Armutsideal und Wirtschatspraxis im Franziskanerorden bis zum Pontifikat Johannes' XXII', *Zeitschrift für Kirchengeschichte*, 124 (2013); and 'Franciscan Obedience and Disobedience in Practice', in M. Breitenstein *et al.*, eds, *Rules and Observance. Devising Forms of Communal Life* (2014).

ACKNOWLEDGEMENTS

The editors of this volume are grateful to the British Academy's Research Awards Committee for their award of a British Academy/Leverhulme Small Research Grant which funded a workshop held for the contributors to this volume at the Institute of Historical Research in January 2017 and to Caroline Barron who generously assisted in the organization of the workshop. The cover image of Gower's tomb and coat of arms comes from Glasgow University Library, MS Hunter 59, folio 129r and is used by permission of University of Glasgow Library, Special Collections. Martha Carlin owes particular thanks to Nick Higham and Cath D'Alton, who prepared Maps 1.1 and 1.2; to the British Historic Towns Atlas for permission to reproduce a detail from *A Map of Tudor London* (2018) in Map 1.3; to the Institute of Historical Research, University of London, for permission to photograph and publish the images in Figs 1.2 and 1.11; to the Yale Center for British Art and its staff for providing the images in Figs 1.3 and 1.5; and to the Lewis Walpole Library (Yale University) and its staff for providing the images in Figs 1.1, 1.6, 1.7, 1.8, and 1.9. Michael Bennett owes thanks to the Huntington Library, San Marino, California, USA for permission to reproduce images from MS. EL 26 A 17, fol. 1r, and The National Archives, Kew, UK, for permission to reproduce its image of the seal from TNA, PRO, DL 27/310. Seb Falk is grateful to the Bodleian Library, University of Oxford, for permission to reproduce images from Bodleian Library MS Digby 147 and Bodleian Library MS Bodley 266, fol. 109v. and to the Morgan Library & Museum for permission to reproduce an image from MS M.126, fol. 157v. Finally, this book is dedicated by the editors to R. F. Yeager in recognition not only of his work in promoting the study of Gower's poetry but, in particular, in gratitude for his generosity in providing detailed comments on draft versions of the chapters included here.

LIST OF ABBREVIATIONS

BL British Library, London
CA *Confessio Amantis*
CCR *Calendar of Close Rolls*
CFR *Calendar of Fine Rolls*
CIPM *Calendar of Inquisitions Post Mortem*
CLB *Calendar of Letter-Books Preserved among the Archives of the Corporation of the City of London at the Guildhall*, ed. Reginald R. Sharpe (eleven volumes; London: Corporation of the City of London, 1899–1912).
CPR *Calendar of Patent Rolls*
CT *Cronica Tripertita*
e.s. extra series
EEBO Early English Books Online
EETS Early English Text Society
EHR *English Historical Review*
Gower, *Complete Works*, I: John Gower, *The Complete Works Volume I: The French Works*, ed. George C. Macaulay (Oxford: Clarendon Press, 1899).
Gower, *Complete Works*, II and III: John Gower, *The Complete Works, Volumes II and III: The English Works*, ed. George C. Macaulay (Oxford: Clarendon Press, 1901).
Gower, *Complete Works*, IV: John Gower, *The Complete Works, Volume IV: The Latin Works*, ed. George C. Macaulay (Oxford: Clarendon Press, 1902).
Gower, *The French Balades*: John Gower, *The French Balades*, ed. Robert F. Yeager (Kalamazoo: Medieval Institute Publications, 2011).
Gower, *Major Latin Works*: *The Major Latin Works of John Gower: The Voice of One Crying and the Tripartite Chronicle*, trans. Eric W. Stockton (Seattle: University of Washington Press, 1962).
Gower, *Minor Latin Works*: John Gower, *The Minor Latin Works with In Praise of Peace*, eds Robert F. Yeager and Michael Livingston (Kalamazoo: Medieval Institute Publications, 2005).
HPHC John S. Roskell, Linda Clark, and Carole Rawcliffe, eds, *The History of Parliament: The House of Commons, 1386-1421* (Stroud, Gloucestershire: Alan Sutton, for the History of Parliament Trust, 1992; four volumes).
LMA London Metropolitan Archives
MED *Middle English Dictionary*

LIST OF ABBREVIATIONS

MO	*Mirour de l'Omme*
n.s.	new series
ODNB	*Oxford Dictionary of National Biography*
o.s.	original series
PMLA	*Publications of the Modern Language Association of America*
PROME	*Parliament Rolls of Medieval England*, eds Chris Given-Wilson, Paul Brand, Seymour Phillips, Mark Ormrod, Geoffrey Martin, Anne Curry and Rosemary Horrox (Woodbridge: Boydell, 2005).
RRC	Ana Sáez-Hidalgo, Brian Gastle, and Robert F. Yeager, eds, *The Routledge Research Companion to John Gower* (London: Routledge, 2017).
SHC	Somerset Heritage Centre, Taunton
SR	*The Statutes of the Realm*, eds Alexander Luders *et al.* (eleven volumes; London: Record Commission, 1810–28).
TNA	The National Archives, London
VC	*Vox Clamantis*

A NOTE ON THE REFERENCES

Gower's Individual Works

Carmen Super Multiplici Viciorum Pestilencia: all references are from Gower, *Complete Works*, IV, pp. 346–54.

Cinkante Balades: all references are from Gower, *The French Balades*, pp. 56–131.

Confessio Amantis: all references are, unless otherwise stated, from Gower, *Complete Works*, II and III.

Cultor in Ecclesia: all references are from Gower, *Minor Latin Works*, pp. 50–1.

De Lucis Scrutino: all references are from Gower, *Minor Latin Works*, pp. 12–17.

Dicunt Scripture: all references are from Gower, *Minor Latin Works*, pp. 52–3.

Ecce Patet Tensus: all references are from Gower, *Minor Latin Works*, pp. 40–1.

Epistola (to Archbishop Arundel): all references to the *Epistola* are from Gower, *Complete Works*, IV, pp. 1–2.

Epistola ad Regem (*Vox Clamantis*, VI.8–18): all references are from Gower, *Complete Works*, IV.

Est Amor: all references are from Gower, *Minor Latin Works*, pp. 32–3.

H[enricus]Aquile Pullus: all references are from Gower, *Minor Latin Works*, pp. 46–7.

In Praise of Peace: all references are from Gower, *Minor Latin Works*, pp. 107–18.

Mirour de l'Omme: all references are from Gower, *Complete Works*, I. All translations, unless otherwise stated, are from John Gower, *Mirour de l'Omme* (*The Mirror of Mankind*, trans. William B. Wilson; revised by Nancy W. Van Baak (East Lansing: Colleagues Press, 1992).

O Deus Immense: all references are from Gower, *Minor Latin Works*, pp. 34–9.

Orate pro Anima. (Armigeri Scutum): all references are from Gower, *Minor Latin Works*, p. 53.

O Recolende: all references are from Gower, *Minor Latin Works*, pp. 44–6.

A NOTE ON THE REFERENCES

Presul Ouile Regis: all references are from Gower, *Minor Latin Works*, pp. 50–1.

Quia Unusquisque: all references are from Gower, *Minor Latin Works*, pp. 38–40.

Quicquid Homo Scribat: all references are from Gower, *Minor Latin Works*, pp. 46–7.

Rex Celi Deus: all references are from Gower, *Minor Latin Works*, pp. 42–4.

Traitié selonc les auctors pour essampler les amantz marietz: all references are from Gower, *The French Balades*, pp. 12–33.

Unanimes Esse Qui Secula: all references are from Gower, *Minor Latin Works*, pp. 50–1.

Vox Clamantis: all references are from Gower, *Complete Works*, IV. All translations, unless otherwise specified, are from Gower, *Major Latin Works*.

Other References

Chaucer's works: All references to Chaucer's works are from *The Riverside Chaucer*, ed. Larry D. Benson (third edition; Oxford: Oxford University Press, 1987).

Biblical references: All biblical references are to *The Holy Bible Translated from the Latin Vulgate (Douay Rheims Version)*. Revised by Bishop Richard Challoner (Rockford: Tan Books, 1971).

PREFACE: GOWER IN CONTEXT

Stephen H. Rigby and Siân Echard

It is a commonplace of modern criticism that a fruitful way of understanding medieval literary texts is to consider the ways in which they engage with the social hierarchies, institutions, conventions, behaviours and ideologies of their day. As Janet Coleman put it, relatively few works of fourteenth-century literature 'were meant merely to entertain but were intended to instruct, exhort and, ultimately, to inspire readers to criticize and eventually to reform social practice, by which was meant the behaviour of church officials and the politically and economically powerful'.[1] As Helen Barr argues, literary language is neither independent of reality nor a passive reflection of it, but is itself a form of social practice or behaviour.[2] Both old and new historicist approaches have been extremely influential amongst scholars of medieval literature, particularly those working on Geoffrey Chaucer.[3] Yet, in many ways, the works of John Gower are even more readily open to historicist readings than are those of Chaucer, against which Gower's verse is so often compared or judged. After all, whilst Chaucer tended to engage with the social, political and religious controversies of the day obliquely or in an allegorical form, Gower explicitly addressed the conflicts which divided his contemporaries. If Chaucer's 'Knight's Tale' provides us with a mirror for princes in the guise of a *roman antique* about Duke Theseus of Athens, then Book VII of Gower's *Confessio Amantis* directly sets out the virtues needed in a king.[4] Whilst Chaucer's 'Miller's Tale' is often read as a peasants' revolt in literary form, with the Miller's bawdy fabliau being pitted against the hierarchical world-view of the 'Knight's Tale' which precedes it,[5]

---

[1] Janet Coleman, *English Literature in History, 1350–1400: Medieval Readers and Writers* (London: Hutchinson, 1981), p. 16.

[2] Helen Barr, *Socioliterary Practice in Late Medieval England* (Oxford: Oxford University Press, 2001), pp. 1–2.

[3] For a survey of historical approaches to Chaucer, see Stephen H. Rigby, 'Reading Chaucer: History, Literature and Ideology', in Stephen H. Rigby and Alastair J. Minnis, eds, *Historians on Chaucer: The General Prologue to the Canterbury Tales* (Oxford: Oxford University Press, 2014), pp. 1–23.

[4] Stephen H. Rigby, *Wisdom and Chivalry: Chaucer's Knight's Tale and Medieval Political Theory* (Leiden: Brill, 2009), p. 274.

[5] For references, see Stephen H. Rigby, *Chaucer in Context: Society, Allegory and Gender* (Manchester: Manchester University Press, 1996), pp. 47–9.

PREFACE

Book I of Gower's *Vox Clamantis* offers us a detailed response to the events of the actual Peasants' Revolt of 1381. Thus, although it would be a mistake to take Gower's works as merely straightforward *reportage*, it remains crucial to acknowledge how Gower addressed the issues of his day. Because Gower's work includes such overt political and social commentary, an understanding of the period in which his work was rooted is particularly important. The aim of this volume is to enable a group of historians to bring their specialist expertise to bear on Gower's poetry and to show what a detailed knowledge of England in the late fourteenth and early fifteenth centuries can add to our understanding of his work. By examining the ideological frameworks which were available to Gower and his contemporaries, by determining the social, religious and political issues which his works tackled, and by ascertaining the assumptions and expectations of his original audience, historians can, it is to be hoped, contribute to the project of helping modern readers to arrive at a greater appreciation of the meanings of his texts.

This is not to say that Gower's works can simply be reduced to the status of vehicles for ideas, values, discourses and ideologies which originated outside them. After all, the meaning of the complex works of imaginative literature which Gower produced is bound up with their poetic and formal qualities and with the specifically literary pleasures which they provide to their readers.[6] Yet, whilst this is undoubtedly the case, we should also be aware that, as Charles Muscatine put it, 'a good deal of the appreciation of beauty in art depends directly on a historical sense, on knowing what the words really mean, what conventions are being invoked and what audience is being addressed'.[7] For instance, when we interpret or judge a work as conforming to or departing from the conventions of a particular literary genre, the horizon of expectation which that genre sets up is itself historically specific.[8] As Paul Miller points out, when the Latin quatrain '*Quam cinxere freta*', which was added to most manuscripts of the *Confessio Amantis*,

---

[6] Derek Pearsall, 'Gower's Narrative Art', in Peter Nicholson, ed., *Gower's Confessio Amantis: A Critical Anthology* (Cambridge: D. S. Brewer, 1991), pp. 62–80, at 63, 67; Arno Esche, 'John Gower's Narrative Art', *Ibid.*, pp. 81–108, at 81–2; James Simpson, *Sciences and the Self in Medieval Poetry: Alan of Lille's Anticlaudianus and John Gower's Confessio Amantis* (Cambridge: Cambridge, 1995), pp. 14–15, 235, 271; Matthew Giancarlo, 'Gower's Governmentality: Revisiting John Gower as a Constitutional Thinker and Regiminal Writer', in Russell A. Peck and Robert F. Yeager, eds, *John Gower: Others and the Self* (Cambridge: D. S. Brewer, 2017), pp. 225–59, at 245; Arthur W. Bahr, 'Reading Codicological Form in John Gower's Trentham Manuscript', *Studies in the Age of Chaucer*, 33 (2011), pp. 219–62, at 261.

[7] Charles Muscatine, *Poetry and Crisis in the Age of Chaucer* (Notre Dame: University of Notre Dame Press, 1972), p. 3; Richard F. Green, *Poets and Princepleasers: Literature and the English Court in the Late Middle Ages* (Toronto: University of Toronto Press, 1980), p. 3; George D. Economou, 'The Character Genius in Alan de Lille, Jean de Meun and John Gower', in Nicholson, *Gower's Confessio Amantis*, pp. 109–16, at 109.

[8] Tony Davenport, *Medieval Narrative: An Introduction* (Oxford: Oxford University Press, 2004), pp. 26–7.

praises Gower as a 'satirist', modern notions of satire have to be abandoned if 'a proper perspective on Gower's achievement' is to be obtained.[9] Similarly, whilst modern readers of Gower have often found the *Confessio Amantis* problematic in its combination of love, ethics, politics and science and of pagan and Christian materials, Alastair Minnis has argued that what 'may appear heterogeneous to the modern reader would have been regarded as quite compatible by the learned medieval reader'.[10]

The exchanges between history and literature documented in these pages are a two-way street for our contributors, as the historical explication which they offer is often matched by their recognition of the rewards which are available for historians from a close engagement with literary texts and with the work of literary scholars. Certainly, in exploring Gower's artistic refraction of contemporary affairs, historians can enrich their own understanding of late medieval England as when James Davis uses Gower's poetry to illuminate the issues and tensions within London political society in the late 1370s and early 1380s. In particular, a number of the contributors to this volume focus on the detail of Gower's language. For instance, in his examination of Gower and the law, Anthony Musson reveals the subtlety and nuance of Gower's use of legal language, something often lost if one reads his work only in modern translation. Similarly, Christopher Fletcher shows that any discussion of masculinity in Gower must remain vigilant to the poet's unusually careful and detailed deployment of language: familiar words can, in Gower's texts, be loaded with very specific social meanings. David Green and Martin Heale both encounter the slipperiness of a crafted voice: Gower's position on the nobility in the *Confessio Amantis* must be disentangled from a multitude of conflicting voices to be found within his text, while the poet's apparently crystal-clear condemnation of monks must take account of the gap between Gower's writings and his own religious practice. The elasticity of many of Gower's views allowed them to be deployed to a variety of different ends, as is demonstrated by Stephen Rigby's discussion of political theory and Jens Röhrkasten's essay on the friars. For Katherine Lewis, too, Gower is no monolith, but rather, an author whose reception by later audiences is as important for an historical understanding of his work as his initial context.

Moreover, whilst relating Gower's work to its contemporary context can enhance our understanding of its meaning, historical context provides no simple court of interpretive appeal since the choice of a specific context in which to make sense of a work is itself the result of a process of interpretation. For instance, Gower's change of the dedicatee of the *Confessio Amantis* from

---

[9] Paul Miller, 'John Gower, Satiric Poet', in Alastair J. Minnis, ed., *Gower's Confessio Amantis: Responses and Reassessments* (Cambridge: D. S. Brewer, 1983), pp. 79–105, at 79; Charles Runacres, 'Art and Ethics in the "Exempla" of "Confessio Amantis"', *Ibid.*, pp. 106–34, at 107, 111–14. For the quatrain, see Gower, *Complete Works*, III, p. 479.

[10] Alastair J. Minnis, 'John Gower, *Sapiens* in Ethics and Politics', in Nicholson, *Gower's Confessio Amantis*, pp. 158–80, at 158, 176.

Richard II in the first version of the work (1390) to Henry Bolingbroke in the revised version of the text will have a very different significance depending on whether we choose to date this change to around 1392–93 or to after 1399, when Bolingbroke had usurped the throne. In turn, even if we could agree that the change of dedication occurred around 1392–93, this change would still have a different meaning for those who see this as a time of harmony and reconciliation within England's political community from those who believe that Richard II was already being perceived as an incompetent ruler at this date (see below pp. 133 and 456–7). Similarly, in relation to intellectual context, whilst an appreciation of the medieval concept of 'natural law' has been seen as crucial for an understanding of Gower's views on love and ethics, we also need to be aware that the poet's sources would have provided him with multiple ambiguous and even contradictory senses of the term.[11] There is thus no singular 'historical context' in which to place Gower's work or which will automatically generate its meaning – which is not to say that all interpretations of the poet's historical context or of the meanings of his work are equally valid.

Whilst the contributors to this volume seek to examine Gower's poetry in the context of his life, of the intellectual culture and of the social, religious and political controversies of his day, they do not see an 'historical' approach in general, or any particular historical approach, as providing a unique master-key which will open up the sense of his work. Nor, as the disagreements between the contributors about the dating or meaning of Gower's poetry reveal, is the purpose of the book to close down debate and discussion. Rather, its aim is simply to offer new information, perspectives and analyses which will help to widen our appreciation of the significance of, and the pleasures provided by, Gower's text. In particular, whilst much modern discussion of Gower's poetry has been produced by specialists in Middle English and so, like early modern responses to his work, has tended to concentrate on the *Confessio Amantis*,[12] the chapters below explore not only the *Confessio* but also the French *Mirour de l'Omme* and the Latin *Vox Clamantis* and *Cronica Tripertita* as well as making use of the poet's shorter works, such as *In Praise of Peace*.

The book is divided into six main parts. It begins by discussing Gower's life and the dating of his works (part I). Gower's life has been a key context for the interpretation of his poetry and yet has often been written on the basis of speculation and supposition. Here Martha Carlin provides a new chronology that lists the archival records of Gower's life and then examines what these

---

[11] Kurt Olsson, 'Natural Law and John Gower's *Confessio Amantis*', in Nicholson, *Gower's Confessio Amantis*, pp. 181–213, at 181; Robert Edwards, *Invention and Authorship in Medieval England* (Columbus: Ohio State University Press, 2017), p. 65.

[12] Robert F. Yeager, 'John Gower's Poetry and the Lawyerly Habit of Mind', in Andreea D. Boboc, ed., *Theorizing Legal Personhood in Late Medieval England* (Leiden: Brill, 2015), pp. 71–93, at 75–6.

sources reveal about Gower's places of residence, his sources of income, his marriage and circle of acquaintances, his testament, and his tomb. The rest of the book then goes on to consider Gower's critique of lay society (part II) and the Church (part III), examine his representations of gender (part IV), discuss his political theory and his commentaries on contemporary political life (part V) and to re-assess his use of medieval scientific learning (part VI). Its fourteen chapters provide original readings of both Gower's life and his views on society, religion and politics. Martha Carlin, for instance, offers a major re-interpretation of Gower's biography, one based partly on newly-discovered sources for the poet's life, whilst Anthony Musson's discussion of Gower and the law also offers new insights into the poet's career. In discussing Gower's views of the secular clergy, monasticism and the friars, David Lepine, Martin Heale and Jens Röhrkasten open up aspects of Gower's work which were central to his social outlook but which have been neglected in modern literary scholarship. Other contributors, including Mark Bailey on attitudes to labour, David Green on the challenges faced by the nobility and Michael Bennett on the reign of Richard II, develop original interpretations of the contemporary historical context which invite us to read Gower's work in new ways, whilst Katherine Lewis's examines context in terms of the reception of Gower's work in her discussion of how his presentation of women might have been received by female owners of the *Confessio Amantis*. Other contributors pursue new methodological approaches, as in Christopher Fletcher's study which adopts the methods of German *Begriffsgeschichte* and the French school of *textométrie* to show how a detailed analysis of lexicon and use of words can illuminate Gower's understanding of masculinity. Some chapters engage with the existing critical literature on Gower to offer new understandings of the poet's work, as in Stephen Rigby's chapter which seeks to show why Gower's political theory has been the source of such contradictory readings. Others offer new sources for Gower's poetry, as in Seb Falk's discussion of Gower's knowledge of astronomy. The book thus seeks to offer fresh insights into Gower's life, into the context needed to understand his work and into modern critical reception of his poetry. Hopefully, this volume not only demonstrates what historians can contribute to our understanding of Gower's work but will also encourage other historians to engage with the debates which literary scholars have initiated about how we should locate medieval literature in its historical context.

PART I

GOWER'S LIFE AND WORKS

CHRONOLOGY OF JOHN GOWER'S LIFE RECORDS

Martha Carlin

Sigla, Abbreviations, and Technical Terms Used

*, **	There was more than one John Gower in the later 1300s, and not all documentary references to 'John Gower' can be identified with certainty. A single asterisk (*) marks uncertain entries in which 'John Gower' is likely to have been the poet; a double asterisk (**) marks uncertain entries in which 'John Gower' is unlikely to have been the poet
' '	Indicates a verbatim quotation or translation (all translations are by Martha Carlin)
&c.	etc.
BL	British Library, London
By p.s.	*Per breve de privato sigillo* (By writ of the privy seal)
Carlin, 'Gower's Life'	Chapter 1 in this volume
CCR	*Calendar of Close Rolls*
CIPM	*Calendar of Inquisitions Post Mortem*
co.	county
CPR	*Calendar of Patent Rolls*
LMA	London Metropolitan Archives
Michaelmas	Feast of St Michael the Archangel (29 September)
NSJB	Feast of the Nativity of St John the Baptist (24 June)
ODNB	*Oxford Dictionary of National Biography* (2004)
Parl Rolls	'Edward III: May 1366', in *Parliament Rolls of Medieval England*, ed. Chris Given-Wilson *et al.* (Woodbridge: Boydell Press, 2005), http://www.british-history.ac.uk/no-series/parliament-rolls-medieval/may-1366
TNA	The National Archives, Kew

Money denominations: One pound (*l.* or £) = 20 shillings (*s.*) = 240 pence (*d.*)

For regnal years, saints' days, and the legal calendar, see *A Handbook of Dates for Students of British History*, ed. Christopher R. Cheney, new edition revised by Michael Jones, Royal Historical Society Guides and Handbooks 4 (Cambridge: Cambridge University Press, 2000).

Chronology

1327 x 1343 Birth of John Gower, most likely in Kent; parents unknown, but seemingly connected with the families of Sir Robert Gower of Brabourne and Sir Roger de Northwode. [See discussion in Martha Carlin, 'Gower's Life'.]

25 Dec. 1364 At Christmas, 38 Edw. III, William, son and heir of Sir William de Septvans, enfeoffed John Gower and his heirs of a moiety of the manor of Aldington (Kent) and certain marshes called 'Lokelyng' and 'Herlyng' in Iwade (Kent), in return for 80 marks (£53 6s. 8d.). [*CIPM 1365–70*, p. 76; *Parl Rolls*.]

25 Dec. 1364 – 29 Sept. 1365 The under-age heir William Septvans 'continually dwelt in the company of Richard de Hurst and the said John Gower, at Canterbury and elsewhere', from Christmas 1364 until Michaelmas 1365, 'and during that whole time he was led and counselled by them to alienate his lands &c.'. [*CIPM 1365–70*, pp. 76–7; *Parl Rolls*.]

15 & 18 Feb. 1365 Inquisition taken at Maidstone (Kent), 18 Feb., 39 Edward III (1365). 'William de Septem Vannis, who held a moiety of the manor of Aldyngton, co. Kent, of the king in chief by knight's service, alienated the same three days ago [*15 Feb.*] to John Gower and his heirs.' [*Calendar of Inquisitions Miscellaneous 1348–77*, p. 221 (no. 596).]

16 Feb. 1365 Writ from Edward III to the escheator of Kent, ordering him to hold an inquisition *ad quod damnum* to learn if it is to the king's or anyone else's damage if John Gower retains a moiety of the manor of Aldington (Kent) with its appurtenances, which he acquired for himself and his heirs, without the king's licence, from William Septvans, who held it of the king in chief 'as it is said' ('*ut dicitur*'); and by what service it is held; and how much it is worth per annum. [TNA, C 143/356/11; *List of Inquisitions ad quod damnum*, part 2, 547.]

6 March 1365 Inquisition taken at Maidstone (Kent) before John de Tye, escheator. The jurors say that it is not to the king's or anyone else's damage that John Gower retain the moiety of the manor of Aldington with its appurtenances, which he acquired, without the king's licence, for himself and his heirs, from William Septvans, who held it of the king in chief. The said manor is held of the king for knight service that they do not know, and for payment of 13s. per annum to the ward of the king's castle of Rochester on the feast of St Andrew. And they say that the said moiety is worth 53s. 4d. per annum, net. Endorsed, 'Let it be, for 53s. etc.' ('*Fiat pro liij s' etc*".). [TNA, C 143/356/11; *List of Inquisitions ad quod damnum*, part 2, p. 547.] The fine of 53s. 4d. was the value of the assize (fixed) rents only; see below under Nov. 1373.

9 March 1365 Moorend (Northamptonshire). 'Pardon, for 53s. paid to the king by John Gower, to him for acquiring in fee from William de Septem Vannis a moiety of the manor of Aldynton by Berghsted [*Bearsted*], co. Kent, held in chief, and entering therein without licence; and restitution of the same to him.' [*CPR 1364–67*, p. 99.]

22 June 1365 William, son and heir of Sir William de Septvans, came before John Pyel, mayor of the staple of Westminster, and acknowledged himself bound to John 'Gouwer' in £60, to be paid at All Saints then next following (1 November 1365). [*CIPM 1365–70*, p. 78.]

23 & 25 June 1365 'Charter of William Sepvauns, son of William Sepvauns, knight, (*militis*), giving to John Gower, his heirs and assigns, a yearly rent of 10*l*. issuing from the manor of Wygebergh [*Wigborough, Essex*] and from all the grantor's lands in Essex, to be taken at Michaelmas and Easter by even portions, with power to distrain for arrears, and the grantor has given the said John 1*d*. in name of seisin; also all the chattels live and dead thereupon, to take and drive whither he will. Dated 23 June 39 Edward III. Memorandum of acknowledgment, 25 June.' [*CCR 1364–68*, p. 185; cf. *Parl Rolls*; *CCR 1369–74*, pp. 9–10.]

[23?] & 25 June 1365 'Writing of William Sepvauns, son and heir of William Sepvauns late deceased, being a quitclaim with warranty to John Gower, his heirs and assigns, of the whole manor of Aldynton with 14*s*. 6*d*. of rent and a rent of one cock, 13 hens and 140 eggs in Maplescompe [*Maplescombe, Kent*], and the homages and all the services of the tenants who ought to render the same. Witnesses: James de Peckham, William Vauls, Richard de Aldynton, Alan de Chelscombe, Richard atte Wode. *Memorandum* of acknowledgment, 25 June.' [*CCR 1364–68*, p. 185.]

17 March 1366 London. Grant by Sir John de Northwode to John Gower, his heirs and assigns, of Northwode's interest in an annual quitrent (fixed rent) of £12, payable by the master of the collegiate church of St Thomas the Martyr of Acon, London, which should revert to Northwode after the death of his stepmother Agnes, widow of Sir Roger de Northwode. (Other sources establish that this quitrent derived from property in the London parish of St Mary Colechurch.) [LMA, HR 94/36 (transcribed in full in Carlin, 'Gower's Life', Appendix 1); Derek J. Keene and Vanessa Harding, 'St. Mary Colechurch 105/19', in *Historical Gazetteer of London Before the Great Fire: Cheapside; Parishes of All Hallows Honey Lane, St Martin Pomary, St Mary Le Bow, St Mary Colechurch and St Pancras Soper Lane* (London, 1987), pp. 518–26, *British History Online*, http://www.british-history.ac.uk/no-series/london-gazetteer-pre-fire/pp518-526.]

21 April 1366 Canterbury (Kent). Proof of age of William, son and heir of Sir William de Septvans. William the son was born on 28 August 1346. The jurors say that William the son has alienated properties. These included

William's enfeoffment on 25 Dec. 1364 of John Gower and his heirs, in return for 80 marks, of the moiety of the manor of Aldyngton (Kent), which is worth £10 per annum; and certain marshes, called 'Lokelyng' and 'Herlyng', in Iwade (Kent), worth 40s. per annum; 'in which moiety is a certain wood, worth one hundred pounds to sell'. John Gower has had possession since then and received the issues. There is no waste. [*CIPM 1365–70*, pp. 75–9; 'L.B.L.' (Lambert B. Larking), '"Probatio Ætatis" of William de Septvans, from the Surrenden Collection', *Archaeologia Cantiana*, 1 (1858), pp. 124–36, at 128; *Parl Rolls*.]

11 May 1366 Westminster (Middlesex). Parliament held 4–11 May, final plenary session (11 May). The case of William, son and heir of Sir William de Septvans, was reviewed, 'the heir himself being present', and 'it appeared to the prelates, magnates and commonalty that he was not of full age. It was therefore resolved that the proof of his age should be of none effect, that his lands should be taken back into the king's hands, that all bonds &c. made by him [*including to John Gower*] should be annulled, and that process should be made by writs of *scire facias* against all persons to whom he had alienated any lands &c. of his inheritance since the proof of his age'. [*CIPM 1365–70*, pp. 77–9; *Parl Rolls*.]

18 July 1366 London. Grant by John Gower to Simon de Benyngton, citizen and draper of London, his heirs and assigns, of the reversion of an annual quitrent of £12, payable by the master and brothers of St Thomas of Acon, London (discussed above under 17 March 1366), which Agnes, widow of Sir Roger de Northwode, holds for life. This quitrent is 'of the inheritance of the said John Gower ('*de hereditate predicti Johannis Gower*'), which the same John Gower has by grant of John de Northwode, knight, son and heir of Roger de Northwode, knight, and which rent after the death of the said Agnes ought to revert to the said John Gower and his heirs'. [LMA, HR 94/107: transcribed in full in Carlin, 'Gower's Life', Appendix 2.]

**16 Oct. 1366 Westminster (Middlesex). 'Commission, pursuant to the ordinance in council, to William Dane and John Wynter, "shipman", to make diligent scrutiny in the town and port of Sandwich, and in the arms of the sea and coasts adjacent, of jewels, gold and silver taken from the realm without licence, and of letters patent, bulls, instruments or other matters taken from, or brought into, the realm to the prejudice of the king or the realm. By testimony of Ralph Spigurnell, the king's admiral. The like to the following:— John Gower, John Abbot of Melcombe [*Dorset*] and John Taillour of Weymouth [*Dorset*]; in the town and port of Melcombe and the arms of the sea and coasts adjacent.' [*CPR 1364-67*, p. 362. This John Gower seems unlikely to have been the poet, since the latter had no other known links with Dorset.]

*1 June 1367 London. 'Writing of John Gravesende citizen and draper of London, giving with warranty to John Gower, his heirs and assigns, 10*l*.

free quit rent to be taken every year at Michaelmas of all the lands of the grantor as well in Kent as in the city of London, with power to distrain therein for arrears and coats. Witnesses: John de Stodeye, John Tornegold, William de Essex citizens of London, John Page, William Galoun of Kent. Dated London, 1 June 41 Edward III. *Memorandum* of acknowledgment, 2 June.' [*CCR 1364–68*, p. 379. John de Gravesende was a witness to William Weston's quitclaim of the manor of Kentwell on 6 March 1376; see below.]

6 Feb. 1368   Westminster (Middlesex). 'Licence for William, son and heir of William de Septvanz, knight, to enfeoff John Gower of a moiety of the manor of Aldyngton, co. Kent, except 6 acres of land therein, which moiety is of his inheritance and is held in chief; notwithstanding that the said William is held to the king by a bond in 3,000*l*. not to alienate, remit or quitclaim any lands or rent of his inheritance to any person or persons in fee or for life. By p.s.' [*CPR 1367–70*, p. 83.]

6 Feb. 1368   Westminster (Middlesex). 'Licence for William, son and heir of William de Septvanz, knight, to enfeoff John Gower of all his marsh in Ywade, 14*s*. 6*d*. of rent and a rent of a cock, 13 hens and 140 eggs in Maplescomp, and a moiety of the manor of Aldyngton, co. Kent, except 6 acres of land therein, all which are of his inheritance, and of which the said moiety and rent are held in chief, notwithstanding that the said William is held to the king by a bond in 3,000*l*. not to alienate, remit or quitclaim any lands or rent of his inheritance to any person or persons, in fee or for life. By p.s.' [*CPR 1367–70*, p. 96.]

10 March 1368   Newington (Kent). Grant by William Septvaunz, son of Sir William Septvaunz, to John Gower, his heirs and assigns, of William's whole marsh in Ywade (Kent). Witnesses: Sir John de Cobeham and Sir John de Northwode, knights, Thomas Brokhull, John Roiston, William Symme, and others. Dated at 'Niewenton', 10 March, 42 Edward III. [BL, Add. Charter 68771.]

28 June 1368   Long Melford (Suffolk). Grant by Thomas Syward, citizen and pewterer of London, and Joan his wife, daughter of Sir Robert Gower, to John Gower, of the manor of Kentwell (Suffolk), with the appurtenances. Dated at 'Melford', Wednesday after NSJB, 42 Edward III. [BL, Harley Charter 56 G. 42.]

4 July 1368   London. Letter of attorney by Thomas Syward, citizen and pewterer of London, and Joan his wife, daughter of Sir Robert Gower, appointing William Cornewaille, John Rouheved, John Thairyoor, and Richard Reed to put John Gower in seisin of the manor of Kentwell (Suffolk). Dated at London, 4 July, 42 Edward III. [BL, Harley Charter 56 G. 41.]

7 July 1368   Writ from the king to the escheator of Suffolk and Essex to hold an inquisition *ad quod damnum* to inquire if it is to the damage of the king or anyone else if John Gower retain the manor of 'Kentewell' (Suffolk), with its appurtenances, which Gower acquired in fee, to himself and his heirs forever, without the king's licence, from Thomas Syward, late citizen and pewterer of London, and Joan his wife, daughter and heir of Sir Robert Gower, who held it of the king in chief, 'as it is said' ('*ut dicitur*'); and by what service the said manor is held, and what it is worth. [TNA, C 143/364/4 (1); *List of Inquisitions ad quod damnum*, part 2, p. 559.]

19 July 1368 Inquisition *ad quod damnum*, held at Melford (Suffolk). The jurors say that it is not to the king's or anyone else's damage if John Gower retain the manor of 'Kentewell' in fee, to himself and his heirs, forever. It is held of the king in chief by service of one knight's fee. It is worth £10 13s. 4d. per annum. [TNA, C 143/364/4 (2); *List of Inquisitions ad quod damnum*, part 2, p. 559.]

22 July 1368 Pardon, dated at Odiham (Hampshire), for 16 marks paid to the king by John Gower, to him of his trespass in acquiring in fee the manor of 'Kentewell', in the counties of Suffolk and Essex, held in chief, from Thomas Syward, late citizen and pewterer of London, and entering therein without licence; and grant that he may hold the same in fee. [*CPR 1367–70*, p. 146.]

23 July 1368 Westminster (Middlesex). 'John Gower to Richard de Ravensere clerk. Recognisance for 20*l*., to be levied, in default of payment, of his land and chattels in Suffolk. *Cancelled on payment*.' [*CCR 1364–68*, p. 482.]

25 x 30 June 1369 Westminster (Middlesex). Final concord, made the morrow of NSJB (25–30 June) 1369, and recorded in the octaves of Michaelmas (6–12 Oct.) 1379, by which John Spenythorn and Joan his wife (deforciants) granted the manor of Kentwell to John Gower, who gave them 200 marks of silver. [BL, Harley Charter 50 I. 13.]

29 Sept. 1373 Otford (Kent). Grant by John Gower to Sir John de Kobham (*sic*), William de Weston, Roger de Asshebournhame, Thomas de Brokhell, and *dom*. Thomas de Preston, rector of the church of Tunstall, of the manor of Kentwell (Suffolk), with all its appurtenances, forever. Dated at 'Otteford', Thursday the feast of Michaelmas, 47 Edward III. [BL, Harley Charter 50 I. 14, with armorial seal of John Gower. A drawing of this seal in W[illiam] Warwick, 'On Gower, the Kentish Poet, His Character and Works', *Archaeologia Cantiana*, 6 (1866), pp. 83–107, at 86, is reproduced in Carlin, 'Gower's Life', Fig. 1.2.]

20 Oct. 1373 Writ from the king to the escheator of Kent to hold an inquisition *ad quod damnum* to inquire if it is to the injury of the king or anyone else if John de Cobham, knight, William Weston, Roger Asshebournham, Thomas Brokhull, and Thomas de Preston, clerk, retain the manor of Aldington, Kent, which they acquired in fee, without licence, from

John Gower, who held it of the king in chief; and by what service it is held, and what it is worth per annum. [TNA, C 143/382/2 (1).]

20 Oct. 1373 Writ from the king to the escheator of Suffolk to hold an inquisition *ad quod damnum* to inquire if it is to the injury of the king or anyone else if John de Cobham, knight, William Weston, Roger Asshebournham, Thomas Brokhull, and Thomas de Preston, clerk, retain the manor of Kentwell, Suffolk, which they acquired in fee, without licence, from John Gower, who held it of the king in chief, as it is said; and by what service it is held, and what it is worth per annum. [TNA, C 143/382/2 (5).]

5 Nov. 1373 'Melford' (Long Melford, Suffolk). Inquisition *ad quod damnum*. The jurors say that it is not to the damage of the king or anyone else if John de Cobham, knight, William Weston, Roger Asshebournham, Thomas Brokhull, and Thomas de Preston, clerk, retain the manor of Kentwell, Suffolk. They say that it is held of the king by service of rendering 65s. per annum to the ward of the king's castle of Norwich. The manor is worth in all its issues, according to its true value, £10 per annum. [TNA, C 143/382/2 (6).]

23 Nov. 1373 Rochester (Kent). Inquisition *ad quod damnum*. The jurors say that it is not to the damage of the king or anyone else if John de Cobham, knight, William Weston, Roger Asshebournham, Thomas Brokhull, and Thomas de Preston, clerk, retain the manor of Aldington. They say that it is held of the king in chief, but 'whether by one knight's fee or by one-half they do not know' ('*utrum per unum feodum militar' seu dj' ignorant*'). The manor contains a capital messuage (manor house) worth nothing per annum net of reprises (fixed payments); 100 acres of arable land worth 34s. 4d. per annum, at 4d. per acre; 40 acres of woodland worth 6s. 8d. per annum, at 2d. per acre; 48 hens worth 8s., at 2d. each; the assize-rents (fixed rents) of the free tenants are 53s. 4d. per annum. [TNA, C 143/382/2 (2).]

4 Dec. 1373 Writ from the king to the escheator of Kent to hold an inquisition *ad quod damnum* to inquire if it is to the damage of the king or anyone else if John de Cobham, knight, William Weston, Roger Asshebournham, Thomas Brokhull, and Thomas de Preston, clerk, retain the moiety (one-half) of the manor of Aldington, Kent, which they acquired in fee, without licence, from John Gower, who held it of the king in chief; and by what service it is held, and what the said moiety is worth per annum. [TNA, C 143/382/2 (3).]

6 Dec. 1373 Rochester (Kent). Inquisition *ad quod damnum* concerning the moiety of the manor of Aldington, Kent. The jurors say that it is not to the damage of the king or anyone else if John de Cobham, knight, William Weston, Roger Asshebournham, Thomas Brokhull, and Thomas de Preston, clerk, retain the said moiety. They say that the said moiety is held of the king in chief by military service, and by service of rendering 13s. per annum at the feast of St Andrew toward the ward of the king's castle of Rochester. And they say that the said moiety is worth 53s. 4d. per annum net of reprises ('*ultra redditum resolutum et seruicia*'). [TNA, C 143/382/2 (4).]

8 April 1374 Westminster (Middlesex). 'Pardon, for 12 marks paid to the king by John de Cobham, "chivaler", to him, William Weston, Roger Asshebournham, Thomas Brokhull and Thomas de Preston, clerk, of their trespasses in acquiring in fee the manor of Kentwell, co. Suffolk, and a moiety of the manor of Aldyngton, co. Kent, held in chief, from John Gower, and entering therein without licence; and grant that they may retain the same.' [CPR 1370–74, p. 425.]

6 March 1376 London. Quitclaim by William de Weston to Thomas de Preston, chaplain, Roger de Asshbornham, and Thomas de Brokhull, their heirs and assigns, of all his right in the manor of 'Kentewell' (Suffolk) with its appurtenances. Witnesses: Geoffrey de Neweton, Nicholas Potyn, William Olyuer, John Burgh, John Grauesende, 'and others'. Dated at London, 6 March, 50 Edward III. [BL, Harley Charter 57 G. 43. In 1373–74 John Gower had transferred Kentwell to Weston, Preston, Asshbornham, Brokhull, and Sir John de Cobham, evidently to hold as feoffees on his behalf (see above). John Gravesende granted an annual quitrent to Gower on 1 June 1367 (see above).]

3 Nov. 1377(?) London. Quitclaim by John, lord of Cobeham, knight, to Thomas de Preston, chaplain, Roger de Asshbornham and Thomas Brokhull, their heirs and assigns, of all right in the manor of 'Kentwelle' with its appurtenances in the counties of Suffolk and Essex. Witnesses: Sir Reginald de Cobham, Sir John de la Pole, Sir Arnald de Seintliger[?], knights, Ralph de Cobeham, William Burton, 'and others'. Dated at London, 3 November, 1(?) Richard II. [BL, Harl. Ch. 48 E. 32. Sir John de Cobham, Preston, Asshbornham, and Brokhull were Gower's feoffees for Kentwell; see comments under entry for 6 March 1376.]

***temp*. Richard II (1377–99)** The arms of John Gower were included in a roll of arms known as the 'County Roll', composed *temp*. Richard II and coloured in the early fifteenth century. It depicted the arms of nobles, knights, and gentry, grouped by county. The original roll does not survive, but a facsimile was made under the direction of Sir William Dugdale c. 1638–40; it is now London, Society of Antiquaries MS 664/4. John Gower's arms are included under the county of Kent on fol. 20r. [Cf. *Dictionary of British Arms: Medieval Ordinary*, vol. 2, ed. Thomas Woodcock, Janet Grant, and Ian Graham (London: Society of Antiquaries, 1996), p. 440.]

21 May 1378 Westminster (Middlesex). Geoffrey Chaucer, about to journey abroad [*to Lombardy on the king's service*] by licence of the king, has the king's letter of general attorney in the names of John Gower and Richard Forester [*to act for Chaucer*] in all the courts of England for one year. Witness the king at Westminster, 21 May, 1 Richard II; William de Burst, the king's clerk, acted in his place ('*attornavit*'). [*Chaucer Life-Records*, eds Martin M. Crow and Clair C. Olson (Oxford: Clarendon Press, 1966), p. 54.]

*18 July 1378   Westminster (Middlesex). 'To the sheriff of Bedford. Writ of *supersedeas*, by mainprise of Edward Clay of Notynghamshire, John de Kirkeby of Yorkshire, John Cauntelo of Wiltesir and William de Huntyngdon of London, in favour of William Bromesforde and Isabel his wife at suit of Agnes who was wife of Henry Huntyngfeld for alleged trespass by them and John Gower.' [*CCR 1377–81*, p. 206. Perhaps connected with the entry below for 3 June 1390, concerning William Brounesford the elder.]

6–12 Oct. 1379   Westminster (Middlesex). Final concord, made the morrow of NSJB (25–30 June) 1369, and recorded in the octaves of Michaelmas (6–12 Oct.) 1379, by which John Spenythorn and Joan his wife (deforciants) granted the manor of Kentwell to John Gower, who gave them 200 marks of silver. [BL, Harley Charter 50 I. 13.]

23 Feb. 1380   Westminster (Middlesex). 'Licence, for 10 marks paid to the king by Katharine, wife of Thomas de Clopton, knight, for John de Cobham, knight, William Weston, Roger Asshebourne [*recte* Asshebourneham], Thomas Brokehull and Thomas Preston, clerk, to grant to the said Katharine, Robert de Bockyng, clerk, Thomas, parson of the church of Haukedon, Robert Clerc, chaplain, and William Scot, in fee, the manor of Kentwell, co. Suffolk, held of the king by the service of rendering 65*s*. yearly for castle-guard of Norwich castle.' [*CPR 1377–81*, p. 444. Cobham, Weston, Asshebourne[ham], Brokehull and Preston had all been Gower's feoffees for Kentwell: see entry for 6 March 1376.]

3 Feb. 1381   [*Enrolled at Westminster.*] 'Isabel daughter of Walter de Huntyngfelde to John Gower and John Bowland clerk. Quitclaim of all lands of her father in the parish of Thrwleye [*Throwley*] and Stalesfeld [*Stalisfield*], co. Kent. Dated 3 February 4 Richard II. *Memorandum* of acknowledgment, 28 March.' [*CCR 1377–81*, p. 505.]

Easter term (1–27 May) 1381, with continuations to 9–15 Feb. 1382   Westminster (Middlesex), court of Common Pleas. John Gower, by Thomas Path[orn] his attorney, sues John Barbour, baker, John Henry, and Roger Bochier, of the parish of 'Neweton' (Newington, near Sittingbourne), Kent, on a plaint that each of them owes him £32. The sheriffs of London are ordered to arrest them and to bring them to court on the quindene of Trinity (beginning 24 June 1381). Further continuations to the octaves of Michaelmas (6–12 Oct. 1381), the morrow of Martinmas (12–17 Nov. 1381), the octaves of Hilary (20–26 Jan. 1382), and the octaves of the Purification of the Virgin (9–15 Feb. 1382). [TNA, CP 40/482, rot. 232r (last entry), http://aalt.law.uh.edu/AALT6/R2/CP40no482/482_0483.htm.]

Michaelmas term (9 Oct.–28 Nov.) 1381, with continuations to 27 Jan.–2 Feb. 1382 Westminster (Middlesex), court of Common Pleas. John Gower, by William Emery his attorney, sues Walter Cook (or Cookes), carpenter, for not fulfilling a contract to build for Gower's use, and at Gower's expense, a new house in the manor of 'Aldyngton' (Kent). Cook does not appear, so the sheriff of Kent is ordered to summon him to be at the Common Pleas in the octaves of Martinmas (18–24 Nov. 1381). Cook does not appear then, either, so the sheriff is ordered to attach him to appear in the quindene of Hilary (27 Jan.–2 Feb. 1382). [TNA, CP 40/483, rots 144d (6th entry), http://aalt.law.uh.edu/AALT6/R2/CP40no483/483_0307.htm, 488r (3rd entry), http://aalt.law.uh.edu/AALT6/R2/CP40no483/483_0999.htm.]

Hilary term (23 Jan.–12 Feb.) 1382 Westminster (Middlesex), court of Common Pleas. John Gower, by Thomas Pathorn his attorney, sues John Barbour, baker, John Henry, and Roger Bochier, of the parish of 'Neweton' (Newington, near Sittingbourne), Kent, on a plaint that each of them owes him £32. The sheriffs of London are ordered to have them outlawed in the court of Husting and to arrest them and have them at Common Pleas in the quindene of Michaelmas (13–19 Oct. 1382). [TNA, CP 40/484, rot. 439r (5th entry), http://aalt.law.uh.edu/AALT6/R2/CP40no484/484_0896.htm.]

Hilary term (23 Jan.–12 Feb.) 1382 Westminster (Middlesex), court of Common Pleas. John Gower of the county of Kent appoints William Repyndon as his attorney to sue John Heylesdon, citizen of London, for debt. (This is the earliest reference to Gower as 'of Kent'.) [TNA, CP 40/484, rot. 492r (18th entry), http://aalt.law.uh.edu/AALT6/R2/CP40no484/484_0979.htm.]

2 March 1382 [*Enrolled at Westminster*.] 'Isabel late the daughter of Walter de Huntyngfeld of Kent to John Gower of Kent. General release of all actions real and personal. Dated 2 March 5 Richard II. *Memorandum* of acknowledgment, 9 March.' [*CCR 1381–85*, 111.]

24 June 1382 Acquittance, in French, by John Gower to Sir John de Cobeham, lord of Cobeham, for 106s. 6d., in full payment of all debts from the beginning of the world until the making of this. Dated Tuesday the feast of NSJB, 6 Richard II (place not given). Sealed with John Gower's octagonal signet. [From a manuscript formerly in the Surrenden MSS, 'lately dispersed', of Sir Edward Dering, Bart., of Surrenden Dering, transcribed in Warwick, 'On Gower, the Kentish Poet', p. 87, n. 3. A drawing of the signet is reproduced in Carlin, 'Gower's Life', Fig. 1.11.]

1 Aug. 1382 [*Enrolled at Westminster*] 'Guy de Rouclif clerk to John Gower esquire of Kent. Charter of the manors of Feltwelle co. Norfolk and Multon co. Suffolk, which the grantor had by feoffment of Thomas de Catherton. Witnesses John Tydde, John Northfolk, Thomas Noreys, John Trace, Walter Clider, John Overton. Dated 1 August 6 Richard II [*1382*].

French. Memorandum of acknowledgment, 28 August.' (This document, and those below of 3 and 4 August 1382, contain the earliest references to John Gower as 'esquire'.) [*CCR 1381–85*, p. 211. A grant of 'the manor of Feltwelle co. Norfolk' made at Feltwell on 18 June 1382 by John de Plays, knight, to William de Beauchamp, knight, and eight other men, their heirs and assigns, concerned the Feltwell manor later known as East Hall, not Gower's manor, which was later known as South Hall. *CCR 1381–85*, p. 202; Francis Blomefield, 'Hundred of Grimeshou: Feltwell', in *An Essay Towards A Topographical History of the County of Norfolk: Volume 2* (London, 1805), pp. 187–200. *British History Online*, http://www.british-history.ac.uk/topographical-hist-norfolk/vol2/pp187-200.]

3 Aug. 1382 [*Enrolled at Westminster*] 'John Gower esquire of Kent to Guy de Rouclif clerk and to his heirs. Release of the warranty contained in a charter, dated 1 August, 6 Richard II, whereby the said Guy gave the manor of Feltwelle co. Norfolk to the said John, his heirs and assigns. Dated 3 August 6 Richard II [*1382*]. *French. Memorandum* of acknowledgment, 28 August.' [*CCR 1381–85*, p. 214.]

4 Aug. 1382 [*Enrolled at Westminster*] 'Elizabeth Dame Luterell of Devon to John Gower esquire. Quitclaim of the manors of Feltewelle co. Norfolk and Multon co. Suffolk. Dated 4 August 6 Richard II [*1382*]. *French. Memorandum* of acknowledgement, 26 October.' [*CCR 1381–85*, p. 220. The original quitclaim, sealed with Dame Elizabeth's armorial seal, is now Somerset Heritage Centre, Taunton, DD\L/P37/41 (Luttrell Family of Dunster MSS, Box 37); see http://somerset-cat.swheritage.org.uk/records/DD/L/P37/41.]

6 Aug. 1382 [*Enrolled at Westminster*] 'John Gower of the one part, Thomas Blakelake parson of St. Nicholas Feltewelle, John Sybile, Edmund Lakynghethe and John Wermyngton of the other part. Indenture of demise to the said Thomas and the others, their heirs and assigns, of the manors of Feltewelle co. Norfolk and Multon co. Suffolk, rendering yearly 40*l.* in the abbey church of the monks at Westminster during John Gower's life, power being reserved to distrain for arrears, and to enter and hold those manors all his life and for seven years longer if the rent shall be six weeks in arrear; and if John Gower, his executors or assigns shall so enter, they shall not be bound to repair any houses thereto pertaining. Dated 6 August, 6 Richard II. *Memorandum* of acknowledgment by the said John Sybile and Edmund, 24 October.' [*CCR 1381–85*, p. 218.]

6 Aug. 1382 [*Enrolled at Westminster*] 'John Gower to Thomas Blakelake parson of St. Nicholas Feltewelle, John Sybile, Edmund Lakynghethe and John Wermyngton, their heirs and assigns. Indenture of demise of the manors of Feltewelle co. Norffolk and Multon co. Suffolk, rendering, to the lessor and his assigns during his life, 40*l.* a year in the convent church of the monks at Westminster, with covenant that it shall be lawful for the lessor and his assigns to enter again and hold the same all his life, and for his executors and assigns seven years after his decease, if the rent be six weeks in arrear, and that after such entry they shall not be bound to repair any houses pertaining to either manor. Dated 6 August, 6 Richard II. *Memorandum* of acknowledgment by John Gower and John Wermyngton, 29 February this year [*1384; see below*].' [*CCR 1381–85*, p. 426.]

17 Feb. 1384   Westminster (Middlesex). Enrollment of Gower's demise dated 6 August 1382 of Feltwell and Moulton. [*CCR 1381–85*, p. 426.]

29 Feb. 1384   '*Memorandum* of acknowledgment by John Gower and John Wermyngton [*of the demise of Feltwell and Moulton dated 6 Aug. 1382*], 29 February this year [*1384*].' [*CCR 1381–85*, p. 426.]

15 March 1385   [*Enrolled at Westminster*] 'John Spenythorn citizen and tailor of London to John Gower esquire of Kent. General release of all actions real and personal, all plaints and demands. Dated 15 March 8 Richard II. *Memorandum* of acknowledgment, 21 April. *Memorandum* that this acknowledgment was taken by John Burton clerk by order of Michael de la Pole the chancellor.' [*CCR 1381–85*, p. 619. John Burton, the Chancery clerk named here, died in 1394 and thus was not Gower's executor of the same name; see discussion in Carlin, 'Gower's Life'.]

10 June 1385   [*Enrolled at Westminster*] 'Isabel daughter and heir of Walter Huntyngfelde of Kent to John Gower of Kent. Release of all actions real and personal, all claims and demands by reasons of debt, account, trespass etc. Dated London, 10 June 8 Richard II. *Memorandum* of acknowledgment, 10 June.' (This is the last reference to Gower as 'of Kent'.) [*CCR 1381–85*, p. 635.] In the original prologue to *Confessio Amantis*, Gower says that while rowing on the Thames at London he met Richard II's barge; the king invited him aboard and bade him write 'some newe thing' (Pro.34–53*). Douglas Gray has tentatively suggested a date of *c.* 1386 for Gower's commencement of the *Confessio*. For the years 1385–87, Richard II and John Gower are recorded in the capital on the same day only once: 10 June 1385. See discussion in Carlin, 'Gower's Life'. [Douglas Gray, 'Gower, John (*d.* 1408)', *ODNB*, http://www.oxforddnb.com/view/article/11176. For Richard II's itinerary for 1385–87, see Nigel Saul, *Richard II* (New Haven and London: Yale University Press, 1997), pp. 470–1.]

*12 Aug. 1386   Westminster (Middlesex). 'Appointment, during pleasure, of Edmund Stapulgate [*formerly Geoffrey Chaucer's ward; lord of Bilsington, near Canterbury*], Thomas Burbage and John Gower to receive and distribute as directed by the Council for the defence of Dover Castle all victuals therein, in whosesoever custody.' [*CPR 1385–89*, p. 208; cf. Ernest P. Kuhl, 'Some Friends of Chaucer', *Proceedings of the Modern Language Association*, 29/2 (1914), pp. 270–6, at 275–6.]

24 Jan. 1387 Westminster (Middlesex). 'Appointment, during pleasure, of John Gower, Thomas Burbache, and Simon Tanner to receive the victuals in Dover Castle and keep and distribute them as advised by the king and Council.' [*CPR 1385–89*, p. 266.]

3 June 1390 'William Brounesforde the elder to John Gower. General release of all actions real and personal, all claims and demands. Dated Friday before Trinity 13 Richard II. *Memorandum* of acknowledgment, 8 June.' [*CCR 1389–92*, p. 181. Perhaps connected with the entry above for 18 July 1378 concerning William Bromesforde.]

5 May 1391 Writ to the escheator of Kent to hold an inquisition *ad quod damnum* to inquire if it would be to the loss or prejudice of the king or others if Thomas Brokhill were to enfeoff John Frenyngham and William Makenade of the manor of Aldyngton [Kent] with its appurtenances, so that they could in turn grant it back to him for his lifetime, with remainder to William Pympe, Joan his wife [*Brokhill's daughter*], and the heirs of their bodies, with remainder to his own right heirs. To inquire also if the manor is held in chief and (if so) by what service, and its annual value. [TNA, C 143/411/15. Thomas Brokhill or Brokhull had been one of John Gower's feoffees for the manor of Aldington. Sometime between Michaelmas term 1381 and May 1391 Gower evidently directed his feoffees to dispose of it, and Brokhull obtained possession of it for himself: see entries above for 8 April 1374 and Michaelmas term 1381.]

21 July 1391 Cherryng (Kent), inquisition *ad quod damnum*. The jury finds that it would not be to the loss or prejudice of the king or others if Thomas Brokhill were to enfeoff John Frenyngham and William Makenade of the manor of Aldyngton [Kent] with its appurtenances, so that they could in turn grant it back to him for his lifetime, with remainder to William Pympe, Joan his wife [*Brokhill's daughter*], and the heirs of their bodies, with remainder to Brokhill's own right heirs. The manor is held in chief by knight service and by service of rendering 14s. annually at the feast of St Andrew the Apostle towards the ward of Rochester Castle. The manor with its appurtenances is worth £4 19s. 7d. per annum in all its issues. [TNA, C 143/411/15. Thomas Brokhull had been one of John Gower's feoffees for the manor of Aldington: see entry above for 5 May 1381.]

22 June 1391 x 21 June 1392 Thomas Brokhill has enfeoffed John de Frenyngham 'and others' of the manor of Aldyngton, Kent, as of ward of Rochester Castle. 15 Richard II. [*Calendarium Inquisitionum Post Mortem sive Escaetarum*, vol. 3 (1377–1413) (London: Record Commission, 1821), p. 142; cf. *CPR 1396–99*, p. 462. Thomas Brokhull had been one of John Gower's feoffees for the manor of Aldington: see entry above for 5 May 1381.]

[autumn 1392] [*Gower travels to Yorkshire and Norfolk; see the following two entries:*]

c. Sept.–Oct. 1392 London. The ledger of the London merchant Gilbert Maghfeld records that in October 1392 Maghfeld paid a shipman 16*d*. on behalf of John Gower for the freight of a brass pot 'sent by letter from Lynne [*King's Lynn, Norfolk*] to London', and previously had paid 4*d*. for carriage of a chest 'to the water' to send to John Gower at Hull (Yorkshire). ('*Memorandum que Gyboun Maufeld' ad paye pour John' Gower Esquier a j. Schippman pur freit dune bras pott' mis par lettre de lynne iesques a loundres - xvi d.*'; '*Item il ad paye deuaunt pur cariage dune chest' al Ewe pur envoier au dit Joh' a hull - iiij d.*'). Gower evidently repaid Maghfeld these sums because both entries are cancelled. Hull was the port for York, where Gower attended the court of Common Pleas in Michaelmas term 1392; see next entry. [TNA, E 101/509/19, fol. 34r; cf. Edith Rickert, 'Extracts from a Fourteenth-Century Account Book', *Modern Philology*, Vol. 24, No. 1 (Aug., 1926): pp. 111–19, at 118; *Chaucer's Life-Records*, ed. Crow and Olson, p. 500.]

Michaelmas term (9 Oct.–28 Nov.) 1392 York, court of Common Pleas. The case between John Gower, plaintiff, and John atte Buttes of Wylton (now *Hockwold-cum-Wilton, Norfolk*) in a plea of debt is 'respited' (continued) until the octaves of Hilary (20–26 January 1393) for lack of jurors, because none came. (Gower is not described here as represented by an attorney, implying that he appeared in person. See entry below for 14 June 1395.) [TNA, CP 40/527, rot. 237r, 3rd entry: http://aalt.law.uh.edu/AALT6/R2/CP40no527/527_0190.htm.]

c. Oct.–Nov. 1393 Order by Hugh Waterton, chamberlain of Henry Bolingbroke, earl of Derby, to William Loveney, clerk of Bolingbroke's wardrobe (and later one of John Gower's executors): 'Deliver 26*s*. 8*d*. to Richard Dancastre for a collar given to him by my lord the earl of Derby, because of another collar given by my said lord to an esquire, John Gower.' ('*Liuerez a Richard Dancastre pur vn Coler luy done par monseigneur le Conte de Derby par cause dvne autre Coler done par monditseigneur a vn Esquier John Gower vynt et sys soldz' oyt deniers. de par Hugh Waterton Chamburlein au Conte de Derby.*') [TNA, DL 41/424 (formerly DL 41/10/43), m. 15r (17 Richard II, 1393–94).]

1393 x 1398 or 1399 Southwark (Surrey). Probable date-range for the design and construction of John Gower's tomb in the chapel of St John the Baptist in the priory church of St Mary Overy, after Gower's receipt of a livery collar from Henry Bolingbroke in 1393, and before Gower's marriage in 1398 or Bolingbroke's accession as Henry IV in 1399. (See discussion in Carlin, 'Gower's Life'.)

30 Sept. 1394 Guildford (Surrey). Assize of *novel disseisin* (Feriby *v.* Gower *et al.*) concerning the sub-lease of a tenement with appurtenances in

Southwark, belonging to the prior of St Mary Overy (probably Gower's own residence in the priory precinct). The plaintiff, Thomas Feriby, accused John Gower (represented by his attorney, William Elyngton), William Weston, Thomas Saundres, and Thomas Hautwysel of unjustly disseising him of this property. Gower and Weston were convicted, and were ordered to be arrested, to forfeit possession of the property, and to pay Feriby damages of 100s. Saundres and Hautwysel were acquitted, and Feriby was fined for falsely accusing them. The case was concluded on 6 Feb. 1395 (see below). [TNA, JUST 1/1503, rot. 56r-d; discussed in Martha Carlin, 'Gower's Southwark', in *The Routledge Research Companion to John Gower*, ed. Ana Sáez-Hidalgo, Brian Gastle, and R. F. Yeager (London and New York, 2017), pp. 132–49 (141–42); and in Martha Carlin, 'Gower's Life', with full translation given in Appendix 3.]

6 Feb. 1395 Southwark (Surrey). Conclusion of case of Feriby *v.* Gower *et al.*: Feriby came before the same justices and declared himself satisfied of the said damages (100s.); Gower was fined 13s. 4d., and William Weston was fined 6s. 8d. [TNA, JUST 1/1503, rot. 56r-d; Carlin, 'Gower's Southwark', pp. 141–2; Carlin, 'Gower's Life', Appendix 3.]

23 June 1395 London. John Gower, esquire, borrows £3 6s. 8d. from Gilbert Maghfeld on the eve of NSJB (23 June), which is to be repaid within three weeks ('*John Gower Esquier doit dapprest par obligacion le veill' de seint John Baptiste a paier deinz iij symaignes prosheinz apres — iij li.vj s.viij d.*'). Gower evidently repaid this loan, because the entry was cancelled. [TNA, E 101/509/19, fol. 55v; cf. Rickert, 'Extracts from a Fourteenth-Century Account Book', p. 119; *Chaucer's Life-Records*, ed. Crow and Olson, p. 501.]

14 June 1395 – Easter term (19 April–15 May) 1396 Westminster (Middlesex), court of Common Pleas (Easter term 1396). A year ago, on 14 June 1395, John atte Buttes of Wylton (*now Hockwold-cum-Wilton, near Feltwell*), Norfolk, was outlawed in Norfolk because he gave a bond for £40, which John Gower has produced here in court, and which Gower recovered against him in the Curia Regis. Last Michaelmas (1395) John Harowedon, at that time sheriff of Northamptonshire (where Buttes evidently had fled), was ordered to arrest Buttes and imprison him and bring him to court in the quindene of Easter (beginning 15 April 1396), but he did not come. Now (in Easter term 1396) the current sheriff of Northamptonshire sends word that he has been distrained on his chattels to the value of 10d. (*sic*). He was mainprised by four men (*names given*) who are thus now to be amerced. And as before the sheriff is ordered to distrain on Buttes by all his lands, and to have him here in court in the octaves of Trinity (beginning 12 June 1396). [TNA, CP 40/541, rot. 228r (2nd entry), http://aalt.law.uh.edu/AALT6/R2/CP40no541a/aCP40no541afronts/IMG_0475.htm.]

Michaelmas term (9 Oct.–29 Nov.) 1395 Westminster (Middlesex), court of Common Pleas. John Gower, in person, sues Thomas Forester and

John Gay to render to him a reasonable account for their respective terms as Gower's bailiff at Feltwell (Norfolk) and as his receiver. They do not appear; the sheriff of Norfolk is ordered to arrest them and to bring them to the court in the octaves of Hilary (20–26 January 1396). [TNA, CP 40/539, rot. 511r (last entry), http://aalt.law.uh.edu/AALT6/R2/CP40no539/539_1202.htm.]

Michaelmas term (9 Oct.–29 Nov.) 1395 Westminster (Middlesex), court of Common Pleas. John Gower, by his attorney John Drake, sues Thomas Forester to render him a reasonable account for his term as Gower's bailiff in Feltwell (Norfolk) and as his receiver, and similarly sues John Gray [*recte* Gay] to render a reasonable account for his term as Gower's bailiff in the same vill and as his receiver . . . [*MS damaged*]. They do not appear; the sheriff of Norfolk is ordered to arrest them and bring them to the court in the quindene of Hilary (27 January–2 February 1396). [TNA, CP 40/539, rot. 535r (5th entry), http://aalt.law.uh.edu/AALT6/R2/CP40no539/539_1259.htm.]

Easter term (19 Apr.–15 May) 1396 Westminster (Middlesex), court of Common Pleas. John Gower, in person, sues Thomas Forester and John Gay to render to him a reasonable account for their respective terms as Gower's bailiff in Feltwell (Norfolk) and as his receiver. They do not appear; the sheriff of Norfolk is ordered to arrest them and to bring them to the court on the quindene of Trinity (week beginning 11 June 1396). [TNA, CP40/541, rot. 46r (4th entry), http://aalt.law.uh.edu/AALT6/R2/CP40no541a/aCP40no541afronts/IMG_0101.htm. Cf. Sebastian Sobecki, 'A Southwark Tale: Gower, the 1381 Poll Tax, and Chaucer's *The Canterbury Tales*', *Speculum* 92 (2017): pp. 630–60, at 636, 658.]

** Easter term (19 Apr.–15 May) 1396 Westminster (Middlesex), court of Common Pleas. John Gower sues John Cov[e]rton for breaking 'with force and arms' ('*vi et armis*') into Gower's close ('*clausum*') in Birnyston (Burniston, North Yorkshire). [CP 40/541 (Easter term 1396), rot. 148d, http://aalt.law.uh.edu/AALT6/R2/CP40no541a/bCP40no541adorses/IMG_0327.htm (last entry).]

24 Oct. 1396 Westminster (Middlesex). Pardon of his outlawry in the court of Husting, London, to John Cook of Feltewell (Norfolk), for not appearing before the justices of the Common Bench to answer John Gower, esquire, touching a debt of 10 marks. *Teste custode*. London. Similar pardon to William Cook of Ixnyng (Exning, Suffolk, near Moulton) for the same. London. [*CPR 1396–99*, p. 128.]

6 Dec. 1397 [*Enrolled at Westminster.*] 'Memorandum of a mainprise under a pain of 40*l.*, made in chancery 6 December this year by John Frenche, Peter Blake, Thomas Gandre, all of London, and Robert Markle serjeant at arms for Thomas Caudre, canon in the priory of St. Mary Overey in Southwerke, that he shall do or procure no hurt or harm to John Gower.' [*CCR 1396–99*, p. 238.]

Late 1397–Jan. 1398? Gower writes 'Est Amor' in anticipation of his marriage to Agnes Groundolf?

25 Jan. 1398 Highclere (Hampshire). Special licence issued by William Wykeham, bishop of Winchester, to William, curate of St Mary Magdalen, Southwark, to marry parishioners John Gower and Agnes Groundolf, without further banns, in the oratory of Gower's townhouse in the priory of St Mary Overy. [Winchester, Hampshire Archives, Reg. William Wykeham, II: fol. 299v; calendared in *Wykeham's Register*, ed. Kirby, II: 477.]

*22 Nov. 1398 Westminster (Middlesex). 'To the sheriff of Kent. Writ of *supersedeas omnino*, and order by mainprise of Thomas Kempe, John Cranewelle of Kent, William Canynges and John Sandeforde of Surrey to set free John Stoffolde of Crundale [*Kent*], if taken at suit of John Gower of Crundale averring threats.' [*CCR 1396–99*, p. 417.]

Michaelmas term (9 Oct.–28 Nov.) 1399 Westminster (Middlesex), court of Common Pleas. John Gower (initially by an unnamed attorney; subsequently in person) sues Walter Clerk (or Clerkes) of Little Cressingham (Norfolk) for a debt of £30 5s. 8½d. (subsequently reduced to £29 5s. 8½d.). [TNA, CP40/555, rot. 73d (1st entry), http://aalt.law.uh.edu/H4/CP40no555/bCP40no555dorses/IMG_0149.htm, and rot. 165d (1st entry), http://aalt.law.uh.edu/H4/CP40no555/bCP40no555dorses/IMG_0347.htm; cf. Sobecki, 'A Southwark Tale', pp. 637–8, 658–60.]

Michaelmas term (9 Oct.–28 Nov.) 1399 Westminster (Middlesex), court of Common Pleas. John Gower, in person, sues William Fisshere of Shropham (Norfolk) and Denise his wife for a debt of 40s. [TNA, CP40/555, rot. 118r (3rd entry), http://aalt.law.uh.edu/H4/CP40no555/aCP40no555fronts/IMG_0249.htm; cf. Sobecki, 'A Southwark Tale', pp. 638, 660.]

21 Nov. 1399 Westminster (Middlesex). 'Grant for life to the king's esquire John Gower of two pipes of wine of Gascony yearly in the port of London. By p.s.' [*CPR 1399–1401*, p. 128.]

5 April 1400 Westminster (Middlesex). 'To the chief butler for the time being, or his representative in the port of London. Order to deliver to John Gower the king's esquire two pipes of wine of Gascony a year for life, to him granted in that port by the king on 21 November last. By K. Et erat patens.' [*CCR 1399–1402*, p. 78.]

1401–2 In the return for the aid levied for the dowry of Henry IV's eldest daughter Blanche, John Gower is listed as holding in Feltwell (Norfolk) one knight's fee of the earl of Arundel, who holds it of the king ('*Johannes Gower tenet in Feltwell j. f. m. de comite Arundellie, et idem de rege*'). [*Feudal Aids 1284–1431*, I: xxvi–xxvii; III: viii–ix, xi, Appendix, p. 654.]

March 1402 The striking appearance of a comet in March 1402 inspires Gower to write *Presul Ouile Regis* (addressed to Archbishop Thomas Arundel)?

[John Gower, *The Complete Works of John Gower*, ed. George C. Macaulay, 4 vols. (Oxford: Clarendon Press, 1899–1902), IV: 368; 420]

12 Jan. 1405 [*Enrolled 12 Jan. 1405. Westminster.*] 'Memorandum of a mainprise under pain of 100*l*., made in chancery 12 January this year by James Norwode of Kent esquire, and John Mokkynge, John Sandyforde and William Kirton of Surrey for John Solas, and of an undertaking by him under the same pain, that he shall do or procure no hurt or harm to John Gower and William Weston his servant.' [*CCR 1402–5*, p. 484.]

15 Aug. 1408 Southwark (Surrey). John Gower dates his testament in the priory of St Mary Overy on the feast of the Assumption of the Virgin, 1408. [Lambeth Palace Library, Reg. Thomas Arundel, Archbishop of Canterbury, vol. 1, fols 256r–257r; transcribed and translated in Carlin, 'Gower's Life', Appendix 4.]

15 Aug. x 24 Oct. (*perhaps 7 Sept.*) 1408 Death of John Gower. Thomas Berthelette reported in his first edition of Gower's *Confessio* (1532) that an annual obit was celebrated for Gower in the priory of St Mary Overy on the Friday after the feast of St Gregory the Pope. The feast of the ordination of St Gregory is 3 September; if the obit marked the date of Gower's actual death, then Gower probably died on Friday, 7 Sept. 1408. ['To the reder', in *Io. Gower de confessione amantis* (London, 1532), *STC* (*A Short-Title Catalogue of Books Printed in England, Scotland, & Ireland and of English Books Printed Abroad, 1475–1640*, ed. Alfred W. Pollard, Gilbert R. Redgrave, *et al.*, 3 vols, second edition, London: Bibliographical Society, 1976–1991) 12143] An apparently contemporary image of Gower's funeral bier, with his shield of arms held up by two angels, his epitaph ('*Armigeri scutum*'), and a summary of the indulgence for those who prayed for his soul ('*Orantibus pro anima*'), is in Glasgow University Library, MS Hunter 59 (T. 2. 17), f. 129r.

24 Oct. 1408 Lambeth (Surrey). The testament of John Gower is proved before Thomas Arundel, archbishop of Canterbury. The executors are listed as: Gower's wife Agnes; Sir Arnald Savage, knight; 'Sir Roger, esquire' ('*dominum Rogerum Armigerum*'); Sir William 'Denne', canon of the king's chapel; and John Burton, clerk. [*For a full and accurate list of the executors, see under Hilary term 1410, below.*] Administration was granted to Agnes. [Lambeth Palace Library, Reg. Thomas Arundel, Archbishop of Canterbury, vol. 1, fols 256r–257r; transcribed and translated in Carlin, 'Gower's Life', Appendix 4.]

7 Nov. 1408 Lambeth (Surrey). Conclusion of probate of Gower's testament; his widow Agnes is executrix of his testament and administratrix of his goods. [Lambeth Palace Library, Reg. Thomas Arundel, Archbishop of Canterbury, vol. 1, fols 256r–257r; transcribed and translated in Carlin, 'Gower's Life', Appendix 4.]

Hilary term (23 Jan.–12 Feb.) 1410 Westminster (Middlesex), court of Common Pleas. Agnes, who was the wife of John Gower, esquire, Arnald Savage, knight, William Loveneye, esquire of the lord King, William Doune, canon of the King's Chapel at Westminster, and John Burton, clerk, executors of the testament of John Gower, esquire, by their attorney, sue Hugh Luterell, knight, son and heir of Elizabeth, late lady of Luterell of the county of Devon, for unjust detinue of 50 marks. Luterell does not appear, 'as before'; the sheriff of Surrey is ordered to arrest him. The sheriff now sends word that Luterell has not been found; the sheriff is ordered to arrest him, so that he appear in Common Pleas in the quindene of Easter (week beginning 7 April 1410). [TNA, CP 40/596, rot. 232d (for this reference I am grateful to Graham Dawson), http://aalt.law.uh.edu/H4/CP40no596/bCP40no596dorses/IMG_1594.htm (5th entry from bottom).]

24 Feb. 1410 'Hugh Lutterell knight to Agnes Gower, late the wife of John Gower, esquire. Gift for her life of a yearly rent of 20*l.* to be taken of his manor of Feltwelle, co. Norfolk, with power to distrain for arrears there and in his manor of Multon, co. Suffolk. Dated 24 February, 11 Henry IV [*1410*]. *French. Memorandum* of acknowledgment, 25 February.' [*CCR 1409–13*, pp. 80–1.]

Figure 1.1: John Gower's tomb, chaplet, and effigy, from Richard Gough, *Sepulchral Monuments in Great Britain*, vol. II, part 2 (1796). (*By courtesy of The Lewis Walpole Library, Yale University.*)

Chapter 1

GOWER'S LIFE

Martha Carlin

Although John Gower was wealthy and long-lived, and was a celebrated poet with ties to the royal court, his life has been something of a mystery. His parentage, date of birth, place of upbringing, education, and professional occupation(s) – if any – are unknown, and his only documented residence is the house in the Augustinian priory of St Mary Overy in Southwark, across the river from London, where he married Agnes Groundolf in 1398, and where the couple probably lived until Gower's death in 1408.

In Chapter 2, below, Stephen Rigby outlines the chronology of Gower's works and discusses what they reveal about the poet's connections with Richard II (r. 1377–99), Henry Bolingbroke (as Henry IV, r. 1399–1413), and other associates such as Geoffrey Chaucer (d. 1400). Gower's poetry, however, reveals little about his personal life. In *Mirour de l'Omme* there are hints of a possible legal career (see Anthony Musson, below, pp. 218–26) and a possible marriage; in *Est Amor*, he writes plainly of his imminent marriage late in life.[1] Elsewhere, Gower writes explicitly of his physical woes and laments the miseries of old age and failing vision. Thus, in the original Prologue to *Confessio Amantis*, completed about 1390, he says that he has long been ill (lines 79–80*); a decade later, in the Latin verse dedication to Thomas Arundel, archbishop of Canterbury, which Gower wrote for a presentation copy of *Vox Clamantis*, he describes himself as old, blind, sick, bent with age, and wretched.[2] Gower makes similar remarks in the poem

---

[1] John Gower, *Mirour de l'Omme*, ll. 8793–6, 17649, in *The Complete Works of John Gower*, ed. George C. Macaulay (four volumes, Oxford: Clarendon Press, 1899–1902) [hereafter cited as *Complete Works*], I (*The French Works*); John Gower, *The Minor Latin Works with In Praise of Peace*, eds Robert F. Yeager and Michael Livingstone (Kalamazoo, Michigan: Medieval Institute Publications, 2005): 'Est Amor', http://d.lib.rochester.edu/teams/text/yeager-gower-minor-latin-works-est-amor [accessed 17 January 2017].

[2] 'Epistola' (heading, and lines 17, 19–20, 27, 29, 32), in *Complete Works*, IV: 1–2. Macaulay identified Arundel's presentation copy with All Souls College, Oxford, MS 98, and believed that it contains text and corrections in Gower's own hand (*Complete*

Quicquid Homo Scribat, where he dates his blindness to the first or second year of the reign of Henry IV (r. 1399–1413).[3] Nevertheless, he continued at least for a time to compose new works, including the very poems in which he lamented his blindness.[4] In the autumn of 1392 Gower was vigorous enough to make a journey to York, and in Michaelmas term 1399 he appeared in person as a plaintiff in lawsuits in the court of Common Pleas at Westminster.[5] He was still writing in March 1402, since his poem *Presul Ouile Regis*, evidently addressed to Archbishop Arundel, described a comet that appeared in that month.[6]

Gower's life-records have been studied by a number of scholars, including Nicholas Harris Nicolas (1828), George Macaulay (1902), John Fisher (1959 and 1965), and John Hines, Nathalie Cohen and Simon Roffey (2004).[7] Recent archival investigations by Graham Dawson, Sebastian Sobecki, and myself have identified additional sources. These contain new evidence about Gower's private life and his circle of associates, and thus may

---

Works, IV: lx–lxi). Malcolm Parkes rejected the identification of All Souls MS 98 as Arundel's presentation copy, and Andrew Watson concurred with Parkes. See Malcolm B. Parkes, 'Patterns of Scribal Activity and Revisions of the Text in Early Copies of Works by John Gower', in Richard Beadle and A. J. Piper, eds, *New Science out of Old Books: Studies in Manuscripts and Early Printed Books in Honour of A. I. Doyle* (Aldershot: Ashgate, 1995), pp. 81–121, and pls. 12–19, at 92–93; Andrew G. Watson, *A Descriptive Catalogue of the Medieval Manuscripts of All Souls College Oxford* (Oxford: Oxford University Press, 1997), pp. 200–3 (MS 98), at 202. Recently Sebastian Sobecki has argued that the hand of Malcolm Parkes' 'Scribe 10' is to be identified as Gower's own hand ('*Ecce patet tensus*: The Trentham Manuscript, *In Praise of Peace*, and Gower's Autograph Hand', *Speculum*, 90 (2015), pp. 925–59, at 951–59).

[3] '*Quicquid Homo Scribat*', in Gower, *The Minor Latin Works with In Praise of Peace* http://d.lib.rochester.edu/teams/text/yeager-gower-minor-latin-works-quicquid-homo-scribat [accessed 30 December 2016].

[4] *Complete Works*, IV: pp. 365–6; Gower, *The Minor Latin Works with In Praise of Peace*, notes by Yeager to '*Quicquid Homo Scribat*'; Isabella Neale Yeager, with additional notes by Robert F. Yeager, 'Did Gower Love His Wife? And What Has It to Do with the Poetry?' *Poetica*, 73 (2010), pp. 67–86, at 69–70.

[5] TNA, CP 40/527, rot. 237r (3rd entry), http://aalt.law.uh.edu/AALT6/R2/CP40no527/527_0190.htm; CP 40/555, rots 118r (3rd entry), http://aalt.law.uh.edu/H4/CP40no555/aCP40no555fronts/IMG_0249.htm, and 165d (first entry), http://aalt.law.uh.edu/H4/CP40no555/bCP40no555dorses/IMG_0347.htm; all discussed below and also in my 'Chronology of John Gower's Life Records'.

[6] *Complete Works*, IV: pp. 368, 420; Gower, *Minor Latin Works with In Praise of Peace*, '*Presul Ouile Regis*', ed. and trans. Robert F. Yeager, http://d.lib.rochester.edu/teams/text/yeager-gower-minor-latin-works-presul-ouile-regis (accessed 3 November 2017).

[7] Nicholas Harris Nicolas, 'John Gower the Poet', *The Retrospective Review, and Historical and Antiquarian Magazine*, second series, 2 (1828), pp. 103–117; *Complete Works* IV: pp. vii–xxix; John H. Fisher, 'A Calendar of Documents Relating to the Life of John Gower the Poet', *The Journal of English and Germanic Philology*, 58 (1959), pp. 1–23; John H. Fisher, *John Gower: Moral Philosopher and Friend of Chaucer* (London: Methuen, 1965); John Hines, Nathalie Cohen, and Simon Roffey, '*Johannes Gower, Armiger, Poeta*: Records and Memorials of his Life and Death', in Siân Echard, ed., *A Companion to Gower* (Cambridge: D. S. Brewer, 2004), pp. 23–41.

provide fresh insights into the biographical context of his works. Gower's most important surviving personal memorials other than his poetry are his testament, written less than ten weeks before his death in 1408, and his tomb. Like his poetry, they are careful images crafted by Gower to serve as public monuments to himself.

This chapter will examine what the newly-expanded corpus of Gower's life-records can reveal about his life, including his Kentish background, his previously-unnoticed claim of descent from the Northwode family, his wealth, his associates, his movements, and his probable sequence of residences. It will consider what Gower's testament and tomb reveal about him, and will also challenge some current assumptions about Gower's marriage and his wife, Agnes Groundolf, and about the location of the chapel of St John the Baptist where they were buried. An Appendix provides the complete texts of four Gower life-records: two deeds of 1366 that link Gower with the Northwode family; a lawsuit of 1394–95 that concerns Gower's house in Southwark; and Gower's testament, made shortly before his death in 1408. For a chronological tabulation of the archival records of Gower's life, see my 'Chronology of John Gower's Life Records', which prefaces this volume.

Gower's Kentish and Family Connections

Scholars have long noted that John Gower had connections with Kent, and have conjectured that Gower's purchase of the manor of Kentwell, Suffolk, which formerly belonged to Sir Robert Gower, of Brabourne, Kent (*d. c.* 1349), and the poet's use of heraldic arms seemingly identical to those of Sir Robert, indicate that he was related to Sir Robert (see Fig. 1.2). However, a roll of arms now in the Bodleian Library reveals that the poet's arms were not quite identical with those of Sir Robert: both used the device of a white or silver (*argent*) shield displaying three golden leopards' heads on a chevron, but Sir Robert's chevron was black (*sable*), while John Gower's chevron was blue (*azure*).[8] New archival evidence expands John Gower's known links

---

[8] Robert Gower's shield ('*Argent on chevron Sable 3 leopard's faces Or*') is depicted in a roll of arms of c. 1345–51 called Powell's Roll (now Bodleian Library, MS Ashmole 804, part IV, p. 55 (old fol. 28r), http://bodley30.bodley.ox.ac.uk:8180/luna/servlet/detail/ODLodl~1~1~31422~108868:Roll-of-arms--Powell-s-Roll--?sort=Shelfmark,Folio_Page&qvq=q:=powell+;sort:Shelfmark,Folio_Page;lc:ODLodl~1~1&mi=29&trs=31 (accessed 5 November 2017). See Thomas Woodcock, Janet Grant, and Ian Graham, eds, *Dictionary of British Arms: Medieval Ordinary* [hereafter *DBA*], volume 2 (London: Society of Antiquaries, 1996), p. 440. John Philipot, Somerset Herald (d. 1645), sketched Sir Robert's memorial brass, including his arms, but with no indication of the colours used in the arms (BL, Harley MS 3917, fol. 77r; reproduced in W[illiam] Warwick, 'On Gower, the Kentish Poet, His Character and Works', *Archaeologia Cantiana*, 6 (1866), pp. 83–107, at 86 (see Fig. 1.2)). The arms of John Gower matched

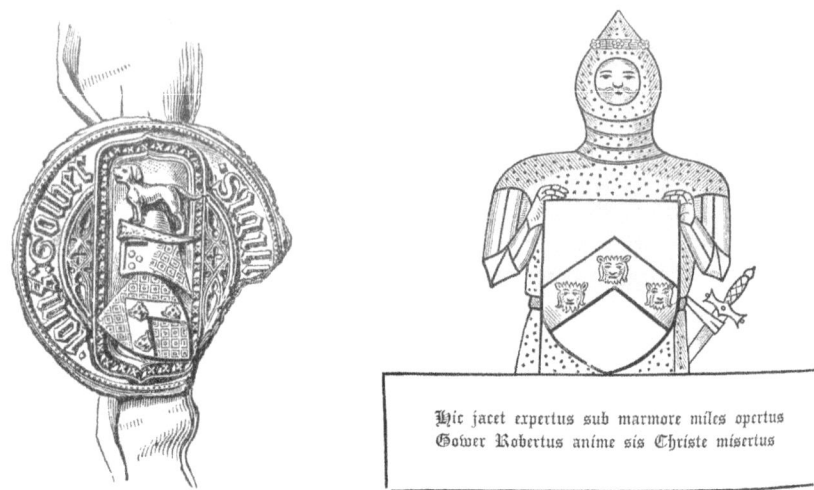

Figure 1.2: *Left*: John Gower's seal, from BL, Harley Charter 50 I. 14 (1373). *Right*: Brass of Sir Robert Gower (d. c. 1349), formerly in Brabourne church, Kent. From William Warwick, 'On Gower, the Kentish Poet, His Character and Works', *Archaeologia Cantiana*, 6 (1866), p. 86. (*Photographs by Martha Carlin, by courtesy of the Institute of Historical Research, University of London.*)[9]

with Kent, and reveals that he claimed descent from another Kentish gentry family, the Northwodes (or Northwoods).

John Gower first occurs in the archival record in Kent, where he was involved in what appears to have been a piece of sharp dealing concerning the

---

those of Sir Robert but had an *azure* (blue) chevron rather than a *sable* (black) chevron. John Gower's were included in a roll of arms known as the 'County Roll', composed *temp.* Richard II and coloured in the early fifteenth century (see *DBA*, II: p. 440), which depicted the arms of nobles, knights, and gentry, grouped by county. The original roll does not survive, but a facsimile was made *c.* 1638–40 under the direction of Sir William Dugdale; it is now London, Society of Antiquaries MS 664/4. John Gower's arms are included under the county of Kent on fol. 20r. John Gower's armorial shield also appeared in a window in the priory church of St Mary Overy, Southwark, where it was sketched in 1611 by two heralds. See BL, Lansdowne MS 874, fol. 82v; reproduced in Francis T. Dollman, *The Priory of St Marie Overie, Southwark* (London: Dryden Press, 1881), plate 39. The same arms are depicted in a memorial page that perhaps dates from around the time of Gower's death in 1408 (Glasgow University Library, MS Hunter 59 [T.2.17], fol. 129r, http://special.lib.gla.ac.uk/manuscripts/search/detail_i.cfm?ID=158 [accessed 9 November 2017]), and in an armorial known as 'Wriothesley's Chevrons', made *c.* 1525 by Sir Thomas Wriothesley, Garter King of Arms (*DBA*, II: p. 440). John Stow described the same arms on Gower's tomb in his *Survey of London*, second edn (1603), ed. Charles L. Kingsford (two volumes; Oxford: Clarendon Press, 1908), II: 58.

9   Sir Robert's brass is taken from a sketch by John Philipot, Somerset Herald (d. 1645), now BL, Harley MS 3917, fol. 77r.

Kentish estates of an under-age heir. On Christmas Day 1364, William, son and heir of Sir William de Septvans, enfeoffed John Gower and his heirs of a 'moiety' (one-half) of the manor of Aldington, and two marshes in Iwade (see Map 1.1). Gower paid Septvans eighty marks (£53 6s. 8d.) for these properties.[10] The 'moiety' had in fact long been an independent manor: by 1066 the former single manor of Aldington had been divided into two manors, later known respectively as Aldington Septvans or West Court (which William de Septvans granted to Gower), and Aldington Cobham or East Court (which was owned by the Cobhams of Sterborough). The two manors lay near Thurnham, where there is still a road called Aldington Lane.[11]

Because William's estates were held 'in chief' (directly of the king), any grant of them to others required a royal licence, and an heir had no legal ability to make such grants until he had reached the age of twenty-one. William's father had died by January 1351, and his mother on 28 October 1356; after her death, an inquisition *post mortem* held at Canterbury (Kent) on 3 December 1356 reported that William was fifteen.[12] In 1364, two inquests held at Canterbury on 18 September and 2 November declared him to be twenty-one.[13] After William had disposed of much of his inheritance, however, another inquest to determine his age was held at Canterbury on 21 April 1366, and it found that, despite the earlier findings that he had been born in 1341 or 1343, he had actually been born on 28 August 1346, and thus would not be of legal age until 28 August 1367.

The same inquest also examined what properties William had alienated and what bonds he had issued while under-age. It found, *inter alia*, that the manor of Aldington that William had granted to Gower was worth £10 per annum, and that it included a wood with a market value of £100, and that the two marshes in Iwade were worth £2 annually. It also found that from Christmas Day 1364 until the following Michaelmas (29 September 1365), William de Septvans had 'continually dwelt in the company of Richard de Hurst and the said John Gower, at Canterbury and elsewhere, and during that whole time he was led and counselled by them to alienate his lands etc.'. In June 1365, while living with Hurst and Gower, Septvans made

---

[10] *Calendar of Inquisitions Post Mortem* [hereafter CIPM], *1365–70*, p. 76.
[11] On Thurnham and the manors of Aldington Septvans (West Court) and Aldington Cobham (East Court), see Edward Hasted, *The History and Topographical Survey of the County of Kent: Volume 5* (Canterbury: W. Bristow, 1798), pp. 525–8. Thurnham lies three miles north-east of Maidstone, at the foot of the North Downs. A trace of Gower's ownership lingered as late as 1642, when one John Gratwicke of Shermanbury (Sussex), yeoman, bequeathed to his son Richard an annuity issuing out of the 'Manor of Aldington West Court alias Aldington Septvans alias Aldington Gower, near Thurnham alias Thernam, co. Kent' (John Comber, 'The Combers of Shermanbury, Chichester and Allington', *Sussex Archaeological Collections*, 49 (1906), pp. 128–56, at 136).
[12] *Calendar of Patent Rolls* [hereafter CPR] *1350–54*, p. 21; CIPM *1352–61*, p. 274.
[13] CIPM *1361–65*, pp. 465, 468.

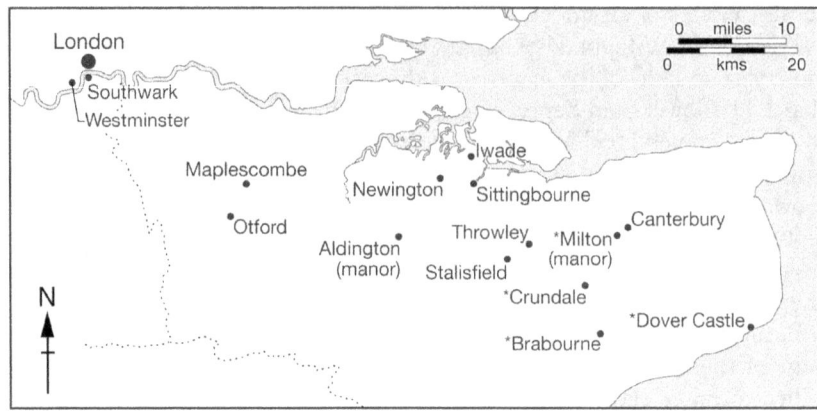

Map 1.1: Places in Kent and metropolitan London where John Gower held property, resided for a time, or visited. Places in which Gower's residence is possible but not certain are marked with an asterisk. (*Source: Tables 1.1 and 1.2. Map courtesy of Nick Higham and Cath D'Alton.*)

additional financial commitments to Gower, quitclaiming to him the manor of Aldington, together with an annual rent of 14s. 6d., a cock, thirteen hens and 140 eggs in Maplescombe (Kent), and the homages and services of the tenants; binding himself to pay Gower £60 by the feast of All Saints (1 November) 1365; and granting to Gower, his heirs and assigns an annual rent of £10 to be taken from his manor of Wigborough (Essex) and other estates in that county. The inquest also found that William had made similar grants to Hurst and others. Evidently, the matter was considered very serious, and the following month (May 1366) it was brought before parliament, which reviewed the evidence of the inquest, annulled all the grants and bonds made to Gower and others by the under-age Septvans, and ordered the properties in question to be seized into the king's hands.[14]

The case concerning Gower was finally resolved in February 1368, a few months after William de Septvans had turned twenty-one, when royal licences enabled Septvans to enfeoff Gower once more with the same properties and rents in Kent, though evidently not the annual rent of £10 in Essex.[15] An original deed, not previously noticed by scholars, by which

---

[14] *CIPM 1365–70*, pp. 75–79; 'Edward III: May 1366', in *Parliament Rolls of Medieval England*, eds Chris Given-Wilson, Paul Brand, Seymour Phillips, Mark Ormrod, Geoffrey Martin, Anne Curry and Rosemary Horrox (Woodbridge: Boydell, 2005) (*British History Online* http://www.british-history.ac.uk/no-series/parliament-rolls-medieval/may-1366, (accessed 17 January 2017); *Complete Works*, IV: p. xi; Fisher, *John Gower*, pp. 50–54. See also *CIPM 1348–77*, 221 (no. 596); TNA, C 143/356/11; *CPR 1364–7*, p. 99; *Calendar of Close Rolls* [hereafter *CCR*] *1364–8*, p. 185; 'L.B.L.' [Lambert B. Larking], '"Probatio Ætatis" of William de Septvans, from the Surrenden Collection', *Archæologia Cantiana*, 1 (1858), pp. 124–36, at 128.

[15] *CPR 1367–70*, pp. 83, 96.

William de Septvaunz granted 'his entire marsh in the parish of Iwade' to John Gower on 10 March 1368, is now British Library, Additional Charter 68771. It is sealed with Septvans' armorial seal, and would have been the actual charter that Gower received from him in 1368.

The Septvans case appears to reflect poorly on Gower's probity. George Macaulay famously agonized over identifying the poet with the 'villanous' and 'disreputable character who for his own ends encouraged the young William Septvans in dishonesty and extravagance'.[16] Not all scholars judge Gower's behaviour harshly. Sebastian Sobecki, for example, has argued that Gower's role in the Septvans case was not discreditable, but rather reflected Gower's legal expertise. Matthew Giancarlo presents a more equivocal view of Gower's role in the Septvans affair, but nevertheless underplays Gower's unethical and illegal pressure on the under-age heir to alienate his patrimony, and represents Gower as having successfully withstood the legal challenges to his property acquisitions.[17] Such interpretations sidestep the judgment implicit in parliament's annulment of all of Septvans' grants, including those to Gower. (For yet another view, see Michael Bennett's discussion of the Septvans affair in Chapter 13, below.)

In addition to shedding some light on Gower's character, the Septvans case provides a few hints about the poet's origins. Because Gower's own age was never at issue, he must have been at least twenty-one by Christmas 1364, and thus was born before Christmas 1343. An inscription on Gower's tomb (discussed at the end of this chapter) recorded that Gower had lived in the reigns of Edward III (r. 1327–77) and Richard II (r. 1377–99). Gower thus probably was born between 1327 and 1343, perhaps sometime in the 1330s. The nine months from Christmas 1364 to Michaelmas 1365 when William de Septvans was living with Richard de Hurst and John Gower in Canterbury 'and elsewhere' represents the earliest record of Gower's physical location. He and Hurst may have stayed at William's townhouse in Canterbury and at his principal manor of Milton, just outside Canterbury, and perhaps also at other Septvans estates that William had not yet alienated or leased out.[18]

Gower's interest in acquiring the Septvans manor of Aldington near Thurnham may have been linked to his relationship with the family of Sir Roger de Northwode (d. 1361), which also had estates in that vicinity. Sir Roger's widow Agnes (d. 1404–5), who was also the widow of John, second Lord Cobham (d. 1355), held dower properties that included lands in both

---

[16] *Complete Works*, IV: pp. xiv–xv.
[17] Sebastian Sobecki, 'A Southwark Tale: Gower, the 1381 Poll Tax, and Chaucer's *The Canterbury Tales*', *Speculum*, 92 (2017), pp. 630–60, at 631–2; Matthew Giancarlo, *Parliament and Literature in Late Medieval England* (Cambridge: Cambridge University Press, 2007), pp. 94–105.
[18] CIPM 1365–70, 75–79; for Kentish properties that William's father had held by knight service, see also *Inquisitions and Assessments relating to Feudal Aids* [hereafter *Feudal Aids*], A.D. 1284–1431, vol. 3, *Kent-Norfolk*, pp. 16, 20, 26, 40, 54; cf. p. 76.

Iwade and Thurnham in Kent.[19] Another of her dower properties was an annual quitrent (fixed rent) of £12 from property in the London parish of St Mary Colechurch. In 1366 Gower claimed to have a reversionary interest in this quitrent by 'inheritance' ('*de hereditate predicti Johannis Gower*': discussed below), as well as by grant from Sir Roger's son and heir Sir John de Northwode (d. 1379).[20] Gower's claim to the quitrent by 'inheritance' implies that he was descended from Sir Roger de Northwode's branch of the Northwode family. Since Gower used arms resembling those of Sir Robert Gower on his own seal by 1373, and later on his tomb (see Figs. 1.2, 1.10), his implied claim of descent from Sir Roger de Northwode's family may mean that Gower's mother (or another female ancestor) was a Northwode.

Other property-holders in this part of Kent in the fourteenth century included Sir John Cobham, third baron Cobham of Cobham (Agnes de Northwode's stepson, d. 1408); his distant cousin Reginald, first lord Cobham of Sterborough (d. 1361); and Sir Arnald Savage of Bobbing (d. 1410). Lord Cobham of Sterborough, Sir Arnald Savage, and (for a time) the Northwodes were among the gentry and magnates from southern counties who maintained residences in Southwark, and this may have been a factor in Gower's eventual decision to move there himself.[21] Southwark, which lay on the south bank of the Thames, across London Bridge from the city of London, was also convenient for travel to and from Kent and other southern counties, and was unaffected by London's nightly curfew, which closed the city's gates, including the gate on London Bridge.

---

[19] *CIPM 1361–5*, pp. 147–8; *CIPM 1377–1413*, p. 301. Agnes, widow of Sir John Cobham, second Lord Cobham of Cobham (d. 1355) and of Sir Roger de Northwode (1307–61), was the daughter of Richard Stone of Dartford. Peter Fleming, 'Cobham family (*per. c.1250–c.1530*)', *Oxford Dictionary of National Biography* [hereafter *ODNB*] (Oxford: Oxford University Press, 2004; online edn, Jan 2008; http://www.oxforddnb.com/view/article/52781, accessed 22 July 2017); Charles L. Kingsford, 'Northwood, John, first Lord Northwood (1254–1319)', rev. Andrew Ayton, *ODNB* (http://www.oxforddnb.com/view/article/20336, accessed 22 July 2017).

[20] London Metropolitan Archives [hereafter LMA], Husting Roll [hereafter HR] 94/36 (17 March 1366), 94/107 (18 July 1366), transcribed in Appendix 1–2; *CIPM 1377–1413*, p. 12; Derek J. Keene and Vanessa Harding, 'St Mary Colechurch 105/19', in *Historical Gazetteer of London before the Great Fire: Cheapside; Parishes of All Hallows Honey Lane, St Martin Pomary, St Mary Le Bow, St Mary Colechurch and St Pancras Soper Lane* (London: Chadwyck-Healey, 1987), pp. 518–26 (*British History Online*, http://www.british-history.ac.uk/no-series/london-gazetteer-pre-fire/pp518-526, accessed 26 June 2017).

[21] On magnate townhouses in Southwark before 1500, see Martha Carlin, *Medieval Southwark* (London: Hambledon, 1996), pp. 25–52. Cf. Elliot Kendall, *Lordship and Literature: John Gower and the Politics of the Great Household* (Oxford: Clarendon, 2008), pp. 37–41.

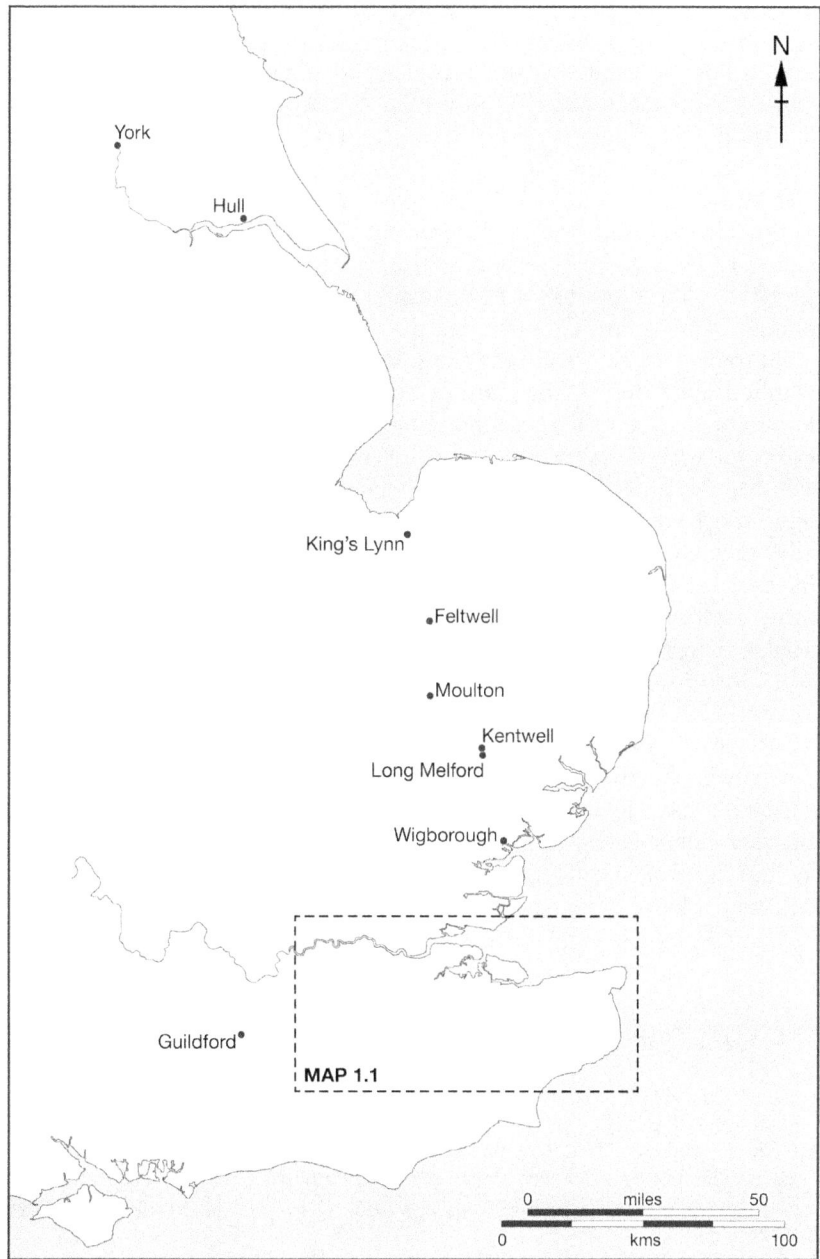

Map 1.2: Places outside Kent and metropolitan London where John Gower held property, resided for a time, or visited. (*Source: Tables 1.1 and 1.2. Map courtesy of Nick Higham and Cath D'Alton.*)

Property Acquisitions: 1364–69, 1381–82

Gower's known acquisitions of income-producing properties all took place in two brief periods: 1364–69 and 1381–82. After obtaining the manor of Aldington and other properties from William de Septvans, Gower's next known acquisition was the annual quitrent of £12 in the London parish of St Mary Colechurch mentioned above. On 17 March 1366 Sir John de Northwode, son and heir of the late Sir Roger de Northwode (d. 1361), granted to Gower the reversion of this quitrent; four months later, on 18 July 1366, Gower granted it to Simon de Benyngton, citizen and draper of London. In his grant, Gower noted that the quitrent was at that time held for life by Sir Roger's widow, Agnes, and that the reversion of it was his by 'inheritance' and by the grant of Sir John (see Appendix 1–2, below).[22] Gower chose to sell the reversion immediately rather than wait for Agnes's death – a wise decision, since she survived for almost forty years (until 1404–5), and only then did her dower properties revert to their respective heirs.[23] On 1 June 1367 Gower acquired another quitrent, of £10 per annum, to be taken from all the lands in Kent and London belonging to John Gravesende, citizen and draper of London.[24] It is not known what became of this latter quitrent; Gower may have disposed of it, or he may have transferred it to feoffees (trustees) acting on his behalf.

In 1368 Gower began the process of acquiring the manor of Kentwell (or Kentwell Hall) in Long Melford, Suffolk. This manor had been held in chief by Sir Robert Gower of Brabourne, Kent, who had died c. 1349. Sir Robert's co-heirs were his two daughters, Katherine and Joan; after Katherine's death in 1366 her sister Joan, wife of William Neve (or Nene) of Weeting, Norfolk, inherited her share.[25] On 28 June 1368, Joan and her second husband, Thomas Syward, citizen and pewterer of London, granted Kentwell to Gower and issued a letter of attorney to put him in seisin of it.[26]

---

[22] LMA, HR 94/36, 107; Keene and Harding, *Historical Gazetteer of London*, property 105/19.
[23] *CIPM 1377–1413*, p. 301.
[24] *CCR 1364–8*, p. 379.
[25] *CCR 1354–60*, p. 358. On Sir Robert Gower and his daughters, see Nicholas Harris Nicolas, 'John Gower, the Poet', *The Retrospective Review, and Historical and Antiquarian Magazine*, 2nd series, 2 (1828), pp. 103–17, at 107; Fisher, *John Gower*, pp. 47–50.
[26] BL, Harley Ch. 56 G. 42 (grant) and 56 G. 41 (letter of attorney). The grant still preserves the two small red seals of Thomas and Joan, and is endorsed on the back in French: '*la Chatre Thomas Syward et Jehane sa / fem[m]e del Manoir de Kentewelle*' ('the Charter of Thomas Syward and Joan his wife of the Manor of Kentewelle'). I am grateful to Jenny Stratford for the information that the hand of this endorsement probably dates from the very end of the fourteenth century or the early fifteenth century, by which time the manor and its title deeds were no longer in Gower's hands.

Table 1.1: John Gower's recorded investment properties and rents (*for sources, see corresponding entries in the 'Chronology of John Gower's Life Records'*)

County	Property or rent	Net value per annum	Notes	Date acquired	Date alienated
Essex	Annual rent from manor of Wigborough and other lands (unspecified) in Essex	£10 rent	Granted to Gower by William de Septvans	23 June 1365	Forfeited to the Crown in 1366
Kent	Manor of Aldington [Septvans]	£10 (valued 21 April 1366); £5 2s. 4d. (valued 23 Nov. 1373)	Granted to Gower by William de Septvans; Gower paid him £53 6s. 8d. for Aldington and the two marshes in Iwade	25 Dec 1364; forfeited to the Crown 1366; re-granted 1368	Michaelmas term 1381 x May 1391
Kent	Marshes of 'Lokelyng' and 'Herlyng' in Iwade	£2 (valued 21 April 1366)	Granted to Gower by William de Septvans	25 Dec 1364; forfeited 1366; re-granted 10 Mar. 1368	Unknown
Kent	Rent in Maplescombe (near Otford)	14s. 6d. and one cock, 13 hens and 140 eggs	Granted to Gower by William de Septvans	June 1365; forfeited 1366; re-granted 1368	Unknown (Gower dated a grant at nearby Otford on 29 Sept. 1373)
Kent	Unspecified lands in Throwley and Stalisfield	Unknown	Quitclaimed to John Gower and John Bowland, clerk, by Isabel daughter of Walter de Huntyngfelde	3 Feb. 1381	Unknown
Kent and London	Rent from unspecified lands	£10 rent	Granted to Gower by John Gravesende, citizen and draper of London	1 June 1367	Unknown

Table 1.1: *Continues*

County	Property or rent	Net value per annum	Notes	Date acquired	Date alienated
London	Quitrent in parish of St Mary Colechurch	£12 rent	Reversion granted to Gower by Sir John de Northwode	17 March 1366	18 July 1366
Norfolk	Manor of Feltwell	£40 rent for the manors of Feltwell (Norfolk) and Moulton (Suffolk) together, 6 Aug. 1382; £20 rent for Feltwell only, 24 Feb. 1410	Granted to Gower by Guy de Rouclif (probably acting as feoffee for Dame Elizabeth Luttrell)	1 Aug. 1382	Rent left by Gower to his wife Agnes, 1408; by 24 Feb. 1410 Feltwell was owned by Sir Hugh Luttrell, who granted the rent to Agnes for her lifetime
Suffolk	Manor of Kentwell	Valued at £10 13s. 4d. per annum by inquisition *ad quod damnum*	Granted to Gower by Thomas Syward, citizen and pewterer of London, and Joan his wife, daughter of Sir Robert Gower	28 June 1368; granted by Gower to feoffees, 29 Sept. 1373	Sold by Gower's feoffees c. Feb. 1380
Suffolk	Manor of Moulton	£40 rent for the manors of Feltwell (Norfolk) and Moulton (Suffolk) together, 6 Aug. 1382	Granted to Gower by Guy de Rouclif (probably acting as feoffee for Dame Elizabeth Luttrell)	1 Aug. 1382	Rent left by Gower to his wife Agnes, 1408; manor owned by Sir Hugh Luttrell by 1410

On 22 July 1368 an inquisition *ad quod damnum* (an inquest held to determine if it would be to the king's damage to allow property held in chief to be alienated, and to assess the property's value and the service due to the king) reported that Kentwell was held of the king in chief by service of one knight's fee, and was worth £10 13s. 4d. per annum. Gower paid the Crown a fine of sixteen marks (£10 13s. 4d.), *i.e.*, one year's income from the manor, for a pardon for obtaining it without licence.[27] Gower appears to have been short of funds at that time, for the very next day (23 July) he issued a recognizance (an acknowledgment of a debt) of £20 to Richard Ravensere, a senior royal administrator, using his 'lands and chattels in Suffolk' (his newly-acquired manor of Kentwell) as collateral for repayment.[28] It evidently took Gower a year to complete his payment for Kentwell to Sir Robert Gower's daughter Joan and her husband, for on 25 June 1369 he paid 200 marks cash (£133 6s. 8d.) to John Spenythorn and Joan his wife – the same Joan, now married to a third husband – and they in turn relinquished all right in Kentwell to Gower.[29]

At Michaelmas (29 September) 1373, Gower transferred his manor of Kentwell to five men: Sir John de Kobham (Cobham), William de Weston, Roger de Asshebournhame, Thomas de Brokhell (Brokhull, Brokhill), and Thomas de Preston, rector of the church of Tunstall,[30] and then or soon after Gower also transferred his manor of Aldington to the same five men.[31] Inquests *ad quod damnum* were held by the escheators of Suffolk and Kent to determine what these manors were worth and what they owed annually to the king. The jurors in Suffolk reported that Kentwell was worth £10 a year and was held of the king by service of 65s. per annum.[32] The jurors in Kent reported that Aldington contained a capital messuage (manor house) of no net value per annum, 100 acres of arable land worth 34s. 4d. per annum, at 4d. per acre, forty acres of woodland (*subbosci*) worth 6s. 8d. per annum,

---

[27] TNA, C 143/364/4; CPR 1367–70, p. 146.
[28] The money was repaid, and the recognizance was cancelled (CCR 1364–68, p. 482). On Ravensere, who at this time was a greater clerk of Chancery and archdeacon of Lincoln, see Alison K. McHardy, 'Ravenser, Richard (d. 1386)', ODNB (http://www.oxforddnb.com/view/article/23173, accessed 7 July 2017).
[29] BL, Harley Ch. 50 I. 13; Nicolas, 'John Gower, the Poet', p. 109. Joan's identification is made clear in deeds of 1369–75, which describe her as Joan, the wife of John Spenythorn (or Spynythorn), citizen and tailor of London, 'sometime the wife of Thomas Syward, late citizen and pewterer of London' (LMA, HR 97/192, 193 (1369), 98/143 (1370), 101/22 (1372), 103/77 (1375)).
[30] BL, Harley Ch. 50 I. 14. This charter retains an excellent impression of Gower's seal. There is a drawing of this seal in Warwick, 'On Gower, the Kentish Poet', p. 86 (see Fig. 1.2; cf. Fig. 1.11). On 8 October 1373 Weston was appointed by the other four feoffees to take seisin of Kentwell on behalf of all of them (BL, Harley Ch. 48 E. 29).
[31] TNA, C 143/382/2 (2) (inquisition *ad quod damnum* concerning the manor of Aldington, Kent, 23 November 1373).
[32] TNA, C 143/382/2 (6) (inquisition *ad quod damnum* held at Melford, Suffolk, 5 November 1373).

at 2*d*. per acre, forty-eight hens (*gall'*) worth 8*s*., at 2*d*. each, and that the assize-rents (fixed rents) of the free tenants came to 53*s*. 4*d*. per annum. It was held of the king in chief by military service and 13*s*. per annum.[33] On 8 April 1374 the five men paid twelve marks (£8) to the Crown as a fine for having acquired these two manors without a licence.[34]

Many scholars, including John Fisher,[35] have assumed that these transfers were outright grants, but in fact the five men to whom the manors were transferred were acting as Gower's feoffees (trustees), and they held the properties on Gower's behalf for some years.[36] Gower probably began the process of selling Kentwell in the autumn of 1379, when he recorded the final concord made a decade earlier by which John and Joan Spenythorn had granted him the manor; this presumably was a way of confirming his title to it.[37] The disposal of Kentwell had begun by 23 February 1380, when Katharine, wife of Thomas de Clopton, knight, paid ten marks (£6 13*s*. 4*d*.) for a licence for Gower's five feoffees to grant to her and to four named men, in fee, the manor of Kentwell, Suffolk, which was held of the king by the service of rendering 65*s*. annually for castle-guard of Norwich castle.[38] The Cloptons' acquisition of Kentwell was complete by 19 June 1380, when Sir Thomas Clopton let the manor to a tenant for five years.[39]

During at least part of this period Gower evidently dwelt, or intended to dwell, at Aldington in Kent, for in Michaelmas term 1381, by his attorney William Emery, he sued Walter Cook, carpenter, in the court of Common Pleas for not fulfilling a contract to build for Gower's use, and at Gower's expense, a new house in the manor of Aldington. Cook did not appear, and the sheriff of Kent was ordered to attach him to appear in the quindene of Hilary (27 January–2 February 1382).[40] By May 1391, however, Gower, through his feoffees, had disposed of Aldington, since by then Thomas Brokhill (or Brokhull), one of Gower's former feoffees, held the manor in

---

[33] TNA, C 143/382/2 (2) and (4) (inquisitions *ad quod damnum* held at Rochester, Kent, 23 November and 6 December 1373).
[34] *CPR 1370–74*, p. 425.
[35] Fisher, *John Gower*, p. 53.
[36] On 6 March 1376 Weston quitclaimed his right in Kentwell to Preston, Asshebournham and Brokhull, and Cobham did the same on 3 November, ?1377 (the year is unclear in the MS, but appears to be 1 Richard II) (BL, Harley Ch. 57 G. 43 and Harley Ch. 48 E. 32).
[37] BL, Harley Ch. 50 I. 13.
[38] *CPR 1377–81*, p. 444.
[39] BL, Harley Ch. 48 D. 2.
[40] TNA, CP 40/483, rots. 144d (6th entry), http://aalt.law.uh.edu/AALT6/R2/CP40no483/483_0307.htm, 488r (3rd entry), http://aalt.law.uh.edu/AALT6/R2/CP40no483/483_0999.htm. Michael Bennett has reached a similar conclusion concerning Gower's tenure and occupation of Aldington. See Michael Bennett, 'John Gower, Squire of Kent, the Peasants' Revolt, and the *Visio Anglie*', *Chaucer Review*, 53 (2018), pp. 258–82.

chief, and Brokhill shortly after settled it on himself for life, with remainder to his daughter and son-in-law and their heirs.[41]

On 3 February 1381 Gower obtained additional lands in Kent. Isabel, daughter of Walter de Huntyngfelde, quitclaimed to John Gower and John Bowlond (or Bouland), clerk (discussed below), all her father's lands in Throwley and Stalisfield, around thirteen to fifteen miles by road to the east of Thurnham.[42] The value of these lands is not known, nor is it known what Gower and Bouland did with them.

In August 1382 Gower acquired his last known investment properties, the manors of Feltwell (later known as South Hall)[43] in Norfolk, and Moulton in Suffolk. The two manors previously had belonged to Dame Elizabeth Luttrell (d. 1395), widow of Sir Andrew Luttrell (d. 1378). She was the daughter of Hugh Courtenay, tenth earl of Devon, and, through her mother Margaret (daughter of Humphrey VII de Bohun, earl of Hereford and Essex), was a great-granddaughter of Edward I.[44] Dame Elizabeth apparently had obtained the manors of Feltwell and Moulton by 1370,[45] and on 20 February 1380 she

---

[41] TNA, C 143/411/15 (inquisition *ad quod damnum*: writ, 5 May 1391; inquest, 21 July 1391). The jurors reported that Aldington was held in chief by knight service and by service of 14s. per annum for the guard of Rochester Castle, and that it was worth £4 19s. 7d. per annum in all its issues. They also reported that it would not be to the loss of the king or others if Brokhill, through feoffees, settled the manor on himself for life, with remainder to William Pympe and Joan his wife (Brokhill's daughter) and the heirs of their bodies, with remainder to his own right heirs. Brokhill duly granted the manor to the feoffees in 15 Richard II (22 June 1391 x 21 June 1392) (*Calendarium Inquisitionum Post Mortem sive Escaetarum*, vol. 3 (1377–1413) (London: Record Commission, 1821), p. 142); cf. *CPR 1396–99*, p. 462.

[42] *CCR 1377–81*, p. 505.

[43] Francis Blomefield, 'Hundred of Grimeshou: Feltwell', in *An Essay Towards A Topographical History of the County of Norfolk: Volume 2* (London: William Miller, 1805), pp. 187–200 (*British History* Online, http://www.british-history.ac.uk/topographical-hist-norfolk/vol2/pp187-200, accessed 12 July 2017).

[44] Robert W. Dunning, 'Luttrell family (*per.* c.1200–1428)', *ODNB* (http://www.oxforddnb.com/view/article/54529, accessed 10 July 2017); Robert N. Swanson, 'Courtenay, William (1341/2–1396)', *ODNB* (http://www.oxforddnb.com/view/article/6457, accessed 15 July 2017). In 1315 William de Beauchamp (*de Bello Campo*) was lord of Feltwell (*CCR 1313–18*, p. 208). The Beauchamps retained an interest both in Gower's manor, which was later known as South Hall, and in another manor in Feltwell, later known as East Hall (*CCR 1381–85*, p. 202; TNA, C 143/409/3 (inquisition *ad quod damnum*, 1390); Blomefield, 'Hundred of Grimeshou: Feltwell', in *An Essay Towards A Topographical History of the County of Norfolk: Volume 2*, pp. 187–200).

[45] Indented deed of covenant by Sir John Chevereston to Dame Elizabeth de Luterell, 1 August 1370 (Taunton, Somerset Heritage Centre [hereafter SHC], DD\L/P37/38 (Luttrell Family of Dunster MSS, Box 37); see http://somerset-cat.swheritage.org.uk/records/DD/L/P37/38. Cf. a final concord between John de Chyuereston, 'Chivaler', querent, and Hugh de Chyuereston, deforciant, concerning five manors including Multon and Feltwell in 1352 (TNA, CP 25/1/287/44, no. 470 (http://aalt.law.uh.edu/AALT4/CP25%281%29/CP_25_1_287/IMG_0879.htm); and the quitclaim[?] by Sir John Chevereston to Dame Elizabeth Luterell of 'all the lands he claimed to hold of

and Sir Matthew Gornay granted them to Thomas de Catherton 'and others', who probably held them as feoffees on her behalf.[46] On 1 August 1382 Guy de Rouclif (Rouclyf, Rouclyff), clerk, who had obtained the two manors by feoffment of Thomas de Catherton, granted them to John Gower, esquire, of Kent.[47] This is the first known reference to Gower as 'esquire'.

Dame Elizabeth Luttrell (née Courtenay) was the sister of Margaret Courtenay (d. 1395), wife of Sir John Cobham, third baron Cobham (d. 1408). Their brother, William Courtenay, was successively bishop of Hereford (1370–75), bishop of London (1375–81), and archbishop of Canterbury (1381–96). Dame Elizabeth died at Bermondsey Abbey near Southwark on 7 August 1395,[48] and it seems likely that in earlier years she had spent time in London, perhaps to visit her sister and brother-in-law, who had a townhouse there, or to see her brother William, who in 1381 would have moved from the episcopal palace in the precinct of St Paul's Cathedral to the archiepiscopal palace across the river in Lambeth.[49] If so, Gower's association with Sir John Cobham, and his own periodic visits to the capital (discussed below), might have resulted in contact with Lady Luttrell that led to his acquisition of these manors.

Within days of acquiring the manors of Feltwell and Moulton, Gower handed them over to tenants. On 3 August 1382 he gave Guy de Rouclif a release of the warranty in the charter whereby Rouclif had granted the manor of Feltwell to Gower, his heirs and assigns; this suggests that Rouclif, like Catherton, had acted as Lady Luttrell's feoffee. On 4 August 1382 Dame Elizabeth quitclaimed the manors of Feltwell and Moulton to Gower.[50] On 6 August Gower demised (leased) both manors, for his lifetime, to Thomas Blakelake, parson of St Nicholas Feltwell, John Sybile, Edmund Lakynghethe and John Wermyngton. According to the terms of the demise, the annual rent

---

her in the manors of Feltewell in Norfolk, of Moleton and of Debenham in Suffolk', 1376 (SHC, DD\L/P37/39, Luttrell Family of Dunster MSS, Box 37, http://somerset-cat.swheritage.org.uk/records/DD/L/P37/39).

[46] SHC, DD\L/P37/40 (Luttrell Family of Dunster MSS, Box 37); see http://somerset-cat.swheritage.org.uk/records/DD/L/P37/40.

[47] *CCR 1381–85*, p. 211. Rouclif was working in the Privy Seal office by 1370 (*Issue Roll of Thomas de Brantingham, Bishop of Exeter, Lord High Treasurer of England*, ed. Frederick Devon (London: John Rodwell, 1835), p. 401). He died in 1392; see n. 192, below.

[48] Rosamund Allen, 'Cobham, John, Third Baron Cobham of Cobham (c.1320–1408)', *ODNB* (http://www.oxforddnb.com/view/article/5744, accessed 12 July 2017); Sir H[enry] C. Maxwell Lyte, *History of Dunster* (two volumes; London: St Catherine Press, 1909), I: 76–7.

[49] On the episcopal palace, see William Sparrow Simpson, 'The Palaces or Town Houses of the Bishops of London', *Transactions of the London and Middlesex Archaeological Society*, n.s. 1 (1905), pp. 13–71.

[50] *CCR 1381–85*, pp. 214, 220. The original quitclaim, with an armorial seal of Dame Elizabeth Luterell, is now SHC, DD\L/P37/41 (Luttrell Family of Dunster MSS, Box 37); see http://somerset-cat.swheritage.org.uk/records/DD/L/P37/41.

of £40 for the two manors was to be paid 'in the abbey church of the monks of Westminster', and the tenants were to be responsible for maintaining and repairing any houses pertaining to the manors.[51] Gower himself is described in these documents as 'John Gower, esquire, of Kent'. The requirement that the rent be paid in Westminster Abbey strongly suggests either that Gower lodged in the vicinity of Westminster Abbey when he visited London, or else that he had an agent who was based in Westminster. Deeds concerning real property that were issued to or by married persons generally were made in the names of both spouses. Since none of the deeds issued to or by Gower mentions a wife, Gower probably was not married during the years 1364–69 and 1381–82.

In Michaelmas term 1395 and Easter term 1396, Gower sued Thomas Forester and John Gay in the court of Common Pleas, accusing each of them of having failed to render a reasonable account for his term as Gower's bailiff of Feltwell and his receiver of monies.[52] Around the same time Gower sued John Cook of Feltwell and William Cook of Exning, Suffolk (near Moulton), for non-payment of a debt of ten marks (£6 13s. 4d.).[53] The suit against Forester and Gay implies that Gower had been managing Feltwell directly, through his own manorial officer, and thus was no longer leasing out the entire manor to a tenant. The suits against John Cook of Feltwell and William Cook of Exning suggest that Gower was in direct contact with affairs in both Feltwell and Moulton, and so may have been managing the latter manor directly as well. Similarly, in Michaelmas term 1399 Gower sued Walter Clerk (or Clerkes) of Little Cressingham, Norfolk (about fourteen miles by road north-east of Feltwell), for a debt of £30 5s. 8½d., and William and Denise Fisshere of Shropham, Norfolk (about twenty-one miles by road east of Feltwell), for a debt of 40s.[54] This may mean that Gower visited Feltwell and was still active in its management. In 1401–02 royal commissioners for

---

[51] *CCR 1381–85*, pp. 218, 426.
[52] In Michaelmas term 1395, Gower appeared twice against Forester and Gay, the first time in person, and the second time by his attorney John Drake. In Easter term 1396, Gower once more appeared in person. On each of these occasions Forester and Gay failed to appear, and the sheriff of Norfolk was ordered to arrest them and to bring them to the court, respectively, on the octaves of Hilary 1396, the quindene of Hilary 1396, and the quindene of Trinity 1396 (TNA, CP 40/539, rots 511r (last entry), http://aalt.law.uh.edu/AALT6/R2/CP40no539/539_1202.htm, and 535r (5th entry), http://aalt.law.uh.edu/AALT6/R2/CP40no539/539_1259.htm; CP 40/541, rot. 46r (4th entry), http://aalt.law.uh.edu/AALT6/R2/CP40no541a/aCP40no541afronts/IMG_0101.htm). The latter case is discussed by Sebastian Sobecki ('A Southwark Tale', pp. 636, 658).
[53] On 24 October 1396 the two men, who had been outlawed in the London court of Husting for non-appearance in the court of Common Pleas in this matter, were pardoned of their outlawry (*CPR 1396–99*, p. 128).
[54] TNA, CP40/555, rots 74d (1st entry), http://aalt.law.uh.edu/H4/CP40no555/bCP40no555dorses/IMG_0149.htm, and 165d (1st entry), http://aalt.law.uh.edu/H4/CP40no555/bCP40no555dorses/IMG_0347.htmCP40/555, rot. 118r (3rd entry),

a feudal aid assessed Gower as holding one knight's fee in Norfolk of the earl of Arundel, who held it of the king, but there is no mention of Gower holding any other manors by military service.[55] Thus in 1401–02 Gower still evidently had title to Feltwell, but perhaps no longer to Moulton.

When Gower made his testament on 15 August 1408, he bequeathed to his wife Agnes the 'farms' (rents) of his manors of '*Southwell*' in the county of '*North*' (evidently a scribal error for Feltwell in Norfolk), and Moulton in Suffolk, 'as can be more fully ascertained in a certain writing made under my seal and the seals of others' (see Appendix 4, below). The actual ownership of both Feltwell and Moulton passed to Dame Elizabeth Luttrell's son and heir, Sir Hugh Luttrell (*d.* 1428).[56] In Hilary term 1410, Gower's widow Agnes and the four men who served with her as executors of Gower's testament, by their attorney, sued Sir Hugh in the court of Common Pleas for the unjust detinue of fifty marks (£33 6s. 8d.). Luttrell failed to appear, 'as before', and the sheriff of Surrey was ordered to arrest him and have him appear in Common Pleas in the quindene of Easter.[57] Sir Hugh then came to terms with Agnes: on 24 February 1410, he granted to 'Agnes Gower, late the wife of John Gower, esquire', during her lifetime, a yearly rent of £20 to be taken from his manor of Feltwell, with power to distrain for arrears there and in his manor of Moulton.[58] This suggests that Agnes by now retained only a single annual rent of £20, from Feltwell.

Gower's Income
(For Sources, See 'Chronology of John Gower's Life Records')

John Gower was already a man of means by December 1364, when he paid eighty marks (£53 6s. 8d.) for the manor of Aldington and two marshes in Iwade. The source of this wealth is unknown; he may have inherited it from parents or other relations, or he may have earned money from mercantile

---

http://aalt.law.uh.edu/H4/CP40no555/aCP40no555fronts/IMG_0249.htm. These cases are discussed in Sobecki, 'A Southwark Tale', pp. 637–8, 658–60.

[55] *Feudal Aids 1284–1431*, vol. 3, *Kent–Norfolk*, Appendix, p. 654; cf. pp. viii–ix, xi. Gower thus did not hold Feltwell in chief: the earl of Arundel was the tenant-in-chief, and Gower owed Arundel an annual quitrent.

[56] 'Luttrell, Sir Hugh (c. 1364–1428), of Dunster, Som.', in *The History of Parliament: The House of Commons, 1386–1421*, ed. John S. Roskell, Linda Clark, and Carole Rawcliffe (Stroud: Alan Sutton, for the History of Parliament Trust, 1993) [hereafter *HPHC*] (http://www.historyofparliamentonline.org/volume/1386-1421/member/luttrell-sir-hugh-1364-1428, accessed 12 July 2017).

[57] TNA, CP 40/596, rot. 232d (5th entry from bottom), (http://aalt.law.uh.edu/H4/CP40no596/bCP40no596dorses/IMG_1594.htm).

[58] *CCR 1409–13*, pp 80–1.

or professional work of some kind.[59] In 1365 his income from the Septvans properties in Aldington, Iwade, Maplescombe, and Essex amounted to about £23, but in May 1366 these lands and rents were confiscated by the Crown. In March 1366 Gower obtained a quitrent in London worth £12 per annum, but disposed of it four months later. Gower's income in 1366 from these lands and rents probably was around £15. In 1367 Gower's only known income was an annual rent of £10 from unspecified lands in Kent and London. In 1368 Gower received a new grant from William de Septvans of the manor of Aldington, a marsh in Iwade, and the rents in Maplescombe but not in Essex. From 1368 to 1380 Gower's income was perhaps around £29 per annum: £8 from the re-granted Septvans properties (Aldington's annual value had fallen by 1373 to £5 2s. 4d.), £10 from the rent in London and Kent, and £10 13s. 4d. from Gower's new manor of Kentwell. Gower sold Kentwell c. February 1380, and a year later he acquired unspecified lands of unknown value in Throwley and Stalisfield. If they were worth about £2 per annum, and if Gower retained his other lands and rents, his income from 1380 to 1382 would have been around £20 per annum. In August 1382, Gower bought the manors of Feltwell and Moulton, which he then leased out for £40 per annum. To help pay for these manors, Gower may have sold off his lands and rents whose disposition is otherwise unknown. If so, and if Gower held onto Aldington until about 1385 (when he was last referred to as 'of Kent'), his annual income from 1382 to 1385 would have reached around £45, or just over 17s. per week. After Gower disposed of Aldington (sometime between autumn 1381 and May 1391), his income from Feltwell and Moulton would have been £40 per annum, or just over 15s. per week. Gower's approximate annual income from his known lands and rents is summarised in Table 1.2.

Table 1.2: Gower's approximate annual income from his known lands and rents (*Sources: Table 1.1 and 'Chronology of John Gower's Life Records'*)

1365	£23
1366	£15
1367	£10
1368–1380	£29?
1380–1382	£20?
1382–1385?*	£45?
1385?*–1408	£40

*Possible date of sale of Aldington (autumn 1381 x May 1391)

[59] On allusions to commerce in Gower's work, see Roger A. Ladd, 'Gower, Business, and Economy', in *The Routledge Research Companion to John Gower*, ed. Ana Sáez-Hidalgo, Brian Gastle, and R. F. Yeager (London: Taylor and Francis, 2017) [hereafter *RRC*], pp. 158–71.

Thus, during the last forty-three years of his life, Gower's yearly income from his known property holdings ranged from about £10 to about £45; during most of that period it was probably about £29–£40. That was a perfectly respectable income for a gentleman or even a knight, but it was no great fortune.[60]

There appears to be a major discrepancy between Gower's known income and his known expenditures. As will be seen in the discussion at the end of this chapter, Gower evidently spent lavishly in the 1390s on his own tomb in the priory church of St Mary Overy; he also endowed a perpetual chantry and obit there, and donated generously to the fabric of the church. The cost of endowing the chantry alone probably was at least £200, and the cash bequests in Gower's testament came to about £138.[61] Altogether, Gower may have spent £500 or more on these projects and legacies, at a time when his recorded rental income was only £40 a year. It thus seems likely that Gower had other sources of income in addition to his known portfolio of rents. He may, for example, have owned properties or rents that have left no trace in the archival record. But the documents that do survive suggest that he also supplemented his rental income with the profits of a very different kind of investment: money-lending.

Gower seems to have needed a year (June 1368–June 1369) to pay the 200 marks (£133 6s. 8d.) in cash for his purchase of Kentwell, and he also borrowed money himself on at least two occasions: in July 1368, when he gave a bond for £20 to Richard Ravensere, using his newly-acquired manor of Kentwell as collateral; and in June 1395, when he briefly borrowed £3 6s. 8d. from Gilbert Maghfeld (discussed below); both debts were duly repaid. There are, however, eight records in which Gower himself is a creditor, either acknowledging the repayment of a debt, or else suing defaulting debtors. These records span more than three decades, from 1365 to 1399, and they probably represent only a portion of Gower's activities as a creditor, since large numbers of court records and other archival sources remain unindexed and little-explored. The largest recorded amount for which Gower sued defaulting debtors was £96, representing debts of £32 each owed by three men from Newington, near Iwade, in Kent, where Gower owned marshland. The smallest amount was 40s., due from a married couple from Shropham, in Norfolk, about twenty miles from Gower's manor of Feltwell. (Forty shillings was the lowest amount for which one could sue someone for debt in the court

---

[60] On aristocratic, knightly and gentry income levels in the early fourteenth and early fifteenth centuries, see Christopher Dyer, *Standards of Living in the Later Middle Ages* (Cambridge: Cambridge University Press, 1989), pp. 29–32.

[61] On the cost of endowing a perpetual chantry from the mid fourteenth century onwards, see Kathleen L. Wood-Legh, *Perpetual Chantries in Britain* (Oxford: Oxford University Press, 1965), pp. 45–6; cf. Richard Barrie Dobson, 'The Foundation of Perpetual Chantries by the Citizens of Medieval York', in *Studies in Church History, volume IV: The Province of York*, ed. G. J. Cuming (Leiden: E. J. Brill, 1967), pp. 22–38, at 26.

of Common Pleas.) The eight records in which Gower appears as a creditor are as follows:

1. 22 June 1365. William, son and heir of Sir William de Septvans, comes before John Pyel, mayor of the staple [of Westminster], and acknowledges himself bound to John 'Gouwer' in £60 to be paid at All Saints (1 November 1365).[62]

2. May 1381–Michaelmas term 1382. John Gower, by Thomas Path[orn] his attorney, sues John Barbour, baker, John Henry, and Roger Bochier, of the parish of 'Neweton' (Newington, near Sittingbourne), Kent, in the court of Common Pleas, on a plaint that each of them owes him £32.[63]

3. Hilary term 1382. Court of Common Pleas. John Gower of the county of Kent appoints William Repyndon as his attorney to sue John Heylesdon, citizen of London, for debt.[64]

4. 24 June 1382. Acquittance by John Gower to Sir John de Cobham for receipt of 106s. 6d., sealed with Gower's signet (see Fig. 1.11).[65]

5. Michaelmas term 1392–Trinity term 1396. In Michaelmas term 1392, John Gower sued John atte Buttes of 'Wylton' (now Hockwold-cum-Wilton, near Feltwell), Norfolk, in the court of Common Pleas; the case was continued to the following Hilary term for lack of jurors. On 14 June 1395 Buttes was outlawed in Norfolk for non-payment of a bond for £40, which Gower produced in court, and which Gower recovered against him in the Curia Regis. In Michaelmas term 1395, the sheriff of Northamptonshire (where Buttes evidently had fled) was ordered to arrest Buttes and imprison him and bring him to court in the quindene of Easter 1396, but he did not come. Now, in Easter term 1396, the sheriff is ordered to have Buttes in court in the octaves of Trinity (1396).[66]

---

[62] *CIPM 1365–70*, p. 78.
[63] TNA, CP 40/482, rot. 232r (last entry), http://aalt.law.uh.edu/AALT6/R2/CP40no482/482_0483.htm; noted by Sebastian Sobecki in his paper on '*Paralegal Chaucer: Attorneys, Guardians, Sureties*' at a conference on 'Chaucer and the Law', Senate House, University of London, 1 July 2017. The continuation to Michaelmas term 1382 can be found in TNA, CP 40/484, rot. 439r (5th entry), http://aalt.law.uh.edu/AALT6/R2/CP40no484/484_0896.htm.
[64] TNA, CP 40/484, rot. 492r (18th entry), http://aalt.law.uh.edu/AALT6/R2/CP40no484/484_0979.htm.
[65] From a document formerly in the Surrenden MSS, 'lately dispersed', of Sir Edward Dering, Bart., of Surrenden Dering (Kent), printed in Warwick, 'On Gower, the Kentish Poet', p. 87, n. 3.
[66] TNA, CP 40/527, rot. 237r (3rd entry), http://aalt.law.uh.edu/AALT6/R2/CP40no527/527_0190.htm; CP 40/541, rot. 228r (2nd entry), http://aalt.law.uh.edu/AALT6/R2/CP40no541a/aCP40no541afronts/IMG_0475.htm.

6. 24 Oct. 1396. Westminster. Pardons to John Cook of Feltwell (Norfolk) and William Cook of Exning (near Moulton, Suffolk), for outlawry in the London court of Husting for not having appeared in the Common Pleas to answer John Gower, esquire, touching a debt of ten marks.[67]

7. Michaelmas term 1399. John Gower, by his attorney, sues Walter Clerk (or Clerkes) of Little Cressingham, Norfolk, for a debt of £30 5s. 8½d. (subsequently reduced to £29 5s. 8½d.).[68]

8. Michaelmas term 1399. John Gower, in person, sues William Fisshere of Shropham, Norfolk, and Denise his wife, for a debt of 40s.[69]

The medieval economy depended heavily on credit and, despite the legal and ecclesiastical condemnation of usury, money-lending was ubiquitous. Gower would have been far from unusual if he did, in fact, lend money at interest. The cases listed above suggest that he lent substantial sums to people of all ranks, ranging from the improvident heir William Septvans and the Kentish baron Sir John Cobham, to Londoners and to townsfolk and villagers who lived in the vicinity of Gower's rural estates.

The picture of Gower's wealth suggested by his pattern of investments in lands and rents during two brief periods (1364–69 and 1381–82), and his role as a creditor throughout most of his adult life (1365–99), may reflect the general fall in property values that was a feature of the period after the Black Death.[70] For example, the annual value of the manor of Aldington was put at £10 in 1366, but by 1373, when Gower transferred Aldington to feoffees, its value had fallen by half, to £5 2s. 4d. per annum.[71] Gower may have felt that it was unsafe to depend for his income entirely on rents and property-holding, and he may have turned to money-lending as a means of diversifying his investments and supplementing his income.

Gower's Movements and Places of Residence

Table 1.3 represents a chronological list of the places where it is likely or certain that Gower can be located. Places where he is likely or certain to have had a residence are identified in capital letters. For example, the under-age Kentish heir William de Septvans is said to have spent the nine months between Christmas 1364 and Michaelmas (29 September) 1365 in

---

[67] CPR 1396–99, p. 128.
[68] TNA, CP40/555, rots 74d (1st entry), and 165d (1st entry).
[69] TNA, CP40/555, rot. 118r (3rd entry).
[70] See, e.g., Dyer, *Standards of Living*, pp. 41–4.
[71] CIPM 1365–70, pp. 75–79; Larking, '"Probatio Ætatis" of William de Septvans', at 128; TNA, C 143/382/2 (2).

Table 1.3: John Gower's itinerary, identifying places where he can be located (*Gower's likely residences are shown in CAPITAL letters*)

Date	Place	Notes	Source
1327 x 1343	unknown (KENT?)	Gower's birth; parents unknown, but seemingly connected with the families of Sir Robert Gower of Brabourne and Sir Roger de Northwode	(see above under 'Gower's Kentish and family connections')
25 Dec. 1364–29 Sept. 1365	living in CANTERBURY (Kent) and elsewhere (perhaps at the townhouse and nearby manor of MILTON of William de Septvans, and at other Septvans estates)	William de Septvans was 'continually in the company' of Gower and Richard de Hurst 'at Canterbury and elsewhere'	*CIPM 1365–70*, pp. 76–77; *Feudal Aids*, vol. 3, pp. 16, 20, 26, 40, 54
18 July 1366	London	Grant by Gower of his reversionary interest in an annual quitrent of £12 in the London parish of St Mary Colechurch, to Simon de Benyngton, draper, dated at London	LMA, HR 94/107 (see Appendix 2)
1–2 June 1367	London and Westminster	Grant to Gower by John Gravesende citizen and draper of London, dated 1 June 1367 at London; enrolled 2 June 1367 at Westminster	*CCR 1364–8*, p. 379
10 March 1368	Newington (Kent)	Grant to Gower by William Septvaunz of marshland in Iwade (Kent), dated at Newington	BL, Additional Ch. 68771
28 June 1368	Melford (Suffolk)?	Grant to Gower by Thomas Syward, citizen and pewterer of London, and Joan his wife, daughter of Sir Robert Gower, dated at Melford	BL, Harley Ch. 56 G. 42

Date	Place	Notes	Source
4 July 1368	London?	Letter of attorney by Thomas Syward and Joan his wife, dated at London	BL, Harley Ch. 56 G. 41
23 July 1368	Westminster	Recognizance by Gower to Richard de Ravensere, clerk, dated at Westminster	CCR 1364–68, p. 482
25 x 30 June 1369	Westminster?	Final concord between Gower, 'querent' (grantee), and John Spenythorn and Joan his wife (widow of Thomas Syward), 'deforciants' (grantors), dated at Westminster	BL, Harley Ch. 50 I 13
29 Sept. 1373	Otford (Kent)	Grant by Gower, dated at Otford	BL, Harley Ch. 50 I. 14
21 May 1378	London or Westminster?	Geoffrey Chaucer appoints John Gower and Richard Forester his general attorneys during his absence abroad	*Chaucer Life-Records*, eds M. M. Crow and C. C. Olson (1966), p. 54
6 x 12 Oct. 1379	Westminster?	Enrollment at Westminster of final concord made 25 June 1369 between Gower and the Spenythorns	BL, Harley Ch. 50 I. 13
Easter term (1–27 May) 1381 (with continuations until Feb. 1382)	vicinity of Sittingbourne (Kent): perhaps ALDINGTON?	Gower, by his attorney, in the court of Common Pleas, sues three men of the parish of Newington (near Sittingbourne), for debt	TNA, CP 40/482, rot. 232r
ante-Michaelmas term (9 Oct.–28 Nov.) 1381	at or near ALDINGTON (Kent)?	Gower, by his attorney, sues Walter Cook, carpenter, in Common Pleas, for not fulfilling a contract to build for Gower's use a new house in the manor of Aldyngton	TNA, CP 40/483, rots. 144d, 488r

Date	Place	Notes	Source
Hilary term (23 Jan.–12 Feb.) 1382	KENT	John Gower of Kent designates an attorney in the court of Common Pleas to act for him in a plea of debt v. John Heylesdon, citizen of London	TNA, CP 40/484, rot. 492r
2 March 1382	KENT	Isabel late the daughter of Walter de Huntyngfeld of Kent, to John Gower of Kent: general release of all actions real and personal	CCR 1381–85, p. 111
1–6 August 1382	WESTMINSTER?	Enrollment at Westminster of grant by Guy de Rouclif to John Gower, esquire, of Kent, of the manors of Feltwell and Moulton, and release by Gower to Rouclif. Demise by Gower of the same manors, with rent payable to Gower and his assigns in the church of Westminster Abbey	CCR 1381–85, pp. 211, 214, 426
Feb. 1384?	WESTMINSTER?	Gower's demise of Feltwell and Moulton, dated 6 Aug. 1382, was enrolled at Westminster 17 Feb. 1384 and acknowledged by the lessees on 29 Feb. Perhaps it was at this time that John Wacche (or Wecche) and Agnes his wife, sub-tenants of an elite house in the priory of St Mary Overy, sub-let the house to Gower, although Gower may not have occupied it until after John Wacche's death in August 1384.	CCR 1381–85, p. 426; Carlin, 'Gower's Southwark', pp. 141–2; TNA, JUST 1/1503, rot. 56r-d (see Appendix 3, below)

Date	Place	Notes	Source
release dated 15 March 1385; acknowledged 21 April 1385	KENT (15 March); Westminster and possibly SOUTHWARK (21 April)	John Spenythorn, citizen and tailor of London, to John Gower, esquire, of Kent: general release of all actions real and personal. Acknowledged at Westminster.	*CCR 1381–85*, p. 619
10 June 1385	London, KENT, and possibly SOUTHWARK	Release (dated at London) to John Gower of Kent by Isabel daughter and heir of Walter Huntyngfelde of Kent of all actions real and personal. (This is the last reference to Gower as 'of Kent'.)	*CCR 1381–85*, p. 635
On or about 10 June 1385? (See Table 1.4 and discussion below)	London	According to Gower's original Prologue to *Confessio Amantis*, while rowing on the Thames at London he met Richard II's barge; the king invited him aboard and bade him write 'some newe thing'.	(For date of commencement of *Confessio Amantis* and dates of visits to London by Richard II and John Gower, see discussion below.)
12 August 1386	DOVER CASTLE (Kent)?	Appointment of Edmund Stapulgate, Thomas Burbage and John Gower to receive and distribute for the defence of Dover Castle all victuals therein	*CCR 1385–89*, p. 208
12 Jan. 1387	DOVER CASTLE (Kent)?	Appointment of John Gower, Thomas Burbache, and Simon Tanner to receive the victuals in Dover Castle and keep and distribute them as advised by the king and Council	*CCR 1385–89*, p. 266

Date	Place	Notes	Source
c. Sept.–Oct. 1392	Hull (Yorkshire)	Gilbert Maghfeld, London merchant, pays for carriage of a chest 'to the water' to send to John Gower, esquire, at Hull	TNA, E 101/509/19, fol. 34r. Cf. E. Rickert, 'Extracts from a Fourteenth Century Account Book', Modern Philology, 24 (1926), p. 118; Chaucer Life-Records, eds Crow and Olson, p. 500
Michaelmas term (9 Oct.–28 Nov.) 1392	York (court of Common Pleas)	Gower, evidently in person, sues John atte Buttes of Wylton (Norfolk) for debt	TNA, CP 40/527, rot. 237r
c. Oct. 1392	Lynn (now King's Lynn, Norfolk)	Gilbert Maghfeld pays on Gower's behalf for freight of a brass pot from Lynn to London	TNA, E 101/509/19, fol. 34r. Cf. Rickert, 'Extracts', p. 118; Chaucer Life-Records, eds Crow and Olson, p. 500
30 June x Nov. 1393	Kent? SOUTHWARK?	Gower is given a livery collar by Henry Bolingbroke, earl of Derby, possibly during Derby's journey from Dover to London, 30 June–5 July 1393 (via Canterbury, Sittingbourne, Newington, Rochester, Ospringe, and Dartford), or else in the capital July x Nov. 1393	TNA, DL 41/424, m. 15 (c. Oct.–Nov. 1393: Gower's collar); Expeditions to Prussia and the Holy Land made by Henry Earl of Derby, ed. L. Toulmin Smith (Camden Society, 1894), pp. lxxix, 254–57

Date	Place	Notes	Source
by Michaelmas 1394	SOUTHWARK?	Feriby v. Gower et al.: assize of novel disseisin concerning a tenement owned by the priory of St Mary Overy, Southwark (probably the house that Gower himself occupied within the priory precinct)	TNA, JUST 1/1503, rot. 56r-d (see Appendix 3 below, and Carlin, 'Gower's Southwark', pp. 141–42)
6 Feb. 1395	SOUTHWARK?	Surrey assizes (Feriby v. Gower et al.: case concluded)	TNA, JUST 1/1503, rot. 56d
23 June 1395	London	Gower borrows £3 6s. 8d. from Gilbert Maghfeld, to be repaid within 3 weeks	TNA, E 101/509/19, fol. 55v. Cf. Rickert, 'Extracts', p. 119; *Chaucer Life-Records*, eds Crow and Olson, p. 501
Michaelmas term (9 Oct.–29 Nov.) 1395	Westminster	Gower, in person, sues John Gay and Thomas Forester in the court of Common Pleas	TNA, CP40/539, rot 511r
Easter term (19 Apr.–15 May) 1396	Westminster	Gower, in person, sues John Gay and Thomas Forester in the court of Common Pleas	TNA, CP40/541, rot. 46r; S. Sobecki in *Speculum* 92 (2017), pp. 636–37, 658
Marriage licence issued 25 Jan. 1397/8 at Highclere, Hampshire; the marriage probably took place at the end of Jan. or early Feb. 1398	SOUTHWARK	Licence by the bishop of Winchester to the curate of St Mary Magdalen, Southwark, to marry his parishioners John Gower and Agnes Groundolf in the private oratory in Gower's house in the priory of St Mary Overy	Hampshire Archives, Reg. Wykeham, vol. II, fol. 299v; cf. *Wykeham's Register*, ed. Kirby, II: 477

Date	Place	Notes	Source
22 Nov. 1398	CRUNDALE? (Kent: between Ashford and Canterbury)	Order to the sheriff of Kent to set free John Stoffolde of Crundale if taken at suit of John Gower of Crundale averring threats	CCR 1396–99, p. 417
Michaelmas term (9 Oct.–28 Nov.) 1399	Westminster	Gower (initially by an attorney; subsequently in person) sues Walter Clerk(es) of Little Cressingham (Norfolk) for debt; and in person sues William Fisshere of Shropham (Norfolk) and Denise his wife for debt	TNA, CP40/555, rots 73d, 118r, 165d; S. Sobecki in *Speculum* 92 (2017), pp. 637–38, 658–60
15 August 1408	SOUTHWARK (house in the precinct of St Mary Overy)	Gower dates his testament in the priory of St Mary Overy, Southwark	Lambeth Palace Library, Reg. Arundel, vol. 1, fols 256r–257r
15 August 1408 x 7 Nov. 1408	SOUTHWARK (house in the precinct of St Mary Overy)?	Gower dies (his testament proved at Lambeth, 7 Nov. 1408)	Lambeth Palace Library, Reg. Arundel, vol. 1, fols 256r–257r (see Appendix 4, below)

the company of Gower and Richard de Hurst 'at Canterbury and elsewhere'. This may mean that Gower was living at Septvans' townhouse in Canterbury and his nearby manor of Milton, and perhaps at other Septvans estates.

The itinerary of Gower's movements, as tabulated in Table 1.3, makes it likely that Gower, who was described in documents as 'of Kent' until at least June 1385, did indeed spend most of his time in Kent until sometime after January 1387, a decade after many scholars have assumed that Gower had taken up permanent residence in Southwark Priory.[72] While he evidently visited the capital on many occasions, he was never described as being 'of' London, Westminster, or Southwark. In a roll of arms composed in the reign of Richard II and organized by county, John Gower's arms were included

---

[72] See, e.g., Robert Epstein, 'London, Southwark, Westminster: Gower's Urban Contexts', in Echard, *A Companion to Gower*, pp. 43–60; and Martha Carlin, 'Gower's Southwark', in *RRC*, pp. 132–49, at 140.

under the county of Kent.⁷³ Gower was not a resident of Southwark at the time of the Southwark poll tax re-assessment in early 1381.⁷⁴ Instead, he probably was living at Aldington, Kent, for in Michaelmas term 1381 he sued a carpenter for failing to build him a house there, for his own use.⁷⁵ He may have lived principally at Aldington since 1368, when William de Septvans re-granted the manor to him.

It is possible that Gower had lodgings at Westminster in August 1382, when he leased out Feltwell and Moulton and specified that their annual rent of £40 was to be paid at Westminster Abbey. Gower may also have been lodging in or visiting Westminster in February 1384, when he had the lease enrolled (17 February) and acknowledged by the lessees (29 February). Perhaps it was at this time that John Wacche (or Wecche) and his wife Agnes, sub-tenants of an elite townhouse that evidently lay within the precinct of the priory of St Mary Overy, Southwark, sub-let the house to Gower 'at will' (*i.e.* at their pleasure, with no fixed term). Gower's sub-tenancy of this house (discussed below) is his first known connection to the priory. Gower may have met John Wacche through his attorney Thomas Pathorn or his feoffees Thomas Preston and Roger Asshebournham, all of whom had had contact with Wacche (for profiles of these men, see below under 'Gower's associates and friends'). Gower paid an annual rent of four marks (£2 13s. 4d.) for the Wacches' house.⁷⁶ He may not have occupied it, however, until after John Wacche's death in August 1384.

In the original prologue to *Confessio Amantis*, Gower wrote that he was being rowed in a boat on the Thames 'under the town of New Troy' (*i.e.*, London) when he met Richard II's barge. The king invited Gower aboard, and bade him write 'some newe thing'. Douglas Gray tentatively dates Gower's conception of the plan of *Confessio Amantis* to 'perhaps *c.* 1386'.⁷⁷ Nigel Saul's itinerary for Richard II shows that the king was at Westminster on twenty-seven days in 1385, thirty-five days in 1386 (plus twelve days at Westminster or Eltham), and on only two days in 1387 (see Table 1.4).

---

73 London, Society of Antiquaries MS 664/4, fol. 20r. See n. 8, above.
74 Discussed in Carlin, 'Gower's Southwark', p. 140.
75 Unfortunately, no detailed poll tax returns survive for Aldington. Gower's name does not appear in the surving returns for Kent, which are printed in *The Poll Taxes of 1377, 1379 and 1381*, ed. Carolyn C. Fenwick, 3 vols, British Academy, Records of Social and Economic History, new series 27, 29, 37 (Oxford: Oxford University Press, 1998–2005), I: 386–433.
76 CCR 1381–85, p. 426; TNA, JUST 1/1503, rot. 56r-d (see Appendix 3). The Wacches' house, the evidence for locating it within the priory precinct, and Gower's occupation of it are discussed in Carlin, 'Gower's Southwark', pp. 140–4.
77 *Complete Works*, II: p. xxix; CA: Pro.34–53; Douglas Gray, 'Gower, John (d. 1408)', ODNB (http://www.oxforddnb.com/view/article/11176, accessed 16 July 2018).

Table 1.4: Dates when Richard II was at Westminster in 1385, 1386, and 1387. (*Source*: Nigel Saul, *Richard II* (New Haven and London: Yale University Press, 1997), Appendix: 'Richard II's Itinerary, 1377–99', pp. 468–74, at 470–1.)

	1385	1386	1387
Jan	–	8–18	–
Feb	11–14	17	9
Mar	7–11	5–9, 17–22	–
Apr	–	–	–
May	–	–	–
June	10–12, 20–22	–	–
July	–	–	–
Aug	–	–	–
Sept	–	8–15, 21	–
Oct	23	2–4, 7–18 (Westminster/Eltham)	–
Nov	5–10, 14–15	–	10
Dec	3, 19–21	–	–

Table 1.4 reveals that between 1385 and 1387 Richard II visited Westminster primarily during the autumn and winter months. Table 1.3 shows that Gower is not recorded in the capital in 1385–87 during those months. The king and Gower may, however, have made overlapping visits to the capital in those years on one occasion: in June 1385. Gower may have visited London (perhaps lodging in his rented townhouse in Southwark) on 10 June to receive the release made to him by Isabel, daughter and heir of Walter Huntyngfelde of Kent; the eighteen-year-old king, who was shortly to depart on a campaign to Scotland (July 1385), was at Westminster on 10–12 and 20–22 June. If Gower's encounter with the king actually took place – and there is no real reason to doubt this – it is thus possible that it occurred on (or about) 10 June 1385.[78] If so (or if Gower met with Richard II during any of the king's other visits to the capital between February 1385 and March 1386), the meeting may have led not only to Gower's composition of *Confessio Amantis*, but also to his only appointment to royal service. In August 1386, Edmund Stapulgate (or Staplegate, of Bilsington, near Canterbury), Thomas Burbage and John Gower were appointed to administer the reception and

---

[78] On the plausibility of Gower's encounter with Richard II, see Joyce Coleman, '"A bok for King Richardes sake": Royal Patronage, the *Confessio*, and the *Legend of Good Women*', in *On John Gower: Essays for the Millennium*, ed. Robert F. Yeager, Studies in Medieval Culture, 46 (Kalamazoo, Michigan: Medieval Institute Publications, 2007), pp. 104–23, and see Michael Bennett in Chapter 13, below, pp. 435–6.

distribution of victuals at Dover Castle; Gower was re-appointed in January 1387, together with Burbage and Simon Tanner.[79] Although there were other men called John Gower during this period, two factors make it likely that the Gower named in these commissions was Gower the poet. The first is that Gower the poet had had strong links to Kent since at least 1364, and perhaps since birth. The second factor is that Gower the poet had a connection with Edmund Staplegate, for in the mid 1370s Staplegate had been the ward of Geoffrey Chaucer.[80]

The evidence of Gower's property acquisitions and itinerary (Tables 1.1 and 1.2) thus suggests that from 1368 until the 1380s Gower's principal residence may have been at Aldington. He disposed of the manor sometime between Michaelmas 1381 and May 1391, perhaps by August 1382, to fund his purchase of Feltwell and Moulton, or perhaps after June 1385, when he is last referred to as 'of Kent'. By April 1385 Gower probably had taken possession of the townhouse in Southwark that he had sub-let from the Wacches. If he then served as a royal commissioner in Dover Castle from late 1386 until sometime in 1387, it may not have been until 1387 or later that Gower became permanently established in the capital. Nothing is known of his movements for the next five years.

In the autumn of 1392 Gower seems to have made a journey to Yorkshire and East Anglia. The ledger of the London merchant Gilbert Maghfeld records, in an undated entry of around October 1392, that Maghfeld paid 16d. to a shipman on behalf of John Gower, esquire, for freight of a brass pot, sent 'by letter' from the port of Lynn (now King's Lynn), Norfolk, to London ('*Memorandum que Gyboun Maufeld' ad paye pour John' Gower Esquier a j. Schippman pur freit dune bras pott' mis par lettre de lynne iesques a loundres - xvi d.'*). Sometime previously, Maghfeld had paid 4d. for carriage of a chest 'to the water' (*i.e.*, to the waterfront) to send to Gower at Hull ('*Item il ad paye deuaunt pur cariage dune chest' al Ewe pur envoier au dit Joh' a hull - iiij d.'*).[81] Hull was the port for the inland city of York, and Gower's actual destination evidently was York, to which Richard II had temporarily moved the Chancery, the Exchequer, the courts of Common Pleas and King's Bench, and the prisoners of the Fleet. The king announced the move to the sheriffs of London in a writ dated 13 May 1392, and on 25 October 1392 he issued the first writ for the return to Westminster of the court of Common Pleas, followed by the return of the other offices of state, the Fleet prisoners,

---

[79] CPR 1385–89, pp. 208, 266; cf. Ernest P. Kuhl, 'Some Friends of Chaucer', *Proceedings of the Modern Language Association*, 29 (1914), pp. 270–6, at 275–6.

[80] Chaucer's wardship of Stapulgate (or Staplegate) was discussed by Sebastian Sobecki in his paper on '*Paralegal Chaucer*' (see n. 63, above). On Staplegate, see *Chaucer Life-Records*, eds Martin M. Crow and Clair C. Olson (Oxford: Clarendon Press, 1966), pp. 294–301.

[81] Edith Rickert, 'Extracts from a Fourteenth-Century Account Book', *Modern Philology*, 24 (1926–27), pp. 111–19, 249–56, at 118; cf. *Chaucer Life-Records*, eds Crow and Olson, p. 500.

and all their rolls and other records.[82] During Michaelmas term 1392, while the court of Common Pleas was in York, Gower was the plaintiff in a plea of debt (noted above) against John atte Buttes of 'Wylton' (now Hockwold-cum-Wilton, Norfolk). Since no attorney is mentioned as appearing on Gower's behalf, he evidently appeared in person, and this accords with the evidence from Maghfeld's ledger of Gower's travels to Hull and Lynn at about this time.[83] After leaving York, Gower probably went by sea to Lynn, from which port he sent the brass pot to London. From Lynn, Gower may have travelled by road to his East Anglian estates at Feltwell, Norfolk (about twenty miles south of Lynn) and Moulton, Suffolk (about thirty miles south-east of Feltwell), before returning to the capital or elsewhere.

During this period Henry Bolingbroke, earl of Derby, the eldest son of John of Gaunt, duke of Lancaster, left England on 24 July 1392 for a crusade in Lithuania and a pilgrimage to the Holy Land, and was gone for almost a year, returning on 30 June 1393.[84] Sometime between his return and the following November, Derby gave John Gower a livery collar. Scholars have long associated Derby's gift of this collar with Gower's change of the dedication of the *Confessio Amantis* from Richard II to Derby (Pro.83–89). The prologue containing the new dedication declares that it was written in the 'yer sextenthe of kyng Richard' (Pro.25).[85] Since that year ran from 22 June 1392 to 21 June 1393, Gower presumably wrote it during Derby's absence, perhaps when there was news of his impending return.[86]

The record of the collar is a document, written on a slip of paper bearing traces of four red wax seals. It is in a file of twenty documents relating to the account for 17 Richard II (22 June 1393–21 June 1394) of William Loveney, clerk of Derby's Wardrobe. Loveney, who later served as one of John Gower's executors (discussed below), had not accompanied Derby abroad. The document is an order by Hugh Waterton, Derby's chamberlain, to deliver 26s. 8d. to Richard Dancastre, an esquire who had attended Derby on both of his recent excursions abroad, 'for a collar given to him by my lord the Earl

---

[82] Caroline M. Barron, 'The Quarrel of Richard II and London 1392-7', in F. Robin H. Du Boulay and Caroline M. Barron eds, *The Reign of Richard II: Essays in Honour of May McKisack* (London: Athlone, 1971), pp. 173–201, at 181–3, 193 and n. 85.

[83] Unfortunately for Gower, the case was 'respited' (continued) until the octaves of Hilary (20–26 January 1393), because none of the jurors had come (TNA, CP 40/527, rot. 237r (3rd entry), http://aalt.law.uh.edu/AALT6/R2/CP40no527/527_0190.htm). I found no entry for this case in the plea roll for Hilary term 1393 (TNA, CP 40/528), but the case recurs in 1395–96 (TNA, CP 40/541, rot. 228r, 2nd entry, http://aalt.law.uh.edu/AALT6/R2/CP40no541a/aCP40no541afronts/IMG_0475.htm), and is discussed above.

[84] *Expeditions to Prussia and the Holy Land Made by Henry Earl of Derby*, ed. Lucy Toulmin Smith, Camden Society, n.s., 52 (London, 1894), p. lxxix.

[85] See *Complete Works*, II: pp. xxii–xxiii, xxv–xxvi, xxix.

[86] *Expeditions to Prussia and the Holy Land*, ed. Toulmin Smith, pp. lxxii–lxxix.

of Derby, because of another collar given by my said lord to an esquire, John Gower':

> Liuerez a Richard Dancastre *pur* vn Coler luy done *par* mons*eigneur* le Conte de Derby *par* cause dvne autre Coler done *par* mondits*eigneur* a vn Esquier John Gower vynt *et* sys soldz' oyt deniers.
>
> de *par* Hugh Waterton Chamburlein au Conte de Derby.[87]

This document is not dated, but its position in the file suggests that it was entered around October–November 1393.[88] Derby arrived at Dover on 30 June 1393, and travelled to London via Canterbury, Sittingbourne, Newington, Rochester, Ospringe, and Dartford, arriving in the capital on 5 July 1393.[89] It is possible that Gower met with Derby shortly upon his return and received the collar at some point during Derby's journey from Dover to London, through those parts of Kent with which Gower had been most closely associated. Otherwise, the granting of the collar to Gower presumably took place later that summer or autumn in the capital.

A year later, in Michaelmas term 1394, Gower was sued in an assize of *novel disseisin* ('recent dispossession') held at Guildford, Surrey. The case concerned the sub-lease of a 'tenement' (a building plot, with or without buildings) in Southwark owned by the priory of St Mary Overy. This tenement probably was an elite townhouse occupied by Gower within the priory precinct (see Map 1.3). I have discussed this case elsewhere,[90] and have provided a translation of the full legal record in Appendix 3, below. The plaintiff was Thomas de Feriby, a clerical pluralist (holder of multiple benefices) who had long been in the service of Richard II's uncle, Thomas of Woodstock, duke of Gloucester, and in 1394 was Gloucester's 'chancellor'.[91] Feriby sued John Gower (represented by his attorney, William Elyngton) and three co-defendants, William Weston (one of Gower's former feoffees

---

[87] TNA, DL 41/424 (formerly DL 41/10/43), m. 15r. (The document has no endorsement.). On Richard Dancastre, see *Expeditions to Prussia and the Holy Land*, ed. Toulmin Smith, p. li and *passim*.

[88] The order is enigmatic, but Fisher, following Macaulay, probably was correct in assuming that Gower had been given Dancaster's collar: in 1393–94 Derby's household accounts record a payment of 56s. 8d. for a silver collar for his butler, John Payne, because Derby had given Payne's collar to another esquire, and in 1396–97 Derby's wardrobe accounts report that Derby gave a collar of rolled SS to his esquire Robert Waterton because he had given Waterton's own collar to another esquire ('*eo quod dominus dederat colerium ipsius Roberti alio armigero*') (Fisher, *John Gower*, p. 68; *Complete Works*, IV: pp. xvi–xvii and nn.; Matthew Ward, *The Livery Collar in Late Medieval England and Wales: Politics, Identity and Affinity* (Woodbridge: Boydell Press, 2016), p. 27, n. 35).

[89] *Expeditions to Prussia and the Holy Land*, ed. Toulmin Smith, p. lxxix.

[90] Carlin, 'Gower's Southwark', pp. 141–2.

[91] Carlin, 'Gower's Southwark', p. 141.

for Kentwell and Aldington), Thomas Saundres, and Thomas Hautwysel (all represented by their bailiff), for dispossessing him of the tenement. According to the court record, both Feriby and Gower said that the tenement had been let by Prior Henry Collingbourne (prior from 27 March 1361 to 15 June 1395)[92] to Thomas and Joan Vynch for their lifetimes, and that thereafter it was held of the Vynches by a series of sub-tenants; unfortunately, no dates are given for the sequence of leases. The Vynches granted their interest in the tenement to Adam de Bury (skinner and mayor of London; d. 1385–86); he granted it to John Wacche (or Wecche; d. August 1384) and Agnes his wife; and they granted it to Gower to hold at will. After John Wacche's death, his widow Agnes married William Olyver (skinner and alderman of London; d. 1396–97). Thomas Vynch then died (date unknown), and Agnes and William Olyver surrendered their lease back to Joan Vynch, which ended Gower's tenancy-at-will.

At this point in the narrative, the accounts of Gower and Feriby diverged. Gower claimed that Joan Vynch, who retained her original life-tenancy of the property, granted the tenement to him, to hold for his lifetime (which would have contravened the terms of her own lease), and then later granted it to Feriby to hold for *her* lifetime, in breach of the grant that she had made 'long before' to Gower. According to Feriby, however, Joan Vynch granted the property to him to hold for her lifetime without having made any intervening grant to Gower.

Feriby won his case against Gower and Weston, but not against their two co-defendants, who were acquitted. He was awarded possession of the property and 100s. in damages from Gower and Weston, who were ordered to be arrested; Feriby in turn was to be fined for his false charge against Saundres and Hautwysel.[93] The case was concluded at Southwark on 6 February 1395, when Feriby came before the same justices and declared that he had been satisfied for the above damages, and Gower and Weston were assigned fines, respectively, of one mark (13s. 4d.) and half a mark (6s. 8d.). If the tenement in the case was the same townhouse in the priory precinct that Gower and his wife Agnes seemingly occupied from 1398 until 1408 (see below), then Gower must have swallowed his pride and obtained a new sub-lease of it from Feriby. Some scholars, including Macaulay, have conjectured that Gower held a corrody from the priory that provided him with lodgings there for life.[94] This case makes it clear that Gower held this property not as a

---

[92] Carlin, *Medieval Southwark*, p. 285.
[93] A note at the foot of the roll records an amercement of one mark (13s. 4d.); this probably represents Feriby's fine. He may also have paid the charge of 20d. for the 'proclamation' similarly noted at the foot of the roll.
[94] *Complete Works*, IV: pp. xix, 390; Robert H. Snape, *English Monastic Finances in the Later Middle Ages* (Cambridge: Cambridge University Press, 1926), p. 141; Robert F. Yeager, 'Chaucer's French Audience: The *Mirour de l'Omme*', *Chaucer Review*, 41/2 (2006), pp. 111–37, at 118–9; Yeager and Yeager, 'Did Gower Love His Wife?', p. 68; Sobecki, 'A Southwark Tale', pp. 639 n. 42, 643 n. 61, 644.

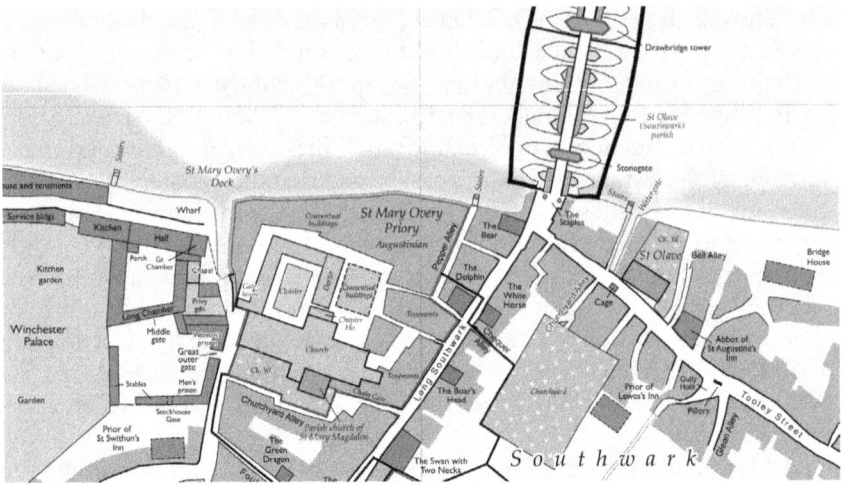

Map 1.3: Southwark: the priory of St Mary Overy and surrounding area near London Bridge, c. 1520, from A *Map of Tudor London*, British Historic Towns Atlas, in association with The London Topographical Society (2018).

corrodian but as an ordinary sub-tenant, and that he paid rent for it to an intervening lay tenant, not to the prior or the priory.

The evidence that the tenement in question was an elite house within the precinct of the priory of St Mary Overy is as follows. In 1375 John Wacche, an administrator of Crown properties, joined the staff of William Wykeham, bishop of Winchester, whose grand Southwark palace (shown in Map 1.3) lay just to the west of the priory of St Mary Overy. However, no women were housed in the bishop's palace, and John Wacche had a family (he was survived by his wife Agnes, two sons, and one daughter). The priory had a number of lay tenants dwelling in its outer close, which faced the high street, between the east-west portion of Pepper Alley (opposite Chequer Alley) on the north and the Chain Gate on the south. It seems likely that the tenement rented by the Wacches (as sub-tenants of the Vynches), and owned by the priory, was a fine house there, conveniently close to the bishop's palace. John and Agnes Wacche evidently were dwelling in the house in 1381, when they and their two servants were listed in the Southwark poll tax return; the Wacches' high assessment placed them among the top fourteen taxpaying households in Southwark.[95]

According to the lawsuit, John and Agnes Wacche granted the property to John Gower, to hold at will at the high annual rent of £2 13s. 4d. This grant must have been made before John Wacche died in August 1384, but it is likely that the Wacche household occupied the house at least until his

---

[95] Carlin, 'Gower's Southwark', pp. 141–3.

death, because his testament (dated 1 August 1384) reveals him to have been a parishioner of St Mary Magdalen, Southwark (see Map 1.3), most of whose residents dwelt within the priory precinct.[96] The Wacches' high tax assessment in 1381, and the high rent that Gower later paid to them, suggest that the house was an elite one. Both its elite status and its location within the priory precinct are supported by an entry dating from 1424 x 1439 in a volume belonging to the priory. It reports that in 1424 the seven bells in the priory's wooden bell tower were replaced with eight bells of better weight, which were hung in the newly-completed crossing tower in the priory church. The wooden bell tower was described as lying in the precinct, between 'the tenement where Richard Merevayle, vintner, lives, and the tenement called *Fynchez place*'. 'Place' was a high-status descriptor, and the property's name suggests that its former tenants were the Vynches.[97]

As noted above, Gower may have chosen to establish a townhouse in Southwark rather than in London or Westminster because it was more convenient for travel to and from Kent, and because some of his Kentish neighbours kept townhouses there. Gower's choice to rent a house within the priory of St Mary Overy may, as some scholars have speculated, reflect an interest in using the priory's library and 'scriptorium', although there is no clear evidence that he did so (or even that the priory had a scriptorium in Gower's day). A different and perhaps stronger motive may have been security. St Mary Overy, like most religious houses, was a gated community, and a tenancy within its precinct would have been a practical arrangement for a gentleman who desired a townhouse to use during visits to the capital, but was concerned to keep the house and its contents secure when he was away. During Gower's occupation of this house, he may have spent much time elsewhere (see Maps 1.1 and 1.2), such as at Aldington (if he retained it as late as 1385 x 1391), at Dover Castle (1386–87), on his journey to Yorkshire and East Anglia (1392), perhaps on periodic inspection tours of his country properties (e.g., Feltwell and Moulton in 1395–96; Feltwell in 1399), and possibly at a house in Crundale in Kent (1398; discussed below). A house situated beside a bell tower, near a busy high street and near major construction works in the priory church, would not have been a quiet retreat. However, the house's security within the priory close, and its convenient location close to London Bridge, to St Mary Overy's dock, and

---

[96] The witnesses to the testament included Southwark residents, and it was proved (on 28 August 1384) in the bishop's Southwark palace. Winchester, Hampshire Archives: Register of Bishop William Wykeham, vol. I, fol. 234r–v; calendared in *Wykeham's Register*, ed. Thomas F. Kirby, 2 vols, Hampshire Record Society, 11, 13 (1896–99), II: pp. 410–1. The parish of St Mary Magdalen consisted of the priory precinct and an area on the east side of the high street opposite the priory. See Carlin, *Medieval Southwark*, pp. 20 (Fig. 1), 95.

[97] Carlin, 'Gower's Southwark', pp. 142–3.

to stairs that gave access to river craft (all shown on Map 1.3), would have been important assets.[98]

Gower's residence in the priory in the last decade of his life is attested in two documents. The first of these is the special licence issued on 25 January 1398 by William Wykeham, bishop of Winchester, in whose diocese Southwark lay, to William, the curate of St Mary Magdalen, Southwark, to solemnize the marriage of his parishioners John Gower and Agnes Groundolf in the private oratory (chapel) within Gower's townhouse (*hospicium*) in the priory of St Mary Overy.[99] The second document is Gower's own testament, dated 15 August 1408 within the priory of St Mary Overy (see discussion below and Appendix 4). In it, Gower bequeathes to his wife, Agnes, his household furnishings including a chalice and a vestment for the altar in the oratory of his townhouse (*hospicij*). The reference in both the marriage licence and the testament to Gower's house having a private oratory suggests that both documents were referring to the same house, which Gower had occupied since at least January 1398. It seems likely that this was the elite house in the lawsuit of 1394–95 discussed above; if not, then Gower must have leased another elite house in the priory precinct after losing that lawsuit.

Gower's residence in Southwark during these years is also suggested by his evident conflicts with two other residents there. Firstly, on 6 December 1397 three Londoners and a serjeant at arms mainprised (stood surety for) Thomas Caudre, a canon of the priory of St Mary Overy in Southwark, 'that he shall do or procure no hurt or harm to John Gower'.[100] It may have been the quarrel with Caudre that prompted Gower to obtain a special licence to be married in his private oratory (see below). Secondly, on 12 January 1405, James Norwode (Northwode) of Kent, esquire, John Mokkynge, John Sandyforde, and William Kirton of Surrey similarly mainprised John Solas 'that he shall do or procure no hurt or harm to John Gower and William Weston his servant'.[101] John Solas (d. 1418), a member of an established Southwark family, was a clerk of the court of King's Bench whose particular responsibility was enrolling the records for Surrey and Sussex. Solas was also an active lawyer with an extensive legal practice, and he served as MP for

---

[98] On building operations at St Mary Overy during Gower's residence there, and the locations of the priory, London Bridge, St Mary Overy's dock, and the river stairs, see Carlin, *Medieval Southwark*, pp. 22–3, 34 (Fig. 6), 68–73.

[99] Winchester, Hampshire Archives: Reg. Wykeham, vol. II, fol. 299v; calendared in *Wykeham's Register*, ed. Kirby, II: p. 477.

[100] *CCR 1396–99*, p. 238.

[101] *CCR 1402–5*, p. 484. James Northwode was a younger son of Sir John de Northwode (d. 1379), with whose father Sir Roger (d. 1361) John Gower implicitly claimed some kind of kinship; see discussion above, under 'Gower's Kentish and family connections'. On the Northwode family, see 'L.B.L.' [Lambert B. Larking], 'Genealogical Notices of the Northwoods', *Archaeologia Cantiana*, 2 (1859), pp. 9–42, with family tree in plate facing p. 42.

Southwark in the parliaments of 1393, 1395, November 1414, and March 1416. The cause of the dispute between Gower and Solas is not known, but Solas evidently was a man of uncertain temper who had a number of other such quarrels.[102]

Although Gower was living in Southwark in the late 1390s, it is possible that he also retained, or re-established, a residence in Kent in this period. On 22 November 1398, a writ was sent from Westminster to the sheriff of Kent, by mainprise of Thomas Kempe and John Cranewelle of Kent, and William Canynges and John Sandeforde of Surrey, 'to set free John Stoffolde of Crundale, if taken at suit of John Gower of Crundale averring threats'.[103] Crundale lies between Ashford and Canterbury, some ten to twelve miles south-east by road from Throwley and Stalisfield. Stoffolde's mainpernors came from both Kent and Surrey, which implies that he, like Gower, had connections with both counties; in 1405 one of Stoffolde's mainpernors, John Sandeforde, also mainperned Gower's Southwark antagonist John Solas.[104] The location of Crundale and the recurrence of Sandeforde as a mainpernor may mean that 'John Gower of Crundale' was indeed the poet, although there is no other evidence associating him with Crundale.

On 21 November 1399 the newly-crowned Henry IV granted to John Gower, 'the king's esquire', two pipes (252 gallons) of Gascon wine yearly for life, to be delivered to him in the port of London, and on 5 April 1400 an order was made to the king's chief butler or his representative in the port of London to deliver the wine as specified in the grant.[105] This would have provided Gower's household with about two-thirds of a gallon of wine daily, a valuable honorarium and mark of esteem for the aging poet, and the only recorded gift, other than the livery collar, that he received from Henry.

Gower's Associates and Friends

From the archival sources for Gower's life, seventeen of his recorded feoffees and other associates and all five of his executors can be identified. Some were neighbours of Gower in Kent and/or Southwark, and Gower may have been on terms of personal friendship with them, as he evidently was with his fellow-poet Geoffrey Chaucer. It is striking, however, that Gower himself is not recorded serving as a feoffee or executor for anyone else. Geoffrey Chaucer, when he was about to go abroad in 1378, appointed Gower to

---

[102] Carole Rawcliffe, 'Solas, John (d. 1418), of Southwark, Surr.', in *HPHC* (http://www.historyofparliamentonline.org/volume/1386-1421/member/solas-john-1418, accessed 27 July 2017).
[103] *CCR 1396–99*, p. 417.
[104] *CCR 1402–5*, p. 484. The recurrence of Sandeforde as a mainpernor was also noted by Fisher in 'A Calendar of Documents', p. 23.
[105] *CPR 1399–1401*, p. 128; *CCR 1399–1402*, p. 78.

be one of his two general attorneys in his absence, but no other record has thus far been found of Gower serving in a position of legal or financial trust on another's behalf. Such service was common among men of standing, including merchants and craftsmen as well as men of gentle or noble status. Apart from his possible service at Dover Castle in 1386–87, Gower seems never to have held any royal commissions or public office, or to have served in local or county administration, all of which were typical elements of gentry careers. Perhaps Gower shunned such obligations; perhaps the stigma of the Septvans case shadowed him for life.

It is also striking that, of Gower's five executors, only his wife Agnes (who is named in the special marriage licence issued in January 1398) previously occurs at all in Gower's life records. At the time of his death, the elderly Gower may have had few surviving friends, and no family other than Agnes. Agnes's co-executors were all men of standing or professional distinction, and may have been chosen largely for this reason rather than because they were personally close to Gower. Of Gower's other known associates, only William de Septvans, Geoffrey Chaucer, and Gower's five feoffees for Kentwell and Aldington (Sir John Cobham, William Weston, Roger Asshebournham, Thomas de Brokhull, and Thomas de Preston) occur in Gower's life records over a period of more than two years. If Gower did have a longstanding circle of personal friends, it is not reflected in the archival record.

The following brief profiles of Gower's known associates are grouped as follows: (1) miscellaneous associates and personal friends; (2) feoffees (trustees who held property on Gower's behalf); (3) attorneys who represented Gower in court; (4) executors.

Miscellaneous Associates and Personal Friends

William (III) de Septvans (Septvauns, Sepvauns, Septvaunz, Sevance, Seyvance, Sevantz, Septemvannis, etc.) (1346–1407)

William was the son and heir of Sir William (II) de Septvans, of Milton (near Canterbury), Kent (d. by Jan. 1351) and his wife Elizabeth (d. 28 Oct. 1356). Born on 28 August 1346, William III was the under-age heir whom Gower and Richard de Hurst (discussed below) and others bilked of much of his patrimony, before parliament and the Crown intervened (discussed at the beginning of this chapter). According to later testimony, Septvans 'continually dwelt in the company of Richard de Hurst and the said John Gower, at Canterbury and elsewhere', from Christmas 1364 until Michaelmas 1365, 'and during that whole time he was led and counselled by them to alienate his lands etc.'. Parliament annulled the various grants that the under-age Septvans had made to Gower and others, but in February and March 1368, a few months after he turned twenty-one, Septvans once more enfeoffed Gower with the manor of Aldington, a marsh in Iwade, and rents in Maplescombe.[106] These are his last recorded contacts with Gower.

William III had been knighted by 18 October 1380, when he was appointed sheriff of Kent; he also served as an MP for Kent at the parliament of 1380. During the Great Revolt of 1381 he was a target of the rebels, and in the months following was appointed to three commissions in Kent to round up and punish rebels and put down unlawful assemblies. In November 1381 he was succeeded as sheriff of Kent by Sir Arnald Savage (discussed below). He died on 31 August 1407.[107]

Richard de Hurst (*fl.* 1351–85)

Richard de Hurst, who was involved with Gower in the Septvans affair, was based in Sussex. In 1351 he acknowledged a debt of forty marks (£26 13s. 4d.), to be levied in Sussex,[108] and he was sheriff of Surrey and Sussex in 1361–62.[109] By Christmas 1364 he and Gower were collaborating in Canterbury in the defrauding of the under-age William de Septvans (discussed above). Septvans alienated his manor of Wigborough (Essex) to Richard de Hurst and his heirs, but after Septvans was found to have been under-age, Wigborough was seized into the king's hands.[110] Richard de Hurst was still active in 1384–85, when he was a commissioner to levy and collect a tenth and fifteenth in Sussex.[111]

John de Northwode, knight (b. c. 1323?; d. 1379)

Sir John de Northwode, who in March 1366 granted Gower the reversion of an annual quitrent of £12, was the eldest son and heir of Sir Roger de Northwode (Northwood) of Kent (*d.* 5 November 1361) and his first wife, Juliana (*married* 1322; *d.* 1329), daughter of Sir Geoffrey de Say. Sir Roger owned extensive estates in northern Kent, including at Thurnham (where Gower's manor of Aldington lay) and Northwode Schepeye (at or near Minster in the isle of Sheppey), and also a townhouse in Southwark (Surrey). Between 1369 and 1371 Sir John disposed of the Southwark

---

[106] *CPR 1350–54*, p. 21; *CIPM 1352–61*, p. 274; *CIPM 1361–65*, pp. 465, 468; *CIPM 1365–70*, pp. 75–9; *CPR 1367–70*, pp. 83, 96; BL, Additional Ch. 68771.
[107] Sir Reginald Tower, 'The Family of Septvans', *Archaeologia Cantiana*, 40 (1928), pp. 105–30, at 111–4; William E. Flaherty, 'The Great Rebellion in Kent of 1381', *Archaeologia Cantiana*, 3 (1860), pp. 65–96; *List of Sheriffs for England and Wales from the Earliest Times to A.D. 1831*, Lists and Indexes 9 (London: Public Record Office, 1898; rpt New York, 1963), p. 68; J. Cave-Browne, 'Knights of the Shire for Kent, from A.D. 1275 to A.D. 1831', *Archaeologia Cantiana*, 21 (1895), pp. 198–243, at 215.
[108] *CCR 1349–54*, p. 388.
[109] *List of Sheriffs for England and Wales*, p. 136.
[110] *CCR 1369–74*, pp. 9–10.
[111] *Calendar of Fine Rolls 1383–91*, p. 69; *CCR 1381–85*, p. 534.

townhouse (called 'Northwodes', on the south side of Tooley Street, opposite St Olave's church), but he retained his father's estates in Kent and acquired others as well. He served in France in 1359, was knighted sometime before his father's death, and was summoned to parliament from 1363 to 1376. Sir John married Joan, daughter of Robert Here of Faversham, Kent, and died on 27 February 1379.[112]

In March 1366 Northwode granted Gower the reversion of an annual quitrent of £12 in the London parish of St Mary Colechurch, which Gower subsequently claimed to possess by 'hereditary right', as well as by Northwode's grant, thus implying a blood relationship with Sir John's family (see Appendix 1 and 2). In April 1366 Sir John was on the jury at Canterbury that heard the case of the under-age heir William de Septvans.[113] In March 1368 he was the second witness to Septvans' grant to Gower of a marsh in Iwade, Kent.[114]

Geoffrey Chaucer, civil servant and poet (c. 1340–1400)

In May 1378 Geoffrey Chaucer appointed John Gower and Richard Forester to be his general attorneys while he was abroad on the king's service on a mission to Lombardy.[115] Chaucer and Gower evidently had a friendly relationship at least into the mid to late 1380s, when they exchanged literary nods in their respective works. Chaucer may have spent some time in Southwark when Gower was living there.[116]

John Bouland (de Boulande, Bowland), clerk (fl. 1379 – d. 1388)

On 3 February 1381 Isabel, daughter of Walter de Huntingfelde, quitclaimed to Gower and to John 'Bowland', clerk, all her father's lands in Throwley and Stalisfield, Kent.[117] Bouland first appears in June 1379 as John de Bouland, clerk, of the diocese of Carlisle, notary public, when he attested a notarial

---

[112] On Sir Roger and Sir John de Northwode, see Kingsford and Ayton, 'Northwood, John, first Lord Northwood (1254–1319)'; *CIPM 1361–5*, pp. 147–8; *CIPM 1377–1413*, pp. 12, 33, 301. On the Northwodes' Southwark property, see Carlin, 'Urban Development of Southwark', pp. 173–5 (gazetteer no. 152), citing abutment references in TNA, E 40/4024 (1369), and BL, Cotton MS Vesp. F. XV, fols 184v–185r (lease of 1371 in cartulary of Lewes Priory). Cf. Carlin, *Medieval Southwark*, pp. 45, 179–80, and Fig. 7 (plan of Tooley Street, property no. 152).

[113] *CIPM 1365–70*, pp. 75–9.

[114] BL, Additional Ch. 68771.

[115] *Chaucer Life-Records*, eds Crow and Olson, pp. 54, 60; TNA, C 76/62, m. 6.

[116] On Chaucer's links to Southwark, his possible sojourn(s) there, and his literary exchanges with Gower, see Caroline M. Barron, 'Chaucer the Poet and Chaucer the Pilgrim', in Stephen H. Rigby and Alastair J. Minnis, eds, *Historians on Chaucer: The 'General Prologue' to the Canterbury Tales* (Oxford: Oxford University Press, 2014), pp. 24–41, at 31, and Martha Carlin, 'The Host', *ibid.*, pp. 460–80, at 475–9.

[117] *CCR 1377–81*, p. 505.

instrument before the king's council in Westminster.[118] By July 1384 he was a canon of the royal chapel at Windsor.[119] In May 1385 Bouland, a king's clerk, was granted an annual salary of twenty marks until he should be provided with a benefice, without cure of souls, of the same value, and by June 1387 he had been provided to the prebend of Flixton in Lichfield Cathedral. By the time he made his will, dated at London on 14 May 1388, he was archdeacon of St David's.[120]

John Wacche (Wacch, Wecche) (*fl.* 1357 – d. August 1384), and Agnes his wife

At some point between 1382 and 1384, John Wacche (or Wecche) and his wife Agnes sub-let their Southwark house to John Gower. Wacche was serving as a royal administrator by 1357[121] and held a variety of appointments.[122] He was still in royal service on 1 May 1375, but by 26 June 1375 he had joined the staff of William Wykeham, bishop of Winchester.[123] It was probably at that time that Wacche and his wife Agnes became the sub-tenants of an elite house in the precinct of the priory of St Mary Overy, Southwark, which lay near the bishop's own Southwark palace and manor.[124] In 1381 John and Agnes Wacche were listed in the Southwark poll tax return along with their servants Walter and Alice. The couple's joint assessment of 6s. placed them among the top fourteen taxpaying households in Southwark; their servants paid 4d. each.[125] The Wacches evidently were still living in their Southwark house in Michaelmas term 1382,[126] but between then and John Wacche's death in August 1384 they sub-let it 'at will' (*i.e.*, at their pleasure, with no fixed term) to John Gower.[127] This may have occurred in February 1384, when Gower evidently was in London on business concerning his manors of Feltwell and Moulton (discussed above).[128]

---

[118] *CCR 1377–81*, p. 267.
[119] *CCR 1381–85*, p. 463.
[120] *CCR 1385–89*, pp. 7, 319, 494.
[121] *CCR 1354–60*, p. 372.
[122] *CPR 1367–70*, p. 139; *CCR 1369–74*, pp. 64, 145; *CCR 1374–77*, p. 222.
[123] *CPR 1374–77*, p. 150; *CCR 1374–77*, pp. 244–5.
[124] The testament of John 'Wecche' was dated 1 August 1384 and was proved on 27 August 1384 before Wykeham; in the probate clause, Wykeham described John 'Wacche' as his '*familiaris servitor*' (Winchester, Hampshire Record Office, William Wykeham's Register, vol. I, fol. 234r–v; calendared in *Wykeham's Register*, ed. Kirby, II: pp. 410–11.
[125] Carlin, *Medieval Southwark*, pp. 172, 269 (Appendix I, nos. 950–956); *The Poll Taxes of 1377, 1379 and 1381*, ed. Fenwick, II: p. 563 (m. 2v, col. 2).
[126] TNA, CP 40/487, rot. 222 (first entry), http://aalt.law.uh.edu/AALT6/R2/CP40no487/487_0467.htm.
[127] Carlin, 'Gower's Southwark', pp. 141–2; TNA, JUST 1/1503, rot. 56r–d (see Appendix 3).
[128] *CCR 1381–85*, p. 426.

In 1377 John Wacche and Roger Assheborham (Asshebournham, *q.v.*) were among the witnesses to a quitclaim at London.[129] In five London Husting deeds of 1377 and 1381, Wacche served as a feoffee for the settlement of some property in London along with Thomas Preston, clerk (*q.v.*), and Thomas Pathorn (*q.v.*), with both of whom Gower was also associated, and in Michaelmas term 1382, Pathorn served as Wacche's attorney. It is possible that it was through these or similar contacts that Wacche came to meet John Gower and to sub-let his house to him.[130]

William Wexham of Southwark (*fl.* 1391–1412)

In February 1395 William Wexham of Southwark was one of the two men who stood surety for Gower at the conclusion of the assize of *novel disseisin* brought by Thomas de Feriby (see Appendix 3, below). William and his wife Cristina were property-owners in Southwark in 1391.[131] In October 1400 a writ of *supersedeas omnino* was sent to the sheriff of Surrey to set free William Wexham if he had been taken at the suit of John Hosyer.[132] Two of Wexham's mainpernors, John Brenchesle (or Brynchele, *d.* 1420) and Thomas Spencer (*d.* 1428), were Southwark residents who were professionals in the writing crafts: Brenchesle was the clerk of the London Tailors' fraternity, and Spencer was a scrivener who claimed to have owned a copy of a 'book called *Troylous*' (presumably Chaucer's *Troilus and Criseyde*) in 1394. Either or both might have known Gower and might even have done some copying for him.[133] Wexham was still alive in June 1412, when he confirmed previous grants that he had made of properties in Southwark.[134]

Feoffees

John (de) Cobham, knight, third baron Cobham of Cobham (c. 1320–1408)

In April 1366 Cobham was one of three men commissioned by Edward III to convene an inquest at Canterbury to investigate the matter of the under-age Kentish heir William de Septvans, including Septvans' illegal grants to

---

[129] CCR 1374–77, p. 521.
[130] LMA, HR 106/59–62 (1377), 110/78 (1381); CCR 1381–85, p. 426; Carlin, 'Gower's Southwark', pp. 141–2; TNA, JUST 1/1503, rot. 56r-d (see Appendix 3).
[131] LMA, E/MW/C/0251 (feoffment, 1391); see also E/MW/C/0252 (abutment reference, 1391), https://search.lma.gov.uk/LMA_DOC/E_MW.PDF (accessed 30 July 2017). The Wexhams do not appear in the Southwark poll tax reassessment of 1381 (*The Poll Taxes of 1377, 1379 and 1381*, ed. Fenwick, II: pp. 558–64).
[132] CCR 1399–1402, pp. 273–4.
[133] See Martha Carlin, 'Thomas Spencer, Southwark Scrivener (*d.* 1428): Owner of a Copy of Chaucer's *Troilus* in 1394?', *Chaucer Review*, 49/4 (2015), pp. 387–401, esp. 393–4; and Carlin, 'The Host', pp. 476–9.
[134] CCR 1409–13, pp. 343–5.

John Gower. Cobham, himself a great-grandson of Joan Septvans, was distantly related to William de Septvans.[135] In March 1368, however, after Septvans came of age, Cobham was the first witness to his grant to Gower of marshland in Iwade,[136] and in 1373 Cobham was the first of Gower's five feoffees for the manors of Kentwell and Aldington.[137] (In legal documents, feoffees and witnesses generally were listed in descending order of their rank or seniority.) Cobham quitclaimed his interest in Kentwell to three of the other feoffees (Thomas de Preston, Roger Asshebournham, and Thomas Brokhull) in November, 1(?) Richard II (1377?).[138] However, he may have remained a feoffee for Aldington until it was acquired by Brokhull sometime between Michaelmas term 1381 and May 1391.[139] In June 1382 Cobham paid off a debt to Gower of 100s. 6d.[140] It may have been through such links with Cobham, whose wife Margaret was the elder sister of Elizabeth, Lady Luttrell, that Gower came to acquire Lady Luttrell's manors of Feltwell and Moulton in August 1382.[141]

Cobham was a prominent national figure. He served on military campaigns in France, was a judge in the court of chivalry, headed diplomatic missions, and was appointed by parliament to be an advisor to Richard II. For more than forty years, beginning in the 1350s, he was also active in local government in Kent, where he held extensive lands. Sir Arnald Savage (q.v.), whose own estates lay in the same part of Kent, served as one of Cobham's major feoffees. During the political crisis of 1387–88 Cobham actively sided with the Lords Appellant and in 1388 was appointed to a committee of five who were to attend continually on Richard II, who was forbidden to do anything without their consent; Cobham himself was to oversee the king's personal affairs. Cobham was still attending parliament in the 1390s, and was at a great council held at Eltham in 1395, but two years later he was among those targeted during Richard's revenge on the Appellants and their supporters. Cobham was arrested in September 1397, and on 28 January 1398 he was impeached in the Shrewsbury parliament for his role in the events of 1387–88. He was sentenced to death, but the king commuted his sentence

---

[135] *CIPM 1365–70*, pp. 75–9; Nigel Saul, *Death, Art and Memory in Medieval England: The Cobham Family and Their Monuments 1300–1500* (Oxford: Oxford University Press, 2001), p. 260.
[136] BL, Additional Ch. 68771.
[137] BL, Harley Ch. 50 I. 14; TNA, C 143/382/2; cf. *CPR 1370–74*, p. 425 (1374).
[138] BL, Harley Ch. 48 E. 32. It is possible that Cobham subsequently resumed his service as a feoffee for Kentwell, because in February 1380 Katharine, wife of Sir Thomas de Clopton, paid for a royal licence for all five feoffees to grant to her and to four named men, in fee, the manor of Kentwell (*CPR 1377–81*, p. 444).
[139] TNA, CP 40/483, rots 144d (6th entry), 488r (3rd entry); TNA, C 143/411/15.
[140] Acquittance by Gower (formerly in the Surrenden MSS, 'lately dispersed'), printed in Warwick, 'On Gower, the Kentish Poet', p. 87, n. 3.
[141] *CCR 1381–85*, pp. 211, 214, 220; SHC, DD\L/P37/41 (Luttrell Family of Dunster MSS, Box 37); see http://somerset-cat.swheritage.org.uk/records/DD/L/P37/41.

to banishment for life to Jersey. Following Henry Bolingbroke's arrival at Ravenspur in June 1399, Cobham also returned. He addressed parliament in October 1399, declaring that Richard II had been rightly deposed, and that the former king and his counsellors should be punished. At the parliament of 1406 he subscribed to the entailing of the crown on Henry IV's sons. Cobham died at Maiden Bradley, Wiltshire, on 10 January 1408.[142]

Of all of Gower's known associates, his longest-documented connection was with Cobham. As noted above, Cobham last occurs in Gower's life records in 1382, although he may have remained one of Gower's feoffees until the disposal of Aldington. After Henry Bolingbroke's accession, Gower wrote glowingly of Cobham as a beacon of justice, virtue, and fidelity, and a 'true friend of the realm' (*Cronica Tripertita*, 2: 213–32). Michael Bennett emphasizes the connection between Gower and Cobham in his analysis of Gower's politics in Chapter 13, below.

William (de) Weston (c.1351–c.1419)

William Weston was the second of Gower's five feoffees in 1373 for the manors of Kentwell (Suffolk) and Aldington (Kent).[143] In March 1376 he quitclaimed his right in Kentwell to three fellow-feoffees (Preston, Asshebournham, and Brokhull).[144] However, he may have remained a feoffee for Aldington until it was acquired by Brokhull sometime between Michaelmas term 1381 and May 1391.[145] William Weston was presumably the man of this name who was a co-defendant with Gower in 1394–95 in the assize of *novel disseisin* brought by Thomas de Feriby (see Appendix 3, below). It may have been Weston's son William who was named with Gower in January 1405, when the Southwark lawyer John Solas undertook, on pain of £100, not to commit or procure any 'hurt or harm to John Gower and William Weston his servant'.[146]

At least three William Westons, all of whom served as members of parliament, were active during the reigns of Richard II and Henry IV,[147] but

---

[142] Allen, 'Cobham, John, Third Baron Cobham of Cobham'.
[143] BL, Additional Ch. 68771; Harley Ch. 50 I. 14; TNA, C 143/382/2; cf. *CPR 1370–74*, p. 425.
[144] BL, Harley Ch. 57 G. 43. It is possible that Weston, like Cobham, subsequently resumed his service as a feoffee for Kentwell; see n. 138, above.
[145] TNA, CP 40/483, rots 144d (6th entry), 488r (3rd entry); TNA, C 143/411/15.
[146] *CCR 1402–5*, p. 484.
[147] For the two contemporary MPs of this name who probably were *not* Gower's associates, see Carole Rawcliffe, 'Weston, William IV (d. c. 1427) of London', in *HPHC* (http://www.historyofparliamentonline.org/volume/1386-1421/member/weston-william-iv-1427, accessed 30 July 2017); and Linda S. Woodger, 'Weston, William II (d. c. 1419), of Dedswell in Send, Surr. and Hindhall in Buxted, Suss.', in *ibid*. (http://www.historyofparliamentonline.org/volume/1386-1421/member/weston-william-ii-1419, accessed 30 July 2017).

the one most likely to have been Gower's associate was the Surrey landowner William Weston of West Clandon (*c*. 1351–*c*. 1419).[148] Three things point to this identification: firstly, the other two MPs of that name cannot be traced before the 1390s; secondly, William Weston of West Clandon was married to a Northwode descendant; and thirdly, only William Weston of West Clandon had a son called William Weston (*fl*. 1415–51), who might have been of suitable age to have served as Gower's 'servant' in 1405.[149]

William Weston of West Clandon was the son and heir of his father of the same name (*d*. by 1353). His career can be traced from April 1371, when he was appointed as an esquire of the body to Edward III with an annuity of forty marks. In July 1373 Weston and John Legge (*d*. 1381) were commissioned to escort the two captive sons of Charles of Blois to Nottingham Castle. A few months later Weston became one of John Gower's feoffees for the manors of Kentwell and Aldington. He was a man of substance, and in 1378, and again in 1392, he was fined 40*s*. for not taking the order of knighthood. By October 1381 Weston had married Joan, daughter and heir of John Legge and his wife Agnes de Northwode, who was the daughter of Sir John's cousin, Sir Robert de Northwode (*d*. 17 July 1360). Weston held a variety of commissions and offices in Surrey between 1380 and 1407, but thereafter served only as a Justice of the Peace (1413–17). He also held office jointly in Surrey and Sussex as sheriff (1382–83), escheator (1388–89, 1400, 1401–02), and aulnager (1394–96). He served as MP for Surrey in November 1380, November 1390, 1393, 1394, January 1397, 1401, 1415, and 1419, and probably died some months later.[150]

Roger (de) Asshebournham (Ashburnham) (*fl*. 1373 – *d*. *c*. 1392)

Asshebournham was the third of Gower's five feoffees in 1373 for the manors of Kentwell and Aldington.[151] He remained a feoffee for Kentwell until it was acquired by Katherine, wife of Sir Thomas de Clopton, in February 1380.[152] He may also have remained a feoffee for Aldington until it was acquired by

---

[148] Carole Rawcliffe, 'Weston, William I (c.1351–c.1419), of West Clandon, Surr.', in *HPHC* (http://www.historyofparliamentonline.org/volume/1386-1421/member/weston-william-i-1351-1419, accessed 30 July 2017).

[149] Carole Rawcliffe, 'Weston, William III, of Ockham, Surr.', in *HPHC* (http://www.historyofparliamentonline.org/volume/1386-1421/member/weston-william-iii, accessed 2 August 2017).

[150] Rawcliffe, 'Weston, William I (c.1351–c.1419), of West Clandon, Surr.'; BL, Harley Ch. 50 I 14; TNA, C 143/382/2. On the genealogy of the Northwode family, see [Larking], 'Genealogical Notices of the Northwoods', pp. 9–42; [Thomas Milbourne], 'Report of Proceedings at Redhill, in July, 1877', *Surrey Archaeological Collections*, 7 (1880), pp. liii–lvii, at lv.

[151] BL, Additional Ch. 68771; Harley Ch. 50 I. 14; TNA, C 143/382/2; cf. *CPR 1370–74*, p. 425.

[152] *CPR 1377–81*, p. 444.

his fellow-feoffee, Thomas de Brokhull, sometime between Michaelmas term 1381 and May 1391.[153] In 1377 Asshebournham and John Wacche (discussed above) were among the witnesses to a quitclaim at London.[154] Roger was a younger son of John Ashburnham (d. 1335), of Ashburnham in east Sussex, and a younger brother of the latter's improvident eldest son and heir John (d. 1371 or later). Roger became a prominent figure in the administration of Sussex, and acquired at least five manors for himself in Sussex and Kent before his death c. 1392.[155]

Thomas (de) Brokhull (Brockhull, Brockhill) (fl. 1368 – d. c. 1411)

In March 1368 Brokhull was the third witness to the grant by William Septvaunz to Gower of his marsh in Iwade, and in 1373 he was the fourth of Gower's five feoffees for the manors of Kentwell and Aldington.[156] He remained a feoffee for Kentwell until it was acquired by Katherine, wife of Sir Thomas de Clopton, in February 1380.[157] He probably remained a feoffee for Aldington until he acquired it for himself sometime between Michaelmas term 1381 and May 1391.[158]

Brokhull was probably a younger son or nephew of Sir Thomas Brockhill of Saltwood, Kent. He was captain of Marck Castle in Picardy from December 1380 to April 1382; MP for Kent in October 1382, 1385, 1395, January 1397, 1399, and 1402; and between 1383 and 1407 held office in Kent many times. Brokhull was employed into the 1390s as a feoffee of landed estates. In addition to Gower's manor of Aldington, Brokhull obtained a manor and other lands at Little Chart (Kent), which he held of the monks of Christ Church, Canterbury.[159]

Thomas de Preston, clerk (fl. 1373–81)

Preston was the fifth of Gower's five feoffees in 1373 for the manors of Kentwell and Aldington.[160] He remained a feoffee for Kentwell until it was

---

[153] TNA, CP 40/483, rots 144d (6th entry), 488r (3rd entry); TNA, C 143/411/15.
[154] CCR 1374–77, p. 521.
[155] Linda S. Woodger, 'Ashburnham, John (d. 1417), of Ashburnham, Sussex', in *HPHC* (http://www.historyofparliamentonline.org/volume/1386-1421/member/ashburnham-john-1417).
[156] BL, Additional Ch. 68771; Harley Ch. 50 I. 14; TNA, C 143/382/2; cf. *CPR 1370–74*, p. 425.
[157] *CPR 1377–81*, p. 444.
[158] TNA, CP 40/483, rots 144d (6th entry), 488r (3rd entry); TNA, C 143/411/15.
[159] Linda S. Woodger, 'Brockhill, Thomas (d.c.1411), of Calehill in Little Chart and Aldington, Kent', in *HPHC* (http://www.historyofparliamentonline.org/volume/1386-1421/member/brockhill-thomas-1411); *Calendarium Inquisitionum Post Mortem sive Escaetarum*, vol. 3 (Richard II-Henry IV) (London: Record Commission, 1821), p. 142.
[160] BL, Additional Ch. 68771; Harley Ch. 50 I. 14; TNA, C 143/382/2; cf. *CPR 1370–74*, p. 425.

acquired by Katherine, wife of Sir Thomas de Clopton, in February 1380.[161] He may also have remained a feoffee for Aldington until it was acquired by his fellow-feoffee Thomas de Brokhull sometime between Michaelmas term 1381 and May 1391.[162]

Preston was rector of the church of Chelsea, Middlesex, in 1368, but by 26 May 1369, when he was ordained a deacon at London by Simon Sudbury, bishop of London, he evidently had exchanged it for the rectory of Tunstall, near Sittingbourne, Kent, and he was still described as rector of Tunstall in Gower's grant of Kentwell in 1373.[163] By 1377 Preston was vicar of Bexley, Kent, and was still so described in 1381. In both 1377 and 1381 Preston served as a co-feoffee for property in London along with two other Gower associates: Thomas Pathorn (*q.v.*), and John Wacche or Wecche (*q.v.*).[164]

Attorneys

William Emery (*fl.* 1381 – d. 1431/2)

Emery served as Gower's attorney in the court of Common Pleas when Gower sued the carpenter Walter Cook in Michaelmas term 1381.[165] During the 1380s he developed a thriving professional career in the court of Common Pleas, specializing in the registering of conveyances of property in Kent, and also began acquiring property for himself in eastern Kent. Between 1404 and his death in 1431/2 he served frequently as bailiff or jurat of Canterbury, and he was MP for Canterbury in 1413. In 1384 he became a feoffee for Roger de Northwode in the sale of the reversion of the manor of Horton, and this property continued to require his attention as late as 1408. He was still active as a feoffee in 1427, and died between Michaelmas 1431 and 26 August 1432.[166]

---

[161] *CPR 1377–81*, p. 444.
[162] TNA, CP 40/483, rots 144d (6th entry), 488r (3rd entry); TNA, C 143/411/15.
[163] 'Appendix: Rectors and Incumbents', in *Survey of London: Volume 7, Chelsea, Part III: The Old Church*, ed. Walter H. Godfrey (London: London County Council, 1921), pp. 84–5 (http://www.british-history.ac.uk/survey-london/vol7/pt3/pp84-85, accessed 26 June 2017); *Registrum Simonis de Sudbiria Diocesis Londoniensis A.D. 1362–1375*, ed. Robert C. Fowler, 2 volumes, Canterbury and York Society, Canterbury and York series 34, 38 (1927–38), I: p. 70; BL, Harley Ch. 50 I. 14.
[164] LMA, HR 106/59–62 (1377), 110/78 (1381); *CCR 1381–85*, p. 426.
[165] TNA, CP 40/483, rots. 144d (6th entry, http://aalt.law.uh.edu/AALT6/R2/CP40no483/483_0307.htm), 488r (3rd entry, http://aalt.law.uh.edu/AALT6/R2/CP40no483/483_0999.htm).
[166] Linda S. Woodger, 'Emery, William (d. 1431/2), of Canterbury, Kent', in *HPHC* (http://www.historyofparliamentonline.org/volume/1386-1421/member/emery-william-14312); *CCR 1405–09*, pp. 360–1, 362–3.

Thomas Pathorn (*fl.* 1372–82)

Thomas Pathorn served as Gower's attorney in the court of Common Pleas in 1381 and 1382.[167] He occurs in Surrey property transactions by 1372.[168] In five London Husting deeds of 1377 and 1381, Thomas Pathorn 'of the county of York' served as one of four feoffees for the settlement of property in London. Two of Pathorn's co-feoffees in these deeds – Thomas Preston, clerk (*q.v.*), and John Wacche or Wecche (*q.v.*)[169] – were also associates of John Gower, and Pathorn served as Wacche's attorney in Michaelmas term 1382.[170]

William Repyngdon (de Repyndoun, Repyngton) (*fl.* 1382–90?)

William Repyngdon served as Gower's attorney in the court of Common Pleas in Hilary term 1382.[171] He is not described as a clerk, so he probably was not the royal clerk William Repyngdon or Repyngton who, between 1399 and 1406, became prebendary of Bridgnorth and Hastings, portioner of Burford, parson of Balsham, and prebendary of Leicester[172] and who, in August 1400, when Henry IV was at Newcastle-on-Tyne, was commissioned, along with two other men, 'to take carriage and horses for carrying the king's jewels'.[173] Gower's attorney may have been the William de Repyndoun of Kent who in June 1390 was a mainpernor in Chancery for William Blosme.[174] Perhaps he was the William Repyngdon who sued Thomas Godyn *alias* Buxhull of Robertsbrigge (Sussex), franklin, in the court of Common Pleas *temp.* Richard II.[175]

William Elyngton of London (*fl.* 1394–95)

William Elyngton served as Gower's attorney at the Surrey assize of *novel disseisin* in Michaelmas term 1394 brought by Thomas de Feriby against Gower and his co-defendants, and he stood surety for Gower at its conclusion in February 1395 (see Appendix 3, below). Several men of this name were active during the reigns of Richard II and Henry IV. Gower's attorney was described as 'William Elyngton of London' when he stood surety for Gower, evidently to distinguish him from William Elyngton of Yorkshire (the most

---

[167] TNA, CP 40/482, rot. 232r (1381); CP 40/484, rot. 439r (1382).
[168] Frank B. Lewis, *Pedes Finium, or, Feet of Fines Relating to the County of Surrey*, Surrey Archaeological Society, extra volume 1 (1894), pp. 141 (no. 94); 142 (no. 104).
[169] LMA, HR 106/59-62 (1377), 110/78 (1381); CCR 1381–85, p. 426.
[170] TNA, CP 40/487, rot. 222.
[171] TNA, CP 40/484, rot. 492r.
[172] CPR 1399–1401, pp. 127, 295, 469; CPR 1401–05, p. 9; CPR 1405–08, pp. 175, 176.
[173] CPR 1399–1401, p. 355.
[174] CCR 1389–92, p. 191.
[175] CPR 1416–22, p. 225.

prominent of the contemporary William Elyngtons), who stood surety on the same occasion for Gower's co-defendant, William Weston. Gower's attorney was not described as a clerk, so he probably was not the William Elyngton, king's clerk, who in October 1386 was presented to the vicarage of Coggeshall, Essex, or who served as a co-feoffee for property in Essex in November 1413.[176] Perhaps he was the William Elyngton who on 2 March 1394 made a recognisance to John Hertilpole, clerk, for £10 to be levied in the city of London, and who was one of a group of six men who stood surety for an armourer to whom the guardianship of a London orphan was committed in September 1395.[177]

John Drake (*fl.* 1381–1401?)

In Michaelmas term 1395, John Drake served as Gower's attorney in the second iteration during that term of his lawsuit against Thomas Forester and John 'Gray' (*recte* Gay) to render him reasonable accounts for their respective terms as his bailiff in Feltwell (Norfolk) and as his receiver.[178] Of the several John Drakes who appear in the records of the reigns of Richard II and Henry IV, only one recurs as an attorney in the court of Common Pleas. This John Drake served as Katherine Sporle's attorney in Hilary, Easter, and Michaelmas terms 1381, and stood surety for a clerk and served as attorney for three different men in Trinity term 1401.[179]

Gower's Executors

The list of executors given in the register copy of Gower's testament (see Appendix 4) is defective, but a complete list survives from Hilary term 1410, when Gower's executors sued Sir Hugh Luttrell in the court of Common Pleas. The plea roll names them as 'Agnes, who was the wife of John Gower, esquire; Arnald Savage, knight; William Loveneye, esquire of the lord King;

---

[176] *CPR 1385–89*, p. 229 (1386); Essex Record Office, D/P 32/25/29 (1413) (https://secureweb1.essexcc.gov.uk/SeaxPAM/ViewCatalogue.aspx?ID=29990).

[177] *CCR 1392–96*, p. 247; *Calendar of Letter-Books ... of the City of London: Letter Book H*, ed. Reginald R. Sharpe (London: John Edward Francis, for the Corporation of London, 1907), p. 424.

[178] TNA, CP 40/539, rot. 535r, 5th entry (http://aalt.law.uh.edu/AALT6/R2/CP40no539/539_1259.htm).

[179] Robert C. Palmer, *English Law in the Age of the Black Death, 1348–1381: A Transformation of Governance and Law* (Chapel Hill: University of North Carolina Press, 1993), p. 333 (citing TNA, CP 40/481, rot. 175d; 482, rot. 423d; 483, rot. 159d); Jonathan Mackman and Matthew Stevens, 'CP40/562: Trinity term 1401', in *Court of Common Pleas: The National Archives, CP40 1399–1500* (London: Centre for Metropolitan History, 2010) (*British History Online*, http://www.british-history.ac.uk/no-series/common-pleas/1399-1500/trinity-term-1401, accessed 22 December 2017), summaries of TNA, CP 40/562, rots 149r, 303d, 308d, 309d, 313d.

William Doune, canon of the King's Chapel at Westminster; and John Burton, clerk'.[180]

Agnes, John Gower's widow (*fl.* 1398–1410)

(Discussed below.)

Sir Arnald (or Arnold) (II) Savage (1358–1410)

Savage's family had long been established at Bobbing (near Sittingbourne), Kent. His father, also Sir Arnald (*d.* 1375), had been a member of the Black Prince's household and a Kentish administrator; his mother Eleanor (*d.* 1375) had nursed the future Richard II in infancy. The second Sir Arnald inherited the manors of Bobbing and Tracies (in Newington), and various small properties nearby, but he was never a man of great wealth. He was knighted in 1385 during Richard II's expedition to Scotland, and served Richard II as a king's knight or chamber knight until the end of his reign. Under both Richard II and Henry IV, Savage was a knight of the shire for Kent and was appointed to various commissions for the county; in 1401 and 1404 the Commons chose him as their Speaker. Savage also served on the councils of the Prince of Wales and of Henry IV. He died on 29 November 1410; his brass survives in St Bartholomew's Church, Bobbing.[181]

Savage's Kentish manors lay in the vicinity of Gower's properties, and he also maintained a substantial house in Southwark that he rented from the Bridge House (the trust that maintained London Bridge). Savage's house lay just outside the Bridge House headquarters on the north side of Tooley Street, and was described in the Bridge House accounts of 1391–92 as 'a certain new inn [*i.e.*, *townhouse*] in the parish of St. Olave's, Southwark, outside the gate of the Bridge House, which Sir Arnold Savage now holds'. In 1405 he and the Bridge wardens shared the cost of some new glass for the private chapel in his house.[182] When Sir Arnald's widow, Joan, made her

---

[180] TNA, CP 40/596, rot. 232d.

[181] John L. Kirby, 'Savage, Sir Arnold (1358–1410)', *ODNB* (http://www.oxforddnb.com/view/article/24712, accessed 18 July 2017); John S. Roskell, 'Sir Arnald Savage of Bobbing: Speaker for the Commons in 1401 and 1404', *Archaeologia Cantiana*, 70 (1956), 68–83; John S. Roskell and Linda S. Woodger, 'Savage, Sir Arnold (1358–1410), of Bobbing, Kent', in *HPHC* (http://www.historyofparliamentonline.org/volume/1386-1421/member/savage-sir-arnold-i-1358-1410, accessed 2 August 2017).

[182] Savage paid the very high annual rent of 68s., which was 14s. 8d. more than the previous tenant had paid, suggesting that the house had been renovated for him. In 1405 the house's chapel was embellished with thirty-two feet of new glass at a cost of 34s. 8d., of which Sir Arnald paid half and the Bridge wardens the other half. See Vanessa Harding and Laura Wright, eds, *London Bridge: Selected Accounts and Rentals, 1381–1558*, London Record Society, vol. 31 (1995, for 1994), no. 137; Martha Carlin, 'The Urban Development of Southwark, c. 1200 to 1550' (unpub. PhD thesis,

testament in April 1413, shortly before her death, she was still living in St Olave's parish, perhaps in the same house.[183] Savage's elder sister, Eleanor, was the wife of Sir Roger Northwode (son and heir of Sir John Northwode, *q.v.*),[184] and Sir Arnald must have been well known to Gower, but he does not occur in Gower's life records until he was named as an executor in Gower's testament. He was still active as Gower's executor in Hilary term 1410, and died on 29 November 1410.[185]

William Loveney(e) (Loueney), king's esquire (*fl.* 1382 – d. 1435)

During Gower's lifetime, William Loveney was a member of Henry Bolingbroke's household, in which he served for more than thirty years. Loveney first occurs as a clerk of Henry's household on 31 March 1382, when Henry was only fourteen years old. In 1385, as a mark of their '*grande affection*', Henry and his wife Mary de Bohun granted him a lifetime corrody at Llanthony Priory, and it was probably Henry's influence that in February 1389 procured Loveney (called William Loveney of Brentford, Essex) a royal pardon for having killed a man at Brentford on 8 September 1387. By 5 May 1390 Loveney was keeper of Henry's Wardrobe, a position he continued to hold until around September 1398. It is possible that Gower met Loveney in the summer or autumn of 1393, when Gower received a livery collar from Henry (discussed above). Loveney had married by September 1397, but in 1398 he followed Henry into exile, and after Henry's return and accession as king, Loveney was keeper of his Great Wardrobe from 28 October 1399 until 8 April 1408. He also served Henry IV throughout his reign in a variety of commissions and other offices, including collector of the cloth subsidy and petty custom at London (1400–01), supervisor of victualling and array on the marches of Picardy (1405), treasurer of the king's daughter Philippa, on her marriage to Erik IX of Denmark (July 1406–May 1408), sheriff of Essex and Hertfordshire (Nov. 1408–Nov. 1409), escheator of Essex and Hertfordshire (Nov. 1409–Dec. 1410), and keeper of the king's ships (1412). Loveney also served as MP for Middlesex in 1401, 1407, and May 1413.[186]

University of Toronto, 1984), pp. 352–4 (property no. 223); Fisher, *John Gower*, pp. 66, 341 n. 1 (citing LMA, Calendar of Bridgemasters' account rolls, nos. 11 and 17). Fisher misunderstood these Bridge House accounts, believing that Savage owned his house, and that the glass was for the chapel on London Bridge.

[183] TNA, PROB 11/2A/428 (testament of Joan, widow of Arnald Savage, knight, dated 15 April 1413, proved 12 May 1413).

[184] Roskell, 'Sir Arnald Savage of Bobbing', p. 69.

[185] TNA, CP 40/596, rot. 232d; Roskell and Woodger, 'Savage, Sir Arnold (1358–1410), of Bobbing, Kent'.

[186] Carole Rawcliffe, 'Loveney, William (d. 1435), of Brentford, Mdx., and Great Wendover, Essex', in *HPHC* (http://www.historyofparliamentonline.org/volume/1386-1421/member/loveney-william-1435, accessed 9 January 2017); *CPR 1388–92*, p. 11;

Loveney was given many marks of favour by Henry IV after 1399. These may have been due entirely to Loveney's hard work, long service and administrative expertise, but it is also possible that the new king was especially endebted to him for one particular service. Early in 1400 Loveney was sent to Pontefract 'by the king's command upon the king's secret affairs' about the time of Richard II's death there, and it is possible that Loveney, with his history of lethal violence, had some role in that event.[187]

After the death of Henry IV, Loveney seems largely to have retired to his estates in Middlesex and Essex. In 1415 Henry V's French campaign brought him two final state commissions: in November the royal council chose Loveney to deliver pay and supplies to the garrison at Harfleur and to report on the town's defences, and the following month the king appointed him to provide for the household expenses of the Dukes of Orleans and Bourbon and of other noble French prisoners taken at the battle of Agincourt and held at Windsor. Thereafter, Loveney took some part in county affairs, including serving as a JP for Middlesex (1404–18) and Essex (1412–16, 1419–23), and, briefly, as sheriff of Essex and Hertfordshire (1422), but he was no longer active in the royal administration.[188] If Loveney had indeed played a role in Richard II's death, Henry V, who had been knighted by Richard and who arranged for Richard's body to be regally re-buried in Westminster Abbey, may have deliberately shunned him. After 1422 Loveney occurs only once in government records: in May 1434 he was listed among the notables of Essex who were required to take an oath not to assist disturbers of the peace. He died in 1435.[189]

Chronicque de la traïson et mort de Richart Deux Roy Dengleterre, ed. Benjamin Williams (London: English Historical Society, 1846), pp. 159–60n.

[187] Rawcliffe, 'Loveney, William (d. 1435)'. The date of Loveney's journey is not given, but sometime between 21 February and 20 March 1400 the Exchequer made the following payment: 'To William Loveney, clerk of the lord king's great wardrobe, sent by the lord king's command upon the lord king's secret affairs (*misso precepto domini Regis in secretis negociis ipsius domini Regis*) to the castle and town of Pountfreyt. In money delivered to him, by his own hands, for his own wages, costs and expenses and those of his men riding and returning with him on account of the lord king's service aforesaid, 66s. 8d.' (*Chronicque de la traïson et mort*, ed. Williams, p. lxi, n. 3; Latin text from the Pell Issue Rolls, Michaelmas term, 1 Hen. IV). Frederick Devon, who printed a translation of this record in *Issues of the Exchequer* (London: John Murray, 1837), p. 276, mistranscribed Loveney's name as 'Loveday'. See also James Hamilton Wylie, *History of England under Henry the Fourth* (four volumes; London: Longmans, 1884–98), I: pp. 115–7; Michael Bennett, *Richard II and the Revolution of 1399* (Stroud: Sutton, 1999), p. 192.

[188] Rawcliffe, 'Loveney, William (d. 1435)'; Devon, *Issues of the Exchequer*, p. 344.

[189] Rawcliffe, 'Loveney, William (d. 1435)'.

William Doune (Doun, de Doune; often printed as Donne) (*fl.* 1386 – d. by 28 May 1414)

A civil servant and clerical pluralist, Doune was a clerk of the Privy Seal from 1386,[190] and in 1389 was presented to the mastership of the hospital of St John at Burford.[191] In December 1392 Thomas Hoccleve and William de Doune were among the members of the Privy Seal staff to whom legacies were bequeathed by their colleague Guy de Rouclif.[192] On 11 October 1397 Doune became parson of Everdon in the diocese of Lincoln, exchanging that benefice on 22 September 1403 for the London church of St Martin Ludgate.[193] He was a canon of the royal chapel of St Stephen, Westminster, from 12 December 1399 until his death.[194] In January 1407 William Doun, parson of St Martin Ludgate, took legal action against John Askewythe, citizen and scrivener of London, averring threats.[195] Doune was dead by 28 May 1414, when his prebend in St Stephen Westminster was granted to a successor.[196]

John Burton, clerk (*fl.* 1405–08?)

At least three clerks called John (de) Burton were active in the reigns of Richard II and Henry IV. On 21 April 1385 a Chancery clerk called John Burton took an acknowledgment that John Spenythorn, citizen and tailor of London, had given John Gower, esquire, of Kent, a general release of

---

[190] Thomas F. Tout, *Chapters in the Administrative History of Medieval England* (six volumes; Manchester: Manchester University Press, 1920–33), V: 88–9, 91, 98; *CPR 1396–99*, p. 38.

[191] Richard H. Gretton, *The Burford Records: A Study in Minor Town Government* (Oxford: Clarendon, 1920), p. 257.

[192] TNA, PROB 11/1/57 (testament of Guy de Rouclif, clerk, dated 3 December 1392, proved 28 December 1392). Rouclif bequeathed to Hoccleve, his under-clerk, five marks and a book called the *Trojan War* ('Item, lego Thome Heccleue [sic] *Clerico meo quinque marcas vna cum vno libro vocato Bello Troie*'); to Doune he bequeathed 40s. In August 1382 Rouclif, probably acting as Dame Elizabeth Luttrell's feoffee, had granted the manors of Feltwell and Moulton to Gower (discussed above). Hoccleve may have begun working as an apprentice in the Privy Seal office about that time or shortly after: Linne Mooney has tentatively identified his hand in a Privy Seal document dated 6 April 1383 (Linne Mooney, 'Some New Light on Thomas Hoccleve', *Studies in the Age of Chaucer*, 29 (2007): pp. 293–340, at 310–1 and n. 45).

[193] *CPR 1396–99*, p. 208; *CPR 1401–05*, pp. 261, 305. The abbot and convent of Westminster were the patrons of the rectory of St Martin Ludgate (Richard Newcourt, *Repertorium Ecclesiasticum Parochiale Londinense* (two volumes; London: Benj. Motte, 1708–10), I: 414.

[194] George Hennessy, *Novum Repertorium Ecclesiasticum Parochiale Londinense* (London: Swan Sonnenschein, 1898), p. CXXVII (*q* 129); *CPR 1413–16*, p. 199. See also Elizabeth Biggs, 'The College and Canons of St Stephen's, Westminster, 1348–1548' (unpublished University of York Ph.D. thesis, 2016), pp. 279–80.

[195] *CCR 1405–09*, p. 243.

[196] *CPR 1413–16*, p. 199.

all actions real and personal.[197] Professor Fisher and others have identified this Burton with Gower's executor, but that is impossible because Burton the Chancery clerk died in 1394. He first occurs, as John de Burton, one of the clerks of 'the late earl of March' (Edmund de Mortimer, d. 1381), on 18 August 1383, when he was presented by the king to the chapel of Sudbury (Suffolk).[198] By July 1384 this John de Burton was parson of North Crawley (Buckinghamshire), and a clerk of Chancery.[199] He was subsequently parson of Over (Cambridgeshire) from at least 1387 to 1389 (perhaps to 1392), and of the London church of St Mary Somerset by 1394.[200] He was a clerk of the rolls of the royal Chancery by October 1384, and was still so described in 1392,[201] although he was appointed as keeper of the rolls on 24 October 1386 and held that office until his death (by 22 July) in 1394. This John de Burton was also keeper of the *Domus Conversorum* in London during those years.[202]

Another 'John de Burton, clerk' who can also be excluded from consideration as Gower's executor was an adherent of Henry Percy, earl of Northumberland, during Percy's rebellion against Henry IV in 1405. In the parliament rolls of March 1406 he is described as having been one of the three men named by Percy on 11 June 1405 as his 'general and special attorneys' to make treasonous alliances on Northumberland's behalf with Robert [III], king of Scotland, and with French ambassadors.[203] It is impossible to believe that Gower would have chosen an adherent of Percy as an executor.

A plausible candidate for Gower's last-named executor, and perhaps the writer of his testament, was 'John Burton, married clerk, of London'. He appears in the papal register on 27 April (5 Kal. May) 1405 as due to be appointed to the office of notary, after examination by the archdeacon of

---

[197] Fisher, *John Gower*, p. 67; *CCR 1381–85*, p. 619. Spenythorn was the third husband of Joan, daughter of Sir Robert Gower of Brabourne, Kent. Gower had paid them 200 marks for the manor of Kentwell in June 1369. Joan is not named in this release, suggesting that she had died.

[198] TNA, SC 8/222/11085.

[199] TNA, SC 8/183/9128.

[200] TNA SC 8/181/9044; C 143/424/12; *CPR 1391–96*, pp. 696–7.

[201] TNA, SC 1/43/84 (October 1384); Durham Cathedral Muniments: Eboracensia. Durham University Library, Archives and Special Collections, 1.6.Ebor.15, m. 10 (10 October 1386) (http://reed.dur.ac.uk/xtf/view?docId=ark/32150_s1xs55mc05t.xml, accessed 3 January 2017); *The Church in London, 1375–1392*, ed. Alison K. McHardy, London Record Society, 13 (1977), nos. 492 (p. 65) and 499 (p. 67).

[202] *CPR 1385–89*, p. 230; *CPR 1391–96*, p. 468; TNA, E 101/250/26-29 (1386–92), E 101/251/1-2 (1392-96). The *Domus Conversorum* was a house for Jews who had converted to Christianity; in 1377 it was annexed to the Mastership of the Rolls. 'Hospitals: Domus conversorum', in *A History of the County of London: Volume 1, London Within the Bars, Westminster and Southwark*, ed. William Page (London, 1909), pp. 551–4 (*British History Online*, http://www.british-history.ac.uk/vch/london/vol1/pp551-554, accessed 5 March 2018).

[203] 'Henry IV: March 1406, Part 2', in *Parliament Rolls of Medieval England* (http://www.british-history.ac.uk/no-series/parliament-rolls-medieval/march-1406-pt-2, accessed 3 January 2017).

Middlesex.[204] A papal notary would have been professionally qualified both to write a testament and to act as a co-executor, and perhaps also appealed to Gower's sense of his own status.

Gower's Marriage

In late January 1398, as Richard II's last parliament was gathering at Shrewsbury, John Gower was planning to marry Agnes Groundolf at his house in Southwark. William Wykeham, bishop of Winchester, in whose diocese Southwark lay, issued a special licence authorizing William, curate of the church of St Mary Magdalen, Southwark (which was attached to the priory church: see Fig. 1.3), to solemnize without further banns the marriage of his parishioners John Gower and Agnes Groundolf, outside the parish church, in Gower's private oratory in his townhouse in the priory of St Mary Overy:

> Willelmus permissione diuina Wyntoniensis Episcopus, dilecto in christo filio domino Willelmo Capellano parochiali ecclesie sancte Marie Magdalene in Suthwerk nostre diocesis salutem graciam et benedictionem. Vt matrimonium inter Johannem Gower et Agnetem Groundolf dicte ecclesie parochianos sine vlteriori bannorum edicione dumtamen aliud canonicum non obstitat extra ecclesiam parochialem in Oratorio ipsius Johannis Gower infra hospicium suum in Prioratu beate Marie de Oueree in Suthwerk predict' situat' solempnizare valeas liciencium tibi tenore presencium quatenus ad nos attinet concedimus specialem. In cuius rei testimonio sigillum nostrum fecimus hijs apponi. Dat' in Manerio nostro de alta Clera vicesimo quinto die Mensis Januarij Anno domini Millesimo CCC^{mo} Nonagesimo septimo Et nostre Consecracionis anno Tricesimo primo.[205]

Wykeham, who was staying at his episcopal manor of Highclere in Hampshire, issued this special marriage licence there on 25 January 1397/8. Highclere is about seventy miles from London Bridge; in Gower's day, this represented a journey of several days – more in bad weather. The wedding thus cannot have taken place before the end of January; its actual date is unknown.[206]

---

[204] *Calendar of Entries in the Papal Registers relating to Great Britain and Ireland: Papal Letters*, vol. 6, A.D. 1404–1415, ed. Jessie Alfred Twemlow (London: H. M. Stationery Office, 1904), p. 93.

[205] Hampshire Archives, Winchester: Reg. William Wykeham, vol. 2, fol. 299v; calendared in *Wykeham's Register*, ed. Kirby, II: p. 477.

[206] For Wykeham's itinerary, see *Wykeham's Register*, ed. Kirby, II: Appendix I (January 1328 is at p. 627). Sebastian Sobecki has mistakenly dated the wedding licence to 2 January and the wedding itself to 23 January 1398 (Sobecki, 'A Southwark Tale', p. 643).

In anticipation of his marriage, Gower evidently wrote a brief poem, *Est Amor* ('This is Love').²⁰⁷ The poem begins wryly, with a list of disparaging literary tropes about love (*e.g.*, 'peaceful fight', 'sweet gall', 'stinging rose'). It then shifts in tone to observe that love is like a great clamour made up of small noises; like life and death, love can seem to wander haphazardly, but has a fixed course. The poem concludes with a declaration that marriage is the safe haven of love, the equivalent of a religious rule or order (like the rule or order of St Benedict) for lovers who hope for salvation. It ends with the couplet:

> Hence I, Gower, old in years, in hope of favour,
> Devote myself to the marriage bed, safe in the order of matrimony.
>
> (*Hinc vetus annorum Gower, sub spe meritorum*
> *Ordine sponsorum tutus adhibo thorum.*)²⁰⁸

Gower's depiction of matrimony as a spiritual safe haven may also reflect a broader concern with safety, because *Est Amor* was written during a time of political terror, when Richard II was taking vengeance on the former Appellants and their supporters, including Gower's former feoffee Sir John Cobham. But the poem also quietly celebrates the sweet domesticity and physical joys of marriage, likening it to the garden rose that is more fragrant than the shoot of the open fields ('*Fragrat ut ortorum rosa plus quam germen agrorum*'), and concluding in hopeful anticipation of the marriage bed.

Gower's Wife: Agnes Groundolf

Little is known of Gower's wife Agnes Groundolf, but much has been conjectured. The special marriage licence issued by Bishop Wykeham identifies both John Gower and Agnes Groundolf as parishioners of St Mary Magdalen, Southwark, but provides no other personal information about them. Scholars have generally assumed that Agnes Groundolf was of humble background, and that Gower probably married her simply to provide himself with a caregiver. Gower's biographer John Fisher argued that:

---

[207] Gower's '*Traitié pour essampler les amantz marietz*', a collection of eighteen French *balades* on the evils of adultery, has also traditionally been dated to the period shortly before his marriage, but Professor Yeager has argued that it is probably contemporary with the *Confessio Amantis*. John Gower, *The French Balades*, ed. Robert F. Yeager (Kalamazoo: Medieval Institute Publications, 2011), 'Introduction' (http://d.lib.rochester.edu/ /text/yeager-gower-french-balades-introduction).

[208] My translation; Latin text from Gower, *The Minor Latin Works with In Praise of Peace, Est Amor* (http://d.lib.rochester.edu/teams/text/yeager-gower-minor-latin-works-est-amor, accessed 1 August 2017).

The introduction of a woman into a monastic establishment would have caused difficulties, and then as now the kind of devoted care the old man needed would have been hard to hire. A wife would have been by all odds the best solution. We hear nothing of Agnes's family – the name of Groundolf is itself suggestive. Such a marriage of convenience between an elderly invalid and his nurse would explain the permission to perform the wedding in Gower's lodgings.[209]

The evidence does not support these assertions. Firstly, Gower's house (discussed above), like that of other lay tenants, was in the public part of the priory precinct (facing the high street), and not in the private portion reserved to the canons (between the priory church and the river; see Map 1.3), so having female servants would not have 'caused difficulties'. Secondly, Agnes's surname (discussed below) was an English one that is not 'suggestive' of anything. Thirdly, while Agnes might indeed have cared for her elderly husband, a wealthy man like Gower could have hired skilled attendants with no difficulty; there was no need for him to marry a caregiver simply to retain her services. Finally, Fisher baselessly dismissed Agnes as a lowly functionary whose marriage was purely one of convenience to Gower, and he mistranslated her epitaph (discussed below) and sneered at her virtues listed there: 'The terms *elemosina* and *casta voluntas* speak volumes.' In fact, in Agnes's epitaph, these terms refer to almsgiving (implying that she was a generous donor, not a receiver of charity) and purity of mind (not Fisher's 'willing chastity'), and they bespeak esteem, not contempt.[210]

In recent years, Eve Salisbury has built on Fisher's assumptions to speculate that, for reasons of propriety in a religious precinct, and in order to devote themselves to prayer and to the revision of Gower's *Confessio*, John Gower and Agnes Groundolf probably committed themselves to a sex-free marriage:

> The marriage between John and Agnes is as likely to have been a chaste marriage as an impersonal quid-pro-quo type business transaction. Such an arrangement would have allowed the couple to devote themselves entirely to doing the work of God in their community while at the same time mitigating the gossipy innuendo that their living arrangement at St Mary Overeys is likely to have generated. So too would they be in a position to spend time in devotional activities and quiet contemplation as well as in the supervision of manuscript production (the *Confessio* was actively undergoing revision when the marriage took place). Moreover, when we recall that the home of John and Agnes was located in a religious establishment governed and occupied by Augustinian canons, a chaste marriage is all the more plausible since sexual activity, whether conjugal or not, was prohibited in sacred space [. . .]

---

[209] Fisher, *John Gower*, p. 65.
[210] Fisher, *John Gower*, p. 65.

That the nuptial arrangement could have been agreed upon for reasons pertaining to mutually determined marital chastity explains why the wedding was granted a special licence and performed by an upper-level ecclesiastical official whose services were required (above and beyond the duties of a parish priest) to sanction vows of marriage that had sacramental implications beyond the ordinary. Married couples who wanted 'to maintain chastity in their homes', according to Dyan Elliott, were 'urged to make their vow into the hands of a bishop'.[211]

Professor Salisbury's speculations here, like those of Professor Fisher, run counter to the evidence. As noted above, Gower's house was in the public part of the priory precinct, where lay tenants led ordinary private lives and where a married couple had no need to consider the propriety of having conjugal relations. The special licence was needed to perform the marriage in a private house, and the officiating priest was to be the curate of the couple's parish church of St Mary Magdalen, not 'an upper-level ecclesiastical official' and certainly not the bishop himself. A curate was a deputy parish priest who had no benefice (tenured stipend), but served the cure of souls of a parish in place of the vicar or rector, who paid him a salary and could dismiss him at will. The priory of St Mary Overy held the rectory of St Mary Magdalen and employed William to serve as curate there.[212] There is no evidence whatsoever to suggest that the Gowers' marriage 'had sacramental implications beyond the ordinary'. A much more plausible explanation for the special marriage licence may lie in John Gower's quarrel with Thomas Caudre, one of the canons of the priory of St Mary Overy. On 6 December 1397 three Londoners and a serjeant at arms stood surety that Caudre would 'do or procure no hurt or harm to John Gower'.[213] The cause of the quarrel between Caudre and Gower is not known, but perhaps this unpleasant episode, which occurred shortly before Gower's marriage, lay behind Gower's wish to be married privately in his own house, rather than in his parish church of St Mary Magdalen, which adjoined the south aisle of the choir of the priory church, where the canons had their stalls (see Fig. 1.3).

Some scholars, puzzling over Agnes's unfamiliar surname, have conjectured that she was a Flemish immigrant, like many poor residents of Southwark. Robert Yeager, for example, dismissed the notion that Gower might have written the *Traitié pour essampler les amantz marietz* (a 'treatise' comprising eighteen French *balades* on marital fidelity) as a wedding gift for Agnes, since

---

[211] Eve Salisbury, 'Promiscuous Contexts: Gower's Wife, Prostitution, and the *Confessio Amantis*', in Malte Urban, ed., *John Gower: Manuscripts, Readers, Contexts* (Turnhout: Brepols, 2009), pp. 219–40, at 226–7.
[212] *Victoria History of the Counties of England: Surrey*, ed. Henry E. Malden (five volumes; Westminster and London: [various publishers], 1902–14), II: 108; IV: 153.
[213] CCR 1396–99, p. 238.

no one has ever asked whether Agnes could speak French—let alone *read* it—or, for that matter, what she might have done about the *Traitié*'s Latin marginalia. Her surname, "Groundolf," is unusual, and probably "Doche"—that is, "brod and case" Flemish, not Walloon. During Gower's years of residence in Southwark, Flemings—mostly Dutch-speaking—constituted a substantial minority of the residents, and while they were engaged in a range of trades, they were commonly stereotyped by contemporaries as brewers, or, if they were female, as prostitutes. So—did "moral Gower" marry Agnes of the Stews?[214]

Others, too, have connected Agnes's presumed Flemish origins with the '*frows de Flaundres*' who worked in Southwark's brothels, and wondered how Gower could have met her. Rosamund Allen speculated that

> it seems not impossible that a priest at St Olave's or the Master or a sister at the hospital might have recommended as a servant for the aged Gower an intelligent girl from a poor family whom they might have been anxious to protect from the life of the brothels.[215]

Eve Salisbury, who quoted this passage, concurred:

> There is a possibility that Gower's wife, Agnes Groundolf, whom he married late in life, may have been Flemish, a young foreign woman whom Gower 'rescued' from a life of prostitution in the Southwark stews.[216]

Sebastian Sobecki has suggested that 'Agnes's social status and reputation' may have 'constituted an affront to the religious house', and that this had been the cause of Canon Caudre's quarrel with Gower.[217]

In reality, Agnes's surname was not Flemish, it was Anglo-Danish: a legacy of Viking settlement in the Danelaw.[218] Families with the surname 'Grundolf(f)' can be found, for example, in Norfolk in 1292,[219] and in the

---

[214] Robert F. Yeager, 'John Gower's Audience: The Ballades', *Chaucer Review*, 40 (2005), pp. 81–105, at 87–8; cf. Yeager and Yeager, 'Did Gower Love His Wife?', p. 75.

[215] Rosamund S. Allen, 'John Gower and Southwark: The Paradox of the Social Self', in Julia Boffey and Pamela King, eds, *London and Europe in the Later Middle Ages* (London: Centre for Medieval and Renaissance Studies, Queen Mary and Westfield College, University of London, 1995), pp. 111–47, at 139–40.

[216] Eve Salisbury, 'Violence and the Sacred City: London, Gower, and the Rising of 1381', in Mark D. Meyerson, Daniel Thiery, and Oren Falk, eds, '*A Great Effusion of Blood*'? *Interpreting Medieval Violence* (Toronto: University of Toronto Press, 2015), pp. 79–97, at 89.

[217] Sobecki, 'A Southwark Tale', pp. 643–4.

[218] John Beddoe, 'The Ethnology of the West Riding', *Yorkshire Archaeological Journal*, 19 (1907), pp. 30–60, at 59.

[219] The name occurs in Martham, on the east coast of Norfolk (Barbara Dodwell, 'Holdings and Inheritance in Medieval East Anglia', *Economic History Review*, n.s. 20

West Riding of Yorkshire in the poll tax return of 1379.[220] Since most adults of independent means in Gower's day married, and many re-married if widowed, it is also quite possible that Agnes was a widow in 1398, and that Groundolf was her late husband's surname, not her maiden name. In Michaelmas term 1395, one John Grundolf of London was the plaintiff in a lawsuit over property in Wethersfield, Essex.[221] One of the six defendants was Edmund Lakyngheth, who in 1382 was one of Gower's lessees of the manors of Feltwell and Moulton.[222] If Agnes was John Grundolf's widow (or daughter), she may well have had property of her own when she married Gower.

Agnes outlived Gower, who made her his principal heir and entrusted her with the execution of his testament and the administration of his goods (discussed below). She was buried separately from him, although seemingly in the same chapel of St John the Baptist. Her tomb no longer survives, but John Leland (c. 1503–52) noted that she was buried in a 'more modest sepulchre' than her husband's.[223] John Bale (1495–1563) left a transcription of Agnes's Latin epitaph, most likely composed by Gower himself:

> Quam bonitas, pietas, elemosina, casta voluntas,
> Sobrietasque fides, coluerunt, hic iacet Agnes,
> Vxor amans, humilis Gawer [sic] fuit illa Ioannis,
> Donet ei summus, caelica regna Deus.[224]

Professor Fisher translated Agnes's epitaph to fit his conception of her as a lowborn caregiver who accepted a chaste marriage to the aged poet:

(1967), pp. 53–66, at 60–1, citing BL, Stowe MS 936, fols 53v–54v.).

[220] [Anon.], *The Returns for the West Riding of the County of York of the Poll Tax Laid in the Second Year of the Reign of King Richard the Second, A.D. 1379*, Yorkshire Archaeological Journal, rpt Yorkshire Archaeological and Topographical Association (London: Bradbury, Agnew, & Co., 1882), pp. 266 (Coniston Cold), 288 (Dent), 290 (Ingleton); these entries can also be found in *The Poll Taxes of 1377, 1379 and 1381*, ed. Fenwick, II: pp. 440 (Coniston Cold), 452 (Dent), 453 (Ingleton).

[221] TNA, CP 40/539, rots 347d (2nd entry, http://aalt.law.uh.edu/AALT6/R2/CP40no539/539_0771.htm), 645d (7th entry above small tear in left margin, http://aalt.law.uh.edu/AALT6/R2/CP40no539/539_1445.htm).

[222] *CCR 1381–85*, pp. 218, 426.

[223] John Leland, *Commentarii de Scriptoribus Britannicis*, ed. Anthony Hall, 2 vols in 1 (Oxonii: E Theatro Sheldoniano, 1709), II: 414–16, at 415 (https://play.google.com/books/reader?id=PLoWAAAAQAAJ&printsec=frontcover&source=gbs_atb_hover&pg=GBS.PA415, accessed 10 August 2017); John Leland, *De viris illustribus/On Famous Men*, ed. and trans. James P. Carley, with Caroline Brett (Toronto and Oxford: The Pontifical Institute of Mediaeval Studies and The Bodleian Library, 2010), no. 493, pp. 694–7, at 696; James P. Carley, 'Leland, John (c.1503–1552)', *ODNB* (http://www.oxforddnb.com/view/article/16416, accessed 10 Aug 2017). For Leland's reference to the tombs of John and Agnes Gower, see n. 245 below.

[224] John Bale, *Index Britanniae Scriptorum*, eds Reginald Lane Poole and Mary Bateson (Oxford: Clarendon, 1902), p. 209.

> 'Her faith enhanced by goodness, piety, charity, willing chastity, and sobriety, here lies Agnes. She was the loving wife of humble John Gower. May God grant her the heavenly kingdom.'[225]

A more accurate translation would be:

> Here lies Agnes, whom goodness, piety, almsgiving, purity of mind (*casta voluntas*),
> good sense (*sobrietas*), and faith (*fides*) adorned (*coluerunt*).
> She was the loving, modest (*humilis*) wife of John Gower.
> May God the highest grant her the heavenly realms.[226]

Thus, depictions of Agnes as a poor, uneducated, immigrant caregiver from the back alleys or even the bordellos of Southwark do not accord in any way with the woman with the English surname – perhaps a widow or heiress with property – with whom Gower looked forward to wedded life in *Est Amor*; or with the loving and gracious wife described in her epitaph; or with the spouse whom the wealthy, status-conscious poet with the rank of esquire made his principal heir, executrix of his testament and administratrix of his goods.

The widowed Agnes appears at least twice in the archival record after the probate of her husband's testament. As noted above, in Hilary term (23 January–12 February), 1410, Agnes and her four co-executors sued Sir Hugh Luttrell, son and heir of Elizabeth, late lady of Luttrell, in the court of Common Pleas, for the unjust detinue of fifty marks (£33 6s. 8d.). Sir Hugh failed to appear in person or by an attorney, and the sheriff of Surrey was ordered to arrest him, and to bring him to court on the quindene of Easter (7 April).[227] On 24 February 1410, however, Luttrell evidently settled with Agnes, granting to her, during her lifetime, a yearly rent of £20 to be taken from his manor of Feltwell.[228] In light of Professor Yeager's questioning of Agnes's language skills, it is worth noting that Luttrell's grant was written in French – perhaps because Agnes could read it?

Gower's Testament (See Appendix 4, Below)

Gower made his testament in the priory of St Mary Overy, Southwark, on the feast of the Assumption (15 August) 1408. He opened with the standard declaration that he was 'of sound mind' but he did not add, as many

---

[225] Fisher, *John Gower*, p. 65.
[226] Rosamund Allen has offered a somewhat similar translation: 'Here lies Agnes, whom goodness, devotion, charity, chaste inclination, sobriety and faith cultivated; she was the loving and humble wife of John Gower; may the supreme God grant her the heavenly kingdom' (Allen, 'John Gower and Southwark', p. 137).
[227] TNA, CP 40/596, rot. 232d.
[228] With memorandum of acknowledgment, dated 25 February (*CCR 1409–13*, pp. 80–1).

testaments did, any reference to his bodily health. The entire document is quite impersonal. Gower left cash bequests to fifteen religious institutions:

- The prior, sub-prior, canons and novices of the priory of St Mary Overy, Southwark, and their valets and grooms (Clauses 2–3; total cash value: around £14)

- The lights and ornaments of Gower's parish church of St Mary Magdalen, Southwark (which was attached to the priory church of St Mary Overy; see Fig. 1.3), and the priest and clerks there (Clause 4; total cash value: £2 15s.)

- The lights and ornaments of the other local parish churches of St Margaret, St George, and St Olave in Southwark, and St Mary Magdalen in nearby Bermondsey, and each resident parish priest or rector serving the cure of souls there (Clause 5; total cash value: about £4)

- The master, priests, professed sisters, women servants, and sick inmates of the Hospital of St Thomas the Martyr, Southwark (Clause 6; total cash value: about £6)

- The professed sisters, women servants, and sick inmates of the London hospitals of St Anthony, Elsing Spital, and St Mary 'Bedlem' (Bethlehem) outside Bishopsgate, and of St Mary Spital (St Mary Rounceval) by Westminster (Clause 7; total cash value: about £5 2s. 0d.)

- Each house of lepers in the suburbs of London (there were four of these, including the Lock in Kent Street on the outskirts of Southwark) (Clause 8; total cash value: £2)[229]

- The prior and canons of Elsing Spital (Clause 9; total cash value: £4)

Gower left bequests of goods to:

- The altar of the chapel of St John the Baptist in the priory church of St Mary Overy (Clause 10: two silk vestments; a new missal and chalice)

- The prior and canons of St Mary Overy (Clause 11: a new *Martilogium* [book of martyrs])

---

[229] Carlin, *Medieval Southwark*, p. 24. The other London-area leper houses recorded in Gower's day were at Westminster (St James), Holborn (St Giles), and at Kingsland near Hackney; there may also have been two others, at Mile End towards Stratford le Bow, and at Knightsbridge (Marjorie B. Honeybourne, 'The Leper Hospitals of the London Area', *Transactions of the London and Middlesex Archaeological Society*, 21 (1967), pp. 4–54 (esp. 5, 7, 20–54).

- His wife Agnes (Clause 12: £100 in cash; the rents of two manors; silver table plate; all beds and chests; the furnishings, vessels, and utensils of the hall, pantry, and kitchen; a chalice and a vestment for the altar in the oratory of Gower's townhouse)

Gower's legacies to members of the clergy required them to pray for him and, in some cases, to have others pray for him as well. The total value of his cash bequests to religious institutions was about £38 (Clauses 2–9), and he also left £100 in cash to his wife, Agnes (Clause 12).

Gower's bequests to his local religious institutions are unsurprising, since he had lived in the precinct of the priory of St Mary Overy in Southwark for some years. However, most testators who left bequests to London leper houses and hospitals included St Bartholomew's in Smithfield, and St Mary Spital outside Bishopsgate, which were the city's largest hospitals, and it is curious that Gower did not mention these. Gower had no known connection with the hospitals in London and Westminster that he did name.[230]

Gower directed that his body was to be buried in the priory church of St Mary Overy, 'in the place specially provided for this'. This was his elaborate tomb in the chapel of St John the Baptist (discussed below). To the chapel's altar Gower bequeathed two silk vestments, a large new missal, and a new chalice, with instructions that they were to 'remain forever to the service of the said altar and not elsewhere'.[231] To the prior and canons of St Mary Overy he gave a large *Martilogium* (book of martyrs), newly compiled at his own expense, stipulating that he was to have daily a special memorial written in it, 'according to their promises'. This meant that a portion of the martyrology would be read out every day (as was usual in religious houses) in Gower's memory, and that the priory had agreed to this.[232] The Tudor antiquary John Leland reported an oral tradition at the priory that Gower had been responsible for repairs to the priory church and its furnishings, partly at the expense of wealthy and powerful friends (unnamed), and partly at Gower's own expense.[233] There is no mention of this in Gower's testament or other extant life records, but a tablet near Gower's tomb that promised an indulgence of 1500 days for all who prayed for Gower's soul (discussed

---

[230] Brief descriptions of all these institutions except the parish church of St Mary Magdalen, Bermondsey, can be found in Caroline M. Barron and Matthew Davies, eds, *The Religious Houses of London and Middlesex* (London: Institute of Historical Research, University of London, 2007).

[231] At one time, the 'Gower Missal' (BL, Additional MS 59855) was tentatively identified as the missal bequeathed by Gower to the priory of St Mary Overy in 1408 (*British Library Journal*, 1978, p. 196, http://www.bl.uk/eblj/1978articles/pdf/article17.pdf), but the British Library's online catalogue now follows Kathleen Scott in re-dating this manuscript to 1440–50.

[232] I am grateful to Donald Logan for information on this use of martyrologies in religious houses.

[233] Leland, *De viris illustribus/On Famous Men*, ed. Carley, no. 493, at pp. 696–7.

below) supports the likelihood that Gower had been a generous donor to the priory church, as did the display of John Gower's shield of arms in a clerestory window on the south side of the nave (now destroyed).[234] Gower's testament makes no mention of a perpetual chantry, or of any other provision for the saying of masses on behalf of his soul. He evidently provided for this separately, however, because in 1532, seven years before the dissolution of St Mary Overy, Thomas Berthelette, who published a printed edition of the *Confessio*, wrote in the preface that in St John's chapel in the priory church, Gower 'hath of his owne foundation a masse dayly songe. And more ouer he hath an obyte yerely done for hym within the same churche on fryday after the feaste of the blessed pope saynte Gregory'.[235] St Gregory's usual feast day is 12 March, but the feast of his ordination is 3 September. If Gower's obit commemorated the actual anniversary of the poet's death (which must have occurred between the dating of his will on 15 August 1408 and its probate on 24 October 1408), then he probably died on Friday, 7 September 1408.

The only beneficiary whom Gower mentioned by name in his testament was his wife Agnes, whom he had married in 1398 (discussed above).[236] She received £100 in cash, silver table plate, a chalice and vestment, and all the furnishings of Gower's townhouse (*hospicij*) in the priory, including his chests (*cistas*) (Clause 12). The chests would have contained Gower's cash, valuables, and important documents, as well as his clothing and other personal effects, probably including his papers and books. The bequest to Agnes of a chalice and vestment 'for the altar that is within the oratory of my townhouse' ('*pro altare quod est infra oratorium hospicij mei*') is significant. Gower had left two sets of vestments together with a new missal and new chalice for use in the chapel of St John the Baptist where he was to be buried (Clause 10), so the bequest of a chalice and vestment to Agnes, expressly for use in the townhouse's oratory, indicates that Gower expected her to continue to reside in the house after his death.

Sebastian Sobecki, in a recent attempt to establish a pre-Dissolution provenance for the 'Trentham' manuscript of Gower's work (BL, Additional MS 59495), has argued that this manuscript, 'together with his [Gower's] writing materials, may have passed to St. Mary Overeys during his last

---

[234] BL, Lansdowne MS 874, fol. 82v; reproduced in Dollman, *The Priory of St Marie Overie*, plate 39. This ink sketch, part of a collection made by two heralds in 1611, notes the colouring of the arms; a caption adds: 'Gower. This standeth in the highest South window of the body of the church nere the roofe therof.'

[235] *Io. Gower de confessione amantis*, Imprinted at London: In Fletestrete by Thomas Berthelette printer to the kingis grace, an. M.D.XXXII. [1532] Cum priuilegio (*A Short-Title Catalogue of Books Printed in England, Scotland, & Ireland and of English Books Printed Abroad, 1475–1640*, ed. Alfred W. Pollard, Gilbert R. Redgrave, *et al.*, 3 vols, second edition, London: Bibliographical Society, 1976–1991) [hereafter STC] 12143), editor's preface ('To the reder.'), available online through EEBO.

[236] This point has also been noted in Yeager and Yeager, 'Did Gower Love His Wife?', p. 70.

years, or it may have reverted to the priory together with his quarters and other personal belongings'. There is no evidence, however, that Gower gave away any books or papers before his death, and the suggestion that Gower's belongings and lodgings reverted to the priory upon Gower's death contradicts the explicit provisions of Gower's testament. Since Professor Sobecki acknowledges that the Trentham manuscript itself contains no evidence linking it to the priory, there is thus no evidentiary support for his contention that this manuscript remained in the priory for more than 130 years until its dissolution.[237] The medieval ownership of the Trentham manuscript must therefore continue to be regarded as unknown.

Gower also bequeathed to Agnes the rent of two manors, 'Southwell' in the county of 'North' (evidently a scribal error for Feltwell in Norfolk), and Moulton in Suffolk. There is no mention of other properties owned or held by Gower or by any feoffees on his behalf, but the disposition of such properties was normally addressed in a last will (*ultima voluntas*) and not in a testament (*testamentum*), which dealt primarily with monetary legacies, chattels, and burial instructions. Unfortunately, no *ultima voluntas* for Gower has been found.

Gower made no reference in his testament to his parents or to other relations, living or dead. He left no bequests to patrons, friends, executors, or servants, and he made no mention of any outstanding debts owed by him or to him. Unusually, for a wealthy and pious townsman, Gower left no legacy to any house of friars, or to the inmates of local prisons. Also unusual is the lack of a bequest to his parish church to make amends for unpaid or 'neglected' tithes, and to his executors to compensate them for their work and expenses, both of which were routine features of testaments of this period. Gower left no bequest to the long-established confraternity of the priory of St Mary Overy, or to the church or poor of his birthplace, or to any chaplain who served the private oratory in his house.[238] In the face of death, the childless Gower's greatest priority, as expressed in his testament, evidently was to ensure the prayers of others on behalf of his soul only. No other souls were to be prayed for, not those of his family, friends, spouse(s) or patron(s), nor even the conventional 'all the faithful departed'. The prayers so expressly besought were to be for Gower alone.

In his poem *Dicunt Scripture*, Gower reflects sombrely on the need for the living to make formal financial provision for post-mortem prayers for their

---

[237] Sebastian Sobecki, '*Ecce patet tensus*: The Trentham Manuscript', pp. 930–2, 933, 954 n.144. As part of this argument, Sobecki also (p. 930) misdates the surrender of the priory to 14 October 1541, two years after its actual surrender on 27 October 1539. See Carlin, *Medieval Southwark*, p. 75.

[238] On the confraternity of the priory of St Mary Overy, see Carlin, *Medieval Southwark*, p. 74.

own soul, because after their death few friends will be mindful of this.[239] Gower seems to have taken his own advice, since he evidently oversaw the construction of his own tomb (discussed below), made arrangements for his own chantry, and provided for a daily memorial to himself to be read by the canons of St Mary Overy, rather than entrusting these matters to his executors.

Gower's testament was proved at Archbishop Arundel's palace at Lambeth, just west of Southwark, on 24 October 1408. The copy of Gower's testament in the archbishop's register names five executors: his wife Agnes; Sir Arnald Savage, knight; 'Sir Roger, esquire' (*dominum Rogerum Armigerum*); Sir William Denne, canon of the king's chapel; and John Burton, clerk. Scholars have long puzzled over the identities of 'Sir Roger, esquire' and of 'William Denne', but the executors' lawsuit against Sir Hugh Luttrell in Hilary term 1410 (discussed above), gives the correct list of Gower's executors: Agnes, who was the wife of John Gower, esquire; Sir Arnald Savage, knight; William Loveneye, esquire of the lord King; William Doune, canon of the King's Chapel at Westminster; and John Burton, clerk (all of them discussed above).[240] The administration of Gower's goods was granted to Agnes, and the probate was concluded two weeks later, on 7 November 1408.

Gower's Tomb

Gower's lavishly decorated stone tomb survives today in Southwark Cathedral, which originally was the priory church of St Mary Overy. The priory was surrendered on 27 October 1539; in 1540 the Southwark parishes of St Margaret and St Mary Magdalen merged to form the new parish of St Saviour, and the parishioners purchased the former priory church from the Crown to serve as their new parish church.[241] In 1905 St Saviour's became the cathedral church of the new diocese of Southwark.

The church was partly rebuilt and heavily restored in the nineteenth century. In 1832, in preparation for a rebuilding of the north aisle and nave, John Gower's tomb was moved from the north aisle of the nave to the south transept, and any remains still in the tomb disappeared at that time. The tomb was restored at the expense of Earl Gower, and in 1894 it was returned to its present location on the wall of the north aisle of the nave, in the second bay west of the crossing.[242] Gower's tomb had been in this location,

---

[239] *Complete Works*, IV: pp. 368, 420; Gower, *Minor Latin Works with In Praise of Peace*, 'Dicunt Scripture', ed. and trans. Robert F. Yeager, http://d.lib.rochester.edu/teams/text/yeager-gower-minor-latin-works-dicunt-scripture (accessed 4 November 2017).
[240] TNA, CP 40/596, rot. 232d (Hilary term, 11 Hen. IV).
[241] Carlin, *Medieval Southwark*, pp. 95–6.
[242] William Taylor, *Annals of St. Mary Overy* (London: Nichols and Son, 1833), p. 73; William Thompson, *The History and Antiquities of the Collegiate Church of St. Saviour*

or nearby, by 1618, when Anthony Munday, in his updated edition of John Stow's *Survey of London*, described it as 'A very faire Tombe in the North Ile of the Church', and quoted an inscription or plaque that said that it had been 'Newly constructed at the expense of the Parish, AD 1615' ('*Noviter constructum impensis Parochiae, Anno Domini 1615*').[243] 'Newly constructed' suggests that the tomb had been moved, since otherwise there would have been no need to rebuild it.

Gower's testament specified that his body was to be buried in the chapel of St John the Baptist. Where was this chapel? Five accounts written before the 'reconstruction' of Gower's tomb in 1615 refer to the tomb's location:

> Thomas Berthelette wrote in 1532 that Gower's tomb was 'on the Northe syde of the fore sayde churche, in the chapell of saynte Iohn'.[244]

> John Leland wrote, c. 1533-45: 'I cannot rightly calculate the date of his [Gower's] death, but this much is certain: that he was honorably buried at London, in the house of the canons of St Mary on the bank of the Thames, where his wife is also buried, though in a humbler sepulchre. He has there a notable statue with two distinctive features: a golden collar, and an ivy wreath interposed with roses, the former the ornament of a knight, the latter of a poet.'[245]

> John Bale (1495–1563) wrote that Gower 'was celebrated under the kings Richard II and Henry IV. He was laid to rest in the house of St Mary de Oueres, distinguished by the poetic laurel, a sign of the flourishing of letters and science, in a noble sepulchre, in the chapel of St John, on the northern side'.[246]

(*St. Marie Overie*), *Southwark* (London: Ash and Company, 1904), pp. 38, 206; *Complete Works*, IV: pp. xix–xx, xxiv.

[243] John Stow, *The Survey of London*, ed. Anthony Munday (London: George Purslowe, 1618), STC 23344, p. '780' (recte p. 776), http://sceti.library.upenn.edu/sceti/printedbooksNew/index.cfm?TextID=stow&PagePosition=792. This addendum to Stow's original text was included in the subsequent edition of Stow's *Survey* by Anthony Munday et al. (London: Nicholas Bourn, 1633), STC 23345.5, p. 451, and in John Strype, *A Survey of the Cities of London and Westminster*, 2 vols (London: printed for A. Churchill et al., 1720), vol. II, Bk iv, Ch. 1, p. 11.

[244] Berthelette, 'To the reder', in *Io. Gower de confessione amantis*, STC 12143.

[245] My translation. '*De tempore ejus obitus non possum recte computare. Hoc interim constat, quod honorifice sepultus sit Londini apud canonicos Marianos in ipsa Tamesis ripa, ubi etiam & ejus uxor sepulchro, sed humiliori, conditur. Habet ibidem statuam duplici insignem nota, nempe aureo torque, & hederacea corona rosis interserta, illud militis, hoc poetae ornamentum.*' (Leland, *Commentarii de Scriptoribus Britannicis*, ed. Hall, II: 415; Leland, *De viris illustribus/On Famous Men*, ed. and trans. Carley, no. 493, p. 696).

[246] My translation. '*Claruit sub regibus, Ricardo secundo et Henrico quarto. Londini tandem quieuit in coenobio ad diuam Mariam de Oueres laurea poetica insignitus in signum florentis literaturae ac scientiae sepulchro nobili, in capella diui Ioannis ad partem septentrionalem.*' (Bale, *Index Britanniae Scriptorum*, pp. 208–9).

John Stow wrote in his *Annales of England* (1592) that Gower 'builded a great part of S. Mary Oueries church in Southwarke, then new re-edified. On the North side of which Church he prepared for his bones a resting place, where somewhat after the olde fashion he lyeth right sumptuously buried in a tombe of stone, with his image also of stone lying over him'.[247]

John Stow wrote in the first edition (1598) of his *Survey of London* that Gower's tomb was 'on the North side of the said church'; in the second edition (1603), he added 'in the chapple of S. Iohn, where hee founded a chauntrie'.[248]

Thus, Berthelette and Stow, both writing before 1615, said that the tomb and chapel were on the north *side* of the church, whereas Anthony Munday (1618, 1633) and later observers, including John Aubrey, who visited St Saviour's around 1670, and John Strype, in his new, expanded edition of Stow's *Survey* (written c. 1702–07; published 1720), described Gower's tomb as in the north *aisle* of the church, where it is today.[249] The tomb is shown in the latter location in the plan of the church published by Concanen and Morgan in 1795 (Fig. 1.3, at no. 29).[250]

Modern scholars have generally assumed that St John's chapel and Gower's tomb have always been in this location. John Hines, Nathalie Cohen, and Simon Roffey, who in 2004 reviewed both the documentary and the structural evidence, argued that the tomb fits its current site so well that it is likely to have been the original location, and that this bay was a liturgically desirable location for a chapel and tomb because it adjoined a doorway that may have been used by the canons of St Mary Overy to process from the cloister into the church. They considered it 'almost certain' that the chapel

---

[247] John Stow, *Annales of England* (London, 1592), STC 23334, p. 518, *sub anno* 1400. The same text can be found in Stow's subsequent editions of the *Annales* (London, 1600, 1601, 1605), STC 23337-23337, pp. 528–9, *sub anno* 1400.

[248] John Stow, *A Survay of London* (first edition; London: John Wolfe, 1598), STC 23341, p. 334; second edition (1603), ed. Kingsford, II: p. 57.

[249] Aubrey's description of Gower's tomb begins: 'In the *Chapel* of St. John, now the North Ile of the Church, was a Chauntry founded by *John Gower*, Esq; where within the North Wall is a fair Free stone Tomb of the *Gothick* Order.' At first glance it would seem that Aubrey's account clinches the location of the chapel of St John in the north aisle of the church. However, Aubrey evidently took his reference to the chapel and chantry from Stow, and so provides no new independent information about the location of the chapel (Richard Rawlinson, *The Natural History and Antiquities of the County of Surrey: Begun in the Year 1673, by John Aubrey, Esq; F.R.S. and Continued to the Present Time*, 5 vols. (London: E. Curll, 1718–19), V: 202, 210. Strype, *Survey of the Cities of London and Westminster*, II.iv.11; Julia F. Merritt, 'Strype's Survey of London: The Creation of the 1720 Edition', https://www.hrionline.ac.uk/strype/introduction.shtml [accessed 7 October 2017]).

[250] Matthew Concanen, Jr, and Aaron Morgan, *The History and Antiquities of the Parish of St Saviour's, Southwark* (Deptford-Bridge, 1795), plate following p. 90.

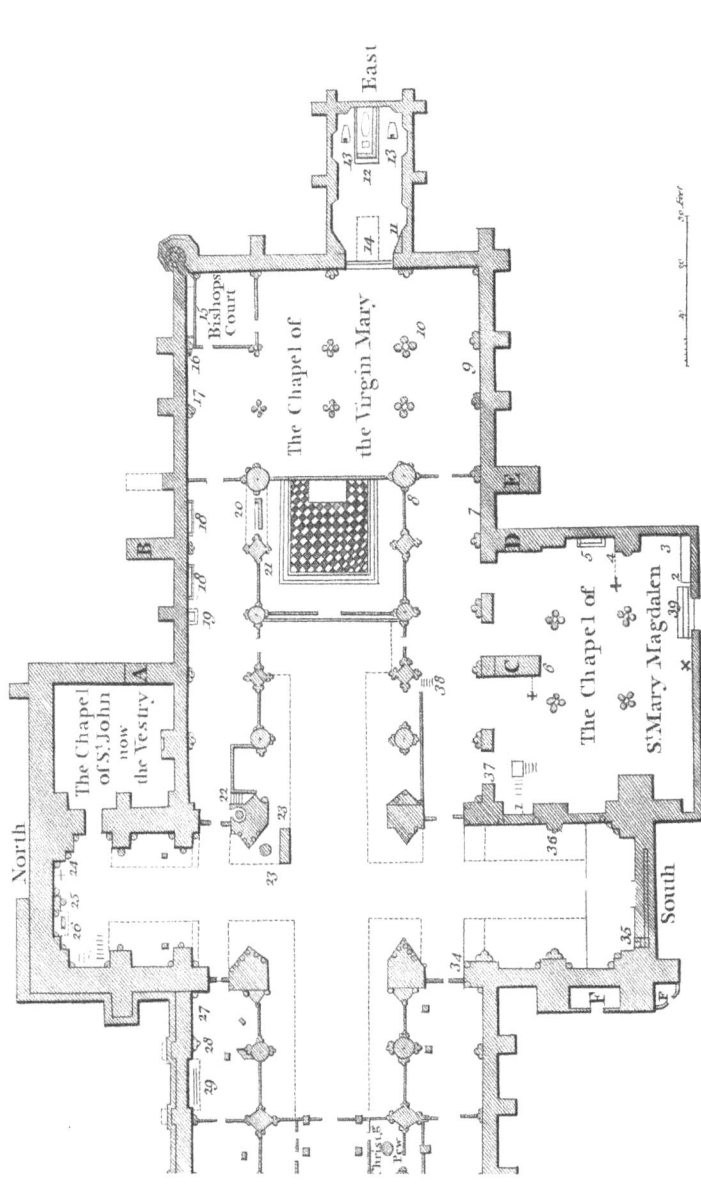

Figure 1.3: Plan of the eastern part of St Saviour's church, Southwark (formerly the priory church of St Mary Overy; now Southwark Cathedral), from Matthew Concanen, Jr and Aaron Morgan, *History and Antiquities of the Parish of St Saviour's, Southwark* (1795), facing p. 175. (By courtesy of the Yale Center for British Art, Paul Mellon Fund, File Number 579092-0001.) Gower's tomb in the north aisle (at no. 29) is in the same location that it occupies today.

itself already existed there 'prior to the construction of the Gower chantry', and conjectured that the chapel of St John consisted of a single bay, probably enclosed by a wooden parclose.[251] These conjectures were subsequently endorsed without further discussion by Nathalie Cohen and Chris Mayo in a study of the fabric of Southwark Cathedral, and by Simon Roffey in a study of chantries and chantry chapels.[252] However, a chapel blocking the east end of the north aisle would have been quite intrusive, and there is strong evidence that the chapel of St John and the Gowers' tombs were actually located elsewhere.

A broadsheet plan of St Saviour's church published by the antiquary Arthur Tiler in 1759, and Concanen and Morgan's very similar plan of 1795 (see Fig. 1.3), both label the chapel on the east side of the north transept as 'The Chapel of St John now the Vestry'.[253] This chapel dates from the twelfth century and is known today as the Harvard Memorial Chapel to commemorate John Harvard, for whom Harvard University is named, who was baptized in the church in 1607. Simon Roffey, Nathalie Cohen, and Chris Mayo have investigated the structural history of this chapel, but not its dedication.[254] Three early histories of St Saviour's – those of Arthur Tiler (1765), Concanen and Morgan (1795), and William Moss and Joseph Nightingale (1820) – identified this chapel as the site of Gower's chantry and thus, by implication, as the chapel of St John the Baptist.[255] In 1904, however, Canon William Thompson, the rector of St Saviour's, published a volume on the church in anticipation of its elevation to cathedral status, in which he referred to this chapel (then still used as a vestry) as 'traditionally known as the chapel of St John-the-Divine' (a post-medieval name for St John the Evangelist).[256] This seems unlikely: dedications to St John the Evangelist were much less common in medieval England than dedications to

---

[251] Hines, Cohen and Roffey, *'Iohannes Gower, Armiger, Poeta'*, pp. 32–41 and Fig. 3.

[252] David Divers, Chris Mayo, Nathalie Cohen, and Chris Jarrett, *A New Millennium at Southwark Cathedral: Investigations into the First Two Thousand Years*, Pre-Construct Archaeology, monograph 8 (London, 2008), Chapters 3–4 (by Cohen and Mayo), pp. 35–100 (at 52, 84); Simon Roffey, *Chantry Chapels and Medieval Strategies for the Afterlife* (Stroud: Tempus, 2008), pp. 132–3, 159.

[253] Tiler's plan of 1759 is reproduced in William Rendle, *Old Southwark and Its People* (Southwark: W. Drewett, 1878), between pp. 156 and 157.

[254] Simon Roffey, 'The Early History and Development of St. Marie Overie Priory, Southwark: The 12th-Century Chapel of St. John', *London Archaeologist*, 8:10 (1998), pp. 255–62; Divers, Mayo, Cohen and Jarrett, *A New Millennium at Southwark Cathedral*, pp. 52–8.

[255] Arthur Tiler, *The History and Antiquities of St Saviour's Southwark* (London: J. Wilkie, 1765, ESTC [online English Short Title Catalogue, 1473–1800, http://estc.bl.uk/F/?func=file&file_name=login-bl-estc] T2795), p. 12; Concanen and Morgan, *The History and Antiquities of the Parish of St Saviour's*, p. 75; William G. Moss and the Rev. Joseph Nightingale, *The History and Antiquities of the Parochial Church of St Saviour, Southwark* (London: J. Taylor, 1820), p. 37.

[256] Thompson, *History and Antiquities of the Collegiate Church of St. Saviour*, p. 122.

St John the Baptist, and I have found no source earlier than Thompson that assigns the dedication of this chapel to the Evangelist.[257]

It is much more likely that the chapel now known as the Harvard Chapel was the chapel of St John the Baptist mentioned in Gower's testament. The main evidence for this is that the Tudor and Jacobean parish records, like the Georgian plans and histories of the church, refer to only *one* chapel or altar of St John. This means that the church did not have both a chapel or altar of St John the Baptist *and* a chapel or altar of St John the Evangelist. For example, inventories of vestments, plate, and other valuables made between 1547 and 1552 by the churchwardens of St Saviour's reported that 'Saynt Johns Altare' possessed five sets of hangings, that two altar cloths 'of redde cloth of gold that was for Saynt Jones altare' had been sold, and that two hangings of blue damask 'for saynt Johns altar' were missing.[258] In 1613 a glazier's bill for repairs to St Saviour's windows included charges for ninety-four feet of new glass, the repair of twenty-six feet of old glass, and the installation of 'a great casment', all in 'St Johns chapell'.[259] Had there been one altar or chapel dedicated to St John the Baptist and another to St John the Evangelist, these records would have needed to differentiate them. There is no evidence in the extant parish records that the bay in the north aisle where Gower's tomb now lies ever contained a chapel at all. The sequence of windows listed in the glazier's bill puts St John's chapel between the north aisle and the north choir aisle – *i.e.*, on the site of the Chapel of St John shown in Fig. 1.3. Therefore, if the church had only one chapel dedicated to St John, then that chapel – the current Harvard Chapel – must have been the chapel of St John the Baptist where John and Agnes Gower were buried.

Two indications that Gower built his tomb in an already-existing chapel are that he does not refer to the chapel in a proprietary way (*e.g.*, as 'my chapel' or as 'the new chapel built at my expense'), and that he left bequests to the chapel and its altar but not to the chaplain. This implies that when Gower made his testament the chapel was already in use, but that it was not Gower's private chantry chapel. Gower may have chosen this chapel as the site for his tomb because of its dedication to St John the Baptist – perhaps his own baptismal saint. The title of Gower's *Vox Clamantis* ('The voice of one crying') evokes the same saint (Matthew 3:3; Mark 1:3; John 1:23). As noted above, Bale reported that Gower's tomb lay on the north side of St John's chapel, and this accords with the orientation of the tomb itself, which was designed to have the effigy facing towards the altar. The evidence thus suggests that John Gower's tomb originally lay on the north side of the chapel

---

[257] I am grateful to Caroline Barron for this information.
[258] John R. Daniel-Tyssen, 'Inventories of the Goods and Ornaments of the Churches in the County of Surrey in the reign of Edward VI', *Surrey Archaeological Collections*, 4 (1869), pp. 1–189, at 83, 85, 89.
[259] LMA, P92/SAV/142.

now known as the Harvard Chapel but whose original dedication was to St John the Baptist.

The churchwardens' accounts for St Saviour's do not survive for the early 1600s, but the vestry minutes for 1557–1628 are extant, and they report the projected move of one stone tomb. On 10 August 1607 a parish tenant called Henry Willson

> was conferred wth all About the takinge downe of the tombe of stone beinge in parte of the Church wch is lett vnto him by lease where laye certaine Oade [i.e., woad], and the placing of the stone in some other parte of the Church, And the said Henrye Willson verye willinglye and friendlye consented to the takinge of the same tombe awaye or anye thinge els the Churchwardens thought fit wch was in any parte of the Church so leased vnto him beinge not preiudiciall vnto him and makinge the places vp againe in anye reasonable sorte.[260]

Henry Willson (or Wilson) was the last of a series of bakers who from 1559 until 1624 leased the chapel of the Virgin Mary, known today as the retrochoir, at the eastern end of the former priory church (see Fig. 1.3), to use as a bakehouse and for other purposes.[261] Unfortunately, the parish lease-book does not survive, and the vestry minutes do not reveal if in 1607 Wilson was also the tenant of St John's chapel. If he was, the entry above probably signals the beginning of the process of moving Gower's tomb. Extensive renovations were carried out at St Saviour's in 1613–14, and it seems likely that the dismantling and moving of Gower's tomb (either in 1607 or later), and its reconstruction in 1615, were part of this broad programme of refurbishment.[262]

Gower's tomb, as it survives today, has been moved more than once and has been heavily restored, but before its reconstruction in 1615 it was described in some detail by Berthelette and in greater detail by Stow.[263] The richly-painted stone tomb with its vaulted canopy portrayed the poet as a prosperous and well-connected gentleman of letters, who proudly displayed the heraldic arms that seemingly connected him with Sir Robert Gower of Brabourne (see Fig. 1.2), and the Lancastrian collar of SS that linked him with Henry Bolingbroke. The recumbent effigy depicted Gower as a man

---

[260] LMA, P92/SAV/450 (St Saviour's vestry minutes, 1582–1628), p. 411.

[261] LMA, P92/SAV/449 (St Saviour's vestry minutes, 1559–81), pp. 10 (1559), 122, 126 (1576); P92/SAV/450, pp. 292, 293 (1594), 411 (1607), 534 (1624).

[262] See, e.g., LMA, P92/SAV/35-146 (bills for repairs to St Saviour's, 1594, 1613–14, 1636, 1651), P92/SAV/450, pp. 450 (1613), 473 (1616).

[263] Berthelette, 'To the reder', in *Io. Gower de confessione amantis*, STC 12143; Stow, *Survey of London* (1603), ed. Kingsford, II: pp. 57–8; Stow, *Annales of England* [fourth edition, 1605], pp. 528–9, *sub anno* 1400. The detailed descriptions of Gower's tomb in John Taylor, *Annals of St Mary Overy* (London: Nichols & Son, 1833), pp. 73–7; *Complete Works*, IV: pp. xx–xxiv; and Hines, Cohen and Roffey, 'Iohannes Gower, Armiger, Poeta', pp. 24, 33–4, 36–9, all contain errors (discussed below).

in his prime, finely garbed in a long, damasked gown, with curling auburn hair that covered his ears and a fashionable forked beard, and crowned with a diadem-like chaplet of roses. The feet of Gower's effigy rested, as was common for male effigies, on a lion, but his head was uniquely pillowed on three large volumes displaying the titles of his major works in French (*Speculum Meditantis*, i.e. *Mirour de l'Omme*), Latin (*Vox Clamantis*), and English (*Confessio Amantis*). Gough's engraving (see Fig. 1.1) shows the volumes stacked in chronological order, with *Speculum* on top, *Vox* in the middle, and *Confessio* on the bottom. In the modern restoration of the tomb, however, *Vox* is on top, followed by *Speculum* and then *Confessio*.

According to Bale, a Latin couplet inscribed somewhere on Gower's tomb offered up these three volumes to the king:

> *De triplici eius opere, hoc carmen est super eius tumbam editum.*
> *Quos uiuens legi, libros nunc offero regi.*
> *Cuius habent legi, secula cuncta regi.*[264]
>
> (This poem concerning his triple work is displayed on his tomb:
> 'Those books that, when living, I compiled, I now offer to the king,
> By whose law all ages must be ruled.')[265]

Gower probably designed his own tomb and oversaw its construction sometime between the autumn of 1393 and the beginning of 1398 or – at the latest – the autumn of 1399 (see discussion below). If so, this couplet can be seen as a canny declaration of allegiance to the king and 'the king's law', which enabled Gower, whose effigy displayed Bolingbroke's livery collar, to represent himself nonetheless as a loyal subject of Richard II.

A prose colophon (*Quia Vnusquisque*) written by Gower after Bolingbroke became king, and surviving in numerous manuscripts, also gives the Latin titles of these three works.[266] The original Latin title of the earliest, *Mirour de l'Omme*, was *Speculum Hominis* ('The Mirror of Mankind') – a literal translation of the French title. It is so called in the first recension of the colophon, but in later versions, as on Gower's tomb, it is called *Speculum Meditantis* ('The Mirror of One Meditating'), evidently to accord with the sound and syntax of the other two titles (*Vox Clamantis* and *Confessio Amantis*).[267]

---

[264] Bale, *Index Britanniae Scriptorum*, ed. Poole, p. 209. These three lines were quoted by Macaulay, who says that Bale's source probably was Nicholas Brigham (*Complete Works*, IV: p. lix).

[265] I am very grateful to Claire Fanger and Leofranc Holford-Strevens for assistance with this translation.

[266] For a list of manuscripts containing copies of *Quia Vnusquisque*, see Derek Pearsall, 'The Manuscripts and Illustrations of Gower's Works', in Echard, *A Companion to Gower*, pp. 73–97 (74–8).

[267] *Complete Works*, III: pp. 479–80, 550; IV: pp. 360, 418–9; Gower, *The Minor Latin Works with In Praise of Peace*, 'Quia Unusquisque' (notes by Robert F. Yeager), http://d.lib.

It seems possible that Gower devised the three short, rhyming Latin titles when he was designing his tomb, so that they would make a pleasing and distinctive triad on the ends of the three volumes that supported the head of his effigy. If so, Gower's tomb would represent an earlier witness to this triad of Latin titles than the surviving manuscripts of the colophon.

The published descriptions of Gower's tomb contain a number of discrepancies and inaccuracies. As many scholars have noted, the Tudor antiquaries disagreed about the appearance of the effigy's chaplet. Berthelette described it as a 'garlande', Leland as 'an ivy wreath interposed with roses', and Bale as a laurel wreath. Stow disagreed with all of them, stating emphatically in his *Survey of London* that the effigy did not have 'any garland of Iuie and Roses but a Chaplet of foure Roses onely', and reiterating that it was 'a chaplet, like a coronet of foure Roses', while in the first edition of the *Annales* (1592) he described it as 'a garland or Chaplet of roses red', to which in the later editions he added 'foure in number'.[268] Stow's descriptions are closest to the monument itself (see below). Richard Gough's influential *Sepulchral Monuments* (1796) includes a written description of the monument that contradicts details of his accompanying engraving of it (see Fig. 1.1). According to the written description:

> the poet's effigy [. . .] is crowned with a chaplet of four roses over his hair reaching to his shoulders, but curling up, and a small forked beard, and a gold collar of SS, fastened in front with a stud adorned with a swan chained (the badge of Richard II) between two portcullices. At his feet a lion. He is habited in a purple gown formerly damaskt with roses, with a standing cape, and buttoned down to his feet, but painted of one dingy colour in the several repairs of this church [. . .].[269]

In Gough's engraving, however, as in the surviving monument, the effigy's hair touches the high collar ('standing cape') of the gown in back, but not the shoulders, and the chaplet has five rosettes, not four.[270] On the monument, the two ends of the collar of SS are fastened together by a link with a swivel (known as a 'torret'), from which hangs a round pendant with the device of a swan.[271] The swan bears no chain, and the collar has no portcullises

---

rochester.edu/teams/text/yeager-gower-minor-latin-works-quia-unusquisque (accessed 8 November 2017).

[268] Berthelette, 'To the reder', in *Io. Gower de confessione amantis*, STC 12143; Leland and Bale, see nn. 245 and 246, above; Stow, *Survey of London* (1603), ed. Kingsford, II: p. 57; Stow, *Annales of England*, editions of 1592, 1600, 1601, and 1605, STC 23334, p. 518 *sub anno* 1400, STC 23335-23337, p. 528 *sub anno* 1400.

[269] Richard Gough, *Sepulchral Monuments in Great Britain* (two volumes in five parts; London: Nichols, 1786–96), II.2: 24.

[270] Hines, Cohen and Roffey, in '*Iohannes Gower, Armiger, Poeta*', p. 38, note that the fifth rosette 'is hidden at the back of the effigy', but it is shown in Gough's engraving.

[271] On the torret or terret (sometimes also spelled 'tiret'), see *MED*, s.v. 'toret', n.(1); *OED*, s.vv. 'torret' and 'terret'.

(see Figs 1.1, 1.4, and 1.5). Thus, Gough's engraving corresponds better than his written description with the evidence of the actual monument.[272] George Macaulay, however, evidently relying on Gough's inaccurate written description rather than on his accurate engraving of the monument, wrote that the effigy's collar of SS was 'fastened in front with a device of a chained swan between two portcullises'.[273] The author of the erroneous description published by Gough, and later canonized by Macaulay, was probably influenced by two eighteenth-century engraved portraits of Gower that included fictitious portcullises on the livery collar (see Figs 1.6 and 1.8). A swan, sometimes shown chained and sometimes unchained, was the badge of the de Bohun family (not, as Gough claimed, of Richard II), and was adopted by Henry Bolingbroke after his marriage to Mary de Bohun; the portcullis later became another important Lancastrian device. Gower's tomb displays an unchained swan and no portcullises.[274]

Modern scholarly descriptions of Gower's tomb have introduced additional errors. For example, Professor Fisher claimed erroneously that in 1724 John Anstis had described Gower's livery collar as 'clasped by a swan between two portcullises'. He also misidentified an engraving of Gower's tomb by George Vertue, published in 1727 (Figs 1.6 and 1.7), as a 'woodcut' printed by William Caxton in 1483 at the end of his edition of *Confessio Amantis*, and he misquoted and failed to understand the significance of the inscription on the ledge of the tomb (discussed below).[275] John Hines, Nathalie Cohen, and

---

[272] In an early manuscript of *Confessio Amantis*, an apparent illustration of Gower's livery collar was added in the 1390s to the figure of 'Amans' (Bodleian Library, MS Fairfax 3, fol. 8r), and this collar similarly shows no portcullises. See Joyce Coleman, 'Illuminations in Gower's Manuscripts', in *RRC*, pp. 117–31, at 124–25 and Fig. 10.3; *Complete Works*, II: p. clvii.

[273] *Complete Works*, IV: p. xx.

[274] For the swan as the badge of the Bohun family, adopted by Henry Bolingbroke after his marriage to Mary de Bohun in 1380, see J. R. Planché, 'On the Badges of the House of Lancaster', *Journal of the British Archaeological Association*, 6 (1851): pp. 374–93, at Plates XXX–XXXII, pp. 383–5; Anthony R. Wagner, 'The Swan Badge and the Swan Knight', *Archaeologia*, 97 (1959): pp. 127–38, at 127, 136, Plates XXXIV, XXXVI–XXXVII; cf. Jenny Stratford, *Richard II and the English Royal Treasure* (Woodbridge: Boydell Press, 2012), pp. 5, 24, 80, 266, 305, 419, and Plates 5(a), 36(a) and (b). The portcullis was adopted by the Beauforts as their family badge by 1439 (Michael P. Siddons, *Heraldic Badges in England and Wales* (three volumes in four parts; London: The Society of Antiquaries of London, 2009), II.1: p. 200.

[275] Fisher, *John Gower*, pp. 25, 40. Anstis refers to 'the Swan which now hangs at the End of the Collar' but makes no mention of any portcullises (*The Register of the Most Noble Order of the Garter*, ed. John Anstis, 2 vols. (London: John Barber, 1724), II: p. 118 (not p. 116, as cited in Fisher's n. 62). One of the British Library's three copies of Caxton's edition of *Confessio Amantis* (1483) (shelf mark IB.55077) has Vertue's engraved portrait of Gower pasted in as a frontispiece, with the lower detail depicting Gower's tomb pasted in facing the last page of text. Fisher evidently mistook the latter for a fifteenth-century woodcut. This copy of Caxton's edition has been reproduced in EEBO.

Simon Roffey report that 'there is now no sign' of a forked beard on the effigy, whereas the forked beard has perhaps been cropped but is still clearly visible (see Fig. 1.4; compare with Fig 1.1).²⁷⁶ Simon Roffey describes the livery chain on Gower's effigy as 'a chain of interlinked 'S's, fastened with a chained swan device beneath twin portcullises to demonstrate the poet's affiliation to the Royal Court of Richard II'.²⁷⁷ However, the 'SS' are not interlinked, the swan is not chained, there are no portcullises, and the livery collar connected Gower with Bolingbroke, not Richard II (see Figs 1.4 and 1.5).

On the effigy's chaplet, the words '*merci*' and '*Ihs*' (*i.e.*, *Jhesus*) in raised letters alternated between the carved rosettes (see Fig. 1.9); these words have been misread by several scholars.²⁷⁸ George Macaulay noted that the memorial brass of Sir Robert Gower in Brabourne church also wore a chaplet of roses (see Fig. 1.2).²⁷⁹ Similar chaplets can be seen on a number of other military effigies and brasses of the period.²⁸⁰ The use of a chaplet of roses on martial monuments such as these suggests that its appearance on Gower's effigy may allude to Gower's status as an esquire rather than to his eminence as a poet.

Gower's tomb was embellished with a variety of ornaments and with texts in Latin and French, all presumably written by Gower himself (see Fig. 1.1). On the wall behind Gower's effigy, the painted figures of Charity, Mercy, and Pity bore French verses in their hands beseeching Jesus to have mercy on his

---

²⁷⁶ Hines, Cohen, and Roffey, '*Iohannes Gower, Armiger, Poeta*', p. 38.

²⁷⁷ Simon Roffey, *Chantry Chapels and Medieval Strategies for the Afterlife* (Stroud: Tempus, 2008), p. 159.

²⁷⁸ Gough's engraving of the chaplet (Fig. 1.9) shows '*Ihs*' with a backwards 's' (similar to 'ʒ'). Taylor misread '*Ihs*' as '*Jh*' (Taylor, *Annals of St. Mary Overy*, pp. 73–4). Macaulay misread Gough's engraving of this word as '*ihi*' (*Complete Works*, IV: p. 20, n. 4). Hines, Cohen, and Roffey misread the four words in Gough's engraving of the chaplet as three words: '*D[o]m[inu]s merci Ih[esu]s*' ('*Iohannes Gower, Armiger, Poeta*', p. 40).

²⁷⁹ *Complete Works*, IV: p. 20, n. 3.

²⁸⁰ See, for example, the effigy of William, fifth baron Willoughby (d. 1409), in Spilsby, Lincolnshire; the brass of Reginald, second lord Cobham of Sterborough (d. 1403) in Lingfield, Surrey; and the alabaster effigy (1419–20) of Ralph Greene, esquire (d. 1417), in Lowick, Northamptonshire (Henry Trivick, *The Picture Book of Brasses in Gilt* (New York: Charles Scribner's Sons, 1971), Plate 23 (cf. Michael Hicks, 'Willoughby family', *ODNB*); John Wickham Flower, 'Notices of the Family of Cobham, of Sterborough Castle, Lingfield, Surrey', *Surrey Archaeological Collections*, 2 (1864), pp. 115–94, at plate following p. 140; Sally Badham and Sophie Oosterwijk, '"Cest Endenture Fait Parentre": English Tomb Contracts of the Long Fourteenth Century', in *Monumental Industry: The Production of Tomb Monuments in England and Wales in the Long Fourteenth Century*, ed. Sally Badham and Sophie Oosterwijk (Donington, Lincolnshire: Shaun Tyas, 2010), pp. 187–236, at 217–24 and plate 5). Other martial effiges and brasses with chaplets include those of John Willoughby, third baron Willoughby de Eresby (d. 1372), in Spilsby, Lincolnshire; Thomas de Braose, fourth baron Braose (d. 1395), in Horsham, Sussex; Sir John Marmion (d. 1386?), in West Tanfield, Yorkshire; and Sir John Dinham (d. 1428), in Kingskerswell, Devonshire; images of these (some under variant names and dates) can be viewed at http://effigiesandbrasses.com/.

Figure 1.4: Gower's tomb: detail of effigy. (*Photograph © Martha Carlin.*)

Figure 1.5: Sketch of the collar of SS from Gower's tomb effigy. From William Thompson, *The History and Antiquities of the Collegiate Church of St. Saviour (St. Marie Overie), Southwark* (London: Ash and Co., 1904), p. 202 (Fig. 52). (*By courtesy of the Yale Center for British Art, Reference Library Collection, File Number 3699195-0001.*)

Figure 1.6: Engraved portrait of John Gower, by George Vertue (1727) (*By courtesy of The Lewis Walpole Library, Yale University.*)

Figure 1.7: Gower's tomb, by George Vertue (1727): detail from Figure 1.6. (*By courtesy of The Lewis Walpole Library, Yale University.*)

Figure 1.8: Engraved portrait of John Gower by John Simco (1792). (*By courtesy of The Lewis Walpole Library, Yale University.*)

Figure 1.9: Chaplet of Gower's tomb effigy, by Richard Gough (1796): detail from Figure 1.1. (*By courtesy of The Lewis Walpole Library, Yale University.*)

soul.[281] On the panel above the effigy's feet were Gower's carved and painted armorial shield, helmet, and crest, the shield tilted as if hanging ('*pendent*') from its right corner, and the helmet and crest facing right (see Fig. 1.10). Gower had used the same design for his arms in his seal (1373), but in the latter the shield hangs from its left corner, and the helmet and crest face left (see Fig. 1.2). In his octagonal signet (1382), Gower used the device from his crest of a standing dog ('talbot'), facing left, over which were his initials 'ig' (see Fig. 1.11).

---

[281] These verses were quoted by Berthelette, Stow, and later antiquarian commentators on Gower's tomb; Macaulay quoted Berthelette's account (1532) and summarized other references to the three allegorical figures (*Complete Works*, IV: pp. xxii–xxiii).

Figure 1.10: Gower's tomb: armorial panel. (*Photograph © Martha Carlin.*)

Figure 1.11: John Gower's signet from his acquittance to Sir John Cobham (1382). From William Warwick, 'On Gower, the Kentish Poet, His Character and Works', *Archaeologia Cantiana*, 6 (1866), p. 86, n.3. (*Photograph by Martha Carlin, by courtesy of the Institute of Historical Research, University of London.*)

In his *Survey of London* (1603), John Stow described Gower's arms as 'a field argent, on a Cheueron azure, three Leopardes heads golde, their tongues gules, two Angels supportars, on the creast a Talbot', and John Aubrey gave a very similar description c. 1670.[282] Both Stow and Aubrey mention Gower's arms as supported by two angels. In the extant armorial panel, however, the carved arms take up almost the entire breadth of the panel, and appear to leave no room for supporting angels (see Fig. 1.10). In one manuscript of Gower's work, what seems to be a memorial page made around the time of Gower's death has a coloured sketch of Gower's upright shield supported by two flying half-angels.[283] According to Stow's *Annales* (1592, 1600, 1601, 1605), Gower's tomb had once displayed 'the likeness of Angels with posies in Latine'. Stow added that the tomb's pious paintings had been white-washed out, and the nose and hands of the effigy struck off.[284] It is not clear

---

[282] Stow, *Survey of London* (1603), ed. Kingsford, II: 58; Rawlinson, *Natural History and Antiquities of the County of Surrey*, V: 204.

[283] Glasgow University Library, MS Hunter 59 (T.2.17), fol. 129r (http://special.lib.gla.ac.uk/manuscripts/search/detail_i.cfm?ID=158). On the same page is a drawing of a funeral bier with lighted tapers at head and foot, together with Gower's epitaph (*Armigeri scutum*) and a summary of an inscription recording an indulgence of 1500 days to those who prayed for Gower's soul (both discussed below).

[284] Stow, *Annales*, editions of 1592 (p. 518), 1600, 1601, 1605 (pp. 528–9), *sub anno* 1400.

where the angels were on the tomb. Perhaps there was a painted shield with supporting angels on the panel at the effigy's head, for which no decoration is otherwise recorded. Possibly the angels with 'posies' (poesies: mottos or short inscriptions) were between the allegorical figures on the back wall, in the space occupied today by a pair of sculpted winged cherub heads atop painted columns, first recorded in Vertue's engraving of 1727 (see Figs. 1.1, 1.7, 1.10).

A painted epitaph in Latin (*Armigeri scutum*), evidently then as now placed below the figures of Charity, Mercy, and Pity, drew attention to Gower's shield and rank of esquire, while acknowledging that these worldly honours evaporated at death:

> Henceforth the shield provides no safety to the esquire;
> Rather, he has rendered up his clay, the common tribute to death.
> His spirit released, may it rejoice to be set free
> Where the kingdom of stainless virtues is established[285]

None of the Tudor descriptions mentions any reference to Gower's name on the tomb, but in 1618 Anthony Munday quoted an inscription that read:

> *Hic jacet Ioannes Gower, Armiger, Anglorum Poeta celeberrimus,*
> *ac huic sacro Aedificio benefactor insignis, vixit temporibus Ed.*
> *3. & Rich. 3.* [sic]

> ('Here lies John Gower, esquire, the most celebrated poet of the English
> and a notable benefactor to this sacred building; he lived in the reigns of Edward III and Richard III [*recte* II].')[286]

Munday did not say where this inscription appeared on the tomb. Rawlinson described the figures of Charity, Mercy, and Pity on the back panel of the tomb, and the armorial panel at the foot, and then noted: 'and underneath is

---

[285] My translation. Cf. 'Orate pro anima (Armigeri Scutum)', in Gower, *Minor Latin Works with In Praise of Peace* (http://d.lib.rochester.edu/teams/text/yeager-gower-minor-latin-works-orate-pro-anima-title, accessed 30 December 2016). The epitaph is quoted by Stow (*Survey of London*, 1603, ed. Kingsford, II: 58), but also appears in Glasgow, MS Hunter 59 (T.2.17), fol. 129r, which appears to be a memorial dating from about the time of Gower's death. It contains a summary of Gower's appeal for prayers ('*Orantibus pro anima Iohannis Gower mille quingenti dies indulgencie misericorditer in domino conceduntur*': discussed below), a coloured sketch of Gower's shield supported by two angels, the epitaph *Armigeri scutum*, and a coloured sketch of a funeral bier with an elegant pall, and with a lighted taper at head and foot.

[286] Stow, *Survey of London*, ed. Munday (1618), p. '780' (*recte* p. 776) (http://sceti.library.upenn.edu/sceti/printedbooksNew/index.cfm?TextID=stow&PagePosition=792) (my translation). This addendum to Stow's original text was included in the subsequent edition of Stow by Munday *et al.* (London: Elizabeth Purslow, 1633), p. 451, and in Strype, *A Survey of the Cities of London and Westminster*, vol. II, Bk iv, Ch. 1, p. 11.

this Inscription', followed by quotations of '*Hic jacet*' and '*Armigeri scutum*'.[287] This may mean that '*Hic jacet*' was painted just above '*Armigeri scutum*'– a very suitable location, especially since both refer to Gower as an esquire. Strype also quoted '*Hic jacet*', but did not say where it was placed.[288] The inscription's reference to Gower as a notable benefactor of the priory church resembles the account in Stow's *Survey* (1598 and later editions), which described Gower as 'an especiall benefactor to that worke'. This may mean that Stow based his comment at least partly on the '*Hic jacet*' inscription, and thus that it was already on the tomb in his day.[289]

Confusingly, John Aubrey reported that he saw 'on a Limb' of the monument a similar but briefer inscription:

> *Johannes Gower, Princeps*
> *Poetarum Angliae, vixit*
> *temporibus Edwardi tertii,*
> *et Richardi secundi*
>
> ('John Gower, most eminent
> of the poets of England: he lived
> in the reigns of Edward III
> and Richard II')[290]

In the seventeenth century, one of the meanings of 'limb' was 'border or edging', and perhaps c. 1670 this inscription was on the front edge (ledge) of the tomb.[291] If so, it was subsequently replaced there by the '*Hic jacet*' inscription. The first line of '*Hic jacet*' was partially quoted in George Vertue's engraved portrait of Gower (1727: see Fig. 1.6), and the entire '*Hic jacet*' inscription appears on the ledge of the tomb in Richard Gough's engraving of 1796 (Fig. 1.1).[292] The '*Hic jacet*' inscription, or something similar, seems likely to have been contemporary with the tomb, because otherwise no inscription on the original monument identified Gower by name. If so, like the other texts on the tomb, Gower probably wrote it himself. In modern restorations of the tomb, Henry IV's name has been added to the '*Hic jacet*' inscription's list of the kings in whose reigns Gower lived. Professor Fisher, who failed to appreciate the significance of the kings in dating Gower's tomb

---

[287] Rawlinson, *Natural History and Antiquities of the County of Surrey*, V: pp. 204–5.
[288] Strype, *Survey of the Cities of London and Westminster*, II.iv.11.
[289] Stow, *Survey of London* (1598), p. 334, (1603), ed. Kingsford, II: 57. In the *Annales*, Stow wrote that Gower 'built a great part of S. Mary Oueries church in Southwarke, then new re-edified'. (Stow, *Annales* (1592), p. 518, (1600, 1601, 1605), p. 528, *sub anno* 1400). Stow, like Leland, may also have drawn on oral tradition for evidence of Gower's generosity to St Mary Overy.
[290] My translation. Rawlinson, *Natural History and Antiquities of the County of Surrey*, V: pp. 204–5.
[291] *Oxford English Dictionary*, s.v. 'limb', n.2.
[292] Gough, *Sepulchral Monuments*, II, part 2: Plate VIII, p. 25.

(see below), misrepresented this inscription as having included Henry IV from the beginning.[293]

Berthelette noted that a 'table' (tablet) hung near the tomb with a Latin inscription that promised to anyone who prayed for Gower's soul an indulgence of 1500 days, 'so oft as he so dothe'.[294] The full text of this inscription (*Orate pro anima*) survives in two manuscripts of Gower's works (BL, Cotton MS Tib. A. IV, fol. 174v, and Harley MS 6291, fol. 158r), and a summary (*Orantibus pro anima*) survives in a third (Glasgow, MS Hunter 59 [T.2.17], fol. 129r).[295]

Gower's tomb must have been designed after the composition of the last of his three great works, *Confessio Amantis* (the first recension of which was completed c. 1390), and after he received the livery collar from Henry Bolingbroke in the summer or autumn of 1393.[296] The lack of any reference in the tomb to Gower's wife Agnes suggests that it was designed, and probably completed, before his marriage early in 1398. If the '*Hic jacet*' inscription recorded by Munday, or the similar inscription reported by Aubrey, was contemporary with the tomb, Gower's tomb must have been completed before the autumn of 1399, since both inscriptions reported that Gower lived during the reigns of Edward III (1327–77) and Richard II (1377–99), and neither mentioned Henry IV (1399–1413). Their reference to the reigns in which Gower lived, rather than to the date of his death, also suggests that the tomb was completed during Gower's lifetime. John Leland's statement that he did not know when Gower died, and Stow's guess in the *Annales* that Gower died around 1400, also imply that no date of death was inscribed on the tomb. In his testament, Gower directed that he was to be buried 'in the place specially provided for this' but left no instructions about constructing or completing his tomb. Thus, the evidence suggests strongly that Gower's tomb was designed and completed during his own lifetime, sometime between the autumn of 1393 and the beginning of 1398 or – at the latest – the autumn of 1399.

Gower's self-focused testament and his elaborate tomb, with its interwoven references to his ancestry, privileged rank, literary attainments, wealth, generosity, and piety, reflect his strong interest in crafting and controlling his own image. The likelihood that Gower commissioned his tomb well before his death, and that he saw it completed while his vision was

---

[293] Fisher, *John Gower*, 38. Fisher has been followed in this by Hines, Cohen and Roffey, 'Iohannes Gower, Armiger, Poeta', p. 24 and n. 4; and by David Griffith, 'A Living Language of the Dead? French Commemorative Inscriptions from Medieval England', *The Medieval Journal*, 3 (2013): pp. 69–136, at 100. I am grateful to Richard Sharpe for alerting me to Griffith's article and sending me a copy of it.

[294] Berthelette, 'To the reder', in *Io. Gower de confessione amantis*, STC 12143.

[295] For the texts, see 'Orate pro anima (Armigeri scutum)', in Gower, *Minor Latin Works with In Praise of Peace* (http://d.lib.rochester.edu/teams/text/yeager-gower-minor-latin-works-orate-pro-anima-title, accessed 30 December 2016).

[296] For the date of the *Confessio*, see Chapter 2, pp. 129–36, below.

still untroubled, means that it is likely to have reflected his personal wishes and even, perhaps, his aesthetic tastes.

Conclusion

This chapter raises many questions and challenges many longstanding assumptions concerning Gower's life, his sources of income, his movements and residences, his associates, his marriage, and the provisions that he made for his death. It introduces new documentary records and re-examines long-familiar ones to see if they can yield new insights. John Gower's world, as seen through the lens of documentary records, was based primarily in Kent until around 1387, and was a world of strategic connections and temporary associations; a litigious world; a world of ruthless financial priorities. For Gower, it may also have been a somewhat isolated world, since his archival record is curiously lacking in evidence of conventional obligations and service, personal friendships, family relationships, collegial ties, and confraternal or parochial affiliations. With the exception of a possible stint disbursing supplies at Dover Castle in 1386–87, Gower seems to have performed no royal service nor held any public office, and no known deed, testament, or other record names him as a feoffee, executor, or legatee. This seems remarkable for one who was a member of the small, interlinked world of the county gentry; an educated man who engaged in financial and legal activities in Kent and the capital for at least thirty-five years (1364–99); and a man of letters who must have been in contact with at least some of the intellectual and cultural elite of his day, and who cultivated connections with Richard II, Henry Bolingbroke, and Archbishop Arundel. Gower's lack of personal engagement in national, county, or local affairs contrasts sharply with the careers of many of his associates, such as Sir John Cobham, Sir Arnald Savage, Sir John de Northwode, William Weston, and Thomas Brockhull, and also contrasts with the vigorous commentaries on contemporary events that figure so largely in his literary works.

Gower's world may have included family members to whom he was close, and a circle of friends with whom he shared affectionate bonds, but if so they are unknown; his life records reflect only two relationships that may have been based on personal esteem or affection. One was his apparent friendship with Geoffrey Chaucer, who is the only person known to have asked Gower to serve in a position of personal trust (as one of Chaucer's general attorneys in 1378), and with whom Gower exchanged literary compliments. The other was his marriage late in life to Agnes Groundolf, to whom Gower evidently addressed at least one poem (*Est Amor*), with whom he spent his final decade, and to whom he confided the fulfillment of his final written work, his testament.

APPENDIX:
FOUR GOWER LIFE RECORDS

1 and 2: Two deeds, 1366 (in Latin)
3: Lawsuit, 1394–95 (in English translation)
4: Testament, 1408 (in Latin and in English translation)

(*In the following Latin transcriptions, standard abbreviations have been silently expanded.*)

1.

London Metropolitan Archives, Husting Roll 94/36
Grant by John de Northwode, knight, to John Gower, his heirs and assigns, of the reversion of an annual quitrent of £12 (17 March 1366)

[*In left margin:*] Scriptum Johannis Gower per Johannem de Northwod militem.

Universis presens scriptum visuris vel audituris Johannes de Northwode Miles salutem in domino. Cum Agnes qui fuit vxor Rogeri de Northwode Militis patris mei tenet ad terminum vite sue duodecim libratas annui liberi et quietus redditus percipiend' annuatim per manus Magistri ecclesie collegiate Sancti Thome Martiris de acon' in civitate london' quod quidem Redditus post decessum dicte Agnetis michi revertere deberet Noveritis me pro me et heredibus meis concessisse per presentes quod predictus annuus redditus cum pertinencijs post decessum dicte Agnetis remaneat Johanni Gower heredibus et assignatis suis imperpetuum percipiend' ad terminos consuetos. Et ego predictus Johannes de Northwode et heredes mei reversionem predictum cum pertinencijs prefato Johanni Gower heredibus et assignatis suis warantizabimus imperpetuum. In cuius rei testimonium huic presenti carte sigillum meum apposui. Dat' london' decimo septimo die Marcij anno regni Regis Edwardi tercij post conquestum Angl' quadragesimo.

2.

London Metropolitan Archives, Husting Roll 94/107

Grant by John Gower of the above quitrent, which he has 'by inheritance' (*'de hereditate'*) as well as by grant of John de Northwode, knight, to Simon de Benyngton, citizen and draper of London (18 July 1366)

[*In left margin:*] Scriptum Simonis de Benyngton' Pannarij per Johannem Gower.

Omnibus christi fidelibus ad quos presens scriptum peruenerit Johannes Gower salutem in domino. Cum Agnes que fuit vxor Rogeri de Northwode Militis teneat duodecim libratas annui liberi et quietus redditus percipiend' de Magistro et Fratribus sancti Thome de Acon' London' ad terminum vite ipsius Agnetis de hereditate predicti Johannis Gower quam idem Johannes Gower habet ex concessione Johannis de Northwode Militis filij et heredis Rogeris de Northwode Militis. et qui quidem redditus post mortem predicte Agnetis ad predictum Johannem Gower et heredes suos reuerti debeat: Remaneat Simoni de Benyngton' Civi et Pannario Ciuitatis predicte heredibus et assignatis suis imperpetuum. In cuius rei testimonium huic presenti scripto sigillum meum apposui. Dat' london' die sabbati proxima ante festum sancte Margarete virginis anno regni Regis Edwardi tercij post conquestum quadragesimo.

3.

Assize of novel disseisin: *Feriby v. Gower et al. (1394–95)*

The National Archives: JUST 1/1503, rotulet 56r-d

Online images are available on AALT (Anglo-American Legal Tradition) at:
http://aalt.law.uh.edu/AALT4/JUST1/Just1no1503/aJUST1no1503fronts/
IMG_3470.htm
(recto)
http://aalt.law.uh.edu/AALT4/JUST1/Just1no1503/bJUST1no1503dorses/
IMG_3639.htm
(dorse)

(*In the following translation, the text has been divided into paragraphs for greater clarity.*)

[ROTULET 56 RECTO]

Pleas of assizes at *Guldeford* before the aforesaid Justices,[297] the Wednesday after Michaelmas, in the aforesaid year [*of 18 Richard II; i.e., 30 September 1394*]:

Surrey. The assize comes to try by jury if John Gower, William Weston, Thomas Saundres, and Thomas Hautwysel unjustly newly disseised Thomas de Feriby, clerk, of his free tenement (*de libero tenemento suo*) in Suthwerk '*post primam etc*'', and wherefore he [*Feriby*] complains that he [*Gower*] has disseised him [*Feriby*] of one messuage with appurtenances, 'etc.'[298]

And the same John [*Gower*] came by William Elyngton his attorney, and the others did not come, but one James Dyuele [*or* Dynele] responded for them as their bailiff (*tanquam eorum balliuus*), and said for them that they had done no injury or disseisin to the said Thomas [*Feriby*], and concerning this they put themselves on the assize. And the said Thomas [*Feriby*] likewise. And so let the assize be taken among them, 'etc.'.

And the said John [*Gower*] responds as the tenant (*vt tenens*) of the said messuage under consideration, and he says that an assize between them should not take place, because he says that one Henry, prior of the church of St Mary *de Ouerey*,[299] was seised of the said messuage with its appurtenances in his demesne as of fee and by right of his said church, and, thus seised thereof, demised that messuage with appurtenances to one Thomas Vynch and Joan his wife to have for term of the lives of Thomas Vynch and Joan, saving the reversion thereof after their deaths to the said prior and his successors.

By virtue of which demise, the said Thomas Vynch and Joan [*his wife*] were seised thereof in their demesne as of a free tenement (*vt de libero tenemento*). And afterwards the said Thomas Vynch granted the said messuage with appurtenances to one Adam de Bury to hold for term of the lives of the said Thomas Vynch and Joan [*his wife*], by virtue of which grant the said Adam [*de Bury*] was seised thereof in his demesne as of a free tenement.

And afterward the said Adam [*de Bury*] granted all his state that he had in the said messuage to John Wacch and Agnes his wife, by virtue of which grant the same John Wacch and Agnes were seised thereof in their demesne as of a free tenement. And afterward the same John Wacch and Agnes [*his wife*] demised the said messuage with appurtenances to the said John Gower, to hold at the will of the said John Wacch and Agnes [*his wife*], rendering for it to the same John Wacch and Agnes [*his wife*] four marks per annum.

---

[297] *rot*. 55r: John Wardham and William Haukeford, Justices of the Lord King at the Surrey assizes.
[298] For Thomas de Feriby, see *Wykeham's Register*, ed. Kirby, I: 192, II: 499.
[299] Henry Collingbourne, prior 27 March 1361–15 June 1395 (Carlin, Medieval Southwark, p. 285).

And afterward the said John Wacch died, after whose death the said Agnes [*his widow*] took as husband one William Olyver. And afterward the said Thomas Vynch died. And afterward the said William Olyver and Agnes [*his wife, widow of John Wacch*] surrendered all their state that they had in the said messuage to the said Joan [*widow of Thomas Vynch*], by virtue of which surrender, the same Joan [Vynch] was seised thereof as in her original (*pristino*) state. And afterward, thus seised thereof, she granted the said messuage with its appurtenances to the said John Gower, to hold for term of the life of the said John Gower [*sic*]. By virtue of which grant, the same John Gower was seised thereof of such state (*de tali statu*).

And afterward the said Joan [Vynch], contrary to her own act (*contra factum suum proprium*), granted the same messuage with appurtenances to the said Thomas de Feriby, to have for term of the life of the same Joan [Vynch]. By virtue of which grant, the same Thomas de Feriby entered into the said messuage with appurtenances, and the said Thomas Hautwysel intruded (*intrusit*) upon the possession of the said Thomas de Feriby, and the said John Gower recently removed him, Thomas Hautwysel, wherefore he [Gower] demands judgment if there ought to be an assize between them, 'etc'. (*et predictus Johannes Gower ipsum Thomam Hautwysel inde recenter ammovit vnde petit iudicium si assisa inde inter eos fieri debeat etc'*).

And the said Thomas de Feriby says that he should not be precluded by something alleged earlier from having the said assize, because he says that it is true that the said Prior was seised of the said messuage with appurtenances as of right of his said church and, thus seised thereof, demised that messuage with appurtenances to the said Thomas Vynch and Joan [*his wife*] for term of the lives of the said Thomas Vynch and Joan [*his wife*], saving the reversion thereof to the said Prior and his successors in the form abovesaid (*in forma predicta*).

By virtue of which demise, the same Thomas Vynch and Joan [*his wife*] were seised thereof in their demesne as of a free tenement (*vt de libero tenemento*), and afterward the same Thomas Vynch granted all the state that he had in that messuage with appurtenances to the said Adam de Bury, to have for term of the life of the said Thomas Vynch and Joan [*his wife*]. By virtue of which grant the same Adam [*de Bury*] was seised thereof in the form aforesaid.

And afterward the same Adam [*de Bury*] granted all the <state> that he had in the said messuage with appurtenances to the said John Wacch and Agnes [*his wife*] in the form aforesaid. By virtue of which grant, the same John Wacch [*and Agnes*] were seised thereof (*ijdem Johannes Wacch* [et Agnes] *fuerunt inde seisiti*) in their demesne in the form abovesaid. And afterward the same John Wacch and Agnes [*his wife*] demised to the said John Gower the said messuage with appurtenances, to hold in the form abovesaid, rendering therefor four marks per annum to the same John Wacch and Agnes [*his wife*]. And afterward the same John Wacch died, after whose death the same Agnes [*his widow*] took as husband the said William Olyver.

And afterward the said Thomas Vynch died, after whose death the same William Olyver and Agnes [*his wife, widow of John Wacch*] surrendered all the state that they had in the said messuage with appurtenances to the same Joan [*widow of Thomas Vynch*]

[ROTULET 56 DORSE]

in the form aforesaid, by virtue of which surrender the said Joan [Vynch] was seised thereof as of her free tenement in the form aforesaid. And he says that the same Joan [Vynch], being in possession of the said messuage, demised that messuage with appurtenances to the said Thomas de Feriby to hold for term of the life of the said Joan [Vynch] in the form aforesaid.

By virtue of which demise, the said Thomas de Feriby was seised of the said messuage with appurtenances as of a free tenement, until the said John Gower and the others named in the writ unjustly and without judgment disseised him thereof, without the said John Gower having anything in the said messuage and appurtenances by demise of the said Joan [Vynch] made thereof to the said John Gower before the said demise made to the said Thomas de Feriby of the said messuage in the form aforesaid. And this he is prepared to prove, wherefore he seeks a trial and that it should proceed to the taking of the assize, 'etc.'

And the said John Gower says that the said Joan [Vynch] demised the said messuage with appurtenances to the same John Gower long before the said demise [*was*] made to the said Thomas de Feryby [*sic*] of that messuage in the form aforesaid. And this he is prepared to prove, wherefore he seeks a trial, 'etc.'

And the said Thomas de Feriby says that the said Joan [Vynch] demised to the same Thomas de Feriby the said messuage with appurtenances for term of the life of that Joan [Vynch] in the form aforesaid, and that the said John Gower before that demise had nothing in that messuage by demise of the same Joan, as the said Thomas alleged above. And he asks that this be inquired into by the assize. And the said John Gower similarly. And therefore let an assize be taken between them, 'etc.'

The jurors (*Recognitores*) come who were chosen, examined, and sworn for this; they say on their oath that the said Joan [Vynch] demised to the said Thomas de Feriby the said messuage and appurtenances under their consideration, to have for term of the life of the said Joan [Vynch], and that the said John Gower before that demise never had anything in that messuage by demise of that Joan [Vynch], as the said Thomas de Feriby previously alleged. And lastly they say that the said Thomas de Feriby was seised of the same messuage with appurtenances as of a free tenement until the said John Gower and William Weston disseised him unjustly and without judgement and with force and arms, to the loss of the said Thomas de Feriby of one hundred shillings. And they say that the said Thomas Saundres and Thomas Hautwysel took no part (*non interfuerunt*) in the said disseisin.

	Therefore, it is considered that the said Thomas de Feriby shall recover his seisin of the said messuage with appurtenances by view of the jurors of the assize, and his said losses assessed above at one hundred shillings. And
Cap'	the said John Gower and William Weston are to be taken into custody
~~misericordia~~	(*capiantur*). And the said Thomas de Feriby is <amerced> for his false claim against Thomas Saundres and Thomas Hautwysell, who are acquitted of the said disseisin. And they are to go *sine die*. Afterwards, namely on the 6th day of February, in the 18th year of the reign of our present lord King [6 Feb. 1395], before the said Justices at Southwark, the said Thomas de Feriby comes and acknowledges that satisfaction has been made to him for the said damages. And upon this the said John Gower and
Fines	William Weston separately pray to be admitted to fines with the lord King in that behalf (*petunt se ad fines cum domino Rege occasione premissa*
~~j marc'~~	*admitti*). And they are admitted; namely, the same John Gower for 13s. 4d., by surety of William Elyngton of London and William Wexham of
~~dj' marc'~~	Southwark; and the same William Weston for 6s. 8d., by surety of William Armeston of the county of Northampton and William Elyngton of the county of York. And so they are to go *sine die*, 'etc.'

Damages, 100s. <u>Wherefore 100s., and amercement 1 mark, and proclamation 20d.</u> (*Dampna C s'* <u>*Vnde C' et misericordia j marc' et proclam' xx d'*</u>)

4.

John Gower's Testament, 1408

Lambeth Palace Library: Register of Thomas Arundel, Archbishop of Canterbury
2 vols (1396–97, 1399–1414), I: folios 256r–257r

[*fol. 256r*] In dei nomine Amen. Ego Johannes Gower compos mentis et in fide catholica ad misericordiam domini domini [*sic*] nostri ihesu christi ex toto me comendans condo testamentum meum sub hac forma. In primis lego [*fol. 256v*] animam meam deo creatori meo et corpus meum ad sepeliendum in ecclesia Canonicorum beate marie de Oueres. in loco ad hoc specialiter deputato. Et lego Priori dicte ecclesie qui pro tempore fuerit quadraginta solidos. Item lego subpriori viginti s'. Item lego cuilibet Canonico sacerdoti deo ibidem servienti xiij s' et iiij d'. ceteris vero canonicis ibidem Nouicijs lego cuilibet eorum sex s' et viij d'. ita ut omnes et singuli exequias sepulture me [*sic*] deuocius colant orantes pro me. Item lego cuilibet valetto infra portas dicti prioratus. Priori et Conuentui seruienti duos solidos. et cuilibet Garcioni xij d'. Item lego ecclesie beate Marie Magdalene xl. s'. ad luminaria et ornamenta dicte ecclesie. Item lego Sacerdoti ibidem paroch' .x. s'. ut oret et orari faciat pro me. Item lego Magistro Clerico ibidem iij s'. Item lego subclerico ij s'. Item lego iiij. ecclesiis paroch' in Soutwerk [*sic*]. videlicet sancte Margarete sancti Georgij. sancti Olaui. et sante Marie Magdalene iuxta Bermundesey cuilibet earum singillatim xiij s' et iiij d'. ad ornamenta et Luminaria vt supra. Et cuilibet Sacerdoti paroch' siue Rectori in cura ibidem pro tempore residenti et ecclesie seruienti sex s' et octo d'. vt orent et orari faciant pro me in suis paroch' faciant et procurent Item lego magistro hospitalis sancti Thome Martiris in Southwerk .xl. s' et cuilibet sacerdoti qui est de gremio dicti hospitalis. in eodem seruienti. vj s' et viij d' vt orent ibidem pro me. Item lego cuilibet sorori professe in dicto hospitali. iij s' et iiij d'. et cuilibet earum ancille infirmos custodienti xx. d'. Item lego cuilibet infirmo infra dictum hospitale. languenti xij d'. Item lego singulis hospitalibus subscriptis videlicet sancti Antoni. Elsingspitell. Bedlem extra Byschopus gat. seint mary spytell iuxta Westm'. cuilibet sorori ubi sunt sorores in dictis hospitalibus professe una cum ancillis et languentibus ibidem vt percipiant singillat' modo vt supra. Item lego cuilibet domui leprosorum in suburbijs London' decem s'. ad distribuend' inter eosdem vt orent pro me. Item lego Priori de Elsingspitell' .xl. s' et cuilibet Canonico sacerdoti ibidem professo sex. s'. et viij. d'. vt orent pro me. Item lego ad seruicium altaris in Capella sancti Johannis Baptiste in qua corpus meum sepeliendum est videlicet duo vestimenta de panno serico cum toto eorum apparatu. quorum vnum est de Blw [*sic*] Baudkyn mixtum de colore albo. Et alium vestimentum est de albo serico. Item lego ad seruicium dicti altaris vnum missale grande et no[u]um eciam et [*sic*] vnum calicem. nouum vnde voluntas mea est quod dicta vestimenta vna cum Missale et Calice maneant imperpetuum tantummodo ad seruicium dicti altaris et non alibi. Item lego Priori et Conuentui. quendam magnum Librum sumptibus meis nouiter compositum qui Martilogium dicitur. sic quod in eodem specialem memoriam scriptam secundum eorum promissa cotidie habere debeo. Item lego Agneti uxore mee C. lj' legalis monete. Item lego eidem iij Ciphos vnum cooperculum duo salaria et xij. Cocliar' de argento. Item lego eidem omnes lectos meos et cistas. una cum apparatu aule panetrie coquine et eorum vasis et omnibus vtensilibus quibuscumque. Item lego eidem vnum calicem et vnum vestimentum pro altare quod est infra oratorium hospicij mei. Item volo quod si dicta Agnes vxor mea diucius me viuat quod tunc ipsa Libere et Pacifice inmediate [sic] post mortem meam percipiat omnes redditus michi debitos de firmis Maneriorum meorum tam de Southwell' in Comitatu North' quam in Multon' in Comitatu Suff' prout in quodam scripto inde confecto sub sigillo meo necnon sub sigillis aliorum plenius constari poterit. Huius autem testamenti mei facio constituo executores meos videlicet Agnetam vxorem meam dominum Arnaldum Sauage Militem dominum Rogerum Armigerum [sic] dominum Willelmum Denne Canonicum Capelle domini Regis et Johannem Burton'. Clericum. Dat' infra Prioratum beate Marie de Oueres in Sutwerk [sic]. in festo assumpcionis beate Marie anno domini Millesimo CCCC.^{mo} viij.

Tenore presencium nos. Thomas etc'. Notum facimus. Vniuersis quod vicesimo quarto die Mensis Octobris anno domini Millesimo CCCC.^{mo} octavo in Manerio nostro de Lamhith' probatum fuit coram nobis testamentum suprascriptum pro eo etc'. cuius pretextu etc'. Administracio que omnium bonorum dictum testamentum concern'. vbicumque etc'. dilecte in christo filie Agneti vxori sue exec' in eodem testamento nominate commissa extitit et per eandem admissa in debita forma iuris. Reseruat' nobis potestate etc'. In cuius rei etc'. Dat' die Loco Mense et anno domini supradictis Et nostre translacionis anno terciodecimo.

[f. 257r] Noverint Vniversi per presentes etc'. quod nos Thomas etc'. de fidelitate dilecte in christo filie Agnetis relicte et executricis testamenti et bonorum administratricis. Johannis Gower nuper defuncti cuius testamentum per nos nuper de prerogatiua nostre Cant' ecclesie pro eo quod idem defunctus nonnulla bona optinuit in diuersis Dioc' nostre Cant' prouinc' dum viuebat et tempore mortis sue legitime extitit approbatum et administracio bonorum eiusdem dicte Agneti commissa. de et super administracione etc'. confidentes ipsam ab vlteriori etc'. In cuius rei etc'. Dat' in Manerio nostro de Lamhith' .vij.^{mo} die Mensis nouembris anno domini Millesimo CCCC.^{mo} octauo. Et nostre translacionis anno terciodecimo.

John Gower's Testament
(Translation)

(*In this translation the clauses of the testament have been numbered for convenience of citation*)

In the name of God, amen. I, John Gower, being of sound mind and catholic faith, commending myself entirely to the mercy of our lord Jesus Christ, make my testament in this fashion:

1. I leave my soul to God my creator, and my body to be buried in the church of the canons of the Blessed Mary *de Oueres*, in the place specially provided for this.

2. To the prior of the said church 40s.; and to the sub-prior 20s.; and to each canon priest serving God there 13s. 4d.; and to the other novice canons there 6s. 8d. each; so that each of them will attend (*colant*) the exequies of my burial, praying devoutly for me.

3. To each valet (*valetto*) within the gates of the said priory, serving the prior and convent, 12d.; and to each groom (*garcioni*) there, 6d.

4. To the church of the Blessed Mary Magdalen 40s. for the lights and ornaments of the said church. To the parish priest there 10s., so that he will pray and have prayers made for me. To the master clerk there 3s.; to the under-clerk 2s.

5. To the four parish churches of *Soutwerk*, viz., St Margaret, St George, St Olave, and St Mary Magdalen by (*iuxta*) Bermundesey, 13s. 4d. each for their lights and ornaments, as above. And to each resident parish priest or rector serving the cure of the church there 6s. 8d., so that they will pray and have prayers procured for me in their parishes.

6. To the master of the hospital of St Thomas the Martyr in *Southwerk* 40s., and to each priest who is of the bosom of the said hospital (*de gremio dicti hospitalis*), serving in the same, 6s. 8d., so that they will pray there for me. To each professed sister in the said hospital 3s. 4d., and to each woman servant (*ancille*) of theirs caring for the sick, 20d. To each sick person (*infirmo*) lying (*languenti*) within the same hospital, 12d.

7. To each of the following hospitals, viz., of St Anthony, *Elsingspitell, Bedlem extra Bischopus gat, seint mary spitell iuxta Westm'*; to each sister where there are professed sisters in the said hospitals, together with the women servants (*ancillis*) and those lying there, so that each of them receive in the manner described above (*vt percipiant singillat' modo vt supra*).

8. To each house of lepers in the suburbs of London 10s. to be distributed among them to pray for me.

9. To the prior of *Elsingspitell* 40s., and to each professed canon who is a priest there 6s. 8d., so that they pray for me.

10. I leave to the service of the altar in the chapel of St John the Baptist in which my body is to be buried two vestments of silk cloth with all their apparel (*apparatu*), of which one is of blue baudekin mixed with white (*de Blw* [sic] *Baudkyn mixtum de colore albo*), and the other vestment is of white silk. I leave to the service of the said altar a large and new missal and a new chalice, and my will is that the said vestments and the missal and chalice remain forever to the service of the said altar and not elsewhere.

11. I leave to the prior and convent a certain large book, newly compiled (*compositum*) at my own expense, which is called a martyrology (*Martilogium*), on the condition that I am to have daily a special memorial written in it, according to their promises (*sic quod in eodem specialem memoriam scriptam secundum eorum promissa cotidie habere debeo*).

12. I leave to Agnes my wife one hundred pounds of legal money. I leave to her three cups, one cover (*vnum cooperculum; i.e., for a cup*), two salts (*salaria*), and twelve spoons of silver. I leave to her all my beds and chests, together with the furnishings (*apparatu*) of the hall, pantry, kitchen, and their vessels and all utensils whatsoever. I leave to her a chalice and a vestment for the altar that is within the oratory of my townhouse (*hospicij*). I will that if the said Agnes my wife should survive me (*diucius me viuat*), that then freely and peacefully, immediately after my death, she should take all rents due to me from the farms (*firmis: fixed rents*) of my manors of *Southwell* in co. *North'* [*sic; evidently a scribal error for the manor of Feltwell in Norfolk*] and *Multon'* in Suffolk, as can be more fully ascertained (*constari*) in a certain writing made under my seal and the seals of others.

13. I make and constitute as executors of my testament Agnes my wife; Sir Arnald Savage, knight; Sir Roger [*blank*], esquire [*dominum Rogerum Armigerum: recte William Loveney, esquire*]; Sir William Denne [*recte Doune*], canon of the king's chapel; and John Burton', clerk. Dated within the priory of B. Mary *de Oueres de Sutwerk*, on the feast of the Assumption of the Blessed Mary [*15 August*], A.D. 1408.

By the tenor of these presents, we Thomas [*Arundel, Archbishop of Canterbury*] make it known to all that on the 24th day of October, AD 1408, at our manor of Lambeth (*Lamhith'*), the above-written testament was proved before us, '*pro eo etc*'', by pretext of which, 'etc.', and the administration of all goods concerning the said testament, wheresoever 'etc.', has been committed to our beloved daughter in Christ, Agnes his wife, named executrix in the same testament, and accepted by her in due form of law. With power reserved to us 'etc.'. In [*witness*] whereof 'etc.'. Dated the day, place, month, and year abovesaid, and in the thirteenth year of our translation.

Know all by these presents, 'etc.', that we, Thomas [*Arundel, Archbishop of Canterbury*], 'etc.'. By the oath of our beloved daughter in Christ, Agnes, relict and executrix of the testament and administratrix of the goods of John Gower, lately deceased (whose testament was duly proved before us, of our prerogative of Canterbury, because during his life and at the time of his death the said deceased was possessed of goods in several dioceses of our province of Canterbury), the administration of the goods was committed to the said Agnes, *de et super administracione etc'. confidentes ipsam ab vlteriori etc'*. In witness whereof 'etc.' Dated at our manor of Lambeth, the 7th day of the month of November, AD 1408, and in the thirteenth year of our translation.

Chapter 2

GOWER'S WORKS

Stephen H. Rigby

The Difficulties of Dating Gower's Works

Given Gower's explicit references to historical events such as the papal schism, the Great Revolt of 1381 and the deposition of Richard II, historians and literary scholars have inevitably sought to relate his poetry to the religious, social and political conflicts and controversies of his day. Yet, a major difficulty in adopting this historical approach to Gower's works is the uncertainty which persists about the chronology of their composition. Some of Gower's poems can be dated with precision. For instance, his *Carmen Super Multiplici Viciorum Pestilencia*, which sets out the 'manifold plague of vices', including heresy, pride, lust, perjury and greed, from which England was supposedly suffering, explicitly states that it was written in the twentieth year of Richard II's reign, i.e. 1396–97 (pr. 8; ll. 312–3). Similarly, in alternative versions of *Quicquid Homo Scribat (In Fine)* in which Gower takes leave of writing in old age, he refers to himself as having gone blind in the first or second year of Henry IV's reign (ll. 1–8), i.e. in 1399–1400 or 1400–01, with the work presumably dating shortly after this date. However, if a marginal note in a manuscript of *Presul Ouile Regis* is to be believed, this poem's account of the misfortunes striking the kingdom can be linked to the great comet visible across Europe in 1402 which was widely interpreted as an omen of disaster.[1] As Yeager points out, Gower's blindness does not, despite the poet's claims to the contrary, seem to have stopped him from writing and his complaints may have been a 'conscious pose for literary purposes' rather than an accurate reflection of his ability to work.[2]

I am grateful to Siân Echard and Robert Yeager for their comments on an earlier version of this chapter.

[1] Gower, *Minor Latin Works*, pp. 79–80.
[2] Gower, *Minor Latin Works*, p. 70. See also Andrew Galloway, 'The Common Voice in Theory and Practice in Late Fourteenth Century England', in Richard W. Kaeuper, ed., *Law, Governance and Justice: New Views on Medieval Constitutionalism* (Leiden: Brill, 2013), pp. 243–86, at 266–7.

Other works by Gower offer a less specific indication of their date of composition, as in the prose headings to three of the four manuscripts of *O Deus Immense* which claim that the poem's warnings about the need for kings to take good counsel, obey the law and win the love of his subjects (ll. 7, 9–18, 58, 65–6) were written whilst Richard II was still alive.[3] Sometimes, biographical details in the poems can help with their dating, assuming, of course, that the first-person voice within the text can be equated with that of Gower himself. For instance, since his *Est Amor* refers to the poet as approaching 'the marriage bed in the order of husbands' (ll. 26–7), it may have been written around the time of his marriage to Agnes Groundolf for which William Wykeham, bishop of Winchester, issued a licence in January 1398.[4] More speculatively, *Dicunt Scripture*, which teaches of the need to be mindful of death and of the good of one's soul, may be linked to the composition of Gower's testament in 1408.[5]

Other works by Gower are even more difficult to date. For instance, the date when Gower composed his *Traitié selonc les auctors pour essampler les amantz marietz*, which offers a defence of married love as being in line with reason, nature and the divine will, is extremely uncertain, with suggestions ranging from as early as 1376–77, when Edward III's relationship with Alice Perrers was a political issue, through 1385–90, 1392 or even the late 1390s.[6] In the absence of a secure date, interpretation can run the risk of becoming circular as scholars speculatively identify a particular period for the composition of a work from its content and then interpret its content from the context of that period. Many of Gower's other works are equally hard to date. For instance, the accusations about simony and clerical corruption which Gower made in his *Cultor in Ecclesia* are, as Robert Yeager pointed out, 'general enough to be applicable at almost any point' in the poet's lifetime.[7] Similarly, whilst Gower's *De Lucis Scrutino* must date from after the papal schism of 1378, to which it refers in its opening lines (ll. 3–4), its complaints about the transgressions of each social order could have been made at virtually any time in Gower's career.

---

[3] Gower, Minor Latin Works, p. 69.
[4] *Wykeham's Register*, volume II, ed. Thomas F. Kirby (London: Simpkin & Co., 1899), p. 477. For Gower's marriage, see Martha Carlin, above pp. 79–80.
[5] Gower, *Minor Latin Works*, p. 81. On Gower's testament, see Martha Carlin, above, pp. 85–90.
[6] Gower, *The French Balades*, pp. 9–10; Cathy Hume, 'Why did Gower Write the Traitié?', in Elizabeth Dutton, with John Hines and Robert F. Yeager, eds, *John Gower, Trilingual Poet: Language, Translation and Tradition* (Cambridge: D. S. Brewer, 2010), pp. 263–75, at 273–4; Bertolet, 'Gower's French Manuscripts', pp. 99–100; Peter Nicholson, 'The French Works: The Ballades', in RRC, pp. 312–20, at 315–17; Yeager, 'John Gower's Audience: The Ballades', pp. 91–2. The Traitié work was translated into a northern dialect of Middle English in the early fifteenth century (Gower, *The French Balades*, pp. 153–73).
[7] Gower, The Minor Latin Works, p. 80.

A further problem is that Gower's poems as we now have them may not be in their original form. For instance, his *Cinkante Balades* which, like his *Confessio Amantis*, criticises the 'madness' of 'foolish love' and praises love within marriage as being in accord with reason, nature and honour (XLIX; L; LI), may originally have been written in the early 1390s. However, other dates have been suggested for this work which, at least in its present form with its dedication to Henry IV, must date from after 1399 (I; II; LI: 27).[8] Similarly, a work such as *Ecce Patet Tenus*, whose description of the power of love has speculatively been linked with the poet's *Est Amor*, could make use of lines written much earlier in the poet's career, in this case drawing on the discussion of love in Book V of the *Vox Clamantis*.[9]

The *Mirour l'Omme*

The first of Gower's major works which has survived is the French *Mirour de l'Omme*, to give it the title which it has in its only surviving manuscript.[10] The poem is an allegorical vision in which Sin, the daughter of the Devil, incestuously marries Death, who is also the offspring of the Devil, and gives birth to seven daughters who are the Seven Deadly Vices (Pride, Envy, Anger, Sloth, Avarice, Gluttony and Lechery). The Flesh of Man is tempted to surrender to the Devil, Sin and the World but then Reason, Fear and Conscience lead the Flesh to be reconciled with the Soul, by whom it should be governed. The World then marries the Seven Vices, each of whom has five daughters, with Pride, for instance, giving birth to Hypocrisy, Vainglory, Arrogance, Boasting and Disobedience, with all thirty-five daughters attacking Man and subjecting him to Sin. In response, God sends the Seven Virtues (Humility, Charity, Patience, Prowess, Generosity, Measure and Chastity) to counter the power of the vices and each of these virtues also has five daughters, as when Humility gives birth to Devotion, Fear, Discretion, Modesty and Obedience. The daughters of the Vices and Virtues then join battle for control of Man, with Sin seeming to gain the upper hand, its effects being examined in each estate, from the pope and emperor downwards. All men seek to blame each other or the world for their failings but Gower insists that man is responsible

---

[8] Gower, *The French Balades*, p. 53; Craig E. Bertolet, 'Gower's French Manuscripts', in RRC, pp. 97–101, at 98; Nicholson, 'The French Works', pp. 312–13; Robert F. Yeager, 'John Gower's Audience: The Ballades', *Chaucer Review*, 40 (2005), pp. 81–104, at 89–93.
[9] Gower, Minor Latin Works, p. 72.
[10] Gower, *Complete Works*, I: lxviii. In the earliest Latin colophons to the *Confessio Amantis* and the *Vox Clamantis*, Gower referred to the *Mirour de l'Omme* as the *Speculum Hominis* but later changed this to the *Speculum Meditantis* (Gower, *Complete Works*, III: 479; John H. Fisher, *John Gower: Moral Philosopher and Friend of Chaucer* (London: Methuen, 1965; first published 1964), pp. 89–90, 311) and it is this latter title which it is given on Gower's tomb (Gower, *Complete Works*, IV: xx).

for his own fate and that he can use his free will to repent and turn to God and so, with the help of the Virgin Mary, achieve salvation. Gower therefore begins an account of the life of the Virgin, although the final leaves of the manuscript have not survived and the text breaks off at line 29945.

The *Mirour de l'Omme* is difficult to date precisely. John Fisher suggested that Gower's denunciation of the king's plundering of the church and his infringement of its rights (22297–22359) was linked to the Good Parliament of 1376 but the criticisms of the king made in this passage may be generic rather than relating to a particular event.[11] Nevertheless, the *Mirour de l'Omme* was probably begun before the death of Edward III (21 June 1377) as it includes Gower's criticism of the disobedient refusal of the French to do homage 'to the one who has the birthright from his mother' (2137–48), a clear reference to Edward III's claim to the throne of France through his mother, Isabella, daughter of Philip IV of France. Another passage which may well have been written before the death of Edward III is that in which Gower says that 'nowadays' (*'meintenant'*) it can be seen that 'woman is powerful' in the land even though 'it is in discord with all laws that a woman should rule in the land and should subject the king to serve her' (22807–12). This is probably a reference to the power at court of Alice Perrers, who had been the king's mistress since 1364, although their relationship only became public after the death of Queen Philippa in 1369. Alice's influence over the king led to her being banished from court by the Good Parliament of 1376, but she was pardoned on 22 October 1376 and then remained with the king until his death.[12]

Yet, although these passages link the *Mirour de l'Omme* to the period of Edward III's lifetime, Gower's reference to the monster with two heads which 'now exists' at Rome and which disfigures the 'noble beauty' of the church (18817–40) must date from after the Great Schism within the western church which began on 20 September 1378, with Urban VI and Clement VII each claiming to be the rightful pope, and lasted until 1417.[13] These lines must thus be a later interpolation into the original text, although since we have only one manuscript of the *Mirour de l'Omme*, it is impossible to trace the stages of production of this work.[14] It is thus likely that Gower was

---

[11] Fisher, *John Gower*, p. 95.
[12] Chris Given-Wilson, 'Perrers, Alice (d. 1400/01)', *Oxford Dictionary of National Biography*, Oxford University Press, 2004; online edition, [http://www.oxforddnb.com/view/article/21977, accessed 24 May 2016]. On Gower and Perrers, see Gardiner Stillwell, 'John Gower and the Last Years of Edward III', *Studies in Philology*, 45 (1948), pp. 454–71, at 456–67.
[13] Howard Kaminsky, 'The Great Schism', in Michael Jones, ed., *The New Cambridge History. Volume VI, c.1300–c.1415* (Cambridge: Cambridge University Press, 2000), pp. 674–96, at 674–7.
[14] Gower, *Complete Works*, I: xlii; Maria Wickert, *Studies in John Gower* (Washington D.C.: University Press of America, 1981), p. 24 n. 38; Fisher, *John Gower*, p. 95. In a later passage in the *Mirour*, Gower refers to the two heads of the city of Rome

working on the *Mirour de l'Omme* from around 1376 to 1379. Robert Yeager has tentatively argued that Gower's decision to write this poem in French may suggest that he began work on it in the late 1350s when Edward III was claiming the French throne, that his efforts may have slowed following the king's renunciation of his claim in the Treaty of Brétigny (1360) and that he resumed work on it in earnest in 1369 when Edward renewed his claim once more.[15] However, there is nothing in the text of the *Mirour de l'Omme* itself to support such an early date for its composition. Yeager has also argued that the final section of the *Mirour de l'Omme*, on the life of the Virgin Mary, may have been a later addition to the text, dating from the time of Gower's residence at the Augustinian Priory of St Mary Overy in Southwark.[16] However, as Martin Heale argues below (pp. 272–4), it is difficult to demonstrate that the content of the *Mirour de l'Omme* is linked to the Augustinians in general, let alone to St Mary Overy in particular. That Gower's denunciation of the peasants and labourers in the *Mirour* includes the prediction that the common people will turn against their superiors in the near future (26425–26532) may suggest that the poem was written before the rising of 1381. Even here, however, there is room for doubt since his criticism of the lesser people who rise up against their superiors 'like savage beasts in a multitude and a tempest against their lords' (27229–38) seems to echo the criticism of the peasants in Book I of the *Vox Clamantis* which Gower wrote after the 1381 revolt. As we shall see below, there may have been other occasions when Gower's seeming prophecies about the future may actually have been written with the advantage of historical hindsight.

The *Vox Clamantis*

The rising of 1381 is explicitly dealt with at length in Gower's second major work, the Latin *Vox Clamantis*, which survives in nine independent manuscripts (along with later copies of two of them) and which contains over 10,000 lines.[17] In its final form, the poem is in seven books. Book I (the *Visio*) provides an allegorical account of the events of the 1381 revolt in which

---

(22158–22212) but this seems to be a reference to the pope and the emperor rather than to the two rival popes.

[15] Robert F. Yeager, 'Politics and the French Language in England during the Hundred Years' War', in Denise N. Baker, ed., *Inscribing the Hundred Years' War in French and English Cultures* (Albany: State University of New York Press, 2000), pp. 127–57, at 137–8; Robert F. Yeager, 'John Gower's French', in Siân Echard, ed., *A Companion to Gower* (Cambridge: D. S. Brewer, 2004), pp. 137–51, at 142.

[16] Robert F. Yeager, 'Gower's French Audience: The Mirour de l'Omme', *Chaucer Review* 41 (2006–07), pp. 111–37, at 118–25; Bertolet, 'The French Works: Mirour de l'Omme', in *RRC*, pp. 321–7, at 322–3.

[17] Derek Pearsall, 'The Manuscripts and Illustrations of Gower's Works', in Echard, *A Companion to Gower*, pp. 72–97, at 78, 84.

the peasants are portrayed as farmyard animals which abandon their true natures and are transformed into wild beasts which turn against humanity. In Book II, Gower denies that Fortune is to blame for the lamentable state of the world and, as in the *Mirour de l'Omme*, asserts that man is responsible for his own fate. He then proceeds to discuss the faults of the estates which make up society including the secular clergy (Book III), the regular clergy (Book IV), the knights, peasants, labourers, merchants and artisans (Book V) and the ministers of the law and royal officials (Book VI.1–6). Book VI also includes a discussion of the duties of the virtuous ruler (VI.7–18). Finally, Gower invokes the image of the statue in Nebuchadnezzar's dream (Daniel: 1–45) to symbolize the decay of the world caused by the power of sin, particularly of lechery and avarice, and reminds his readers of death and of the judgement that follows in order to bring about the repentance needed for salvation (Book VII).

The *Vox Clamantis* went through a number of stages of composition. The fact that one of the surviving versions of the poem, that in MS Laud 719, lacks the allegorical account of the 1381 rising found in the other manuscripts has been cited as evidence that Gower may have begun writing the poem before the revolt took place and that the account of the revolt offered in Book I was a later addition to it. Carlson has dated the *Visio* to late 1381 or 1382 although Fisher suggested that it may actually have been inserted into the *Vox* as late as 1386.[18] However, even the text of MS Laud 719 begins with the reference to Gower's dream-vision of society as having taken place in June 1381 (i.e., at the time of the revolt) that is found in the other manuscripts of the poem (I.1.1–2), which suggests that Gower's account of the revolt was deliberately omitted from this particular manuscript rather than that it had yet to be written.[19] Nevertheless, other pieces of textual evidence *do* support the view that the *Visio* may have been added to the work after the estates satire of its later books had been written. For instance, the prologue to what is now Book II of the *Vox Clamantis*, which invokes the help of God, uses the humility topos to apologize for any shortcomings in the work that follows and announces that 'the name of this volume shall be *The Voice of One Crying*' (II.Pro.5–30, 83), reads as if it originally formed the introduction to the poem as a whole. The fact that Book II is much shorter than the books which follow has also been seen as indicating that it had originally functioned as a prologue to the entire work. However, if this were the case, the headnote at the start of Book II, which refers to the narrator having awoken from

---

[18] David R. Carlson, 'Gower's Early Latin Poetry: Text-Genetic Hypotheses of an *Epistola ad regem* (ca. 1377–1380) from the Evidence of John Bale', *Medieval Studies*, 65 (2003), pp. 293–317, at 294; Fisher, *John Gower*, p. 108; Ian Cornelius, 'Gower and the Peasants' Revolt', *Representations*, 131 (2015), pp. 22–51, at 25–6.

[19] One of the other manuscripts of the *Vox Clamantis* (Lincoln Cathedral Library, A.72) also lacks the *Visio* but this is a sixteenth-century copy of MS Laud 719 (Macaulay, *The Latin Works*, pp. xxxi–ii, lxvii–ix; Fisher, *John Gower*, pp. 101–3, 306).

his dream-vision, must have been added to make sense of the subsequent insertion of Book I.[20]

If the suggestion that the *Visio* was a later addition to the existing text of the *Vox Clamantis* remains a speculative if plausible hypothesis, the surviving manuscripts do nevertheless reveal some other definite revisions to the original text. One occurs at the start of Gower's critique of the secular clergy at the beginning of Book III, Chapter 1, which exists in three different forms, one of which makes no mention of the Great Schism, whereas the other two both refer to the existence of a 'proper' ('*bonus*') pope, who was supported by England (i.e. Urban VI) and a 'schismatic' one (i.e. Clement VII), favoured by the French. This suggests that the original version of this part of the text was written before 1378 (thus adding further weight to the theory that the *Visio* was a later insertion) and that Gower then added the reference to the Schism after this date.[21] If this was the case, Gower may have been working on (or at least revising) both the *Mirour de l'Omme* and the *Vox Clamantis* at around the same time.[22]

A more significant revision of the *Vox Clamantis* occurs in two important passages of Book VI. Following his condemnation of the abuses of the lawyers, judges, sheriffs and bailiffs (VI.1–6), Gower laments the discord which he saw as running throughout society (VII.7.1–544) and then addresses an 'epistle' to Richard II on the nature and duties of kingship (VI.8–17). The epistle includes a section in which Richard's late father, the Black Prince, who had died on 8 June 1376, is set up as a model for the king to follow as his people's 'defender in arms' (VI.13.917–68) and it is possible that this praise of the Black Prince draws on an earlier eulogy of him by Gower.[23] The text here exists in two different versions with the main body of the epistle itself being the same in both but with its introduction and conclusion expressing very different attitudes towards the king. Fisher speculatively suggested that the epistle may have been written between 1381 and 1386 but Carlson dated it to the first four years of Richard II's reign.[24] Michael Bennett, however, argues below that the epistle seems to address the king as though he were

---

[20] Gower, *Complete Works*, IV: pp. xxxi–ii; Fisher, *John Gower*, pp. 102–3.
[21] Gower, *Complete Works*, pp. 105–6; Gower, *Major Latin Works*, pp. 116, 397; Wickert, *Studies in John Gower*, pp. 11–14; Fisher, *John Gower*, p. 103. The reference to 'schisms in the churches' at the end of some manuscripts of Book IV, Chapter 24 seems to refer to the divisions caused by heresy rather than to the Great Schism whilst the allusion to the divisions which caused the downfall of Rome (V.16.1007–10) refers to conflicts within ancient Rome, rather than to the contemporary papacy (Gower, *Complete Works*, IV: 199–200; Gower, *The Major Latin Works*, pp. 193–5, 219, 440; Fisher, *John Gower*, p. 103).
[22] Cornelius, 'Gower and the Peasants' Revolt', p. 25.
[23] David R. Carlson, 'Gower's Early Latin Poetry: Text-Genetic Hypotheses of an *Epistola ad regem* (ca. 1377–1380) from the Evidence of John Bale', *Medieval Studies*, 65 (2003), pp. 293–317, at 310–15.
[24] Fisher, *John Gower*, p. 108; Carlson, 'Gower's Early Latin Poetry', p. 315.

married, in which case it must have been written later than January 1382 when Richard married Anne of Bohemia (below, pp. 432–3). In the original introduction to the epistle, Gower absolves the young king (who was ten years old at the time of his accession in 1377) of any responsibility for the lack of justice in the land or for the corruption of the royal court, saying that 'the boy is free of blame' and that 'not the king but his council is the cause of our sorrow'. It was the 'elders' who were responsible for the vices which afflicted the land: 'if the king were of mature age, he would set right the scale which now is without justice' (VI.7.545–80*). In a similar vein, the original conclusion to the epistle looks optimistically to the future, praying that, with divine aid, the handsome young king would one day be a 'healthy old man' and that God would 'direct his actions for the better'. Gower hopes that the king would be honoured for his virtue and that he would protect his subjects, thereby winning the praises of posterity in this world and achieving salvation in the next. He concludes by praising the goodness that was within the king before bidding him farewell (VI.18.1159–1198*).

By contrast, the revised version of the introduction to the epistle is much more critical of the king: he is an 'undisciplined boy' who 'neglects the moral behaviour from which a man might grow up from a boy'; rather than pursuing virtue, the king is 'childish' in his behaviour, being ruled by his own whims, egged on by 'youthful company' and led astray by 'older men of greed' who tolerate his sinful and evil ways (VI.7.545–80). The epistle's revised conclusion reveals a similar shift in attitude to the king and adopts a much more cautionary tone, calling upon the king to 'return to God' and to exercise justice, pacifying his subjects 'not by means of terror but rather through love'. If the king followed this advice, he would please God and would win the hearts of his people but if he failed to rule justly, seeking only his own profit, then the people would 'turn itself away' from him (VI.18.1159–1200).

The dates of these alternative versions of the introduction and conclusion to the epistle to the king are uncertain, partly because all of the surviving manuscripts of the *Vox Clamantis* date from after 1399.[25] Fisher dated the earlier version, in which the young king was addressed with affection and hope, to the years between 1381 and 1386, with the revisions to the text being made in the 1390s, with Stockton likewise suggesting a date of around 1393 for the changes.[26] Michael Bennett by contrast argues that these changes may have been made in the late 1380s, in the period when Richard began to face open criticism and resistance in parliament and from leading members of the nobility (see below, pp. 434–5). If Gower's comments about the king's character defects were made at this time, they were extremely

---

[25] Joel Fredell, 'The Gower Manuscripts: Some Inconvenient Truths', *Viator*, 41 (2010), pp. 231–50, at 245.
[26] Fisher, *John Gower*, pp. 102, 108; Gower, *Major Latin Works*, p. 13; Judith Ferster, *Fictions of Advice: The Literature and Politics of Counsel in Late Medieval England* (Philadelphia: University of Pennsylvania Press, 1996), p. 111.

pointed and forthright and Bennett suggests below that they may not have had a wide circulation outside Gower's immediate circle (below, pp. 446, 451–2).[27] Another possibility, although it certainly remains open to debate, is that Gower's alterations to the text, including its extremely outspoken criticisms of the king, were actually introduced after Richard's deposition in 1399, allowing Gower to pose as an explicit critic of the king at an early date and casting himself in the role of a prophet who had foreseen the fate which the king would suffer if he did not heed Gower's advice.[28] Certainly, as we shall see, further changes to the text of the Vox Clamantis were made following Richard's deposition. It thus seems that Gower began the Vox Clamantis at some date before the Peasants' Revolt of 1381, perhaps even before the Great Schism of 1378; that he added Book I, with its account of the revolt, sometime in the early 1380s; and that he continued to make changes to the text through to perhaps the early years of the fifteenth century.

The Confessio Amantis

Like the Vox Clamantis, the text of Gower's third major work, the Confessio Amantis, underwent a series of revisions, the dating and political significance of which are extremely controversial. The Confessio Amantis is mainly in Middle English, although it also contains verses and explicatory glosses in Latin.[29] The complete text has survived in forty-nine manuscripts (as well as a number of manuscripts which are fragmentary or which include extracts from the text) and is divided into a prologue and eight books.[30] The Prologue echoes the themes of Gower's earlier works in lamenting the decline of society from the harmony and virtue of olden times and in asserting that

---

[27] Janet Coleman, *English Literature in History, 1350–1400: Medieval Readers and Writers* (London: Hutchinson, 1981), p. 153.

[28] Christopher Fletcher, *Richard II: Manhood, Youth and Politics, 1377–99* (Oxford: Oxford University Press, 2008), pp. 17–18; Nigel Saul, 'John Gower: Prophet or Turncoat', in Dutton, Hines and Yeager, *John Gower, Trilingual Poet*, pp. 86–97, at 89–90.

[29] Derek Pearsall, 'Gower's Latin in the *Confessio Amantis*', in Alastair J. Minnis, ed., *Latin and Vernacular: Studies in Late-Medieval Texts and Manuscripts* (Cambridge: D. S. Brewer, 1989), pp. 13–25; Siân Echard, 'With Carmen's Help: Latin Authority in the *Confessio Amantis*', *Studies in Philology*, 95 (1998), pp. 1–40. For public reading as the means by which the meaning of these Latin passages were conveyed to the audience for Gower's text, see Joyce Coleman, 'Lay Readers and Hard Latin: How Gower May Have Intended the *Confessio Amantis* To Be Read', *Studies in the Age of Chaucer*, 24 (2002), pp. 209–35.

[30] Pearsall, 'The Manuscripts and Illustrations of Gower's Works', pp. 74–7; Jane Griffiths, 'Gower's *Confessio Amantis*: A "New" Manuscript', *Medium Aevum*, 82 (2013), pp. 244–59. There were also two early printed editions of the *Confessio Amantis* (Norman F. Blake, 'Early Printed Editions of *Confessio Amantis*', *Mediaevalia*, 16 (1990), pp. 289–306).

humanity is responsible for its own fate. Book I then announces a change of theme, to that of romantic love. It recounts how when the narrator, Amans (i.e. the lover), was out walking in the woods, lamenting the woes of love, Venus and her son, Cupid, the goddess and god of love, appeared to him and how Venus sent her chaplain, Genius, to hear his confession concerning his sins in love. Genius then questions Amans about his failings in love, seeking to correct him with the help of exemplary tales, many of which are drawn from the poetry of Ovid. Genius's questions are organized in relation to the Seven Deadly Sins and their sub-parts. He begins with pride (Book I), before examining Amans in relation to envy (Book II), wrath (Book III), sloth (Book IV), avarice (Book V) and gluttony (Book VI). The confession is then interrupted by a lengthy digression in which Genius sets out Aristotle's teachings to Alexander concerning the branches of knowledge, cosmography, and the virtues needed by a king (Book VII). Then, in Book VIII, Genius returns to the task of hearing Amans's confession, although he does so not by examining him about lechery in general, which is the seventh deadly sin, but, more specifically, by addressing the sin of incest. He concludes by urging Amans to renounce the wilfulness and blindness of love and to turn instead to reason, but Amans is still unable to abandon his love. Finally, Venus appears once more and, by reminding Amans (who is now revealed to be John Gower himself) of his old age, succeeds in putting an end to his desire and so allows reason to triumph over the folly and 'unwise fantasie' of love (VIII.2865–6).

Critics have spent much time discussing the various stages of revision which the *Confessio Amantis* underwent although, as Fredell noted, a focus on the variant forms of the work in the surviving manuscripts can lead us to overlook the overwhelming similarities that exist between their texts, even if the manuscripts do differ in their layout of verses and glosses and in their inclusion of tables of contents.[31] Macaulay's account of the revisions which Gower made to this work, which distinguished three main recensions of the work as well as three separate variants of the first recension and two of the second, has remained extremely influential.[32] As we shall see, Macaulay's classification of the manuscripts is problematic but, nonetheless, his analysis does provide a useful starting point for discussion even if his classification is not eventually retained. The Prologue to the 'first recension' of the *Confessio Amantis* describes it as a book which was written 'for king Richardes sake'. Here Gower recounts how, 'par chaunce', he had met Richard II whilst rowing on the River Thames. The king then invited Gower to join him

---

[31] Richard K. Emmerson, 'Reading Gower in a Manuscript Culture: Latin and English in Illustrated Manuscripts of the *Confessio Amantis*', *Studies in the Age of Chaucer*, 21 (1999), pp. 143–86, at 145; Joel Fredell, 'John Gower's Manuscripts in Middle English', in *RRC*, pp. 91–6, at 93; Siân Echard, 'Pre-Texts: Tables of Contents and the Reading of John Gower's *Confessio Amantis*', *Medium Aevum*, 66 (1997), pp. 270–87.

[32] Gower, *Complete Works*, II: cxxvii–clxvii.

on his barge where he had requested that the poet should write 'Som newe thing' for him, a request which Gower, who pledges his allegiance and obedience to the king in the text, sought to fulfil, even though he had long been suffering from sickness (Pro.24–92*). We cannot know for certain whether this meeting actually took place although, as Nicholson says, 'there is no reason to doubt' Gower's account of it or to disbelieve that the king made such a request (see also below, pp. 435–6).[33] Book VIII of this recension ends with Gower presenting his work to Richard whom he praises for being just, merciful and generous to his subjects (VIII.2971–3053*). Many of the manuscripts of the first recension contain a marginal date of 1390 beside line 331 of the Prologue, which gives the earliest date at which the first version of the text was completed, although it is possible that Gower actually began work on the 33,444 lines of the text at some point in the mid-1380s with Martha Carlin (above, pp. 52–3) and Michael Bennett (below, pp. 435–6) suggesting that the meeting on the Thames probably took place in 1385 or early 1386.[34] However, all of the manuscripts of this recension of the *Confessio Amantis*, with its praise of Richard II, were actually produced after Richard's deposition by Henry Bolingbroke in 1399, with some copies even being owned by Bolingbroke's own younger sons.[35]

In the manuscripts of what Macaulay identified as the second recension of the *Confessio Amantis*, there are some alterations to the text of Books V, VI and VII.[36] More significantly, the epilogue was changed, with the passages in praise of Richard II found in the first recension being replaced by a general prayer for the state of England (VIII.2941–3172). Some manuscripts of this recension of the *Confessio Amantis* also alter the Prologue, replacing the account of Gower's meeting with Richard II on the Thames with a general lament about the world's decay. They also alter the dedicatee of the work from the king to Henry Bolingbroke (i.e., the future Henry IV, the son of John of Gaunt, duke of Lancaster), whom Gower addresses as his 'oghne lord'

---

[33] Dhira B. Mahoney, 'Gower's Two Prologues to the *Confessio Amantis*', in Robert F. Yeager, ed., *Re-Visioning Gower* (Asheville: Pegasus Press, 1998), pp. 17–37, at 19, 36; Peter Nicholson, *Love and Ethics in Gower's Confessio Amantis* (Ann Arbor: The University of Michigan Press, 2005), p. 108. See also Joyce Coleman, '"A Bok for King Richardes Sake": Royal Patronage, the *Confessio* and the *Legend of Good Women*', in Robert F. Yeager, ed., *On John Gower: Essays at the Millennium* (Kalamazoo: Medieval Institute Publications, 2007), pp. 104–23, at 106–7; Robert F. Yeager, 'The Body Politic and the Politics of Bodies in the Poetry of John Gower', in Piero Boitani and Anna Torti, eds, *The Body and The Soul in Medieval Literature* (Cambridge: D. S. Brewer, 1999), pp. 145–65, at 161.

[34] See also Fisher, *John Gower*, p. 116; Douglas Gray, 'Gower, John (d. 1408)', *Oxford Dictionary of National Biography*, Oxford University Press, 2004, online edition [http://www.oxforddnb.com.manchester.idm.oclc.org/view/article/11176, accessed 18 August 2017].

[35] Joel Fredell, 'Reading the Dream Miniature in the *Confessio Amantis*', *Medievalia et Humanistica*, 22 (1995), pp. 61–93.

[36] Pearsall, 'The Manuscripts and Illustrations of Gower's Works', pp. 93–4.

and whom he praises as being 'Ful of knyhthode and alle grace' (Pro.24–92). However, at least one manuscript of this supposed recension retained the original version of the Prologue with its dedication to King Richard, whilst two others whose opening leaves are now defective may also have taken this form. As a result of such variations, critics have questioned the utility of this 'recension' as a coherent or useful category and have challenged the assumption that it chronologically preceded the third recension.[37]

The manuscripts of the 'third recension' of the *Confessio Amantis* omit the changes to Books V, VI and VII found in works of the 'second recension', but retain the revised versions of the Prologue, with its dedication to Henry of Lancaster, and of the epilogue, in which all reference to Richard II has been removed.[38] Some manuscripts of the second and third recensions date the prayer for the state of England in the epilogue to Book VIII to the fourteenth year of Richard II's reign, i.e., 22 June 1390 to 21 June 1391.[39] However, the Prologue to the second and third recensions is dated in the text to the sixteenth year of the reign (Pro.25), i.e., between 22 June 1392 and 21 June 1393. Significantly, in the autumn of 1393, Gower was presented with a livery collar by Bolingbroke, perhaps as a reward for the poet's presentation to him of a copy of the revised version of the *Confessio Amantis*. This collar was probably the Lancastrian 'collar of esses' which Gower is shown wearing both on his tomb effigy and in a miniature in the Fairfax manuscript of the *Confessio Amantis*.[40]

The changes which Gower made to the Prologue and to the ending of the *Confessio Amantis*, along with Bolingbroke's gift of a collar to Gower in 1393, have sometimes been understood as a sign that by this date the poet was becoming disillusioned with Richard II's rule and that he had shifted his political allegiance towards Bolingbroke.[41] However, this remains a contro-

---

[37] Gower, *Complete Works*, III: pp. cxxix, cxxxiv; Fisher, *John Gower*, p. 120; Pearsall, 'The Manuscripts and Illustrations of Gower's Works', p. 94; Peter Nicholson, 'Poet and Scribe in the Manuscripts of Gower's *Confessio Amantis*', in Derek Pearsall, ed., *Manuscripts and Texts: Editorial Problems in Later Middle English Literature* (Cambridge: D. S. Brewer, 1987), pp. 130–42, at 139–42.

[38] Pearsall, 'The Manuscripts and Illustrations of Gower's Works', p. 93.

[39] Gower, *Complete Works*, II: cxviii; Gower, *Complete Works*, III: 468; Fisher, *John Gower*, pp. 117, 120; Peter Nicholson, 'The Dedication of Gower's *Confessio Amantis*', *Mediaevalia*, 10 (1984), pp. 159–80, at 172.

[40] Gower, *Complete Works*, IV: xvi–xvii, xx; Fisher, *John Gower*, p. 68; Jeremy Griffiths, '*Confessio Amantis*: The Poem and its Pictures', in Alastair Minnis, ed., *Gower's Confessio Amantis* (Cambridge: D. S. Brewer, 1983), pp. 163–79, at 165. Alternatively, Yeager suggests that the collar was a reward for Gower's presentation of the original version of the *Cinkante Balades* to Bolingbroke (Gower, *The French Balades*, p. 53).

[41] Russell A. Peck, *Kingship and Common Profit in Gower's Confessio Amantis* (Carbondale and Edwardsville: Southern Illinois University Press, 1978), pp. 8–10; Gower, *Major Latin Works*, p. 13; Nigel Saul, *Richard II* (New Haven: Yale University Press, 1997), pp. 436–7; John Hines, Nathalie Cohen and Simon Roffey, 'Johannes Gower, Armiger, Poeta: Records and Memorials of his Life and Death', in Echard, *A Companion to*

versial issue. On the one hand, even in the first 'Ricardian' recension of the text, a number of manuscripts of the *Confessio Amantis* conclude by addressing the work to Henry Bolingbroke, who was then earl of Derby.[42] On the other, Gower is unlikely to have been radically alienated from Richard during this period, which was one of relative political peace between the king and his former opponents (although Richard was at odds with the city of London in 1392), and Bolingbroke would hardly have been seen as an 'alternative' to Richard at this early date. It has even been suggested that the changes which were apparently made to the text of the *Confessio Amantis* in the early 1390s were actually introduced after 1399.[43] Indeed, Lindeboom has speculated that the version of the text dedicated to Henry Bolingbroke was actually produced *before* that which was dedicated to Richard II, although it is hard to reconcile this re-ordering of the versions of the poem with Gower's claim that the *Confessio Amantis* was written in response to the king's request for a new poem from him at their meeting on the Thames (Pro.48–56*).[44] Given the similarities between all the versions of the *Confessio Amantis*, the problems in identifying a coherent second recension of it, and the strong possibility that many of the variant readings in its manuscripts are the result of scribal rather than authorial revision, it may be best to conclude that we are actually confronted with one basic version of the text but with two different dedications.[45] The earlier of these, with its dedication to Richard II, may date from 1390 whilst the other, which refers to Bolingbroke as Henry of Lancaster and as earl of Derby, rather than as duke of Hereford (as he was from 1398) or as the king (as he was from 1399), may be from some time in the 1390s but probably before the middle of 1393.

Gower, pp. 23–42, at 26. Allen even suggests that Gower's Lancastrian loyalty was formed as early as the mid-1380s (Rosamund S. Allen, 'Gower and Southwark', in Julia Boffey and Pamela King, eds, *London and Europe in the Later Middle Ages* (London: Centre for Medieval and Renaissance Studies, Queen Mary and Westfield College, 1995), pp. 111–47, at 126–7.

[42] Gower, *Complete Works*, II: xxi; Gower, *Complete Works*, III: 478, 549; Nicholson, 'The Dedication of Gower's *Confessio Amantis*', pp. 159–80.

[43] Gower, *Complete Works*, II, pp. xxiii–iv; Lynn Staley, 'Gower, Richard II, Henry of Derby and the Business of Making Culture', *Speculum*, 75 (2000), pp. 68–96, at 78–9; Caroline M. Barron, 'The Quarrel of Richard II with London, 1392–7', in Francis R. H. Du Boulay and Caroline M. Barron, eds, *The Reign of Richard II: Essays in Honour of May McKisack* (London: The Athlone Press, 1971), pp. 173–201; Nicholson, *Love and Ethics in Gower's Confessio Amantis*, p. 111; Carlson, *John Gower, Poetry and Propaganda in Fourteenth-Century England*, p. 215; Fredell, 'John Gower's Manuscripts in Middle English', p. 91; Terry Jones, 'Did John Gower Rededicate his *Confessio Amantis* before Henry IV's Usurpation?', in Simon Horobin and Linne Mooney, eds, *Middle English Texts in Transition* (York: York Medieval Press, 2014), pp. 40–74.

[44] Wim Lindeboom, 'Rethinking the Recensions of the *Confessio Amantis*', *Viator*, 40 (2009), pp. 319–48.

[45] Fredell, 'The Gower Manuscripts', pp. 242–3. On the scribal revisions, see Peter Nicholson, 'Gower's Revisions to the *Confessio Amantis*', *Chaucer Review*, 19 (1984–85), pp. 123–43.

A final significant change made by Gower to the later versions of the *Confessio Amantis* also occurs in the epilogue to Book VIII in relation to Gower's references to Geoffrey Chaucer. In the first recension of the *Confessio Amantis*, when Venus appears to Gower, she asks him to 'gret wele Chaucer whan ye mete' and adds some complimentary comments about Chaucer as her 'owne clerk' (VIII. 2941–2957*) but these sixteen lines do not appear in the later versions of the work. By 1390, when the first recension of the *Confessio Amantis* may have been written, Gower and Chaucer had already been closely associated for a number of years. As early as 1378 (around the time when Gower was finishing the *Mirour de l'Omme* and perhaps beginning work on the *Vox Clamantis*), when Chaucer left on a royal embassy to Italy, he appointed Gower and Richard Forester as his attorneys to act on his behalf in his absence.[46] At the end of *Troilus and Criseyde*, which was completed by 1387 at the latest, Chaucer famously 'directs' his text to the 'philosophical' Ralph Strode and to 'moral Gower' for correction (V.1856–9).[47] Four of the exemplary stories from Gower's *Confessio Amantis*, those of Constance (II.587–1598), of Florent (I.1407–1864), of Virginia (VII.5131–5306) and of Phebus and the crow (VII.768–817), are included in Chaucer's *Canterbury Tales* in the form of the tales told by the Man of Law, the Wife of Bath, the Physician and the Manciple, respectively. However, of these, only the 'Man of Law's Tale' is closely related to the story in the form that it has in the *Confessio Amantis*.[48] Since the eighteenth century, Gower's removal of the passage in the *Confessio Amantis* which referred to Chaucer, along with the disparaging comments made by Chaucer's Man of Law in the 'Introduction' to his tale (II.77–89) about the stories of Canace and Apollonius, versions of which appear in Gower's *Confessio Amantis* (III.143336; VIII.2712008), has sometimes been read as evidence of a quarrel between the two poets, but such claims are extremely speculative.[49]

---

[46] Gower, *Complete Works*, IV: xv–xvi; Fisher, *John Gower*, pp. 61, 337 n. 79; *Chaucer Life-Records*, eds Martin M. Crow and Clair C. Olson (Oxford: Clarendon Press, 1966), p. 54.

[47] Barry Windeatt, *Oxford Guides to Chaucer: Troilus and Criseyde* (Oxford: Clarendon Press, 1992), pp. 3–11; Robert F. Yeager, '"O Moral Gower": Chaucer's Dedication of Troilus and Criseyde', *Chaucer Review*, 19 (1984–85), pp. 87–99.

[48] Helen Cooper, *Oxford Guides to Chaucer: The Canterbury Tales* (Oxford: Clarendon Press, 1999), pp. 13, 123–4, 127–8, 157, 250, 385.

[49] Fisher, *John Gower*, pp. 26–34; Derek Pearsall, *The Life of Geoffrey Chaucer: A Critical Biography* (Oxford: Blackwell, 1992), pp. 123–3. One problem here is that Chaucer may not have been specifically alluding to Gower's versions of the stories of Canace and Apollonius since these tales were also available in other sources (*The Riverside Chaucer*, ed. Larry D. Benson (third edition; Oxford: Oxford University Press, 1987), p. 856). Ironically, Fisher interpreted Gower's removal of his reference to Chaucer not as a sign of a breach between the two men but rather as an 'act of consideration' on Gower's part since it avoided associating Chaucer with Gower's shift of allegiance towards Bolingbroke which Fisher believed was expressed by the revised versions of the *Confessio Amantis* (Fisher, *John Gower*, pp. 119–20).

The surviving manuscripts of the *Confessio Amantis* have been central to debates about how the texts of Gower's works were produced. Fisher argued that the scriptorium of the Priory of St Mary Overy in Southwark where Gower was certainly living in the final years of his life and, as Martha Carlin argues, from perhaps the mid-1380s (above, p. 54) may have been responsible for producing some of the manuscripts of Gower's works.[50] However, more recent work has been critical of this suggestion and it has been argued that the manuscripts were more likely to have been written by a large number of commercial scribes working independently on specific quires of each manuscript.[51] Even more recently, Mooney and Stubbs have suggested, on the basis of a palaeographical analysis, that many of the manuscripts of Gower's poems were, like those of other Middle English works including Chaucer's *Canterbury Tales* and Langland's *Piers Plowman*, copied out by clerks associated with the London Guildhall. For instance, they identify John Merchaunt, a London chamber clerk who eventually rose to be the city's common clerk from 1399 to 1417, as the 'Scribe D' who was involved in the production of seven manuscripts of Gower's *Confessio Amantis*.[52] However, their scribal attributions have proved to be contentious and while it is possible that Guildhall clerks were involved in the writing of Gower's manuscripts, it is possible that freelance commercial clerks, clerks of the Temple and royal clerks, such as Thomas Hoccleve, a clerk of the Privy Seal who was one of the five scribes who were responsible for producing Cambridge, Trinity College MS R.3.2 of the *Confessio Amantis*, were also involved in their production.[53]

---

[50] Fisher, *John Gower*, pp. 58–60, 93, 101. For some of Gower's sources, see H. C. Mainzer, 'A Study of the Sources of the *Confessio Amantis* of John Gower' (Unpublished University of Oxford D.Phil. thesis, 1968); Robert F. Yeager, *John Gower's Poetic: The Search for a New Arion* (Cambridge: D. S. Brewer, 1990), p. 53; Lynn Arner, *Chaucer, Gower and the Vernacular Rising: Poetry and the Problem of the Populace after 1381* (University Park: The Pennsylvania State University Press, 2013), p. 49.

[51] Pearsall, 'The Manuscripts and Illustrations of Gower's Works', p. 93; Nicholson, 'Poet and Scribe in the Manuscripts of Gower's *Confessio Amantis*', pp. 130, 138; Anthony I. Doyle and Malcolm B. Parkes, 'The Production of Copies of the *Canterbury Tales* and the *Confessio Amantis* in the Early Fifteenth Century', in Malcolm B. Parkes and Andrew G. Watson, eds, *Medieval Scribes, Manuscripts and Libraries: Essays Presented to N. R. Ker* (London: Scolar Press, 1978), pp. 163–209, at 165, 167, 196–200; Malcolm B. Parkes, 'Patterns of Scribal Activity and Revisions of the Text in Early Copies of Works by John Gower', in Richard Beadle and Alan J. Piper, eds, *New Science Out of Old Books: Studies in Manuscripts and Early Printed Books in Honour of A. I. Doyle* (Aldershot: Scolar Press, 1995), pp. 81–121, at 82, 94, 97; Jean-Pascal Pouzet, 'Southwark Gower: Augustinian Agencies in Gower's Manuscripts and Texts: Some Prolegomena', in Dutton, Hines and Yeager, *John Gower, Trilingual Poet*, pp. 11–25, at 11–16, 23–4.

[52] Linne R. Mooney and Estelle Stubbs, Scribes and the City: London Guildhall Clerks and the Dissemination of Middle English Literature, 1375–1425 (York: York Medieval Press, 2013), especially pp. 38–9, 60–5.

[53] Jane Roberts, 'On Giving Scribe B a Name and a Clutch of London Manuscripts from c. 1400', *Medium Aevum*, 80 (2011), pp. 247–70, Lawrence Warner, 'Scribes

A manuscript of the first recension of the *Confessio Amantis* was used to translate the poem into Portuguese, this being the earliest known translation of any major English literary work into another European language. The only surviving manuscript of the Portuguese text states that the work was 'copied' in 1430 but it is possible that the original translation, which was carried out by Robert Payn, an Englishman, was perhaps produced under the patronage of Philippa, the daughter of John of Gaunt, who arrived in Portugal in 1386, where she married King João I and where she remained until her death in 1415. In turn the Portuguese version of Gower's work was translated into Castilian, by John of Cuenca, 'householder of the city of Cueta', perhaps under the patronage of Catherine, Philippa's half-sister, who in 1388 married Enrique, the heir to the Castilian throne, where she reigned as queen from 1390 to 1406, and where she lived until her death in 1418.[54]

Gower and the 'Revolution' of 1399

If, as we have seen, it is controversial whether Gower shifted his political allegiance to Henry Bolingbroke as early as 1392–93 – or even whether such a choice would have been necessary at this date – there can be no doubting his support for the Lancastrian cause once Bolingbroke had seized the throne in 1399. Richard's reign officially ended on 29 September and as early as the following 21 November the new king awarded Gower two pipes (i.e. 252 gallons) of Gascon wine a year from the king's chief butler or his deputy at the port of London. As the *Mirour de l'Omme* had said, 'wine gives the heart perception and gladness when one takes it soberly' (16423–6). This grant refers to Gower as a 'king's esquire', which by this date could mean that he was a member of the king's affinity rather than that he was actually resident in the royal household.[55] Gower's close connections to Henry IV can also be seen in three of the series of short Latin poems which Gower wrote in the early years of Henry IV's reign: *Rex Celi Deus*, *O Recolende* and *H. Aquile Pullus*. Fisher referred to these as the 'laureate group' and they may have been written for, respectively, Henry's assumption of the throne on 30

Misattributed: Hoccleve and Pimkburst', *Studies in the Age of Chaucer*, 37 (2015), pp. 55–100; Matthew W. Irvin, 'The Merchant's Tale: Beryn and the London Company of Mercers', *Studies in the Age of Chaucer*, 40 (2018), pp. 55–100, at 115–16, 127–8; Sonja Drimmer, *The Art of Allusion: Illumination and the Making of English Literature* (Philadelphia: University of Pennsylvania Press, 2019), pp. 37–42.

[54] Ana Sáez-Hidalgo, 'Iberian Manuscripts of Gower's Works', in *RRC*, pp. 110–16.

[55] *CPR 1399–1401*, p. 128; Fisher, *John Gower*, p. 68; Chris Given-Wilson, *The Royal Household and the King's Affinity: Service, Politics and Finance in England, 1360–1413* (New Haven: Yale University Press, 1986), pp. 21–2, 64, 212. The reference to drinking in *O Recolende* (21) led Fisher to see the poem as a response to the king's gift of wine (Fisher, *John Gower*, pp. 68–9) but the text actually refers to the heavenly reward which awaits the king if he 'drinks in the deeds of mercy' (15–21).

September 1399, his coronation (on 13 October 1399) and the elevation of Henry's son, the future Henry V, as Prince of Wales (on 15 October) or as Duke of Aquitaine (on 23 October).[56] It is likely that Gower's *Unanimes Esse Qui Secula*, with its praise of love as the key to the kingdom's strength and happiness and its call for me to learn the lessons of 'yesterday' about the dangers of division (l. 8), also dates from this period, although, of course, this had also been one of the themes of the Prologue to the *Confessio Amantis* (Pro.121–9142–50168–71, 338, 573–7, 849–52, 892–6, 967–1089).

Another work dating from the start of Henry IV's reign was the English poem *In Praise of Peace*, which survives only in one manuscript (British Library Additional MS 59495, also known as the 'Trentham Manuscript').[57] In this poem, which Sobecki has argued was written before the renewal of the peace between England and France on 18 May 1400, Gower calls upon the king, 'who was chosen by Christ', to maintain peace, which is 'the chief of al the worldes welthe' (1, 71, 78).[58] Gower's loyalty to the new king is also evident from the *Cinkante Balades*, whose only copy is also preserved in the Trentham Manuscript, with the poem being dedicated to the 'good and pious King Henry' (26), although some of it may originally have been composed much earlier (see above, p. 123).[59] As we have seen (above, p. 128), it is also possible, although by no means certain, that the changes which Gower made to the introduction and conclusion to the epistle to Richard II in the *Vox Clamantis* were added after the king's deposition.

However, perhaps the clearest expression of Gower's loyalty to the new regime can be seen in the justification of Bolingbroke's usurpation which he offers in the *Cronica Tripertita*. This verse account of Richard's reign has survived in five manuscripts, in four of which it is presented as a continuation to the *Vox Clamantis*.[60] One of the manuscripts of the combined text of the *Vox Clamantis* and the *Cronica Tripertita* also includes the dedicatory *Epistola* to Thomas Arundel, whom Henry IV had restored to the archbishopric of Canterbury from which he had been removed by Richard II in 1397. Part I of the *Cronica* offers an account of the events of 1387–88 when Bolingbroke was one of the five Lords Appellant who sought to reform the government of the realm, although its focus is on Thomas, duke of Gloucester (designated as 'the Swan'), Richard, earl of Arundel ('the Horse') and Thomas, earl of Warwick ('the Bear'); Part II shows how Richard took revenge on his opponents during his so-called 'tyranny' which began in 1397; Part III tells how Richard was deposed and replaced by Henry IV in 1399. The text of

---

[56] Fisher, *John Gower*, pp. 99–100; Gower, *Minor Latin Works*, p. 7.
[57] Sobecki argues that this manuscript is written in Gower's own hand (Sebastian Sobecki, '*Ecce patet tensus*: The Trentham Manuscript, In Praise of Peace and John Gower's Autograph Hand', *Speculum*, pp. 925–59, at 951–59).
[58] Gower, *Minor Latin Works*, pp. 89, 93; Sobecki, '*Ecce patet tensus*', pp. 933–42.
[59] Gower, *The French Balades*, pp. 56–7.
[60] Pearsall, 'The Manuscripts and Illustrations of Gower's Works', p. 78.

the *Cronica* has usually been seen as a single work which was composed soon after the death of Richard which may have occurred in mid-to-late February 1400, a death which Gower claimed was the result of Richard's grief and self-starvation (III.431–49).[61] However, Michael Bennett argues below (see pp. 440–7, 467–73) that the first and second parts of the text may actually have been written much closer to the events which they recount before being incorporated into a single work following Richard's deposition.

Gower's works bring together individual ethics with political and social theory and contain both grand statements of principle and responses to specific historical incidents. The chapters below seek to explore Gower's moral and social outlook in more detail. Key issues which the contributors focus on include how coherent was Gower's overall ideological position? Does the multiplicity of voices contained in Gower's poems, particularly in the *Confessio Amantis*, make it impossible to identify Gower's own viewpoint? To what extent did the poet's works rehearse traditional moral and social values and employ inherited conventions and stereotypes and how far did he arrive at, or even desire to set out, his own personal stance in response to specific contemporary events and controversies? Did Gower remain consistent in his political principles between the composition of the *Mirour de l'Omme* (c. 1376) and the *Cronica Tripertita* (c. 1400) or did he alter his views in response to the deposition of Richard II in 1399?

---

[61] On Richard II's death, see Saul, *Richard II*, pp. 425–6.

PART II

GOWER AND LAY SOCIETY

Chapter 3

NOBILITY AND CHIVALRY

David Green

Contexts and Competing Interpretations

Throughout his work, John Gower showed a deep concern with the roles and responsibilities the secular aristocracy should undertake and how the chivalric ethic might be properly applied. Given the socio-political environment in which he wrote, this is hardly surprising. The English position in the Hundred Years War (1337–1453) became increasingly parlous as Gower's life drew on and this brought with it a general sense of war weariness. In addition, over the course of the 1380s and 1390s, disillusionment grew with Richard II (1377–99), his court and the military community at large. Difficulties with dating Gower's works mean, however, that it is often difficult to link his opinions to specific historical events.[1] As a result, a number of intriguing questions arise regarding Gower's attitudes to the chivalrous elite and how these attitudes may have evolved over time.

Various scholars have considered Gower's work in relation to the secular elite, the political world which its members inhabited, and the chivalric ethic that shaped their behaviour. Elliot Kendall, for example, has argued persuasively that a knowledge of the structures and intricacies of aristocratic households and of the wider world of retinues and affinities is vital when seeking to understand *Confessio Amantis* and suggests that Gower's opinions regarding the importance of a divinely-ordained social hierarchy can be explored in microcosm through imagery associated with the lordly *domus magnificencie*.[2] Gower's works have also been used to suggest that a sense of disillusionment pervaded England in the final quarter of the fourteenth century and he is said by scholars such as Ben Lowe and Winthrop Wetherbee to have attributed the debilitating prolongation of the Hundred Years War

---

My thanks to Siân Echard and Stephen Rigby for their very helpful comments on this chapter.

[1] See Chapter Two, above.
[2] Elliot Kendall, *Lordship and Literature: John Gower and the Politics of the Great Household* (Oxford: Oxford University Press, 2008), pp. 3, 115–17.

and the degenerate conduct of the *bellatores* to the failings of the aristocracy and the corruption of chivalry.[3] 'I do not know how this happened', Gower tells us in the Mirour de l'Omme (c. 1376–78), 'nor whence the evil has come, but everyone alive nowadays can see that knighthood has been ruined [or lost]' [*Car ce voit bien cil q'ore vit, / Chivalerie est trop perdue*] (23977–80). Many of Gower's remarks imply that when nobles waged war, their motives were sinful and that the consequences were often disastrous for the nation. In *Confessio Amantis* Genius warns us, repeatedly and emphatically, about the evils of warfare as well as the absurdity of knightly endeavours motivated by love and romantic ideals.

Such comments were far from unusual: a good deal of later medieval 'complaint literature' suggested that the military and chivalric elite had fallen far from the standards set in some earlier age. Thus, in *Piers Plowman*, Langland has Lady Meed, a potent symbol of bribery and corruption, rallying Edward III's forces in France whilst in Chaucer's 'Tale of Melibee' the wise man says that 'There is ful many a man that cryeth "werre! werre!" That woot ful little what werre amounteth'.[4] Similarly, in his *Songe du Vieil Pelerin* (1389), Philippe de Mézières accused English knights of destroying Christendom: they were intoxicated, he said, with knighthood and galvanized to wickedness by stories of Lancelot and Gawain.[5] Yet, it is also clear that Gower did not condemn all violence out of hand, nor criticize every aspect of chivalry. Indeed, on various occasions he described knighthood (of a particular sort) as a grand aspiration and, even within the *Confessio Amantis*, a number of tales suggest warfare can be justified and that love may provide a worthy spur for action.

Because of the diverse attitudes expressed within and between Gower's works, it is difficult to establish his opinion on the conjoined subjects of chivalry and nobility. Indeed, it may be that his readers (then and now) should not seek to resolve the apparent incongruities which can be found

---

[3] For such opinions see B. Lowe, *Imagining Peace: A History of Early English Pacifist Ideas, 1340–1560* (Philadelphia: University of Pennsylvania Press, 1997), pp. 35–41, 80–9; Nigel Saul, 'A Farewell to Arms? Criticism of Warfare in Late Fourteenth-Century England', in Chris Given-Wilson, ed., *Fourteenth Century England*, II (Woodbridge: Boydell Press, 2002), pp. 131–45 at 132–4, 142–3; Winthrop Wetherbee, 'John Gower', in David Wallace, ed., *The Cambridge History of Medieval English Literature* (Cambridge: Cambridge University Press, 1999), pp. 589–609.

[4] William Langland, *The Vision of Piers Plowman: A Compete Edition of the B-Text*, ed. Aubrey V. C. Schmidt (London: Everyman, 1987), III: 196–205; Geoffrey Chaucer, 'The Tale of Melibee' (VII: 1037–8).

[5] Philippe de Mézières, *Le Songe du Vieil Pelerin*, ed. G. W. Copeland (two volumes; Cambridge: Cambridge University Press, 1969), I: 185–6, 397. See also Maurice Keen, 'Chaucer and Chivalry Re-Visited', in Matthew Strickland, ed., *Armies, Chivalry and Warfare in Medieval Britain and France* (Stamford: Paul Watkins, 1998), pp. 1–12 at 6–7; Yoshiko Kobayashi, 'Letters of Old Age: The Advocacy of Peace in the Works of John Gower and Philippe de Mézières', in Russell A. Peck and R. F. Yeager, eds, *John Gower: Others and the Self* (Cambridge: D. S. Brewer, 2017), pp. 204–22.

in his writings, or expect his works to provide straightforward answers to intricate questions. Diane Watt, for instance, has suggested that various passages in *Confessio Amantis* invite 'multiple interpretations' and encourage 'complex, often contradictory… (mis)readings'.[6] Similarly, Patricia Batchelor has spoken in terms of the 'dynamic ambiguity' of the *Confessio Amantis*, noting how the glosses and texts sometimes support but on other occasions subvert one another, requiring readers to interpret meaning for themselves.[7] Such analyses offer a challenge to earlier readings which suggested that Gower's works offer a remarkably clear moral position, as when John Fisher claimed that '[t]he most striking characteristic of Gower's literary production is its single-mindedness…inner consistency of purpose and point of view'.[8]

An Aristocracy in Crisis?

However Gower is to be interpreted, there is no doubt that as he explored the character, roles and responsibilities of the nobility, the context in which he was writing was changing and fluid. It is likely that the population of England fell by about 50% in the years between 1300 and 1400. Depopulation from famine, war and plague meant that the coercive powers of aristocratic landlords, secular and ecclesiastic, diminished, villeinage declined, and the demand for labour increased markedly. As traditional seigneurial powers decayed, wage rates escalated and prices fell. Lords undertook less direct management of their estates and rented out larger areas to the peasantry and to demesne farmers.[9] As a result, those peasants and labourers who survived the middle years of the century made substantial socio-economic gains: their scarcity in a new world made them valuable. Consequently, a significant redistribution of wealth took place alongside what was, for some, an uncomfortable blurring of social boundaries.

Because of these developments, such barriers as there had been between the lower levels of the aristocracy (the gentry) and the upper levels of the peasantry became increasingly porous and a new potential for social mobility

---

[6] Diane Watt, *Amoral Gower* (Minneapolis: University of Minnesota Press, 2003), p. 17. See also Jonathan Hsy, 'Gower and Theory: Old Books, New Matters', in *RRC*, pp. 9–20.

[7] Patricia Batchelor, 'Feigned Truth and Exemplary Method in the *Confessio Amantis*', in Robert F. Yeager, ed., *Re-Visioning Gower* (Asheville: Pegasus Press, 1998), pp. 1–16 at 1, 9.

[8] John H. Fisher, *John Gower: Moral Philosopher and Friend of Chaucer* (New York: New York University Press, 1964), p. 135. For detailed references to the debate about the consistency of Gower's views, see Stephen Rigby, below, pp. 384–5.

[9] Richard M. Smith, 'The English Peasantry, 1250–1650', in Tom Scott, ed., *The Peasantries of Europe: From the Fourteenth to the Eighteenth Centuries* (London: Longman, 1998), pp. 339–71, at 360–1. For the economic and social change of this period, see also chapter four, below.

emerged. In this context, it became increasingly important to seek to differentiate and designate those of different ranks, but it also became increasingly difficult to do so. Membership of the gentry depended on a complex mix of factors including birth, wealth, service (especially, although not exclusively, military in nature) and land/property ownership.[10] This diverse group had a collective identity and occupied a space between the free peasantry and the peerage with whom they shared many characteristics including chivalry and co-membership of the order of knighthood. However, in the later Middle Ages, the increasing diversity of the sub-knightly ranks of the aristocracy, which came to include the esquire and gentleman, made this space increasingly indistinct, especially given the emergence of a newly wealthy upper stratum of the peasantry in the years after the plague. The yeoman was the most significant of this new group and he sat only a little below the lowest of the gentry. Furthermore, the very existence of a sub-knightly aristocracy suggests a change had taken place in conceptions of chivalry and the composition of those who comprised the chivalrous elite. In earlier years, knighthood had been one of the key elements that bound the aristocracy together despite the very considerable differences in wealth, influence and status which separated its lowliest and most eminent members.[11] This was no longer the case and many chose not to assume knightly status because of the expenses and obligations it potentially involved. Gower himself was one of those who might have taken on the mantle of knighthood, although his reasons for not doing so are not certain.

The nobility was also becoming increasingly diverse in this period. Over the course of the fourteenth century, the peerage, those sixty to seventy lords entitled to individual summons to parliament, emerged as a group at the apex of English political society, but even this was not a homogenous collective, as Chris Given-Wilson has noted:

> Social distinctions...became more rigidly defined, more blatantly advertised, and more jealously guarded...The development of ranks within the peerage [such as duke (from 1337) and marquis (from 1385)], the popularity of books of courtesy (which, *inter alia*, clarified rules of social precedence), and the blatant social overtone of, for example, the livery

---

[10] Peter Coss, *The Origins of the English Gentry* (Cambridge: Past and Present Publications, 2003), esp. pp. 9–11; Philippa Maddern, 'Gentility', in Raluca Radulescu and Alison Truelove, eds, *Gentry Culture in Late-Medieval England* (Manchester: Manchester University Press, 2005), pp. 18–34, at 18–19, 23. See also Peter Coss, 'Knights, Esquires and the Origins of Social Gradation in England', *Transactions of the Royal Historical Society*, sixth series, 5 (1995), pp. 155–78.

[11] David Crouch, *The English Aristocracy, 1070–1272: A Social Transformation* (New Haven: Yale University Press, 2011), pp. 3–19.

laws, or sumptuary legislation, all point to the fact that status was becoming ever more defined.[12]

It was for this reason that Richard II's appointments of a number of men to the upper echelons of the nobility in 1397 were the cause of so much strife and division.[13] Many of the established noble families virulently opposed these social upstarts, whom contemporaries derided as 'duketti' and who were associated with and held responsible for Richard's failing regime. Concerns with rank, therefore, were widespread and were not confined only to the differences between aristocracy and peasantry, but also to those within these internally differentiated groups.[14]

Gower, then, saw a society in flux. For him, as for many of his contemporaries, this proved deeply unsettling.[15] He complained in the *Mirour de l'Omme* that the wage demands of the peasantry were leading to the impoverishment of the nobility and, consequently, to an inversion of the social order (26437–484). Similarly, in *Vox Clamantis*, again and again, he expressed his disgust that peasants were now demanding so much more than their station should permit. As society fractured, so peasants lost sight not only of their status but also of those things – food, clothing and drink, as well as wages – which it was appropriate for them to enjoy (I.2.181–98; I.3.242–55; I.4.359–70). The exclusivity of the aristocracy, expressed and perhaps even defined by its members' lifestyle and code of social conduct as well as their wealth, was compromised as a result.[16]

Such concerns were shared by the elite, both secular and ecclesiastic. In the post-plague period, the visual expression of status became a matter of increasing importance. For the higher nobility, demonstrations of wealth in their households and among their retinues were vital. Edward III recognised the need to ensure the social distinctiveness of key members of the nobility

---

[12] Chris Given-Wilson, *The English Nobility in the Late Middle Ages* (London: Routledge, 1987), p. 57.

[13] Sylvia Federico, 'The Chivalry of Richard II: 1381 and 1399', in Gwilym Dodd, ed., *The Reign of Richard II* (Stroud: Tempus Publishing, 2000), pp. 51–6.

[14] Chris Given-Wilson, 'Richard II and the Higher Nobility' in Anthony Goodman and James L. Gillespie, eds, *Richard II: The Art of Kingship* (Oxford: Clarendon Press, 1999), pp. 107–28, at 117–19, 127–8.

[15] Similar attitudes may be found in some of Geoffrey Chaucer's works as well as those of Nicholas Bozon (fl. c.1320), Robert Mannying (d. 1338), John Bromyard (d. c.1352), and Thomas of Wimbledon (fl. c.1388). See Stephen H. Rigby, 'Reading Chaucer: Literature, History and Ideology', in Stephen H. Rigby and Alistair Minnis, eds, *Historians on Chaucer: The 'General Prologue' to The Canterbury Tales* (Oxford: Oxford University Press, 2014), pp. 1–23 at 4–6. See further, Janet Coleman, *English Literature in History, 1350–1400: Medieval Readers and Writers* (London: Hutchinson, 1981), p. 136.

[16] As Mathew Giancarlo has remarked, 'loss of property [in this period] was tantamount to a loss of noble identity' (*Parliament and Literature in Late Medieval England* (Cambridge: Cambridge University Press, 2007), p. 114).

and he made a substantial number of grants to ensure that his 'new men' (those he appointed earls in and after 1337) could maintain themselves in appropriate style.[17] For the lesser gentry, as socio-economic conditions changed, legal measures were taken to seek to re-establish their social inimitability and prevent those now wealthy peasants expressing their spending power publically. These measures included the labour legislation (from 1349), the sumptuary laws (from 1363) and later the game laws (1390). The Ordinance (1349) and Statute (1351) of Labourers formed desperate attempts to buttress the socio-economic status of the aristocracy in the immediate aftermath of plague as peasants left their manors and offered their services to the highest bidder. The 1351 statute was designed to prevent this wilful disruption of the proper order and what the Crown described as the 'malice of servants'. The sumptuary laws, in a similar fashion, although short-lived, aimed to restrict 'the excess of dress of people beyond their estate' that was said to have led 'to the very great destruction and impoverishment of the land'.[18] Gower, therefore, was far from alone in seeing social mobility as being both a symptom and a cause of national misfortune.

Attempts were also made, in the form of the game laws of 1390, to legislate to maintain the social distinctiveness of hunting and hawking, pastimes beloved by and emblematic of the aristocracy. Hunting played a key part in a nobleman's education. It required a fine sense of observation, placed a young man in a potentially perilous situation, giving him a taste of battle, and developed skills in riding. It might also help with tactical awareness given the need to organise men and hounds in the field.[19] Gower used hunting as a device to describe the devastating social disruption he witnessed during the Peasants' Revolt (1381). In *Vox Clamantis* he depicted diabolical peasants transformed into beasts and insects, predating upon the realm. Those rebels who were turned into hounds rejected all social propriety

---

[17] James Bothwell, *Edward III and the English Peerage: Royal Patronage, Social Mobility, and Political Control in Fourteenth-Century England* (Woodbridge: Boydell Press, 2004), pp. 31–7; Christopher Woolgar, *The Great Household in Late Medieval England* (New Haven: Yale University Press, 1999), pp. 8–30.

[18] *SR*, I: 307, 380; Chris Given-Wilson, 'Service, Serfdom and English Labour Legislation, 1350–1500', in Anne Curry and Elizabeth Matthew, eds, *Concepts and Patterns of Service in the Later Middle Ages* (Woodbridge: Boydell Press, 2000), pp. 21–37; Negley B. Harte, 'State Control of Dress and Social Change in Pre-Industrial England', in Donald C. Coleman and Arthur H. John, eds, *Trade, Government and Economy in Pre-Industrial England: Essays Presented to F. J. Fisher* (London: Weidenfeld and Nicholson, 1976), pp. 132–65 at 139–40; W. Mark Ormrod, 'The Politics of Pestilence: Government in England after the Black Death', in W. Mark Ormrod and Phillip G. Lindley, eds, *The Black Death in England* (Stamford: Paul Watkins, 1996), pp. 147–81 at 156.

[19] Nicholas Orme, *From Childhood to Chivalry: The Education of the English Kings and Aristocracy, 1066–1530* (London: Methuen, 1984), pp. 191–8. See also Emma Griffin, *Blood Sport: Hunting in Britain since 1066* (New Haven: Yale University Press, 2007), pp. 61–3.

and proper behaviour: 'well-bred dogs were not in company with them', we are told, 'they were worthless ones which had no training. They neither went hunting not rejoiced at the [sound of the] horn' (I.5.387–90). As this suggests, Gower considered the failure to perform one's duty and undertake one's proper social function an affront to a divinely ordered society.

Yet the legislative measures of this period failed to arrest the forces of change and, rather than ensuring a return to pre-plague conditions, they, alongside the more immediate pressures of successive poll taxes, only brought about resentment and anger which, as Gower had predicted, finally erupted in revolt. He remarked in the *Mirour de l'Omme* that the 'nettle' of the common people would 'sting' landlords if they failed to manage their tenants effectively (26491–95).[20] Furthermore, the perceived failure of the nobility to fulfil its chief responsibility and defend the realm against potential invasion in the 1370s as the war with France faltered may have encouraged the hostility of the peasantry in 1381.[21] While Gower decried revolt, he shared the rebels' disappointment with the impotence of the nobility.

Gower's revulsion at peasant uprisings was far from unique. A similar sense of social dislocation pervaded the works of writers such as Henry Knighton (d. c. 1396), Jean le Bel (d. 1370) and, later, Leonardo Bruni (d. 1444) as revolts broke out in England, France and elsewhere. A concerted assault seemed to have been launched which threatened the aristocracy's position of authority in the supposedly divinely ordained social hierarchy.[22] Thus the *Anonimalle Chronicle* described the rioting in London in 1381, noting how the rebels released all those incarcerated in the Fleet and Westminster prisons and burned legal and church records as well as John of Gaunt's Savoy Palace and many other 'fine and pleasant buildings'. The rebels demanded 'that henceforth no man should be a serf nor make homage of any type of service to any lord'.[23] Although, as will become clear, many of Gower's works suggest there was a dire need to reform the chivalry of England, he also felt

---

[20] Steven Justice, *Writing and Rebellion: England in 1381* (Berkeley: University of California Press, 1994), p. 141; Coleman, *English Literature in History*, p. 132. On the outbreak of the 1381 revolt see Christopher Dyer, *Making a Living in the Middle Ages: The People of Britain 850–1520* (New Haven: Yale University Press, 2009), pp. 286–93; Alastair Dunn, *The Great Rising of 1381: The Peasants' Revolt and England's Failed Revolution* (Stroud: Tempus Publishing, 2002), pp. 57–71.

[21] Eleanor Searle and Robert Burghart, 'The Defense of England and the Peasants' Revolt', *Viator*, 3 (1972), pp. 365–88.

[22] *The True Chronicles of Jean Le Bel, 1290–1360*, trans. Nigel Bryant (Woodbridge: Boydell Press, 2011), pp. 235–7. See further, Samuel K. Cohn, *Lust for Liberty: The Politics of Social Revolt in Medieval Europe, 1200–1425* (Cambridge, Mass.: Harvard University Press, 2008), esp. pp. 25–52; Justice, *Writing and Rebellion*, pp. 208–18; Rigby, 'Reading Chaucer', p. 8.

[23] *The Peasants' Revolt of 1381*, ed. R. Barrie Dobson (second edition; Houndmills: Macmillan Press, 1983), pp. 155–61.

beholden to protect a threatened social order which they surmounted and to stand against the revolutionary tendencies of the 1381 revolt.[24]

Chivalry and Military Service

Economic change, social mobility and peasant discontent were not the only threats to nobles and their position in later medieval England and elsewhere. Roles were also shifting in the military sphere and this, too, had major implications for the secular elite and the ways in which its members identified with the chivalric ethic. The later Middle Ages saw substantial changes in military practice and organisation that some historians have even considered 'revolutionary'.[25] Whether or not this is an appropriate description, there is no question that the early phases of the Hundred Years War saw the increasing professionalisation of English armies. Contracts (indentures) replaced traditional 'feudal' means of raising armies: troops were recruited and properly armed for particular periods of service and for clearly designated rates of pay. Although nobles were often central to this process, either serving as commissioners of array or by bringing members of their own retinues and households into national service, their image from within and outside their ranks altered. The 'revolution' saw a greater proportion of infantrymen, especially archers, employed in English expeditionary forces and they undertook an increasingly important tactical role that changed the composition of the military community.[26] Infantrymen had played an important part in armies from earliest times, but for much of the Middle Ages their role had usually been secondary to that of cavalry. This was no longer the case. The Scottish campaigns of the 1330s and the expeditions to France from the 1340s onwards saw dismounted knights, fighting side by side with archers and regular infantrymen. This trend continued over the course of the Hundred Years War. When, in the *Gesta Henrici Quinti* (c. 1417),

---

[24] In a similar fashion, when Mordred usurps the throne in the *Alliterative Morte Arthure* (c.1400), his army is described as a rabble lacking nobility – a clear picture of an inverted social order (*King Arthur's Death: The Middle Stanzaic Morte Arthur and Alliterative Morte Arthure*, ed. Larry D. Benson and Edward E. Foster (Kalamazoo: Medieval Institute Publications, 1994), ll. 3569–78). My thanks to Siân Echard for this observation.

[25] See Clifford J. Rogers, 'The Military Revolutions of the Hundred Years War', *Journal of Military History*, 57 (1993), pp. 241–78.

[26] Matthew Bennet, 'The Medieval Warhorse Reconsidered', in Stephen Church and Ruth Harvey, eds, *Medieval Knighthood V: Papers from the Sixth Strawberry Hill Conference 1994* (Woodbridge: Boydell Press, 1995), pp. 19–40, esp. 33–4; Kelly DeVries, *Infantry Warfare in the Early Fourteenth Century: Discipline, Tactics and Technology* (Woodbridge: Boydell Press, 1996), pp. 112–28, 155–87; Michael Prestwich, *Armies and Warfare in the Middle Ages: The English Experience* (New Haven: Yale University Press, 1996), esp. pp. 12–57, 334–46.

Walter Hungerford bemoaned the small size of Henry V's army at Agincourt (1415), it is indicative of English military priorities that he wished not for more knights but rather 'ten thousand of the best archers in England'.[27] Shared service in arms with those of lesser status recast an aristocratic social position that had been established, in part, on the basis of its members' status as warriors whose role was essential to the defence of the realm.

The professionalisation of arms brought with it the chance for advancement into the ranks of the secular elite from outside. In his *Scalacronica*, written c. 1355–63, Sir Thomas Gray described deeds of arms performed by those who began their careers as archers before becoming knights 'and some of them captains'.[28] While some of those who won promotion to the ranks of men-at-arms were the cousins and younger sons of minor gentry families, others, such as Sir Robert Knolles, who almost certainly began his career as an archer before his accession into knightly ranks, were the sons of burgesses or yeomen.[29] Military service, then, might be a means of social elevation. As Nicholas Upton commented in *De Studio Militari* (c. 1440), 'In these days we see openly how many poor men, labouring in the French wars, are becoming noble: one by prudence, another by valour, a third by endurance.'[30] Despite this, service in arms continued to retain a certain glamour: as longbowmen and infantrymen fought alongside the military aristocracy they acquired the sheen of chivalry. Yet, in now being shared between all those who fought, this veneer proved rather thin. It is in this context that we see the development of the Robin Hood ballads, which were certainly in existence by around 1377, and with them a particular image of the yeoman archer.[31] Undoubtedly a fine warrior, but one outside the ranks of the aristocracy, the literary Robin, 'a gode yeman', appropriated some of the cultural space conventional knightly heroes had formerly occupied. He was courteous on occasion, but could also be brutal. More importantly, he utterly rejected traditional notions of service and, hence, of hierarchy. Robin's encounter with the poor knight in the *Gest of Robyn Hode* (c. 1400–c. 1450) is instructive.[32] While it suggests that no inherent antipathy existed between yeomen and those of higher social status,

---

[27] *Gesta Henrici Quinti: The Deeds of Henry the Fifth*, eds Frank Taylor and John S. Roskell (Oxford: Oxford University Press, 1975), p. 79.

[28] Sir Thomas Gray, *Scalacronica, 1272–1363*, ed. Andy King (Woodbridge: Surtees Society, 2005), pp. 156–7.

[29] Michael Jones, 'Knolles, Sir Robert (d. 1407)', *Oxford Dictionary of National Biography* (Oxford: Oxford University Press, 2004; online edn, 2009); Adrian R. Bell, Anne Curry, Andy King and David Simpkin, *The Soldier in Later Medieval England* (Oxford: Oxford University Press, 2013), pp. 162–7.

[30] Cited by Maurice Keen, *Origins of the English Gentleman: Heraldry, Chivalry and Gentility in Medieval England, c.1300–c.1500* (Stroud: Tempus Publishing, 2002), pp. 76, 80.

[31] See Langland, *Piers Plowman*, V: 403.

[32] Textual and linguistic analysis of the *Gest* suggest a possible date of composition as early as c.1400 (Anthony J. Pollard, *Imagining Robin Hood: The Late Medieval Stories in Context* (London: Routledge, 2004), p. 6).

it also indicates that rank no longer provided an exact indication of wealth or power. The very fact that Robin could assist the knight poses questions about their relative positions.[33]

Under these circumstances, military service could no longer only be portrayed as an act of *noblesse oblige*. Nor was it the *sine qua non* of the nobility, many of whom began to seek careers away from the battlefield as opportunities arose in local and central government. Gower did not approve of this trend either. In the *Mirour de l'Omme*, written before his opposition to the Hundred Years War had hardened, he rebuked 'those rogues who do not take up arms', saying that they 'shall not enjoy the privileges of the knight, since they stay at home' (23797–800). While they might serve as jurors and court officials, they should not be exempt from paying taxes or share in the honours that service in arms provides. As this suggests, in the later Middle Ages the very nature of the military aristocracy, those descendants of the first *bellatores*, underwent significant change on account of new recruitment practices and a restructuring of expeditionary forces. As Gower remarked, 'Arms are [now] used by everyone, but not everyone whom we see taking arms is knightly [chivalrous]' (MO: 24001–2).

Here Gower, of course, may also be referring to conduct on the battlefield itself. There is no question that this, too, came under scrutiny, partly as a result of changing military tactics. French defeats at encounters such as Crécy (1346), Poitiers (1356), and later at Agincourt can be attributed, in part, to an outmoded reliance on (knightly) cavalry and individual (chivalric) attempts to win glory rather than on more prosaic but effective qualities such as collective discipline and the use of missile weapons. When the English implemented a strategy that relied on such elements they also compromised the ability of soldiers on all sides to capture and hold for ransom knights, nobles and other valuable members of the chivalric elite.[34] Ransoming had been at the heart of chivalry as it was exercised on the battlefield and, therefore, changes in military practice such as these called into question the roles, responsibilities and sense of mutual respect among all those who now bore arms.

---

[33] 'A Gest of Robyn Hode' in, *Rymes of Robyn Hood: An Introduction to the English Outlaw*, eds R. Barrie Dobson and John Taylor (Gloucester: Alan Sutton, 1989), p. 80. See also Colin Richmond, 'An Outlaw and Some Peasants: The Possible Significance of Robin Hood', *Nottingham Medieval Studies*, 37 (1993), pp. 90–101; Richard Almond and Anthony J. Pollard, 'The Yeomanry of Robin Hood and Social Terminology in Fifteenth-Century England', *Past & Present*, 170 (2001), pp. 52–77; R. W. Hoyle, 'A Re-Reading of the *Gest of Robyn Hode*', *Nottingham Medieval Studies*, 61 (2017), pp. 67–113 at 76–80, 94–6.

[34] David Green, *The Hundred Years War: A People's History* (New Haven: Yale University Press, 2014), pp. 33–5; Rémy Ambühl, *Prisoners of War in the Hundred Years War: Ransom Culture in the Late Middle Ages* (Cambridge: Cambridge University Press, 2013), esp. pp. 12–18, 28–39.

Such changes did not, however, signify the 'death of chivalry' as Johan Huizinga and Raymond Kilgour once argued.[35] Chivalry was reshaped, certainly, and those who comprised 'the chivalry of England' were not necessarily cut from the same cloth as previous generations, but, as Maurice Keen, Richard Barber, Richard Kaeuper and others have shown, the chivalric ethic remained in rude health. The fourteenth century saw the development of important institutions such as the Order of the Garter (founded 1348) whilst increasing jurisdiction was afforded to the Court of Chivalry. At the same time the chivalric Saint George emerged as the nation's patron, while the reading public demonstrated a voracious appetite for a wide range of chivalric texts, old and new.[36] Even Richard II, who is rarely accounted a great knight, deployed the trappings of chivalry to bolster his authority. Although he himself did not joust, he sponsored tournaments, hunted regularly, and took a close interest in heraldry, as did many of his subjects as we can see from legal cases such as the Scrope-Grosvenor controversy (1389). Indeed, 'the chivalric values of knighthood' have been considered 'an essential ingredient of Ricardian kingship'.[37] Richard also used chivalry to try and ensure loyalty among his subjects, for example in his appointments to the Garter and, most famously, in his dubbing of four Irish kings in 1394. Although these efforts proved, respectively, counter-productive and a failure, they also reveal the value many contemporaries placed on chivalric bonds.[38]

Criticism and Reform

Just as chivalry retained its cultural currency, so Gower believed it vital to maintain the status of the chivalric elite at the apex of a clearly defined and stable social hierarchy. Yet Gower was far from being a simple mouthpiece of the nobility: in *Vox Clamantis* the failures of the secular elite cause almost

---

[35] Johan Huizinga, *The Autumn of the Middle Ages*, trans. Rodney J. Payton and Ulrich Mammitzsch (Chicago: University of Chicago Press, 1996), esp. pp. 61–125 (originally published in 1919); Raymond Kilgour, *The Decline of Chivalry as Shown in the French Literature of the Late Middle Ages* (Cambridge, Mass.: Harvard University Press, 1937).

[36] Richard Barber, *The Knight and Chivalry* (revised edition; Woodbridge: Boydell Press, 2000), pp. 137–40, 147–52; Richard Barber, *Edward III and the Triumph of England: The Battle of Crécy and the Company of the Garter* (London: Allen Lane, 2013), pp. 67–96, 259–339; Richard W. Kaeuper, *Medieval Chivalry* (Cambridge: Cambridge University Press, 2016), pp. 216, 225–7, 312; Maurice Keen, *Chivalry* (New Haven: Yale University Press, 1984), pp. 196–7; Green, *Hundred Years War*, pp. 38, 41–2. See further: Craig Taylor, *Chivalry and the Ideals of Knighthood in France during the Hundred Years War* (Cambridge: Cambridge University Press, 2013), esp. pp. 19–53.

[37] James L. Gillespie, 'Richard II: Chivalry and Kingship', in James L. Gillespie, ed., *The Age of Richard II* (Stroud: Sutton Publishing, 1997), pp. 115–38, at 120–2, 125–6. See further Federico, 'Chivalry of Richard II: 1381 and 1399', pp. 51–6.

[38] Gillespie, 'Richard II: Chivalry and Kingship', pp. 126, 130–1; Darren McGettigan, *Richard II and the Irish Kings* (Dublin: Four Courts Press, 2016), pp. 143–57.

as much distress and seem nearly as unnatural as the monstrous violence of the 1381 rebels. The nobility could, it seems, no longer undertake the responsibilities its station demanded – its members were indolent and lacked courage and wisdom. 'In former times', Gower tells us, 'knighthood was prompt in service, but now their service is slow in coming, since their life is evil' (VC: VII.23.1257–8).[39]

The need to reform the chivalrous while at the same time maintaining their social standing resulted in a number of tensions in Gower's writings. While he clearly articulated the importance of social rank, he was also acutely aware of how many people fail to perform their duties as they should. These tensions are given form in the various contending opinions offered by exemplars and narrators and in tales told throughout his works. To some degree, these differences expressed those wider anxieties that had always existed around knighthood and its associated ideology. Gower was far from alone in describing the secular elite of his own age as degenerate or at least falling far from the standards set by the luminaries of the past and some of his criticisms had been raised against knights and nobles for hundreds of years – they formed the stock in trade of moralists and preachers. Thus, authorities from Bernard of Clairvaux (d. 1153) onwards, would have us believe that chivalry, perhaps from its very inception, had been in a state of decline or even entropy.[40]

Gower was particularly keen to criticise those chivalric attributes which encouraged dispute and discord and could lead to corruption. As Matthew Irvin has noted, Book V of *Vox Clamantis* deals almost entirely with the dangers which love and fame pose to chivalry.[41] There we read that 'if a knight makes war for the sake of vain praise, his praise is unwarranted'. We are also reminded that 'The end will bring nothing but inevitable folly upon the man for whom Venus initially leads the way to arms' (V.1.25–6). A similar moral can be found in the 'Tale of Actaeon' and the 'Tale of the False Bachelor' in *Confessio Amantis* (I.333–78; II.2501–782). Indeed, Winthrop Wetherbee goes so far as to say that such criticisms form part of a broader assault on knightly ethics: 'Chivalry is ... the villain of the *Confessio*', he argues, 'at odds with Genius' teaching in virtually every area.' Various tales 'set chivalric values in an adversary relation to the nascent institutions of civil law and parliamentary government...*Vox Clamantis*, too, [dwells] at length on how sexual love corrupts knighthood, goading the chivalric spirit

---

[39] See also Wetherbee, 'John Gower', pp. 595, 597.

[40] Bernard of Clairvaux, *In Praise of the Knighthood: A Treatise on the Knights Templar and the Holy Places of Jerusalem*, ed. M. Conrad Greenia (Kalamazoo: Cistercian Publications, 2000); Barber, *Knight and Chivalry*, pp. 371–83; Richard W. Kaeuper, *Holy Warriors: The Religious Ideology of Chivalry* (Philadelphia: University of Pennsylvania Press, 2009), pp. 9–17; Kaeuper, *Medieval Chivalry*, pp. 288–9; Keen, *Chivalry*, pp. 5, 49, 61.

[41] Matthew W. Irvin, *The Poetic Voices of John Gower: Politics and Personae in the Confessio Amantis* (Cambridge: D. S. Brewer, 2014), p. 102.

to spend itself in a reckless quest for empty glory, to the detriment of public spirit and true *probitas* [goodness].'[42] In a similar fashion, Gower's *In Praise of Peace* invites its dedicatee, Henry IV, to view the famous Nine Worthies as being more akin to fallen rulers than to enduring chivalric heroes – they provide cautionary examples rather than models to emulate with Alexander being compared unfavourably with Solomon who ruled with reason rather than the sword (29–49, 281–87).[43]

Many of Gower's contemporaries, French as well as English, were similarly critical of the supposed shortcomings of the aristocracy, often explaining defeat in battle as the consequence of knights' cowardice or their undue concern with things vain and unimportant.[44] The condemnation of England's military elite began in earnest as the resumption of the Hundred Years War in 1369 was soon followed by the loss of almost all that had been gained in the glory years of Crécy and Poitiers. The monastic chronicler Thomas Walsingham, as well as decrying the members of Richard II's chamber as knights of Venus rather than Mars,[45] attributed the abandonment of French territories to the effeminacy and feebleness of English men-at-arms. 'Heavens above!', he remarked in an entry for 1383, 'the land which once produced and gave birth to men that demanded the respect of all men who dwelt near them and the fear of those from afar, now spewed out men lacking manly courage, who were a laughing stock to the enemy.'[46] The French military reforms which Charles V (1364–80) and Bertrand du Guesclin had initiated and the power vacuum associated with Edward III's declining years and Richard II's minority were not, of course, factors which Walsingham thought worthy of consideration in explaining French successes in this period. The denigration of knights and men-at-arms, then, was commonplace. The end of the fourteenth century saw soldiers, nobles especially, castigated

---

[42] Wetherbee, 'John Gower', p. 602.
[43] See also Jenni Nuttall, *The Creation of Lancastrian Kingship: Literature, Language and Politics in Late Medieval England* (Cambridge: Cambridge University Press, 2007), p. 57.
[44] This was also the case in France where criticism was especially bitter after the defeat at Poitiers. See Charles de Beaurepaire, 'Complainte sur la bataille de Poitiers', *Bibliothèque de l'école des chartes*, 12 (1851), pp. 257–63. For Gower's thoughts regarding the sin of vainglory see CA: I.2670–720, where he refers to the vanity associated with clothing, dancing, food, and emphasises the importance of humility. For further discussion see Wendy Scase, *Literature and Complaint in England, 1272–1553* (Oxford: Oxford University Press, 2007), esp. pp. 62–87.
[45] *The St Albans Chronicle: The Chronica Maiora of Thomas Walsingham, Volume 1: 1376–1394*, eds John Taylor, Wendy R. Childs, and Leslie Watkiss (Oxford: Clarendon Press, 2003), p. 814 (entry for 1387). See further, W. Mark Ormrod, 'Knights of Venus', *Medium Aevum*, 73 (2004), pp. 290–305; Christopher Guyol, '"Let Them Realize What God Can Do": Chivalry in the *St Albans Chronicle*', in James Bothwell and Gwilym Dodd, eds, *Fourteenth Century England*, IX (Woodbridge: Boydell Press, 2016), pp. 87–108.
[46] *St Alban's Chronicle*, Volume 1, pp. 704–5.

repeatedly. And if the military aristocracy's failure to fulfil its responsibilities was not blamed on its members' degeneracy and cowardice, then their over zealousness, characterised by the depredations of the (mercenary) Free Companies and the English *chevauchée* (raiding) strategy, was seen as causing reprehensible misery (VC: V.7; VI.13).[47]

Such disparate concerns suffuse Gower's works and lead to some apparent anomalies. He sought to maintain the social hierarchy and yet also wished to reform the aristocratic elite. That elite comprised, in essence, a warrior caste that delighted in a chivalric ethic at the centre of which was the worship of 'prowess' – of martial physicality and deeds of arms.[48] This was particularly problematic as the ultimate demonstration of prowess was to be made in war, as Geoffroi de Charny argued in his 'Book of Chivalry' (*Livre de Chevalerie*, c. 1350). Here he told his readers (including members of King Jean II's newly formed Company of the Star) that 'one should value and honor men-at-arms engaged in war more highly than any other men-at-arms…You should love, value, praise, and honor all those whom God by his grace has granted several good days on the battlefield'.[49] Although there is no evidence that Gower had read Charny's *Livre*,[50] ideas of this sort were in wide circulation and may have posed particular difficulties for Gower if, as Nigel Saul has argued, he was one of those who called most passionately for peace in the period when the war with France was renewed following the collapse of the treaty of Brétigny in 1369.[51]

In the *Mirour de l'Omme*, Gower seems to support the war in France and complains about those knights who 'seek not their honour in France but rather stay at home and make war on their neighbours' (23666–7). However, it has been argued that in the decade after this he shifted to a position that might be described, perhaps awkwardly, as militant pacifism.[52] John Barnie and Ben Lowe have suggested that Gower first raised objections to the Anglo-French war in response to demands for clerical taxation, but at that time (1376–79) he also supported Edward III's claim to the French throne which had come to him through Queen Isabella. As he wrote in the

---

[47] Nigel Saul, *For Honour and Fame: Chivalry in England, 1066–1500* (London: Bodley Head, 2011), pp. 129–34.
[48] Richard W. Kaeuper, *Chivalry and Violence in Medieval Europe* (Oxford: Oxford University Press, 1999), esp. pp. 129–60.
[49] *The Book of Chivalry of Geoffroi de Charny: Text, Context, and Translation*, eds Richard W. Kaeuper and Elspeth Kennedy (Pennsylvania: University of Pennsylvania Press, 1996), pp. 89–91.
[50] See Craig Taylor, 'English Writings on Chivalry and Warfare during the Hundred Years War', in Peter Coss and Christopher Tyerman, eds, *Soldiers, Nobles and Gentlemen: Essays in Honour of Maurice Keen* (Woodbridge: Boydell Press, 2009), pp. 64–84, at 72 and n. 39. Interestingly, no comparable manuals of chivalry were written in England at this time.
[51] Saul, 'A Farewell to Arms?', pp. 132–4.
[52] Saul, *For Honour and Fame*, pp. 128–9. See also Robert F. Yeager, 'Pax Poetica: On the Pacifism of Chaucer and Gower', *Studies in the Age of Chaucer*, 9 (1987), pp. 97–121.

Mirour de l'Omme, 'The people of France should know that God hates the disobedience of those who, contrary to their allegiance, avoid, by war, doing homage and obedience to the one who has the birthright from his mother' (2139–49). Subsequently, they argue, Gower's objections to war took on a more 'moral' dimension and he began to see the Anglo-French conflict as unjust and an offence against charity and natural law.[53] Thus, in *Confessio Amantis* he wrote:

> After the lawe of charite, / Ther schal no dedly werre be: / And ek nature it hath defended / And in hir lawe pes comended, / Which is the chief of mannes welthe, / Of mannes lif, of mannes helthe. / Bot dedly werre hath his covine / Of pestilence and of famine, Of poverte and of alle wo (III.2261–69).[54]

Gower thus seems to suggest that although war could be waged for just reasons, for many of the second estate it was often no more than a violent expression of vanity, a manifestation of the sin of Pride (considered in *Confessio Amantis*, Book I), and a contravention of the sixth of the Ten Commandments ('Thou shalt not kill'). Those in power who were in a position to begin a just war often abused their authority or were unsuitable to wield that authority. If the king and his nobles were wrathful, avaricious and incapable of self-restraint then any war they sanctioned was likely to be unjust. Gower had already argued, in Book 5 of *Vox Clamantis*, that, commonly, wars were fuelled by the greed of the knightly aristocracy and any national interest had been lost to its members' avarice:

> the knight whom the sake of gain moves to enter into battle will have no righteous honor. It is the vulture's ghastly nature to want [to eat] men, and to follow the camps of war in order to seize upon its food. Those who want war and who follow the camps and are eager for spoils and thirsting for loot are similar…[H]onour is now neglected for gold (V.8.535–53; see also CA: III.2352–60).

As a result, many of the secular elite who should have maintained law, order, and justice now sowed discord and destruction instead. Gower went on to contend in *In Praise of Peace* (1399–1400) that war could be the 'modir of the wronges alle' (l. 106). The poem is structured around the opposing qualities and effects of war and peace with peace being seen as a stabilising force

---

[53] Lowe, *Imagining Peace*, esp. pp. 36–7, 82–7; John Barnie, *War in Medieval Society: Social Values and the Hundred Years War* (London: Weidenfeld and Nicolson, 1974), pp. 122–3.

[54] Saul suggests that *Confessio Amantis* reveals 'Gower's strengthening conviction that war – even a Just War – is contrary to most Christian convictions' (Saul, 'A Farewell to Arms?', p. 143).

and war as the reverse. As Gower says, 'The fortune of the werre is evere unknown' (l. 290).

Similar sentiments were expressed at different stages of the Hundred Years War by clerical authors such as John Bromyard (d. c. 1352), Richard FitzRalph (d. 1360), and Thomas Brinton (d. 1389).[55] Geoffrey Chaucer also expressed his disquiet concerning unjust war and uncontrolled violence in various works including *Lak of Stedfastnesse* and *A Former Age*.[56] Intriguingly, despite Gower's criticisms of John Wyclif and the Lollards (VC: VI.19.1267; CA: Pro.348–51), it is a perspective which Wyclif also shared and his attitudes to war and peace may have followed a similar trajectory to Gower's.[57] Wyclif expressed his increasing fury about unlawful violence in a series of works. He first became concerned with the subject in 1375 when seeking to reconcile the reality of warfare with the commandment against killing in *De Mandatis Divinis* ('On the Divine Commandments'). Soon after, he became convinced that such violent conflicts were pointless, as he argued in *De Civili Dominio* ('On Civil Lordship', c. 1375), and by 1378 he saw those who perpetrated war needlessly, particularly the mercenary Free Companies, as 'hateful to God'. By this stage, England's war in France had become 'the sin of the kingdom'. He grew even more indignant when Bishop Despenser launched his 'crusade' to Flanders in 1383, against the supporters of the Avignon antipope, and argued in *De Cruciata* ('On Crusade', 1382) that, having offered indulgences, remissions from sins and the chance of martyrdom, the papacy was culpable of having promoted an inherently corrupt endeavour.[58]

In France, as the fourteenth century drew to a close, calls for peace also resounded. By this time, the devastation of the nation and the failure of the nobility to defend the realm had become familiar refrains. The brutality soldiers on all sides inflicted was recognised and lamented. In *L'arbre des batailles* (1387) Honoré Bonet pleaded with his readers, arguing that: 'Valiant men and wise…who follow arms should take pains, so far as they can, not to bear hard on the simple and innocent folk but only on those who make

---

[55] As John Bromyard said, 'Victory in battle is not achieved by the size of one's army but by the help of God. Yet now, alas, princes and knights and soldiers go to war in a different spirit; with their cruel actions and desire for gain, they incline themselves more to the ways of the devil than to those of God…nor do they fight at the expense of the king or of themselves, but at that of the Church and of the poor, despoiling both (cited in Rory Cox, 'Natural Law and the Right of Self-Defence According to John of Legnano and John Wyclif', in Chris Given-Wilson, ed., *Fourteenth Century England*, VI (Woodbridge: Boydell Press, 2010), pp. 149–69 at 154).

[56] John Scattergood, 'Social and Political Issues in Chaucer: An Approach to "Lak of Stedfastnesse"', *The Chaucer Review*, 21 (1987), pp. 469–75; Andrew Galloway, 'Chaucer's Former Age and the Fourteenth-Century Anthropology of Craft: The Social Logic of a Premodernist Lyric', *English Literary History*, 63 (1996), pp. 535–48.

[57] For Gower and Wyclif, see David Lepine below, pp. 264–6.

[58] Rory Cox, *John Wyclif on War and Peace* (Woodbridge: Royal Historical Society, 2014), pp. 90, 104–8.

and continue war and flee peace.'⁵⁹ Christine de Pizan (d. 1430), driven by similar concerns, advocated the need for Roman-style military discipline among French troops and argued that 'no honour can accrue to a prince in killing, overrunning, or seizing people who have never borne arms nor could make use of them, or poor innocent people who do nothing but till the land and watch over animals'.⁶⁰ Gower's concern with the dreadful consequences of intemperate, unrestrained aggression in war was shared, therefore, by many on both sides of the Channel.

Justifying War and Chivalry

However, while it is clear that, as Wetherbee has shown, Gower expressed revulsion with unjust violence, it is equally apparent that he did not decry all wars. It may be, as Ben Lowe has suggested, that Gower believed a just war should be 'an extraordinary and extremely rare occurrence',⁶¹ but it was far from an impossible one and, indeed, he argued on several occasions that war might be a necessary prelude to peace. We are presented, therefore, with varying perspectives on the subject of war throughout Gower's works. For example, he tells us that 'Arms bring peace; arms curb the rapacious. A worthy king should bear arms so that the guilty man may fear them' (VC: IV.6.713–14). In a similar fashion, it is permissible for knights to fight in self-defence and to keep the peace.⁶² As Genius says in *Confessio Amantis*:

> And over this for his contre / In time of werre a man is fre /
> Himself, his hous and ek his lond / Defende with his oghne hond,
> / And slen, if that he mai no bet, / After the lawe which is set
> (III.2235–40).

Such attitudes can even be seen in his *In Praise of Peace*. Despite the main thrust of the poem, this is perhaps not surprising given it was composed

---

[59] *The Tree of Battles of Honoré Bonet*, trans. George W. Coopland (Liverpool: Liverpool University Press, 1949), p. 154.
[60] Christine de Pizan, *The Book of Deeds of Arms and of Chivalry*, eds Sumner Willard and Charity Cannon Willard (University Park: University of Pennsylvania Press, 2003), p. 171.
[61] Lowe, *Imagining Peace*, p. 84.
[62] Sara V. Torres, 'In Praise of Peace in Late Medieval England', in Joanna Bellis and Laura Slater, eds, *Representing War and Violence, 1250–1600* (Woodbridge: Boydell Press, 2016), pp. 95–115 at 106–9; Stephen H. Rigby, *Wisdom and Chivalry: Chaucer's Knight's Tale and Medieval Political Theory* (Leiden: Brill, 2009), p. 186. See also Fletcher, below, pp. 373–4, and Rigby, below, pp. 389–90, 423.

essentially as propaganda for a ruler (Henry IV) who had come to the throne through violence.[63] Gower stated:

> Good is t'eschure werre, but natheles / A kyng may make werre upon his right, / For of bataile the final ende is pees. / Thus stant the lawe, that a worthi knight / Uppon his trouthe may go to the fight. / Bot if so werre that he might chese, / Betre is the pees, of which may no man lese (64–70).

By contrast with some of the opinions Gower advanced elsewhere, this was a traditional approach to the issue of just war. Following St Augustine (d. 430), Thomas Aquinas had argued that certain conditions needed to be fulfilled for a war to be considered 'just': first, it should be instigated on the authority of a sovereign prince; second, those attacked must deserve punishment; and, third, the belligerents needed to be motivated appropriately. In *Summa Theologiae* (1265–74), Aquinas wrote, 'The desire to [cause] harm, the cruelty of revenge, the unforgiving and inflexible spirit, the arrogance of the contestant, the desire to dominate, and all such motives, are rightly to be condemned when it comes to war.'[64] Ideas such as these clearly influence Gower's comments regarding just war.

However, a different perspective can be discerned when Gower praises particular individuals for their bloody deeds. This is perhaps most apparent when Richard II is exhorted to recall and emulate the achievements of his father, Edward, the Black Prince (Prince of Wales and Aquitaine, 1330–76). According to Gower, the prince's 'feats of arms':

> excelled Hector's…He plundered foreign lands while he protected his own…France felt the effects of him; and Spain…was fearful of him… He pursued and destroyed [his enemies]…just as a wolf driven by hunger scatters a sheepfold. He was always sober in his actions but his sword was often drunk with the blood of the enemy…His hostile blade was sated with enemy gore; a torrent of blood slaked the thirst of his weapons… He attacked strongholds annihilating the people (VC: VI.13.917–84).

Although claiming, somewhat unconvincingly, that Edward was 'always sober in his actions', Gower appears to delight in the prince's savagery, writing in terms reminiscent of a *chanson de geste*.[65] Furthermore, while, in

---

[63] David R. Carlson, *John Gower: Poetry and Propaganda in Fourteenth Century England* (Woodbridge: Boydell Press, 2012), pp. 204–5, 207; Torres, 'In Praise of Peace in Late Medieval England', p. 113; Nigel Saul, 'John Gower: Prophet or Turncoat?' in Elisabeth Dutton with John Hines and Robert F. Yeager, eds, *John Gower, Trilingual Poet: Language, Translation and Tradition* (Cambridge: D. S. Brewer, 2010), pp. 85–97.

[64] *Aquinas: Selected Political Writings*, ed. Alessandro P. D'Entrèves (Oxford: Basil Blackwell, 1965), pp. 159–61.

[65] Coleman, *English Literature in History*, p. 146.

general, he condemned fighting and military action motivated by avarice,[66] he also writes with a certain admiration that 'In order to seize booty [the Black Prince] boldly penetrated his antagonists' [lands]' (VC: VI.13.956).

Just as Gower offered a range of views on the legitimacy of warfare, his attitudes to other aspects of knightly behaviour also appear somewhat fluid. Certainly, a number of tales in the *Confessio Amantis* give very positive views of deeds of arms performed for love and renown as in Book I, where although Florent seeks 'the fame of worldes speche' (I.1415), he is not without merit. Furthermore, in Book IV, after delivering a blistering reprimand of chivalry, 'Genius returns, to tales of romance and gives an enthusiastic and rollicking praise of knighthood and deeds of arms [see IV.1627–44] as the best way to win fame and…a woman's regard.'[67] Similarly, when Gower explored questions of love, its quandaries and its relationship with chivalry in his *Cinkante Balades*, which may have been written in the early 1390s (see above, p. 123), he seems to contradict opinions that he himself presented elsewhere. For example, in *Balade* 44 (1–2, 9), the lady describes her love in glowing terms – he is 'Vailant, Courtois, gentil et renomée / Loial, verrai, certain de vo promesse' [Valiant, courteous, honourable and renowned, / Loyal true, unwavering in [his] promise]. She praises his 'valor et…grant prouesse' [valour and great prowess].[68] On this occasion, a knight's chivalry is praiseworthy and guarantees a lady's high regard.

Gower, therefore, does not offer an unambiguous view of chivalry. As Kurt Olsson has argued with regard to *Confessio Amantis*, '[a]lthough one might combine Genius's opposed stances in a single consistent view – "chevalerie" ideally serves the cause of peace – the confessor does not attempt to reconcile them.'[69] Perhaps this should not surprise us: the state of knighthood, the role of chivalry and the responsibilities of the nobility had always been subjects of debate. The priorities an author such as Jean Froissart (d. 1405) advocated for knights were not the same as those which Christine de Pizan advanced, just as Thomas Gray differed from Geoffroi de Charny in his understanding

---

[66] A view Thomas Hoccleve shared in *The Regiment of Princes* (c.1411), cited by Stephen H. Rigby, 'Worthy but Wise? Virtuous and Non-Virtuous Forms of Courage in the Later Middle Ages', *Studies in the Age of Chaucer*, 35 (2013), pp. 329–71 at 367.

[67] Peter Nicholson, *Love and Ethics in Gower's Confessio Amantis* (Ann Arbor: University of Michigan Press, 2005), p. 226. Contrastingly, Rigby argues that Gower maintains a clearer line of argument throughout his works. According to this reading, problems arise when one fights solely in order to win a lady's love. Similarly, one should not fight for honour, but a knight should, nevertheless, be honoured when he is brave. See Rigby, 'Worthy but Wise?', pp. 359–60.

[68] However, it is important to note that the *Cinkante Balades* develops into a consideration of the link between legitimate love with honour and reason, before turning to an even more celebrated form of love, namely that which should be given to the Virgin.

[69] Kurt Olsson, *John Gower and the Structures of Conversion: A Reading of the Confessio Amantis* (Cambridge: D. S. Brewer, 1992), p. 126, n. 26.

of the importance of chivalric duties.[70] In part, this was because the chivalric ethic comprised various qualities that might not always be compatible with one another. It was often difficult to establish the correct balance between prowess, courtesy and piety, for example, when it came to matters of knightly honour, given that the ultimate defence of one's honour was likely to be made with sword in hand.[71] Deeds of arms performed in order to gain or defend one's honour were central to many chivalric conventions. Gower's works suggest that violence of this sort could undermine (unity within) the sacred order of knighthood, although he also acknowledged that it might be vital to defend one's honour. Maintaining self-control while at the same time preserving one's honour required a highly refined sense of balance. If a clear message for the nobility can be discerned in Gower's writings, it is a call for the awareness of the need for such balance and, consequently, moderation and self-control. For this reason, Genius recommends that Amans cultivate 'Fair speche' (CA: III.604) as well as patience.[72] Patience allows one to temper one's responses, and so prevent an escalation of violence and a possible cycle of vengeance. In a similar fashion, one should exercise restraint in matters of love or the consequences can be deeply sinful.[73] Personal restraint blended with courtesy to create a refined form of knightly *gentilesse* may be seen as Gower's ideal in most instances.[74] This was not merely a courtesy that dictated relationships between men and women but one which ensured violence between members of the chivalric elite was kept to a minimum and that the prowess of the nobility remained dedicated to the service of the common good.

Chivalric Ideals and Noble Responsibilities

In general, while Gower's works express a range of viewpoints, they suggest that the chief responsibilities of the nobility were based on the maintenance of order in a broad sense. First, order should be preserved through the

---

[70] Barber, *Knight and Chivalry*, pp. 147–9; Taylor, *Chivalry and the Ideals of Knighthood in France*, pp. 44–6, 66–7, 179–80; Andy King, 'The Ethics of War in Sir Thomas Gray's *Scalacronica*' in Chris Given-Wilson, Ann Kettle and Len Scales, eds, *War, Government and Aristocracy in the British Isles, c.1150–1500: Essays in Honour of Michael Prestwich* (Woodbridge: Boydell Press), pp. 148–62; Kaeuper, *Chivalry and Violence*, pp. 284–8.

[71] Julian Pitt-Rivers, 'Honour and Social Status', in Jean G. Peristiany, ed., *Honour and Shame: The Values of Mediterranean Society* (London: Weidenfeld and Nicholson, 1965), pp. 19–77; Taylor, *Chivalry and the Ideals of Knighthood in France*, pp. 54–90. See also Christopher Fletcher, below, pp. 371–2.

[72] Rigby, 'Worthy but Wise?', pp. 349–50. Patience is also personified in the *Mirour* as an individual who opposes revenge (Torres, 'In Praise of Peace in Late Medieval England', pp. 101–2). See also Olsson, *Gower and the Structures of Conversion*, p. 124 and n. 23.

[73] When Venus cannot control her own appetites, she commits incest with her son (Kendall, *Lordship and Literature*, pp. 162–6).

[74] Alan T. Gaylord, 'Gentilesse in Chaucer's *Troilus*', *Studies in Philology*, 61 (1964), pp. 19–34 at 23; Olsson, *Gower and the Structures of Conversion*, pp. 2–3.

protection of the church at home and perhaps also overseas. Gower's position with regard to crusading, as with broader knightly duties, is not unambiguous. While he did not decry crusades, *per se*, he appears to have been somewhat wary of them and his attitudes may have changed over time. In *Confessio Amantis* the dialogue between Genius and Amans in Book IV reveals a range of opinions on the subject and, indeed, some profound divisions (1615–1723).[75] The internal debate in Gower's works puts one in mind of more recent discussions concerning the character of Chaucer's Knight and the continuing appeal of crusading in the later Middle Ages.[76]

Many English knights, including Gower's hero, Henry Bolingbroke, took the cross in the later fourteenth century. Philippe de Mézières was another who sought to maintain the crusading impulse within Europe through his 'Order of the Passion' which he hoped would be at the heart of a combined Anglo-French enterprise to the Holy Land.[77] Nevertheless, although the crusading movement remained highly popular, it endured a series of blows following the loss of the Holy Lands (1291), the dissolution of the Order of the Temple (1314), and, later, the disastrous Nicopolis campaign (1396). Furthermore, because the crusading ideal itself remained so potent, it became very apparent when that ideal was seen to be debased as in Despenser's 1383 'crusade' to Flanders.[78] In such a context, crusading was an activity to be balanced against other responsibilities and one needed to be sure of the

---

[75] Yeager, 'Pax Poetica', p. 105.
[76] While it seems most unlikely that Chaucer's description of the Knight is a satirical one or that the Canterbury pilgrim should be considered a mercenary, as some have argued, there is no doubt that the conduct of the Free Companies in the later fourteenth century called into question the rectitude of individual knights, if not the order of knighthood in general. See Terry Jones, *Chaucer's Knight: The Portrait of a Medieval Mercenary* (second edition; London: Methuen, 1994); Maurice Keen, 'Chaucer's Knight, the English Aristocracy and the Crusade', in *Nobles, Knights and Men-at-Arms in the Middle Ages* (London: Hambledon Press, 1996), pp. 101–20; John H. Pratt, 'Was Chaucer's Knight Really a Mercenary?', *The Chaucer Review*, 22 (1987), pp. 8–27; Stephen H. Rigby, 'The Knight', in Rigby and Minnis, *Historians on Chaucer*, pp. 42–62. Concerning the Free Companies see Kenneth Fowler, *Medieval Mercenaries, Volume 1: The Great Companies* (Oxford: Wiley-Blackwell 2000).
[77] Philippe de Mézières, *Letter to King Richard II: A Plea made in 1395 for Peace between England and France*, trans. George W. Coopland (Liverpool: Liverpool University Press, 1975); Adrian Bell, 'English Members of the Order of the Passion: Their Political, Diplomatic and Military Significance', in Renate Blumenfeld-Kosinski and Kiril Petkov, eds, *Philippe de Mézières and his Age: Piety and Politics in the Fourteenth Century* (Leiden: Brill, 2012), pp. 321–48. See further, Lowe, *Imagining Peace*, pp. 37-8.
[78] Gillespie, 'Richard II: Chivalry and Kingship', pp. 123–4; Timothy Guard, *Chivalry, Kingship and Crusade: The English Experience in the Fourteenth Century* (Woodbridge: Boydell Press, 2013), esp. pp. 123–42, 182–207. Housley notes that 'the shedding of Christian blood at clerical command was [seen as] increasingly distasteful' in this period (Norman Housley, *The Later Crusades, 1274–1580: From Lyons to Alcazar* (Oxford: Oxford University Press, 1992), pp. 248, 264).

motives of the individual crusader (MO: 23893–964; CA: IV.1630–8) as well as the 'justice' of the expedition in question.[79]

The next key responsibility of the nobility was to maintain domestic order both socially and legally. Gower noted in the *Cronica Tripertita* that when Henry IV took the throne, 'all the nobles sat allied with him [in parliament], and the wisest commoners were present' (III.342–6). Representatives of the community of the realm were, thus, joined together in common cause and in support of a truly legitimate monarch.[80] Gower also called on the nobility to maintain order and law throughout the kingdom. To fulfil this responsibility, it might well be necessary to use force, particularly if an event like the Peasants' Revolt should take place. When Gower's rigidly elitist conception of the social order was threatened, he saw violence as being entirely justified. For him, the bestial peasants had committed horrendous acts, and their crimes demanded a very firm response. The mayor of London, William Walworth (d. 1385) is thus presented as being completely vindicated when he cuts down Wat Tyler (VC: I.1861–2).[81] For Gower, the line between the maintenance of patient, moderate, restrained authority and the use of coercive brutality might well be contingent on circumstances. So, he remarks in *Confessio Amantis*:

> Lo thus, my Sone, to socure / The lawe and comun riht to winne, / A man ma sle withoute Sinne, / Ande do therof a gret almesse, / So forto kepe rihtwisnesse (III.2229–34).[82]

In less turbulent times, nobles might ensure order in the kingdom through the provision of wise counsel to the king. Gower emphasised the necessity of such counsel to ensure balance between and within the estates and to help the king arbitrate disputes.[83] Richard II's inability to manage arguments with and between his nobles and his failure to listen to the counsel of his nobility contributed to his deposition. The opening passages of the *Cronica Tripertita* suggest, somewhat unfairly, that Richard had listened to 'the base, immature counsel of fools [and] the poisonous counsels of brash youths to the

---

[79] See Gower, *In Praise of Peace*, ll. 239–52; Guard, *Chivalry, Kingship and Crusade*, pp. 177–8.

[80] See further, W. Mark Ormrod, '"Common Profit" and "The Profit of the King and Kingdom": Parliament and the Development of Political Language in England, 1250–1450', *Viator*, 46 (2015), pp. 219–52; Giancarlo, *Parliament and Literature in Late Medieval England*, pp. 122–5.

[81] Eve Salisbury, 'Violence and the Sacrificial Poet: Gower, the *Vox*, and the Critics', in Robert F. Yeager, ed., *On John Gower: Essays at the Millennium* (Kalamazoo: Medieval Institute Publications, 2007), pp. 124–43, at 125–6, 128–9.

[82] Gower also supported the use of capital punishment for robbery, murder and treason (CA: III.2208–14).

[83] Samantha J. Rayner, *Images of Kingship in Chaucer and his Ricardian Contemporaries* (Cambridge: D. S. Brewer, 2008), pp. 15, 18.

effect that he was to prey upon the goods of his nobles, whom he reduced to a state of weakness' (I.13–18).[84] By so doing, Gower implies that the king himself undermined the financial and political status of the nobility and thus threatened the social order. Given the economic pressure the peasantry exerted from below, such an assault from on high could not be tolerated. A concern with good counsel was, of course, a commonplace of late medieval political exchange in many contexts and media. Given that Gower saw himself as a public poet and sought to have his opinions heard by those in positions of power, it is hardly surprising that he spent a good deal of time ruminating on this subject.[85] 'Solomon the wise is dead', he lamented in *Vox Clamantis*, 'and Rehoboam lives again, whereby young men are above the prudent counselling of their elders' (VI.20.1295–6).[86]

Gower's conception of his status as a public spokesman and his connections to the nobility are evident in his remarkable tomb and effigy at Southwark.[87] The monument, famously, shows his head resting on his three major literary works and he wears around his neck a Lancastrian collar of linked esses with a swan pendant. Collars were among the most prestigious of symbols granted to members of noble households and 'bastard feudal' retainers. Often given as special reward or to show particular favour or status, they suggested an enduring relationship between giver and receiver. The author himself received just such a collar from Henry Bolingbroke in 1393 costing 26s. 8d. In the *Cronica Tripertita*, Gower refers to Bolingbroke as 'he who wore the S' (I.52).[88] This is a further indication that while the author denounced the actions of many nobles and denigrated the failings of individual knights, he still championed the nobility as the social elite and maintained an idealised conception of the order of chivalry.

---

[84] On the subject of Richard's supposed susceptibility to wicked counsel see Christopher Fletcher, *Richard II: Manhood, Youth and Politics, 1377–99* (Oxford: Oxford University Press, 2008), pp. 75–6, 272–3.

[85] 'The poet's role becomes that of a moderator, a common voice among and above the voices trying to direct the discussion and common clamour toward some form of *remede*' (Giancarlo, *Parliament and Literature in Late Medieval England*, pp. 90–128). See also Derek Pearsall, 'The Gower Tradition', in Alastair Minnis, ed., *Gower's Confessio Amantis: Responses and Reassessments* (Cambridge: D. S. Brewer, 1983), pp. 179–97; Lynn Staley, *Languages of Power in the Age of Richard II* (Philadelphia: University of Pennsylvania Press, 2005), pp. 27, 346–54; Watt, *Amoral Gower*, pp. 1–11.

[86] See further, Anthony Goodman, 'Richard II's Councils', in Goodman and Gillespie, *Richard II: The Art of Kingship*, pp. 59–82 at 63–4.

[87] See Martha Carlin, above, pp. 55–6. Gower's conception of himself as a member of the lesser nobility is also evident in his brief Latin poem *Orate pro anima (Armigeri scutum)*. My thanks to Siân Echard for this suggestion.

[88] See further, Matthew Ward, *The Livery Collar in Late Medieval England and Wales: Politics, Identity and Affinity* (Woodbridge: Boydell Press, 2016), pp. 19, 45.

Conclusions

In one reading of Gower's work, it would seem that, with regard to the actions of the nobility and to their proper use of arms, all that truly mattered was one's motivation for fighting. Although Gower abhorred violence for the most part, he also recognised the need for members of the secular elite to fight in certain circumstances: to protect the rights of the people (including their own rights); to defend the realm; and, if their inspiration was just, to defend the church by going on crusade. As a result, although he condemned bloodshed in most instances, Gower praised those 'flowers of chivalry' who took up arms for the right reasons and with an awareness of the need for restraint. A true knight would fight for justice – justice being defined as that which delivers to all men their due – and by his deeds he would maintain the social order and prevent such nightmarish episodes as the Peasants' Revolt from recurring. Those who would fight in such causes and with such pure motives were, however, few and far between. For the most part, we seem to be told, the nobility of England has been consumed with avarice and weakened by lust. Reform was necessary.

Yet, it is evident that Gower's writings were more sophisticated than this reading suggests. Certainly, it is too easy to think of Gower as a simple moralist – a tag suggested by Chaucer's famous appellation of him as the 'moral Gower' – and so assume he projected a consistent didactic certainty throughout his works.[89] If, instead, we consider Gower's poems, especially the *Confessio Amantis*, to be compilations (*florilegia* of sorts) then we should not expect his works to offer unambiguous responses to complex subjects. The author garnered material from an array of classical and medieval sources, wrote in assorted genres with a range of readers in mind and couched his ideas accordingly.[90] We should not be surprised, therefore, when Gower offered contradictory or somewhat dissonant discussions of the same subject. Kurt Olsson has argued that such 'shifts of meaning have the effect of weaning readers away from the false security of a single-valenced argument, or from a facile morality and illusory wisdom'.[91] Like the competing viewpoints presented by Chaucer in *The Canterbury Tales* in which the pilgrims' stories reproduce the social conflicts of the age, Gower's readers may not have been presented with definite conclusions but, instead, with questions to which they must find their own answers. Even if we do not see in Gower such 'a multitude of contending conceptions', as Paul Strohm suggested with regard to Chaucer,[92] might we be better thinking of Gower's

---

[89] Geoffrey Chaucer, 'Troilus and Criseyde', V: 1856.
[90] Coleman, *English Literature in History*, p. 126.
[91] Olsson, *Gower and the Structures of Conversion*, pp. 5–7, 11–12, 15.
[92] Paul Strohm, *Social Chaucer* (Cambridge, Mass.: Harvard University Press, 1989), pp. 181–2. See also Rigby, 'Reading Chaucer', pp. 17–19; Stephen H. Rigby, *Chaucer in Context: Society, Allegory and Gender* (Manchester: Manchester University Press,

readers not as passive recipients of some unvarnished truth but as active participants in a dialogue from which they must draw their own conclusions and take responsibility for them?

Perhaps, then, Gower's rhetoric had a degree of pliability even if it was set within certain moral parameters. Thus, while we would be wrong to seek a clear, single, simplistic perspective on the subjects of chivalry and nobility in his works, he does provide us with a general direction of moral travel. Gower was clearly indignant at the failings of the nobility, but his works do not suggest that its members were beyond redemption (CA: Pro.514–28): while knighthood may have been in need of reform, England and Christendom at large remained very much in need of knighthood.

1996), pp. 53–72. Geoffroi de Charny adopted this approach when writing for a French aristocratic audience in his *Les demandes pour la joute, les tournois et la guerre* (c.1350). See Steve Muhlberger, *Charny's Men-at-Arms: Questions Concerning the Joust, Tournaments and War* (Wheaton: Freelance Academy Press, 2014).

Chapter 4

THE PEASANTS AND THE GREAT REVOLT

Mark Bailey

Gower the Conservative

For modern readers, John Gower is likely to appear as a thinker who was 'conservative' in his outlook, being rigidly elitist in his views and relentlessly condemnatory to those whom he saw as challenging the existing social hierarchy.[1] Barrie Dobson, for instance, awarded him 'the title of Jeremiah of late fourteenth-century England' and bemoaned his 'monotonous, heavy-handed and extremely pessimistic approach to his theme'.[2] If Gower's reputation is justified then it owes a good deal to his treatment of peasants in general and to his response to their participation in the Great Revolt of 1381 in particular, where he portrays the rebels as vicious animals who are without reason or merit.[3] Gower was writing during a period of tumultuous

---

I am most grateful to Robert Yeager, Siân Echard and, especially, Steve Rigby, whose comments greatly improved this essay.

[1] Eve Salisbury, 'Violence and the Sacrifical Poet: Gower, the *Vox* and Critics', in Robert F. Yeager, ed., *On John Gower: Essays at the Millennium* (Kalamazoo: Institute of Medieval Studies, 2007), pp. 124–43 at 125. See also Winthrop P. Wetherbee, 'John Gower', in David Wallace, ed., *The Cambridge History of Medieval English Literature* (Cambridge: Cambridge University Press, 1999), pp. 589–609 at 589–90; Helen Barr, *Socioliterary Practice in Late-Medieval England* (Oxford: Oxford University Press, 2001), p. 121. It cannot be emphasized too strongly that the term 'conservative' is used here simply to refer to those thinkers who seek to justify and maintain the social hierarchy of their own day rather than referring to any specific form of modern conservatism.

[2] R. Barrie Dobson, ed., *The Peasants' Revolt of 1381* (second edition; London: Macmillan, 1983), p. 387.

[3] Nigel Saul, 'John Gower: Prophet or Turncoat?', in Elisabeth M. Dutton, John Hines and Robert F. Yeager, eds, *John Gower Trilingual Poet: Language, Translation and Tradition* (Cambridge: D. S. Brewer, 2010), pp. 85–97 at 94; Gower, *Major Latin Works*, pp. 10, 20; Kurt Olsson, 'John Gower's *Vox Clamantis* and the Medieval Idea of Place', *Studies in Philology*, 84 (1987), pp. 134–58, at 134 (quote), 143–56; Paul Freedman, 'The Miller', in Stephen H. Rigby and Alastair J. Minnis, eds, *Historians on Chaucer: The General Prologue to the Canterbury Tales* (Oxford: Oxford University Press, 2014), pp. 368–85, at 380, 384.

change in English society and economy, following successive devastating outbreaks of plague after 1348. Here we set out the reality of the changes which English society underwent during this period and examine the intellectual framework that Gower employed to make sense of them. The abundance of central government and local sources which has survived from this period has allowed historians in recent years to recover a great deal about the lives of the lowest ranks of society, to reassess the changes after the Black Death and to re-interpret the causes of the Great Revolt. It will be argued here that fundamental changes to the labour market shook the ideological and moral framework of society, and that the attempts of the ruling elite to make sense of what was happening – and their inability to prevent it – informed the development of a poetic common voice in Ricardian England. The historical evidence indicates that Gower was not only a conservative thinker but was backwards looking even by the standards of his own day.

The Peasants and the Third Estate

Of the estimated 2.8m people in England in the 1370s, the overwhelming majority – perhaps 85% or more – belonged to what contemporary social commentators defined as the third estate, the *laboratores* whose ordained role was to provide food, clothing and shelter through manual labour for the other two estates: the *oratores*, who prayed for society and sought to bring it salvation, and the *bellatores*, whose task was to provide physical protection and justice. Gower's discussion of the peasantry can only be understood within the context of this conventional theory of society. Each estate, and every individual within it, was responsible for discharging its function for the common profit of society, so that any neglect of the collective duty by one estate diminished and damaged that group, and had an adverse impact upon the others (MO: 18421–26604).[4] More than any other contemporary poet, Gower emphasized the 'common profit' accruing from this mutual interdependence and from the commitment of the individual to the collective good.[5] Indeed, he even created a new word to describe a love of the common profit: '*conjoye*'.[6] Like many medieval social commentators, he made use of the body as a metaphor for the political community, which could only function when

---

[4] Gower, *Major Latin Works*, p. 23. For the tripartite theory, see Stephen H. Rigby, 'England: Literature and Society', in Stephen H. Rigby, ed., *A Companion to Britain in Later Middle Ages* (Oxford: Basil Blackwell, 2003), pp. 497–520 at 500–4.
[5] Russell A. Peck, *Kingship and Common Profit: Gower's Confessio Amantis* (Carbondale: South Illinois University Press, 1978), pp. xix–xxv.
[6] Kellie Robertson, *The Laborer's Two Bodies: Literacy and Legal Productions in Britain 1350–1500* (Basingstoke: Palgrave Macmillan, 2006), pp. 84–6.

it was an integrated whole.[7] Whilst emphasizing the reciprocal duties of the three estates, Gower, like other tripartite theorists, stressed that whilst the *laboratores* were indispensable in providing subsistence for the rest of society, they were also located firmly at the base of the social hierarchy, as the feet of the social body, and so should be obedient and deferential to the ruling elite.[8] Just as Thomas of Wimbledon in his famous sermon 'Give account of thy stewardship' (*c.* 1388) stressed the need for servants and bondsmen to live in fear of displeasing their lord, and to be 'suget and lowe', so Gower wrote of 'the little common people who are called labourers' (MO: 26425–6).[9] To challenge the social hierarchy, or even to seek individual mobility within it, was sinful and would lead to personal damnation, because its structure was fixed and divinely ordained.[10] Rejection of the roles assigned to each estate would also cause the social fabric to unravel: 'concord causes the smallest enterprise of the people to prosper, discord causes the greatest affairs to sink to nothing' (VC: V.11.671–2). The themes of *Vox Clamantis* are those of traditional estates theory, namely the requirement of the king and the ruling elite to provide protection and justice, and the necessity for all people to fulfil their estates function.[11] Gower emphasized how the social order was disintegrating because of a collective relinquishing of social responsibility by all three estates. His principal targets for criticism were actually the shortcomings of the first and second estates, but his condemnation of the peasantry was short and stinging.[12]

The vast majority of members of the third estate lived in the countryside. Despite their overwhelming numerical importance in England's population, these peasants do not feature prominently in Gower's works. Their appearance is largely confined to *Vox Clamantis* Book I (also known as the *Visio Anglie*, in which he offers an allegory of the Great Revolt of 1381) and Book V,

---

[7] Robert F. Yeager, 'The Body Politic and the Politics of Bodies in the Poetry of John Gower', in Piero Boitani and Anna Torti, eds, *The Body and Soul in Medieval Literature* (Cambridge: D. S. Brewer, 1999), pp. 145–65.

[8] Stephen Knight, 'The Voice of Labour in Fourteenth-Century English Literature', in James Rothwell, P. Jeremy P. Goldberg, and W. Mark Ormrod, eds, *The Problem of Labour in the Fourteeenth Century* (York: York Medieval Press, 2000), pp. 101–22 at 104–5; Jennifer Hole, 'The Justification of Wealth and Lordship versus Rulers' Exploitation in Medieval England', *Parergon*, 27 (2017), pp. 25–47 at 27–35.

[9] *Wimbledon's Sermon: A Middle English Sermon of the Fourteenth Century*, ed. Ione K. Knight (Pittsburgh: Duquesne University Press, 1967), p. 67.

[10] Lawrence W. Clopper, 'Need Men and Women Labor? Langland's Wanderer and the Labor Ordinances', in Barbara A. Hanawalt, ed., *Chaucer's England* (Minneapolis: University of Minnesota Press, 1992), pp. 110–29 at 116.

[11] Andrew Galloway, 'Gower in his Most Learned Role and the Peasants' Revolt of 1381', *Mediaevalia*, 6 (1993), pp. 329–47 at 329.

[12] Siân Echard, 'Gower's "Bokes of Latin": Language, Politics, and Poetry', *Studies in the Age of Chaucer*, 25 (2003), pp. 123–56, at 141; Olsson, 'John Gower's *Vox Clamantis* and the Medieval Idea of Place', pp. 136–7; Pamela L. Longo, 'Gower's Public Outcry', *Philological Quarterly*, 92 (2013), pp. 357–87.

and also to short sections of the *Mirour de l'Omme* and *Confessio Amantis*.¹³ When discussing the third estate in the *Mirour de l'Omme*, Gower concentrates more upon those who lived in towns, devoting around 1,300 lines to urban merchants, craft workers and retailers (MO: 25177–26424) whilst allocating scarcely 100 of the poem's 30,000 lines to the rural peasantry (MO: 26425–26518). Peasants feature so infrequently in Gower's work that their brief appearances have been characterized as plebian intrusions into the minds and the lives of the upper classes, yet this lack of attention also reflects Gower's concentration on the shortcomings of the ruling groups within contemporary society.¹⁴

Where he does discuss peasants, Gower focuses mainly upon the requirement for them to labour for the common profit of society. Labour is an essential element in the human condition, although its nature and function are differentiated according to each estate (MO: 23617–22).¹⁵ Gower adopts the conventional stance that the duty of the third estate is to produce the food and drink to sustain the rest of society: while such menial labour is humiliating and a consequence of Adam's original sin, it is also personally and socially beneficial when performed properly (VC: V.9.561–620; MO: 14435–6, 14533–14556). Peasants who are lazy or who withhold their labour undermine the common good, are disobedient and constitute a threat to social harmony (MO: 5487–90).¹⁶ By contrast, the tasks of the first and second estates (ruling, fighting, praying and interceding on behalf of humanity) are presented as being superior to those performed by the *laboratores*.¹⁷ Gower's belief in the superiority of these forms of labour is sketched out in the *Mirour de l'Omme* (MO: 14569–80) and then established unequivocally in the *Confessio Amantis*, where manual labour is depicted as a common necessity but mental labour is presented as a matter of choice on the part of those individuals who are aware of their talent.¹⁸ This is, of course, a talent possessed by Gower himself, who has enlisted in the army of mental labourers. Gower imagined himself as a poet detached from the socio-economic order and therefore able to comment upon it as a teacher or

---

13 George G. Coulton, *The Medieval Village* (Cambridge: Cambridge University Press, 1931), p. 237; Ian Cornelius, 'Gower and the Peasants' Revolt', *Representations*, 131 (2015), pp. 22–51 at 24, 33.
14 David Aers, '*Vox Populi* and the Literature of 1381', in Wallace, *Cambridge History of Medieval English Literature*, pp. 432–53 at 432, 435–6; Longo, 'Gower's Public Outcry', p. 361; Cornelius, 'Gower and the Peasants' Revolt', p. 24.
15 Gregory M. Sadlek, *Idleness Working: A Discourse on Love's Labour from Ovid through Chaucer and Gower* (Washington: Catholic University of America Press, 2004) p. 188; Matthew W. Irvin, *The Poetic Voices of John Gower: Politics and Personae in the Confessio Amantis* (Cambridge: Cambridge University Press, 2014), p. 169.
16 Sadlek, *Idleness Working*, pp. 184–7; Irvin, *Poetic Voices of John Gower*, pp. 172–5; Robertson, *Laborer's Two Bodies*, pp. 85–6.
17 Irvin, *Poetic Voices of John Gower*, p. 172.
18 Nicola Masciandaro, *The Voice of the Hammer: The Meaning of Work in Middle English Literature* (Notre Dame: University of Notre Dame Press, 2007), pp. 84–8.

preacher.[19] He allies himself with the members of the second estate – indeed, in the *Visio* he escapes from the rebels with the nobles in a ship – but he also presents himself as a learned counsellor to them rather than actually being one of their number.[20] The task of the nobility is to rule over the third estate, using violence if necessary, because otherwise the peasantry will lapse from their social duty and will fail to perform their ordained role within estates theory.[21] The natural disposition of peasants is to deny the value of culture and law, so they must be controlled by the rational and morally-capable first and second estates: 'Peasants are not at all honest, courteous or gentle unless they are obliged by force to be so' (MO: 26471–2).[22]

Although Gower outlines the diversity of economic function, wealth and social standing of town dwellers among the third estate and conveys some sense of the variety within urban society (MO: 25177–26436), his work provides no sense of the diversity among that estate's rural dwellers. Yet, in reality, the latter comprised a fluid and varied social group which consisted mainly of agriculturalists working upon their own holdings but also included craft workers, labourers and servants of various sorts. The growing commercialization of the economy since the twelfth century had stimulated the development of the land, labour and commodity markets throughout the countryside, together with the expansion of towns and trade, both of which created greater diversification and specialization in the labour market.[23] Skilled artisans – such as textile workers, carpenters, brewers and bakers – were concentrated in towns, but they were also liberally sprinkled around rural communities. Overall, it has been estimated that by 1381 57% of the labour force worked in agriculture, 19% in industrial activities and 24% in services.[24] In the countryside, most peasants held agricultural landholdings of between about half a dozen acres and 40 acres, those with smaller holdings having to augment the produce of their holdings with additional income from wage labour and those with more land requiring additional hired labour to help them work their holdings. The majority of these landholders were personally free, while a minority, perhaps as few as

[19] Ann W. Astell, 'The Peasants' Revolt: Cock Crow in Gower and Chaucer', *Essays in Medieval Studies*, 10 (1993), pp. 53–60 at 53; Masciandaro, *Voice of the Hammer*, p. 189, n. 89.
[20] Galloway, 'Gower in his Most Learned Role', p. 345; Cornelius, 'Gower and the Peasants' Revolt', p. 28.
[21] Irvin, *Poetic Voices of John Gower*, pp. 44–5, 170–5.
[22] Galloway, 'Gower in his Most Learned Role', p. 333; Cornelius, 'Gower and the Peasants' Revolt', p. 33.
[23] Bruce M. S. Campbell, 'Factor Markets in England Before the Black Death', *Continuity and Change*, 24 (2009), pp. 79–106; John Langdon and James Masschaele, 'Commercial Activity and Population Growth in Medieval England', *Past and Present*, 190 (2006), pp. 35–81.
[24] Stephen Broadberry, Bruce M. S. Campbell, Alexander Klein, Mark Overton and Bas van Leeuwen, *British Economic Growth 1270–1870* (Cambridge: Cambridge University Press, 2015), p. 195.

20%, were hereditary serfs. The relative abundance of land after the Black Death (1348–49), and the spread of more flexible and advantageous tenurial conditions, caused the proportion of smallholdings to fall and encouraged a small elite of peasants to accumulate larger holdings and exert greater social control over their community.[25] Gower's analysis, by contrast, skates over the complexity and heterogeneity of rural society in the late fourteenth century. He does occasionally distinguish cultivators (VC: V.9.569, 629), labourers and servants (VC: V.9.575) among the rustics,[26] but in general he does not differentiate between the heterogenous sub-groups which made up the rural component of the third estate.[27]

Gower uses terms to describe the peasantry which convey a sense of an anonymous, amorphous and bucolic mass: usually *rustici* (VC: V.9.560, 603–4, 612, 620), *rusticitas* (VC: V.9.596, 609, 615), *rustica proles* (VC: I.2.174; V.9.607), and *plebs* (VC: I.2.171), but also *rurales* (VC: V.9.560), *serui* (VC: V.9.600, 621, 623, 628), and *coloni* (VC: V.9.573, 593).[28] These nouns emphasise the peasants' rural and agricultural backgrounds, and their coarse and unpolished demeanour, and are chosen deliberately to place as much social distance as possible between them and the poet.[29] By contrast, contemporary non-literary sources seldom employ the narrow and pejorative descriptors adopted by Gower, and instead use a specialized vocabulary to identify the precise occupational or tenurial status of a peasant or town dweller. The poll tax listings of 1381, for example, organize taxpayers into categories such as *agricole* (agriculturalists), *cultores* (cultivators), *artifices* (artisans), *servientes* (servants), and *laboratores* (labourers). Similarly, parliamentary petitions and government statutes refer routinely to labourers, servants, artisans and, sometimes, 'bondsmen'.[30] The word *rustici*, which

---

[25] The population estimate is from Christopher Dyer, 'Villeins, Bondsmen, Neifs and Serfs', in Paul Freedman and Monique Bourin, eds, *Forms of Servitude in Northern and Central Europe: Decline, Resistance and Expansion* (Turnhout: Brepols, 2005), pp. 419–36 at 433. For the disappearance of serfs see Mark Bailey, *The Decline of Serfdom in Late Medieval England: From Bondage to Serfdom* (Woodbridge: Boydell Press, 2014), pp. 3–61. For changes in rural society, see Richard H. Britnell, 'Land and Lordship: Common Themes and Regional Variations', in Ben Dodds and Richard H. Britnell, eds, *Agriculture and Rural Society after the Black Death* (Hertford: University of Hertford Press, 2008), pp. 149–67; Mark Bailey, 'The Ploughman', in Rigby and Minnis, *Historians on Chaucer*, pp. 352–67, at 353–8.

[26] Labourers and servants – 'those unwilling to serve anyone by the year' – attract 25 separate lines at VC: V.10.629–654.

[27] The urban classes are sketched at VC: V.11.655–704.

[28] Barr, *Socioliterary Practice*, p. 103; Irvin, *Poetic Voices of John Gower*, p. 170.

[29] Barr, *Socioliterary Practice*, pp. 107–8, 110, 130–57.

[30] See, for example, *The Poll Taxes of 1377, 1379 and 1381: Part 2, Lincolnshire to Westmoreland*, ed. Carolyn C. Fenwick (Oxford: British Academy, 2001); *Parliament Rolls of Medieval England 1275–1504*, ed. Chris Given-Wilson (Woodbridge: Boydell Press, 2005) (hererafter PROME), *volume V: Edward III, 1351–1377*, pp. 337, 339; SR, II: 11, 57.

Gower so often uses, hardly ever appears in manorial documents which instead designate people according to tenurial or personal status, such as a freeman (*liber homo*) or free tenant (*liber tenens*); serf of the lord by blood (*nativus/nativa domini de sanguine*); unfree tenant (*villanus, customarius, nativus tenens*) or tenant of unfree land (*tenens terra nativi*). The fact that Gower does not make visible the real distinctions within rural society underlines how the members of the third estate serve a symbolic function in his poetry and how little he attempts to understand them.[31]

The Impact of the Black Death

The Black Death of 1348–49, and the second national outbreak of plague in 1361–62, killed around half the population of England, which showed no signs of renewed growth until the later fifteenth century. The result was a massive fall in the productive capacity of the economy and in the output of its main sector, agriculture. Recent estimates suggest that between the early 1340s and the late 1370s population fell by 46%, GDP fell by around 25% and customary land values fell by a third. The complaints about shortages of workers indicate, however, that the economy still possessed some buoyancy and did not contract as much as the population and, according to one estimate, GDP per capita rose by around 25% over the same period whilst the proportion of the population below the poverty line fell from 41% to 22%.[32]

Those people fortunate enough to have survived the succession of national and local epidemics were on the whole better off, especially wage labourers. Before the plague, many villagers had been either landless or insufficiently provided with land but thereafter they could acquire a foothold on the property ladder and expand the size of their landholdings if they so desired, and could do so on favourable terms. In addition, Braid postulates that the economic behaviour of workers changed following the experience of mass mortalities and that they now preferred consumption strategies – such as buying better food and clothing, and enjoying leisure time – instead of using their new wealth to save or invest.[33] These two forces caused the pool of available wage labourers and servants to shrink faster than the fall in

---

[31] Michael Bennett, 'John Gower, Squire of Kent, the Peasants' Revolt and The *Visio Anglie*', *The Chaucer Review*, 53 (2018), pp. 258–82, at 278–9.

[32] Broadbery et al., *British Economic Growth*, p. 320 and table 5.03; Bailey, *Decline of Serfdom*, p. 316.

[33] Robert Braid, 'Economic Behaviour, Markets and Crises: The English Economy in the Wake of Plague and Famine in the Fourteenth Century', in Simonetta Cavaciocchi, ed., *Economic and Biological Interactions in Pre-Industrial Europe from the Thirteenth to the Eighteenth Centuries* (Florence: Firenze University Press, 2010), pp. 335–72 at 354–61.

population, which explains why wage rates for skilled and unskilled workers soared during the epidemic of 1348–49 and remained high thereafter.[34]

The chronic shortage of workers after 1348–49 was felt acutely by members of the first and second estates, many of whom depended upon customary and hired labour to cultivate their large demesnes (i.e. the land which had not been permanently leased out to peasant tenants). Chroniclers wrote repeatedly and bitterly about the high cost of obtaining workers, their arrogance and their taste for better food and more leisure.[35] To the modern observer, the higher remuneration of the lower orders was a predictable and justifiable economic response to a fundamental shift in the supply of labour, but to medieval social ideologists these underlying economics were irrelevant. The expectations and requirements of menial labour were clearly articulated in estates theory, so any failure to conform to them was a moral problem, one which provoked outraged laments in literature, sermons, chronicles and even parliamentary legislation.[36] For instance, formal petitions to parliament complained about the 'wickedness', 'outrageous demands' and 'malice' of labourers and servants, and targeted the 'able-bodied scoundrels [who] beg and will not labour…for the ease of their bodies'.[37] Legislation passed in 1388 was prefaced with the complaint that labourers would not serve 'without outrageous and excessive hire…to the great damage and loss' of the lords and commons.[38]

Gower shared this hostility to the rising expectations and aspirations of the lower orders. As we have seen, estates theory required deference to one's social superiors, but Gower expresses a commonly-held concern among the ruling elite that the lower orders were increasingly disobedient and unruly: 'it is a great wrong to see the upper class in the power of the peasant class' (MO: 26483–4); 'when the foot rises up against the lord, this is very dishonorable; and likewise when the people rise up like savage beasts in a multitude against the lords, this is a great error' (MO: 27229–34). Indeed, Gower's stance was particularly extreme in its portrayal of the peasantry as a dark and menacing force, innately rebellious and ready to strike if not properly governed.[39] They are 'an impatient nettle' ready to sting the nobility (MO: 26482–26506),

---

[34] Braid, 'Economic Behaviour, Markets and Crises', pp. 354–7.
[35] David L. Farmer, 'Prices and Wages 1350–1500', in Edward Miller, ed., *The Agrarian History of England Wales, Volume III: 1348–1500* (Cambridge: Cambridge University Press, 1991), pp. 431–525 at 484; John Hatcher, 'England in the Aftermath of the Black Death', *Past and Present*, 144 (1994), pp. 3–35 at 11–12; *The Black Death*, ed. Rosemary Horrox (Manchester: Manchester University Press, 1994), pp. 79–80.
[36] Hatcher, 'England in the Aftermath of the Black Death', pp. 10–19; Horrox, *Black Death*, pp. 70, 72–3, 79.
[37] *PROME, volume V*, pp. 211, 337–8; *PROME, volume VI, Richard II 1377–1384*, pp. 36–7.
[38] SR, II: 57.
[39] Olsson, 'John Gower's *Vox Clamantis*', pp. 140–1; Cornelius, 'Gower and the Peasants' Revolt', p. 33.

and likened to a flood or fire in their capacity for 'merciless destruction' (VC: I.12.841–2). Their growing assertiveness following the catastrophe of the Black Death is arrogantly misplaced: 'it is not for anyone from the class of serfs to set things right' (VC: V.9.627–8).[40] Such behaviour is portrayed as irrational and stupid, because it involves a willful rejection of the lower orders' ordained place and role within society. The 'asinine behaviour [of the rebels in 1381] labeled them as stupid and wild, for they had no power of reasoning' (VC:I.2.237–8) and labourers would 'never be gladly subject to reason' (MO: 26425). The populace is comprised of 'unreasoning brutes' (VC: I.2.178) and is 'so lacking in reason as to be as beasts' (VC: V.10.651).[41]

These sharp criticisms of the peasantry were a consequence of a perceived deterioration in their behaviour following the Black Death and, in particular, their 'aggressively appetitive' taste for higher standards of living.[42] Gower reinforces their shortcomings by evoking a bygone golden age when society was organic and harmonious and the lower orders knew and accepted their place (CA: Pro.93–100).[43] 'In olden days the workers were not accustomed to eat wheat bread; instead their bread was made from other grains or from beans. And likewise they drank only water. And they feasted on cheese and milk, but rarely on anything else. Their clothing was of grey material. At that time the world was well ordained for people of their estate. But custom and old usages have now been turned upside down' (MO: 26449–26461). Now the peasants had become greedy and reluctant to work, thus rejecting their proper place in society and threatening its essential fabric.[44] Gower is conventional in depicting their behaviour as sinful, and he identifies gluttony, sloth and pride as particular vices. Gluttony is reflected in their

---

[40] Gower, *Major Latin Works*, p. 209.
[41] Karla Taylor, 'Inside Out in Gower's Republic of Letters', in Dutton, Hines and Yeager, *John Gower Trilingual Poet*, pp. 169–81 at 180; See also Paul Freedman, *Images of the Medieval Peasant* (Stanford: Stanford University Press, 1999), p. 142; Steven Justice, *Writing and Rebellion: England in 1381* (Berkeley: University of California Press, 1994), p. 212.
[42] Hatcher, 'England in the Aftermath of the Black Death', p. 24; Andrew Galloway, 'Reassessing Gower's Dream Visions', in Dutton, Hines and Yeager, *John Gower Trilingual Poet*, pp. 288–303 at 292–5.
[43] Coulton, *Medieval Village*, p. 236; Gower, *Major Latin Works*, pp. 17–18, 208–11; Aers, 'Vox Populi', p. 440; Masciandaro, *Voice of the Hammer*, pp. 86–7; Longo, 'Gower's Public Outcry' pp. 370–1.
[44] For the peasantry in the generation after the Black Death, see Hatcher, 'England in the Aftermath of the Black Death', pp. 3–35; Edmund B. Fryde, *Peasants and Landlords in Later Medieval England* (Stroud: Alan Sutton Publishing, 1996), pp. 29–53; Christopher Dyer, *Making a Living in the Middle Ages: The People of Britain 850–1520* (New Haven: Yale University Press, 2002), pp. 271–97; Peter L. Larson, *Conflict and Compromise in the Late Medieval Countryside: Lords and Peasants in Durham 1349–1400* (New York: Routledge, 2006); Mark Bailey, 'The Myth of the Seigniorial Reaction in England', in Maryanne Kowaleski, John Langdon and Phillipp R. Schofield, eds, *Peasants and Landlords in the Medieval English Economy: Essays in Honour of Bruce Campbell* (Turnhout: Brepols, 2015) pp. 147–72.

desire for higher wages, their increased consumption of domestic goods, their appetite for more and better food and drink, and for social advancement (VC: V.15.850–60): they now demanded 'things for their bellies like a lord' (VC: V.10.648).[45] Sloth is witnessed in their reluctance to work: 'the poor lesser folk, who should stick to their work, demand to be better fed than those who hired them' (MO: 26510–12). The sin of pride is evident in their new-found taste for fine clothing, especially the 'women who have seized upon ermine and grey furs for trimming' (MO: 25681–25704). Gower criticizes 'the poor lesser folk' who now 'clothe themselves in fine colours and handsome attire, whereas formerly they were clothed without pride and without conspiracy in sack cloth' (MO: 26510–18). Such criticisms echo the sumptuary legislation of 1363, which sought to discourage the fashion of 'outrageous and excessive apparel of divers people against their estate and degree', as the lower orders sought to emulate the dress of their betters.[46]

Although Gower criticizes the rising expectations of the lower orders generally, he rarely specifies these failings as being characteristic of the landholding peasantry but rather, like other contemporary social commentators, focuses his criticism on the labourers and servants (MO: 26425–26461; VC: V.10.629–56): they 'are sluggish, they are scarce and they are grasping. For the very little they do, they demand the highest pay…yet a short time ago one performed more service than three do now' (VC: V.9.577–8, 581–2). In this age of labour shortage workers could now be choosy about whether to work or not, and if they did choose to work they could demand higher wages and other perks, such as food and drink. Landlords felt obliged to offer better food and drink at harvest time to entice them, and to accept worker demands for daily or weekly contracts rather than their own preference for longer-term contracts which would restrict labour mobility.[47] Recent analysis of some exceptionally detailed manorial accounts has provided a clear insight into the productivity of agricultural workers employed by lords: the inducements necessary to persuade them to work increased after the Black Death, yet their productivity had undoubtedly fallen.[48] Labourers were now working more slowly and less efficiently for landlords, yet were being paid more money, food

---

[45] Gower, *Major Latin Works*, p. 201; Sylvia Federico, 'A Fourteenth-Century Erotics of Politics: London as a Feminine New Troy', *Studies in the Age of Chaucer*, 19 (1997), pp. 121–55, at 51–2; Sadleck, *Idleness Working*, pp. 183–7; Craig E. Bertolet, *Chaucer, Gower, Hoccleve and the Commerical Practices of Fourteenth-Century London* (Farnham: Ashgate, 2013), pp. 67–8, 150.

[46] Hatcher, 'England in the Aftermath of the Black Death', pp. 11, 18; Horrox, *Black Death*, p. 312.

[47] Hatcher, 'England in the Aftermath of the Black Death', pp. 19–32; Farmer, 'Prices and Wages', p. 484.

[48] David Stone, 'The Productivity of Hired and Customary Labour: Evidence from Wisbech Barton in the Fourteenth Century', *Economic History Review*, 50 (1997), pp. 640–56; David Stone, *Decision-Making in Medieval Agriculture* (Oxford: Oxford University Press, 2005), pp. 101–11.

and drink to do so, just as Gower had complained. One suspects they were more industrious and productive when working for themselves or in trades.

The Evolution of the Labour Laws

The immediate response of the government to the shortages of wage labour had been to introduce the Ordinance (1349) then the Statute of Labourers (1351), which sought to reduce the costs of labour and increase its supply by setting statutory maximum wage levels and forcing able-bodied people to work.[49] This was an extraordinarily ambitious body of legislation, one whose purpose was to ensure that the peasantry adhered to the social contract ordained by estates theory. It was novel, too, because the government had not previously regulated the labour market.[50] The legislation embodied an optimism that royal intervention could be used to restore the conditions of the 1340s, so that the post-plague labour shortages and higher wages would prove to be a temporary abnormality.[51] As one prominent legal historian argues, the labour legislation was illustrative of a radical new governmental social policy whose aim was to coerce ordinary people to stand to their duties in the traditional manner.[52]

At first the statute proved reasonably successful, but its effectiveness and enforcement soon diminished, especially after the second great outbreak of pestilence in 1361–62.[53] By the 1360s the vast majority of employers – including the greatest landlords – were openly paying cash wages in excess of the unrealistic maxima specified by the labour laws, and were generously

---

[49] Farmer, 'Prices and Wages', pp. 483–90; Hatcher, 'England in the Aftermath of the Black Death', pp. 10–11.
[50] Horrox, *Black Death*, pp. 287–9, 312–16.
[51] Middleton, 'Acts of Vagrancy: the C-Version Autobiography and the Statute of 1388', in Steven Justice and Kathryn Kerby-Fulton, eds, *Written Work: Langland, Labour and Authorship* (Philadelphia: University of Pennsylvania Press, 1997), pp. 208–317 at 233–9.
[52] Robert C. Palmer, *English Law in the Age of the Black Death, 1348–1381: The Transformation of Governance and Law* (Chapel Hill: University of North Carolina Press, 1993), pp. 294–305.
[53] Bertha H. Putnam, *The Enforcement of the Statutes of Labourers during the First Decade after the Black Death 1349–1359* (New York: Columbia University Press, 1908), pp. 178, 221; Farmer, 'Prices and Wages', pp. 484–5, 489; Anthony J. Musson and W. Mark Ormrod, *The Evolution of English Justice: Law, Politics and Society in the Fourteenth Century* (Basingstoke: Macmillan, 1999), pp. 94–5; Chris Given-Wilson, 'Service, Serfdom and English Labour Legislation 1350–1500', in Anne Curry and Elizabeth Matthew, eds, *Conceptions and Patterns of Service in the Later Middle Ages* (Woodbridge: Boydell Press, 2000), pp. 21–37 at 22–5; Fryde, *Peasants and Landlords in Later Medieval England*, pp. 33–6, 64–5, 118; Given-Wilson, 'Problem of Labour', p. 98; Dyer, *Making a Living*, pp. 278–86.

supplementing these with inducements of food and drink.[54] Many labourers had sufficient land, food and cash to meet their needs, and so were reluctant to work except on their own terms.[55] Data relating to the wages of English workers are plentiful and reliable, and reveal that the wage rates of agricultural reapers, for example, rose 39% between 1341–45 and 1371–75.[56] It became increasingly apparent to everyone, including chroniclers such as Henry Knighton, that the Statute of Labourers had not succeeded in turning back the clock to the 1340s; Gower himself acknowledged this when he said of the labourers and servants that 'the established law is no help to one, for there is no ruling such men' (VC: V.10.647–9).[57] The ineffectiveness of the labour laws and the shortage of workers forced society to ponder the relative importance and value of labour – all forms of labour, including that of poets – in ways that had never been necessary before.[58] It also triggered a debate among the ruling elite: since the disobedience of the third estate constituted a moral outrage, what could be done about it?

The evolving response to this question can be charted through the contents of petitions to parliament addressing the subject of labour and through changes to the legislation, because these reveal better than any other source the burning issues of the day among the merchant and gentry classes.[59] From the early 1350s to the early 1370s the focus of the labour laws remained unerringly upon the key objectives laid out in 1351: capped wages, contracts by the year (to reduce labour mobility) and compelling all able-bodied people to work. Prosecutions under the statute reveal that breaches of wage caps, and to a lesser extent of contracts, were the main targets for enforcement.[60] Concerns about the effectiveness of the statute were first aired in 1368.[61] In 1372 a petition complained that tougher punishments were needed to deter contract breakers whilst another petition in 1376 bemoaned the widespread evasion of the legislation, analysed the likely reasons why, and proposed

---

[54] Farmer, 'Prices and Wages', pp. 438, 469–70; Hatcher, 'England in the Aftermath of the Black Death', pp. 21–4.
[55] Hatcher, 'England in the Aftermath of the Black Death', p. 27.
[56] John. H. Munro, 'The Late Medieval Decline of English Demesne Agriculture: Demographic, Monetary and Political-Fiscal Factors', in Mark Bailey and Stephen H. Rigby, eds, *England in the Age of the Black Death: Essays in Honour of John Hatcher* (Turnhout: Brepols, 2012), pp. 299–350, at table 20A.
[57] See also Horrox, *Black Death*, pp. 79–80.
[58] Robertson, *Laborer's Two Bodies*, p. 4, 39.
[59] For an earlier attempt at this approach, see Durant W. Robertson, 'Chaucer and the Economic and Social Consequences of Plague' in Francis X. Newman, ed., *Social Unrest in the Later Middle Ages* (Binghampton: Medieval and Renaissance Texts and Studies, 1986), pp. 49–74, at 58–62.
[60] Putnam, *Enforcement of the Statutes of Labourers*, pp. 78, 174–84; Judith M. Bennett, 'Compulsory Service in Late Medieval England', *Past and Present*, 209 (2010), pp. 7–51.
[61] PROME, volume V, p. 211; Anthony R. Bridbury, *The English Economy from Bede to the Reformation* (Woodbridge: Boydell Press, 1992), p. 33.

some radical solutions.[62] Both cited the underlying difficulties caused by the mobility of labourers and servants, too many of whom were able to break contracts then pick up better-paid work elsewhere with impunity, whilst that of 1376 expressed a fear that this led to idle begging and requested the prohibition of alms to, and the arrest and imprisonment of, able-bodied vagrants and beggars.[63] Although no new legislation immediately resulted from this petition, it nonetheless represented a watershed in the debate on labour and changes in policy soon followed.[64] In the 1380s reiterations of the labour laws included the usual directives about wages and contracts, but now included specific clauses designed to address particular concerns about vagrants and those wandering without proper purpose. In 1383 parliament passed a statute empowering royal officials and constables to stop and question 'vagabonds', the first time this word had been used in an official context, who were to be imprisoned if they did not possess sureties for their good behaviour.[65] In 1388 parliament passed the most wide-ranging revision of the labour legislation since 1351, introducing powers to return able-bodied vagrants to their home village and put them to work, obliging travelling peasants to carry testimonials cleared by Justices of the Peace to explain their need to travel, and introducing penalties upon employers guilty of breaches of the legislation.[66] Its provisions were couched in uncompromising language, but proved largely impractical and virtually unenforceable: even so, the breathtaking scope signaled the government's desire to extend its remit to a new social policy relating to mobility and vagrancy.[67]

Attitudes towards labour thus evolved between the 1350s and 1380s, beginning with the assumption in the 1350s and 1360s that legislation could be deployed successfully to restore the labour market to the conditions of the 1340s; then the tempering of this assumption in the 1370s with the growing acceptance that the legislation had failed in its objective, prompting debate about what next to do; and finally, in the 1380s, the development of a new policy of targeting the able-bodied poor and vagrants, who were deemed to have no excuse for their supposed idleness in a world of abundant employment.[68] This is not to argue that attempts to control wages and contracts

---

[62] PROME, volume V, pp. 264, 337–40.
[63] PROME, volume V, pp. 264, 337–40; Given-Wilson, 'Problem of Labour', pp. 88–9. A petition in October 1377 called for the imprisonment of destitute vagrants (PROME, volume VI, pp. 36–7).
[64] Middleton, 'Acts of Vagrancy', pp. 224–8; Given-Wilson, 'Problem of Labour', p. 86.
[65] SR, II: 32–3; Farmer, 'Prices and Wages', p. 486; Marjorie K. McIntosh, Controlling Misbehaviour in England 1370–1600 (Cambridge: Cambridge University Press, 1998), pp. 89–90, 130; Given-Wilson, 'Problem of Labour', p. 89.
[66] SR, II: 56–8; Middleton, 'Acts of Vagrancy', pp. 225–39; Given-Wilson, 'Problem of Labour', pp. 87–9; McIntosh, Controlling Misbehaviour, pp. 89–90.
[67] Given-Wilson, 'Problem of Labour', p. 89; Given-Wilson, 'Service, Serfdom and English Labour Legislation', pp. 21, 24, 28, 30, 34.
[68] Hatcher, 'England in the Aftermath of the Black Death', p. 32.

disappeared after 1380, nor that the idle poor did not feature before 1380: after all, the latter are mentioned explicitly in the Ordinance of Labourers in 1349, and in a London civic ordinance of 1359.[69] But there was a shift in *emphasis*, from a generic belief that normal service would soon be resumed after the Black Death to a more targeted policy when it became apparent that it would not, which resulted in the appearance of the able-bodied beggar as a 'common bogeyman'.[70]

Social commentators in the post-plague period could approach the problem of labour in one of three main ways: they could castigate the third estate in general for its failure to perform its ordained function within society; they could encourage the third estate to carry out its duties by means of an idealized role-modelling of productive labour; or they could denounce the worst excesses of particular categories of offenders.[71] The latter two approaches were readily compatible with the emerging pragmatism of the 1370s and 1380s. Indeed, during those decades, rather than simply bemoaning the shortcomings of the peasants and labourers a growing number of commentators consciously chose to emphasize the positive ideal of industrious and praiseworthy labour.[72] Thus the followers of John Wycliffe glorified productive labour, and both Langland and Chaucer chose a virtuous ploughman to exemplify their ideal for the third estate.[73] The choice of a ploughman for this purpose was highly significant, because it was this category of workers which was most commonly prosecuted under the statute.[74] Similarly, the problem of the able-bodied poor began to loom larger in contemporary literature. Langland engages with it when discussing 'wastours' in the B-text of *Piers Plowman*, written in the late 1370s, but his subsequent changes to the C-text, written in the early 1380s, suggest that he had embarked upon a dialogue on the topic at exactly the time when it was foremost in contemporaries' minds.[75]

---

[69] SR, I: 307–8; Given-Wilson, 'Service, Serfdom and English Labour Legislation', pp. 29–30; Clopper, 'Need Men and Women Labor?', pp. 118–19; McIntosh, *Controlling Misbehaviour*, p. 129.

[70] Andrew Galloway, 'The Economy of Need in Late Medieval English Literature', *Viator*, 40 (2009), pp. 309–31, at 317, 321.

[71] Hatcher, 'England in the Aftermath of the Black Death', pp. 13–19; Middleton, 'Acts of Vagrancy', pp. 227–36; Knight, 'Voice of Labour', pp. 103–6; Barr, *Socioliterary Practice*, pp. 130–57; Sadelek, *Idleness Working*, pp. 175–6; Robertson, *Laborer's Two Bodies*, pp. 3–7; Bailey, 'The Ploughman', pp. 360–7; Longo, 'Gower's Public Outcry' p. 372.

[72] Sadlek, *Idleness Working*, pp. 175–6, 183–5; Bailey, 'The Ploughman', pp. 360–7.

[73] Sadelek, *Idleness Working*, pp. 175–6; Barr, *Socioliterary Practice*, pp. 135–6, 145.

[74] Bailey, 'The Ploughman', pp. 358–9.

[75] Clopper, 'Need Men and Women Labor?', pp. 110–29; Anna P. Baldwin, *The Theme of Government in Piers Plowman* (Cambridge: D. S. Brewer, 1981), pp. 356–63; Middleton, 'Acts of Vagrancy', pp. 208–317; Derek Pearsall, '*Piers Plowman* and the Problem of Labour', in Rothwell et al., *Problem of Labour*, pp. 123–32 at 127–32; Bennett, 'Compulsory Service', pp. 26–8.

Gower – no less than Langland and Chaucer – held conventional views on labour.⁷⁶ It is necessary for sustenance (MO: 14461), and people should be sufficiently industrious to avoid poverty but not so industrious as to acquire excessive riches (MO: 14401–24, 14533–44): 'He who tries to be industrious merely in order to amass wealth…converts the virtue of industry into the vice of covetousness' (MO: 14485–9). Yet there are strong indications that Gower's approach to the contemporary problem of manual labour was even more conservative than many of his contemporaries. His views on the peasantry remained overwhelmingly negative, offering 'no concessions to mutuality nor concern for their well-being'.⁷⁷ He often alluded to a golden past when peasants were docile and industrious, and a central theme of the *Confessio Amantis* is the superiority of the good old days.⁷⁸ Unlike Langland and Chaucer, Gower did not depict a praiseworthy ploughman, but instead singled them out for criticism, claiming that they sowed 'an evil disposition widespread among the common people' (VC: V.9.574). 'The servants of the plow, contrary to the law of the lord, seek to make a fool of the land. They desire the leisures of great men, but they have nothing to feed themselves with, nor will they be servants' (VC: V.9.584–8). Indeed, Gower attacks contemporary ills to a far greater extent than did Chaucer.⁷⁹

A sharpening focus upon supposedly able-bodied beggars forced many contemporaries to ponder the complex issue of the nature and degree of human need, and, by extension, to reassess the charitable giving of alms to the poor.⁸⁰ Langland explores carefully the tension between the Christian duty to be charitable to beggars and the legal prohibition upon giving alms to able-bodied beggars, and Chaucer extensively examined the wider concept of need, but these knotty issues do not feature as explicitly or substantially in Gower's works.⁸¹ In a short passage in the *Confessio Amantis* he explores how charity offers spiritual enhancement to the donor and material enhancement to the recipient (2049–2232), but does not develop the theme further.⁸² The sin of idleness is explored generically

---

[76] Sadelek, *Idleness Working*, pp. 170–1.
[77] Freedman, *Images of the Medieval Peasant*, p. 20. See also, Barr, *Socioliterary Practice*, pp. 131, 145; Hatcher, 'England in the Aftermath of the Black Death', p. 13.
[78] Masciandro, *Voice of the Hammer*, pp. 84–7.
[79] Robert F. Yeager, *John Gower's Poetic: The Search for a New Arion* (Cambridge: D. S. Brewer, 1990), p. 200.
[80] Given-Wilson, 'Service, Serfdom and English Labour Legislation', pp. 31–2; Galloway, 'Economy of Need', pp. 314–17.
[81] David Aers, *Community, Gender and Individual Identity: English Writing 1360–1430* (London: Routledge, 1988), pp. 35–72; Baldwin, *Theme of Government*, pp. 57–63; Anne M. Scott, *Piers Plowman and the Poor* (Portland: Four Courts Press, 2004), pp. 231–5; Robertson, *Laborer's Two Bodies*, pp. 45–50, 68–77; Galloway, 'Economy of Need', pp. 323–8.
[82] Galloway, 'Economy of Need', pp. 318–20.

(MO: 5125–6180), including the specific observations that the idle do not contribute to the common good (MO: 5487–90) and should be denied alms and aid (MO: 14425). Similarly, he observes that 'God is pleased with those who eat no idle bread' (MO: 14509–10) and vagrants are noted for their arrogance (MO: 26473–4). Other than these isolated remarks, Gower offers few explicit comments about the idle and the vagrant. His solution for society's ills is through the agency and example of the ruling elite, not the moral self-reform of the lower orders.

In sum, contemporary commentators depicted society as a hierarchy of interdependent parts, binding everyone into a social contract of mutually supporting and beneficial relationships.[83] Gower's ideas were deeply rooted in this convention, and in particular he promoted the importance of maintaining a unified social body and the common profit that would accrue from it. From the 1370s even conservative thinkers were opening up debates about, and shifting their attitudes towards, labour and poverty, but Gower's writings convey little sense of engagement with these live issues, despite the clear opportunities to do so in his later revisions to the Vox Clamantis or in the Confessio Amantis. Instead, he simply reasserted his belief that the political community should respond to the rapid social changes by restoring the traditional hierarchy and harmony through individual and collective reform.[84] His nostalgia for the past, his focus upon sin, and his indifference to evolving contemporary debates, indicate an attitude staunchly aligned with a wistful desire to turn the clock back.

The Great Revolt of 1381

A passage within the Mirour de l'Omme, which was written in the mid- to late 1370s (see above, pp. 124–5), laments the lethargy of the first and second estates and portrays them as being asleep in the face of the threat posed by the growing rebelliousness of the third estate (MO: 26482–26506).[85] In June 1381 this threat became a reality through a mass uprising, which provided Gower with an opportunity to showcase his views on the ills of society and to map the route to redemption.[86] Vox Clamantis had been originally drafted in the late 1370s as a poem about the responsibilities and sins of the three estates, in which Gower wrote little about the peasantry.

---

[83] For good summaries, see Stephen H. Rigby, English Society in the Later Middle Ages: Class, Status and Gender (Basingstoke: Macmillan Press, 1995), pp. 306–10; and Hole, 'Justification of Wealth', pp. 27–44.
[84] Longo, 'Gower's Public Outcry' pp. 358–9, 361, 373.
[85] John H. Fisher, John Gower: Moral Philosopher and Friend of Chaucer (London: Methuen), pp. 95, 99; Dobson, Peasants' Revolt, pp. 97–9.
[86] Galloway, 'Reassessing Gower's Dream Visions', pp. 298–301; Salisbury, 'Violence and the Sacrifical Poet', pp. 128–31; Astell, 'Peasants' Revolt', pp. 53, 58.

After the dramatic events of 1381, however, Gower added a new first book (the *Visio Anglie*) whose dream vision offered an allegorical account of the revolt.[87] Gower describes this section of the poem as a 'waking sleep' whose dreams and messaging contain clear portents for the future (VC: I.2.143–4), thus presenting himself as a prophetic and detached voice speaking authoritatively to the ruling elite.[88] The revolt was a sharp illustration of the consequences of the breakdown in social cohesion about which Gower had warned his readers, and provided him with another opportunity to propose the fulfilment of one's duties to society, the cohesion of the body politic, and obedience to a wise king as the remedy for the social ills of his day.[89]

Gower is sometimes portrayed as an eye-witness to the insurrection in London, perhaps because he depicts himself as being on the ship that is also the Tower of London, but also because he is assumed to have been resident in Southwark at the time, an assumption which has been effectively challenged by Michael Bennett and Martha Carlin.[90] Indeed, Eric Stockton long ago sketched out various grounds for arguing that the allegorical *Visio* was not actually an eye-witness account of the events in London.[91] Certainly, Gower's narrative lacks the detailed observation we might expect from an eye-witness, providing only a fleeting treatment of most of the key events of the revolt in London, such as the destruction of John of Gaunt's Savoy Palace, the burning of Clerkenwell Priory, the murder of the archbishop of Canterbury, the attacks on Flemings in London, the storming of the Tower of London, and the death of the rebel leader, Wat Tyler (VC: I.11.798–19.1860). Bennett has made a persuasive case that Gower probably did witness some of the rural unrest near his home in Kent, and the experience may have affected him deeply.[92]

Besides, even if the *Visio* did constitute a first-hand account of the revolt, Gower's narrative reveals far more about his ideological biases and moral

---

[87] Yeager, *John Gower's Poetic*, pp. 201–2; Justice, *Writing and Rebellion*, p. 209; Galloway, 'Reassessing Gower's Dream Visions', p. 300; Longo, 'Gower's Public Outcry', pp. 357–8.

[88] Galloway, 'Reassessing Gower's Dream Visions', pp. 291–2, 296; Gower, *Major Latin Works*, p. 11; Justice, *Writing and Rebellion*, pp. 208–9; Masciandaro, *Voice of the Hammer*, p. 189.

[89] Saul, 'John Gower', p. 93; Yeager, ' The Body Politic', pp. 162–5; Longo, 'Gower's Public Outcry' pp. 357–9, 366–79.

[90] Fisher, *John Gower*, p. 60; Eve Salisbury, 'Violence and the Sacred City: London, Gower and the Rising of 1381', in Mark D. Meyerson, Daniel Thiery and Oren Falk, eds, '*A Great Effusion of Blood?' Interpreting Medieval Violence* (Toronto: 2004), pp. 79–97 at 81; Salisbury, 'Violence and the Sacrificial Poet', p. 136; Longo, 'Gower's Public Outcry', p. 374; Robert Epstein, 'London, Southwark, Westminster: Gower's Urban Contexts', in Siân Echard, ed., *A Companion to Gower* (Cambridge: D. S. Brewer, 2004) pp. 43–60, at 53, 57; Justice, *Writing and Rebellion*, p. 209; Bennett, 'John Gower, Squire of Kent', pp. 258–66; and Martha Carlin, above p. 54.

[91] Gower, *Major Latin Works*, p. 16.

[92] Bennett, 'John Gower, Squire of Kent', pp. 268–74, 281–2.

purposes than it does about the detail of the rising. Thus, although the *Visio* captures the terror, frenzy and brutality of the tumult, it is notable for its lack of detail about the participants themselves. In his allegory, Gower depicts the rural population as animals, which was not an uncommon convention of the time.[93] In the *Visio*, however, these animals are transformed into furious beasts bringing confusion and slaughter to London. The rebels screech, bray, moo, grunt, bark, foam, stomp and rampage through seven whole chapters of the *Visio* before any of the actual events of the revolt begin (VC: I.2–8.164– 678).[94] Gower's focus is upon the behaviour of the peasant-animal mob – noisy, uncontrolled, mad, bestial and sinful (VC: I.10.782; 13.880–936) – not its social composition.[95] The rusticity of Gower's rebels does not accord with the findings of modern research, which has revealed that they actually came from a wide variety of social and occupational backgrounds, including members of the clergy, gentry and the village elite.[96] He describes the revolt as a rising of the 'unfree peasants' against freemen and nobles (VC: I.Pro.), whereas in fact its epicentres were towns, and parts of the south-east and East Anglia, where the vast majority of the population were personally free.[97] Likewise, the *Visio* contains no specific references to the events of the revolt outside London, whereas many of the chronicle accounts of the rising cover in some detail the widespread rural unrest throughout Kent, Essex, Hertfordshire, Cambridgeshire and East Anglia, as well as the

[93] Paul Strohm, *Hochon's Arrow: The Social Imagination of Fourteenth-Century Texts* (Princeton: University of Princeton Press, 1992), pp. 36–8; Justice, *Writing and Rebellion*, pp. 212–13; Craig E. Bertolet, 'Fraud, Division and Lies: John Gower and London', in Yeager, *On John Gower*, pp. 43–70 at 44; Hole, 'The Justification of Wealth', pp. 36–7.

[94] Kim Zarins, 'From Head to Foot: Syllabic Play and Metamorphosis in Book I of Gower's *Vox Clamantis*', in Yeager, *On John Gower*, pp. 144–60 at 144; Cornelius, 'Gower and the Peasants' Revolt', pp. 23–4.

[95] Derek Pearsall, 'Interpetative Models for the Peasants' Revolt', in Patrick J. Gallacher and Helen Damico, eds, *Hermeneutics and Medieval Culture* (Albany: State University of New York Press, 1989), pp. 63–70 at 66; David R. Carlson, 'Gower's Beast Allegories in the 1381 *Visio Anglie*', *Philological Quarterly*, 87 (2008), pp. 257–75; Galloway, 'Gower in his Most Learned Role', p. 334; Zarins, 'From Head to Foot', p. 157; Taylor, 'Inside Out in Gower's Republic of Letters', p. 180; Irvin, *Poetic Voices of John Gower*, pp. 40–4. For a view that Gower does represent some of the sub-groups within peasant society, see Cornelius, 'Gower and the Peasants' Revolt', pp. 40–4.

[96] Dobson, *Peasants' Revolt*, pp. 27–8; Herbert Eiden, 'Joint Action against Bad Lordship. The Peasants' Revolt in Essex and Norfolk', *History*, 93 (1998), pp. 5–30, at 10, 23–8; Minjie Xu, 'Disorder and Rebellion in Cambridgeshire in 1381' (Unpublished Cambridge University Ph.D. thesis, 2016), pp. 67–81.

[97] The exact phrase is '*seruiles rustici impetuose contra ingenuous et nobiles regni insurrexerunt*' whose terms Stockton translates as 'lowly peasants' and 'freemen and nobles' (Gower, *Major Latin Works*, p. 49); see also Barr, *Socioliterary Practice*, p. 107. The point about freedom was first made by Michael M. Postan, 'Medieval Agrarian Society in its Prime: England', in Michael M. Postan, ed., *The Cambridge Economic History of Europe, Volume 1: The Agrarian Life of the Middle Ages* (Cambridge: Cambridge University Press, 1966), pp. 549–632, at 608–10.

violent outbreaks in towns such as Beverley, Bury St Edmunds, Canterbury, Cambridge, St Albans, Scarborough and York.[98]

The *Visio* portrays the leaders of the revolt as base criminals who incite others to destroy property and the nobility (VC: I.9.710–30; 12.831–50).[99] Their behaviour is repeatedly dismissed as irrational and mad, and, once having abandoned reason, they are reduced to the level of animals. The depictions of the rebels as rustics and their actions as base were widespread among the ruling elite, although Gower's tone and condemnation are more extreme than most contemporary commentators.[100] The *Visio* has been rightly described as 'among the most vitriolic anti-peasant documents of the entire Middle Ages', and as 'a piece of virtuoso contempt' emphasizing the peasantry's 'animal inarticulacy': among the chroniclers of the revolt, only Thomas Walsingham, a monk of the abbey of St Albans, which was one of the main targets of the rebels, is as hostile.[101] Since the rebels are denied their own voice, Gower's audience is provided with no sense of their grievances, their organization or the sophistication of the ideas which they advanced at their meetings with Richard II at Mile End and Smithfield.[102] Whereas a number of the chroniclers note occasional acts of restraint on the part of the rebels, such as their prohibition of looting from the Savoy Palace, which was burnt to the ground instead, with even Thomas Walsingham recording the rebels' strong stance against theft and allowing 'that they were not motivated by avarice', Gower has no such insight into how the rebels understood their own actions.[103] Gower also skates over the complexities of the revolt and its causes. He scarcely mentions the careful targeting of unpopular royal and municipal figures in London, and only refers obliquely to the attacks on

---

[98] Dobson, *Peasants' Revolt*, pp. 235–304.

[99] Yoshiko Kobayashi, 'The Voice of an Exile: From Ovidian Lament to Prophecy in Book I of John Gower's *Vox Clamantis*', in Andrew Galloway and Robert F. Yeager, eds, *Through a Classical Eye* (Toronto: Pontifical Institute, 2009), pp. 339–62 at 339–40; Longo, 'Gower's Public Outcry', pp. 375–6.

[100] Legislation passed in late 1381 described the insurrection as 'against God, good faith and reason' (SR, II: 20). See also Dobson, *Peasants' Revolt*, p. 131; Pearsall, 'Interpetative Models', pp. 65–6; Yeager, 'The Body Politic', pp. 151–8; Strohm, *Hochon's Arrow*, pp. 36–45; Barr, *Socioliterary Practice*, p. 111; Longo, 'Gower's Public Outcry', pp. 374–5.

[101] Pearsall, 'Interpetative Models', pp. 65–6; Freedman, *Images of the Medieval Peasant*, pp. 62, 142; Justice, *Writing and Rebellion*, p. 211; for Walsingham, see Dobson, *Peasants' Revolt*, pp. 171–2.

[102] Strohm, *Hochon's Arrow*, p. 51; Justice, *Writing and Rebellion*, pp. 210–13; Echard, 'Gower's "Bokes of Latin"', pp. 133–7; Longo, 'Gower's Public Outcry', pp. 374–5; Dobson, *Peasants' Revolt*, pp. 159, 161, 183–4; Pearsall, 'Interpetative Models', p. 66; Aers, 'Vox Populi', p. 441; Justice, *Writing and Rebellion*, pp. 193–254; Anthony J. Musson, *Medieval Law in Context: The Growth of Legal Consciousness from Magna Carta to the Peasants' Revolt* (Manchester: Manchester University Press, 2001), pp. 84–5, 243.

[103] See the observations made by six different chroniclers in Dobson, *Peasants' Revolt*, pp. 157, 161, 164–5, 169–70, 183–4, 186, 188, 200, 206.

Flemings (to which Chaucer famously refers in the 'Nun's Priest's Tale'), yet recent research has shown that the complex political currents swirling within the capital in the years before 1381 explain why these specific targets were purposely chosen.[104]

Following the lead of Gower and the chroniclers, early historians depicted the revolt narrowly as an explosive outburst by rural serfs against exploitative manorial lordship, triggered by frustration with a losing war and heavy taxation.[105] However, more recent work portrays a widespread but selective assault on royal officials and the judicial establishment as being at the heart of the revolt.[106] Certainly, the chancellor's opening speech to parliament in 1383 blamed the rising on the behaviour of lesser officials of the Crown, whom he accused of 'grievous oppressions' and of acting 'like kings in the country, so that justice and law are scarcely administered to anyone'.[107] While this claim conveniently deflected blame from the government's own shortcomings, it is supported by recent historical research. The main targets of the rebels were political and legal figures, especially those associated with the management of royal finances, in particular with the collection of the poll taxes which the government had introduced since 1377 in order to pay for the war with France, and with the enforcement of the Statute of Labourers. In Cambridgeshire the majority of all acts of violence in the revolt recorded in legal documents were committed against local political and legal office holders, thus underlining its 'primarily political rather than feudal and manorial' orientation.[108] Exasperation and frustration with a system of royal justice that had increasingly intruded into the lives of ordinary people, and which had become administered by a narrowing group of self-serving officials, exploded into anger in 1381 and briefly united a diverse group of people most affected by these developments.[109] This was a varied and complex movement, triggered by the heavy-handed enforcement of the third poll tax in early

---

[104] Salisbury, 'Violence and the Sacred City, pp. 80–4, 88–9; W. Mark Ormrod, 'The Peasants' Revolt and the Government of England', *Journal of British Studies*, 29 (1990), pp. 1–30 at 4–5; Bart Lambert and Milan Pajic, 'Immigration and the Common Profit: Native Cloth Workers, Flemish Exiles, and Royal Policy in Fourteenth-Century London', *Journal of British Studies*, 55 (2016), pp. 633–57; Geoffrey Chaucer, 'The Nun's Priest's Tale', VII: 3394–6.

[105] Charles Oman, *The Great Revolt of 1381* (London: Greenhill Books, 1989; first published 1906), pp. 5–12.

[106] Larry R. Poos, *Rural Society after the Black Death: Essex 1350–1525* (Cambridge: Cambridge University Press, 1991), p. 239.

[107] J. Anthony Tuck, 'Nobles, Commons and the Great Revolt of 1381', in Rodney H. Hilton and Trevor H. Aston, eds, *The English Rising of 1381* (Cambridge: Cambridge University Press, 1984), pp. 194–212 at 205.

[108] Xu, 'Disorder and Rebellion', p. 169

[109] Alan Harding, 'The Revolt against the Justices', in Hilton and Aston, *English Rising of 1381*, pp. 165–93 at 180; Ormrod, 'Peasants' Revolt', pp. 13–14; Musson and Ormrod, *Evolution of English Justice*, p. 97; Musson, *Medieval Law in Context*, p. 242.

May 1381, and involving a range of military, political, judicial, social and economic grievances.[110]

Gower was alert to the heightened contemporary concerns about the administration of justice, and in *Vox Clamantis* (VI.9.649–50) highlights the baleful influence of those at the head of government in promoting war and unpopular taxation, and 'the need to purge the kingdom from such influence'.[111] He observed that 'there are those who in serving the king bring suffering upon the poor by taking too much for his benefit' (VI.9721–22). A king had to act as the just defender of his people (*'defensor plebis'*) by tempering justice with mercy, and by protecting the weak from the abuses of government.[112] Yet, although Gower was very aware of these generic abuses, he does not link them explicitly to the causes of the revolt. Instead, he blames the inactivity of the nobility in the face of profound changes around them, and the lack of love within society (VC: I.21.2101–2).[113] Much of his criticism is levelled at the ruling elite, not at the peasants themselves, which was a common theme among contemporary moralists.[114]

The Peasants' Revolt was thus as complex and eclectic as Gower's account of it was over-simplified and narrow. His extreme caricature of the participants as bestial, mad, criminal, irrational and diabolical rustics distances them from any civilized discourse and has been interpreted as oppressively de-humanizing.[115] The details of the uprising were unimportant to Gower because, as Fisher commented, he was not offering history: his use of what has been seen as a 'heavy' and 'incongruous' allegorical mode in the *Visio*

---

[110] Nicholas Brooks, 'The Organization and Achievements of the Peasants of Kent and Essex in 1381', in Henry Mayr-Harting and Robert I. Moore, eds, *Studies in Medieval History Presented to R. H. C. Davis* (London: Bloomsbury, 1985), pp. 260–8; Harding, 'Revolt against the Justices' pp. 165–93; Christian D. Liddy, 'Urban Conflict in Later Fourteenth-Century England: the Case of York in 1380–1', *EHR*, 118 (2003), pp. 1–32.

[111] Yoshiko Kobayashi, '*Principis umbra*: Kingship, Justice and Pity in John Gower's Poetry', in Yeager, *On John Gower*, pp. 71–103 at 87. See also Robert J. Meindl, 'Gower's *Speculum Ludicis*: Judicial Corruption in Book VI of the *Vox Clamantis*', in Russell A. Peck and Robert F. Yeager, eds, *John Gower: Others and the Self* (Cambridge: D. S. Brewer, 2017), pp. 260–82.

[112] Kobayashi, '*Principis Umbra*', pp. 87–9. See also Andrew Galloway, 'The Literature of 1388 and the Politics of Pity in Gower's *Confessio Amantis*' in Emily Steiner and Candace Barrington, eds, *The Letter of the Law: Legal Practice and Literary Production in Medieval England* (Ithaca: Cornell University Press, 2002), pp. 105–14, at 105.

[113] Strohm, *Hochon's Arrow*, p. 53; Tuck, 'Noble, Commons and the Great Revolt', pp. 194–5; Galloway, 'Reassessing Gower's Dream Visions', p. 300; Justice, *Writing and Rebellion*, p. 216.

[114] Echard, 'Gower's "Bokes of Latin"', p. 140; Hole, 'The Justification of Wealth', pp. 28–38.

[115] Carlson, 'Gower's Beast Allegory', pp. 257–70; Barr, *Socioliterary Practice*, p. 108–111; Cornelius, 'Gower and the Peasants' Revolt', p. 39; Ethan Knapp, 'John Gower: Balzac of the Fourteenth Century', in Ana Sáez-Hidalgo and Robert F. Yeager, eds, *John Gower in England and Iberia* (Cambridge: D. S. Brewer, 2014), pp. 215–28 at 223.

was meant to distance his audience from the actual events of the revolt, and frames a poet's meditation on what happens to society when order is not maintained.[116] The rebels' world view is irrelevant to Gower, because their irrational behaviour emanates from the collapse of the social order that occurs when the ruling elite fail to provide authority, social responsibility and appropriate leadership.[117] He is unequivocal that 'evils proceed from the highest status in life' (VC: VII.1.243) and will recur for as long as there is no improvement in the behaviour of the first and second estates. While Gower emphasizes the link between personal and collective wrongdoing and political misfortune, he does offer hope: energetic reform and resourceful action can make a difference (VC: I.19.1881–21.2150). The restoration of proper lordship, a good king, penitence and prayer to God – 'the awakening of the Christian subject' – will in turn restore the social order.[118] The revolt brought home the scale of the problems facing society and reinforced to the ruling elite that they lacked sufficient public and private powers to coerce the third estate; thereafter greater emphasis needed to be placed on winning hearts and minds through exhortation, literature and preaching about the importance of the 'common profit'.[119]

Gower the Conservative Conservative

As Robert Yeager points out, an understanding of historical context is especially important in understanding Gower's work, because he was 'a more reactive writer than most, whose verse seems to have come in response to

---

[116] Fisher, *John Gower*, p. 173; Pearsall, 'Interpetative Models', p. 65; Galloway, 'Gower in his Most Learned Role', p. 332.

[117] Olsson, 'John Gower's *Vox Clamantis*', pp. 137–8; Yeager, *John Gower's Poetic*, p. 205; Astell, 'Peasants' Revolt', p. 53; Cornelius, 'Gower and the Peasants' Revolt', pp. 28, 44; Hole, 'The Justification of Wealth', pp. 38–44.

[118] Olsson, 'John Gower's *Vox Clamantis*', pp. 143–56; Astell, 'Peasants' Revolt', p. 57; Cornelius, 'Gower and the Peasants' Revolt', pp. 30–1; Galloway, 'Reassessing Gower's Dream Visions', p. 301.

[119] Anthony Musson, 'New Labour Laws, New Remedies? Legal Reaction to the Black Death Crisis', in Nigel Saul, ed., *Fourteenth-Century England*, 1 (Woodbridge: Boydell Press, 2000), pp. 73–88 at 74; Given-Wilson, 'Problem of Labour', p. 98. For a highly imaginative attempt to argue that the *Confessio Amantis* seeks to address this message to radical elements of non-ruling urban elites in the wake of the uprising, see Lynn Arner, 'History Lessons from the End of Time: Gower and the English Uprising of 1381', *Clio*, 31 (2002), pp. 237–55 and Lynn Arner, *Chaucer, Gower and the Vernacular Rising: Poetry and the Problem of the Populace after 1381* (University Park: Penn State University Press, 2013). In fact, there is little evidence that this layer of urban society was especially radical in the 1380s or even that they comprised a sizeable group outside the largest half dozen English towns, but there is clear evidence that fiscal pressures and royal officeholding created a crisis of government in such places (Liddy, 'Urban Conflict', pp. 1–32).

people and events around him'.[120] Gower himself claimed to represent 'not so much his own private opinion as the general opinion of his place and time', meaning the opinion of the literate and politicized gentry and the urban elite who could understand his Latin and French works.[121] That literate and intellectual elite was attempting to make sense of the peasantry's reluctance to work, and the soaring costs of employing labourers and servants. Gower makes no attempt to understand this behaviour from the perspective of the peasantry themselves, and shows very little interest in them as people: for example, he does not capture their wide social differentiation and scarcely acknowledges the existence of the landholding peasantry. The lack of visibility of the third estate in Gower's poetry emphasizes that its members are performing a symbolic function within his work, with the focus not upon who they were but on how they should behave, with such ideal behaviour viewed through the lens of traditional social theory rather than of contemporary economic reality.

The demographic decline following the Black Death created a shortage of manual labour, and the scale and speed of this change posed huge challenges of adjustment for society. The government responded quickly by introducing legislation to restore pre-plague norms for wages and contracts, and to require peasants and labourers to work when required. The Statute of Labourers of 1351 was designed to impose upon the peasantry and wage-earners the model of menial labour ordained in estates theory, and its introduction soon after the plague had struck represented a tacit acknowledgement that the ruling elite was incapable of imposing that model through either physical coercion or moral compulsion. Gower blamed this incapacity on human sin and the relinquishing of social responsibility by all sections of society, but especially by the ruling elite. To modern eyes, however, the explanation for the changes and tensions in the society of his day is clear: by the time plague arrived in 1348 English landlords no longer had manual labour at their beck and call through either personal service, physical compulsion or moral diktat; rather, labour was now a commodity which was bought and sold for wages according to market forces and regulated through legal contracts. Over-population on the eve of the Black Death had skewed market forces heavily in favour of landlords, effectively obscuring the economic implications of the creeping commoditization of labour. The introduction of labour laws in the wake of the Black Death reflected a contemporary optimism that legislation would be effective in reforming work habits and so restore the *status quo ante*. By the 1370s, however, it was increasingly obvious that the legislation had failed in this objective, such that peasants and labourers could be neither compelled to work nor relied upon to conform to the behaviours ordained in estates theory. Irreversible socio-economic changes and the shock of the Great

---

[120] Yeager, *John Gower's Poetic*, p. 199.
[121] Coulton, *Medieval Village*, pp. 235–6; Justice, *Writing and Rebellion*, pp. 210–11; Galloway, 'Reassessing Gower's Dream Visions', pp. 289–91.

Revolt posed a clear imminent threat to the traditional fabric of society and the 'common profit'. The ensuing debate grappled with issues (such as justice and labour) that pierced the heart of contemporary society, and offered social commentators an urgent and relevant platform for their views, both of which helped to stimulate the emergence of a poetic tradition addressing common themes – even if it did not always arrive at common answers.[122]

The labour legislation reflected the dominant conservatism within contemporary social thought, although the initial confidence of the ruling elite in the power of legislation to re-impose the traditional social order eventually gave way to pragmatism, characterized by subtly different messages about labour and a focus upon the able-bodied poor, which in turn raised difficult questions about charity and need. There is little evidence that Gower himself engaged with these evolving debates on labour and poverty, and for him the revolt and the failure of the legislation reinforced the existence of major divisions within society and the mounting threat that they posed to what he saw as the 'common profit'. Gower directed much of his criticism at the ruling elite, and his inattentiveness to the third estate implies that he regarded their particular shortcomings as being more of a symptom of society's woes than their cause. His remedy applied to all estates, whom he exhorted to reform their behaviour and to return to a world in which people committed to their social calling as a matter of duty, although in this regard the lower orders required leadership from their betters because they were incapable of self-reform. This powerful but conventional message changed little, even as he wrote and re-wrote his works in the 1380s and 1390s, confirming him as a social conservative even by the standards of his own age.

---

[122] Anne Middleton, 'The Idea of Public Poetry in the Reign of Richard II', *Speculum*, 53 (1978), pp. 94–114; Steven Justice, 'The Idea of Public Poetry in the Reign of Richard II', in Steven Justice, ed., *Anne Middleton: Chaucer, Langland and Fourteenth-Century Literary History* (Farnham: Variorum, 2013), pp. 1–26.

Chapter 5

TOWNS AND TRADE

James Davis

Gower's Commercial Anxieties

It has often been suggested by scholars that John Gower, like other contemporary poets, found it hard to reconcile his conception of an ideal social order with the realities and complexities of a new commercial world.[1] In this view, Gower was a conservative voice fighting anachronistically against the tide of recent socio-economic change, his attitude towards merchants being seen as at best equivocal whilst his stance towards retailers was one of strident antipathy.[2] Janet Coleman, for instance, suggests that writers such as Gower were 'fearful of the traditional world being turned upside down by the rising third estate'.[3] Ethan Knapp presents Gower's views on towns and trade as constituting a response to 'the emergent economic forces (and their social agents) in his own day' and argues that even though Gower accepted the need for trade, he also had a 'deep ambivalence' about the effects of growing commercialisation which was corroding traditional social structures.[4] Yet,

---

I should like to thank Steve Rigby, Robert Yeager, Siân Echard and Stephen Kelly for their invaluable comments on drafts of this chapter.

[1] Janet Coleman, *English Literature in History, 1350–1400: Medieval Readers and Writers* (London: Hutchinson & Co, 1981), pp. 51, 136; Arthur B. Ferguson, *The Articulate Citizen and the English Renaissance* (Durham, NC: Duke University Press, 1965), p. 51; James M. Dean, *The World Grown Old in Later Medieval Literature* (Cambridge, Mass.: Medieval Academy of America, 1997), pp. 239–40.

[2] Winthrop Wetherbee, 'John Gower', in David Wallace, ed., *The Cambridge History of Medieval English Literature* (Cambridge: Cambridge University Press, 1999), pp. 589–609 at 590; Coleman, *English Literature in History*, p. 127; Jill Mann, *Chaucer and Medieval Estates Satire: The Literature of Social Classes and the General Prologue to the Canterbury Tales* (Cambridge: Cambridge University Press, 1973), pp. 99–102; cf. Roger Ladd, *Antimercantilism in Late Medieval English Literature* (New York: Palgrave Macmillan, 2010), pp. 49, 89.

[3] Coleman, *English Literature in History*, p. 129.

[4] Ethan Knapp, 'John Gower: Balzac of the Fourteenth Century', in Ana Sáez-Hidalgo and Robert F. Yeager, eds, *John Gower in England and Iberia: Manuscripts, Influences, Reception* (Cambridge: D. S. Brewer, 2014), pp. 215–28 at 216–18, 227.

in reality, the 'emergence' of a mercantile elite and of a monetised and commercialised economy had been in train for nearly two hundred years by the time Gower was writing.[5] Indeed, the kinds of criticisms of commerce made by Gower were already evident in the work of social commentators of the thirteenth and early fourteenth centuries as much as they were in the post-Black Death era.

More recent scholarship on Gower, merchants and the city has sought to reassess the late-fourteenth-century context for his writings and suggests that the poet was more aware of the contemporary concerns of his audience than has often been recognised. Thus, Jonathan Hsy argues that while the detailed description of London's trade offered in the *Mirour de l'Omme* ostensibly adopts the framework of traditional anti-mercantile tropes such as the figure of 'Triche', the poet's flexible linguistic style produced a more nuanced perspective on the urban milieu than he is often given credit for.[6] Roger Ladd has similarly examined the sophisticated ways that Gower critiqued mercantile practices and notes that while the *Mirour de l'Omme* lists the frauds which trade could involve, it also presents trade as a social good, a view which would have appealed to its likely mercantile audience as would Gower's criticisms of alien merchants.[7] In both of these approaches, there is an understanding that in order to comprehend fully the historical context for Gower's views on towns and trade, we need to go beyond general notions about commercial mentalities and the rise of a money economy and instead develop a more detailed understanding of the post-Black Death commercial environment. In particular, this chapter explores how a focus on the 1370s, when Gower was writing *Mirour de l'Omme*, can add to our understanding of *Mirour de l'Omme* and how it would have resonated with contemporaries.

Much has been written about Gower's affinity with London's wholesale merchants and the wool staplers and his adoption of contemporary anxieties about the role of foreign merchants in England's trade, and those well-worn arguments do not need to be repeated here.[8] Instead, this chapter will focus on the extensive discussion in *Mirour de l'Omme* (some 400 lines) of the retail trades and the selling of artisanal goods, a topic which has attracted surprisingly little attention. One exception to this neglect is Craig Bertolet's exploration of regulation of trade in the capital as a context for understanding

---

[5] The best analysis of the commercialisation of pre-Black Death England is offered by Richard H. Britnell, *The Commercialisation of English Society, 1000–1500* (second edition; Manchester: Manchester University Press, 1996).

[6] Jonathan Hsy, *Trading Tongues: Merchants, Multilingualism, and Medieval Literature* (Columbus: Ohio State University Press, 2013), pp. 105–7, 111.

[7] Ladd, *Antimercantilism in Late Medieval English Literature*.

[8] Ladd, *Antimercantilism in Late Medieval English Literature*, pp. 87–101; Craig E. Bertolet, '"The Slyeste of Alle": The Lombard Problem in John Gower's London', in Malte Urban, ed., *John Gower: Manuscripts, Readers, Contexts* (Turnhout: Brepols, 2009), pp. 197–218.

the *Mirour de l'Omme*. Bertolet scoured London's records for examples of laws and cases that mirrored Gower's accusations about commercial malpractice in order to establish the 'interpretative frameworks' that shaped people's attitudes towards retail trade. He argued that, for Gower, 'the commercial polity is unstable, difficult to govern, and exclusionary' and that the poet was seeking to praise those who worked against fraud and for civic harmony.[9] However, whilst Bertolet's work does much to illuminate Gower's viewpoint, his approach still relies on broad notions of the common good and public order and invokes general diatribes against commercial fraud. Whilst these ideas were undoubtedly integral to how medieval trades were represented in both the law and in literary works, they were also abstract conceptions that were very long-lived. Focusing on these broader moral principles can reinforce the idea of a Gower living in a golden past of an idealised social order, rather than engaging with the pressing issues of his own day.

In order to provide some better sense of the commercial and political issues of the 1370s which formed the context for the *Mirour de l'Omme*, we need to examine three main topics. Firstly, we have to assess the impact of the Black Death and the population decline of the period. The upheavals of the plague undoubtedly affected the organisation of the artisanal and retail trades as much as it did the labour supply, but the key issues of the 1370s, particularly high retail prices and a lack of small coin, are little recognised in analyses of Gower. Secondly, we need to look at the Good Parliament of 1376 as Gower was writing when London was undergoing significant political change, fostered by the events of the Good Parliament and by accusations of corruption among London aldermen. Discussions about civic governance and the common good were prominent, and this led to significant constitutional reform in the capital. Finally, we need to examine the role of John Northampton, who emerged as the standard bearer of civic complaints in the 1370s. During his later mayoralty (1381–83) he pursued a range of policies designed to curry popular favour among all Londoners, including regulations aimed at price control and currency shortages. Northampton's mayoralty is also notable for the increased use of the pillory and its accompanying theatre of punishment. As we shall see, the moral outlook and anxieties underlying his campaign bear strong resemblance to the concerns which Gower had expressed a few years earlier. Although Gower made little attempt to provide specific names, dates or narratives when discussing retail trade, instead setting out his views in an abstract and allegorical form, this does not mean that he was unresponsive to the events and anxieties of his day. Rather, Gower was offering a conservative, popular programme for market reform, one in which conventional paradigms were weaved together with some of the pressing issues of his day.

---

[9] Craig E. Bertolet, *Chaucer, Gower, Hoccleve and the Commercial Practices of Late Fourteenth-Century London* (Farnham: Ashgate, 2013), p. 14.

The Audience for the *Mirour de l'Omme*

The *Mirour de l'Omme* was probably written between 1376 and 1379 (see pp. 124–5, above). As many scholars have shown, Gower was writing within the traditions of estates satire and drawing upon customary literary stereotypes. The three main estates of those who pray, fight and work are dealt with in order, with the broadly defined third estate being comprised of legal professionals, merchants, artisans, taverners, victuallers and, lastly, peasants and agricultural labourers. According to medieval estates theory, townspeople had to undertake their estate functions dutifully and virtuously within their allotted place in the social hierarchy in order for the community to prosper. There is no indication that Gower questioned the veracity of this model of society; his complaint was rather the failure of individuals to fulfil their expected tasks. Gower thus borrowed traditional views without compunction, including those found in thirteenth-century pastoral and scholastic texts.[10] This has led many scholars to claim that Gower rarely challenged prevailing conceptions; with his work being seen as conservative and generic and as lacking the subtle ironies and complexities of the verse of Chaucer or Langland.[11] It may indeed be the case that Gower was reiterating accepted ideology, yet this also reminds us that his writing was firmly embedded in contemporary perceptions and ideals and this has its own value for those studying Gower's work. Moreover, as we shall see, Gower was also able to adapt traditional ideas to the specific context in which he was writing in the 1370s.

London is the undoubted setting for Gower's discussion of trade in *Mirour de l'Omme*, even if direct references to the capital are few, as when 'Triche' is associated with 'the noble city on the Thames, which Brutus founded' (MO: 25249–60). Critics have thus discussed whether Gower's text expresses a London 'voice'.[12] Robert Epstein suggests that the passages in *Mirour de l'Omme* on merchants and traders 'must derive from first-hand observation of the bustle of fourteenth-century London'. Indeed, Gower is often viewed as a representative of London's 'middle class' or bourgeoisie, although these terms are not exactly applicable to the society of the time.[13] Gower himself hints that he is aiming at a mercantile audience with whose members he was

---

[10] Wetherbee argues that *Mirour de l'Omme* is indebted to penitential manuals such as Deguileville's *Pilgrimage of Human Life* (Wetherbee, 'John Gower', p. 592).

[11] Knapp, 'John Gower', p. 216; Claire B. Sponsler, 'Society's Image: Estates Literature in Fifteenth-Century England', *Semiotica*, 63 (1987), pp. 229–38 at 232–3.

[12] Ethan Knapp, 'Towards a Material Allegory: Allegory and Urban Space in Hoccleve, Langland, and Gower', *Exemplaria*, 27 (2015), pp. 93–109 at 101.

[13] Coleman, *English Literature in History*, pp. 71, 128–30; Anne Middleton, 'The Idea of Public Poetry in the Reign of Richard II', *Speculum*, 53 (1978), pp. 94–114; Gardiner Stillwell, 'John Gower and the Last Years of Edward III', *Studies in Philology*, 45 (1948), pp. 454–71 at 469; c.f. Roger Ladd, 'Gower, Business, and Economy', in *RRC*, pp. 158–71 at 161, who notes this problem of the applicability of these terms.

familiar: 'I know not why I should preach to such merchants ... Therefore one of them said to me the other day ...' (MO: 25909–20). By the time Gower was writing Vox Clamantis, he presented himself as expressing the 'vox populi', but his literary approach in the Mirour is very much to align himself with the merchant and ruling elite.[14] He claims to be a frequent attendee at wine taverns, while avowing little knowledge of alehouses or bakers: 'But I do not know the details except that everyone in the city complains and cries out about them' (MO: 26197–208). He suggests he knows the common voice and understands their concerns, but presents himself as apart from them and his literary style is very much in keeping with his likely intended audience.

The Anglo-French of Mirour de l'Omme once led critics to speculate that it was written for the royal court and common lawyers. However, the scholarly consensus is now that the work was intended for a broader urban audience.[15] Certainly, London French was a dialect used in merchant circles well into the fifteenth century, as can be seen in guild ordinances, borough proclamations and public oaths.[16] As Richard Britnell has shown, it was also regarded as the appropriate language in which burgesses and craftsmen petitioned their mayor and council, as well as a high-status language with which to communicate with the king, even if the use of French as an official civic language raised issues of practicality about how these administrative materials were to be transmitted to the public. Gower was thus writing in a language that was the preferred medium for merchant companies and burgesses in outlining their regulatory and administrative rhetoric.

Gower's Depiction of Retail Trades

In an approach that owes a lot to stock conventions, Gower's Mirour de l'Omme readily identified traditional malpractices and frauds within the professions, offering few remedies but bemoaning the dishonest intent of

---

[14] See VC: VII.25.1469: 'what I have set down is the voice of the people, but you will also see that where the people call out, God is often there.'

[15] Coleman, English Literature in History, pp. 21–2, 127; Andrew Galloway, 'Gower's Kiste', in Sáez-Hidalgo and Yeager, eds, John Gower, pp. 193–214 at 197.

[16] Richard H. Britnell, 'Uses of French Language in Medieval English Towns', in Jocelyn Wogan-Browne, ed., Language and Culture in Medieval Britain: The French of England, c.1100–c.1500 (York: York Medieval Press, 2009), pp. 81–9 at 82–3; Hsy, Trading Tongues, p. 113; Ladd, Antimercantilism in Late Medieval English Literature, p. 54; Craig E. Bertolet, 'The French Works: Mirour de l'Omme', in RRC, pp. 321–7 at 322–3; Robert F. Yeager, 'Gower's French Audience: The Mirour de l'Omme', Chaucer Review, 41 (2006), pp. 111–37. For examples, see: Munimenta Gildhallae Londoniensis, ed. Henry T. Riley (three volumes; London: Roll Series, 1859), I: 306–19, 358–61, 367–73, 377–85, 387–91, 408–9, 417–33, 457–67, 470–8, 494–6, 505–28; Memorials of London and London Life in the XIIIth, XIVth and XVth Centuries, AD1276–1419, ed. Henry T. Riley (London: Longmans, 1868), pp. 244–65.

so many vendors: '... of all those who live off money by buying and selling I will not except a single one as not attending on Fraud [*'Triche'*] – neither merchant, nor victualler, nor retail shopkeeper. Everyone who knows how to beguile, beguiles others in his trade; so whoever considers the present time with a critical eye can see the strangest things.' (MO: 26341–52). Although *Mirour de l'Omme* appears to be a virulent anti-commercial text, its complaints about traders were a commonplace of estates satire and Gower's target was individual fraud rather than trade per se.[17] Indeed, Gower consistently reiterates the necessity and legitimacy of both wholesale and retail trade for the common good ('bien commun'), reflecting a sentiment that was long established in scholarly thought, as in the works of Thomas Aquinas and Peter Olivi, and which was becoming entrenched in civic language (MO: 25501–12, 25981–92).[18]

Yet, whilst Gower's complaints were often conventional, there are some aspects of his outlook that do need further explanation. His focus on the wool trade, the wine trade and other retail activities is comparatively unusual, while other trades are excluded that we might expect to have been covered. In particular, the fishmongers are not included in his attack on victuallers in *Mirour de l'Omme* and only merit a brief mention in *Vox Clamantis* (VC: V.14.807–8). Martha Carlin argues that Gower was not yet living in Southwark at the time that he was writing the *Mirour de l'Omme*. Certainly, this section lacks references to cooks, innkeepers, tailors, shoemakers and prostitutes, which were the dominant trades of this suburb according to the 1381 poll tax assessment.[19] Either way, it reminds us that Gower's purpose in

---

[17] Craig E. Bertolet, 'Fraud, Division, and Lies: John Gower and London', in Robert F. Yeager, ed., *On John Gower: Essays at the Millennium* (Kalamazoo: Medieval Institute Publications, 2007), pp. 43–70; Ladd, *Antimercantilism in Late Medieval English Literature*, pp. 49–75; Robert Epstein, 'Dismal Science: Chaucer and Gower on Alchemy and Economy', *Studies in the Age of Chaucer*, 36 (2014), pp. 221–2; Joel Kaye, *Economy and Nature in the Fourteenth Century: Money, Market Exchange, and the Emergence of Scientific Thought* (Cambridge: Cambridge University Press, 2000), pp. 82–3.

[18] Ladd, *Antimercantilism in Late Medieval English Literature*, p. 51. For the common good in civic documents, see James Davis, 'The Common Good and Common Profit in the Trade Regulations of Medieval English Towns', in Jesús Ángel Solórzano Telechea, Beatriz Arízaga Bolumburu and Jelle Haemers, eds, *Los Grupos Populares en la Ciudad Medieval Europea* (Logroño: Instituto de Estudios Riojanos, 2014), pp. 133–50; Christopher Fletcher,'De la communauté du royaume au common weal: les requêtes anglaises et leurs stratégies au XIVe siècle', *Revue Française d'Histoire des Idées Politiques*, 32 (2010) pp. 359–72.

[19] Martha Carlin, 'Gower's Southwark', in *RRC*, pp. 132–49 at 137 and see above, pp. 51–2. For the older view on Gower and Southwark, see John H. Fisher, *John Gower: Moral Philosopher and Friend of Chaucer* (London: Methuen, 1965), pp. 37–70, 97. Some of these subjects are tackled in the abstract by Gower. Cooks in noble households are mentioned in *Mirour* in an earlier section in relation to delicacy and gluttony (MO: 7789–8112) whilst prostitution is considered in the context of lechery and wantonness (MO: 9193–636).

the *Mirour* was not to offer a mimetic or comprehensive discourse about his surroundings. Rather he was providing an interpretation of popular anxieties about fraud, price and the common good, some of which were permeating contemporary civic discourse. What were the main themes he raised?

Gower suggests that he knows little about the ale trade, since it was a daily drink for poor people, but he did regard it as important enough to include in *Mirour de l'Omme* as part of his complaints about poor quality and high prices (MO: 26161–72). There is no mention of the assize processes intended to regulate the price of ale, nor the assize of bread, though he again expresses concern about short weight and high prices for bread (MO: 26173–208). There is an underlying concern about value for money and whether some vendors were cutting corners in order to make more money from the stipulated prices. However, for other commodities, Gower was more direct, whether the price of a penny for a cut of meat or the trebling of poultry prices. One detailed list of poultry prices was published by the London authorities on 24 December 1370, including those for mallards, woodcocks, curlews, larks, swans, geese, capons, hens, partridges, plovers and pheasants, and even for eggs.[20] This list is strikingly similar to Gower's outline in *Mirour*: 'such rich birds as partridges, pheasants, plovers, and swans, whereby Fraud collects his evil gain ... the poulterers have hurt me in another way by raising the prices of capon and goose with their falsification, so that nowadays eggs have become as expensive as hens used to be' (MO: 26293–304). It is perhaps no coincidence since such lists of prices would have been proclaimed publicly in the marketplaces and possibly pinned to a prominent place such as the market cross. Were Gower's complaints thus influenced by contemporary ordinances that were common knowledge?

Gower uses a rhetorical device which was often used within the genre of complaint literature when he states that: 'In the city I hear common people say everywhere that there is no honesty in these bakers; on the contrary, it is entirely wanting' (MO: 26173–84). Nevertheless, there is a more specific context within which we should understand Gower's claim and his attempt to present himself as a legitimate voice speaking out on behalf of the people and their concerns. The wellbeing of the community and 'poor common people' were strong themes in his demand for sales in small lots to aid the poor.[21] Excessive prices are here stated to be detrimental to the common good and thus, it is implied, to social order. Beef and mutton are so overpriced that 'the poor common people curse and say that such victuallers know not the value of a halfpenny', demanding a penny for a cut of meat or else withdrawing

---

[20] CLB, G, pp. 273–4 (24 Dec 1370).
[21] In an interesting aside, Gower does mention that poultry might be bought on credit (MO: 26257–92). Langland too was concerned about bakers and brewers who sold their products at an excessive price, or deceived customers about their substance (William Langland, *Piers Plowman: The B Version*, eds George Kane and E. Talbot Donaldson (Berkeley: University of California Press, 1988), III: 79–94; IX: 396–400).

their product, even allowing it to degrade into dogfood (MO: 26221–56). Current concerns thus stand alongside the more established tropes within Gower's work, with anxiety about high prices and the value of a halfpenny. Similarly with the poulterers, Gower discusses the tripling of prices for birds that are not fresh (MO: 26269–80). There is little focus on hygiene and the waste products of butchers and poulterers, which was a frequent concern within contemporary national and civic legislation and, indeed, pastoral literature.[22] Instead, Gower concentrates on the claimed quality of the product, its price and the ability of the poor to buy it. At the heart of his concern about shopkeepers, who primarily serve the poor, is the accusation that they are making excessive profit with little care for the good of the community: 'they make a penny out of a farthing' (MO: 26305–40).

Prices and Money

Gower's diatribe seemingly says little that is new yet, in fact, his focus on the particular issues of prices, quality, coin and the common good was specifically relevant to the commercial conditions of 1370s London. The reasons for this can be found in the economic aftermath of the Black Death and subsequent plague epidemics which had resulted in a substantial and sustained population decline in London from c.80,000 in 1300 to half that in 1400, even though the city continued to attract immigrants.[23] Most historians agree that the consequent shortages in manpower meant a real rise in wages for labourers and artisans. Many commodity prices also rose, but the general trend was towards an increase in per capita wealth and real wages. Indeed, greater spending power was driving up demands from the lower strata of society for better quality foodstuffs, clothing and manufactures and stimulated growing imports of semi-luxury manufactures. There was also a burgeoning of victuallers who became increasingly professionalised in the second half of the fourteenth century, pushing *ad hoc* traders, often women, into the margins of huckstering.[24] This trend was reflected in greater

---

[22] SR, I: 203 (51 Henry III? or 13 Edward I? (*Statutum de Pistoribus*)); *Beverley Town Documents*, ed. Arthur F. Leach (London: Selden Society, 1900), pp. 28–9; *Monumenta Juridica: The Black Book of the Admiralty*, ed. Travers Twiss (London, 1873), volume II, pp. 144–7, cap. 58 [57].

[23] Caroline M. Barron, *London in the Later Middle Ages: Government and People 1200–1500* (Cambridge: Cambridge University Press, 2004), pp. 45, 237–42, 303.

[24] Maryanne Kowaleski, 'A Consumer Economy', in Rosemary Horrox and W. Mark Ormrod, eds, *A Social History of England, 1200–1500* (Cambridge: Cambridge University Press, 2006), pp. 238–59; Mark Bailey, 'Historiographical Essay: The Commercialisation of the English Economy, 1086–1500', *Journal of Medieval History*, 24 (1998), pp .297–311 at 299–300; James Davis, 'Selling Food and Drink after the Black Death', in Mark Bailey and Stephen Rigby, eds, *Town and Countryside in the*

numbers of cooks, innkeepers and shopkeepers in a city like London, as well as complaints about the detritus from meat and fish processing.[25]

However, in the bustle of the medieval marketplace the niceties of improved consumer spending power may not have been fully appreciated by urban consumers who were experiencing significant price inflation. John Munro's revision of the Phelps Brown and Hopkins price data shows how, after the Black Death, wheat prices remained stable or buoyant until 1376, before falling away. Concurrently, prices for pigs, mutton, fish, malt and cloth were all relatively high throughout the 1360s and 1370s.[26] Like wages, these price trends did not go unnoticed. As soon as the Black Death hit England, the Ordinance of Labourers (1349) expressed concern over the rise in artisanal wages, and stated that victuals should be sold for a 'reasonable price', 'so that such sellers have a moderate profit and not excessive, as shall be reasonably required by the distance of the places wherefrom such victuals are carried.'[27] The statute of 1363 is often cited in terms of its attention to sumptuary laws and clothing, but the legislation also noted the inflationary pressure on poultry prices due to 'great dearth' and the subsequent need for the enforcement of lower prices.[28] In London, these concerns were specifically addressed by the civic authorities in a range of ordinances. Added to this, there was a broader concern that victuallers in the city were misinterpreting their privileges and interfering with the influx of victuals brought by outsiders. As a result, in 1357, the mayor and aldermen of London were given authority to look as closely at the activities of fishers, butchers and poulterers, as they had previously examined bakers, brewers and wine sellers.[29]

Price controls in retail markets had a long pedigree, dating back to at least the early thirteenth century for the assizes of bread and ale.[30] The London

---

Age of the Black Death: Essays in Honour of John Hatcher (Turnhout: Brepols, 2012), pp. 351–406 at 353, 356.

[25] Martha Carlin, *Medieval Southwark* (London: Hambledon Press, 1996), pp. 192–200; Gervase Rosser, *Medieval Westminster, 1200–1540* (Oxford: Clarendon Press, 1989), pp. 122–33; Ernest L. Sabine, 'Butchering in Mediaeval London', *Speculum*, 8 (1933), pp. 335–53; Barron, *London in the Later Middle Ages*, pp. 23, 58–9, 263. Studies of Winchester and Colchester show that after an initial fall in brewers immediately after 1349, there was then a surge in numbers and production until the end of the fourteenth century (Derek Keene, *Survey of Medieval Winchester* (two volumes; Oxford: Clarendon Press, 1985), I: 268–9; Richard H. Britnell, *Growth and Decline in Colchester, 1300–1525* (Cambridge: Cambridge University Press, 1986), pp. 90–3, 194; Marjorie K. McIntosh, *Working Women in English Society, 1300–1620* (Cambridge: Cambridge University Press, 2005), pp. 152–4.

[26] 'The Phelps Brown and Hopkins 'basket of consumables' commodity price series and craftsmen's wage series, 1264–1700: Revised by John H. Munro', at: https://economics.utoronto.ca/munro5/ResearchData.html.

[27] SR, I: 307–8, 23 Edw. III c.6 (1349).

[28] SR, I: 378–9, 37 Edw. III c.3 (1363).

[29] SR, I: 351, 31 Edw. III st.1 c.10 (1357); see also CCR 1349–54, pp. 360–1.

[30] James Davis, *Medieval Market Morality: Life, Law and Ethics in the English Marketplace, 1200–1500* (Cambridge: Cambridge University Press, 2012), pp. 222–50.

authorities regularly produced detailed price lists, such as that in 1300 for bulls, cows, pigs, sheep, eggs and certain fish; any who refused to abide by these could lose their right to sell in the city's markets.[31] The admission of a new mayor was often followed by the publication of new schedules of prices for poultry and meat.[32] However, the decades after the Black Death saw a noticeable surge in ordinances and public proclamations concerned with the enhanced cost of victuals and the rhetoric of a 'reasonable' price or profit.[33] In 1361, London officials sought to cap prices of victuals in order 'that the sellers may gain a reasonable but not excessive profit', and 'the city by their efforts and diligence may be brought again to its due estate'.[34] This language was also used in the statutory legislation of 1363.[35] In 1378, roasted fowl was included in price controls, and in 1380 the pies that contained rabbit and goose.[36] Such regulatory reiteration and stringency was as much a barometer of anxiety as it was a salve.[37] As with labour costs, the authorities were struggling to counteract price inflation in the new economic environment. The butchers in April 1377 responded to claims of high prices for their lambs by claiming 'that they could not sell them for less without loss'.[38] It was in this environment, where prices were seen to be inflationary, that customers were becoming more sensitive to the quality of goods; these were exactly the issues on which Gower himself concentrated in the *Mirour de l'Omme*.

The problems caused by rising prices were exacerbated by a shortage of lower denomination silver coin. An increase in English gold coins in the 1350s sustained the value of the overall currency, but this could not conceal the shortage of silver coin in the mid to late fourteenth century. The volume of silver coinage had reached its peak in the early fourteenth century, and then fell steadily and significantly in the decades either side of the Black Death. This was partly the result of a general European silver bullion famine, but was also the product of the lack of issue of halfpenny and farthing coins. There were numerous commons petitions through the 1360s

[31] *Munimenta Gildhallae Londoniensis*, II/i, pp. 192–3, 304–5; Robert Braid, 'Behind the Ordinance of Labourers: Economic Regulation and Market Control in London before the Black Death', *Journal of Legal History*, 34 (2013), pp. 3–30 at 13.
[32] CLB, H, pp. 108, 110–11 (1378), 348–9 (1389); CLB, G, pp. 102–3 (1357), 270–3 (1370).
[33] CLB, F, p. 212 (1350); CLB, G, p. 242 (c. 1369); *Memorials of London*, pp. 253–8 (1350), 347–8 (1370). For a broader perspective, see Gwen Seabourne, *Royal Regulation of Loans and Sales in Medieval England* (Woodbridge: Boydell and Brewer, 2003), pp. 160–1.
[34] CCR 1360–4, pp. 284–5 (1361); Davis, *Medieval Market Morality*, p. 226.
[35] SR, I: 378–9, 37 Edw. III c.3 (1363). See also SR, II: 63, 13 Ric. II st.1 c.8 (1389–90).
[36] *Memorials of London*, pp. 426, 438.
[37] This had also been the case with animal prices in the 1310s (Buchanan Sharp, 'Royal Paternalism and the Moral Economy in the Reign of Edward II: The Response to the Great Famine', *Economic History Review*, 66 (2013), pp. 628–47).
[38] CLB, H, pp. 61–2 (23 April 1377).

and 1370s about this shortage of smaller coin for the purchase of foodstuffs.[39] By 1380, there was a specific concern about the lack of coins to buy small lots of bread and ale.[40]

In general, changing patterns of consumption were beginning to reshape urban retail markets, with certain trades benefitting from the demand for better quality foodstuffs and petty manufactures. However, after the initial arrival of the plague, price inflation was sustained until the mid-1370s. By the time Gower was writing *Mirour de l'Omme*, there had been twenty-five years of complaints and regulation about prices and quality, alongside anxiety about buoyant retail markets. This historical context adds texture to our reading of Gower's sections on artisans and retailers. His catalogue of deceptions, unreasonable prices and a lack of goods available for small change replicated the prejudices of his intended audience, without having to address the underlying economic realities. For Gower, the answer lay partly in individual redemption but also in better civic governance.

The Good Parliament and Civic Governance

Gower was writing *Mirour de l'Omme* after the events of the Good Parliament in July 1376, which sought to tackle the corruption of certain royal officials and supporters. At this Parliament, three London aldermen, Richard Lyons, Adam Bury and John Pecche, were impeached by the Commons for having abused their positions for personal gain. Lyons, along with William Latimer, was specifically upbraided for how he exploited staple licenses and wool customs.[41] John Pecche and Adam Bury were both previous mayors of London and they were accused, alongside Lyons, of having corruptly manipulated the sweet wine monopoly of the city. The three impeached London men were subsequently abandoned by the Council of Aldermen, who removed them from their office.[42] It was perhaps these men that Gower had in mind in the *Mirour* when he commented about citizens and rulers who committed fraud in their search for personal advancement: 'an evil burgher ['*burgois*'] should

---

[39] Martin Allen, *Mints and Money in Medieval England* (Cambridge: Cambridge University Press, 2012), pp. 332–7, 343–5, 360–1; Martin Allen, 'The Proportions of the Denominations in English Mint Outputs, 1351–1485', *British Numismatic Journal*, 77 (2007), pp. 190–209 at 192–4.

[40] *Parliament Rolls of Medieval England*, eds Chris Given-Wilson, Paul Brand, Seymour Phillips, Mark Ormrod, Geoffrey Martin, Anne Curry and Rosemary Horrox (Woodbridge: Boydell Press, 2005), (cited below as *PROME*) at British History Online http://www.british-history.ac.uk/no-series/parliament-rolls-medieval, Richard II: November 1380, no. 32 [accessed 12 October 2017].

[41] George Holmes, *The Good Parliament* (Oxford: Clarendon Press, 1975), pp. 108–14; Pamela Nightingale, 'Capitalists, Crafts and Constitutional Change in Late Fourteenth-Century London', *Past and Present*, 124 (1989), pp. 3–35 at 14–15.

[42] *CLB, H*, pp. 30–1, 38–40 (1376).

be cut off severely before he brings the city to ruin ... I tell you that when a citizen turns away from right and allies himself with wrong, he should be hanged or drowned, before the people go astray because of him and the city becomes divided' (MO: 26389–412).

John Pecche was a vintner, fishmonger and draper who had served as mayor in 1361 and acted in concert with Richard Lyons, not only in raising loans for the Crown but also in the organisation of the sweet wine monopoly, which Pecche obtained from Lyons in November 1373.[43] It is notable that taverners and wine occupy an inordinate amount of space in *Mirour de l'Omme* compared to other retail trades. Gower himself implies his personal interest as a frequent consumer, but there may also be more to this passage relating to the events of 1376, about which some of his audience were only too aware. At first glance, Gower's criticisms of taverners are steeped in convention, echoing the complaints of many medieval pastoral and moral texts about the mixing of new wine with old, the blending of different varieties, or the watering down of the product. The false friendship of taverners in order to elicit more sales is recurrent (MO: 25993–26124).[44] However, it is noticeable that Gower does not, directly, make the traditional complaint in this section that the tavern was akin to a devil's school in enticing people from church and teaching them sin; though it is alluded to in the vignette of city ladies 'trotting with mincing steps to the tavern in the morning before going to church or to the market'.[45] Rather, he was more concerned with the quality of the wine, practices of concealment, and excessive prices: 'He who thus keeps a tavern is not exempt from falseness' (MO: 26005–16). In London, taverners and vintners could be amerced for refusing to allow their customers to see the wine being drawn; presumably a precaution against mixing or watering-down of wine.[46] Wine was one of

---

[43] See Roger L. Axworthy, 'Pecche, John (d.1380)', *Oxford Dictionary of National Biography* (Oxford University Press, 2004, online edition, January 2008) [http://www.oxforddnb.com/view/article/52212].

[44] *Middle English Sermons*, ed. Woodburn O. Ross (EETS, o.s. 209 (1940)), pp. 234 (ll. 22–31), 235 (ll. 19–24), 236 (ll. 1–9); John de Bromyard, *Summa Predicantium* (Nuremburg, 1518), cap. 20, 'Amor'; *Dan Michel's Ayenbite of Inwyt*, ed. Richard Morris (EETS, o.s. 23, (1866)), pp. 44–5, 56–7.

[45] *Robert of Brunne's 'Handlyng Synne'*, AD 1303, ed. Frederick J. Furnivall (EETS, o.s. 119 (1901)), p. 37 (ll. 1017–1034); *The Book of Vices and Virtues*, ed. W. Nelson Francis (EETS, o.s. 217 (1942)), pp. 53 (l. 26), 54 (l. 19); *Jacob's Well: An English Treatise on the Cleansing of Man's Conscience*, ed. Arthur Brandeis (EETS, o.s. 115 (1900)), pp. 147 (l. 25), 148 (l. 12). Earlier, when discussing the sins of gluttony and drunkenness, Gower does state: 'the tavern, rightly speaking, is the devil's church' (MO: 8257–68).

[46] *Munimenta Gildhallae Londoniensis*, II/i, pp. 303–4, 425 (1320–1). This was reiterated in 1370 (*Memorials of London*, pp. 341–3). For more on the wine trade, see Margery K. James, *Studies in the Medieval Wine Trade*, ed. Elspeth M. Veale (Oxford: Clarendon Press, 1971); Seabourne, *Royal Regulation of Loans and Sales in Medieval England*, pp. 76–7, 79, 85. For a case in 1353 involving two Genoese tavern-keepers in London

the main items that were subject to assize legislation demanding that food and drink should be sold at a reasonable price and without excessive profit, which was reinforced in the decades after the Black Death.[47] On 19 May 1376, around the time that Gower was writing *Mirour de l'Omme*, a London proclamation ordered that no taverner should sell Gascon wine (or 'Ryve') for no more than 10d per gallon or wine of la Rochelle for 8d.[48]

However, Gower's specific iteration of sweet wines also hints at another agenda. In one section, Gower's taverner offers: 'vernage wine, Greek wine, and Malmsey. In order to make them spend more he names many kinds of wines to them: Candy, Ribole, Romanian, Provençal, and Montross; and he claims to have Rivere and Muscatel in his possession for sale. But he has not a third of these; rather he says this as a novelty, in order to induce them to drink' (MO: 26089–100). These were all sweet wines and in London the retail of such wines was a purchased monopoly, one held firstly by Richard Lyons at three taverns in Cheap, Walbrook and Lombard Street from 26 August 1365 (when Adam Bury was also mayor) to November 1373, and thereafter by Pecche. Lyons' original grant (1365) at an annual rent of £200 stipulated that his sweet wines should be sold at a reasonable price, and stipulated the prices as: 'a gallon of fine vernage at 32d, other vernage at 2s., Malvesyn, Romanye, Ryvere, Rybole, Candy, Clarre and all other sweet wines at 16d.'[49] The consternation caused by the monopoly grant is evident in the inquiry called just three months later to scrutinise Lyons 'to see that the wines are sound, and to condemn such as they find to be bad'.[50] In a similar fashion, there appears to have been some ambiguity as to whether the monopoly purchased by Pecche in 1373 went against a recent parliamentary ordinance.[51] Two weeks later, a royal writ was sent to the mayor, Adam Bury, demanding that he set a reasonable price for sweet wines and to publicly proclaim it: 'vernage at 2s a gallon, 'Ryvere', 'Mawvesie' and 'Romeneye' at 16d; Candye, Trubidiane, Mountrosse, Greek, Creet, Province and Clarre at 12d.'[52] This built upon an ordinance from the previous September, which included non-sweet wines from Gascony and the Rhine and ordered that customers should be able to see their wine being drawn from sealed casks. It was in this proclamation that the authorities encouraged customers to complain if they were concerned about

---

who were selling red, white and sweet wine and thus faced suspicions of mixing, see *Memorials of London*, p. 270.

[47] *Memorials of London*, pp. 341–3 (1370). For the longer history of the assize of wine, see Britnell, *Commercialisation of English Society*, p. 94; Davis, *Medieval Market Morality*, pp. 248–51.

[48] *CLB, H*, p. 27 (19 May 1376).

[49] Thomas Rymer, *Foedera* (ten volumes; third edition; The Hague, 1739–45), volume iii, part ii, p. 768; *CLB, G*, p. 199 (1365).

[50] *CLB, G*, p. 204 (30 Nov 1365).

[51] *CLB, G*, p. 318 (30 Nov 1373).

[52] *CLB, G*, pp. 318–19 (13 Dec 1373).

the price or quality of wine.[53] By the time of the Good Parliament, Pecche was accused of taking an excessive profit of 40d on every butt he sold.[54] He denied the charge and claimed that he had the approval of the mayor and fifteen aldermen, but he was nevertheless condemned by both the parliament and his fellow aldermen.[55] The judgement was reversed by February 1377, but Pecche (like Lyons) remained excluded from any office. By 1382, the sweet wine monopoly was formally ended by statute.[56] Although Gower makes no direct reference to Lyons, Pecche or Bury, his mercantile readership would surely have been aware of the monopoly on sweet wine and the associations with those impeached in 1376.

In discussing the events of 1376, the city's Letter Books recorded that 'the commonalty have further complained that for many years past they have been badly treated' by the city's mayors and aldermen who had used office for their own personal gain.[57] Permeating through the proceedings of the Good Parliament were not just issues relating to royal offices, but also concerns about civic governance. This included long-standing demands for constitutional reform in the city, aimed especially at the main governing body of the Court of Aldermen but also at the composition of the Common Council. Rule by members of the elite was an accepted paradigm in medieval urban society, since they were considered the better and able sort for this role. However, in turn, they were expected to serve the common good, including the poor, and corrupt officials could, in theory, be justly opposed.[58] Indeed, in many late medieval English towns, civic governance tended to generate antagonism and complaint.[59]

For Londoners, the constitutional repercussions of the Good Parliament were significant since they paved the way for London's Common Council to achieve a more prominent position alongside the Council of Aldermen, with election by ward being replaced with elections of representatives of the 'misteries', or crafts, according to their size. This allowed a broader

---

[53] CLB, G, p. 311 (14 Sep 1373). This, in turn reiterated an ordinance of 1 November 1372 that had explicitly condemned mixing of wines (CLB, G, p. 301). A London ordinance of 21 August 1377 decreed that six trustworthy men of the vintners' craft should survey the wine sold in taverns, ensure that a mark was used on vessels to distinguish certain wines, and 'that no taverner hang any cloth or other obstacle in front of his cellar door, or sell wine beyond the price at which it had been appraised' (CLB, H, p. 74).
[54] CLB, H, p. 39 (1376).
[55] CLB, H, pp. 40, 44 (August 1376); PROME, Edward II: April 1376, no. 33.
[56] SR, II: 28, 6 Ric. II st.1 c.7 (1382).
[57] CLB, H, p. 38 (1 August 1376).
[58] Susan Reynolds, *An Introduction to the History of Medieval English Towns* (Oxford: Oxford University Press, 1977), pp. 171–7; Rosser, *Medieval Westminster*, pp. 243–8; Davis, *Medieval Market Morality*, pp. 163–5.
[59] Stephen H. Rigby, 'Urban "Oligarchy" in Late Medieval England', in John A. F. Thomson, ed., *Towns and Townspeople in the Fifteenth Century* (Gloucester: Sutton, 1988), pp. 62–86.

range of trades to attend. Over forty guilds thus provided Common Council members, who swore that 'for no favour shall you maintain an individual benefit against the common weal of the City, preserving for each mistery its reasonable customs'.[60] Indeed, both the aldermen and commons were enjoined to consult at least eight times a year 'about the common necessities of the city'.[61] By March 1377, there were changes to the way in which aldermen were elected; the Common Council decreed that an alderman removed from office for misbehaviour should not be re-elected, while others might be reconsidered after the gap of a year.[62] The driving force behind such changes was a widespread perception that certain aldermen had been too self-interested in their actions: 'whereas the commonalty have further complained for many years past they have been badly treated by reason of divers mayors and aldermen, disregarding their oath and the needs of the people, having made ordinances for their own private advantage.'[63] This was also a common theme of Gower's work as when he denigrated the ambitions of members of the city elite: 'it is an abuse when one single man, in the foolish belief that he is superior to the others, seeks honors for himself alone and thereby produces a division in the city' (MO: 26365–76). It would be a mistake to identify a single individual as Gower's target here since his complaint is about how the sins of individuals might usurp the common good.[64] However, for his audience, the Good Parliament had demonstrated that specific examples were readily available.

At one point in *Mirour de l'Omme* Gower makes a subtle allusion when he states that 'There is no trade of any sort in which Fraud (if he is so inclined) does not have twenty-four hirelings ['*soldoiers*'] who have refused to do good; and this troubles us in the city – both burghers and officials' (MO: 25957–68). This is an interesting comment upon the governance of the city, and Gower goes on to assert that crafts can be substantially good if they operate under the right direction (MO: 25969–80). It is worth considering why Gower chose the number 'twenty-four' in this passage about civic governance. A contemporary London audience may well have made an immediate connection with the Council of Aldermen, a body of twenty-four individuals who were facing immense criticism at the time that Gower

---

[60] *CLB*, H, p. 42 (9 August 1376). Only briefly in 1351 had the misteries previously elected members in this way (*CLB*, F, pp. 237–8).
[61] *CLB*, H, p. 40 (1 August 1376).
[62] Ruth Bird, *The Turbulent London of Richard II* (London: Longmans, Green & Co, 1949), pp. 7–13, 36–42; Frank Rexroth, *Deviance and Power in Late Medieval London* (Cambridge: Cambridge University Press, 2007), pp. 134–5; *CLB*, H, pp. 38–41, 60. The decree that aldermen should serve only one year at a time revived an earlier practice that had lapsed (*Munimenta Gildhallae Londoniensis*, I: 269; *CLB*, E, pp. 104–5 (1319)).
[63] *CLB*, H, p. 38 (1 August 1376).
[64] Robert Epstein, 'London, Southwark, Westminster: Gower's Urban Contexts', in Siân Echard, ed., *A Companion to Gower* (Cambridge: D. S. Brewer, 2004), pp. 43–60 at 50.

was writing. Indeed, Gower is critical of the burghers and rulers of London, regarding them as disruptive to the common good as much as the individual traders who commit fraud (MO: 26353–64). He states: 'so there is no one who does justice to our city, and thus Fraud goes everywhere creating trouble throughout the city' (MO: 26413–24). Gower repeated a number of these themes in his next major work, *Vox Clamantis*, reminding the mayor that 'it is the onerous responsibility of his office to uphold the laws' and thus bring together the merchants and artisans of the city (VC: V.9.655–76). There is perhaps a hint here of the factional politics that was rife in London at this time, but Gower makes no explicit comment and the discussion remains broad-brush in encouraging unity and honesty. Nevertheless, it is worth considering this context more fully, especially the reforms of John Northampton, as it highlights how Gower's criticisms of urban governance and trading practices were akin to the anxieties of many contemporary Londoners.

The Reforms of John Northampton

There has been much scholarly discussion of the civic upheavals in London in the 1370s and 1380s involving John Northampton and Nicholas Brembre.[65] George Unwin saw these conflicts as between the victuallers (headed by the grocer Nicholas Brembre) and non-victuallers (headed by the draper John Northampton), while Ruth Bird distinguished the struggle as between the elite and the rest, with Northampton being presented as a rather manipulative figure.[66] However, it is simplistic to view the unrest as being between two clearly defined factions. As Pamela Nightingale has shown, allegiances and aims shifted and varied over time, with victuallers and non-victuallers appearing on both sides.[67] Indeed, the council reforms of August 1376 were the result of a cross-alliance between drapers, mercers, goldsmiths and grocers, with the latter possibly satisfied that the Calais staple seemed secure. If there was a central issue in the dispute it was the privileges enjoyed by exporters, which benefitted rich London merchants so long as the staple was overseas, along with the complaint that the elite were dismissive of the needs of retail trade in the city. This was, of course, part of Gower's criticism of alien merchants (MO: 25429–88), which again suggests that he was tapping

---

[65] Bird, *Turbulent London of Richard II*, pp. 63–101; Pamela Nightingale, *A Medieval Mercantile Community: The Grocers' Company and the Politics and Trade of London, 1000–1485* (New Haven: Yale University Press, 1995), pp. 244–317; Nightingale, 'Capitalists, Crafts and Constitutional Change', pp. 3–35. See also Lianna Farber, *An Anatomy of Trade in Medieval Writing: Value, Consent, and Community* (Ithaca: Cornell University Press, 2006).

[66] George Unwin, *The Gilds and Companies of London* (London: Methuen, 1908); Bird, *Turbulent London of Richard II*.

[67] Nightingale, 'Capitalists, Crafts and Constitutional Change', pp. 19–20.

into issues of common consensus among Londoners, rather than favouring one side or another in political skirmishes.

There has been a tendency to assume that Gower would have been naturally opposed to John Northampton and his policies, particularly because of the comments Gower makes about the unruly commons in the Prologue to the *Confessio Amantis* (Pro.499–528) and because of his allusion in *Vox Clamantis* to a 'rude, untutored man' who is unexpectedly elevated to power in the city and who wins the 'adulation of fools' (VC: V.15.845–50, 863–70), which has been viewed as a reference to John Northampton.[68] However, there is no real sense that in *Mirour* Gower was commenting directly on this aspect of the fluctuating fortunes of civic politics, such as Northampton's temporary loss of influence after February 1377. Other matters were more prominent at this time, particularly those raised at the Good Parliament.

The approach of some studies of London politics in this period is perhaps coloured by the downfall of Northampton from 1383, his loss of royal support, agitation in the streets, and his trial in August 1384, which shaped his later reputation. At that trial, Thomas Usk, who had served Northampton from 1381–83, denigrated Northampton because of his appeal to the 'smale people' and vernacular proclamations, arguing that he misled them and stirred them towards sedition.[69] This was a *post hoc* attempt to tarnish Northampton with the stigma of the 1381 revolt, even though there is no indication that he was party to it. Nevertheless, this was a theme taken up by Thomas Walsingham, who also entwined these accusations of sedition with ideas of Lollardy and heresy.[70] Similarly, in 1384, a complaint was made that the Common Council was acting with more noise than reason and so elections were returned to the ward while the restrictions on aldermanic elections were relaxed.[71] This was another step towards stemming Northampton's influence and reshaping his legacy. It is important to note, however, that at the time Gower was writing *Mirour de l'Omme*, Northampton had not yet gained a toxic reputation.

---

[68] Sheila Lindenbaum, 'London Texts and Literate Practices', in Wallace, *The Cambridge History of Medieval English Literature*, pp. 284–309 at 292; Bertolet, 'Fraud, Division and Lies', p. 57.

[69] Helen Carrel, 'Food, Drink and Public Order in the London *Liber Albus*', *Urban History*, 33 (2006), pp. 176–94 at 181; *A Book of London English, 1384–1425*, eds Raymond W. Chambers and Beatrice M. Daunt (Oxford: Clarendon Press, 1931), pp. 22–31; *Knighton's Chronicle 1337–1396*, ed. Geoffrey H. Martin (Oxford: Clarendon Press, 1995), pp. 298–307; Paul Strohm, *Hochon's Arrow: The Social Imagination of Fourteenth-Century Texts* (Princeton: Princeton University Press, 1992), pp.145–60.

[70] *The St Albans Chronicle: The Chronica Maiora of Thomas Walsingham, Volume I, 1376–1394*, eds John Taylor, Wendy R. Childs and Leslie Watkiss (Oxford: Clarendon Press, 2003), pp. 612–15.

[71] *CLB, H*, pp. 228–31 (1383–84); Carrel, 'Food, Drink and Public Order', p. 180; c.f. *CLB, H*, p. 364 (1391?) for an ordinance that forbade discussion of Brembre or Northampton so as to heal division.

Before 1383, John Northampton was undoubtedly mired in city politics and factionalism and was at the forefront of the civic reforms of 1376–77, but he was also an established member of the merchant elite who was later elected to the mayoralty in 1381 with little or no contestation.[72] As part of his attempt to curry favour in the aftermath of the revolt, one of his first acts was to reinforce the city's gates against future incursions.[73] In 1382, Richard II openly supported Northampton's renewed candidacy.[74] We should not assume that all of his policies were the product of factional differences or that his appeal to 'populism' necessarily outraged all the staplers in the early months. On some issues concerning trades, prices and aliens there was, initially at least, a degree of unity among Londoners and Gower's text was part of that pervasive urban mentality. Certainly, the ordinances promulgated by John Northampton during his mayoralty were deliberately intended to appeal to a broad audience within London; parallels could be drawn here with Gower's claim to represent the popular voice. Helen Carrel notes that 'contemporary assessments of the efficiency and success of civic authorities were based upon their ability to administer the food trade fairly, a belief that John Northampton had been able to capitalize upon in 1382'.[75] A city's liberties might even be forfeit to the king if it failed to adequately feed and regulate its food trades, as London had been threatened with in 1354.[76] As such, the ordinances during Northampton's mayoralty reflected concerns that had been bubbling under the surface for some time. They provide an interesting insight into contemporary concerns, upon which Gower had previously commented at length, about prices and regulation of the retail trades.

In early 1382, Northampton and the Common Council responded to concerns about inflated prices of foodstuffs and the shortage of coin, alongside accusations that certain traders were making excessive profits.[77] The very matters that were so prominent in *Mirour de l'Omme* – high prices, value for money, proper measures, and feeding the poor – were now addressed by the city's government. Bakers were ordered to make farthing loaves and brewers to sell ale in farthing measures for the aid of the poor; the implication being that previously the smallest item was sold for a halfpenny. Farthing measures were made and distributed to assist in this production. To address the lack of small denomination coinage, the mayor even ordered a batch of farthings from the London mint to the total value of £80 (76,800 farthings in total). Soon after, on 10 May, another ordinance sought to stop the

---

[72] Nightingale, 'Capitalists, Crafts and Constitutional Change', p. 25.
[73] *CLB, H*, pp. 171–3 (1–2 Nov 1381).
[74] Nightingale, 'Capitalists, Crafts and Constitutional Change', p. 34; Nightingale, *Medieval Mercantile Community*, p. 245; Barron, *London in the Later Middle Ages*, p. 31.
[75] Carrel, 'Food, Drink and Public Order', p. 184.
[76] *PROME*, Edward II: April 1354, no. 26; Carrel, 'Food, Drink and Public Order', pp. 184–5.
[77] *CLB, H*, pp. 183–4 (May 1382); Rexroth, *Deviance and Power in Late Medieval London*, pp. 341–3.

re-selling of ale, even in inns.[78] This provision was reinforced ten days later along with a reminder of the intent that farthings should be used.[79] Further proclamations in 1382 reiterated the need for proper and full measures in sales made by brewers and innkeepers; an issue that had consternated Gower (MO: 26305–28).[80] Early in Northampton's mayoralty, there was also a number of proclamations regarding the sale of wine and selling above the prescribed price. In particular, vintners were warned against placing old wine into cellars where new wine was also being stored.[81]

Nevertheless, the principles underlying these orders were not radical. Northampton was drawing upon older concerns, such as that addressed by the inquiry of September 1379 into the scarcity of bread in the city.[82] In that same year, hostelers were warned about the price and weight of their commodities, and against keeping old wine with new.[83] However, Northampton was pursuing his aims with more rigour and was expressing his policies in the language of morality and civic order.[84] Similarly, the exclusion of victuallers from public office (or, at least, their pursuit of such trade while in office) was promoted by the majority of civic officials, and it drew upon older precedents.[85] Nonetheless, one can also see the revival of this measure as an attempt to address some of the criticisms aimed at civic officials in Mirour de l'Omme. Modern historians have questioned Northampton's political motives but, as a means to an end, he did seek to curry popular support and presented himself as a defender of the common good.[86] His appeal to morality cut across sectional divides just as Gower's had.[87]

Gower also demanded in Mirour de l'Omme that victuallers should face stronger penalties for their deceptions and high prices.[88] The taverner should be hanged on the gallows 'if he were given justice', for he endangers life (MO: 25993–26004). The baker too should have been hanged, 'for bread is man's sustenance, and he who offends against bread (contrary to the common laws) takes people's lives away' (MO: 26173–96). Such assertions went beyond the legal options, but for his audience it would have reflected

---

[78] Rexroth, *Deviance and Power in Late Medieval London*, pp. 343–5.
[79] Rexroth, *Deviance and Power in Late Medieval London*, pp. 346–7.
[80] CLB, H, p. 201 (18 October 1382).
[81] CLB, H, pp. 163 (26 April 1381), 173 (16 Nov 1381); *Calendar of Plea and Memoranda Rolls of the City of London, 1381–1412*, ed. Arthur H. Thomas (London: His Majesty's Stationery Office, 1932), p. 2 (29 Nov 1381).
[82] CLB, H, p. 136 (21 Sep 1379). On this occasion, problems with the water supply were identified.
[83] CLB, H, p. 140 (15 Dec 1379).
[84] Rexroth, *Deviance and Power in Late Medieval London*, p. 159.
[85] SR, I: 178, 12 Edw. II c.6 (1318); II: 28, 6 Ric. II st.1 c.9 (1382).
[86] Rexroth, *Deviance and Power in Late Medieval London*, pp. 138–40.
[87] Rexroth, *Deviance and Power in Late Medieval London*, pp. 143–4.
[88] For this rhetoric see also Langland, *Piers Plowman: The B Version*, III: 76–100; *The Simonie: A Parallel-Text Edition*, eds Dan Embree and Elizabeth Urquhart (Heidelberg: Carl Winter Universititslag, 1991), pp. 65 (B25–6), 98–100 (B427–80).

a concern that punishments were too lenient or not enacted to the extent they could be, such as through a more regular use of the pillory or hurdle. Just two years later, Northampton was enacting the types of reform that Gower had called for and exerting a strong punitive response. During his mayoralty, there were more examples of the use of the pillory than any other fourteenth-century mayor (bar a slight surge in 1364). Frank Rexroth estimates that in previous years just two to four cases a year led to the pillory, but during Northampton's first year as mayor there were sixteen.[89] One example from 24 August 1382 demonstrates the spectacle that was intended, when Reginald atte Chaumbre was sentenced to be punished for selling unwholesome fish by standing in the pillory for one hour on six market days while the fish was burnt beneath him.[90]

Punishments could now be more spectacular and visually striking. In a proclamation of 13 October 1382, any broker who was found guilty of false dealing or usury was to be carried to the pillory on Cornhill with 'his head uncovered, his feet bare, without a girdle, and sitting on a horse without a saddle, his head to the horse's tail, to remain there for an hour, and thence to be carried back to prison, where is to remain four weeks, unless he pay to the Chamberlain the sum of £20 for the use of the Commonalty'.[91] In this expansion of the use of corporal punishment, Northampton was critical of the previous laxity of the Council of Aldermen and declared that it was his duty to protect the poor; in such matters it appears that he and Gower were in tune with the zeitgeist.[92]

Gower also recommended the dragging of bakers down the street as a necessary means to bring them back to honesty (MO: 26173–96). William atte Settle was to face this fate in April 1383 when he was drawn on the hurdle towards the pillory, while the short-weight loaf hung from his neck.[93] This punishment was thus occasionally employed in London, even though such painful humiliation was usually reserved for those sent to the gallows for treason.[94] Proclamations and humiliating corporal punishment were the public face of market regulation, which included a reading of the verdict. The worst excesses of traders were vilified for all to see, such as in the pillory on Cornhill. This was the type of visual display of fraudulent behaviour that

---

[89] Rexroth, *Deviance and Power in Late Medieval London*, p. 147.
[90] Reginald held a royal office and so this sentence was deferred until a decision was made by the king, with the outcome now not being known (CLB, H, p. 197 (24 August 1382)).
[91] CLB, H, p. 199 (13 October 1382). See also Rexroth, *Deviance and Power in Late Medieval London*, pp. 146–7; *Munimenta Gildhallae Londoniensis*, III, pp. 425–6.
[92] Rexroth, *Deviance and Power in Late Medieval London*, p. 153.
[93] *Calendar of Plea and Memoranda Rolls*, p. 41. For similar punishments, see also *Munimenta Gildhallae Londoniensis*, III, pp. 83–4; *Memorials of London*, p. 498.
[94] James Davis, 'Spectacular Punishment: Capital Punishment in Medieval English Towns', in Joëlle Rollo-Koster, ed., *Death in Medieval Europe: Death Scripted and Death Choreographed* (London: Routledge, 2017), pp. 130–48.

informed Londoners' expectations of trade, and Gower's strident language about punishment suggests that he too was stirred by such spectacles. Northampton's ordinances and punishments reveal a broader sense within the civic elite that the current state of London society was lacking and needed reform, but this was not particular to a so-called rising urban middle class. As much as Gower was previously promulgating a message of reformation in social mores and practice, so Northampton too was seeking to address popular perceptions about trade and morals within the city that cut across sectional divides.

Gower's London

The analysis offered here has suggested that, in establishing a context for Gower's discussion of trade, we should shift away from claims about the moral anxieties generated by a supposedly new money economy and instead focus on the more immediate context in which the poet was writing. As scholars like Bertolet, Ladd and Hsy have all recently noted, traditional anti-mercantile concerns were undoubtedly an underlying foundation for *Mirour de l'Omme*, but in many ways Gower took the existence of the commercial system for granted and even highlighted its potential benefits. A closer view of the specific anxieties of the 1370s allows us to delve more deeply into why Gower concentrated on certain topics and not others, and provides an insight into the urban anxieties that resonated at that time. Gower was certainly conservative, iterative and nostalgic, and, in expressing his social views, he drew upon old tropes, worn rhetoric and traditional paradigms. However, this does not mean that he was out of step with the concerns and issues of late fourteenth-century London; issues that mattered to merchants and non-merchants alike. Even as he reiterated the conventions of estates satire, reminding readers and listeners of the importance of saving their souls, he touched upon contemporary disquiet regarding prices, the coinage, quality, governance and corruption. Gower enthusiastically stressed the need to heighten the existing regulatory framework, while reinforcing accepted concepts around open markets, transparency of transactions, honest dealings and just prices. These were age-old concepts, but in some ways they took on new urgency for the inhabitants of 1370s London who were facing a time of price inflation, coin shortages, war and political upheaval. Gower was writing *Mirour de l'Omme* just as the governance of London was experiencing reforms in order to excise corruption and widen participation.

The *Mirour de l'Omme* thus provides an insight into some of the prevalent attitudes and concerns of the time, concerns which help explain why, a couple of years later, John Northampton's attempts to reform London's retail trade were so popular. Northampton instigated legislation to soothe popular anxieties about prices and the currency, whilst also proposing a lower threshold of tolerance for commercial abuses that resulted in a surge in the use of corporal punishment. Whether this was effective or not is debatable, but the policies were as much about perception as practicalities. Gower was promulgating his ideas about the immediate need for reform in the governance of London's retail trade; John Northampton demonstrates that such pleas did not fall on deaf ears.

CHAPTER 6

MEN OF LAW

Anthony Musson

An Evolving Legal System

Gower's works were written during a formative period in the evolution of the judicial system and the legal profession. In particular his poetry was influenced by, and bears witness to, an expansion in the legal system and concomitantly of those staffing its institutions and facilitating the resolution of disputes. This expansion flowed from a heightened intensity in royal governance during the course of the thirteenth and fourteenth centuries with the number of judicial commissions and the amount of parliamentary legislation steadily increasing with a corresponding growth in the level of the supervision and regulation of daily life. New laws, notably the labour legislation and a range of economic and criminal offences required strict enforcement at the local level in order to be effective. Unsurprisingly, searching inquiries frequently revealed corruption and injustices on the part of royal and local officials.[1]

Richard II's reign saw fresh expectations about the legal system fuelled by enhanced accessibility of legal mechanisms and the greater availability of legal practitioners. They were expectations that could not wholly be met, however, as the system was already creaking under the weight of the public and private business which was coming before the courts. While royal government attempted to respond to the social and economic challenges of the period with new legislation, it ended up confounding these new expectations by confirming stereotypes and prejudices as well as perpetuating injustices. In particular there was much criticism by contemporaries of the outlay necessary for pursuing litigation, of the remuneration required by lawyers for their services and of the profits available for those involved in the administration of justice. Legitimate relationships with patrons and payment

---

I am most grateful to Stephen Rigby and Robert Yeager for their helpful comments.
[1] Anthony Musson and W. Mark Ormrod, *The Evolution of English Justice: Law Politics and Society in the Fourteenth Century* (Basingstoke: Macmillan, 1999), pp. 1–7. See also *The 1341 Royal Inquest in Lincolnshire*, ed. Bernard W. McClane (Lincoln Record Society, 78 (1988)).

for work done led to a focus not only on the processes of law (which were oiled by gifts and fees) but also on their social consequences: an accumulation of wealth evidenced by conspicuous consumption and social mobility. In an adversarial legal system where there were bound to be winners and losers, dissatisfaction inevitably centred on those within the system who gained whatever the outcome: the judges and lawyers. It is not surprising therefore, that the legal system and the legal profession were the subjects of voluble complaint, biting satire and suggestions for reform even before Gower entered the fray.[2]

The extent to which Gower was voicing contemporary concerns about fairness and injustice as well as the efficacy and efficiency of the judicial machinery of his day is as important for historians as it is for literary scholars.[3] Studying his writing within an historical context enables us to explore Gower's own engagement with the events, conflicts and processes of his day and to establish the conventions, discourses and sources which he drew upon in his criticisms of judicial structures and of the people who administered them. Furthermore, an examination of how Gower absorbed contemporary discourses and the language of law and justice, as well as of stylistic patterns in mooting, advocacy and drafting of petitions, allows us to evaluate the legal consciousness of both the author and his audience. In this respect an assessment of the sensibility of modern translators to the contemporary legal nuances of Gower's texts is also necessary. Finally, an analysis of Gower's literary works, allows us to compare the poet's presentation of the experience of the law with historical reality and so to appraise the identity, independence, consistency and authority of the poet's 'voice' and of the agenda that underlay it.

The Legal Profession

As we shall see, a number of scholars have speculated that Gower himself had enjoyed a legal training and that he practised as a lawyer at some point in his life. Indeed, there have even been suggestions that Gower should be seen as a real-life model for Chaucer's Man of Law.[4] However, in order to assess such claims, we need to consider what it meant to be a

---

[2] See, for example: 'A Song on the Venality of the King's Judges' in *Thomas Wright's Political Songs*, ed. Peter Coss (Cambridge: Cambridge University Press, 1996), pp. 224–8; 'An Outlaw's Song of Trailbaston' in *Anglo-Norman Political Songs*, ed. Isabel S. T. Aspin (Anglo Norman Text Society, 11 (1953)), pp. 73–6.

[3] Richard W. Kaeuper, 'Debating Law, Justice and Constitutionalism', in Richard W. Kaeuper, ed., *Law, Governance and Justice: New Views on Medieval Constitutionalism* (Leiden: Brill, 2013), pp. 1–14 at 4–6.

[4] John H. Fisher, *John Gower: Moral Philosopher and Friend of Chaucer* (New York: New York University Press, 1964), pp. 56–7; Matthew Giancarlo, *Parliament and Literature in Late Medieval England* (Cambridge: Cambridge University Press, 2007), p. 99.

'man of law' in the fourteenth century. Gower refers generically to 'men of law' ('gens du loy') (MO: 24185, 24292, 24295, 24315 *passim*) although he was also aware of 'apprentices' and 'serjeants' as gradations within the legal hierarchy (VC: VI.4.249; MO: 24361, 24373, 24386–7, 24421).[5] On the basis of contemporary governmental sources (including royal commissions, legislation and petitions) it is apparent that 'man of law' was a phrase which could be used without special differentiation when referring to lawyers generally.[6] In particular, the term was used to describe the preferred appointments to the 'quorum' of the peace commission and other such posts where legal knowledge was insisted upon.[7] The term is also employed in the royal ordinance of 1372 in respect of 'men of law' (*gents de ley*) elected to parliament as knights of the shire.[8] Application of the term by contemporaries in other documents or scenarios, however, demonstrates that things were not quite so straightforward and that the phrase 'man of law' could also be used in a much more specific sense to denote a 'serjeant', i.e., a high-ranking specialist advocate in the royal courts (VC: VI.4.2.49–50).[9] Thus, whilst Chaucer's pilgrim is referred to as the 'Sergeant of the Law' in the 'General Prologue' to *The Canterbury Tales*, the Host subsequently addresses him as 'Sire Man of Lawe'.[10] Similarly, Gower himself refers to both 'sergants

---

[5] In *Vox Clamantis* Gower employs the word 'causidicus' continuously (e.g. VI.1.42, 51, 56; VI.2.108, 111, 119, 137, 151). According to Meindl it was not a term commonly used in Gower's England and derives from usage in the courts of ancient Rome where it had contemptuous connotations. It may be used neutrally by Gower as a synonym for 'pleder' (reflecting the similarity of the text here to that of the *Mirour*) though it may gain resonances of the earlier sense through its repetition. It is translated by Eric Stockton simply as 'lawyer', which Meindl also feels captures the broader spectrum of the legal profession (including the civil and ecclesiastical sides) encompassed by the word (Robert Meindl, '*Semper Venalis*: Gower's Avaricious Lawyers', *Accessus*, Vol. I, No. 2 (2013), pp. 1–56 at 23–5 (Available at: http://scholarworks.wmich.edu/accessus/vol1/iss2/2.)

[6] Musson and Ormrod, *Evolution of English Justice*, pp. 56–7.

[7] Edward Powell, 'The Administration of Criminal Justice in Late Medieval England: Peace Sessions and Assizes', in Richard Eales and David Sullivan, eds, *The Political Context of Law* (London: Hambledon, 1987), pp. 49–60 at 55–6; Simon Walker, 'Yorkshire Justices of the Peace, 1389–1413', *EHR*, 108 (1993), pp. 281–313 at 291–8.

[8] 'Men of law' ought not to come to parliament as representatives because, as 'attorneys for private individuals', they 'procure and cause to be put forward in parliament many [private] petitions in the name of the commons' (*Parliament Rolls of Medieval England*, ed. C. Given Wilson *et al*. (Leicester: Scholarly Editions, 2005), Parliament of April 1372 (Cited below as PROME); *SR*, I. 394); Kathleen L. Wood-Legh, 'Sheriffs, Lawyers and Belted Knights in the Parliaments of Edward III', *EHR*, 46 (1931), pp. 372–88, at 381.

[9] Anthony Musson, 'Centre and Locality: Perceptions of the Assize Justices in Late Medieval England', in Kaeuper, *Law, Governance and Justice*, pp. 211–41 at 224–5.

[10] Geoffrey Chaucer, 'The General Prologue', I: 309 and 'Introduction' to the 'Man of Law's Tale', II: 33. For a more detailed analysis of Chaucer's treatment of this pilgrim, see Anthony Musson, 'The Sergeant-at-Law' in Stephen H. Rigby and Alastair J.

du loy' and 'gens du loy' in a way that implies that he understood these terms to be interchangeable (MO: 24421, 24315).[11]

This medieval ambiguity in terminology is reflected in debates amongst modern historians about those to whom the term lawyer or 'man of law' can justifiably be applied and about whether there was a single, all-embracing legal 'profession'.[12] Some historians have adopted a narrow focus and have concentrated on the elite, the serjeants-at-law and higher judiciary, whose practice was, as Gower himself recognised (MO: 24277–82; 24349–53), largely focussed on the Westminster courts.[13] Certainly, by the time that Gower was writing, the judiciary was a closed group and achieving the rank of serjeant-at-law was essential for promotion to the bench.[14] Others have favoured a broader perspective, one which explores the whole spectrum of the legal profession and incorporates the activities of men of law in the provinces, including those employed in a variety of legal roles as local officials (e.g. stewards, bailiffs, under-sheriffs, coroners, town clerks) or who were involved, in a judicial, administrative or representative capacity, in the assizes, gaol deliveries, peace sessions and the shire, hundred, urban and manorial courts.[15] One problem of definition here is that, unlike the degrees in Roman civil law and canon law available in the universities, no specific

---

Minnis, eds, *Historians on Chaucer: The General Prologue of the Canterbury Tales*, (Oxford: Oxford University Press, 2014), pp. 206–26.

[11] See also William Langland, *The Vision of Piers Plowman: A Critical Edition of the 'B' Text*, ed. Aubrey V. C. Schmidt (London: J. M. Dent, 1978), VII: 39.

[12] As Sir John Baker said in the early 1980s, 'When we contemplate lawyers as a whole, we are bound to wonder whether these diverse men of law can properly be regarded as constituting a single profession' (John H. Baker, *The Legal Profession and the Common Law* (London: Hambledon Press, 1986), p. 76).

[13] Paul Brand, 'The Serjeants of the Common Bench in the Reign of Edward I: An Emerging Professional Elite', in Michael Prestwich, Richard Britnell and Robin Frame, eds, *Thirteenth Century England VII* (Woodbridge: Boydell Press, 1999), pp. 81–102; *The Order of Serjeants at Law*, ed. John H. Baker (Selden Society, Supplementary Series, 5 (1984).

[14] *Select Cases in the Court of King's Bench VII*, ed. George O. Sayles (Selden Society, 87 (1971), p. xli.

[15] Eric W. Ives, 'The Common Lawyers in Pre-Reformation England', *Transactions of the Royal Historical Society*, 5th series, 18 (1968), pp. 145–63; Robert C. Palmer, 'County Year Book Reports: The Professional Lawyer in the Medieval County Court', *EHR*, 91 (1976), pp. 776–801; Nigel Ramsay, 'What Was the Legal Profession?' in Michael Hicks, ed., *Profit, Piety and the Professions in Later Medieval England* (Gloucester: Alan Sutton, 1990), pp. 62–71; Nigel Ramsay, 'Scriveners and Notaries as Legal Intermediaries in Later Medieval England', in Jennifer I. Kermode, ed., *Enterprise and Individuals in Fifteenth Century England* (Stroud: Alan Sutton, 1991), pp. 118–31; Timothy Haskett, 'Country Lawyers: the Composers of English Chancery Bills', in Peter Birks, ed., *The Life of the Law* (London: Hambledon Press, 1993), pp. 9–24; Anthony Musson, *Medieval Law in Context: the Growth of Legal Consciousness from Magna Carta to the Peasants' Revolt* (Manchester: Manchester University Press, 2001); Simon J. Payling, 'The Rise of Lawyers in the Lower House, 1395–1536', *Parliamentary History*, 23 (2004), pp. 103–20.

academic qualifications were available or required in order to work in the common law courts in this period.[16]

Thus, whilst Paul Brand and Robert Palmer have defined 'professional lawyers' not only in terms of a man's possession of legal knowledge or expertise, a willingness to offer legal advice or services to others, and an expectation of remuneration but also in terms of the full-time and long-term nature of such work,[17] this definition may fail to take into account the fact that many of those within the legal profession may not have worked on a full-time basis or may have had other sources of income.[18] Social historians have thus preferred a broader conception of the legal profession and have focused not on its internal ranks but rather on the way in which men of law were distinguished and united by their technical know-how and common ethos, irrespective of the level at which they operated.[19] Certainly, when Gower attacks the 'gens du loy' who corrupt the legal system, his use of both 'pleader' and 'advocate' (MO: 24258–59; 24339; 24810), the technical terms denoting those speaking for litigants in the royal and the ecclesiastical courts respectively,[20] suggests that his own conception of the legal profession was a broad one. Indeed, although there may have been fewer serjeants called to the order in the later fourteenth century than were in evidence earlier in the century, there seems to have been an explosion in the ranks below the elite in this period given that there were three separate bands accorded to 'apprentices' of law in the 1381 poll tax schedule.[21] It was the professional

---

[16] Sir John Baker, ed., *The Men of Court 1440 to 1550. A Prosopography of the Inns of Court and Chancery and the Courts of Law* (Selden Society, Supplementary Series, 18 (2012)), I: 14; James A. Brundage, *The Profession and Practice of Medieval Canon Law* (Aldershot: Ashgate, 2004), Chapters I, VII–VIII.

[17] Paul Brand, *The Origins of the English Legal Profession* (London: Blackwell, 1992) p. vi; Robert Palmer, *The County Courts of Medieval England, 1150–1350* (Princeton: Princeton University Press, 1982), p. 89; Charles Donahue, Jr, 'The Legal Professions of Fourteenth-Century England: Serjeants of the Common Bench and Advocates of the Court of Arches' in Susanne Jenks, Jonathan Rose and Christopher Whittick, eds, *Laws, Lawyers and Texts: Studies in Medieval Legal History in Honour of Paul Brand* (Leiden: Brill, 2012), pp. 227–51 at 227.

[18] Eric W. Ives, *The Common Lawyers of Pre-Reformation England* (Cambridge: Cambridge University Press, 1983), pp. 12–16, 20; Matthew Tompkins, '"Let's Kill All the Lawyers": Did Fifteenth-Century Peasants Employ Lawyers When they Conveyed Customary Land?', in Linda Clark, ed., *Identity and Insurgency in the Late Middle Ages* (Woodbridge: Boydell Press, 2006), pp. 73–87, at 83–5. See also essays in *Concepts and Patterns of Service in the Later Middle Ages*, eds Anne Curry and E. Matthew (Woodbridge: Boydell Press, 2001).

[19] These arguments are set out more fully in Anthony Musson, 'Men of Law and Professional Identity in Late Medieval England', in Travis R. Baker, ed., *Law and Society in Later Medieval England and Ireland* (Abingdon: Routledge, 2017), pp. 225–53.

[20] Donahue, 'Legal Professions', pp. 229–30.

[21] *PROME*, Parliament of April 1379; *The Poll Taxes of 1377, 1379, and 1381*, ed. Carolyn C. Fenwick (three volumes: Oxford: Oxford University Press, 1998–2005), I: xv.

activities of the amorphous categories of 'apprentices' and 'attorneys' for which there was comparatively little formal regulation. Aside from an ethical code of conduct enshrined in the First Statute of Westminster (1275) which governed relations with litigants and lawyers' duty to the court (largely policed by the judges, but sometimes yielding royal action as a result of petitions to king), reliance was largely placed on personal integrity.[22] One of the consequences of the expansion in the ranks of the legal profession was considered to be its woeful social impact. As Gower put it, 'the more of them there are, the more they gulp down their community, thirsting for more profit' (VC: VI.3, headnote). As we shall see, Gower offered a lengthy critique on those in the legal profession 'whom the sin of avarice leads astray' (VC: VI.1.17–18) but before we look at his complaints about the abuses of the age, we need first to ask if Gower himself should be seen as a man of law.

John Gower: Man of Law?

The ubiquity of legal themes in Gower's works and his use of legal terminology and structures have often been seen as a sign that he possessed extensive legal knowledge and even as suggesting that the poet had some personal experience of legal practice, even though the historical sources provide no real evidence about this area of his life.[23] John Fisher, for instance, argued that Gower had enjoyed some legal training and his views have influenced the outlook of subsequent commentators, such as Matthew Giancarlo.[24] Candice Barrington, too, holds the poet up as being legally qualified, but sees him as having subsequently turned away from practice: 'Gower the man-of-law became Gower the poet as he moved from the courtroom's public world to the priory's private space.'[25] She suggests this 'retirement' can be explained as a form of spiritual conversion similar in manner to that described of John Thorpe (d.1421), by the author and mystic, Walter Hilton (d.1396), who himself gave up the practice of canon law to enter the priory of Thurgarton (Lincolnshire).[26] In fact, as Martha Carlin shows above (p. 54), Gower was a poet long before any known connection with Southwark or with

---

[22] Anthony Musson, 'Legal Ethics in the Age of Bracton', in Kim Economides *et al.*, eds, *Fundamental Values* (Oxford: Hart Publishing, 2000), pp. 15–30.

[23] Meindl, '*Semper Venalis*', pp. 1–2; Matthew Giancarlo, 'Gower's Courts', in *RRC*, pp. 150–7, at 151.

[24] Fisher, *John Gower*, pp. 55–8; Giancarlo, *Parliament and Literature*, pp. 99–100. See also John Hines, Nathalie Cohen and Simon Roffey, 'Johannes Gower, Armiger, Poeta: Records and Memorials of his Life and Death', in Siân Echard, ed., *A Companion to Gower* (Cambridge: D. S. Brewer, 2004), pp. 23-41, at 25.

[25] Candice Barrington, 'The Spectral Advocate' in Andrea D. Boboc, ed., *Theorizing Legal Personhood in Later Medieval England* (Leiden: Brill, 2015), pp. 94–118, at 96.

[26] See also Candice Barrington, 'John Gower's Legal Advocacy and *In Praise of Peace*' in Elizabeth Dutton, John Hines and Robert F. Yeager, eds, *John Gower, Trilingual Poet:*

the Priory of St Mary Overy. Conrad van Dijk, by contrast, considers it unlikely that Gower was a lawyer given the poet's vehement attacks on the legal profession and concludes, as does Robert Yeager, that whilst Gower undoubtedly possessed an understanding of legal terminology and familiarity with the business of the different courts, evidence for a 'link between Gower's literary reflections on law and his own life experiences remains tantalizingly elusive'.[27] This debate has recently been re-ignited by Sebastian Sobecki who, as we shall see below, has argued that 'there exists new evidence to support the theory of Gower's training as a lawyer'.[28]

Whilst, as we have seen, Gower has sometimes been suggested as a model for Chaucer's 'Sergeant of the Law', it is unlikely that the poet ever worked at this level of the legal hierarchy. The elite serjeants-at-law are a comparatively well-documented group as records exist of their calls to the bar.[29] They alone had rights of audience in the court of Common Pleas and their arguments in court are frequently recorded in the Year Books, reports of cases taken down apparently verbatim by law students or other practitioners observing court hearings.[30] Yet the only Gower appearing in the Year Books is a 'Nicholas Gour', who was called as a serjeant in 1354 and was appointed two years later as Chief Justice of the King's Bench in Ireland.[31] Nicholas died around 1360 and is commemorated by an effigy in his coif and legal robes at Pembridge (Herefordshire).[32] There is no evidence, however, that he and John Gower, the poet, were related or that the poet himself ascended to this level of the profession. There was a John Gour (who died

---

Language, Translation and Tradition (Cambridge: D. S. Brewer, 2010), pp. 112–25, at 113–14.

[27] Conrad van Dijk, *John Gower and the Limits of the Law* (Cambridge: D. S. Brewer, 2013), pp. 2, 5; Robert F. Yeager, 'John Gower's Poetry', in Boboc, *Theorizing Legal Personhood*, pp. 71–93, at 73. For a detailed overview see: Robert F. Yeager 'John Gower (ca. 1335–1408) and the Law', in Candice Barrington and Sebastian Sobecki, eds, *The Cambridge Companion to Medieval Law and Literature* (Cambridge: Cambridge University Press, 2018).

[28] Sebastian Sobecki, 'A Southwark Tale: Gower, the 1381 Poll Tax and Chaucer's Canterbury Tales', *Speculum*, 92 (2017), pp. 630–60, at 636.

[29] See Baker, *Serjeants-at-Law*, pp. 140–250. However, as Baker acknowledges, some of the calls are probably missing and the lists are not always complete.

[30] Paul Brand, 'The Beginnings of Law Reporting', in Chantal Stebbings, ed., *Law Reporting in England* (London: Hambledon Press, 1995), pp. 1–14; *The Earliest English Law Reports IV*, ed. Paul Brand (Selden Society, 123 (2007)), pp. xi–xxi.

[31] Baker, *Serjeants at Law*, pp. 71, 157, 514. This appointment, like a number of others to the Irish bench during Edward III's reign, was abortive (Paul Brand, 'The Birth and Early Development of a Colonial Judiciary: The Judges of the Lordship of Ireland, 1210–1377', in W. N. Osborough, ed., *Explorations in Law and History* (Dublin: Four Courts Press, 1995), pp. 1–48 at 24). Macaulay argued that Gower the poet would have been too young to have been the Year Book Gower in the 1350s (Gower, *Complete Works*, IV: ix; Fisher, *John Gower*, pp. 57–8).

[32] Nigel Saul, *English Church Monuments in the Middle Ages* (Oxford: Oxford University Press, 2011), pp. 275–6.

around 1380), who was probably Nicholas Gour's son, who, from his effigy (also at Pembridge), was an apprentice-at-law.³³ This John Gour served as steward to the second earl of March (d.1360) and served on various judicial commissions (including as a justice of the peace and justice of labourers) in Herefordshire and Shropshire.³⁴ Again, there is nothing to suggest that this man should be identified with Gower the poet.

In the *Mirour de l'Omme*, the narrator describes himself as 'not a cleric clothed in scarlet and blue' but rather as someone who wore a 'striped sleeve' (*raye mance*) (21772–5) which has sometimes been understood as indicating his status as a man of law. Certainly, like other groups in medieval society, lawyers, whether they were practitioners of common or civil law, were recognisable through their distinctive clothing, their 'l'abit du loy', as Gower calls it (MO: 24268–9), which could include such striped garments.³⁵ Indeed, if we see this striped sleeve as a reference to membership of the legal profession then we may understand Gower to be hinting at the similarities between the lawyers' dress and the striped clothing that prostitutes were required to wear whilst plying their trade in the Stews around Southwark.³⁶ After all, he explicitly likens lawyers to prostitutes ('if you give gold to him, you can have his body') and accuses them of being constantly available to all for hire (VC: VI.1.43–6).³⁷ The image, though distasteful, has some resonance with

---

33 Saul, *Church Monuments*, pp. 244–6. This John Gower appears to have held the manor of Pudlesdon (half a knight's fee) in Herefordshire (*CIPM 1365–70*, p. 13) and was probably the man granted lands and tenements in Jugington, Leominster, in the same county, in 1364 by the abbot of Reading (*The Retrospective Review and Historical and Antiquarian Magazine*, eds Henry Southern and Nicholas Harris Nicolas, second series, 2 (London: Baldwin and Cradock, 1828), pp. 108–9).

34 *CPR 1350–4*, p. 274; *CPR 1354–8*, pp. 227, 554; *CPR 1358–61*, p. 67; *CPR 1361–4*, pp. 64, 292; *1364–7*, pp. 145, 148, 434; *CPR 1367–70*, pp. 192, 196; *CPR 1374–7*, p. 136; George Holmes, *Estates of the Higher Nobility in Fourteenth-Century England* (Cambridge: Cambridge University Press, 1957), pp. 45, 46, 69; Saul, *Church Monuments*, pp. 245–6. This John Gower was nominated attorney in Ireland in 1352 for John Hakelut and his wife Agnes, who was the daughter of Roger Mortimer, first earl of March (*CPR 1350–4*, p. 261) and was appointed attorney of Elizabeth Audley in 1367 to sue for the award of damages and costs in a case before the king's council (*CCR 1364–8*, pp. 344–5). John Gower the poet should also be distinguished from the John Gower who was bailiff of Whitby in the 1390s (TNA, Special Collections, Ancient Petitions, SC 8/212/10560) and who was probably the man of this name who was involved in litigation in the court of Common Pleas during the 1390s, bringing a suit of trespass against John de Cokston (TNA, Court of Common Pleas, Plea Rolls, CP 40/541 m.148d.).

35 William N. Hargreaves-Mawdsley, *Legal Dress in Europe until the End of the Eighteenth Century* (Oxford: Clarendon Press, 1963); Maria Hayward, *Rich Apparel: Clothing and the Law in Henry VIII's England* (Farnham: Ashgate, 2009); pp. 207–10.

36 Martha Carlin, *Medieval Southwark* (London: Hambledon, 1996), pp. 213–22; Barbara Hanawalt, *Of Good and Ill Repute: Gender and Social Control in Medieval England* (Oxford: Oxford University Press, 1998), pp. 26–7.

37 'Causidicus' and 'meretricis' also have a similar ring to them.

Chaucer's 'Sergeant'[38] and with serjeants-at-law more generally, who could be found soliciting for or consulting with clients at St Paul's Cathedral.[39]

Gower's reference to his striped sleeve could be equated with the particoloured garment worn by serjeants and apprentices-at-law which, at least by the late fifteenth century, acted as 'a publication and notice to the people, so that they might know who were able to plead'[40] and so suggests that Gower himself enjoyed the legal status of serjeant. However, the serjeant's formal attire was not yet settled at this time.[41] It is also significant that Gower does not claim to have worn the coif, a garment imbued with its own iconology and later the symbol of the order of serjeants-at-law (MO: 24375–8; 24413–14).[42] As we saw above, there is no evidence that Gower was considered worthy of call to the order. Moreover, even if Gower himself did practise law, his striped sleeve need not indicate that he was a serjeant-at-law. After all, 'rayed' (i.e. striped) gowns could be part of the official clothing of lawyers and officers in other late medieval courts, including those of the city of London in the later Middle Ages, as well as of those in the royal courts. Linne Mooney and Estelle Stubbs have thus speculated that Gower occupied some position at the London Guildhall in the 1360s and 1370s.[43] However, given that Gower himself points out how lawyers earn food and clothing through their retainer (livery) for their service (MO: 24287), a more plausible interpretation of Gower's striped robes, if they are to be understood in a legal context, would be that they represent the livery of an institution or patron since the receipt of 'fees and robes' was a normal natural reward for service rendered, as in the 1380s when the earl of Devon distributed clothing in his livery to legal advisors on his baronial council including both serjeants and locally-based men of law.[44] However, since the passage referring to Gower's striped sleeve

---

[38] Chaucer, 'General Prologue', I: 310.
[39] Baker, *Serjeants at Law*, pp. 102–4.
[40] Sergeant Catesby in 1471, cited in Baker, *Serjeants-at-Law*, p. 67.
[41] Saul, *Church Monuments*, pp. 275–9.
[42] The coif was a garment of white linen covering the head and tied underneath the chin. For its significance see Laura F. Hodges, *Chaucer and Clothing: Clerical and Academic Clothing in the General Prologue to the Canterbury Tales* (Woodbridge: Boydell Press, 2005), pp. 101–25.
[43] G. R. Corner, 'Observations on Four Illuminations Representing the Courts of Chancery, King's Bench, Common Pleas and Exchequer, at Westminster, from a MS of the Time of King Henry VI', *Archaeologia*, 39 (1862–63), pp. 357–72, at 358–61, 365–6, 369–71; Musson, 'The Sergeant of Law', p. 223; Laura F. Hodges, *Chaucer and Costume: The Secular Pilgrims in the General Prologue* (Cambridge: D. S. Brewer, 2000), pp. 106, 112–17, 120–1; Fisher, *John Gower*, pp. 55–6; Baker, *Serjeants-at-Law*, pp. 73–4; Linne R. Mooney and Estelle Stubbs, *Scribes and the City: London Guildhall Clerks and the Dissemination of Middle English Literature, 1375–1425* (York: York Medieval Press, 2013), pp. 135–6. Barrington's suggestion that Gower's striped sleeve is the livery of a seigneurial attorney who specializes in conveyancing seems rather too precise (Barrington, 'Gower's Legal Advocacy', p. 122).
[44] Elliot Kendall, *Lordship and Literature: John Gower and the Politics of the Great Household* (Oxford: Clarendon Press, 2008), pp. 116–17; Franklin J. Pegues, 'A Monastic Society

in the *Mirour de l'Omme* also tells us that its author knows 'little Latin or French' (21775), it may be unwise to equate the first-person voice within the text with that of John Gower himself who was, after all, the author of this poem's 30,000 lines of French verse and whose next major work consisted of 10,000 lines of Latin. Besides, it was not only men of law who wore particoloured robes in this period. The members of other social groups could also be dressed in this manner, as was Chaucer's Merchant in the 'General Prologue', who was dressed in 'mottelee', similar to the Serjeant who was 'hoomly in a medlee cote'.[45]

An alternative context in which to understand Gower's striped sleeve has been suggested by Sebastian Sobecki, who places Gower within the environs of royal government and the central courts and suggests, in particular, that 'he worked at the Court of Chancery during the 1360s and 70s'.[46] While he argues that Gower's garb, inclination and handwriting puts him there, the capacity in which Sobecki envisages him is somewhat anachronistic since the Chancery equity court was in its infancy in the later fourteenth century and the Inner Temple miniature (c. 1460) he cites as evidence of his robes and deployment depicts the court and personnel as they were almost a century later.[47] Thus, while there is evidence that petitions to the king in parliament requesting remedy for the wrongs allegedly committed against them according to 'good faith and conscience' were directed to the chancellor from at least the mid-fourteenth century, the personnel of the court were not 'Chancery barristers' (as Sobecki anachronistically puts it), and in fact were not even common lawyers as such, but rather were clerks trained in the procedures of the 'learned laws' of the Romano-canonical tradition. Indeed, the Chancery was largely a secretariat and predominantly dispensed 'administrative' rather than 'discretionary' justice until the late fourteenth century. While hearings before the chancellor did occur, they often included judges from the other senior courts and there are very few records of such proceedings. In other words, it was largely a bureaucratic body dealing with written submissions rather than an active tribunal dispensing equitable justice.[48]

Although Gower does refer to himself disparagingly as 'a burel clerk' (CA: Pro. 53), this need not mean that he was a clerk in the technical sense of the term (i.e. in holy orders), but could merely mean that he was

---

at Law in the Kent Eyre of 1313–1314', *EHR*, 87 (1972), pp. 548–64; BL, Additional Roll 64320.

[45] Chaucer, 'General Prologue', I: 271, 328.
[46] Sobecki, 'Southwark Tale', 640.
[47] Sobecki, 'Southwark Tale', 633–6.
[48] Bertie Wilkinson, *The Chancery under Edward III* (Manchester: Manchester University Press, 1929); Anthony Musson, 'The Influence of Canon Law on the Administration of Justice in Late Medieval England' in Mathias Schmoeckel, Orazio Condorelli and Franck Roumy, eds, *Der einfluss der Kanonistik auf die Europäische Rechtskultur IV: Verfahrensrecht* (Cologne: Böhlau, 2013), pp. 323–41.

literate. Certainly, at this date, 'clericus' was a term used for those in a wide variety of occupations that could include local legal practitioners in private practice, civic administrative officials and those practising in the local ecclesiastical and secular courts.[49] Chancery clerks were usually in holy orders (even if minor orders) at this time, a vocation which Gower would seem not to have entered. Indeed, several Chancery 'clerks' were well qualified as doctors in canon and/or civil law and a number of them were promoted as king's clerks and appointed to diplomatic roles or served as advocates in the ecclesiastical appeal court, the Court of Arches, or in the royal prerogative Court of Chivalry.[50] It has been estimated that in 1400 at least 120 clerks were employed in the secretarial business of the Chancery. Given the sheer number of clerks, it is quite possible that Gower at some point gained experience in this position, thereby not only becoming familiar with the business of parliament, in which Chancery clerks were probably engaged, but more especially with parliamentary petitions with which Gower seems to have been familiar.[51] Indeed, Gower's knowledge of, and reference to, petitions and legislation lends credence to his having had training in the business of royal administration, either on the job, at one of the flourishing business academies, or at the burgeoning Inns of Chancery, where the *ars dictaminis* (the art of composing letters) was taught and the rudiments of legal procedure formed a natural corollary.[52] Tantalisingly, however, the surviving Chancery records only provide the names of the 'greater clerks', rather than those in lower grades, and do not reveal Gower as having been employed in the Chancery at this level.[53] Gower did have connections with various Chancery personnel, including John Burton and William Donne, the Chancery clerks who were mentioned by Gower in his will, and also with Guy Roucliff (d.1392), clerk of the privy seal, who brokered the sale of the manors of Feltwell and Multon to Gower in 1382, but there is no evidence that Gower himself had this status.[54]

---

[49] Elizabeth Rutledge, 'Lawyers and Administrators: the Clerks of Late Thirteenth-Century Norwich' in Christopher Harper-Bill, ed., *Medieval East Anglia* (Woodbridge: Boydell Press, 2005), pp. 83–98 at 93–4.
[50] Wilkinson, *Chancery under Edward III*, pp. 175, 178.
[51] An association with Chancery was earlier proposed by Janet Coleman (*English Literature in History, 1350–1400: Medieval Readers and Writers* (London, Hutchinson, 1981), p. 127).
[52] Gwilym Dodd, 'Writing Wrongs: The Drafting of Supplications to the Crown in Later Fourteenth-Century England', *Medium Aevum*, 80 (2011), pp. 217–46 at 222–9.
[53] Wilkinson, *Chancery under Edward III*, p. 147.
[54] CCR 1381–5, p. 211. See also, *Ibid.*, p. 110 and Norfolk Record Office (Norwich), MR 287 242 x 4 (1382). A John Gower was associated on several documented occasions (including acting as feoffee, witnessing deeds and taking recognisances), with John Bishopsden. He was usually described as 'clerk' and in one instance was designated as 'of Westminster' but this was possibly the man of this name who was the Herefordshire apprentice of law (CCR 1354–60, p. 641; CCR 1364–8, p. 465; CIPM 1361–5, pp. 16–17).

A final explanation of the striped sleeve which Gower says that he wears in the *Mirour* is that parti-coloured robes could be distributed to guests at the call ceremonies for serjeants-at-law.[55] Gower himself may possibly have been present at such an occasion. Many contemporaries seem to have been unwilling to accept promotion to the level of serjeant, perhaps because of the 'grete expenses and costes' associated with the call ceremony, of which William Ayscough vociferously complained in 1441.[56] The giving of gold rings, such as the five rings handed over by Thomas Morice in 1362, and provision of a sumptuous feast (for which those called usually pooled their resources) could certainly set a serjeant back £100 or more.[57] Gower himself envisaged that serjeants would 'give gold' at their call ceremony in Westminster Hall but also implied that they would be able to recoup the expenditure by reaping the rewards of legal practice thereafter, a claim challenged by Sir John Baker (MO: 24385–92).[58] Like Chaucer's Doctor who 'especially loved gold',[59] Gower sarcastically accentuates the restorative properties of such gold for the serjeants: It 'heals the intelligence they have lost' and makes them 'healthy and understanding of pleas' (MO: 24421–32).[60] That Gower may have observed one of these ceremonies first hand is suggested by the fact that he is one of the few observers to provide contemporary evidence for the ritual outside of reports of it in speeches given by the chief justices who presided at these events and the names of those 'giving gold' recorded for administrative purposes.[61]

Yet, if we cannot show that Gower held any specific legal or clerical position, the poet does seem to put himself in the shoes of one who is legally educated when he professes that: 'No one can understand the terms and expressions of the law unless he has studied them' (MO: 24493–4). However, evidence of those who experienced legal training or who were members of the Inns of Court (and thus of access to legal learning) is extremely sparse before

---

[55] Baker, *Serjeants-at-Law*, pp. 70, 90–1.
[56] S. Lysons, 'Copies of Three Remarkable Petitions to King Henry the Sixth with that King's Sign Manual, Preserved among the Records in the Tower; with a Schedule Annexed to One of Them, Containing an Account of the Robes Provided for the Royal Colleges of our Lady of Eton, and of our Lady and St. Nicholas of Cambridge', *Archaeologia*, 16 (1812), pp. 3–8 at 3–4.
[57] Baker, *Serjeants-at-Law*, pp. 94–5, 99. Sir John Fortescue considered the sum of such expenditure to be as much as £266 13s 4d (Sir John Fortescue, *De Laudibus Leges Anglie*, ed. Stanley B. Chrimes (Cambridge: Cambridge University Press, 1942), p. 122).
[58] Baker, *Serjeants-at-Law*, pp. 35–7.
[59] Chaucer, 'General Prologue', I: 444.
[60] John Gower, *Mirour de l'Omme (The Mirror of Mankind)*, trans. William Burton Wilson, rev. Nancy Wilson van Baak (East Lansing, MI: Colleagues Press, 1992), p. 320.
[61] In the Year Books, John Middleton was described as 'giving gold' in 1375–76, as was Thomas Pinchbeck in 1383 (Baker, *Serjeants-at-Law*, p. 94, n. 8).

the early fifteenth century.[62] For instance, we may only suspect that Richard Forester, who was appointed alongside Gower as attorney for Geoffrey Chaucer in 1378, was a member of the Middle or Inner Temple because of his later testamentary bequest to his 'colleagues at the Temple'.[63] Given the evidence that not everyone who attended the Inns of Court even at this early stage in their development went on to the higher echelons of the profession, it is certainly possible that Gower may have attended legal debates at one of the Inns, or listened to cases being pleaded in the courts (see below) thereby gaining an understanding of the nuances of the substantive common law and its procedures.[64] Even if Gower were not a student at one of the Inns of Court or Chancery, the close relationships between members of the legal fraternity employed in the courts, baronial affinities, ecclesiastical institutions and civic government, strongly suggest his acquisition of a pragmatic legal literacy through a combination of private reading and practical experience, perhaps enhanced by mentoring and coaching from other lawyers.[65]

Sobecki has argued that Gower did have some legal training on the basis that the poet did not retain an attorney for three (of four) cases which he brought in the court of Common Pleas in 1396 and 1399 but rather preferred to sue in his own person. However, this was not the only litigation in which Gower was involved and which may have contributed to his experience of the legal system.[66] For instance in 1381–82, he brought several other cases in the court of Common Pleas mainly for debts owed to him, but also for breach of covenant.[67] In none of these suits, however, did Gower represent himself

---

[62] Michael J. Bennett, 'Provincial Gentlefolk and Legal Education in the Reign of Edward II', *Bulletin of the Institute of Historical Research*, 57 (1984), 203–7; Paul Brand, 'Courtroom and Schoolroom: The Education of Lawyers Prior to 1400', *Historical Research*, 60 (1987), pp. 145–65.

[63] *Chaucer Life-Records*, eds Martin M. Crow and Clair C. Olson (Oxford: Clarendon Press, 1966), p. 54. A Richard Forester was appointed a justice of the peace in Oxford in 1382 (*CPR 1381–5*, pp. 140, 195). He is described as being 'of London' and was attorney of the prioress of Dartford (*CCR 1392–6*, p. 19) and John de Windsor (TNA, SC 8/22/1060). He was feoffee for a number of clients (e.g. *CCR 1381–5*, p. 219; *CCR 1385–9*, pp. 433, 680; *CCR 1392–6*, p. 109. For his bequest, see TNA, Prerogative Court of Canterbury and related Probate Jurisdictions: Will Registers, PROB 11/2A/388.

[64] It was once believed that Chaucer himself was a member of the Inner Temple, though this is now thought to be unlikely (Joseph A. Hornsby, 'Was Chaucer Educated at the Inns of Court?', *Chaucer Review*, 22 (1988), pp. 255–68).

[65] Musson, *Medieval Law in Context*, pp. 67–9, 120–4; Ramsay, 'What was the Legal Profession', pp. 68–9; Deborah Youngs, *Humphrey Newton (1466–1536): An Early Tudor Gentleman* (Woodbridge: Boydell Press, 2009), pp. 42–6; Peter Coss, *The Foundations of Gentry Life: The Multons of Frampton and their World, 1270–1370* (Oxford: Oxford University Press, 2010), pp. 209–29.

[66] Martha Carlin discusses the suit brought against Gower and three other feoffees concerning property in Southwark by Thomas Feriby in 1394–5 in Martha Carlin, 'Gower's Southwark', in *RRC*, pp. 132–49, at 141–2. See also above, pp. 56–7.

[67] TNA, CP 40/483 mm.153d, 483; CP 40/484 mm.439d, 483d.

but rather employed attorneys to sue on his behalf, including William Emery, who gave counsel to the city of Canterbury and several priories and was active both as an attorney in the court of Common Pleas and at the Kent assizes held in Canterbury, Dartford and Rochester.[68] Moreover, the poet's appointment as Chaucer's attorney does not in itself denote that Gower had some legal status or training since it was not unusual for close friends or prominent citizens to be entrusted with such tasks.[69]

The professional status of many contemporary men of law can be seen in their wills and monumental inscriptions. These can provide details of rank or of posts which these men had held in the service of the king or a local magnate and family considered necessary (or fitting) for posterity.[70] By contrast, neither John Gower's will nor his monumental inscription in Southwark Cathedral offer any indication either that he had an affiliation with the Inns of Court or an institution/patron he had served in a legal capacity, nor that he wished to be remembered posthumously as a man of law. In short, whilst there has been much recent emphasis on Gower's legal knowledge and his association with the legal profession (and thus on Gower's viewpoint as an 'insider' of the system that he criticised), there is, as yet, no unequivocal evidence which definitively confirms his status as a lawyer.

Gower's Legal Language and Knowledge

Whatever the extent of Gower's legal training, a familiarity with legal terminology and aspects of substantive law is clearly displayed in his works.[71] His reference to the penalty for traitors invoked as a result of levying an army and adhering to the king's enemies ('and so forth after be the lawe') implies he knew the definition in the Statute of Treasons of 1352 (CA: III.2103).[72] He was also aware that it would be justifiable homicide if a man killed someone while defending himself, his property or his country in time of war (CA: III.2232, 2237–8, 2240). Aspects of common law procedure are also highlighted in his verse. For instance, Gower's identification of 'tort' (wrong) and 'fort' (strong) as two words that 'lawyers in their pleading (it seems to me) have set up' (MO: 24241–52) explicitly recognises the significance of the legal phrase 'tort et force' (derived from the Latin *vi et armis*) which was

---

[68] TNA, CP 40/483 mm.153d, 483; *HPHC*, III: 21–2. For Emery, see Martha Carlin, above, pp. 36, 71. Gower called on the services of William Repingdon and Thomas Matthew as his attornies.
[69] See, for instance, *HPHC*, III: 734.
[70] Musson, *Professional Identity*, pp. 227–8, 236–9.
[71] Conrad van Dijk, 'Gower and the Law: Legal Theory and Practice', in *RRC*, pp. 75–87.
[72] van Dijk, *Limits of the Law*, pp. 163, 167–8; Musson and Ormrod, *Evolution of English Justice*, pp. 103, 108–9, 154–5.

employed in accusations of trespass so as to have the case heard in the king's courts and which was commonly used in bills and petitions.[73]

Yet, although commentators have long recognised Gower's facility with legal language, modern translators of his work have not always picked up on the legal nuances of the terms which he uses and their rendering of particular words or phrases in modern English sometimes obscures the complexity and ambiguities of the text.[74] For example, when Wilson translates Gower's 'et pour sa cause maintenir' as 'in order to win their case' (MO: 242003), he misses the resonance of this phrase with 'conspir' in the previous line and thus the link with 'maintenance': the twin legal abuses of maintenance and conspiracy[75] having frequently been the subject of common petitions and legislation since Edward II's reign.[76] Equally, while Meindl frequently provides a nuanced reading of Gower's text, he too misses the technical point with his translation of Gower's use of *conspiracio* (i.e. conspiracy) simply as 'plots' (VC: VI.3.239).[77] Similarly, Wilson's somewhat bland rendering of 'si la querelle false soit' (MO: 24205) as 'if the case is a false one' loses both the literal sense of 'quarrel' and the specific legal sense of 'querelle' as complaint, as in the schedules of 'querula' (oral complaints) on the rolls of the general eyre.[78] Likewise 'Qe povre gent est sanz garant' (MO: 24610) is translated by Wilson as 'without protector', thereby overlooking that 'sanz garant' is a specific legal term meaning 'without warrant(y)/guarantee' (i.e. without legal protection).[79] Even van Dijk misses Gower's play on the word 'terms' (MO: 24493–4) which, following Wilson, he renders straightforwardly as 'terms' (i.e. legal terminology) but which is actually a punning reference to the Year Book law reports, which were colloquially known as 'terms'.[80]

---

[73] Paul Brand, 'The Languages of the Law in Later Medieval England', in D. A. Trotter, ed., *Multilingualism in Later Medieval Britain* (Cambridge: D. S. Brewer, 2000), pp. 63–76; Alan Harding, 'Plaints and Bills in the History of English Law, Mainly in the Period 1250–1350', in Dafydd Jenkins, ed., *Legal History Studies, 1972* (Cardiff: University of Wales Press, 1975), pp. 68–74.

[74] The sophistication of Gower's vocabulary is highlighted by Barrington in 'Gower's Legal Advocacy', pp. 114–17.

[75] 'Maintenance' was a generic term for abuse of the judicial system, but in its more specific form encompassed the harbouring of criminals, packing and intimidating juries and bribing lawyers and judges. 'Conspiracy' was classed both as a civil and a criminal wrong. It constituted agreements to pervert the course of justice by making malicious accusations or bringing in false verdicts (and included those who retained persons to carry out their schemes).

[76] Musson, *Crime, Law and Society*, pp. 248, 264–6; see also Jonathan Rose, *Maintenance in Medieval England* (Cambridge: Cambridge University Press, 2017).

[77] Meindl, 'Semper Venalis', p. 57.

[78] Wilson, *Mirour de l'Omme*, p. 317. The general eyre was an omnicompetent royal court that travelled around the kingdom on circuits. It entertained complaints initiated by written bill or, more informally, by oral plaint, in addition to the more formal actions commenced by writ (Musson, *Medieval Law in Context*, pp. 138–9, 162–3).

[79] Wilson, *Mirour de l'Omme*, p. 322.

[80] Wilson, *Mirour de l'Omme*, p. 321; van Dijk, *Limits of the Law*, p. 4.

Another word whose subtlety has been overlooked by modern translators of the *Mirour de l'Omme* is 'pecunes' (MO: 24350–61), which is rendered simply as 'money' by both Macaulay (in his glossary) and Wilson.[81] While this undoubtedly involves a double meaning and pun on the Latin derivation (*pecunia*), the plural form used by Gower points towards the colloquial sense used amongst members of the legal profession to refer to the gallery positioned above the courts themselves, otherwise known as 'the Crib'.[82] Gower was clearly aware of it (as someone who had visited the courts in Westminster Hall), but perhaps had experienced hearings from the vantage point, enabling him to observe the law and lawyers in action. Through Gower's allusion, therefore, historians have been able to make the connection between the 'pecunes' and 'the Crib' and to make sense of an early seventeenth-century sketch of the courts in Westminster Hall, thereby identifying and contextualising a significant feature of early legal education.

Although Gower's allusions are predominantly to the substance and procedure of English common law, his knowledge of 'the law' is broader than that which a common lawyer would normally have or require. How should we account for his knowledge of canon law or Roman civil law procedures? Although Gower's understanding of the legal system is underpinned by his absorption of philosophical ideas about the basis of the law familiar from the key treatises of the period ('Master Aristotle teaches me this' (MO: 24714)) there is no record of him having attended an English university. We should not assume of course that English common law lawyers had absolutely no understanding of the 'learned laws' since we know that some early fourteenth-century serjeants and judges were trained in, or at least had some knowledge of, them.[83] There are also references to men trained in Roman law employed in the legal administration of New Romney in the 1390s and of Lynn in the early fifteenth century.[84] It was clearly possible to be a hybrid legal professional, trained in one area, but working in another.

The context in which Gower encountered civil and ecclesiastical law is important. Sobecki suggests that the poet was 'a Chancery lawyer' and that he was closely linked with William Wykeham, who was keeper of the privy seal (1363–67) and then twice served as the royal chancellor (1367–71, 1389–91), during his time as bishop of Winchester (1367–1404).[85] For Gower to have enjoyed a close connection with Wykeham or work in the Chancery, it would mean that the poet was part of the nexus of royal clerks who accompanied or were employed by the bishop/chancellor. Many of

---

[81] Gower, *Complete Works*, I: 536; Wilson, *Mirour de l'Omme*, p. 319.
[82] Baker, *Legal Profession*, pp. 173–5.
[83] For examples, see Paul Brand, 'Sir Edmund Passele, c.1267–1327', *ODNB*; and Paul Brand, 'Hervey Stanton, c.1260–1327', *ODNB*.
[84] HPHC, I: 518, 600; IV: 782.
[85] Sobecki, 'Southwark Tale', pp. 635, 639 n. 43. For Wykeham, see Virginia Davis, *William Wykeham: A Life* (London: Hambledon Continuum, 2007).

these, especially those appointed as king's clerks, served on royal commissions, were employed as diplomats, and acted in connection with the courts of Chivalry and Admiralty, which unlike the central common law courts of King's Bench and Common Pleas used the procedures of the Continental *ius commune*.[86] Gower may have had some experience of these,[87] but the case Sobecki makes is rather circumstantial and not entirely clear chronologically. It is based partly on Wykeham's presence at the episcopal London residence at Winchester House in Southwark, his friendship with Lord Cobham, on Gower's residence in Southwark and his links with Cobham and Chaucer; and partly, too, on the chancellor's favourable finding in the Septvans case in 1369 and Gower's supposed experience of Chancery practice.[88] As with the claims for Gower's status as a man of law in general, so the contention that he was a Chancery lawyer remains extremely conjectural.

The Abuses of the Legal Profession and the 'Common Clamour'

Whatever Gower's own legal status, his poetry engages in detail with issues relating to the conduct and role of men of law in the contemporary administration of justice and seeks to highlight the need for reform. His analysis reveals both the profession's physical expansion (MO: 24315) and the growing provision of legal education (VC: VI.4.289), which went hand in hand with society's increasing resort to the courts. As the poet saw it, however, justice was being undermined by, on the one hand, a lack of impartiality on the part of royal judges owing to their greed and social ties and, on the other, by the lawyers' exploitation of their linguistic skills and of legal technicalities to manipulate the outcome of proceedings. Gower especially drew attention to the profits accumulated through their various types of legal work, which facilitated lawyers' own social mobility but which, he maintained, eroded their concern for the less fortunate. Thus, in privileging their own gains above the common good ('*le bien commun*') they demonstrated a lack of personal ethics and social conscience: 'the lawyer wants people to be contentious, so that he can enjoy prosperity through their disputes' (MO: 24341, 24345; VC:

---

[86] *Courts of Chivalry and Admiralty in Later Medieval Europe*, eds Anthony Musson and Nigel Ramsay (Woodbridge: Boydell Press, 2018).
[87] For example, John Gower may be linked with the Admiralty through a series of documents relating to the appointment of a man of that name as an Admiralty searcher (for jewels, gold, silver, letters patent, bulls and other instruments) at the port of Melcombe Regis in 1366 and his certification of the arrest of a Breton ship to the chancellor, William Wykeham, in 1369 (TNA, SC 8/305/15214; *CPR 1364–7*, p. 362; TNA, Special Collections, Ancient Correspondence, SC 1/56/38). However, there is a strong possibility that this man was not the poet, but a namesake local to Weymouth.
[88] Sobecki, 'Southwark Tale', pp. 642–52.

VI.2.123–4).[89] As in his criticisms of the clergy (CA: Pro.431–41), so when Gower denounces 'men of law' he is reluctant to tar everyone with the same brush but, nevertheless, does claim that those who truly deserve the name for their devotion to law and justice are now few in number (VC: VI.1.1–20).

Gower justified his complaints by claiming that they were not merely his own personal point of view but rather expressed the common rumour heard throughout the country (MO: 241882–3; VC: I.1.15–16). As the 'comun clamour' of the outraged public (CA: Pro.514–15), such rumour took on specific legal connotations since it referred to the notoriety required for public vilification or impeachment and was often used in parliamentary petitions and legislation.[90] In 1341, for instance, the disgraced Chief Justice Richard Willoughby appeared before a special tribunal having been accused, 'by clamour of the people' (rather than on the basis of an indictment or bill), of selling laws 'as if they had been oxen or cows'.[91] 'Common clamour' was also a phrase used in various parliamentary contexts.[92] For instance, the preamble to the Statute of Provisors of January 1380 states that the statute was a response by the king to 'the complaints of his faithful liege people and by their clamour by diverse petitions delivered in diverse parliaments before this time'.[93] By using this phrase, the royal administration was acknowledging that notice had been taken of such clamour. Indeed, reforms were sought, and in some cases had already been implemented (or existing measures re-iterated) in the 1370s in relation to a number of aspects of professional practice, such as the ordinance of 1372 concerning sheriffs and lawyers or the statute of 1378 concerning maintenance.[94] Such efforts at legal reform gave the lie to Gower's claim that, no matter how hard the people clamoured, nobody was listening (MO: 24222). While it may be true that the effectiveness of such measures was often short-lived and that it took the Peasants' Revolt of 1381 to usher in further legislation against retaining and regarding the allocation of assize circuits, the *Mirour*, in its relentless jeremiad about

---

[89] Russell A. Peck, *Kingship and Common Profit in Gower's Confessio Amantis* (London: Southern Illinois University Press, 1977), pp. xx–xxi.

[90] W. Mark Ormrod, 'Murmour, Clamour and Noise: Voicing Complaint and Remedy in Petitions to the English Crown, c.1300–c.1460', in W. Mark Ormrod, Gwilym Dodd and Anthony Musson, eds, *Medieval Petitions: Grace and Grievance* (York: York Medieval Press, 2012), pp. 135–55 at 148–52.

[91] *Year Books of Edward III: 14 and 15 Edward III*, ed. Lionel O. Pike (London: Rolls Series, 1889), pp. 258–63; Musson, *Medieval Law in Context*, pp. 57–9.

[92] Theodore F. T. Plucknett, 'The Origins of Impeachment', *Transactions of the Royal Historical Society*, 24 (1942), 47–71 at 48–50, 69–71; W. Mark Ormrod, 'The Trials of Alice Perrers', *Speculum* (2008), pp. 366–96 at 370–1; PROME, Parliament of October 1362; PROME, Parliament of November 1381; PROME, Parliament of January 1377 (petition 96); *The Register of Edward, the Black Prince, 1346–1365*, ed. Michael C. B. Dawes (four volumes; London: HMSO, 1930–33), II: 103.

[93] PROME, Parliament of January 1380.

[94] PROME, Parliament of April 1372; SR, I: 394: the Ordinance of 1372 (concerning sheriffs and lawyers); SR, II: 9–10: the statute of 1378 (concerning maintenance).

contemporary abuses, makes no mention of the positive developments which were taking place.

The Abuse of Legal Language

Discontent voiced by contemporaries about legal practitioners, upon which Gower draws, was derived in large part from an exaggeration of key features of their professional work, especially their motives for deploying their advocacy skills. Naturally, a lawyer was entitled to be paid for his legal services. Nevertheless, Gower was critical of lawyers' focus on moneymaking. For instance, like Langland, Gower focused on the connection between payment in advance and a serjeant's pleading in court. As Gower put it, 'His tongue remains mute and his lips do not move unless suitably rewarded' (MO: 24438–9). Langland's memorable image of the greater likelihood of being able to measure the mist on the Malvern Hills than of a lawyer unlocking his lips without payment,[95] is echoed by Gower when he highlights the need for payment upfront in order to ensure the lawyer will speak on one's behalf (VC: VI.1.7–8). Certainly, serjeants controlled who spoke (at least in the higher courts) because they alone possessed rights of audience. Interestingly, Gower's complaint that 'Bot such word cam ther non to mowthe/ That he for gifte or for beheste/ Mihte eny wise his deth areste' (CA: Pro.1642–4) attests to the fact that the defendant in a criminal case could have access to counsel (at least in the eyre or king's bench), a privilege largely unrecognised by historians as having existed in the medieval period.[96]

Gower criticises the lawyers' use of their knowledge of legal procedure to make money: 'the men of law obtain their delays and put their client in fear, in order to get more of his money' (MO: 24310–12). In particular, however, he was critical of the lawyers' use of technical language (MO: 24437, 24439, 24447) and linguistic trickery to win a case. Words are the natural tools of the lawyer's trade, with Gower referring to a skill with them as the lawyer's 'ars' (VC: VI.2.19). Of course, in one sense, exploitation of legal loopholes might simply be seen as the lawyer doing his job. After all, a serjeant's alchemy or 'skilful chicanery' with words (VC: VI.1.39) is part and parcel of an adversarial legal system in which what one party might see as 'pleading a lie' (VC: VI.1.35) may well be the basis of the other side's case and even eventually be adjudged to be true. Yet Gower frowned upon such tactics which he criticised as dishonest 'trickery' and 'sophistry' (VC: VI.2.27–9, 37–8).[97] Lawyers' technical language, cross-examination techniques and eloquence in court all come under scrutiny from Gower, for instance, when

---

[95] Langland, *Piers Plowman*, ed. Schmidt, B text, Pro. 212–16; C text, Pro. 160–4.
[96] David Seipp, 'Crime in the Year Books', in Stebbings, ed., *Law Reporting in Britain*, pp. 15–34, at 22–6.
[97] van Dijk, *Limits of the Law*, pp. 46–7.

he highlights their ability to turn things on their head and twist both the law and litigants' words. Here, the 'vigour of their tongue' and the power of their words to beguile has a sinister and subversive aspect, suggesting that justice itself is obfuscated and not well served by such behaviour (VC: VI.2.21–2; VI.3.225–30, 245–6). For Gower, such abilities were potentially able not simply to bend the law, but actually to transform it away from its true nature (VC: VI.1.21–2).[98] His words here resonate with the complaints of contemporary preachers about lawyers' propensity for twisting meanings. As Wycliffe put it, 'Many men of lawe ben comyn mysdoeris, for comynly thei meynteynen the false pert, for money or favour or drede of men, and letten the treuthe bi all here witt and power, and bi suteltes turnen the cat in the panne...', with the phrase 'turning the cat in the pan' referring to lawyers' ability to debate tortuous cases and use their oral skills to deliver unexpected or counter-intuitive legal victories.[99]

The poet thus defends 'plain speech' on the grounds that linguistic artifice produces a lack of intelligibility and reduces accessibility. It would appear that in any 'disputeisoun' Gower's interest is that there should be clarity and that the advocate should avoid sophistry and so 'pronounce/ His tale plein withoute frounce' (CA: VII.1593–4, 1635, 1638–9). Gower makes the same point with reference to Cicero who despite using 'Rhetoriques eloquences' avoided language which was misleadingly ambiguous (CA: VII.1631). Thus, in the story of the 'Cataline Revolt', while Gower's source (Brunetto Latini) shows admiration for Caesar's rhetoric, the poet himself contrasts the approach of the Roman consuls who 'spieken plein after the lawe' (CA: VII.623) with Caesar's speech, which he 'coloureth'.[100] 'Colouring' was a technical term in pleading (meaning the use of exceptions and examples),[101] but Gower employs it here to suggest language which involves unethical manipulation. His criticism of the lawyers' learned 'sotelty' not only echoed the views of preachers and religious dramatists, who condemned legal

---

[98] Translated by Stockton as: 'When lawyers can twist this kind of law, they transmute the justice begotten of their own word' (*The Major Latin Works of John Gower: The Voice of One Crying and The Tripartite Chronicle*, trans. Eric W. Stockton (Seattle: Washington University Press, 1962), p. 220) and by Meindl as: 'When they can twist such a lex around, the shysters/Can change created iura by their words' (Meindl, 'Semper Venalis', p. 20).

[99] John Wyclif, 'The Great Sentence of Curs Expounded', in *Select English Works of John Wyclif*, ed. Thomas Arnold (three volumes; Oxford: Clarendon Press, 1871), III: 332; Gerald R. Owst, *Literature and Pulpit in Medieval England* (revised edition; Oxford: Blackwell, 1961), pp. 341–4, 347–8, 495–6.

[100] Brunetto Latini, *The Book of the Treasure (Li Livres dou Tresor)*, eds Paul Barrette and Spurgeon Baldwin (New York: Garland Publishing, 1993), pp. 304–9.

[101] Donald W. Sutherland, 'Legal Reasoning in the Fourteenth Century: The Invention of "Color" in Pleading', in Morris S. Arnold, Thomas A. Green, Sally A. Scully and Stephen D. White, eds, *On the Laws and Customs of England: Essays in Honor of Samuel E. Thorne* (Chapel Hill: University of North Carolina Press, 1984), pp. 182–94.

cunning 'which made the law a bane for the poor and simple',[102] but also reflected the sophisticated training of advocates and the complexities of legal language.

The Abuse of Lordly Influence

Gower's scrutiny is equally cast on the judiciary. In *Confessio Amantis* the poet echoes *Bracton*, the foremost treatise on the common law (which was itself at this point following the Roman legist Ulpian),[103] when he declares that: 'Justice, whose nature, uncorrupted by law, distributes to each person with an equal weight what is properly his' (CA: gloss at 2797).[104] Whilst Gower emphasises the king's role as lawgiver and upholder of justice, he also recognised that, in practice, the king's authority was delegated to the royal justices appointed to the central courts and to the provincial assizes (CA: VII.2740–52).[105] As a result, it is the reliability, integrity and impartiality of the king's judges and the need for them to be 'lerned', 'trewe' and 'wise' which is Gower's main concern (CA: VII.2751, 2753).[106] Clause 45 of Magna Carta (1215) had emphasised that only justices who knew the law of the land ought to be appointed to the bench and although this stipulation was omitted in subsequent reissues of the charter, there is no evidence that common law judges, who by the late fourteenth century were promoted directly from the ranks of the serjeants-at-law, were unlearned. This lack of formal qualification for the judiciary was also evident in the Continental legal tradition: unlike the university degree qualifications expected of an advocate or proctor, there was no stipulation about the degree of legal expertise required for judges of the *ius commune*. 'Men without formal legal training could act as judges, provided they knew the law.'[107] However, while Gower suggests that the quality and integrity of judges 'is not to be seen at the present day' (VC: VI.5.415–16), his claim is at odds with the view of Chief Justice William Thirning who, in 1389–90, commented to John Markham

---

[102] Owst, *Literature and Pulpit*, pp. 496, 520 (quotation at 496).
[103] 'Justice is the constant and everlasting will to give each man his right' (*Bracton on the Laws and Customs of England*, ed. Samuel E. Thorne (four volumes; Cambridge, Mass.: Harvard University Press, 1968–77), II: 22).
[104] van Dijk, *Limits of the Law*, p. 110.
[105] For developments during the fourteenth century see Musson and Ormrod, *Evolution of English Justice* pp. 12–74.
[106] This is discussed in detail in Robert J. Meindl, 'Gower's *Speculum Iudicis*: Judicial Corruption in Book VI of the *Vox Clamantis*', in Russell A. Peck and R. F. Yeager, *John Gower: Others and the Self* (Cambridge: D. S. Brewer, 2017), pp. 260–82.
[107] Richard H. Helmholz, 'Magna Carta and the ius commune', *University of Chicago Law Review*, 66 (1999), 297–371 at 346–7.

(a serjeant appearing before him) about the calibre of judges/lawyers that the Chief Justice had had the good fortune to observe in the recent past.[108]

Gower uses the stock symbol of the scales to symbolize the even-handedness required of the judiciary (CA: I.45; VII.2741). He suggests that, in one sense, arriving at legal judgements is a purely logical academic process: as long as legal rules are balanced against *ius* or right and the law is applied rationally and on the basis of previous precedents, the requirements of justice will be fulfilled (CA: VII.2759, 2761).[109] Yet, Gower was also worried that justice might not be done when judgement became simply an abstract exercise in legal logic (VC: VI.5.288) since the law necessarily deals with real people and their varying circumstances. Citing the judicial oath, which was set out in the Ordinance of Justices of 1346 and confirmed in the statute of 1384,[110] Gower stresses the requirement for judges to deal with rich and poor equally (MO: 24689–94), thereby reminding his audience what the judiciary have sworn to uphold and should be putting into practice. Failure to abide by these standards and an arbitrary application of the legal rules unrestrained by conscience were, in Gower's view, directly responsible for public dissatisfaction and uprisings of the common people (MO: 24646), as was indeed to be the case in the 1381 revolt when the judiciary were amongst the rebels' main targets.[111]

Susceptibility to bribery and unjust judgements by judges on account of their relationship with the nobility and gentry were the main accusations levelled against the judiciary by Gower and other social commentators (VC: VI.4.271–2).[112] It is of course difficult from a historian's perspective to discern precisely what was regarded as acceptable and what was frowned upon as an undue influence on proceedings. Distinctions should be made between legal chicanery, forgery and clear manipulation of the system at one end of the spectrum and subtle exercise of favour, use of legal knowledge and the strengthening of existing symbiotic relationships at the other. In a society where gifts and favours were an expected and accepted feature of social transactions, the receiving of gifts by men of law may simply have been regarded as one of the entitlements of office with little attention paid to the

---

[108] *Year Books of Richard II: 13 Richard II*, ed. Theodore F. T. Plucknett, Ames Foundation, 7 (London: Spottiswoode, Ballantyne & Co Ltd, 1929), p. 82.

[109] 'There is no reason why serjeants and justices should not already have been refreshing their memories of past cases by looking at reports that they or others had made' (Brand, 'Law Reporting', p. 14).

[110] The text was included in the chronicle of Adam Murimuth (*Adae Murimuth Continuatio Chronicarum. Robertus de Avesbury de Gestis Mirabilibus Regis Edwardi Tertii*, ed. E. M. Thompson (London, Rolls Series, 1889), pp. 193–4; SR, II: 37 (8 Richard II, c.3).

[111] Alan Harding, 'The Revolt Against the Justices' in Rodney H. Hilton and Trevor H. Aston, eds, *The English Rising of 1381* (Cambridge: Cambridge University Press, 1984), pp. 165–93.

[112] Owst, *Literature and Pulpit*, pp. 341–5, 348.

motives of the giver. To an extent, the abuse was embedded in the nature of medieval society itself, which was in turn subject to relationships created or developed within 'bastard feudalism'. The malign effects of this phenomenon have been traditionally understood as responsible for perverting the course of justice, but since the late twentieth century historians have recognised the ambiguities and paradoxes within the system.[113]

Perceptions of corruption were heightened by judges who purchased lands and enlarged their estates and who acted as retained advisors for major provincial landowners. Yet, whilst Gower believed that such close relationships could lead to favour to the rich and the denial of justice to the poor (VC: VI.4.265–70), it was actually royal policy to appoint assize justices, who presided over land litigation and tried prisoners in gaols, to serve in areas where they were known and had influence themselves. Chief Justice William Shareshull (d.1370), for example, the target of criticism in the poem *Wynnere and Wastoure*,[114] began his career as an assize justice on the circuit that included his native Staffordshire, but spent much of his time on the south-western circuit, which included Glastonbury Abbey, on whose affairs he advised, and the Duchy of Cornwall estates of the Black Prince, whom he served as a member of his council.[115] Similarly, Robert Belknap (d.1401), retained by both Westminster Abbey and John of Gaunt in the 1370s before becoming the king's chief justice of Common Pleas (1374–88), was a prosperous landowner, with a house in Queenhithe, London, and estates in Hertfordshire, Sussex and Kent. His influence in the locality was clearly considerable with Bilsington Priory later claiming that it had not dared to sue him for arrears of rent because 'he was a royal justice and most powerful in the county of Kent'.[116] Gower's criticism of the judges in the *Mirour de l'Omme* is in line with the content of parliamentary petitions of the 1370s, which reveals the commons' concern for impartiality in the conduct of judicial sessions. A common petition of 1376, for example, urged against the appointment of lawyers as assize justices in their own home county on the grounds that they were too closely associated with the people there, which would cause their judgements to be biased. It thus advocated the appointment of 'justices from distant places' whom, it was claimed (subtly

---

[113] Christine Carpenter, 'The Beauchamp Affinity: a Study of Bastard Feudalism at Work', *EHR*, 95 (1980), pp. 514–32; John G. Bellamy, *Bastard Feudalism and the Law* (London: Routledge, 1989); Peter Coss, 'Bastard Feudalism Revised', *Past & Present*, 125 (1989), pp. 27–64; Simon Walker, *The Lancastrian Affinity, 1368–1399* (Oxford: Clarendon Press, 1990), pp. 235–61.

[114] *Wynnere and Wastoure*, ll. 149–55, in *Alliterative Poetry in the Later Middle Ages: An Anthology*, ed. Thorlac Turville-Petre (London: Routledge, 1989).

[115] Bertha H. Putnam, *The Place in Legal History of Sir William Shareshull* (Cambridge: Cambridge University Press, 1950), pp. 24–5, 87.

[116] John L. Leland, 'Sir Robert Bealknap (d.1401)', *ODNB*; Thomas F. Tout, *Chapters in the Administrative History of Medieval England* (six volumes; Manchester: Manchester University Press, 1920–33), III, p. 423, n.1.

echoing, like Gower, the judge's oath of office), would be more likely to 'do justice to the small as well as the great, and to the poor as well as the rich'.[117]

It is not surprising, given the anti-judicial feeling that erupted during the Peasants' Revolt of 1381, that appointments to the assize circuits and the relationship between landowners and judges continued to be a live issue during the following decade. Now, however, parliamentary attention was increasingly focussed on the broader subject of the retaining of judges by great lords and others and the derogation from justice that was assumed to flow from it. Gower's views were clearly in line with, indeed actually anticipated, the legislative urge with a petition of 1382 being the first to take up the baton in urging that 'no justice of the law shall be appointed a justice of assize, delivery or any other inquests in the county where he lives, because of close alliances with the lords and great men of the county, as well as various gifts; as a result of which the poor commons cannot obtain justice'. This time, in the post-1381 climate, the royal response made it clear that the matter would not be ignored, as had previously been the case.[118] Two years later, further allegations were made about assize justices who 'when they are in their own country, take fees and robes from many lords in the same country, and have great alliances and other affinities there, from which serious troubles and grievances arise in different ways for the people'.[119] In light of the strength of such anti-judicial feeling, the government took the hint and a legislative response was elicited in the form of a statute enacting 'that no man of law should henceforth be appointed to commissions as a justice of assize or general gaol delivery in his own locality'.[120]

At one point, Gower's narratorial voice does suggest that the poet's criticisms of the legal system may have been the product of his own experience of the law (VC: VI.4.283–4). More generally, however, the anti-judicial sentiment of the *Mirour de l'Omme* and *Vox Clamantis* echoes that to be found in the parliamentary petitions. Gower shared the petitions' fears about a lack of judicial impartiality and, in particular, emphasised the pressure which great lords could bring to bear: 'when a great man's letter strikes the judge's ears, the might of his pen abrogates the justice which ought to ensue' (VC: VI.4.277–78).

Social Mobility

For medieval philosophers, theologians and preachers, society consisted of a divinely ordained hierarchy in which persons should carry out the duties of their specific estate for the common good of all. Those who adopted this

---

[117] *PROME*, Parliament of April 1376 (petition 75).
[118] *PROME*, Parliament of October 1382 (XV, petition 38).
[119] *PROME*, Parliament of November 1384 (petition 17).
[120] 8 Richard II, c.2 (*SR*, II, p. 36).

outlook were inevitably hostile to social mobility, which they saw as the product of pride and greed, preferring instead that each man should remain in the social position to which God had called him (1 Corinthians 7:20).[121] Yet, in reality, despite the disapproval of moralists, many people did seek to improve their social position and to use within, or even between, their social estates. In particular, a legal career was one of the main ways in which clever men of humble or even peasant background could progress in society, achieve positions of influence and even, in some cases, enter the aristocracy.[122] Their success reflected the new opportunities and advantages (including social mobility) which resulted from consumer demand for lawyers in this period coupled with the economic and social repercussions of the Black Death in terms of cash-flow/enrichment and new opportunities to purchase lands. For example, the fruits of the professional career of one of Gower's own attorneys, William Emery, enabled him to become established as a landowner. He is recorded from 1382 onwards making purchases of parcels of land and other properties scattered throughout east Kent, but concentrated in the main on Harrietshaw and Canterbury. According to the assessments made in 1412 for the purposes of taxation, his landed holdings then provided him with an annual income of £20 6s. 8d., placing him on a par with an esquire in social terms.[123] As Gower himself noted, the property acquisitions of those who had profited from the law could be extremely significant in their own localities (VC: VI.2, headnote).

Yet, for contemporary social commentators, the ascension of the social ladder by men of law, aided in many cases by marriage into gentry families and made visible through the acquisition of knighthood or the trappings of gentility, the purchase of houses and country estates and the adoption of the latest architectural innovations, could only have been achieved by ambition, avarice and corrupt practices.[124] Inevitably, Gower, who was extremely critical of social mobility in general (VC: V.15.859–60), saw the social climbing of men of law as self-interested and as a perversion of

---

[121] Stephen H. Rigby, 'England: Literature and Society', in Stephen H. Rigby, ed., *A Companion to Britain in the Later Middle Ages* (Oxford: Blackwell, 2003), pp. 497–520, at 500–7.

[122] Anthony Musson, 'Legal Culture: Medieval Lawyers' Aspirations and Pretensions' in W. Mark Ormrod, ed., *Fourteenth Century England III* (Woodbridge: Boydell Press, 2004), pp. 17–30; Youngs, *Humphrey Newton*; Stephen H. Rigby, 'English Society in the Later Middle Ages: Deference, Ambition and Conflict', in Peter Brown, ed., *A Companion to Medieval English Literature and Culture, c.1350–c.1500* (Oxford: Blackwell, 2007), pp. 25–39, at 32; Michael Bennett, 'Careerism in Later Medieval England', in Joel Rosenthal and Colin Richmond, eds, *People, Politics and Community in the Later Middle Ages* (Gloucester: Alan Sutton, 1987), pp. 19–39; Ives, *Common Lawyers*, pp. 350–93.

[123] HPHC, III: 22. On Emery, see also Martha Carlin, above pp. 36, 71.

[124] Owst, *Literature and Pulpit*, pp. 345–6, 352–3; Anthony Musson, *Lawyers Laid Bare: The Private Lives of Medieval and Tudor Lawyers* (forthcoming).

the natural order (VC: VI.2.138–44; VI.5.375–402).[125] He was particularly critical of those who used the law to rise from a humble station, claiming that it was 'unworthy' for a shoemaker to send his son off to learn 'that which he himself cannot understand' and arguing that it was not in the nature of a villein to understand legal right; such men cared little for justice and were only interested in money (MO: 24274–7). Instead, he implies that a wealthy background was necessary in order for a man not to be swayed by money (MO: 24535–40), thereby echoing similar arguments made in parliament about the need for property qualifications for jurors, sheriffs, coroners and other office-holders.[126]

Ideal and Reality

Of course, lawyers are not alone in being subjected to Gower's barbed scrutiny: the perceived shortcomings and fraudulent malpractices of the medical profession, merchants and ecclesiastics are equally exposed to his satirical censure. Nevertheless, the concentration on lawyers in all three of his major works chimes with contemporary political and social concerns about the legal profession and with specific developments in its evolution during this period. Yet, for all his criticisms of contemporary men of law, Gower offered no practical reforms for the system other than a tax on lawyers' profits (MO: 24325). He was thus reliant primarily on the personal integrity of men of law, especially their concern for their souls on the day of reckoning, i.e. on much the same ethos of the self-regulating legal profession itself.[127] Gower's social ideal was one in which all men, of whatever social degree, were united in 'love' (CA: Pro.1053–86). Thus, although a litigant has a right to an 'advocat' to put his case (CA: VII.2067), in an ideal world there would be no need for legal representation in litigation: 'if the people would stand united in enduring love, then the status of the lawyer would be meaningless' (VC: VI.6.235–6). This might seem to have been the case if disputes were taken out of the formal court-based system and settled not by 'law', but through 'love'. Yet, ironically, informal methods such as arbitration or mediation, known as 'lovedays' (see CA: Pro.1047),

---

[125] John Bromyard, *Summa Predicantium* cited in Owst, *Literature and Pulpit*, p. 558.
[126] For example: jurors: SR, I: 89, 113; escheators: PROME, Parliament of May 1368 (item 14); sheriffs: PROME, Parliament of February 1371 (item 39) and Richard Gorski, *The Fourteenth Century Sheriff: English Local Administration in the Late Middle Ages* (Woodbridge: Boydell Press, 2003), pp. 68–9.
[127] For displays of conscience in lawyers' wills and on their funerary monuments, see Anthony Musson, 'Medieval English Lawyers Wills and Property Strategies', in M. Korpiola and A. Lahtinen, eds, *Planning for Death: Wills and Death-Related Property Arrangements in Europe, 1200–1600* (Leiden: Brill, 2018), pp. 121–52.

themselves increasingly included lawyers as arbiters and judges as umpires.[128] In reality, as opposed to Gower's ideal, it was clearly impossible to escape the reaches of the legal profession.

---

[128] Anthony Musson, 'Arbitration and the Legal Profession in Late Medieval England', in David Ibbetson and Matthew Dyson, eds, *Law and Legal Process: Substantive Law and Procedure in English Legal History* (Cambridge: Cambridge University Press, 2013), pp. 56–76.

PART III

GOWER AND THE CHURCH

CHAPTER 7

THE PAPACY, SECULAR CLERGY AND LOLLARDY

David Lepine

An Anti-Ecclesiastical Gower?

Presenting his verse as the voice of 'all Christian people', Gower's authorial stance was one of indignant complaint, moral lament and outrage, a stance whose consistently aggressive protest and dissent sought to 'bring evil to light' (VC: III.Pro.57).[1] Because 'our fate nowadays is quite adverse because of our vices' and 'things have gone so badly', he prayed that his labour might 'accomplish much' and that others might profit from his work (VC: III.Pro.3, 62, 70). Gower was unfailingly hostile to and critical of the Church, which he believed was corrupt and had fallen away from the ideals of the Gospels (MO: 18445–8). It is not surprising, therefore, that the Church was a major concern throughout his life, as can be seen from all three of his major works. He wrote about it at great length in the *Mirour de l'Omme* (18420–21780) and in Books III and IV of the *Vox Clamantis* and it features in the Prologue and some of the tales in Book II of the *Confessio Amantis*. The condition of the Church is also discussed in some of his later short Latin poems such as his dedicatory *Epistola* to Archbishop Arundel, the *Carmen Super Multiplici* and *De Lucis Scrutino*. It is not surprising that, as a political and public poet, Gower was preoccupied with an institution that had great authority and influence in medieval England and was second only to the Crown in its power. As the means to salvation through its teaching and sacraments it permeated all aspects of life. The great wealth it accumulated and its role as an agent of social control through the church courts reinforced its influence. Its clergy were not only part of an international order but also provided an

---

I am grateful to Sian Echard and Robert Yeager for their comments on an earlier draft of this chapter and to Steve Rigby for his editorial insight and care.

[1] Sian Echard, 'Introduction: Gower's Reputation', in Sian Echard, ed., *A Companion to Gower* (Cambridge: D. S. Brewer, 2004), pp. 1–22 at 8; J. Allan Mitchell, *Ethics and Exemplary Narrative in Chaucer and Gower* (Cambridge: D. S. Brewer, 2004), pp. 151–3.

active, articulate and sometimes critical voice in the English medieval polity. To set Gower's preoccupation with the Church in its historical context three central questions will be addressed here: firstly, how much does his work owe to the clerical stereotypes of the medieval estates satire tradition?; secondly, how radical was Gower in his criticisms of the Church?; finally, can Gower be seen as part of what has been described as a 'new anticlericalism' of the later fourteenth century?

Despite the importance of the Church in Gower's social outlook and the recent renewal of scholarly interest in his work, Gower's views on the Church and secular clergy (those who did not live according to a religious rule as monks and friars did) have attracted surprisingly little attention from literary scholars. One notable exception is Larry Scanlon's discussion of the Tales of Boniface and of Constantine and Sylvester which appear in Book II of the *Confessio Amantis*. He argues that in these tales Gower produced a coherent 'anticlerical' (i.e. hostile to the clergy) critique of the Church, one that not only challenged the basis of papal authority and its claims to temporal power but also sanctioned the use of royal power to constrain the pope's exercise of temporal power. Scanlon reads the fundamental attacks on papal authority in these tales as demonstrating that Gower believed that the Church should be restricted to the spiritual sphere, 'a realm entirely separate from the structures of lay power'. His conclusion is that while Gower's position is an extreme form of anticlericalism, it is not 'anti-ecclesiastical' (i.e. hostile to the Church as an institution) as it accepts clerical authority in spiritual matters.[2]

David Aers, however, is highly critical of Scanlon's distinction between an 'anticlerical' and an 'anti-ecclesiastical' position.[3] He argues that Scanlon's reading is anachronistic and misunderstands orthodox Christian concepts of power and authority as they were 'instituted, understood and enforced' in late fourteenth-century England, a time when Wyclif and the Lollards were attacking papal and clerical claims to divine authority. Any claim that secular monarchs could challenge the ecclesiastical hierarchy when it was judged to be in serious error was thus a 'distinctly anti-ecclesiastical' position. More generally, Aers challenges those scholars who have claimed that Gower was coherent in his moral and political thought.[4] He is critical of Gower's failure to acknowledge and explore the contradictions in his own outlook in his discussions of Lollardy, the Church and authority and points out a number of such inconsistencies, particularly when Gower attacks the Church for its many failings and yet defends it against the Lollards. Whilst Wyclif claimed

---

[2] Larry Scanlon, *Narrative, Authority, and Power: The Medieval Exemplum and the Chaucerian Tradition* (Cambridge: Cambridge University Press, 1994), pp. 256–67.

[3] David Aers, *Faith, Ethics and Church: Writing in England, 1360–1409* (Cambridge: D. S. Brewer, 2000), pp. 111–18, at 112–13.

[4] His targets include Alastair Minnis, Robert Yeager and James Simpson (Aers, *Faith, Ethics and Church*, pp. 102–4).

to be returning to the purity of the Gospels, Gower presents Lollardy as a new and counterfeit doctrine and argues that following the existing Church was the only true way because it was the successor of apostolic foundations and ancient tradition. Yet, he also claims that the contemporary Church had fallen away from its founding ideals. Similarly, whilst Gower attacks prelates he is happy to put his faith in Archbishop Arundel. Literary scholars continue to discuss the Tales of Boniface and Constantine and Sylvester but do so in order to explore wider questions of ethics, justice and law rather than to examine Gower's attitudes to the Church.[5]

Whatever their differences, scholars have long accepted that Gower's work, like that of Chaucer, developed the estates satire tradition and was part of the contemporary 'literature of complaint'. More than forty years ago Jill Mann's pioneering study firmly rooted both Chaucer and Gower in the estates tradition.[6] A decade later Janet Coleman identified seven categories of literary complaint, the sixth of which involved attacks on the Church.[7] More recently Wendy Scase has identified what she has termed a 'new anticlericalism', one that adapted the well-established anticlericalism found in estates satire to the condition and concerns of the later fourteenth-century Church.[8] She contends that new uses and meanings were found for the conventions of this tradition in order to address current issues such as royal and papal taxation of the Church, the increasing numbers of unbeneficed secular clergy and wider questions about clerical poverty and the nature of clerical authority. This 'new anticlericalism' was particularly radical since, unlike earlier forms which had attacked particular groups of clergy, it criticised all clerics. More recently, whilst scholars have continued to read Gower's work as estates satire, they have acknowledged his debt to the pastoral and penitential literature of the thirteenth and fourteenth centuries, especially preaching manuals.[9] Building on the work of Maria Wickert, Peter Nicholson and Matthew Irvin have drawn attention to Gower's use of

---

[5] J. Allan Mitchell, 'Gower's *Confessio Amantis*, Natural Morality and Vernacular Ethics', in Malte Urban, ed., *John Gower: Manuscripts, Readers, Contexts* (Turnhout: Brepols, 2009), pp. 135–54; Matthew W. Irvin, *The Poetic Voices of John Gower* (Cambridge: D. S. Brewer, 2014), pp. 136–44.

[6] Jill Mann, *Chaucer and Medieval Estates Satire: The Literature of Social Classes and the General Prologue to the Canterbury Tales* (Cambridge: Cambridge University Press, 1973). See also Gerald R. Owst, *Literature and Pulpit in Medieval England* (second edition; Oxford: Blackwell, 1961), pp. 213–86.

[7] Janet Coleman, *English Literature in History 1350–1400: Medieval Readers and Writers* (London: Hutchinson & Co., 1981), pp. 65–7.

[8] Wendy Scase, *Piers Plowman and the New Anticlericalism* (Cambridge: Cambridge University Press, 1989), pp. ix–x, 4–14, 137–49.

[9] Irvin, *Poetic Voices of John Gower*, pp. 17–18, 169–75; Roger Ladd, 'Gower, Business and Economy' in eds Ana Saez-Hidalgo, Brian Castle and Robert Yeager, *The Routledge Research Companion to John Gower* (London: Routledge, 2017), pp. 158–71.

sermons on the virtues and vices.[10] But before addressing Gower's relationship with estates satire, the extent of his radicalism and whether he forms part of a 'new anticlericalism', it is necessary to outline the condition of the English Church in the second half of the fourteenth century.

The *Ecclesia Anglicana* in the Later Fourteenth Century

The later fourteenth century was a troubling time for the English Church, one when it faced not only an increasing level of caustic complaint but also growing demands from an increasingly literate laity and a radical challenge from John Wyclif (d. 1384) and his followers, known as the Lollards.[11] Critics, Gower among them, attacked the secular clergy for their pluralism (the practice of holding several benefices simultaneously) and absenteeism and for their ambition, greed, ignorance, immorality and worldliness. Nevertheless, most medieval anticlerical complaint, however fierce, did not amount to a fundamental attack on the Church itself or on sacerdotalism (the central role of priests in the Church). On the contrary, many of these complaints were written by the clergy themselves in an attempt to reform the Church. Even when directed towards the wealth of the Church and to tithes (i.e. the tenth of their income which people owed to the Church which though unpopular were usually paid), only the most radical critics called for disendowment of the Church. Rather than being evidence of falling standards of clerical behaviour, anticlerical complaint was often the product of rising expectations resulting from increased lay literacy and piety: it was a plea for better priests rather than for none at all. In the fourteenth century, encouraged by the pastoral reforms of the twelfth and thirteenth centuries, the laity sought to develop their inner spiritual lives through devotional and instructional literature in the vernacular.[12] The production of vernacular texts raised questions such as how much theological knowledge the laity should have and whether Latin satires on clerical abuses should be translated. Gower's response was to write his anticlerical complaints in both French and Latin. The issue of whether the Bible should be translated from Latin into the vernacular raised even more fundamental questions about what the laity should know. To meet the growing demands of a better educated laity, including those such as Gower himself, pastoral handbooks aimed at raising

---

[10] Peter Nicholson, *Love and Ethics in Gower's Confessio Amantis* (Ann Arbor: University of Michigan Press, 2005), pp. 4–8; Irvin, *The Poetic Voices of John Gower*, pp. 17–18.
[11] Peter Heath, *Church and Realm 1272–1461* (London: Fontana Press, 1988), pp. 103–66.
[12] Andrew Brown, *Church and Society in England, 1000–1500* (Basingstoke: Palgrave Macmillan, 2003), pp. 153–6; Jonathan Hughes, *Pastors and Visionaries: Religion and Secular Life in Late Medieval Yorkshire* (Woodbridge: Boydell Press, 1988), pp. 251–97; William A. Pantin, *The English Church in the Fourteenth Century* (Toronto: University of Toronto Press, 1980), pp. 220–62.

the educational standards of the clergy proliferated alongside devotional literature. The Church's response to these challenges was made more difficult by the Papal Schism from 1378 to 1417, when there were two, and sometimes three, rival popes and which raised difficult questions about where authority in the Church lay.

Gower and Estates Satire

In his examination of the Church in the *Mirour de l'Omme* and the *Vox Clamantis* Gower closely follows the structure and conventions of estates satire.[13] The purpose of estates satires was to censure vice and to promote virtue, with such vices and virtues being seen as specific to particular social estates and occupations. They sought to expose the faults of the members of each of the three classic estates of medieval social theory (those who pray, those who fight and those who work) so as to bring about the moral improvement that would enable them to live in harmony. Estates satires were essentially conservative because their aim was not to overthrow but to correct the existing social order. In both the *Mirour de l'Omme* and *Vox Clamantis*, Gower systematically discusses the vices of the specific groups within each estate in hierarchical order, from the top down.[14] In keeping with the estates satire tradition, Gower often looks back to a golden age, the unspecified 'daies olde' when the clergy set an example of virtue and wisdom (CA: Pro.193–7, 228–9; MO: 20437; VC: III.3.161; III.4.279–80). Attacking those churchmen who fail to perform their duties rather than the 'office' of the clergy itself, he describes a corrupt and fallen church riddled with faults and failing in its pastoral duties. The clergy fall short of the priestly ideal, do not practice what they preach or set an example and neglect their pastoral responsibilities, whether through idleness or through absence in the service of the king or a lord (CA: Pro.417–18, 312–13; VC: III.18.1491–1502; MO: 19069–81). Gower repeatedly contrasts the wealth of the clergy and their failure to reprove the rich and powerful with their neglect of the poor (VC: III.18.1501–2; MO: 19093–105; CA: Pro.315–19). The personal moral failings of the clergy, another central trope of estate satire, are relentlessly castigated, especially the sin of simony, i.e. the buying and selling of ecclesiastical benefices and offices for personal gain (CA: Pro.204–11). Their 'swinish living', lechery, drunkenness and boasting are all condemned, as is their luxurious and worldly lifestyle (MO: 20341–6, 20689–700; VC: III.16.1330). Clerical ambition in all its forms, whether for another benefice, a position at court, a bishopric, or worldly power, is another central concern

---

[13] Paul Miller, 'John Gower, Satiric Poet', in Alastair Minnis, ed., *Gower's Confessio Amantis: Responses and Reassessments* (Cambridge: D. S. Brewer, 1983), pp. 79–105 at 87–90.

[14] Miller, 'John Gower, Satiric Poet', pp. 91–9.

(MO: 20245–68, 20293–304; VC: III.16.1345–7). As well as rehearsing these traditional themes, Gower also adopts the familiar imagery of estates satire, including the biblical imagery of the shepherd and his sheep and the hireling and the wolf (John: 10.1–16; CA: Pro.390–424; MO: 20161–9; VC: III.3.173–4, 190–5), as well as the traditional paradigm of the seven deadly sins (sloth, lust, gluttony, avarice, pride, envy and wrath).

Gower is particularly close to traditional estates satires in his discussion of the episcopate and the beneficed clergy; bishops appear particularly frequently in them. Despite dedicating a copy of the Vox Clamantis to Archbishop Arundel, whom he praised lavishly in its dedicatory Epistola and in the Cronica Tripertita, Gower had little faith in the episcopate of his day. He subjects bishops to extended criticism in the course of ten chapters in Book III of the Vox Clamantis and a thousand lines of the Mirour de l'Omme (19057–20088) because, as he points out, they are the most powerful of the clergy. In a lengthy and somewhat convoluted simile in the Mirour de l'Omme (19345–488) bishops are compared with bees. Inverting medieval writers' usual praise of bees for their loyalty and sociability, he likens bishops to bees who are small, have a voice bigger than their bodies, sting, hoard wealth and live in beautiful houses hiding themselves and their wealth in holes and corners.[15] Widening his criticisms, Gower complains that the bishops do not carry out their pastoral duties, are hypocrites and fail to live by example. Soft on the 'evils and misrule' of lords they are harsh on the minor sins of the poor whom they neglect (MO: 19093–104). Their wealth and luxurious lifestyles involve a catalogue of sins: gluttony, lechery, avarice, greed, envy and pride. Motivated by ambition, their advancement facilitated by simony, they seek worldly power, secular office in the 'chancery and royal treasury' (MO: 19489–500) and accumulate material possessions. In Gower's view the episcopate of his own day fell a long way short of the apostolic ideals they were supposed to uphold.

In fact, whatever the collective shortcomings of the later fourteenth-century episcopate, few individual bishops were as completely worldly, lax and sinful as Gower's polemic suggests. Historians have generally been less censorious than Gower, concluding that Edward III's episcopate was 'remarkably competent and increasing in scholarship and expertise'.[16] About seventy per cent of them were university educated, though most had studied canon or civil law rather than theology, and there were few 'scholar bishops' who owed their promotion solely to their learning. The episcopate was largely Erastian in its outlook, i.e. it accepted the de facto supremacy of the state in ecclesiastical matters. The Crown used bishoprics to reward its senior ministers and as a result the episcopal bench was tamed, becoming amenable

---

[15] Stephen H. Rigby, Wisdom and Chivalry: Chaucer's Knight's Tale and Medieval Political Theory (Leiden: Brill, 2009), pp. 224–5.
[16] Heath, Church and Realm, pp. 138–42; W. Mark Ormrod, Edward III (Stroud: Tempus Publishing, 1990), pp. 92–105, 143–4.

to royal wishes and so vulnerable to the charge of 'Caesareanism' (acting as secular lords rather than pastors) made by Gower and a wide range of other critics including Wyclif. For most of Edward III's reign the two highest offices of state, that of chancellor and treasurer, were held by bishops. In addition, a second tier of bishops were employed in other senior offices such as the keepership of the privy seal or serving on diplomatic missions. Under Richard II a similar pattern was followed, although more bishops served the king personally in the royal household, as confessor or secretary, rather than administratively in the major offices of government, which were increasingly filled by laymen.[17] Throughout the fourteenth century the episcopate was an important source of advice and expertise for the king. Consequently, appointments to the episcopal bench were of great importance to the Crown and so were carefully controlled.

Examples of the 'Caesarian' bishops criticised by Gower are numerous. Famous examples include William Edington, bishop of Winchester (1345–66), an innovative treasurer and subsequently chancellor, Thomas Brantingham, bishop of Exeter (1370–94), the treasurer, and William Wykeham, bishop of Winchester (1367–1404), the chancellor. High office, however, did not preclude being an effective bishop. Diocesan administration was sufficiently sophisticated to enable a bishopric to run smoothly even in the absence of its bishop. Some, like Edington, were almost continually absent from their dioceses. Others, like Brantingham, successfully combined government service with pastoral care by spending long periods in their dioceses diligently administering them when not in office.[18] Although Wykeham was frequently absent from his diocese his register shows his careful oversight of diocesan officials.[19] Archbishop John Thoresby of York (1352–73) had the rare distinction of being both an able chancellor and an outstanding episcopal pastor.[20] Both John Buckingham, bishop of Lincoln (1363–99), and Henry Wakefield, bishop of Worcester (1375–95), gave up royal service on their promotion to the episcopate and devoted the rest of their lives to their dioceses.[21] A handful of the most prominent bishops, including Wykeham,

---

[17] Heath, *Church and Realm*, pp. 218–20.

[18] Richard G. Davies, 'Brantingham, Thomas (d. 1394)', *Oxford Dictionary of National Biography*, Oxford University Press, 2004; online edn, Jan 2008 [http://www.oxforddnb.com/view/article/3278, accessed 10 May 2017].

[19] Virginia Davis, *William Wykeham* (London: Hambledon Continuum, 2007), pp. 108–9, 113, 116.

[20] Jonathan Hughes, 'Thoresby, John (d. 1373)', *Oxford Dictionary of National Biography*, Oxford University Press, 2004 [http://www.oxforddnb.com/view/article/27333, accessed 10 May 2017].

[21] Alison K. McHardy, 'Buckingham, John (c.1320–1399)', *Oxford Dictionary of National Biography*, Oxford University Press, 2004; online edn, Jan 2008 [http://www.oxforddnb.com/view/article/2786, accessed 10 May 2017]; Richard G. Davies, 'Wakefield, Henry (c.1335–1395)', rev. *Oxford Dictionary of National Biography*, Oxford University Press, 2004 [http://www.oxforddnb.com/view/article/37532, accessed 10 May 2017].

and Archbishops Sudbury, Courtenay and Arundel, had a political as well as an administrative role in government.[22]

The wealth and luxurious lifestyles of the bishops that Gower contrasts so sharply with the apostolic poverty of the Gospels (VC: III.2.83–112) is certainly evident in the wills, inventories, palaces and surviving material culture of the contemporary episcopate.[23] In 1291–92 even poorer English sees such as Rochester and Lichfield had incomes of between £300 and £400 and the richest £2000 or more (Winchester £2977, Ely £2000) at a time when most barons had incomes of between £200 and £500.[24] At his death in 1404 Bishop Wykeham had a personal estate valued at more than £6000.[25] Bishops amassed large quantities of cash, plate, fine clothes and other domestic luxuries and their household accounts reveal their luxurious diet, generous hospitality, and the large retinues which attended on them.[26] Such conspicuous consumption was easily satirised but medieval attitudes to wealth were more complex than the literature of complaint would suggest. Moralists such as Giles of Rome justified the possession of wealth provided that it was used to benefit others through hospitality and charity rather than being sought as an end in itself.[27] A fitting degree of display and magnificence, liberality and hospitality for their rank and office was expected by contemporaries of all lords including bishops. However, the wealth needed for the liberality and lifestyle expected of medieval bishops also made them vulnerable to Gower's charges of greed, luxury and worldliness.

In keeping with the conventions of estates satire Gower's criticisms of the episcopate in the *Mirour de l'Omme* and *Vox Clamantis* are not applied to named individuals. Only in the *Cronica Tripertita* of c. 1400 does he name and discuss two prelates: Thomas Arundel, successively bishop of Ely (1373–88), archbishop of York (1388–96) and archbishop of Canterbury (1396–97, 1399–1414), and Alexander Neville, archbishop of York (1373–88).[28] Here

---

[22] Ormrod, *Edward III*, pp. 48–9.
[23] Christopher Woolgar, 'Treasure, Material Possessions and the Bishops of Late Medieval England', in Martin Heale, ed., *The Prelate in England and Europe 1300–1560* (York: York Medieval Press, 2014), pp. 173–90.
[24] www.hironline.ac.uk/taxatio, accessed 14 October 2017; Christopher Dyer, *Standards of Living in the Later Middle Ages: Social Change in England c. 1200–1520* (Cambridge: Cambridge University Press, 1989), p. 29.
[25] Peter Partner, 'Wykeham, William (c.1324–1404)', *Oxford Dictionary of National Biography*, Oxford University Press, 2004; online edn, May 2009 [http://www.oxforddnb.com/view/article/30127, accessed 10 May 2017].
[26] Christopher M. Woolgar, *The Great Household in Medieval England* (New Haven: Yale University Press, 1999), pp. 12, 111–35, 23–9.
[27] Rigby, *Wisdom and Chivalry*, pp. 47–53.
[28] Jonathan Hughes, 'Arundel, Thomas (1353–1414)', *Oxford Dictionary of National Biography*, Oxford University Press, 2004; online edn, May 2007 [http://www.oxforddnb.com/view/article/713, accessed 10 May 2017]; R. Barrie Dobson, 'Neville, Alexander (c.1332–1392)', *Oxford Dictionary of National Biography*, Oxford University Press, 2004 [http://www.oxforddnb.com/view/article/19922, accessed 10 May 2017].

Arundel, 'a worthy churchman ... virtuous, pleasing to Christ and celebrated among the people', is contrasted with Neville, 'a trafficker in his cure of souls and a spoilsman ... this plunderer of the clergy' (CT: II.242–3; I.101–3). Gower admired Arundel's principled opposition to the 'tyranny' of Richard II. By contrast, Neville owed his promotion solely to his noble birth (his father was Ralph, Lord Neville of Raby) and his primacy was characterised by a succession of acrimonious disputes. It came to an abrupt end in 1388 when, having become a prominent member of Richard II's court circle, he was declared guilty of treason in the Merciless Parliament and was translated to a Scottish see which, being outside England, he had no real prospect of gaining; he died in exile in 1392. In general, the later fourteenth-century episcopate was a wealthy, largely Erastian, cadre of professional administrators who ran their dioceses efficiently and, though personally devout, were not primarily gifted pastors. Few were renowned preachers like Thomas Brinton, bishop of Rochester (1373–89), whose sermons echoed many of Gower's complaints.[29] Fewer still were like Ralph Shrewsbury, bishop of Bath and Wells (1329–63), who is described in Ralph Higden's chronicle as 'a man of hie perfeccion' and who gained a reputation for saintliness.[30]

The beneficed clergy, both the higher clergy and rectors and vicars, were as much the targets of Gower's invective as they had been in earlier estates satires. Gower rarely distinguished the higher clergy, the *sublimes et literati* employed in royal and ecclesiastical service, as a separate group but when he did so, he sharply criticised them. They are accused of simony in their accumulation of prebends and dignities in cathedral and collegiate churches (CA: Pro.209–10). The pluralism, absenteeism and extravagant lifestyle he condemned the clergy for were particularly applicable to them. Using papal provisions (the pope's claim to make appointments to English benefices), 'bribery and petition' (MO: 20281–92), they accumulated benefices, especially valuable ones, and abandoned their pastoral responsibilities in pursuit of profit at the 'courts of important men' around whom they fawn and dance attendance (VC: III.16.1356–60). Gower mocks their dress, fine scarlet gowns lined with white and grey fur, and the delicacies found on their tables: more like knights or bishops than pastors, they prosper like rich men (MO: 20473–8; VC: III.16.1329–95). Archdeacons, bishops' officials and rural deans are singled out for their venality; they 'follow profit and put sin on sale' (MO: 20101–2).

---

[29] Henry Summerson, 'Brinton, Thomas (d. 1389)', *Oxford Dictionary of National Biography*, Oxford University Press, 2004 online edn, May 2008 [http://www.oxforddnb.com/view/article/3442, accessed 10 May 2017].

[30] David N. Lepine, 'Shrewsbury, Ralph (c.1286–1363)', *Oxford Dictionary of National Biography*, Oxford University Press, 2004 [http://www.oxforddnb.com/view/article/23058, accessed 10 May 2017]; *Polychronicon Ranulphi Higden monachi Cestrensis: Together with the English Translations of John Trevisa and of an Unknown Writer of the Fifteenth Century*, ed. Joseph R. Lumby (nine volumes; London: Rolls Series, 1865–86), VIII: 436.

Such clergy, an elite of a few hundred of the richest and most successful clerics of their day, were very familiar to Gower and may well have formed a significant part of his audience.[31] They were acquisitive and ambitious in the scramble for preferment and usually rewarded for their service with canonries in cathedral and collegiate churches and with wealthy rectories, which served as a cheap alternative to salaries for the kings, bishops and magnates who employed them. The steep rise in papal provisions in the first half of the fourteenth century was as much driven by the demands of these ambitious clerics and their royal, episcopal and magnate patrons as it was by papal aggrandisement. In their accumulation of lucrative benefices the higher clergy often used advantageous exchanges, sometimes holding a benefice for very short periods of a few weeks or months. These so- called 'chop churches' drew particular opprobrium and in 1392 Archbishop Courtenay issued a mandate against them.[32] Although cases of simony were rare in the ecclesiastical courts, the use of 'chop churches', especially in exchanges of benefices of unequal value, and the payment of annates (the first year's income that successful provisors rendered to the pope) raised suspicions of it.[33] These practices, along with the payment of generous pensions to retiring incumbents, the purchase of the next presentation to a benefice and the fees paid to diocesan offices for institution and induction to a church, lie behind Gower's repeated vehement denunciation of clerical simony.

Gower's knowledge of the higher clergy came in part from his personal dealings with some of them. In 1382 he acquired two East Anglian manors from Guy Rouclif, a king's clerk.[34] Rouclif, whose career is broadly typical of the higher clergy, was probably in royal service by 1369 when he was presented by the Crown to a particularly lucrative benefice, the rectory of Hurworth in the diocese of Durham, which was worth £54 a year.[35] He served as a clerk of the privy seal from 1376 to 1389 and as master of the king's mints from 1388 until his death in 1392. His career displays the ambition and the suspicion of simony that Gower so disapproved of (CA: Pro.209–11). Like so many, Rouclif sought a papal provision and in 1372 was granted one to a Lincoln canonry but was unable to effect it.[36] In 1378 he exchanged

---

[31] David N. Lepine, 'England: Church and Clergy' in Stephen H. Rigby, ed., *A Companion to Britain in the Later Middle Ages* (Oxford: Blackwell, 2003), pp. 361–80 at 370–1.
[32] Heath, *Church and Realm*, p. 153.
[33] Robert N. Swanson, *Church and Society in Late Medieval England* (Oxford: Basil Blackwell, 1989), pp. 65–6; Peter Heath, *English Parish Clergy on the Eve of the Reformation* (London: Routledge & Kegan Paul, 1969), pp. 32–8, 183–4.
[34] *CPR 1381–5*, p. 211.
[35] Thomas F. Tout, *Chapters in the Administrative History of Mediaeval England: The Wardrobe, the Chamber and the Small Seals* (six volumes; Manchester: The University Press, 1920–30), V: 112; *CPR 1367–70*, p. 258; *CPR 1385–9*, p. 462.
[36] *Accounts Rendered by Papal Collectors in England, 1317–1378*, eds William E. Lunt and Edgar B. Graves, (Philadelphia: American Philosophical Society, 1968), p. 462.

Hurworth for the much less valuable prebend of Wisborough in Chichester worth only £13 6s. 8d., perhaps in return for a fee or a pension.[37] His presentation by the king to the prebend of Horton in Salisbury on 13 September 1388 was contested.[38] On the same day the Crown also presented a rival who took possession but Rouclif ousted him and was installed on 12 October. By 30 October his rival, Giles Wenlock, a fellow royal clerk, was presented to his Chichester prebend. Yet, though Rouclif was an ambitious cleric, his will also reveals an interest in literary culture.[39] He bequeathed five marks and a book called the '*Bello Troie*' (The Trojan War) to the poet Thomas Hoccleve, a fellow privy seal clerk, whom he calls his clerk. Although not known to have been a member of Gower's circle, Rouclif may well have been one of his readers. Gower later had much closer dealings with William Doune, another privy seal clerk and associate of Rouclif, whom he trusted sufficiently to make his executor. Doune was at the privy seal office from 1388 until 1399 and was rewarded by the Crown with several benefices: St John's Hospital Burford in 1389, the rectory of Everdon (Northamptonshire) in 1397 and a prebend in St Stephen's, Westminster in 1399.[40] Doune and to a lesser extent Rouclif confirm how close Gower's connections with the royal clerks at Westminster were. They also show that the higher clergy were more complex figures than the stereotypes derived from estates satire that Gower presents to us in his poetry.

Beneath the *sublimes et literati* were the beneficed clergy with cure of souls, rectors and vicars who are as harshly portrayed by Gower as the higher clergy though with an emphasis on different faults. Gower singles out idle scholars who are absent pretending to study divinity (MO: 20221–44) and those who reside in their parishes but are preoccupied with worldly matters (VC: III.19.1525–45; MO: 20305–16). The latter spend their time buying and selling, drinking in taverns and fornicating. Some hunt the fox in the woods so often that they are more familiar with the halloo of the horn than sacred chant (MO: 20314–16; VC: III.18.1504–10), a very familiar trope from estates satires such as the early fourteenth-century *The Simonie*. They neglect their flocks, especially the poor, just as much as the absentee higher clergy and scholars were said to do (MO: 20329–30; VC: III.1501–3).

A lack of evidence makes it hard to assess the standard of pastoral care offered by the late fourteenth-century clergy and the quality of their parochial ministry. What evidence there is largely consists of visitation returns for the triennial visitations of the parishes in their dioceses that bishops were expected to undertake. They suggest that, despite individual failings and

---

[37] J. Le Neve, *Fasti Ecclesiae Anglicanae 1300–1541, Volume VII: Chichester Diocese*, compiled Joyce M. Horn (London: Athlone Press, 1964), p. 50.
[38] J. Le Neve, *Fasti Ecclesiae Anglicanae 1300–1541, Volume III: Salisbury Diocese*, compiled Joyce M. Horn (London: Athlone Press, 1964), p. 61.
[39] London, TNA, PROB 11/1/57.
[40] Tout, *Chapters in the Administrative History*, V: 111.

scandals, the parish clergy generally satisfied their parishioners and met their expectations. For instance, the returns for the diocese of Hereford in 1397 are surprisingly uncritical of the clergy.[41] In almost half the 243 parishes visited, no criticisms of the clergy were made. Most complaints about the clergy, roughly two-thirds, concerned their failure to maintain church buildings or to provide liturgical equipment such as service books and vestments. A quarter of all complaints that were made do allege sexual misdemeanours and drunkenness. Thus, at Eardisley the vicar was accused of living with two female servants and of refusing the sacraments to his parishioners as well as being guilty of usury and perjury. There were strikingly few complaints about the failure to perform pastoral and liturgical duties such as visiting the sick, dispensing charity, preaching and instructing. Most clergy of Hereford diocese were resident. Only seven incumbents were said to be absent from their benefices although a further four farmed (i.e. rented out) their benefices.[42] Two caveats should, however, be made about these sources, even though they do not invalidate their evidence. Firstly, the faults identified in the returns do not necessarily relate to the rector or vicar of the benefice because much of the pastoral work in parishes was carried out by deputies, parish chaplains and other unbeneficed stipendiary priests, rather than the rector himself. Secondly, in some cases the 'all is well' returns seem to have glossed over failings which did exist, as at Aston where no one knew where the rector was but everything else was said to be well; presumably there was a capable parish chaplain.[43] Other surviving visitation returns reveal similar faults and shortcomings but also contain relatively few complaints from parishioners.[44] The economic and commercial activity of rectors and vicars, the 'buying and selling all kinds of temporal goods ... just like merchants', of which Gower complained was much more visible to contemporaries than it is to historians (VC: III.19.1523–43). Many rural rectors were actively engaged in agriculture; as their inventories show, their rectorial estates were working farms.

In both the *Mirour de l'Omme* and the *Vox Clamantis*, after discussing the episcopate and the beneficed clergy, Gower goes on to excoriate two other groups of clergy: the unbeneficed priests and scholars. The inclusion of these two groups, neither of whom appear very frequently in earlier estates satires, shows Gower adapting the genre to the conditions of his own time. Even

---

[41] Arthur T. Bannister, 'Visitation Returns of the Diocese of Hereford in 1397', *EHR*, 44 (1929), pp. 279–89, 444–53; *Ibid.*, 45 (1930), pp. 92–101, 444–63. For a more critical but selective interpretation see William J. Dohar, *The Black Death and Pastoral Leadership: The Diocese of Hereford in the Fourteenth Century* (Philadelphia: University of Pennsylvania Press, 1995), pp. 118–48.

[42] Bannister, 'Visitation Returns', 44: 283–4, 286–8, 444–5, 447, 449, 452; 45: 92–3, 96, 98, 446–7, 449, 457–8, 461.

[43] Bannister, 'Visitation Returns', 44: 447; 45: 446–8.

[44] *The Register of John Chandler Dean of Salisbury 1404–17*, ed. Thomas C. B. Timmins (Wiltshire Record Society, 39 (1984)), pp. xvi–xxi.

so, he discusses them entirely within its conventions. Gower is thus highly critical of the unbeneficed clergy who are discussed at length in two chapters of Book III of the *Vox Clamantis* (III.20–1) and almost 300 lines in the *Mirour de l'Omme* (20497–784). He paints a vivid picture of their faults which are said to be grounded in four of the seven deadly sins, avarice, gluttony, sloth and lust as they 'hop and rush', 'going about the city on foot as if they were masters' (MO: 20636–4; VC: III.20.1561–2). Seeking an easy life, they say mass for money but do not discharge their intercession for the dead properly (MO: 20537–40). Being avaricious, they earn three or four times as much as the priests of former times and accumulate wealth (MO: 20521–7). Jug in hand, full of laughter and dressed in fashionably short coats, they spend freely in taverns and on whores and brawl (MO: 20665–712; VC: III.20.1606–10).

The unbeneficed make up most of the 25,000 secular clergy recorded in the poll taxes of 1377–81.[45] There were thus far more clergy than benefices. With roughly 8–9,000 parishes in the kingdom, and allowing for the pluralism of the higher clergy, fewer than a third of the clergy were likely to gain a benefice. Instead, most survived as parish, chantry or guild chaplains with uncertain prospects, were employed on a temporary basis 'singing' for a year or a quarter (MO: 20500) and lived an insecure hand to mouth existence. Though there were increasing opportunities and rising incomes for those who survived the recurrent outbreaks of plague after 1348, there were repeated attempts to fix their stipends. However, these attempts to ensure they did not earn 'four times than formerly' were only partially successful (MO: 20524–7).[46]

Although Gower discusses the unbeneficed clergy, he has little to say about the large numbers of curates and other priests who carried out much of the day to day pastoral work in parishes. Instead, he focuses on those who prayed for the souls of the dead, whom he calls 'annuellars' in the *Mirour de l'Omme* and stipendiary priests (*presbiteris stipendaris*) in the *Vox Clamantis* (MO: title to 20497; VC: title to III.20). His emphasis reflects the substantial growth of post-mortem commemoration during the fourteenth century as the doctrine of Purgatory, formally promulgated in 1274, took root. The increasingly elaborate strategies devised to avoid the pains of Purgatory often involved the multiple celebration of masses as rapidly as possible, the mass being the most efficacious method of shortening such pains. Chantries, both temporary and permanent, which provided daily masses, obits (annual masses for the dead), trentals (a succession of thirty masses) and requests for a hundred or even a thousand masses in quick succession immediately after death proliferated. These 'mass priests', who like all priests were only allowed to say mass once a day, were becoming more numerous and more visible: Gower speaks of a 'flood' of them (MO: 20513–15). They were

---

[45] Lepine, 'England: Church and Clergy', pp. 361–80.
[46] Heath, *Church and Realm*, pp. 150–2, 288–9.

especially numerous and visible in London where there was a preponderance of rich city parishes offering employment. A lucky few were presented to a permanent chantry (one with its own endowments) and thereby became beneficed, but most had no security of employment. The insecurity of their lives contrasts sharply with the widespread assumption, shared by Chaucer and Langland, as well as by Gower, that those who sought chantries did so for an easy life.[47] Many chantry priests made an important contribution to the enrichment of parish worship.[48] They enabled a more elaborate liturgy to be performed and many contributed to education in their parishes. For all Gower's criticism of 'mass priests', it was his own social estate that employed many of them, as the chantry and obit he himself founded in his will attest.

Whilst mockery of the value of learning, as opposed to true faith and charity, is a standard trope of estates satire, scholars as a social group are rarely singled out for extensive criticism within this genre.[49] When they are, they are presented as garrulous, drunken and lecherous, and as being more interested in gambling than study. In general, however, they are portrayed as being poor and usually unworldly: learning rarely leads to advancement.[50] Gower devotes a considerable amount of space to scholars, three chapters of Book III of the *Vox Clamantis* (VC: III.17, 28–9) and forty-seven lines of the *Mirour de l'Omme* (20785–832), whilst the deception of Pope Celestine in Gower's the Tale of Boniface is carried out by a 'clergoun', a young scholar (CA: II.2850). Gower's criticism of scholars, whilst repeating some existing stereotypes of them as lazy, lustful and inebriated (VC: III.28.2070), goes significantly further than traditional criticism. Inverting the standard anticlerical trope of clerical ignorance, he warns that learning leads to pride and expresses his distrust of educated clergy: 'An innocent priest however untaught in letters is worth more than eloquence in letters that takes pride in its learning and talks the idle speech of sin' (MO: 29557–68). In both the *Mirour de l'Omme* and *Vox Clamantis* absentee rectors and vicars are chided for pretending to study to avoid their pastoral duties (MO: 20221–44; VC: III.17.1402–86). Gower questions their motives: some sought to escape the common law by claiming benefit of clergy, some sought benefices and others advancement in secular courts (VC: III.29.2095–2113).

Gower's concerns reflect the growth of universities in the thirteenth and fourteenth centuries when scholars became more numerous and began to claim membership of an intellectual aristocracy.[51] Most studying at university

---

[47] Geoffrey Chaucer, 'General Prologue', I: 5–7–10; William Langland, *The Vision of Piers Plowman: A Compete Edition of the B-Text*, ed. Aubrey V. C. Schmidt (London: Everyman, 1987), Pro. 83–6.
[48] Clive Burgess, *The Right Ordering of Souls: The Parish of All Saints Bristol on the Eve of the Reformation* (Woodbridge: Boydell Press, 2018), pp. 191–51.
[49] Mann, *Chaucer and Estates Satire*, pp. 203–6.
[50] Mann, *Chaucer and Estates Satire*, pp. 74–85.
[51] Charles F. Briggs, 'The Clerk', in Stephen H. Rigby and Alastair J. Minnis, eds, *Historians on Chaucer: The General Prologue to the Canterbury Tales* (Oxford: Oxford

had clerical status but for many this status was only temporary. They were ordained to minor orders, which gave them benefit of clergy (exemption from sentence in a lay court), but did not go on to enter major orders, the diaconate and priesthood which committed them to celibacy and a clerical career, and so possessed an ambiguous status that Gower criticised. The number of beneficed clergy who were absent studying increased significantly after Boniface VIII's promulgation in 1298 of the apostolic constitution *Cum ex eo* which allowed them to use the revenue from their benefices to support their study at university. A recent survey of the diocese of Lincoln in the first half of the fourteenth century has revealed not only that this practice was widespread, with more than 1200 licences for absence being granted between c. 1300 and c. 1350, but also that most clergy did return to their parishes afterwards.[52] For those who stayed on to study at a higher level, especially in canon or civil law, the rewards could be considerable as episcopal and royal administration was increasingly recruited from graduates.

In his attack on university-educated clergy, Gower does not simply rely on inherited stereotypes but rather engages with contemporary reality, updating the traditional convention of the poor, lecherous and inebriated scholar to reflect the growing numbers of graduates among the higher and beneficed clergy in the later fourteenth-century Church.[53] In most cases, however, Gower relies on the traditional stereotypes of estates satire to express his moral outrage at the corruption and worldliness of the clergy. His attacks on the faults of bishops, archdeacons, rural deans and the beneficed clergy conform particularly closely to the conventions of the genre. Similar attacks can be found in thirteenth-century Latin and French poems such as *Totum regit saeculum* and *Mult est diableis curteis*.[54] The late twelfth-century *Speculum Stultorum*, a work Gower knew well and from which he often quoted, has a vigorous denunciation of luxurious episcopal lifestyles (2717–46).[55] Although Gower updates the genre by adding a new group of clergy, the unbeneficed, and including new criticisms of scholars, he remains conventional in his approach and he treats the unbeneficed clergy and scholars in the same way as the other clergy he discusses. Gower's criticisms of the clergy also drew on the anticlerical 'literature of complaint' identified by Janet Coleman, such as *The Simonie*, which attacked the wealth and corruption of the Church, its absentee bishops and the failure of its clergy to provide pastoral care.[56] Having established that much of Gower's discussion of the secular clergy

---

University Press, 2014), pp. 187–205, at 190–2.

[52] Donald F. Logan, *University Education of the Parochial Clergy in Medieval England: the Diocese of Lincoln c. 1300 to c. 1350* (Toronto: Institute of Pontifical Studies, 2014).

[53] Stephen H. Rigby, *English Society in the Later Middle Ages: Class, Status and Gender* (Basingstoke: Macmillan, 1995), pp. 230–1.

[54] Mann, *Chaucer and Medieval Estates Satire*, pp. 203–6, 304, 309.

[55] *Nigel de Longchamps Speculum Stultorum*, eds John H. Mozley and Robert R. Raymo (Los Angeles: University of California Press, 1960).

[56] Coleman, *English Literature in History*, pp. 66, 113–17.

relied on existing estates satire traditions and its stereotypes, it is necessary to consider the extent to which these traditional concerns were, as Larry Scanlon argued, combined with a more radical approach.

Gower and the Papacy

If Gower's anticlericalism owes a great deal to the tradition of estates satire, his criticism of the papacy is significantly more radical. He was a major antipapal voice and his unrelenting criticism of the papacy recurs in all three of his major works. Following the estates satire tradition of such works as the *Speculum Stultorum* and *The Simonie*, Gower is fierce in his denunciation of the luxury and veniality of the papal court: the avarice there is a sure sign of the presence of the Antichrist (VC: III.14.title). He satirises those who seek to justify papal luxury and worldliness (VC: III.10.821–40) and singles out cardinals for their pomp and adornment, their 'great horses and retinues' and their huge wealth derived from the bribes of foreigners seeking favours (MO: 18841–912, 18961–72). Yet, as well as drawing on these familiar antipapal themes, Gower makes a fundamental attack on the authority of the pope and it is here that he is at his most radical, although whether he is as radical as Scanlon contends is a more open question.

Gower's hostility to the papacy was a response to the increasingly wide scope of its claims, to papal policy in the later thirteenth and fourteenth centuries to effect these claims, and to the pope's direct involvement in the English church during this period. During the eleventh and twelfth centuries, the papacy had undergone a revolution, one which still resonated in Gower's time.[57] As a result of the Gregorian reform movement and the investiture contest (a struggle between the conflicting authorities of the emperor/king and the pope over who was to appoint senior ecclesiastical officials such as bishops and abbots), the power, status and authority of the papacy increased massively. A 'papal monarchy' developed resting on the theory of the pope's 'plenitude of power' which asserted that the pope was the sole source of authority in the Church. The exercise of this plenitude of power by fourteenth-century popes – particularly in relation to papal provisions, to reserving appeals to the papal court and to taxation – provoked widespread popular anti-papalism in England, a trend to which Gower himself contributed. He fully and radically engaged with the wider questions about authority and the Church that these papal claims raised.

The legacy of the pontificate of Boniface VIII (1294–1303) and Anglo-papal relations in the fourteenth century, especially in the 1370s, were crucial in shaping Gower's anti-papal stance. Boniface's reputation was so low and

---

[57] Brett E Whalen, *The Medieval Papacy* (Basingstoke: Palgrave Macmillan, 2014), pp. 111–51.

his alleged notoriety so widespread that he was an obvious choice for an antipapal exemplum and appears as such in Boccaccio's *Decameron* and Dante's *Inferno* as well as in the *Confessio Amantis*. In asserting the superiority of spiritual power over temporal power, Boniface came into conflict with several European monarchs, most notably Philip IV of France but also Edward I of England and Frederick of Aragon in Sicily.[58] Two papal bulls issued by Boniface in the course of his struggle with Philip IV, though they made no new claims, constituted an extreme statement of the papacy's plenitude of power. *Clericis Laicos* (1296) prohibited royal taxation of the clergy without papal permission and *Unam Sanctam* (1302) affirmed papal authority over all other human authority, including temporal authority, concluding that it was 'absolutely necessary for salvation that every human creature be subject to the Roman Pontiff'. It was perhaps *Unam Sanctam* that Gower was satirising when he has the pope say 'we now propose a decree that we shall insist upon by the sword, namely that our name henceforth be preeminent in all the earth' (VC: III.10.913–4).

English complaints about the papacy in the fourteenth century, fuelled by the perception that the papacy (which was based at Avignon rather than Rome between 1309 and 1377) was pro-French, focused on three main issues. The first was papal provisions, justified by the pope's plenitude of power, which rose sharply under the Avignon popes.[59] This steep rise triggered vociferous parliamentary complaints in the 1340s. Provisions were blamed – somewhat unjustly – for filling lucrative English benefices with foreigners who siphoned off their wealth and neglected their pastoral responsibilities. In reality, relatively few foreigners were appointed to English benefices but those who were tended to hold several.[60] The second source of complaint was appeals to the papal courts which had developed as the final court of appeal in Christendom. Despite the growing demand for the court to settle disputes there was considerable resentment of appeals to Rome which were expensive and often protracted. Finally, papal taxation of the English Church also led to criticisms, even though it largely operated to the advantage of the king who received much of the revenue in return for his consent to such taxes being levied. All three issues were at least temporarily settled during the 1360s as papal taxation became infrequent and legislation in 1351 and 1353 restricted provisions and appeals.[61]

However, anti-papalism flared up again in the 1370s, reaching a peak as Gower began writing the *Mirour de l'Omme*.[62] It was largely driven by

---

[58] Whalen, *Medieval Papacy*, pp. 154–60.
[59] There were 630 papal provisions in England in the seven-year pontificate of John XXII (1328–34) and an average of about 150 a year under Clement VI (1342–52) (Ormrod, *Edward III*, p. 138).
[60] Heath, *Church and Realm*, pp. 125–33.
[61] Heath, *Church and Realm*, pp. 132–5.
[62] Heath, *Church and Realm*, pp. 142–3.

the determination of Gregory XI (1370–78) to uphold his control of the Papal States and to return permanently to Rome and by his willingness to undertake large-scale expensive wars to achieve this, but it was also fuelled by papal support for John of Gaunt's unsuccessful pursuit of the Castilian crown.[63] The high cost of Gregory XI's wars with Milan, from 1371 to 1375, and with Florence, the War of Eight Saints, in 1375–77, resulted in increasing and pressing financial demands by the papacy. The success of Arnaud Garnieri, the new papal collector in England, in tripling the income generated from *servitia* and annates (the payments due from those appointed to benefices by papal provision) between 1371 and 1374 caused resentment and led to complaints in the 1373 parliament. Concern also grew that the Statutes of Provisors (1351) and of Praemunire (1353) against provisions and appeals were not being effectively enforced. Anti-papal complaint reached a peak in the Good Parliament of 1376, during which the Commons presented two anti-papal petitions to the king seeking redress for a long list of familiar and longstanding grievances. As well as complaints about provisions and appeals there was resentment about the papal subsidy granted by the Crown in 1375, the first direct tax since 1362, and discontent over the terms of the Treaty of Bruges (1375), the peace settlement with France which had been negotiated by the papacy.

Even though, like almost all medieval Christians, Gower did not question the papal office or reject its place at the heart of the traditional order of Christendom, in the *Mirour de l'Omme* (18433–41) he was fiercely critical of how that office was exercised and in his later work, Book II of the *Confessio Amantis*, seems to go further. Whilst acknowledging the pope's spiritual authority and accepting that, as St Peter's successor, he 'can open the heavens and shut the foul pit of hell' (VC: III.9.595; Matthew 16:18–19), Gower nevertheless satirises wider papal claims: 'I reign with the highest diadem, I free or fetter everything … I tread all the earth as if I were a second God … we are great within the Church and even greater in the world' (VC: III.10.851–8). He is especially critical of the pope's claims to temporal power, arguing that, although the pope should not 'assume Caesar's command', he has taken over 'all the kingdoms of this world' (VC: III.9.600–10). Indeed, in the Tale of Boniface in Book II of the *Confessio Amantis* (II.2803–3040), Gower does not simply attack the papacy but seems to challenge the basis of papal authority and by implication clerical authority in general. In this tale Gower tells how Boniface VIII (1294–1303) usurped the papacy by trickery, fabricating the voice of God to persuade Pope Celestine V to resign. On becoming pope Boniface seeks to place royal authority under that of the Church by demanding homage from King Lowyz (the name Gower gives to Philip IV of France in the tale) and becomes involved in a political struggle.

---

[63] George Holmes, *The Good Parliament* (Oxford: Clarendon Press, 1975), pp. 7–20, 144–9.

The tale ends with the capture of Boniface, his imprisonment and death from starvation in captivity. For some scholars, the tale should be read not only as an indictment of papal entanglement in worldly affairs but also as a more radical attack on the basis of papal authority. Scanlon, for instance, sees the falsification of the voice of God in the tale as a powerful metaphor for the falsity of the Church's wider claims and the role of King Lowyz as sanctioning royal power as a constraint, a truly radical position.[64] However, with the exception of the Lollards, few fourteenth-century readers would have gone so far and it is doubtful whether Gower himself intended this interpretation. Elsewhere in the tale he confines his attack on the pope to the person rather than the office. Thus, he has Sire Guillam de Langharet, King Lowys's knight, say 'We pleigne noght ayein the Pope' and call Boniface a 'Misledere of the Papacie' (II.3016–23). But he also makes an explicit distinction between the spiritual authority of Boniface which King Lowyz will 'honoure and magnefie' and the 'Pride temporal' which 'stonden in debat' (II.2985–91).

In the Tale of Constantine and Sylvester, which immediately follows the Tale of Boniface, Gower is also clear in his rejection of papal claims to temporal power. He condemns the Donation of Constantine, a ninth-century forgery which was widely accepted as genuine, which claimed that the Emperor Constantine had granted the pope temporal power over Rome and the western empire, and describes its effects as a poison spreading within the Church (CA: II.3490–2; MO: 18637–660; VC: III.5.285–8). Nevertheless, although Gower is explicit in his repudiation of papal claims to temporal power, the poet's equivocation about how such claims should be countered undermines Scanlon's reading of the Tale of Boniface. Even in his fiercest extended attack on papal temporal power in the *Vox Clamantis* Gower makes no royal call to arms to resist it (III.9). Thus, critical though he could be of the papacy, the radicalism of Gower's rejection of the pope's temporal power was limited by his ambiguity about how it should actually be limited in practice.

Whilst Gower's anti-papalism grew out of the hostility to the papacy in contemporary England, his attacks were more radical and more sweeping than most contemporary complaints, which tended to focus on specific unpopular policies. Thus, he made only passing references to papal taxation, appeals to the papal courts and papal provisions (VC: III.3.195–200, III.14.1221–9; MO: 18481–92; CA: Pro.207–10; VC: III.16.1375–80). Instead, rather than merely criticising particular papal policies, Gower expressed his outrage at what he saw as the papacy's fundamental failings: its financial corruption, its claims to and exercise of temporal power and its warlike behaviour (VC: III.9.578–620, 690–705; MO: 18541–76, 18601–732). If the

---

[64] Scanlon, *Narrative, Authority, and Power*, p. 260. For alternative readings which focus on Gower's ideas of ethics, justice and authority and the role of conscience see Irvin, *Poetic Voices of John Gower*, pp. 136–44, and Allan Mitchell, 'Gower's *Confessio Amantis*, Natural Morality and Vernacular Ethics', pp. 135–54.

fundamental failings identified by Gower were reformed it would, as Scanlon contends, restrict the papacy's authority to 'entirely spiritual' matters.[65]

Although the Papal Schism of 1378 has often been discussed in relation to Gower's work and, in particular, to the dating of the *Vox Clamantis*, the poet does not examine it at length. Indeed, he devotes more space to the pontificate of Boniface VIII (1294–1303) than to this central religious and diplomatic issue of his own day. All three of his major works make reference to the Schism but in the *Mirour de l'Omme* and Book III of the *Vox Clamantis*, these are relatively brief and not central to his argument. This suggests that both were substantially written before the Schism occurred. In the *Mirour de l'Omme* Gower explicitly denounces the 'two-headed' monster at Rome (18817–40) but this comes at the end of a lengthy critique of the papacy (18421–816) and these lines may have been a later addition. Similarly, in Book III of the *Vox Clamantis* the clearest reference to the Schism comes in revisions to the beginning of the first chapter (III.1.2–3) and one manuscript includes no reference to it at all. Whilst Gower's reference to 'one now called Clement' at the end of Chapter 10 of Book III can be interpreted as a literary pun (III.10.958), it may also be a reference to the anti-pope Clement VII, but even this is far from an outright denunciation of the Schism.[66] More tellingly, chapter 14, entitled 'how signs of the Antichrist have appeared in the Court of Rome', makes only one generic reference, to 'confound heresies and destroy schisms' (III.14.1242), rather than using the Schism as evidence of the Antichrist's presence. Although Gower continued to revise the *Vox Clamantis* he did not add a stronger condemnation of the Schism. Only in his later work, written several years into the Schism, is he more explicit. In the *Confessio Amantis* (Pro.347–50), this split within the Church is said to have caused Lollardy whilst *De Lucis Scrutino*, written towards the end of his life, contains a denunciation of it (ll. 3–4, 29–30). The outrage he felt about the continuing scandal of the Schism may have prompted Gower to be more radical in his criticism of the papacy in the Tale of Boniface, written about a decade after the Schism began, than he had been in his earlier works.

Bellicose Clergy

Gower's radicalism can also be seen in his condemnation of warlike clergy. This theme was rarely touched on in earlier estates satires but Gower devotes four chapters to it in Book III of the *Vox Clamantis* (III.5–6, 8, 10) whilst in the *Mirour de l'Omme* he complains that the pope is warlike and collects the riches and wealth of the world to pay his troops (MO: 18649–64). The policies adopted by the Avignon papacy help explain Gower's repeated

---

[65] Scanlon, *Narrative, Authority, and Power*, p. 262.
[66] Gower, *Major Latin Works*, p. 398.

emphasis on the Church's bellicosity.[67] During the 'Babylonian captivity', when the papacy was based in Avignon (1309–76), successive popes sought to pacify and regain control of Rome and the Papal States; in 1309 Clement V defeated Venice to secure control of Ferrara; John XXII's struggle with the emperor Louis of Bavaria resulted in fighting in Lombardy in 1323, Modena and Bologna in 1326–27 and the temporary establishment of an anti-pope in Rome in 1328; and Innocent VI began a sustained military campaign in the Papal States in 1353. Urban V's determination to return the papacy to Rome intensified this struggle and it was a warlike prelate, Cardinal Albornoz, whose campaigns in 1353–57 and 1358–64 subdued the Papal States sufficiently for Urban to return to Rome briefly between 1367 and 1370. Only after further wars with Milan and Florence was his successor Gregory XI (1370–78) able to move the papacy back to Rome permanently.

However, the 'warrior bishops', of whom Gower disapproved so strongly, were rare in England, the few exceptions being northern bishops with responsibility for the Scottish border. William Zouche, archbishop of York, defeated the Scots at the battle of Neville's Cross in 1346 and Thomas Hatfield, bishop of Durham (1345–81), took part in the French campaigns of 1346 and 1355 and was repeatedly charged with the defence of the northern border, although he also had a reputation for generosity to the poor.[68] Henry Despenser, bishop of Norwich (1370–1406), could be described as a 'warrior bishop' with more justice.[69] His father and his brother fought in France and he himself was said to 'take such delight in deeds of arms'. He fought alongside his brother against Milan on behalf of Pope Urban V in the mid-1360s, led a force of 8000 men on the 'crusade' to Flanders in 1383 when England backed Ghent against the supporters of the Avignon anti-pope, Clement VII, and accompanied Richard II on his Scottish campaign in 1385, but even he spent the bulk of his long episcopate in his diocese. A marginal note at line 375 of Chapter 6 in one of the manuscripts of the *Vox Clamantis* which refers to the Flanders Crusade suggests that Gower's attack on warlike clergy resonated with the scribe.[70] Gower's extended complaint about warlike clergy may also be a response to the Crown's attempt to mobilise the clergy in the defence of the realm against foreign invasion despite the prohibition in

---

[67] David S. Chambers, *Popes, Cardinals and War: The Military Church in Renaissance and Early Modern Europe* (London and New York: I. B. Tauris, 2006), pp. 24–37; Whalen, *Medieval Papacy*, pp. 160–8.

[68] Nicholas Bennett, 'Zouche, William (d. 1352)', *Oxford Dictionary of National Biography*, Oxford University Press, 2004 [http://www.oxforddnb.com/view/article/30303, accessed 10 May 2017]; Roy M. Haines, 'Hatfield, Thomas (c.1310–1381)', *Oxford Dictionary of National Biography*, Oxford University Press, 2004; online edn, Jan 2008 [http://www.oxforddnb.com/view/article/12598, accessed 10 May 2017].

[69] Richard G. Davies, 'Despenser, Henry (d. 1406)', *Oxford Dictionary of National Biography*, Oxford University Press, 2004 [http://www.oxforddnb.com/view/article/7551, accessed 10 May 2017].

[70] Gower, *Major Latin Works*, p. 126.

canon law of them bearing arms.[71] Royal writs were issued at regular intervals from 1368 instructing bishops to array their clergy (assemble them with arms and armour). Although there is evidence that the arrays held in the diocese of Lincoln were met with resistance from some clerics, elsewhere clergy appeared as instructed and wills confirm that some clergy possessed weapons and armour. These criticisms of clerical bellicosity and of the papacy's temporal power and ambitions offer some support for Scanlon's contention that Gower sought to confine clerical power to the spiritual realm. However, it is much less clear that, as Scanlon claims, Gower envisaged monarchical power as the means of achieving this. As Aers has pointed out, Gower held conflicting positions on the nature of authority in the Church and offered no programme of reform for the abuses he so relentlessly exposed. Though radical in his condemnation of papal temporal power and warlike clergy, this radicalism was limited in its scope and in its practical application. This is particularly clear in Gower's response to the most radical critics of the English Church of his own time: Wyclif and the Lollards.

Gower, Wyclif and Lollardy

With the emergence of Wyclif and the Lollards, the often stinging anticlericalism of the estates satire tradition and of the 'literature of complaint' became potentially much more radical, even revolutionary, in its implications. By contrast, Gower's own anticlericalism did not lead him into heresy and although he shared some of Wyclif's criticisms of the Church, the poet was explicit and vehement in his condemnation of Lollardy. Wyclif's challenge to the Church went much further than even the most trenchant anticlerical complaint. He questioned the nature of authority in the Church, particularly that of the pope, and was scathing about what he regarded as the corruption of the institutional Church.[72] He attacked not only the abuses of the contemporary Church but rejected many of its practices *per se*, including indulgences, images, pilgrimages and prayers for the dead, and adopted the Donatist view that celebration of the mass by an unworthy priest invalidated the sacrament. He also advocated a disendowed Church, one that relied on the authority of scripture rather than canon law and the pope, a loosening of the clergy's monopoly of the sacraments and greater access for the laity

---

[71] Bruce McNab, 'Obligations of the Church in English Society: Military Arrays of the Clergy 1369–1418', in William C. Jordan, Bruce McNab and Teofilo F. Ruiz, eds, *Order and Innovation in the Middle Ages* (Princeton: Princeton University Press, 1976), pp. 293–314; Alison K. McHardy, *The Age of War and Wyclif: Lincoln Diocese and its Bishop in the later Fourteenth Century* (Lincoln: Lincoln Cathedral, 2001), pp. 33–7.

[72] Anne Hudson and Anthony Kenny, 'Wyclif, John (d. 1384)', *Oxford Dictionary of National Biography*, Oxford University Press, 2004; online edn, Jan 2008 [http://www.oxforddnb.com/view/article/30122, accessed 10 May 2017].

to scripture through the translation of the Bible into the vernacular. Wyclif ceased to be a radical critic of the Church and became a heretic when he denied the doctrine of transubstantiation; and his ideas were condemned in 1382. After his death in 1384, Wyclif's views were spread at a local level by the Lollards. As a result, they were persecuted by the ecclesiastical and secular authorities and in 1401, after Henry IV had linked heresy with political rebellion against him, the death penalty was introduced for heresy.

The *Mirour de l'Omme* and *Vox Clamantis*, which were written before the public condemnation of Wyclif in 1382, only refer to heresy generically. Gower first directly attacked Lollardy in the Prologue to the *Confessio Amantis* where he refers to 'This newe secte of Lollardie/And also many an heresie/Among the clerkes in hemselve' (Pro.349–51). The *Carmen Super Multiplici Viciorum Pestilencia* of 1396–97, which may have been written soon after a Lollard petition of 1395 to disendow the Church began to circulate, also contains a sustained denunciation of the 'demonic guile' of Lollardy but does not discuss any specific Lollard beliefs. Finally, towards the end of his life, in the dedicatory *Epistola* to Archbishop Arundel in a presentation copy of the *Vox Clamantis*, probably written around 1400, Gower expressed his admiration for the chief scourge of the Lollards.

Yet despite the vehemence of Gower's condemnation of Lollardy, he shared some of Wyclif's radical (though not heretical) ideas including his anti-papalism and criticism of the wealth of the Church.[73] In 1376–77, as Gower started writing the *Mirour de l'Omme*, Wyclif was preaching publicly in London against the pope. Both men attacked the authority of the pope, papal taxation and appeals to Rome and both considered papal provisions to be simoniacal. Both saw the Donation of Constantine as a fatal error and subsequently denounced the Schism (MO: 18637–48). Nonetheless, despite these similarities and his concerns about the use of religious images, Gower was very far from being a Wycliffite.[74] Though highly critical of the papacy's temporal role he did, unlike Wyclif, accept the pope's spiritual authority (VC: III.9.590–8).[75] On most crucial questions, including the disendowment of the Church, the vernacular Bible and transubstantiation, he disagreed with Wyclif. Nor, unlike the Lollards, did he criticise such mainstream practices as the cult of saints, indulgences, pilgrimages and prayers for the dead. Indeed, Gower's testament is entirely orthodox in its affirmation of Purgatory and its strategies to shorten his time there.[76] In it, he made extensive provisions for

---

[73] Holmes, *Good Parliament*, pp. 165–78.
[74] Peter Brown, 'Images', in Peter Brown, ed., *A Companion to Middle English Literature and Culture c. 1350–c. 1500* (Oxford: Blackwell, 2007), pp. 307–12; Anne Hudson, *The Premature Reformation: Wycliffite Texts and Lollard History* (Oxford: The Clarendon Press, 1988), pp. 330–4, 408–11.
[75] For a fuller discussion of Wyclif's views on the papacy see Takashi Shogimen, 'Wyclif's Ecclesiology and Political Thought', in Ian C. Levy, ed., *A Companion to John Wyclif, Late Medieval Theologian* (Leiden: Brill, 2006), pp. 199–240 at pp. 210–20.
[76] For Gower's testament, see Martha Carlin's analysis, pp. 85–90 above.

prayers for his soul by local clergy and at religious houses and hospitals – the prayers of the poor and the sick were considered particularly efficacious. Like almost all of his contemporaries, he sought the intercession of the saints. His choice of the chapel of St John the Baptist in Southwark Priory for his burial place may well reflect a devotion to his namesake patron saint and the *Mirour de l'Omme* ends with an appeal to the Virgin Mary (27361–480) and breaks off in the middle of a hymn of praise to her (29845–945).

Both the *Mirour de l'Omme* and the *Vox Clamantis* were written before Wyclif's condemnation at the Blackfriars Council in 1382 and the subsequent association of heresy with sedition and so were the product of a period when the distinctions between orthodoxy and heresy were blurred.[77] Wycliffite ideas appealed to the same ascetic, evangelical spiritual interests as did orthodox movements such as the 'mixed life' and Carthusian monasticism and grew out of the dissatisfaction with the current failings of the Church that Gower himself shared. Gower's own radicalism was confined to two issues: the temporal claims of the papacy and the warlike behaviour of senior clergy. In all other respects his anticlericalism was mainstream rather than radical. It focused on the failings of the clergy and did not present a fundamental challenge to either the structure or the doctrines of the Church.

Gower, the 'New Anticlericalism' and 'Present-Day Evils'

If Gower's anticlericalism was largely mainstream, remaining close to the traditions of estates satire and the 'literature of complaint', can it be considered part of the 'new anticlericalism' which Wendy Scase has identified in the literature of this period?[78] A central convention of medieval satire was that vices were not discussed simply as abstract faults or in the form of attacks on named individuals but rather were castigated as being typical of particular social groups in specific social contexts.[79] Medieval satirists thus addressed the specific context in which they found themselves and which they sought to reform. This is exactly what Gower himself sets out to do in the Prologue to Book III of the *Vox Clamantis* where he explicitly set out to address 'present-day evils' (VC: III.Pro.54). Without such contemporary relevance satire lacked 'bite'. In this respect all estates satire was 'new', even though its authors often relied on and repeated existing stereotypes, as Gower himself did in his criticisms of the bishops and beneficed clergy. In focusing his indignation on the specific context of the condition and problems of the later fourteenth-century Church Gower thus was following a well-established convention. His inclusion of unbeneficed clergy who are rarely found in

[77] John A. F. Thomson, 'Orthodox Religion and the Origins of Lollardy', *History*, 74 (1989), pp. 39–55.
[78] Scase, *Piers Plowman and the New Anticlericalism*, pp. 4–14, 137–49.
[79] Miller, 'John Gower', p. 89.

earlier estates satires and new criticisms of university educated clergy adapted the genre to the social context of his day, to the growing numbers and the changing nature of the fourteenth-century clergy, but kept its traditional purpose: moral improvement through the correction of vice.

The key characteristic of the 'new anticlericalism' Scase discusses is that it 'developed and unified' existing anticlericalism into 'a new polemic which opposed all clerics' and made it dangerous to the Church.[80] In the later fourteenth century traditional forms of anticlericalism, such as anti-papalism and anti-fraternalism, and earlier debates on clerical poverty and pastoral care were given a new urgency and made more threatening by Wyclif's ideas, especially those on dominion.[81] Wyclif's most radical ideas, disendowment, the primacy of scriptural rather than papal authority, a vernacular Bible and his denial of transubstantiation were indeed a fundamental attack on clericalism and the Church. Gower undoubtedly shares some of the characteristics of Scase's 'new anticlericalism'. His unusually comprehensive denunciation of the clergy, which includes friars and monks as well as all ranks of the secular clergy, and his attacks on unbeneficed clergy are similar to the new anticlerical 'gyrovague' satire on wandering secular priests discussed by Scase.[82] However, unlike Wyclif, Gower did not use his often scathing criticisms of the clergy to make a fundamental attack on the Church. Overall, therefore, it is difficult to place Gower's work within a late fourteenth-century 'new anti-clericalism'.

Nevertheless, in his writings on the clergy, Gower is very much a voice of the later fourteenth century. The events of the 1370s, when Gower was writing the *Mirour de l'Omme* and the *Vox Clamantis*, are particularly important as a context for his invective and for an understanding of his concerns about the state of the Church. His preoccupation with the financial corruption of the Church, with the papacy and its warlike nature, and with the worldly concerns of the episcopate all reflect the problems of this decade during which an unsuccessful and expensive war, high levels of taxation (including increased papal taxation on the English Church), and an unpopular truce mediated by the papacy culminated in a political crisis, a serious attack on the Crown in the Good Parliament of 1376.[83] The influence of these events on Gower can be seen in the parallels between his works and the complaints expressed in this period in parliamentary petitions and ecclesiastical legislation. Gower's works thus echo the two anti-papal petitions which were presented to the king in the Good Parliament of 1376 which contrasted the contemporary Church, corrupted by simony, with a golden age in which worthy, clean-living clergy resided in their parishes, preaching

---

[80] Scase, *Piers Plowman and the New Anticlericalism*, pp. ix–x.
[81] Scase, *Piers Plowman and the New Anticlericalism*, pp. 13, 84–93.
[82] Scase, *Piers Plowman and the New Anticlericalism*, pp. 137–49. For Gower and the regular clergy, see chapters 8 and 9, below.
[83] Ormrod, *Edward III*, pp. 44–53.

and distributing alms. Like Gower, these petitions complained about papal appointments to bishoprics and cathedral dignities. In particular, they paralleled Gower's criticisms of the warlike clergy: 'as soon as the pope wants to have money to maintain his wars in Lombardy or elsewhere, to spend, or for the ransom of his friends, French prisoners taken by the English, he wants a subsidy from the clergy of England.'[84] Gower's hostile description of the unbeneficed clergy in the *Mirour de l'Omme* and the *Vox Clamantis* also has similarities with the tone and language of the 1378 reissue by Archbishop Sudbury of *Effrenata Generis*, the constitution which set maximum stipends for these clergy. Just as Gower satirises their greed, inflated salaries – three or four times what they used to be – and the way they 'hop and rush' around the city drinking, brawling and whoring (MO: 20521–7, 20636–4, 20665–712; VC: III.20.1561–2, 1606–10), so *Effrenata Generis* condemns those 'so tainted with the vice of cupidity' that 'they claim and receive excessive wages'.[85] It continues 'These greedy and fastidious priests vomit from the burden of excessive salaries ... they run wild and wallow and ... after gluttony of the belly, break forth into a pit of evils'.

'A Voice Crying in the Wilderness'?

Gower's sustained and systematic assault on the Church expresses, albeit in an extreme form, the increasing expectations of the laity of his day. His attack on the faults of the clergy, especially in the *Mirour de l'Omme* and the *Vox Clamantis*, was close to the anticlericalism of the estates satire tradition. Like all estates satires, Gower set his criticisms in a specific context, the condition of and problems facing the Church in the later fourteenth century, particularly the issues of the 1370s. In doing so he was following a well-established convention rather than developing a 'new anticlericalism'. Although socially and politically conservative, on one major issue, that of the papacy, Gower was radical. Here his criticism and his rejection of papal claims to temporal power went much further than the standard estates satire trope of papal avarice and venality or than the anti-papal literature of complaint about provisions, appeals and taxation. Even here, however, Gower's radicalism was limited in its scope and to read his Tale of Boniface as a challenge to all papal authority or as promoting royal power to constrain it would be anachronistic. With the exception of Wyclif, late fourteenth-century ecclesiastical and political thought had no concept of such a supreme secular monarch and, unlike Wyclif, Gower accepted the spiritual authority of the pope. Nor did Gower concern himself with other controversial issues of his day such

---

[84] *The Parliament Rolls of Medieval England 1275–1504: Edward III, 1351–77*, ed. W. Mark Ormrod (Woodbridge: Boydell Press, 2005), pp. 331–7.
[85] 'Archbishop Sudbury Raises the Wages of Priests, 1378', in *English Historical Documents 1327–1485*, ed. Alec R. Myers (London: Eyre and Spottiswood, 1969), pp. 728–9.

as tithes, the disendowment of the Church or the production of vernacular texts including the Bible. Whilst Gower's radicalism can also be seen in his repeated condemnation of warlike clergy, such radicalism was undermined by his conflicting positions on the Church and its authority, conflicts which, as Aers points out, remained unacknowledged and unexplored in his work. Even so, Gower succeeded in his aim of being a voice raised against what he saw as the manifest corruption of the clergy from the pope himself down to the lowliest mass priest, a voice railing against how far they had fallen from the apostolic ideals by which he expected them to live.

CHAPTER 8

MONASTIC LIFE

Martin Heale

John Gower and the Monastic Orders

John Gower's writings about monasticism present a paradox. On the one hand, they appear to cohere closely with the anticlerical discourses circulating in late fourteenth-century England.[1] Indeed Gower's stern critiques of the late medieval clergy were sufficient to earn him a place in John Foxe's sixteenth-century roll call of proto-Protestant members of the 'true church'.[2] Yet, on the other, what details we know of John Gower's later life, and of the preparations he made for his death, imply a strong regard for monastic practices and prayers. He spent his final years dwelling within the precinct of St Mary Overy Priory in Southwark. He requested, and was accorded, interment in a prominent location within that monastery's conventual church;[3] and there is no reason to doubt his subsequent reputation as, in the words of the inscription on his tomb, a 'distinguished benefactor of this building'.[4] Gower also established a chantry within the monastery centred on his tomb, presumably to be served by the Southwark canons; and he made generous bequests to the prior, subprior and brethren of the house for their attendance and prayers at his funeral.[5] Indeed, of the major literary figures

---

I am most grateful to Stephen H. Rigby, Robert F. Yeager, Siân Echard and David Lepine for their comments on earlier drafts of this chapter. They bear, of course, no responsibility for the shortcomings which remain.

[1] Wendy Scase, *Piers Plowman and the New Anticlericalism* (Cambridge: Cambridge University Press, 1989).
[2] *The Unabridged Acts and Monuments Online* (1570 edition) (HRI Online Publications, Sheffield, 2011): http//www.johnfoxe.org, pp. 5, 1004.
[3] For Gower's testament, see Gower, *Complete Works*, IV: xvii–xviii. See also John Hines, Nathalie Cohen and Simon Roffey, '*Iohannes Gower, Armiger, Poeta*: Records and Memorials of his Life and Death', in Siân Echard, ed., *A Companion to Gower* (Cambridge: D. S. Brewer, 2004), pp. 23–41, at 27 and Martha Carlin, above, pp. 85–90.
[4] See Hines, Cohen and Roffey, '*Iohannes Gower*', pp. 36–41.
[5] Gower, *Complete Works*, IV: xvii–xviii.

at work in late medieval England, only the Benedictine monk John Lydgate is known to have had stronger personal connections to the religious orders.

The monastic context of John Gower's writings, and its potential significance for their coverage and dissemination, has received episodic attention from scholars. John Fisher argued that the Augustinian canons of St Mary Overy played a central role in Gower's literary career, placing their facilities at his disposal.[6] Fisher's suggestion that Gower's works were produced in the monastery scriptorium has more recently been strongly challenged by detailed manuscript studies, which point instead to London scribes – whether commercial or otherwise – as the most likely copyists.[7] Yet debate continues over the relative importance of John Gower's connections with court, city and monastery in the shaping and spreading of his oeuvre. While several scholars regard a London literary community of civil servants and minor courtiers as the principal context for Gower's work, Jean-Pascal Pouzet and – more cautiously – Robert F. Yeager have sought to reassert the significance of the poet's monastic associations.[8]

Pouzet has made the case for a 'Southwark Gower', whose literary activities were heavily influenced by his connections with the priory of St Mary Overy. He contends that Gower made extensive use of the book collections held by the regular canons, and notes that the poet drew heavily on two Augustinian authors – Peter Riga and Alexander Neckham – in his earlier writings.[9] Pouzet also argues that Augustinian networks were influential in the dissemination of Gower's writings. Both Bisham Priory and Leicester Abbey are known to have possessed manuscripts containing his work, which – it is contended – may well have spread through Augustinian channels such as the order's provincial chapter.[10] Yeager, meanwhile, has embraced Fisher's conclusion that Gower took up residence in the Southwark priory in the late 1370s, and has argued not only that the *Mirour de l'Omme* was completed in the monastery but also for 'the likely influence of the Austin canons on the ultimate shaping of the poem'. In particular, he suggests that the final section of the *Mirour de l'Omme*, with its invocation of the Virgin Mary, might be attributed to a decision on Gower's part to redirect his work from a

---

[6] John H. Fisher, *John Gower: Moral Philosopher and Friend of Chaucer* (New York: New York University Press, 1964), pp. 59–60.

[7] For references to this literature and debate, see Rigby, above, p. 135.

[8] Jean-Pascal Pouzet, 'Southwark Gower: Augustinian Agencies in Gower's Manuscripts and Texts – Some Prolegomena', in Elizabeth Dutton, John Hines and Robert F. Yeager, eds, *John Gower, Trilingual Poet. Language, Translation and Tradition* (Cambridge: D. S. Brewer, 2010), pp. 11–25, esp. 12; Robert F. Yeager, 'Gower's French Audience: the *Mirour de l'Omme*', *Chaucer Review*, 41/2 (2006), pp. 111–37; Robert F. Yeager, 'John Gower's French and his Readers', in Jocelyn Wogan-Browne et al., eds, *Language and Culture in Medieval Britain: The French of England c.1100–c.1500* (York: York Medieval Press, 2009), pp. 135–45.

[9] Pouzet, 'Southwark Gower', pp. 12–17.

[10] *Ibid.*, pp. 17–21.

courtly to a monastic audience, adding that the choice of Latin for the *Vox Clamantis* may have had a similar motivation. Yeager further posits that the brief section on regular canons in the *Mirour de l'Omme* (21157–68) may have been added after Gower took up residence in St Mary Overy Priory.[11] He also proposes that the 'Quixley' who translated into Yorkshire-dialect English John Gower's *Traitié pour essampler les amantz marietz* was Robert de Quixley, the Augustinian prior of Nostell, noting potential links between this Yorkshire priory and the Austin canons of Southwark.[12]

These various arguments are intriguing, but ultimately remain speculative. Pouzet's attempts to connect John Gower's writings with specific manuscripts known to have been held by St Mary Overy Priory have produced, it must be said, rather inconclusive results. For instance, the *De Vita Monachorum*, which Gower drew upon for the *Vox Clamantis*, was probably not written by the Augustinian canon Alexander Neckham.[13] The precise timing of John Gower's re-location to the Southwark priory also remains uncertain, with Martha Carlin suggesting that Gower moved there only in the mid-1380s, i.e. after the composition of the *Mirour de l'Omme* and the *Vox Clamantis* (see above p. 54). Similarly, the inclusion of regular canons in Gower's critique of the religious orders in the *Mirour de l'Omme* and the *Vox Clamantis* is not necessarily suggestive of personal connections: both Chaucer and Langland also wrote of monks and canons alike.[14] Nor is the evidence for the prominence of the Augustinian canons as readers and disseminators of Gower's works very decisive. Gower manuscripts seem often to have circulated among wealthy lay readers, and it is not even clear that his writings attracted a wider readership among the Austin canons than other branches of the religious orders.[15] In their search for Augustinian associations, moreover, both Pouzet and Yeager sometimes overplay potential connections, for instance including

---

[11] Yeager, 'Gower's French Audience', pp. 118–27.
[12] Yeager, 'John Gower's French and his Readers', pp. 135–45.
[13] George Watson, ed., *The New Cambridge Bibliography of English Literature. Volume 1: 600–1660* (Cambridge: Cambridge University Press, 1974), p. 770; Joseph Goering, 'Neckam [Neckham, Nequam], Alexander (1157–1217), Scholar and Abbot of Cirencester', *Oxford Dictionary of National Biography* (online edition; Oxford: Oxford University Press, 2004).
[14] Geoffrey Chaucer, 'General Prologue', I: 187–8; Geoffrey Chaucer, 'The Canon's Yeoman Tale', VIII: 972, 992–5; *The Vision of Piers Plowman: A Critical Edition of the B-Text based on Trinity College, Cambridge MS B.15.17*, ed. Aubrey V. C. Schmidt (London: J. M. Dent & Sons, 1987), X: 316; XV: 320 (cited below as *Piers Plowman: B-Text*); *Piers Plowman by William Langland: An Edition of the C-Text*, ed. Derek Pearsall (London: Arnold, 1978), V: 156 (cited below as *Piers Plowman: C-Text*).
[15] Derek Pearsall, 'The Manuscripts and Illustrations of Gower's Works', in Echard, *A Companion to Gower*, pp. 73–97, at 95–7; Kate Harris, 'Ownership and Readership: Studies in the Provenance of the Manuscripts of Gower's *Confessio Amantis*' (Unpublished University of York PhD thesis (1993)); and see Fisher, *John Gower*, p. 92, which draws attention to Gower manuscripts in the possession of (the Benedictine) Bury St Edmunds Abbey and (the Cistercian) Fountains Abbey.

Halesowen Abbey (a Premonstratensian house, with only tenuous links to the Austin canons) or John Waldeby (an Augustinian *friar*, not canon) in their reckonings.[16] Yet John Gower's monastic associations should not be dismissed out of hand as a factor in his literary career. Even if Gower was not resident in the Southwark priory until the mid-1380s, this would not preclude a prior relationship with the canons of St Mary Overy. Thus, although the Augustinian canons may not have been central figures in shaping and disseminating Gower's works, they nonetheless represent one of several spheres in which he operated.

While John Gower's biographical links to monastic institutions have been carefully examined, neither literary scholars nor historians have shown very much interest in his actual writings on the monastic life.[17] It is symptomatic that Gower receives no mention in Derek Pearsall's analysis of the monastic ideal in later medieval English literature, which focuses instead on Chaucer, Langland and Lydgate.[18] Similarly, David Knowles made no reference to John Gower in his chapter-length account of 'criticism of the religious in the fourteenth century', and Gower's work features only in passing in Wendy Scase's *Piers Plowman and the New Anticlericalism*.[19] This state of affairs might be attributed to a number of factors, including the dominance of the *Confessio Amantis* in Gower studies and the apparently conventional nature of the poet's treatment of the monastic life. Moreover, in contrast to Gower's writings on the Peasants' Revolt or the rule of Richard II, there is little eye-catching material of immediate contemporary relevance here.

Nevertheless, John Gower's own monastic connections, and the fact that he wrote more about the religious orders than almost any other poet in late medieval England, render his evaluation of the monks, regular canons and nuns of his day worthy of closer examination. A number of questions in particular suggest themselves, in the light of the aims of this volume and the state of current scholarship on the subject. How should we reconcile Gower's apparently hostile assessment of contemporary monastic life with his personal support for the religious orders in practice? To what extent was his

---

[16] Pouzet, 'Southwark Gower', p. 18; Yeager, 'John Gower's French and his Readers', p. 139n. The Augustinian friars, established as a religious order in 1256, maintained no particular connections (formal or otherwise) with the Augustinian canons.

[17] For partial exceptions, see Yeager, 'Gower's French Audience', pp. 124–5; Robert R. Raymo, 'Vox Clamantis, IV, 12', Modern Language Notes 71.2 (1956), pp. 82–3; and Matthew Irvin, 'Genius and Sensual Reading in the *Vox Clamantis*', in Dutton, Hines and Yeager, *John Gower, Trilingual Poet*, pp. 196–205.

[18] Derek Pearsall, '"If Heaven be on this Earth, it is in Cloister or in School": the Monastic Ideal in Later Medieval English Literature', in Rosemary Horrox and Sarah Rees Jones, eds, *Pragmatic Utopias: Ideals and Communities, 1200–1630* (Cambridge: Cambridge University Press, 2001), pp. 11–25.

[19] Dom David Knowles, *The Religious Orders in England* (three volumes; Cambridge: Cambridge University Press, 1950–59), II: 90–114; Scase, *Piers Plowman and the New Anticlericalism*, pp. 8, 90.

portrait of monastic life drawn from older literary models and tropes? What was his detailed treatment of the religious orders designed to achieve? Finally, what (if anything) might Gower's writings on this subject reveal about the author and the monastic life of his day? It will be argued that there is, in fact, little in Gower's work that appears to have been drawn directly from close observation of monastic practices, with his treatment of the monastic life and cloistered men and women apparently deriving instead from conventional, written sources.

John Gower on Monastic Life: the *Mirour de l'Omme* and the *Vox Clamantis*

John Gower's treatment of monasticism is largely concentrated in lines 20833–21180 of the *Mirour de l'Omme* and in Book IV of the *Vox Clamantis*, although he made occasional reference to the religious orders at other points in his oeuvre.[20] Both the *Mirour de l'Omme* and the *Vox Clamantis* belong to the earliest phase of his literary career, with Gower apparently working on these poems in the late 1370s (see above, pp. 124–5, 127). There was considerable overlap between these two works, with each addressing the vices of different sections of fourteenth-century society in the manner of a traditional 'estates satire'.[21] However, differences in the structure and design of these works mean that the *Vox Clamantis* offers a more extended – and more balanced – discussion of the monastic orders than the *Mirour de l'Omme*.[22] The lengthy sections on the secular and regular clergy in the *Vox Clamantis*, along with Gower's choice to write in Latin, may indicate that he had a clerical audience more firmly in mind for this poem.[23]

In line with the broader purpose of the *Mirour de l'Omme*, i.e. of highlighting the triumph of vice over virtue among each order of medieval society, Gower's treatment of the monastic life in this work sets out an unremittingly negative picture (20833–21180). Making no distinction between the different monastic orders, he opined that the monks of his day wholly failed to live up to the elevated ideals of their way of life. They neglected their duty to pray for the world (20836–40), disregarded monastic rules and vows (20857–80, 20941–52), and evaded the life of renunciation to which they had supposedly committed themselves (20857–62). They strove covetously to enlarge their house's endowments and to live

---

[20] For other brief asides concerning the religious life in Gower's writings, see MO: 9093, 9157–68, and CA: I.607–45.
[21] For Gower's place within this tradition, see Paul Miller, 'John Gower, Satiric Poet', in Alastair J. Minnis, ed., *Gower's Confessio Amantis: Responses and Reassessments* (Cambridge: D. S. Brewer, 1983), pp. 79–105.
[22] For an overview of these two works' purpose and coverage, see Rigby, above, pp. 123–9.
[23] Cf. Fisher, *John Gower*, pp. 105–6, 157.

in comfort (20841–4), indulging in gluttonous eating to please their 'fat bellies' (20863–5), excessive drinking (20881–5, 20899–900), and sartorial luxury with their 'furred cloaks' (20866–8, 20998–21000) and fine jewellery (21020–2). The asceticism of former times was no longer practised in monasteries. Whereas the monks of old had dwelt in caves and lived in great simplicity, members of religious houses now lived 'like kings ... in great halls' (21109–17). In effect, Gower concluded, they had not withdrawn from the world at all, and were still fixated on creature comforts, worldly honour and social advancement.

Gower also complained in the *Mirour* that monks paid little heed to their enclosure, venturing out to engage in secular activities such as hunting (20845–7, 21043–7). Particularly at fault in this regard were those senior obedientiaries who acted as wardens, stewards or treasurers, and thus routinely left the cloister on monastery business. Such monks were condemned as greedy, lordly and worldly, neglecting their rule and oppressing the weak in their desire for gain (20953–88). Brethren who sought after material advantage in this way were little different from merchants or other laymen: 'only a wife is lacking', though many sired illegitimate children (21037–60). However bad was the behaviour of those monks who absented themselves from the cloister, Gower viewed the internal life of the monastery as little better. This was characterised by 'murmuring, ill will, envy and disobedience', not to mention ignorance (21073–84). Gower considered that worldly monks were to be much pitied since they lost both the joys of the world and the heavenly rewards they ought to have received as members of monastic communities (21061–72). He also implied that such brethren were the majority in the monasteries of his day, with few monks observing the original laws of their orders (21118–20). The regular canons, meanwhile, may have followed tolerably the outward requirements of their order, observing their hours and chapters, but their internal condition was no better than that of the monks (21157–68).

Gower's depiction of the monastic orders in Book IV of the *Vox Clamantis* rehearsed many of the criticisms advanced in the *Mirour* but at considerably greater length. His central theme here was the *waywardness* of the religious orders – an errancy which (as the conclusion to Book IV makes clear) he believed was leading the wider population astray (IV.24.1220–32).[24] The monastic ideal was itself good and holy: 'God is present among the monks who are willing to enter monasteries apart from mankind, and the fellowship of heaven is theirs' (IV.1.11–12). But the many worldly monks who failed to live up to that ideal, and who 'look back from the plow' (IV.4.245–6), betrayed the monastic way of life. Gower's critique of errant and worldly monks again focused particularly on those who embraced 'the delights of

---

[24] Gower's section on each of the monks, the regular canons and the nuns begins with charges of waywardness (VC: IV.1.8, 13). For a similar critique of the secular clergy, see VC: III.29.2141–2.

the flesh'. They devoted themselves to satisfying their swelling bellies and consuming fine food and wine, ordering all their affairs to facilitate their gluttony. As a result, they neglected monastic duties in order to satisfy their appetites, feeding their bodies while their souls went hungry. The drunkenness in which they are said to have frequently indulged, moreover, invariably led to sloth and debauchery (IV.2–3).

Contemporary monks and canons, Gower claimed, found monastic rules displeasing and accordingly disregarded, or at least mollified, them wherever possible. This point was driven home relentlessly with a series of puns. The 're' [essence] had been subtracted from 'regula' [rule] leaving behind only 'gula' [gluttony] (IV.3.127–8); Benedict has been replaced by malediction (IV.4.243–4; IV.7.341); and the canons regular do not observe the canons (IV.8.359–60). Nor, we are told, did monks take seriously their vows of poverty, chastity and obedience. The result was a 'feigned religion', practised by monks who observed the religious life only in its externals of tonsure and habit. Gower repeatedly highlighted the hypocrisy of members of the monastic orders who appeared holy on the outside but were sinful on the inside (IV.2.43–52; IV.3.195–6, 201–6; IV.6.313–14; IV.8.361–6; cf. MO: 21157–68, CA: I.607–45). Monks were also prone to the deadly sins of pride, wrath and envy, which extinguished brotherly love within the monastery. They were grasping, seeking any opportunity to extend their property at the expense of benefactors, the poor, or their fellow-monks. In their worldliness, they freely roamed outside the monastery, seeking honour and status. Consequently – as Gower had stressed in the *Mirour de l'Omme* – errant monks deprived themselves of the blessings of both the world and the cloister by their evil living (IV.9.377–88), while also leading layfolk astray.

The result of all this waywardness and neglect was, Gower concluded, a monstrous charade of the true monastic life.[25] Indeed, he recurrently asserted the *unnatural* state of contemporary monasticism with a series of striking images. Monks were ruled by their bellies and not by their heads (IV.3.127–8) whilst, in their determination to retain the pleasures of the life they had supposedly renounced, they were like the dead returned to life (IV.2.41–2). Gower's deployment of the hackneyed description of the monk outside of his precinct as a 'fish out of water' also emphasised the monstrous nature of this abuse:

> If there were a fish that forsook the waters of the sea to seek its food on land, it would be highly inappropriate to give it the name of fish; I should rather give it the name of monster. Such shall I call the monk who yearns for worldly delights and deserts his cloister for them. He

---

[25] For a discussion of the theme of monstrosity in Gower's works, see Eve Salisbury, 'Remembering Origins: Gower's Monstrous Body Politic', in Robert F. Yeager, ed., *Re-Visioning Gower* (Asheville: Pegasus Press, 1998), pp. 159–84.

should not rightly be called a monk but a renegade, or what God's wrath brands as a monster of the Church (IV.5.281–90).

A member of a religious order who lacks a monk's true nature, moreover, was as unsightly and unnatural as a 'field without grass', 'a plant without leaves' or 'a head without hair' (IV.6.311–12).

Book IV of the *Vox Clamantis* also includes three chapters on nunneries (IV.13–15), a branch of the late medieval Church mentioned only in passing in the *Mirour de l'Omme* (9157–68). For Gower, the monastic life for women, as for men, was praiseworthy and a sure route to heaven when lived virtuously. However, the waywardness of nuns, according to Gower's strictures, consisted almost entirely in the neglect of their vow of chastity. This failure was a product of feminine weakness, 'for a woman's foot cannot stand as steady as a man's can' (VC: IV.13.555–7). Nevertheless, nuns' lapses in chastity were more serious than those committed by men, since 'if the brides of men should be pure, how much more ought the brides of Christ remain chaste in pure conduct for God' (VC: IV.14.637–8; cf. MO: 9157–68). In this emphasis on the centrality but also precariousness of nuns' chastity, John Gower was expressing wholly conventional late medieval attitudes towards female monasticism.[26]

More distinctively, Gower asserted that the sexual immorality of nuns was fostered not only by their inherent womanly frailty but also by inadvisable dabbling in the scriptures by those sisters with some education: 'the very women whom their order thinks most sensible'. By their simplistic and sensual reading of the Bible, without recourse to learned glosses, religious women were led astray into moral lapses (VC: 13.562–74).[27] In this critique of nuns' learning, it is not clear whether Gower had in mind the reading of the Latin Vulgate or vernacular translations of scripture. From the slender evidence that survives regarding the libraries of late medieval English nunneries, it is clear that biblical texts (in addition to the psalter) in Latin, French and – following the Wycliffite translations of scripture in the late fourteenth century – English might be available to religious women.[28]

---

[26] Nancy Bradley Warren, *Spiritual Economies: Female Monasticism in Later Medieval England* (Philadelphia: University of Pennsylvania Press, 2001), pp. 3–9; Elizabeth M. Makowski, *Canon Law and Cloistered Women: Periculoso and its Commentators, 1298–1545* (Washington: Catholic University of America Press, 1999).

[27] For a discussion of Gower's emphasis on sensuality in this passage, see Irvin, 'Genius and Sensual Reading', pp. 196–205.

[28] Latin texts of various sections of the Bible were held by the nuns of Barking and Swine, whereas the small community of Easebourne owned a French bible in the mid-fifteenth century. The nuns of late medieval Barking (the books of Tobit and Susanna) and Thetford (the New Testament) each possessed a volume containing Wycliffite translations of scripture (David N. Bell, *What Nuns Read: Books and Libraries in Medieval English Nunneries* (Kalamazoo, Michigan: Cistercian Publications, 1995), pp. 107–20, 136, 168–70, 211–12, 227, 245; Mary C. Erler, *Women, Reading and Piety*

Moreover, the nunnery of St Mary's, Winchester (Nunnaminster), possessed Latin commentaries on certain books of the Bible in the first half of the fourteenth century; and some of the scriptural texts at late medieval Barking and Swine were accompanied by Latin glosses.[29] It is unlikely, however, that Gower was making an informed comment on reading habits in late fourteenth-century nunneries, about which he could presumably have had little knowledge. Rather, his views seem to have been part of a more general criticism of female learning and its purportedly baleful consequences.[30]

In his discussion of moral failings within nunneries, however, John Gower judged that the greatest blame lay not with 'light-minded' religious women but with the nuns' clerical overseers. In a highly allusive and innuendo-laden passage – in which Gower draws on a range of texts, including Ovid's *Ars Amatoria* and the *Roman de la Rose* – the male confessors, visitors and teachers of nuns are chastised for abusing their authority by preying on weak and vulnerable religious women (IV.13.585–94; IV.14.595–610).[31] As Gower's section on nuns concluded: 'How heavy a crime in our judgment does a man commit who takes it upon himself to violate another's bride!' (IV.15.673–4). It has been suggested that John Gower treated nuns more sympathetically than monks and friars, since their lapses were largely attributed to their exploitation by others and to their own frailty.[32] Yet the emphasis on the abuses of male overseers in chapters 13–15 of Book IV means that the *Vox Clamantis* has strikingly little to say about the lives and activities of the nuns themselves. Even as a conventional satirical portrait of late medieval religious women, Gower's treatment is very limited. There is no sign here of such standard stereotypes of nuns as (in Jill Mann's summation) 'quarrelsome or recalcitrant, deceitful, fond of luxury, unable to keep a secret, lacrimose, and hungry for praise'.[33] His relatively brief discussion of nuns extends little beyond the importance (and fragility) of their chastity, a state of affairs

---

in *Late Medieval England* (Cambridge: Cambridge University Press, 2002), p. 31). See also David N. Bell, 'What Nuns Read: the State of the Question', in James G. Clark, ed., *The Culture of Medieval English Monasticism* (Woodbridge: Boydell Press), pp. 113–33.

[29] *Registrum Anglie de Libris Doctorum et Auctorum Veterum*, eds Richard H. Rouse and Mary A. Rouse, Corpus of British Medieval Library Catalogues, 2 (London: British Library, 1991), p. 264; Bell, *What Nuns Read*, pp. 111–12, 169.

[30] Cf. *Piers Plowman: B-Text*, III: 332–48. This section might also be compared with Gower's concerns about the misreading of scripture by Lollards, as expressed in his *Carmen super multiplici viciorum pestilencia* of 1396–97, a point I owe to Robert F. Yeager.

[31] This complex passage – which features the figures of Genius and Venus in very different roles from their function in the *Confessio Amantis* – is insightfully discussed in Irvin, 'Genius and Sensual Reading', pp. 196–205.

[32] *Ibid.*, p. 202; Gower, *Major Latin Works*, p. 20.

[33] Jill Mann, *Chaucer and Medieval Estates Satire* (Cambridge: Cambridge University Press, 1973), pp. 128–37, esp. 129.

which seems to indicate a distinct lack of interest in female monasticism on Gower's part.

Sources, Stereotypes and Distinctive Themes

In his extended treatment of the monastic life in the Vox Clamantis, Gower drew on a small number of works from the later twelfth and early thirteenth centuries, including Peter Riga's Aurora,[34] Godfrey of Viterbo's Pantheon, the Speculum Stultorum of Nigel Wireker (or de Longchamps),[35] and the De Vita Monachorum. However, as is now widely acknowledged, he did not simply recycle material from these works or from his other sources, but instead wove their ideas and criticisms into his writings in a skilful and subtle manner. A further indication that Gower did not re-use material unthinkingly can be seen in the way that he applied the criticisms of the religious made by their monastic fellows to other sections of society, as when he adapted warnings about monastic avarice from the De Vita Monachorum to judges in the Vox Clamantis (VI.5.313–98).

There are, nonetheless, a number of conventional themes and tropes in Gower's treatment of the religious orders in the Mirour de l'Omme and Vox Clamantis. The emphasis on monastic gluttony, drunkenness and luxurious dress, so prominent in Gower's work, was of course a commonplace of the goliardic and moralistic writing of the previous 250 years.[36] This included long-familiar barbs about monks shaving their heads lest long hair should obstruct their guzzling, and wearing loose garments to conceal their fat bellies (VC: IV.3.135–6, 141–2).[37] The complaint that the habit (or tonsure) does not make the monk (MO: 21085–96; VC: IV.6.313–14), and that a monastic out of his cloister was like a fish out of water (MO: 20845–7; VC: IV.5.281–2), were also ubiquitous clichés.[38] Gower's criticism of the hunting monk in the Mirour de l'Omme (21043–8) was equally predictable.[39] He also adopted the common technique of personifying monastic vices, utilised by Langland and others. Thus 'Dan Envy', 'Dan Hate', 'Dan Pride', 'Dan Incontinence', 'Dan Gluttony', 'Dan Avarice' and their ilk overran religious houses (MO: 21133–56, 21169–80), while 'Abbot World', 'Abbot

---

[34] Paul E. Beichner, 'Gower's Use of Aurora in Vox Clamantis', Speculum, 30 (1955), pp. 582–95.
[35] Robert R. Raymo, 'Gower's Vox Clamantis and the Speculum Stultorum', Modern Language Notes, 70.5 (1955), pp. 315–20.
[36] See Mann, Chaucer and Medieval Estates Satire, pp. 17–24.
[37] E.g. Apocalipsis Goliae, in The Latin Poems commonly attributed to Walter Mapes, ed. Thomas Wright (Camden Society, old series, 16 (1841)), ll. 401–4.
[38] Chaucer, 'General Prologue', I: 179–81; Piers Plowman: B-Text, X: 293–6; Piers Plowman: C-Text, V: 148–51; Mann, Chaucer and Medieval Estates Satire, pp. 29–31.
[39] Mann, Chaucer and Medieval Estates Satire, pp. 24–5.

Grumbler', 'Abbot Inconstancy', 'Abbot Lust' and 'Abbot Deceit' had driven out 'Abbot Patience', 'Abbot Chastity' and 'Abbot Gentle' (VC: IV.7).

It is possible to discern what is commonplace and what is more distinctive in Gower's writing on the religious orders through a comparison with the particular themes elaborated by Chaucer and Langland. Gower may have been familiar with the B-text version of *Piers Plowman* (c.1377x1379), and Chaucer evidently drew on Gower's critique of contemporary monasticism for the 'General Prologue' of the *Canterbury Tales*.[40] There was, in fact, considerable common ground in the three poets' depiction of contemporary monasticism. All praised the monastic ideal itself – with Gower and Langland in particular stressing the high value of the religious life when lived well – but all were sharply critical of departures from rules and vows.[41] All three poets dwelt on the luxurious living of the regular clergy, particularly their gluttony and lavish dress, and their pursuit of inappropriate pastimes such as hunting.[42] Each also specifically targeted the 'lordly' monk, and especially the senior obedientiary – or 'outrider' – who left the cloister to transact the monastery's external business. Such brethren, they agreed, were more preoccupied with their own dignity and comfort than with the welfare of others or the monastic order's rules and ideals.[43] Gower, Chaucer and Langland were also alike in their lack of differentiation between individual religious orders.

Other components of Gower's treatment of the monastic life, however, were more distinctive. These included his emphasis on monks' social climbing, a recurring topic in both the *Mirour de l'Omme* and the *Vox Clamantis* which is found neither in Langland nor Chaucer, and was not commonplace in earlier satirical works.[44] Gower repeatedly railed against the low-born monk who entered a monastery not to withdraw from the world but rather to seek to advance his position within it. The coarse and uncouth inmate might readily attain a position of honour in his house and enjoy a lavish lifestyle, 'and yet a shepherdess was his mother, and probably his father was a servant without nobility' (MO: 21031–3; cf. VC: II.57–60, IV.4.237–8, 6.315–20). In this way not only was the monastic ideal flouted, but the social order threatened: 'But when the base mounts on high, and the

---

[40] See Robert R. Raymo, 'The General Prologue', in *Sources and Analogues of the Canterbury Tales*, eds Robert M. Correale and Mary Hamel (two volumes; Cambridge: D. S. Brewer, 2003–05), II: 1–86.
[41] E.g. *Piers Plowman: B-Text*, X: 297–8; *Piers Plowman: C-Text*, V: 152–3.
[42] Chaucer, 'General Prologue', I: 165–207; *Piers Plowman: B-Text*, X: 303–10; *Piers Plowman: C-Text*, V: 160.
[43] Chaucer, 'General Prologue', I: 166, 172, 200; Chaucer, 'Shipman's Tale', VII: 1–434, esp. 65–6; *Piers Plowman: B-Text*, X: 303–8; *Piers Plowman: C-Text*, IV: 116. Cf. Pearsall, 'Monastic Ideal', pp. 11–25, where the author plausibly attributes this late-medieval literary focus on outriders to their visibility to the lay observer.
[44] This charge was also made in the sixteenth-century evangelical tract *Rede Me and be nott Wrothe* (Jerome Barlow and William Roy, *Rede Me and be nott Wrothe*, ed. Douglas H. Parker (Toronto: University of Toronto Press, 1992), 2527–32, 2540–1).

poor is in wealth, there is nothing in the world so evil' (MO: 21034–6).[45] These complaints correspond closely to Gower's criticism of social mobility in London ('Nothing is more troublesome than a lowly person when he has risen to the top – at least when he was born a serf' (VC: V.15.853–4)); and also to his complaints about the poor peasant, nourished on water from wells, who 'demands things for his belly like a lord' (VC: V.10.647–8). Here would seem to be an example of how Gower's social conservatism shaped his views of the monastic life, which could unquestionably be a promising avenue for social mobility in late medieval England.[46]

We might also note that Gower devoted relatively little attention to monastic maltreatment of the poor, even though this was a theme which featured prominently in Langland's poetry and in several other fourteenth-century critiques of the religious orders.[47] Gower did not wholly ignore this issue. In the *Mirour de l'Omme*, he criticised monastic wardens and stewards for taking the best grain and 'leaving the chaff for others, such as the peasants' (20959–60), and bemoaned how Dan Avarice 'does not let Dan Almsgiving give any largess at all' (21176–8). Similarly in the *Vox Clamantis*, he criticised the religious orders for hoarding wealth which really 'belongs to the needy' (IV.4.229). Such concerns, however, are not particularly emphasised in either work. Nor did Gower anywhere advance the standard contemporary complaint that monasteries were generous hosts to the powerful but were far less attentive to humble visitors.[48] Instead, he simply warned against dining in monasteries, where the (presumably wealthy) guests risked being separated from their possessions by ingratiating monks (VC: IV.4.215–20). In fact, the social functions of the religious orders – as dispensers of alms, hosts, employers and landlords – featured relatively little in Gower's portrait of the monastic life. Although he claimed to be speaking with 'the voice of the people' throughout the *Vox Clamantis* (e.g. III.Pro.23–8, IV.1.19–20,

---

[45] In chapter 6 of Book IV of the *Vox Clamantis*, Gower's comments about social climbing follow on directly from his complaint about those in religious orders who lack 'a monk's true nature'. The implication here seems to be that monks who sought to rise in the world through joining a religious house were another manifestation of the unnatural and monstrous nature of contemporary monasticism.

[46] See Martin Heale, *The Abbots and Priors of Late Medieval and Reformation England* (Oxford: Oxford University Press, 2016), pp. 51–4.

[47] E.g. *Piers Plowman: B-Text*, X: 312–14, 326–7; *Piers Plowman: C-Text*, V. 166; *The Simonie: A Parallel Text Edition*, eds Dan Embree and Elizabeth Urquhart (Heidelberg: Winter Universitätsverlag, 1991), 127–32; *Mum and the Sothsegger. Edited from the Manuscripts Camb. Univ. Ll. Iv. 14 and Brit. Mus. Add. 41666*, eds Mabel Day and Robert Steele (EETS, o.s. 199 (1936)), 540–52. This was also a prominent theme in Wycliffite critique of the monastic orders (Thomas Renna, 'Wyclif's Attacks on the Monks', in Anne Hudson and Michael J. Wilks, eds, *From Ockham to Wyclif*, Studies in Church History Subsidia 5 (Oxford: Blackwell, 1987), pp. 267–80).

[48] See Gerald R. Owst, *Literature and Pulpit in Medieval England* (second edition; Oxford: Blackwell, 1961), p. 262; Heale, *Abbots and Priors*, pp. 252–3.

16.709–10, VI.1.15), there is little sense of the concerns of less elevated sections of society finding expression in his writings on the religious orders.

A further notable element of Gower's writings on the monastic life is his frequent complaints about the regular clergy of 'nowadays' ('au present jour', or 'a ore' (MO: 20995, 21115); 'iam', 'nunc' or 'modo' (e.g. VC: IV.2.49; IV.3.128; IV.4.223; IV.5.304; IV.7.336, 340, 345). This emphasis of course dovetails with Gower's general critique of contemporary society, with his apprehension that 'no estate is as holy as in days gone by' (VC: III.Pro.14). Regarding the religious orders, his central concern, as we have seen, was that present-day monks and canons did not observe the rules and precepts of their 'original founders'. Yet it is not wholly clear that Gower considered his own generation of monks and regular canons to be specially vicious or unworthy, or having fallen away from a recent golden age.[49] He did criticise 'new fashions', the 'new type of religious order' and also the undoing of monastic rules 'in recent times' (VC: IV.3.125; IV.4.236), but this theme was not developed or substantiated with particular examples of harmful modern innovations. Instead, Gower regularly returned to generalised and conventional accusations of sinfulness within the monastic order.

In fact, it seems that John Gower regarded many of the monastic abuses he bemoaned to have been in place for many centuries.[50] In the *Mirour de l'Omme*, he included a story of St Macarius of Egypt (c.300–391) which recounts how the devil spread envy in a monastery in the form of a powder diffused into the monks' hoods, 'so, that burning of envy naturally remains in the monks' hearts, and shall remain forever' (20905–28). Gower, moreover, envisaged a long-lost age of monastic purity 'in early times' ('jadis'), when 'the monks lived in deep caves and exalted the right faith of Jesus Christ; they wore sackcloth and hair shirts; they drank water and ate herbs' (21109–14). Returning to this theme in the *Vox Clamantis*, he contrasted the harshly ascetic homes, diet and dress of the first monks with the luxuries enjoyed by the religious orders of his day (IV.2.83–124). These early exponents of the monastic life, Gower affirmed, had lived in holiness, unity and charity, without envy or grumbling; but that ancient Arcadian purity and simplicity had long since evaporated, as monks gave into 'the weakness of flesh'. Gower seems here to have had in mind the desert fathers and other early hermits, and his treatment of this theme is reminiscent of Langland's approving reference to St Anthony and St Giles, who 'Woneden in wildernesse among wilde beestes; / Monkes and mendinaunts, men by hemselve / In spekes

---

[49] Since Gower drew many of his criticisms of the religious orders from satirical and exhortatory works of the late twelfth and early thirteenth centuries, it would presumably have been difficult for him to romanticise that era of monastic history.

[50] Gower's notion of a golden age appears to have differed according to social estate. Thus the secular clergy were deemed to have been virtuous in an unspecified bygone era (e.g. VC: III.8.555–6; III.15.1273–4) whereas the moral decline of knights was presented as a more recent development (VC: V.1.11–12).

and in spelonkes, selde speken togideres'.[51] This appeal to the eremitical origins of monasticism pointed monks to an ideal rather more austere than the regulations of their orders' founding fathers, creating some tension with Gower's frequent plea to the religious to observe their own rules and vows.

John Gower's reference to the desert fathers suggests a possible intersection with contemporary controversies about the religious life, which particularly focused on the history of early monasticism. One way in which monastic writers in fourteenth-century England sought to defend their way of life was to emphasise its ancient pedigree.[52] This included the argument that the early monks in the Egyptian desert were following directly in the traditions of the apostles, highlighting the biblical credentials of the monastic life questioned by some of its critics. Detractors of late fourteenth-century monasticism, by contrast, pointed to the disjuncture between the first monks and their present-day equivalents, in order to argue for the need for wholesale reform. In particular, William Langland, John Trevisa, John Wyclif and others openly discussed the possibility that the secular power might restore the religious orders to their pristine state through some degree of disendowment.[53] Such measures seem to have been too radical for Gower, however. He did relate, in both the *Mirour de l'Omme* and the *Vox Clamantis*, the well-known story of the angelic prophecy that the endowment of the Church by Constantine would spread poison within it (MO: 18637–48; VC: III.5.283–8). But in neither work did he hint that taking away clerical property was an appropriate response to this state of affairs.[54] Similarly, although Gower criticised monks for their greed in pursuing new grants of property (VC: IV.4.217–20, 231–2), he stopped short of Langland's call for laymen to cease endowing the over-wealthy religious orders.[55]

John Gower's discussion of the desert fathers as exemplars of pristine monasticism does not appear, therefore, to have been a pointed intervention in contemporary controversies about the antiquity of the religious life or the legitimacy of monastic wealth. Nor did he engage directly with John Wyclif's critique of monasticism. Gower was presumably cognisant of Wyclif while composing the *Mirour de l'Omme* and the *Vox Clamantis*, as the 'evangelical doctor' came into prominence at precisely the time these works were written. However, Gower's only reference to Wyclif in Book IV of the *Vox* was a later

---

[51] *Piers Plowman: B-Text*, XV: 272–5.
[52] William A. Pantin, 'Some Medieval English Treatises on the Origins of Monasticism', in Veronica Ruffer and Arnold J. Taylor, eds, *Medieval Studies Presented to Rose Graham* (Oxford: Oxford University Press, 1950), pp. 189–215.
[53] *Piers Plowman: B-Text*, X: 322–5; *Piers Plowman: C-Text*, V: 144; Scase, *Piers Plowman and the New Anticlericalism*, pp. 88–119; Margaret Aston, 'Caim's Castles: Poverty, Politics and Disendowment', in R. Barrie Dobson, ed., *The Church, Politics and Patronage in the Fifteenth Century* (Gloucester: Sutton, 1984), pp. 45–81.
[54] Nor, contrary to Stockton's translation of VC: III.5.293–4, did Gower link this story explicitly to *monastic* endowments.
[55] *Piers Plowman: B-Text*, XV: 318–43.

addition to its final section, which declared him a schismatic akin to Arius and Jovinian (IV.24.1227*–1228*; cf. VI.19.1267–8). Nor did Gower refer to Wycliffite criticisms of the monastic life when condemning Lollardy in his later writings (e.g. CA: V.1803–24).[56]

Indeed, the lack of any clear resonance with topical monastic controversies is one of the more striking elements of Gower's depiction of the religious life in both *Mirour de l'Omme* and *Vox Clamantis*. The relatively few references which he made to specific monastic abuses – such as the monks' creative definitions of meat which allowed them to by-pass the dietary requirements of the Benedictine Rule (MO: 20869–80); their use of sign language to overcome regulations concerning silence (VC: IV.3.171–4); and the strict claustration of women (VC: IV.13–15) – were in fact long-running issues with no special currency in Gower's day.[57] Nor did Gower align himself with any particular programme of monastic reform, other than a general return to pristine observance. He was deeply concerned with the renewal of the monastic life, as he was for the correction of other sections of society. However, what Gower's writings offered were timeless remedies to perpetual difficulties in living up to the monastic ideal, articulated from a conservative and somewhat elitist perspective.

Exhortation and Reform

As we have seen, the overall evaluation of the monastic orders which John Gower put forward in the *Vox Clamantis* was far from positive. He seems to have concluded that the large majority of contemporary monks, canons and nuns were failing to live up to their ideal: 'there are only a few at present who do not give over their errant hearts to sensual pleasures' (IV.5.299–300; cf. MO: 21118–20). Nevertheless, there are enough disclaimers and sympathetic asides in Gower's treatment of the religious orders to imply some ambivalence on his part. He repeatedly praised the monastic ideal itself, pointing to the 'rightful rewards' of the cloister (e.g. IV.1.5–8; IV.5.294) and began Book IV (like other sections of the *Vox Clamantis*) by stressing that his criticism was directed only at the guilty (IV.1.15–18). Similarly, his section on the regular canons began in a somewhat apologetic manner, while acknowledging the saintly reputation that the canons held (albeit undeservedly) among the population, and the presence of 'those who innocently remain in their cloisters' (IV.8).

---

[56] See also the *Carmen super multiplici viciorum pestilencia*.
[57] Barbara F. Harvey, *Living and Dying in Medieval England, 1100–1540: The Monastic Experience* (Oxford: Clarendon Press, 1993), pp. 39–41; Scott Gordon Bruce, *Silence and Sign Language in Medieval Monasticism: The Cluniac Tradition, c.900–1200* (Cambridge: Cambridge University Press, 2007), esp. pp. 161–9; Makowski, *Canon Law and Cloistered Women*.

In other parts of Book IV, Gower evaded condemning the whole body of monks by singling out one particular group of brethren for criticism: senior obedientiaries. In chapter 4 he attacked the inequality of provision within the monastery: 'A hundred monks waste away just so two or three may have fat faces while they are in positions of authority. "Everything is ours," they say; but the balance does not weigh equitably, as long as one man alone gets more than three' (IV.4.273–6). Gower also exhorted claustral priors – the monastic officers responsible for ensuring correct observance of the rule – to treat young monks kindly and without harshness, conquering 'evil through a humble heart' (IV.12.533–6). We might here draw a parallel with late medieval monastic complaints spoken by individual brethren against malefactors during episcopal or chapter visitations, which frequently singled out those monks who abused their internal office to the harm of the rest of the community.[58] Such comments display sympathy on Gower's part with more junior inmates of religious houses, and arguably some understanding of the internal dynamics of monastic life.

We might also note that Gower did not overtly criticise the heads of religious houses in either the *Vox Clamantis* or the *Mirour de l'Omme*. This is perhaps surprising, since monastic superiors were common targets in medieval satire,[59] and Gower himself referred elsewhere in his work to the general principle that a sick head would inevitably corrupt the body's limbs (VC: III.9.737–8, VI.7.498). Thus, while the vices are personified as abbots in chapter 7 of Book IV of the *Vox*, this was less a comment on the particular failings of superiors than a reference to the primacy of these offences in the monastery. Moreover, those monks accused by Gower of *proprietas* – the illicit holding of personal property – were said explicitly to be acting without the knowledge of their superior (VC: heading to IV.4). Nor is there any sense in Gower's writing on the religious orders that their moral problems resulted from poor leadership, in contrast to his critique of secular prelates in Book III of the *Vox*. Once again, we might conclude that Gower's critique of the monastic orders was not as wholesale as it first appears.

Furthermore, a significant part of John Gower's treatment of monasticism in the *Vox Clamantis* has the character of moral exhortation rather than a simple anatomy of abuses. This exhortatory flavour is particularly marked in the final chapters of Book IV (IV.10–12; IV.15). Indeed this section – which draws quite heavily on the *De Vita Monachorum* – reads much like a sermon or moral tract, urging on the religious to better observance.[60] Gower began

---

[58] See, for instance, *Visitations of Religious Houses in the Diocese of Lincoln, 1420–1449*, ed. Alexander H. Thompson (three volumes; Canterbury and York Society, 17, 24, 33 (1915–27)), passim.

[59] See Mann, *Chaucer and Medieval Estates Satire*, pp. 17–37; Heale, *Abbots and Priors*, pp. 250–6.

[60] The correspondence between the *Vox Clamantis* and sermon literature has long been observed. See Owst, *Literature and Pulpit*, pp. 230–1; Maria Wickert, *Studies in John*

chapter 10 thus: 'Being an educated man, I have pondered the writings of the saints, which ought to be well heeded for your instruction. Holy words are more effective, when they are more clearly set forth. Therefore, you monks, see what is in them' (IV.10.391–4). Monks and canons were urged to keep their vows, truly turn away from the world, embrace a simple life of renunciation and activity, and flee the dangerous company of women. Gower's elaboration of this final theme, again drawn largely from the *De Vita Monachorum*, emphasised the vulnerability of monks to women, whom he depicts as dangerous prattlers, venomous serpents, temptresses, she-wolves, and 'the death of the soul'. This is a stark contrast to the stock image of womanising monks found in medieval estates satires. Chapter 12 was aimed explicitly at the 'good monk', who had truly renounced the world and who was encouraged to embrace ascetic practices and the monastic virtues of humility and obedience. The concluding chapter of Gower's short section on nuns, moreover, exhorted female religious to grasp the radiant and glorious rank of virgin, which 'transcends bands of angels and abides more in heaven than even the Triple Crown' (IV.15:655–6).

This switch from censure to exhortation was by no means unique to Book IV of the *Vox Clamantis*. Gower's avowed purpose in the *Vox* was 'that [every] man might examine himself within' (VII.25.1458).[61] His discussion of the parish priesthood followed a similar pattern to his section on monasticism, with the strong criticism of clerical immorality in chapters 16–23 of Book III succeeded by four chapters highlighting the priest's honourable vocation. However, we might note by way of contrast that no such urging to reform was held out to the mendicants, and that Gower offered only fleeting encouragement to the 'good bishop' (III.13.1169–92). Thus, although the criticism directed at the monastic orders in the *Vox Clamantis* was powerful, it was also tempered in various ways. Indeed, there was probably a good deal in Gower's discussion of monastic abuses with which committed members of the religious orders would themselves have agreed.

Conclusions: John Gower and Monasticism

The apparent contradiction between John Gower's literary treatment of contemporary monasticism on the one hand and his personal piety and close personal connections with the regular canons of St Mary Overy on the other cannot be easily reconciled. He represented the monasteries of his day as a shadow of their former selves, with the majority of their inhabitants

---

Gower (Washington: University Press of America, 1981), pp. 69–130; Winthrop Wetherbee, 'John Gower', in David Wallace, ed., *The Cambridge History of Medieval English Literature* (Cambridge: Cambridge University Press, 1999), pp. 589–609, at 594.

[61] Cf. Yeager, 'Gower's French Audience', p. 125, on the ameliorative purpose of Gower's treatment of the religious orders in the *Mirour de l'Omme*.

scorning the rules and vows to which they were committed, a perception he apparently shared with Langland and Chaucer. There is also some irony in his warnings against insinuating and grasping monks, who were keen to part potential benefactors from their money, in the light of his own generous patronage of the Southwark community. The value of monastic life and practices in assisting the salvation of souls, in Gower's estimation, also comes across more clearly in his final acts of patronage to the Augustinian canons of Southwark than in his writings. He considered that the principal function of monasteries – 'the office of their order' – was to pray 'for us who are in the world' (MO: 20833–40). However, the monks' moral failings had imperilled that role: 'But that ancient salvation of souls, which religious orders once possessed, has perished, undermined by the weakness of the flesh' (VC: IV.2.123–4). Yet this is not a concern that Gower laboured in either the Mirour de l'Omme or the Vox Clamantis, and indeed he had rather more to say about the jeopardy monks brought to their own souls by failing to live up to their monastic vocation and ideal (e.g. MO: 20852–6, 21067–72; VC: IV.1.37–40; IV.5.291–6; IV.9.371–88). This emphasis chimes with the poet's general conviction that 'individual repentance, moral reform and self-regulation' was the key to the welfare of both society and soul.[62]

Nevertheless, it is clear that Gower remained an enthusiastic believer in the monastic ideal and that he regarded reform of the religious orders to be an achievable ambition, one to which his own writings might contribute. His discussion of the religious life in both the Mirour de l'Omme and the Vox Clamantis also indicates a sturdy regard (at least in theory) for *traditional* forms of monasticism. Aside from his glowing appraisal of the desert fathers, Gower evidently respected the Benedictine Rule and the form of cenobitic living it prescribed (e.g. VC: IV.4.225–6, 243; IV.7.341; IV.24.1209–10). It is of interest that the more fashionable forms of regulated community life in later fourteenth-century England and London received no mention in Gower's writings. The Carthusian order, in particular, was sharply rising in prominence during the very years when Gower was working on the Mirour and the Vox. The London Charterhouse was founded by Sir Walter Manny in 1371, and swiftly attracted the patronage of prominent courtiers and citizens.[63] The establishment of urban charterhouses in Kingston-upon-Hull (1377) and Coventry (1381) soon followed.[64] The secular college was also becoming increasingly popular over the second half of the fourteenth century,

---

[62] Cf. Stephen H. Rigby's chapter on political theory below, from which the quotation is taken (p. 391).

[63] For the foundation and patronage of London Charterhouse, see William H. St John Hope, *The History of the London Charterhouse from its Foundation until the Suppression of the Monastery* (London: Macmillan, 1925), and cf. Martin Heale, *Monasticism in Late Medieval England, c.1300–1535* (Manchester: Manchester University Press, 2009), pp. 160–4.

[64] David Knowles and Richard Neville Hadcock, *Medieval Religious Houses. England and Wales* (second edition; London: Longman, 1971), pp. 133–6.

with a number of notable foundations made in London and Kent during John Gower's life-time, including Cobham (1362), Guildhall College (1368), St Michael's College, Crooked Lane (1381) and Maidstone (1395).[65] Gower's preference for what might be regarded as more mainstream and traditional forms of monastic life, evinced in both his poems and his patronage of St Mary Overy Priory – despite the wide range of ecclesiastical institutions (secular, mendicant and monastic) in early fifteenth-century London to which he could have turned for the welfare of his soul – again implies a rather conservative religious outlook. Arguably the monastic preferences and interests he displayed also reflected gentry, more than bourgeois, tastes.[66]

Whether John Gower's writings on the religious orders can be used to shed light on his life and literary career remains questionable. Robert F. Yeager has argued that both the *Mirour de l'Omme* and the *Vox Clamantis* may have been completed while Gower was resident in St Mary Overy Priory, and were partially shaped by that milieu.[67] However, as we saw above, it is by no means clear that Gower was resident at St Mary's at the time of the composition of these works. Moreover, whilst it is true that Gower's works seem to display some understanding of the internal dynamics of monastic life, the conventional nature of much of his writing on the religious orders (finding inspiration in earlier satiric or homiletic works, or generic moralising), and the striking lack of reference to topical monastic developments, imply a detachment from the everyday life of the cloister. Nor do the more distinctive elements of Gower's treatment of the religious orders – such as his distaste for monks' social climbing and nuns' learning – seem to stem from keen personal observation of contemporary monasticism, but rather appear to be an expression of his broader social attitudes and preconceptions. The particular significance of John Gower's monastic associations to his literary output is likely to remain enigmatic. However, his writings on the religious orders serve as a reminder of the complex relationship between anticlerical literature and lay attitudes towards, and interactions with, the institutional Church in the later Middle Ages.

---

[65] Ibid., pp. 411–46.
[66] See, for instance, Nigel Saul, *Lordship and Faith: The English Gentry and the Parish Church in the Middle Ages* (Oxford: Oxford University Press, 2017), pp. 68–82; John A. F. Thomson, 'Piety and Charity in Late Medieval London', *Journal of Ecclesiastical History*, 16 (1965), pp. 178–95.
[67] Yeager, 'Gower's French Audience', pp. 111–37.

CHAPTER 9

THE FRIARS

Jens Röhrkasten

Studies of Antifraternalism

Despite the rapid development of Gower studies in recent decades, the poet's views on the mendicant orders have attracted surprisingly little interest from modern scholars.[1] John Fisher, for instance, did not regard the mendicants as one of the poet's major concerns, although he did compare Gower's attitudes towards the friars in *Vox Clamantis* and in the *Mirour de l'Omme* with those expressed in Chaucer's work. His discussion thus focused on the

---

I should like to thank Dr Martin Heale and Professor Stephen Rigby for their helpful comments and suggestions.

[1] Scholars of Gower's work generally neglect his views on the mendicants whilst those writers who discuss the mendicants in late-medieval literature rarely mention Gower. See for instance, Maria Wickert, *Studien zu John Gower* (Cologne: Kölner Universitätsverlag, 1953), p. 28; William R. J. Barron, *English Medieval Romance* (London: Longman, 1990), p. 52; Winthrop Wetherbee, 'John Gower', in David Wallace, ed., *The Cambridge History of Medieval English Literature* (Cambridge: Cambridge University Press, 1999), pp. 589–609; *Selections from John Gower*, ed. Jack A. Bennett (Oxford: Clarendon Press, 1968), pp. xi–xiv; Judson Boyce Allen, *The Friar as Critic* (Nashville: Vanderbilt University Press, 1971), p. 60–2; Janet Coleman, *English Literature in History, 1350–1400: Medieval Writers and Readers* (London: Hutchinson, 1981), pp. 126–7; Jean-Pascal Pouzet, 'Southwark Gower: Augustinian Agencies in Gower's Manuscripts and Texts – Some Prolegomena', in Elizabeth Dutton, with John Hines and Robert F. Yeager, eds, *John Gower, Trilingual Poet: Language, Translation and Tradition* (Cambridge: D. S. Brewer, 2010), pp. 11–25; John A. Burrow, *Ricardian Poetry: Chaucer, Gower, Langland and the Gawain Poet* (Harmondsworth: Penguin Books, 1992), p. 10; Siân Echard, 'Introduction: Gower's Reputation', in Siân Echard, ed., *A Companion to Gower* (Cambridge: D. S. Brewer, 2004), pp. 1–22, at 3; A. George Rigg, *A History of Anglo-Latin Literature, 1066–1422* (Cambridge: Cambridge University Press, 1992), pp. 289–93; Linne Mooney and Estelle Stubbs, *Scribes and the City. London Guildhall Clerks and the Dissemination of Middle English Literature 1375–1425* (York: York Medieval Press, 2013), pp. 1–3; Stephen H. Rigby, *Chaucer in Context: Society, Allegory and Gender* (Manchester: Manchester University Press, 1996), p. 21; Wendy Scase, *Piers Plowman and the New Anticlericalism* (Cambridge: Cambridge University Press, 1989), pp. 3–4.

literary setting for Gower's criticism of the friars rather than examining it in its historical context.[2] This neglect of Gower's views of the friars may be partly due to the fact that critical interest tends to focus on the *Confessio Amantis*, which is the only one of Gower's three main works which does not contain verses on the Dominicans, Franciscans and other mendicant orders, and partly because his attitudes towards nobles, lawyers, townspeople and peasants have been seen as more significant. However, whilst literary critics have found little interest in Gower's remarks on the friars, historians of religious orders have turned to poetry as a source for the study of attitudes to the mendicant orders in the thirteenth and fourteenth centuries, especially in times and places when these new orders were involved in disputes and scandals.[3] Such disputes occurred when there were conflicts of interest and tensions about resources, influence and prestige, but they also raised more general theological and ecclesiological concerns.[4]

By Gower's time, there were four main mendicant orders: the Franciscans, the Dominicans, the Austin Friars and the Carmelites. Unlike the Austin Friars and the Carmelites, the Franciscans and the Dominicans could justify their existence with a reference to their charismatic founders and the Dominicans were linked to tradition by the adoption of an existing rule (i.e.

---

[2] Nigel Saul, 'John Gower: Prophet or Turncoat?', in Dutton, Hines and Yeager, *John Gower, Trilingual Poet*, pp. 85–97; John H. Fisher, *John Gower. Moral Philosopher and Friend of Chaucer* (New York: New York University Press, 1964), pp. 155, 157, 179, 265–9.

[3] Palémon Glorieux, 'Prélats français contre religieux mendiants. Autour de la bulle "Ad fructus uberes" (1281–1290)', *Revue d'histoire de l'église de France*, 11 (1925), pp. 309–31, 471–95; Richard W. Emery, 'The Second Council of Lyons and the Mendicant Orders', *The Catholic Historical Review*, 39 (1953), pp. 257–271; Micheline de Fontette, 'Les mendiants supprimés au 2e concile de Lyon (1274). Frères Sachets et Frères Pies', in *Les mendiants en pays d'Oc au XIIIe siècle*, Cahiers de Fanjeaux, 8 (Toulouse: Privat, 1973), pp. 193–217.

[4] Alexandre Corneille Saint-Marc, *Étude sur la vie et les ouvrages de Guillaume de St-Amour* (Lons-Le-Saunier: Gauthier Frères, 1865), pp. 13–16, 20–2; Max Bierbaum, *Bettelorden und Weltgeistlichkeit an der Universität Paris: Texte und Untersuchungen zum literarischen Armuts- und Exemtionsstreit des 13. Jahrhunderts (1255–1272)* (Münster: Aschendorff, 1920), pp. 1–36; Anastase van den Wyngaert, 'Querelles du Clergé séculier et des Ordres mendiants à l'Université de Paris au XIIIe siècle', *La France Franciscaine*, 5 (1922), pp. 257–81, 369–96; 6 (1923), pp. 47–70; Christine Thouzellier, 'La place du De periculis de Guillaume de Saint-Amour dans les polémiques du XIIIe siècle', *Revue Historique*, 156 (1927), pp. 69–83; Michel-Marie Dufeil, *Guillaume de Saint-Amour et la polémique universitaire parisienne, 1250–1259* (Paris: Éditions A. et J. Picard, 1972), pp. 183–4; Gert Melville, 'Due novae conversationis ordines. Zur Wahrnehmung der frühen Mendikanten vor dem Problem institutioneller Neuartigkeit im mittelalterlichen Religiosentum', in Gert Melville and Jörg Oberste eds, *Die Bettelorden im Aufbau. Beiträge zu Institutionalisierungsprozessen im mittelalterlichen Religiosentum*, Vita Regularis, 11 (Münster: LIT Verlag, 1999), pp. 1–23; Ramona Sickert, 'Wenn Klosterbrüder zu Jahrmarktsbrüdern werden'. Studien zur zeitgenössischen Wahrnehmung der Franziskaner und Dominikaner im 13. Jahrhundert*, Vita regularis, 28 (Münster: LIT Verlag, 2006), pp. 11–12, 43–4, 71–3, 102–3, 150–2, 301–3.

of St Augustine). However, the friars often provoked criticism from other churchmen since their organizational structures, which had only been created in the thirteenth century, paid no attention to existing political or ecclesiastical boundaries.[5] Furthermore, doubts arose about their role in the Church. The ensuing disputes had an influence on poets, first of all in France and later also in other parts of Europe, notably England.[6] The analysis of this literature – which expressed an attitude later known as 'antifraternalism' – began in the first half of the twentieth century. In 1915 Tiberius Denkinger published his work on the treatment of the mendicants in thirteenth-century French didactic literature, focusing on the poems of Rutebeuf and the *Roman de la Rose*. A few years later Joseph Spencer Kennard drew a connection between such earlier criticism of the mendicants and their portrayal by Langland and Chaucer.[7] Kennard could not decide upon a perspective and consequently his approach lacked focus, but the initial idea of studying the portrayal of the friars in imaginative literature was taken up by other literary scholars with historical interests. In an important article published in 1953, Arnold Williams pointed out that Geoffrey Chaucer had used arguments expressed by Richard FitzRalph, archbishop of Armagh (1346–1360), who had turned from being a supporter of the friars, particularly of the Franciscans, into a stern critic of the mendicant orders. Williams linked the arguments used by FitzRalph to earlier attacks on the mendicants which had originated in the 1250s, in a dispute between secular masters at the University of Paris and the Dominicans.[8] This work was further developed by Penn Szittya, who in 1974 began with an analysis of the allegations made against friars from the mid-thirteenth century onwards and showed that they were not just conflicts about resources but also raised wider ecclesiological issues in which the friars' critics used biblical texts to argue that the mendicants did not have a legitimate place within the Church.[9]

---

[5] Hans-Joachim Schmidt, *Kirche, Staat, Nation. Raumgliederung der Kirche im mittelalterlichen Europa*, Forschungen zur mittelalterlichen Geschichte, 37 (Weimar: Hermann Böhlaus Nachfolger, 1999), pp. 391–3; Melville, 'Due novae conversationis ordines', pp. 3–4.

[6] Dufeil, *Guillaume de Saint-Amour*, pp. 148–50, 307–8, 316–22, 324, 352; Penn Szittya, *The Antifraternal Tradition in Medieval Literature* (Princeton: Princeton University Press, 1986), p. 9; Peter Nicholson, *An Annotated Index to the Commentary on Gower's Confessio Amantis*, Medieval and Renaissance Texts and Studies, 62 (Binghampton: Bagwyn, 1989), p. 3.

[7] Tiberius Denkinger, 'Die Bettelorden in der französischen didaktischen Literatur des 13. Jahrhunderts, besonders bei Rutebeuf und im Roman de la Rose', *Franziskanische Studien*, 2 (1915), pp. 63–109, 286–313, at 99, 107, 287–93; Joseph Spencer Kennard, *The Friar in Fiction. Sincerity in Art and Other Essays* (New York: Books for Libraries Press, 1923), pp. 8, 11–16.

[8] Arnold Williams, 'Chaucer and the Friars', *Speculum*, 28 (1953), pp. 499–513, at 503.

[9] Penn Szittya, 'The Friar as False Apostle: Antifraternal Exegesis and the *Summoner's Tale*', *Studies in Philology*, 71 (1974), pp. 19–46, at 35–44; Penn Szittya, 'The Antifraternal Tradition in Middle English Literature', *Speculum*, 52 (1977), pp. 287–313, at 293.

Whilst Williams had seen the accusations made against the mendicants as being realistic and as reflecting the decline of the orders from their original integrity, Szittya recognised that the charges made against them were more conventional and stereotypical. He showed that the anti-mendicant allegations were based on two types of argument, theological and literary, with the latter then being used by 'poets obsessed with the decay of human society' who developed and re-arranged the traditional accusations made against the friars.[10] Research into what had by now been firmly established as 'antifraternal literature' was taken further by Guy Geltner, who examined the charges against the friars and the sometimes violent action taken against them.[11] Geltner pointed out that criticism of the mendicants was published with a range of different objectives in mind. Thus, whilst some of their critics, such as William of St Amour, argued for the complete abolition of the mendicants, others sought only a revision of their privileges or a reform of the orders. However, Geltner's interest was focused mainly on Chaucer, a feature he shares with Williams, Fleming and other scholars of antifraternalism.[12] This leaves room for a more detailed investigation of Gower's treatment of the subject, an analysis of his arguments and their history.

The mendicant orders do not constitute a central element in John Gower's works. However, he regarded them as sufficiently important to dedicate a lengthy section to them in each of two of his major texts, the *Mirour de l'Omme* and *Vox Clamantis*, poems in which he covered all key sections of society including the clergy, combining the tradition of estate satire with

[10] Szittya, *The Antifraternal Tradition*, pp. 4, 203, 206–7, 210, 214, 218–20.
[11] Guy Geltner, 'Faux Semblants: Antifraternalism Reconsidered in Jean de Meun and Chaucer', *Studies in Philology*, 101 (2004), pp. 357–80, at 357 (it should be noted that Boccaccio's Brother Cipollo is not a mendicant but a member of the order of St Anthony of Vienne, see also Nick Havely, 'Chaucer, Boccaccio, and the Friars', in Piero Boitani, ed., *Chaucer and the Italian Trecento* (Cambridge: Cambridge University Press, 1983), pp. 249–68, at 259, 262); Guy Geltner, 'William of St. Amour's De periculis novissimorum temporum: A False Start to Medieval Antifraternalism?' in Guy Geltner and Michael Cusato, eds, *Defenders and Critics of Franciscan Life: Essays in Honor of John V. Fleming* (Leiden: Brill, 2009), pp. 105–118; Guy Geltner, 'Brethren Behaving Badly: a Deviant Approach to Medieval Antifraternalism', *Speculum*, 85 (2010), pp. 47–64; Guy Geltner, *The Making of Medieval Antifraternalism: Polemic, Violence, Deviance, and Remembrance* (Oxford: Oxford University Press, 2012).
[12] John Fleming, 'The Antifraternalism of the Summoner's Tale', *Journal of English and Germanic Philology*, 65 (1966), pp. 688–700; John Fleming, 'The Friars and Medieval English Literature', in Wallace, *The Cambridge History of Medieval English Literature*, pp. 349–75, at 374–5; Havely, 'Chaucer, Boccaccio, and the Friars', p. 259. A section of *Vox Clamantis* relating to the mendicant orders was published in Robert P. Miller, ed., *Chaucer: Sources and Backgrounds* (New York: Oxford University Press, 1977), pp. 264–8. See also Arnold Williams, 'Two Notes on Chaucer and the Friars', *Modern Philology*, 54 (1956), pp. 117–20; Peter Taitt, *Incubus and Ideal: Ecclesiastical Figures in Chaucer and Langland*, Salzburg Studies in English Literature, 44 (Salzburg: Institut für englische Sprache und Literatur, 1975), pp. 4–24, 84–100.

characteristics of the penitential sermon.[13] Despite a degree of respect shown to the two founding saints of the Dominicans and Franciscans, and to the early generations of friars, Gower's presentation highlights the orders' destructive influence on society and the damage they inflict on individuals as well as the Church. Gower manages to convey his largely negative image by drawing on a rich array of allegations and accusations which had their roots in the thirteenth century.

Early Criticisms of the Friars

Much of Gower's material is ultimately derived from the polemical literature produced by William of St Amour and other secular masters at the University of Paris who were engaged in a dispute with the Dominicans and the Franciscans in the 1250s. This confrontation was initially an internal dispute within the university, but it developed into a more fundamental conflict, eventually involving the orders, the papacy and King Louis IX of France.[14] The main cause of the dispute was the presence of mendicant friars among the masters of theology in the university. The dispute had its origins in 1230 when the Dominican Roland of Cremona obtained his chair in theology. A further change affected the Dominican presence at the university shortly afterwards, when the regent master, John of St Giles, joined the order in a dramatic public scene, during a sermon on the benefits of voluntary poverty which he interrupted so that he could take the order's habit. Another secular master, the English theologian Alexander of Hales, soon followed suit by resigning his English benefices and joining the Franciscans.[15] The balance

---

[13] Wickert, *Studien zu John Gower*, pp. 71–2; Jill Mann, *Chaucer and Medieval Estates Satire* (Cambridge: Cambridge University Press, 1973), p. 17. The didactic purpose of the poems is highlighted by Nicholson, *An Annotated Index*, p. 3; Wetherbee, 'John Gower', p. 591.

[14] Frederick M. Powicke and Alfred Emden, eds, *The Universities of Europe in the Middle Ages by the Late Hastings Rashdall* (Oxford: Oxford University Press, 1936), I: 376–85. Chronologies of events are presented in Edmond Faral, 'Les Responsiones de Guillaume de Saint-Amour', *Archives d'Histoire doctrinale et littéraire du Moyen Âge*, 25/26 (1950–51), pp. 337–94, at 369–74 and Palémon Glorieux, 'Le conflit de 1252–57 à la lumière du Mémoire de Guillaume de Saint-Amour', *Recherches de Théologie ancienne et médiévale*, 24 (1957), pp. 364–72, at 366–72. See also Gordon Leff, *Paris and Oxford Universities in the Thirteenth and Fourteenth Centuries* (New York: Wiley, 1968), pp. 34–45. A comparison with other disputes within the medieval Church is made by Sita Steckel, '"Gravis et clamosa querela". Synodale Konfliktführung und Öffentlichkeit im französischen Bettelordensstreit 1254–1390', in Christoph Dartmann, Andreas Pietsch and Sita Steckel, eds, *Ecclesia disputans. Die Konfliktpraxis vormoderner Synoden zwischen Religion und Politik*, Historische Zeitschrift, Beihefte, N.F., 67 (Berlin: de Gruyter, 2015), pp. 159–202, at 162–3.

[15] Palémon Glorieux, 'D'Alexandre de Halès à Pierre Auriol. La suite des maîtres franciscains de Paris', *Archivum Franciscanum Historicum*, 26 (1933), pp. 257–81.

between seculars and members of religious orders among the masters further shifted when other orders, among them the Premonstratensians, began to follow the friars' practice of sending their most able members to the university, where some reached the position of master in the theology faculty. Innocent IV's instruction to the chancellor in 1250 to grant the licence in theology to suitable candidates from religious orders exacerbated existing tensions and may have resulted in the promulgation of new statutes on 2 February 1252 which were directed against the promotion of regular religious in general – the mendicants were not mentioned specifically. However, there is no doubt that they, and particularly the Dominicans who held two chairs at the time, were targeted because in future each college was to have only one regent master.[16] When the secular masters proclaimed a teaching boycott after a serious clash between a group of students and the civic authorities about a year later, the two Dominican masters and their Franciscan colleague did not join in. This caused an open rift between the two factions. Soon after, the masters passed a decree which contained sharp criticism of the mendicants' decision to continue their courses and introduced measures designed to ensure compliance with majority decisions: new masters were to give an oath to observe the university's privileges and its internal legislation, to protect its secrets and to ensure that all future bachelors would act in the same manner. Infringements were to be punished by exclusion from the university.[17] The Dominicans' decision to appeal against this decision to the pope and the count of Poitiers, who was regent of France, the subsequent excommunication and expulsion of the mendicant masters from the university, and the lifting of this sanction by Innocent IV on 21 July 1253 gave a new dimension to the dispute.[18] Although the pope tried to bring about a reconciliation between the parties, the quarrel escalated further, resulting in a long open letter by the secular masters, published in February 1254. It contained a detailed account of the dispute, including a description of the Dominicans' allegedly fraudulent and violent behaviour in 1253 when they had deceived the pope, who was a supporter of the mendicants. In addition, a new type of

---

Powicke and Emden, *The Universities of Europe*, I: 373–4; Clifford Hugh Lawrence, 'Hales, Alexander of (*c*.1185–1245)', *Oxford Dictionary of National Biography*, Oxford University Press, 2004, [http://www.oxforddnb.com/view/article/327, accessed 1 May 2017]; Rolf Köhn, 'Monastisches Bildungsideal und weltgeistliches Wissenschaftsdenken. Zur Vorgeschichte des Mendikantenstreites an der Universität Paris', in Albert Zimmermann, ed., *Die Auseinandersetzungen an der Pariser Universität im XIII. Jahrhundert*, Miscellanea Mediaevalia, 10 (Berlin/New York: Walter de Gruyter, 1976), pp. 1–37, at 30–1.

[16] It was decided 'ut de cetero religiosus aliquis non habens collegium et cui est a jure publice docere prohibitum, ad eorum societatem nullatenus admittatur', *Chartularium Universitatis Parisiensis*, eds Heinrich Denifle and Emile Chatelain (Paris: Delalain, 1889–97), I: 226–7, no. 200; Leff, *Paris and Oxford*, p. 39; Szittya, *The Antifraternal Tradition*, p. 13.

[17] *Chartularium Universitatis Parisiensis*, Denifle and Chatelain, I: 242–4, no. 216.

[18] *Ibid.*, I: 248–9, no. 224.

criticism was introduced: the friars' piety, humility and their contribution to the common good was called into doubt.[19]

Up to this point Innocent IV had been a supporter of the mendicants, but this changed dramatically in the summer of 1254 when he was given a copy of the millenarian *Liber introductorius ad Evangelium aeternum*, by the Franciscan theologian, Gerard of Borgo San Donnino.[20] Even before a papally appointed commission condemned more than thirty statements made in this book in 1255, Innocent IV had decided to switch sides. Scandalised by the treatise he now backed the secular masters in the dispute at Paris. With the publication of the bull *Etsi animarum* on 21 November 1254 he went even further and revoked privileges affecting the mendicants' ministry which infringed the rights of the prelates and of the parish clergy.[21] This document is significant because it anticipated the approach later used by William of St Amour by not explicitly naming the mendicants even though they were its target. Instead it was addressed to all religious of whatever profession or order. It then referred to some of the disadvantages and even dangers associated with the mendicants' ministry, thoughts reflected in much of the later polemical literature and poetry, including the works of John Gower. The pope stated that the arbitrary intrusion into confessional practices by itinerant mendicant priests was disrespectful to the parish clergy and that it prevented them from being acquainted with the sins of their parishioners, which meant that they could not heal what was diseased. This practice also carried serious dangers for the parishioners because it was easier for them to confess their sins to someone they might never encounter again rather than to undergo the embarrassment of revealing their failures to the local priest. In addition an itinerant confessor might be inclined to be more lenient, thus seemingly endorsing the insignificance of the transgression, a practice which jeopardised the spiritual welfare of the laity because this implied a degree of tolerance towards sinful behaviour. Itinerant priests were also accused of approaching those afflicted

---

[19] Ibid., I: 252–8, no. 230, at 253. The friars' claim to the title of 'magister' was seen as incompatible with their claim to humility.
[20] Marjorie Reeves, *The Influence of Prophecy in the Later Middle Ages. A Study in Joachimism* (Oxford: Clarendon Press, 1969), pp. 59–66.
[21] *Chartularium Universitatis Parisiensis*, eds, Denifle and Chatelain, I: 267–70, no. 240; Gratien de Paris, *Histoire de la Fondation et de l'évolution de l'Ordre des Frères Mineurs au XIIIe siècle* (Paris: Société et librairie S. François d'Assise, 1925), pp. 205–10; Grado Merlo, *Nel nome di San Francesco: storia dei frati minori e del francescanesimo sino agli inizi del XVI secolo* (Padua: Editrici francescane, 2003), pp. 163–4; Leonardo Pisanu, *Innocenzo IV e i Francescani (1243–1254)*, Studi e Testi Francescani, 41 (Rome: Edizioni francescane, 1968), pp. 226–7; Dieter Berg, *Armut und Wissenschaft. Beiträge zur Geschichte des Studienwesens der Bettelorden im 13. Jahrhundert* (Düsseldorf: Pädagogischer Verlag Schwann, 1977), pp. 89–94; John Moorman, *A History of the Franciscan Order from its Origins to the Year 1517* (Oxford: Clarendon Press 1968), pp. 125–31; Heribert Holzapfel, *Handbuch der Geschichte des Franziskanerordens* (Freiburg/Br.: Herder, 1909), pp. 273–5; Bert Roest, *A History of Franciscan Education c. 1210–1517* (Leiden: Brill 2000), p. 55.

by serious illness, trying to entice them to choose burial in their churches and attempting to influence the drafting of their wills. This offended God and denigrated religion. Consequently there needed to be restrictions on the itinerant priests' ministry in order to end this practice.

The bull *Etsi animarum* marked the resounding victory of the secular masters of Paris over the mendicants. However, another dramatic shift occurred soon afterwards following the death of Innocent IV on 7 December 1254 and his replacement by Alexander IV, a former protector of the Franciscans. The new pope immediately resumed the policy of support for the mendicants. Only ten days after his election, on 22 December 1254, he revoked the bull *Etsi animarum* and later confirmed all previous mendicant privileges.[22] Further papal interventions on behalf of the friars culminated in the excommunication of the secular masters in June 1255.[23] Already at this time, even before William of St Amour launched his attack on the whole idea of the mendicants' form of religious life, Rutebeuf participated in the dispute, publishing a short poem in which he criticised the Dominicans' claim to two chairs of theology. He contrasted their proud behaviour with the image of humility which they sought to convey and drew attention to the sharp contrast between their pious talk and their aggressive actions, their claims of poverty and their greed.[24]

The affair took a new turn in the autumn of 1255 with the publication of treatises by both sides. It was at this point that William of St Amour, who began his dispute with the Franciscan theologian and future minister general, Bonaventure of Bagnoregio, called into question the doctrinal as well as ecclesiological concept of the new orders.[25] The original dispute about the mendicants' role at the University of Paris now turned into a polemic about the concepts developed by St Francis and St Dominic. In a series of *quaestiones* and sermons William developed the ideas which he then merged into his treatise *De periculis novissimorum temporum*, a fundamental attack on the very existence of the mendicant orders. Without a single direct reference to the friars, and relying entirely on the exegesis of biblical texts, he was able to argue that the Church was threatened by great imminent dangers which were caused by those who wanted to censure others but who were not prepared to submit to the authority of the prelates. Like the '*antichristi*' denounced by St Paul, they entered the houses of others like thieves ('*penetrantes domos*',

---

[22] *Chartularium Universitatis Parisiensis*, eds, Denifle and Chatelain, I: 276–7, no. 244; Ludovico Pellegrini, *Alessandro IV e i Francescani, 1254–1261*, Studi e testi francescani, 34 (Rome: Edizioni francescane, 1966), pp. 33, 76, 78.

[23] The texts are in *Chartularium Universitatis Parisiensis*, eds, Denifle and Chatelain, I: 'Quasi lignum vite' (pp. 279–85, n. 247); 'Controversiam dudum' (pp. 292–6, n. 256).

[24] *Oeuvres complètes de Rutebeuf*, eds Edmond Faral and Julia Bastin (two volumes; Paris: Éditions A. et J. Picard, 1959–60), II: 238–41.

[25] Yves Congar, 'Aspects ecclésiologiques de la querelle entre mendiants et séculiers dans la seconde moitié du XIIIe et le début du XIVe', *Archives d'Histoire doctrinale et littéraire du Moyen Age*, 36 (1961), pp. 35–151, at 56–7, 63.

2 Timothy 3:6[26]), seducing the laity into abandoning the advice given by their proper prelates. They were pseudo-preachers (*'pseudo-praedicatores'*)[27] who did not form part of the ecclesiastical hierarchy which was based on the twelve apostles and the seventy-two disciples (Luke 10:1). Falsely appearing to be pious (they only have *'speciem pietatis'*)[28] they deceived the laity with their fraudulent claim to live like the apostles. These accusations, largely derived from Matthew 23:5, were part of William of St Amour's use of the three biblical figures, the Pharisees, the pseudo-apostles and the *'antichristi'*, to represent the mendicants.[29] St Amour claimed that both men and women revealed their confessional secrets to the friars and abandoned the obedience owed to the prelates. These deceivers thus subverted the Church, like the messengers of Antichrist, and consequently it was the duty of the prelates to take action against them. Denying the mendicants' claim that they were following the apostolic life, William of St Amour argued the direct opposite: they live *contra doctrinam apostoli*,[30] because they roam through the world, they do not work, and they intrude themselves into other people's business. The fact that they live by begging, even though they could provide for their material needs, gives them the character of thieves because they are taking away charity from the needy. Since it was nowhere written that Christ ever was a beggar, their claim to follow him by acting in this way was heretical.[31]

Papal Legislation against the Friars

Despite William of St Amour's personal failure – he lost his teaching position and ecclesiastical benefices[32] – the accusations against the mendicants which he set out in the 1250s served as a quarry for future critics of the friars. However, criticism of the mendicant orders also emerged in other contexts and Guy Geltner's demand for a closer analysis of the role of antifraternal allegations in later texts needs to be heeded.[33] Discussion during the Second Council of Lyons (1274) about a reform of the Church included demands for measures against the mendicant orders. This led to a radical decision: while the Dominicans and the Franciscans were exempted from the conciliar

---

[26] Bierbaum, *Bettelorden und Weltgeistlichkeit*, pp. 5, 8; Szittya, *The Antifraternal Tradition*, p. 77.
[27] Bierbaum, *Bettelorden und Weltgeistlichkeit*, p. 9.
[28] Ibid., p. 14.
[29] Szittya, *The Antifraternal Tradition*, pp. 32, 35.
[30] Bierbaum, *Bettelorden und Weltgeistlichkeit*, pp. 28–9.
[31] Ibid., p. 34. This position was adopted in the fourteenth century by Pope John XXII (James Dawson, 'William of St Amour and the Apostolic Tradition', *Medieval Studies*, 40 (1978), pp. 223–38, at 226–37).
[32] Dufeil, *Guillaume de Saint-Amour*, pp. 304–7; Steckel, 'Synodale Konfliktführung', pp. 169–70.
[33] Geltner, *The Making of Medieval Antifraternalism*, p. 42.

decision because of their obvious benefit for the Church, the status of the Carmelites and the Austin Friars was only confirmed with the proviso that their fate was to be determined at a later date. A papal confirmation occurred piecemeal in 1286 and 1298, when Boniface VIII lifted all restriction on the latter two orders.[34] All other mendicant orders, among them the well-known Fratres de Poenitentia Jhesu Christi, were denied further recruitment. It is significant that future pastoral activities of the Fratres de Poenitentia (Friars of the Sack) and less well known smaller organisations were prohibited and that reference was made to the friars' precarious economic status: their existence was based on the uncertainty of begging.

Although these anti-mendicant measures were clearly a result of a hostility towards the friars in some sections of the Church, a hostility which had even led to demands for their abolition, these restrictions actually had the effect of benefitting the Dominicans and the Franciscans, the two largest orders. Indeed, in the *Opus tripartitum*, even the Dominican master general Humbert of Romans expressed fears about the increasing number of friars and the economic burdens imposed on the laity by the voluntary poor.[35] Certainly, it was in the interest of the two established orders to protect themselves from such competition. Similarly, the Franciscan chronicler Salimbene di Adam approved of the actions taken at the 1274 Council and had few kind words for the Apostle Friars, accusing them of being idle vagabonds who performed no service for Christianity.[36] Humbert and Salimbene were not the only ones to voice unease about the growth of the mendicant movement since other writers were also aware that an increase in the number of mendicant orders would exacerbate the dispute with the secular clergy. In France measures against the friars were organised by a faction of the episcopate who intended to stem what they regarded as mendicant encroachments on the privileges of the secular clergy after the publication of the bull *Ad fructus uberes* (1282), which allowed the superiors of the orders to examine and appoint friars to the ministry.[37] Some French prelates voiced their opposition to the mendicants' pastoral privileges, especially the friars' confessional practices. The

---

[34] 'Religionum diversitatem', in *Decrees of the Ecumenical Councils. Volume 1: Nicea I to Lateran V*, ed. Norman Tanner (Washington: Georgetown University Press, 1990), pp. 326–7; Joachim Smet, *The Carmelites: A History of the Brothers of Our Lady of Mount Carmel* (Darien: Carmelite Spiritual Center, 1988), I: 15; Steckel, 'Synodale Konfliktführung', pp. 177–8.

[35] Burkhard Roberg, *Das Zweite Konzil von Lyon [1274]* (Paderborn: Schöningh, 1990), p. 331–2; Emery, 'The Second Council of Lyons', p. 259.

[36] *Cronica Fratris Salimbene de Adam ordinis minorum*, ed. Oswald Holder-Egger, MGH, Scriptores, 32 (Hanover and Leipzig: Hahn, 1905–13), p. 255: 'congregationem illorum ribaldorum et porcariorum et stultorum et ignobilium'.

[37] De Fontette, 'Les mendiants supprimés' p. 195; *Bullarium Franciscanum*, ed. Johannes Hyacinth Sbaralea (Rome: Typis Sacrae Congregationis de Propaganda Fide, 1759), III: 480; Jeffrey Sikes, 'Jean de Poulli and Peter de la Palu', *EHR*, 49 (1934), pp. 219–40, at 220.

opposition was silenced and an attempt to find a compromise was made by Boniface VIII in *Super Cathedram* (1300).[38] This required the Franciscans and Dominicans to obtain a licence from the local bishop in order to preach and to hear confessions of lay people and to share income from the ministry with the local parish clergy.

Conflicts within the Mendicant Orders

Ironically, anti-mendicant authors could also draw on another tradition: material produced by friars who criticised their own particular orders, material which has received little attention from scholars interested in late-medieval estates satire.[39] Most of these texts were produced by Franciscans who were suspicious about the discrepancies between their order's ideals and the reality of its practice in its more than thirty provinces. Signs of uncertainty among the friars about the implementation of the rule had already emerged before 1230, when Pope Gregory IX was approached by some representatives of the order who requested an authoritative papal interpretation of the *Regula bullata*. Although this was given in 1230 in the bull *Quo elongati*, questions remained. While the simple set of norms set in the twelve chapters of the 1223 rule had been sufficient for the early community of friars, the order's rapid transformation into a structured and sophisticated institution which was active in all parts of Christendom began to change its character. *Quo elongati* was the first in a succession of papal interpretations of the Franciscan rule which culminated in the bull *Exiit qui seminat* in 1279. There were other early signs of crisis. For instance, when Thomas of Celano wrote his second life of St Francis in the 1240s, he related how the saint foresaw that some of the friars would become proud of their learning and that they would be attacked for this failing by critics outside the order.[40]

Much more severe complaints were voiced in the last quarter of the thirteenth century when a dispute arose within the Franciscan order about the best way to ensure observance of its rule. Two main factions emerged. On the one hand were the 'community' or Conventuals, who wanted to make full use of the legal devices contained in papal privileges so as to ensure formal compliance with the original ideals and who wanted the order to

---

[38] Thomas Izbicki, 'The Problem of Canonical Portion in the Later Middle Ages: The Application of "Super cathedram"', in Peter Linehan, ed, *Proceedings of the Seventh International Congress of Medieval Canon Law*, Monumenta Iuris Canonici, Series C, 8, (Rome: Biblioteca Apostolica Vaticana, 1988), pp. 459–73; Szittya, *The Antifraternal Tradition*, p. 74.

[39] Fleming, 'The Antifraternalism of the Summoner's Tale', p. 691.

[40] Thomas of Celano, 'Vita secunda S. Francisci Assisiensis', in *Legendae S. Francisci Assisiensi saeculis XIII et XIV conscriptae*, Analecta Franciscana, 10 (Quaracchi: PP. Collegii S. Bonaventurae, 1926–41), pp. 157–8.

remain a functioning tool of the papacy. On the other were the Spirituals, a small faction, partly consisting of Franciscan intellectuals, which began to emerge after 1274 following a false rumour according to which the friars were to be forced to accept the ownership of property. The Spirituals criticised the emphasis placed by the order on formal theological education which raised issues such as the friars' ownership of books, the need for them to take academic examinations, their quest for privileges and the tendency for the order's economy to be based on burial rights and income from wills, thereby undermining the ideal of poverty.[41]

The disagreements between the two factions led to a debate in which each side accused the other of disobedience, decadence and the failure to observe the rule. The central theme of this dispute was the practice of poverty which, together with humility, was one of the cornerstones of Franciscan spirituality. Ubertino of Casale, one of the most important of the Spirituals, criticised the grandeur of Franciscan architecture in around 1310.[42] His fellow Spiritual, Angelo Clareno, complained in the 1320s how sumptuous buildings had been constructed in convents of the March of Ancona less than twenty years after the death of St Francis, whilst in the 1340s an unknown Spiritual Franciscan composed a detailed treatise on the clean, long and hence decadent habits worn by the Conventuals, who were forcing all friars to wear similar clothing, in contrast with Francis and the early friars who had worn short, patched garments of poor quality.[43] Such concerns had arisen as early as the 1240s and criticism of decay within the Franciscan order was not restricted to the Spirituals.[44] In the 1250s Bonaventure of Bagnoregio, the most prominent of all Franciscan ministers general, admonished the friars to avoid scandals because the order was being regarded with disgust in some parts of the world, a reference to the dispute at the University of Paris but also a more general warning.[45] He mentioned not only the imprudent acceptance of coins in contravention of the order's supposed poverty, but

---

[41] David Burr, *The Spiritual Franciscans. From Protest to Persecution in the Century after St Francis* (University Park: Pennsylvania State University Press, 2001), p. 44. Fleming argued that Chaucer was influenced by the Spirituals, however, these groups were not present in England (Fleming, 'The Antifraternalism of the Summoner's Tale', p. 691). This is also a problem for Clopper's claim that William Langland was indebted to, or even in support of, the Franciscan Spirituals (Lawrence M. Clopper, *'Songes of Rechelesnesse': Langland and the Franciscans* (Ann Arbor: The University of Michigan Press, 1997), pp. 6–8, 15, 20).

[42] Burr, *The Spiritual Franciscans*, p. 54; Clopper, *'Songes of Rechelesnesse'*, p. 11.

[43] *Angeli Clareni Historia Septem Tribulationum Ordinis Minorum*, eds Orietta Rossini and Hanno Helbling, Fonti per la Storia dell'Italia medievale. Rerum Italicarum Scriptores, 2 (Rome: Istituto Storico Italiano per il Medio Evo, 1999), p. 147; 'Fraticelli cuiusdam Decalogus evangelicae paupertatis. An. 1340–1342 conscriptus', ed. Michael Bihl, *Archivum Franciscanum Historicum*, 32 (1939), pp. 279–411.

[44] Burr, *The Spiritual Franciscans*, pp. 20–4.

[45] *Doctoris Seraphici Bonaventurae Opera Omnia* (Quaracchi: PP. Collegii S. Bonaventurae, 1898), VIII: 468: 'in diversis orbis partibus in taedium vertitur et contemptum'.

also the laziness of some friars which was the root of all vices. Begging friars were feared like robbers, elaborate buildings were constructed which exposed the friars to the criticism of outsiders, there was too much intimacy with members of the laity, too much interference in parish business, which led to conflicts about burials, while the frequent relocation of convents resulted in unrest and high expenses.[46] As a result, Bonaventure – like his Dominican contemporary Thomas Aquinas – did not merely defend his order against external attacks but also tried to reform it.[47] The disputes between the majority and the Spirituals about the friars' way of life became a permanent feature of the Franciscan order. Neither the attempts by Pope Clement V to resolve the dispute at the Council of Vienne (1311–12) nor John XXII's forceful interventions in the 1320s put an end to these conflicts, although they did raise public awareness of the tensions among the Franciscans which eventually led to the official recognition of separate observant groups within the order.[48]

Although conflicts were most prominent amongst the Franciscans, they were not the only order in which such tensions emerged. Around 1270, when the dispute at Paris was coming to an end, Nicholas, the former general of the Carmelites, criticised his own order in the treatise *Ignea sagitta*. Originally a community of hermits on Mount Carmel, the Carmelites had only arrived in Europe in the 1240s when they were still following their eremitical tradition, their first convents being located in remote rural areas. Their transformation into a mendicant order made it impossible to continue their eremitical lifestyle of quiet contemplation because the friars were given new tasks in urban locations. In a passionate plea to abandon the mendicant way of life and to return to the eremitical tradition, Nicholas deplored the changes which affected the Carmelites who, as hermits, should be occupied with prayers in their cells rather than running about in public squares.[49] Having abandoned a truly holy life they were now trying to please the laity whom

---

[46] *Ibid.*, p. 469: 'ut eis timeant quasi praedonibus obviare'; 'aedificiorum constructio sumtuosa et curiosa'; 'mutatio locorum frequens et sumtuosa cum quadam violentia et perturbatione terrarum'. This was further developed by Olivi and other Franciscan authors. See *Petrus Ioannis Olivi. De usu paupere. The Quaestio and the Tractatus*, ed. David Burr, The University of Western Australia: Italian Medieval and Renaissance Studies, 4 (Florence: Olschki, 1992), p. 90.

[47] Decima Douie, 'St. Bonaventura's Part in the Conflict Between Seculars and Mendicants at Paris', in *S. Bonaventura 1274–1974* (Grottaferrata: Collegio S. Bonaventura, 1973–74), II: 585–612, at 593–6; James Weisheipl, *Friar Thomas d'Aquino. His Life, Thought and Works* (Oxford: Basil Blackwell, 1975), pp. 89–91.

[48] Moorman, *History of the Franciscan Order*, pp. 369–73.

[49] 'Nicolai prioris generalis ordinis Carmelitarum Ignea sagitta', ed. Adrianus Staring, *Carmelus*, 9 (1962), pp. 237–307, at 274: 'dum in caritate non ficta coniuncti et cementati, votum emissae professionis dedignabantur transgredi, sed in cellis suis permanentes, non per plateas discurrentes, in lege Domini meditari et in orationibus vigilare, non quasi ex necessitate, imo ex motu spiritualis gaudii hilariter satagebant'.

they scandalised with their infamy.[50] The urban environment made them proud and arrogant.[51] He questioned their ability to preach on two grounds, firstly because they lacked the necessary learning and secondly because they were no longer leading a holy life. Thus they destroyed by their example whatever they constructed with their word. They were similarly unsuitable as confessors.[52] This text highlights the fact that internal criticism of the friars did not only emerge in the Franciscan order and that the texts produced in these internal debates formed a genre in their own right, polemical treatises whose contents could become known beyond the circle of regular religious for whom they were intended.

FitzRalph's Attack on the Friars

Whilst French poets became involved in the early dispute between mendicants and seculars, as is shown by the intervention of Rutebeuf at Paris, there is little evidence of anti-mendicant feeling in English poetry of this period, although the late thirteenth-century Anglo-Norman poem *Ordre de Bel-Eyse* did criticise the mendicants for their rich diet and their close contact with nuns and other female religious.[53] Similarly, the turbulent phase in Franciscan history, between Clement V's failure to find common ground between the factions in the order with *Exivi de paradiso* (1312) and the intensification of the tensions after John XXII's intervention which led to the dramatic pronouncement in the bull *Cum inter nonnullos* (1323) that the claim that Christ and the apostles had held no possessions was heretical, had no immediate responses in English literature. These issues were important in parts of Italy where the Franciscan Spirituals and the even more radical Fraticelli came under pressure and had to rely on the support provided by king Robert of Naples, but they do not seem to have been significant for the friars in England.[54]

However, this was to change when the dispute about the legitimacy of the mendicants resurfaced in the 1350s, first in Avignon and then in London. The protagonist was Richard FitzRalph, archbishop of Armagh, a distinguished theologian who had been chancellor of Oxford University and who had originally been an admirer of the mendicants' scholarship and the protector of the Franciscans in Ireland. Katherine Walsh has suggested that FitzRalph's change of attitude was a result of his experience in Ireland from

---

[50] *Ibid.*, p. 279.
[51] *Ibid.*, p. 287.
[52] *Ibid.*, p. 280: 'Qui quidquid verbo aedificant, destruunt per exemplum. Nam inter lepram et lepram discernere nescientes tamquam scientiae et iuris ignari, solvunt quae solvi non expedit, ligant quae ligari utique non oportet'.
[53] Sickert, 'Wenn Klosterbrüder zu Jahrmarktsbrüdern werden', p. 49.
[54] Havely, 'Chaucer, Boccacio, and the Friars', p. 253.

1346, where he was confronted with practical problems in the administration of his diocese, although, as Michael Haren has argued, even before this period FitzRalph had belonged to the circle of Bishop Grandison of Exeter, a group sceptical of the mendicants' role in the Church.[55] This background may explain his reaction to the scene he witnessed on his visit to Avignon in 1349–50, when representatives of the mendicants at the Curia attempted to dilute the provisions of the bull *Super cathedram* (1300).[56] His sermon before Pope Clement VI in July 1350 seems to have been the starting point of his confrontation with the friars. Here he attacked their attempts to begin negotiations on *Super cathedram*, and, in particular, their efforts to have its supposedly unnecessary sections removed and its most rigid clauses mitigated. Although his language was conciliatory, his message was not: the mendicants should have no role in the ministry unless they are called upon to help by the local bishop under whose control they should act.[57] FitzRalph argued that the traditional ecclesiastical structures had been in existence for twelve hundred years before the arrival of the friars and that the Church had not asked for the creation of new orders and had not handed over the ministry to them, an argument which had been originally formulated with even greater precision by William of St Amour, who had traced the legitimate ecclesiastical hierarchy back to Christ and his first vicar, i.e. the papacy, the followers of the twelve apostles – the episcopal hierarchy – and those who followed in the footsteps of the seventy-two disciples: the priesthood.[58]

Even before the summer of 1350, when FitzRalph began to target the mendicants, he had criticised priests who were careless in granting absolution, but now he repeated these criticisms with direct reference to the friars and declared their activities to be damaging to Christian society. He argued that the friars' profession of individual as well as institutional poverty prohibited them from demanding any part of the income of the secular Church. Their ministry interfered with the work of the secular clergy who were responsible for the spiritual wellbeing of their parishioners and strict controls on the friars' activities should be imposed as a consequence. Mendicant sermons were to be allowed only outside the preaching hours of the secular 'prelates' unless a special licence had been granted. FitzRalph here defined 'prelates' as all members of the secular Church ordained to the priesthood, even chaplains:

---

[55] Michael Haren, 'Diocesan Dimensions of a Die-Hard Dispute: Richard FitzRalph and the Friars in Evolving Perspective', in Howard Clarke and Seymour Phillips, eds, *Ireland, England and the Continent in the Middle Ages and Beyond: Essays in Memory of a Turbulent Friar, F .X. Martin OSA* (Dublin: University College Dublin Press, 2006), pp. 164–76, at 166.
[56] Katherine Walsh, *A Fourteenth-Century Scholar and Primate: Richard FitzRalph in Oxford, Avignon and Armagh* (Oxford: Clarendon Press, 1981), pp. 359–63.
[57] Louis Hammerich, 'The Beginning of Strife between Richard FitzRalph and the Mendicants', *Det Kgl. Danske Videnskabernes Selskab, Historiskfilologiske Meddelelser* 26/3 (Kopenhagen: Levin & Munksgaard, 1938), p. 59: 'tenerentur episcopo obedire'.
[58] Bierbaum, *Bettelorden und Weltgeistlichkeit*, p. 9.

in the ecclesiastical hierarchy they were all superior to mendicant priests.[59] The friars' ministry in the confessional was just as superfluous as mendicant sermons and should be abolished because members of the laity should make their confessions to the parish clergy rather than to mendicant priests who had no jurisdiction and who had commercialised this activity.[60] FitzRalph presented several arguments in support of these assertions. For instance, he claimed that the confessor's absolution was only effective if restitution was made, something the friars could not ensure, and he added that the granting of flawed absolutions detracted from the friars' state of perfection and was consequently against their own rule.[61] Furthermore it was better for the sacraments to be administered by a person who was familiar with the parishioners' problems and the process was more effective if confession involved a degree of shame which would be absent because of the anonymity of the often unknown mendicant priest.[62] In a similar way the archbishop argued against the burial of laypeople in mendicant churches. This was detrimental to the parish clergy as well as to the friars themselves, because it involved them in litigation, sometimes with the ecclesiastical establishment, sometimes with the families of the deceased, a state of affairs which was once more contrary to their own ideals. FitzRalph's conclusion was simple: these and other papal privileges enjoyed by the four mendicant orders should be revoked.[63]

Although the archbishop's sermon in Avignon before the pope had been a public event, it is unlikely that it found much interest in England or Ireland, to where Richard FitzRalph returned in 1351. It is true that occasional disputes about burials between parochial or diocesan clergy and the friars of one or the other mendicant convent had occurred in England, but such incidents were normally resolved and they did not lead to profound arguments about ecclesiological principles.[64] In the British Isles the controversy had so far been a distant event, of interest only to theologians and prelates, to academics at the universities. This changed when the archbishop came to London in the summer of 1356, using his time in the city for a public reiteration of his views. In his London sermons between June 1356 and March 1357 he introduced a wider public to the 'mendicant problem'. He found support in the city and he preached to a wide public audience, including at St Paul's Cross.[65]

---

[59] Hammerich, 'The Beginning of Strife between Richard FitzRalph and the Mendicants', pp. 56–7.
[60] Ibid., pp. 58–9, 63.
[61] Ibid., p. 64.
[62] Ibid., p. 65.
[63] Ibid., p. 73.
[64] Arnold Williams, 'Relations Between the Mendicant Friars and the Secular Clergy in England in the Later Fourteenth Century', Annuale Mediaevale, 1 (1960), pp. 22–95, at 54–5.
[65] Aubrey Gwynn, 'The Sermon-Diary of Richard FitzRalph, Archbishop of Armagh', Proceedings of the Royal Irish Academy, 44 (1937/8) section C, pp. 1–57, at 31; Coleman, English Literature in History, p. 40.

The anti-mendicant arguments in these sermons were not original but were largely derived from William of St Amour.[66] Nevertheless the archbishop's activities functioned as a catalyst which set off a wide-ranging debate which, as we shall see below, was reflected in the works of Gower.

Criticism of the mendicants and the portrayal of friars as comic, hypocritical, even deceitful figures in English literature post-dates FitzRalph's public appearances in London and is clearly linked to his sermons. Earlier anti-mendicant polemics must have attracted some attention and, through works such as the encyclopaedia *Omne bonum*, had begun to reach a wide English audience, whilst manuscripts of William of St Amour's works can be shown to have appeared in English libraries.[67] However, FitzRalph's intervention was important for two reasons. The first was the public nature of his attacks, which led to a response from the London mendicants who compiled a list of errors found in his statements, which was delivered to him by John Arderne, the prior of the London Austin Friars, and which, in turn, provoked a further justification of FitzRalph's views, again in the form of a public sermon.[68] The second was the introduction of a new element into the English debate: the reopening of the question of the poverty of Christ. The notion that Christ and the apostles had held no property was of particular importance to the Franciscans, who justified their own form of religious life with their desire to follow Christ's example.[69] Following his measures to suppress the Franciscan Spirituals, John XXII had reopened this question even though the Minorites claimed that it had already been conclusively settled in the bull *Exiit qui seminat* (1279) and, as we saw above, declared that it was heretical to postulate absolute poverty for Christ and the apostles.[70] The

---

[66] James Dawson, 'Richard FitzRalph and the Fourteenth-Century Poverty Controversies', *Journal of Ecclesiastical History*, 34 (1983), pp. 315–44, at 341–2. FitzRalph's original contribution is highlighted by Scase, *Piers Plowman and the New Anticlericalism*, pp. 50–2.

[67] Penn Szittya, 'Kicking the Habit: The Campaign Against the Friars in a Fourteenth-Century Encyclopedia', in Guy Geltner and Michael Cusato, eds, *Defenders and Critics of Franciscan Life: Essays in Honor of John V. Fleming* (Leiden: Brill, 2009), pp. 159–75, at 159–67; Szittya, *The Antifraternal Tradition*, pp. 63–4, 72; *Omne Bonum: A Fourteenth-Century Encyclopedia of Universal Knowledge*, ed. Lucy Sandler (two volumes; London: Harvey Miller, 1996) I: 46; II: 195.

[68] Walsh, *A Fourteenth-Century Scholar*, p. 417; Katherine Walsh, 'Fitzralph [FitzRalph], Richard', *Oxford Dictionary of National Biography*, ref:odnb/9627, http://www.oxforddnb.com/view/article/9627, accessed 12 May 2017.

[69] Walsh, *A Fourteenth-Century Scholar*, p. 377.

[70] Moorman, *History of the Franciscan Order*, pp. 310–17; Livarius Oliger, 'Fr. Bonagratia de Bergamo et eius Tractatus de Christi et Apostolorum Paupertate', *Archivum Franciscanum Historicum*, 22 (1929), pp. 292–335, 487–511, at 298–9; Charles Davis, 'Le Pape Jean XXII et les spirituels: Ubertin de Casale', in *Franciscains d'Oc: Les 'Spirituels' (ca.1280–1324)*, Cahiers de Fanjeaux, 10 (Toulouse: É. Privat, 1975), pp. 263–83, at 264–6; Giacomo Todeschini, 'Oeconomica franciscana. Proposte di una nuova lettura delle fonti dell'etica economica medievale', *Rivista di storia e letteratura religiosa*, 12/1 (1976), pp. 15–77, at 29, 44.

ensuing rift between the pope and the order's leadership under the minister general Michael of Cesena acquired a political dimension when Franciscan intellectuals – among them William of Ockham – began to support the German king, Ludwig the Bavarian, against the pope, a dispute which had subsided towards the middle of the fourteenth century but was then revived in Britain by FitzRalph's polemics.

John Gower and Antifraternalism

The views on the mendicant orders publicised by Archbishop FitzRalph became widely known, in contrast with the efforts by London Franciscans and other mendicants to defend themselves against his attacks.[71] FitzRalph's treatise *De pauperie salvatoris* had a profound influence on John Wyclif and there was a Middle English translation of it by John Trevisa (c.1380).[72] Many of the views expressed by the Anglo-Irish theologian were to influence English poetry and, in particular, were to be used by John Gower in his polemics against the mendicants.[73] For instance, in relation to the friars' ministry, FitzRalph had called for a total abolition of mendicant privileges, a point Gower repeated in *Mirour de l'Omme* with his claim that the orders were outside the law and not under ecclesiastical control: 'N'est qui les puet au droit reuler: La loy commune n'ad poer, Car ils ne sont pas seculier, Ne sainte eglise en son degre, Leur privileges attempter, Ne voet' (21462–8, 21482–92). The archbishop demanded that the friars should practise poverty, an argument also picked up on by Gower (21193–201, 21511–2). Their confessional practice was lax (21259–63, 21282–3) and they were not part of the original structure of the Church (VC: IV.22.1097), even though FitzRalph acknowledged that the orders had been accepted by the papacy.[74] Like FitzRalph, Gower was often implicitly referring to the Franciscans, even when explicitly speaking of the mendicants in general, a simplification which failed to take into account the differences which existed between the four mendicant orders in the late fourteenth century.[75] While the archbishop was

---

[71] Michael Haren, 'Bishop Gynwell of Lincoln, Two Avignonese Statutes, and Archbishop FitzRalph of Armagh's Suit at the Roman Curia against the Friars', *Archivum Historiae Pontificiae*, 31 (1993), pp. 275–92.

[72] Walsh, *A Fourteenth-Century Scholar*, p. 378; John Trevisa, *Dialogus inter militem et clericum*, ed. Aaron Perry (EETS, o.s. 167, (1925)). FitzRalph's own sources are discussed in Dawson, 'Richard FitzRalph and the Fourteenth-Century Poverty Controversies', pp. 317–29.

[73] Walsh, *A Fourteenth-Century Scholar*, p. 365; Williams, 'Relations Between the Mendicant Friars and the Secular Clergy', p. 26.

[74] Hammerich, 'The Beginning of Strife between Richard FitzRalph and the Mendicants', pp. 43, 55, 58, 61, 64, 66.

[75] Although Gower was, of course, aware of the Dominican and Franciscan founders and does mention 'Jacobin, Carme et Menour' (MO: 21760), he also speaks of the

clearly aware of the different attitudes to poverty between the orders and the different legal settings provided by their rules, with the Franciscans and the Carmelites following rules of their own while the Dominicans and the Austin Friars were at least technically following the rule of St Augustine, Gower merely seems to have known the basic institutional differences between those orders which constituted the 'mendicants'. In *Mirour de l'Omme* he does refer to 'Jacobin, Carme et Menour' (i.e. Dominicans, Carmelites and Franciscans) (21760) but he showed little interest in the individual history and identity of these orders. Instead he focused on their present state and on the effects they allegedly had on contemporary society.

Gower's criticism is vociferous and is drawn from an impressive number of sources, but it is neither well organised nor based on any real knowledge of the orders' internal organisation. The relevant sections in his works are characterised by repetition and there is no clear direction. *Mirour de l'Omme* begins with a complaint about the mendicants' possessions (21199–200), the friars' failure to work (21210), their greed despite their preaching of poverty (21217–20), their elaborate architecture (21229), their deceit in confession (21249–52), their social selectivity (21277) and lechery (21296). In these stanzas Gower plays with personified friars, Flattery and Hypocrisy, largely to show their moral failings. He then returns to the theme of mendicant architecture (21403–4, 21411–40) and moves on to their political ambitions (21445), their privileged status (21462) and their pride (21493), then returns to their greed, which contrasts with their claim to poverty (21311), their falseness: 'fals semblant' (21594), their hypocrisy (21615) and the fact that they have no role in the Church. Gower concludes by labelling them with the term 'Pseudo' (21627, 21631, 21637) and he illustrates this with their deceit, their corrupt practices, their failure to practise what they preach (21720) and the bad example they give to the laity (21738). In *Vox Clamantis* Gower begins with the accusation of the mendicants' fictitious poverty (IV.16) and their hypocrisy in sermons and in the ministry in general (IV.17–18). He continues with the observation that they have no role in the Church (IV.19-20), then castigates their corrupt recruitment practices (IV.21) and their hypocrisy (IV.22). This is followed by criticism of their mobility – their refusal to live enclosed in a monastery – and their large and increasing numbers (IV.23) before Gower returns to the ecclesiological problem he had addressed earlier (IV.19–20; IV.24), although here he uses new material.

Even though Gower drew together a wide range of accusations, his criticisms can be grouped into a mere three categories. Although there are parallels, these categories differ from the three biblical figures presented by William of St Amour, who saw the friars as Pharisees, pseudo-Apostles and

---

ordo fratrum (VC: IV.19.891) or castigates the failings of the 'fratrum ordinis mendicancium' (IV.22). See Terry Dolan, 'Langland and FitzRalph: Two Solutions to the Mendicant Problem', *The Yearbook of Langland Studies*, 2 (1988), pp. 35–45, at 35.

'Anti-Christi'.[76] Instead, Gower arranged his criticisms around three linked arguments which were firstly ecclesiological, secondly moral and thirdly social, arguing that the friars have no role in the Church, that they are morally corrupt and that they are a danger to society.

Firstly, Gower presents the mendicants as an eschatological phenomenon, a threat associated with the approaching end of the world. In *Vox Clamantis* he alleges that there have been warnings and prophesies against the friars (IV.17.766) and his statement that God's rule does not know the friar (IV.22.1021) denies the mendicants' right to exist.[77] Gower insinuated that the mendicant orders are identical with those whose arrival marks the end of time, which had been William of St Amour's key argument in his treatise *De periculis novissimorum temporum*. The statement in *Mirour de l'Omme* (21482–92, 21527–8) that their focus is on their food, their clothing, their physical comfort and their pride gives them some of the qualities attributed in 2 Timothy 3:1–7 to such '*antichristi*'.

This association of the mendicants with those who announce the coming of the Antichrist leads Gower to his second point, their moral corruption. They preach poverty to others but they advance themselves,[78] views found in *Mirour de l'Omme* (21193–21201, 21511–2) as well as *Vox Clamantis* (IV.16.715–6, 721–2), where Gower added that they praise God with their mouths, but with their hearts they worship gold (IV.17.793–4). In *Mirour de l'Omme* it is claimed that the friars are drawn to the world instead of to religion and that they want to protect their privileges rather than follow God because they only pay attention to their food, their clothing and their physical comforts (21188–93, 21232, 21482–92), features which also later characterised Chaucer's Friar Huberd.[79] The friars' moral decay gives them the quality of being false apostles, hypocrites who endanger the souls of Christians. People should make their escape when their habits come into view.[80] This theme occurs repeatedly, both in the *Mirour de l'Omme* (21250, 21256–60, 21289–21300, 21314–6, 21367, 21580–8, 21615, 21619, 21625–7) and in *Vox Clamantis* (IV.17.751–72; IV.22.1062–3). Arriving in pairs as Hypocrisy and Flattery, the mendicants are really wolves in sheep's clothing (Matthew 7:15; MO: 21629–36; VC: IV.17.798).

Both *Vox Clamantis* and *Mirour de l'Omme* agree that the proof of this corruption is the friars' greed and their desire to enjoy wealth, because whatever the friar touches with his hand sticks to it (MO: 21217–20; VC: IV.16.740–4; IV.17.763; 22.1134). Gower claims that this obsession with wealth and physical comfort is reflected in mendicant architecture. The claim 'Ils ont maison celestial' in *Mirour de l'Omme* (21229) is later repeated in the

---

[76] Szittya, *The Antifraternal Tradition*, pp. 32–5.
[77] Ibid., pp. 62–122; Scase, *Piers Plowman and the New Anticlericalism*, p. 3.
[78] Geltner, 'William of St. Amour's De periculis novissimorum temporum', p. 107.
[79] Williams, 'Two Notes on Chaucer and the Friars', p. 117.
[80] See Romans 16:17–8.

same text (21403–437) and also appears in *Vox Clamantis* (IV.22.1141–9, 1151–2, 1154, 1165–6, 1173–4). The elaborate nature of their architecture with its beautiful cloisters, intricate carvings and vaultings, exquisite metalwork and windows, reveals the true nature of the friars. It naturally follows that they are socially selective, favouring the children of the rich as novices, and that they carry out their spiritual work only for material gain, an assessment again found in *Mirour de l'Omme* (21340, 21373–84, 21472–80, 21571–6) and *Vox Clamantis* (IV.16.737–40). The characterisation is refined in *Mirour de l'Omme*: their corruption extends to plotting and scheming and the spreading of falsehoods, even in their sermons (21222, 21233–4, 21385–96, 21610, 21638), practices to which they are well suited because their eloquence allows them to hide poison under honey (VC: IV.20.976; IV.22.1076).[81] The ability to adapt to their environment, like chameleons, permits them to perform different roles in different places, at court or in the intimacy of the bedchamber (VC: IV.18.824–6, 831–4), a quality reminiscent of *Faus Semblanz* in the *Roman de la Rose*, who has been seen as representing the completely corrupt friar, although Sickert and Geltner both argue that this character is a much more multi-faced figure than a mere mendicant.[82] Since the friars are servants of vice, a label applied in *Mirour de l'Omme* (21237–8, 21419–20, 21441, 21610–12) as well as in *Vox Clamantis* (IV.22.1024–5), it is not surprising to find a degree of sexual innuendo in Gower's criticisms along with allegations of adultery and duped husbands (MO: 21305, 21318–9, 21325, 21332–6, 21338, 21349; VC: IV.18.836–7, 853–4, 863, 865–70): Gower here deplores that, unlike bees, the friars do not lose their sting after using it once (VC: IV.18.877–88).[83] Another sign of decline is the friars' pride, an attitude largely due to their academic education. Thus they demand to be called masters instead of displaying humility (MO: 21493–8; VC: IV.18.809–21). They cause strife and conflicts, they destroy peace and social harmony, they wear linen under coarse woollen cloth and hide viciousness under a cloak of virtue, and they often proliferate *zizania* – heresies (VC: IV.22.1036–7, 1038–9, 1047, 1051–2, 1083). This rich array of accusations is enhanced by repetitions in the text.

Gower's third point is the friars' superfluousness; they have no role in the Church or in society at large. This claim is based not only on the mendicants'

---

[81] The friars' falsity is a key characteristic in the *Roman de la Rose* (Szittya, 'The Friar as False Apostle', pp. 36–7).

[82] Sickert, *'Wenn Klosterbrüder zu Jahrmarktsbrüdern werden'*, pp. 46–8; Geltner, 'Faux Semblants', p. 360. The complexity of the character was partly caused by alterations introduced into the text by later medieval editors (Sylvia Huot, *The Romance of the Rose and its Medieval Readers: Interpretation, Reception, Manuscript Transmission*, Cambridge Studies in Medieval Literature, 16 (Cambridge: Cambridge University Press, 1993), pp. 38–40).

[83] Carolly Erickson, 'The Fourteenth-Century Franciscans and Their Critics', *Franciscan Studies*, 35 (1975), pp. 107–35: 36 (1976), pp. 108–47, at 35 (1975), p. 125; Fisher, *John Gower*, p. 266.

absence in the ecclesiological model originally favoured by William of St Amour, but also on their individual as well as institutional corruption. Before the existence of the *ordo fratrum* (IV.19.889–96) the Church had possessed a clear hierarchical structure with the pope at the top, an argument clearly derived from the earlier anti-mendicant ecclesiological model of William of St Amour who, as we saw above, had argued that the mendicants had no legitimate place in the ecclesiastical hierarchy which had its roots in Christ, the twelve apostles and the seventy-two disciples. This argument was taken up a century later by Richard FitzRalph and although it is impossible to say for certain whether Gower was acquainted with the debate at Paris in the 1250s, it is more likely that the poet was making use of FitzRalph's sermons rather than that he knew the works of William of St Amour at first-hand.[84]

For Gower, the mendicants are ineffective and disruptive in the Church and harmful to society. This is shown by a number of examples. The mendicants' ministry is lax and flawed, a fault recently emphasised by Richard FitzRalph. Like the archbishop, Gower associates all mendicants with the original Franciscan ideal, claiming that they now disregard the principles and norms which had originally been set by St Francis. Thus, while St Francis had abandoned the world, they are seeking it and are guilty of the sin of greed (MO: 21522). Gower goes as far as suggesting that the granting of absolution is merely a business for the friars. They do not want contrition ('ce n'est pas de son affaire' (MO: 21259–63)), they want money, thus turning the confessional into a commercial enterprise and subverting the whole purpose of confession (MO: 21265–76, 21282–3; VC: IV.16.734–8). Absolution is granted in return for the contents of the rich man's purse and penance is redeemed with silver, circumstances which invalidate the whole process (MO: 21277–88). Other parts of the mendicants' ministry correspond to this perversion of the confessional. In *Vox Clamantis*, Gower claims that whilst sin is condemned in the friar's sermon, he privately condones it in the confessional; thus the sinner administers sins to others (IV.17.751–60). It follows that moral decay and corrupt procedures render the mendicants' spiritual intercession ineffective (IV.22.1137–8, 1169–71, 1179–82). Without a legitimate place in the Church the friars are like ravens among the white birds (VC: IV.19.903–6). Like the figure of Burnell the Ass in Nigel of Longchamps' *Speculum Stultorum*, they had to found a religious order of their own – even though there was no need for it (VC: IV.24.1190–1210).[85] Worse, they meddle in parish business, claiming the right to hear confessions and to conduct burials (MO: 21469–71). Their failure to lead a proper religious life, travelling through the world, is castigated (MO: 21501–4; VC: IV.17.780; IV.22.1113–5). *Vox Clamantis* adds that even though they are

---

[84] Szittya, *The Antifraternal Tradition*, p. 200.
[85] 'Hinc est quod statuo me tradere religioni, Cujus ero primus doctor et auctor ego' (*Nigel de Longchamps Speculum Stultorum*, eds John Mozley and Robert Raymo (Berkeley: University of California Press, 1960), ll. 3259–60).

not part of the clergy, they try to usurp that status (IV.19.906; IV.20.945–7). Failing to submit to discipline, they corrupt the secular clergy and they control the papacy, obtaining privileges by fraud (IV.16.725–8; IV.19.919–22).[86] The mendicant privileges, a traditional target of the friars' critics, which are referred to in both *Mirour de l'Omme* (21462–8) and *Vox Clamantis* (IV.20.961–2; IV.22.1097), give them a state outside society and they are neither under the control of ecclesiastical nor of secular law. This allows them to usurp papal authority by granting dispensations in reserved cases (VC: IV.19, 917–24).

If they are detrimental to the Church, the mendicants are equally harmful to society. Gower claims in both the *Mirour* and the *Vox* poems that their danger is exacerbated by the large number of friars and the way in which the number of friars increases whilst the observance of their rule declines is 'contre la commune pes' (MO: 21522, 21540, 21562-8; VC: IV.20.951–6; IV.21.981–1014; IV.22.1129). They tend to recruit young boys through flattery and deceit, increasing their membership beyond measure. Just as one cannot count the stars, so it is impossible to count the friars; they are like the waves and they multiply just as hair grows.[87] In *Mirour de l'Omme* Gower argues that since the friars do no manual work ('ils n'ont cure de charue') (21210, 21529–40), they do not contribute to society, an accusation already made by William of St Amour who, referring to 2 Thessalonians 3, had pointed out that the *gyrovagi* were lazy and ought to live by their own work.[88] In a society where the shortage of labourers had led to denunciations of those who refused to work (see above, pp. 179–82), such an argument may have been particularly powerful. Certainly, both *Vox Clamantis* (IV.20.957–8, 965–6; IV.22.1121) and *Mirour de l'Omme* (21223–4) repeatedly invoke the scenario in which a large number of friars are said to enjoy the fruits of the labour of others without themselves being willing to make a contribution. Should they not work in the fields like the villeins do?[89] In *Vox Clamantis* Gower draws the logical conclusion: since the friars do not contribute to the common good, they have no role in the world (IV.20.950; IV.22.1023).

Gower also raises the question of the mendicants' real objectives. According to both *Mirour de l'Omme* (21599–600) and *Vox Clamantis*

---

[86] Douie, St. Bonaventura's Part in the Conflict Between Seculars and Mendicants at Paris', pp. 587–8 draws attention to the secular masters' claim in a letter to French bishops issued in February 1254 that the friars had obtained a papal bull by fraud.

[87] Erickson, 'The Fourteenth-Century Franciscans and Their Critics', p. 112; Fisher, *John Gower*, p. 265.

[88] *Magistri Guillielmi de S. Amore Opera Omnia quae reperiri potuerunt* (Constance: Ad Insigne Bonae Fidei apud Alithophilos, 1632); 'De periculis novissimorum temporum', p. 47; Bierbaum, *Bettelorden und Weltgeistlichkeit*, pp. 28–9; Faral, 'Les Responsiones de Guillaume de Saint-Amour', p. 378; Kathryn Kerby-Fulton, 'Hildegard of Bingen and Anti-Mendicant Propaganda', *Traditio*, 43 (1987), pp. 386–99, at 394.

[89] David Aers, *Community, Gender and Individual Identity: English Writing, 1360–1430* (London: Routledge, 1988), pp. 31–5.

(IV.17.802–4), whilst the friars' cunning has already perverted so many people, even worse is to come: they have ulterior motives and want to rule the world. There is not a king, prince or magnate who does not entrust their secrets to them. The consequences of this familiarity with state secrets are spelled out in *Vox Clamantis*: the friars will gradually usurp all political power, even that of the pope (IV.16.725–32). This danger is underlined by the fact that they have even killed an emperor (MO: 21450–4), a reference to the death of the Holy Roman Emperor Henry VII in 1313, who was allegedly killed by a Dominican friar when receiving communion, an allegation which had already been refuted by the emperor's son, King John of Bohemia.[90]

Gower thus presents a formidable array of arguments against the mendicants. No other author of medieval estates satire seems to have collected such a vast quantity of antifraternal material. However, Gower failed to arrange his accusations into a sequence of coherent arguments or to arrive at clear conclusions. Furthermore, his objectives are not entirely clear because whilst some of his arguments (the friars are superfluous, have no place in the Church, and represent the imminent end of the world) point to the need for the abolition of the mendicant orders, others (their orders have undergone a moral decline) merely suggest the need for their reform. His own views remain obscure until he introduces long sections about the friars in the 'good old days', when they still adhered to their founders' ideals. Both *Mirour de l'Omme* (21460, 21505–8) and *Vox Clamantis* (IV.16.699–700) refer to this supposed glorious past when the orders' aims were good and holy and their founders were pious people who wanted to be – rather than merely to seem to be – good.[91] Francis is thus said to have stayed away from the world and had never asked for the cure of souls, preferring a life of poverty and simplicity (MO: 21522–6; VC IV.19.925–30) and neither he nor Dominic had wanted young boys to join their communities. The founding ideals of these saints were still valid and honour is due to the true followers of St Francis (MO: 21545–61; VC IV.20.978–9). Gower differentiates between the good friars, who take their vocation seriously and who attempt to adhere to the ideals of their founders, and those who are corrupt (MO: 21266). Both *Mirour de l'Omme* (21649–59, 21673–84) and *Vox Clamantis* (IV.22.1015) contain reminders that the mendicant orders in their original state were beneficial, that the founders' intentions were good, a clear effort to distinguish between the positive influence of good friars and the negative effect of those who fail to live up to the required standard.

---

[90] Maria Franke, *Kaiser Heinrich VII. im Spiegel der Historiographie. Eine faktenkritische und quellenkundliche Untersuchung ausgewählter Geschichtsschreiber der ersten Hälfte des 14. Jahrhunderts*, Forschungen zur Kaiser und Papstgeschichte des Mittelalters, Beihefte zu J. F. Böhmer, Regesta Imperii, 9 (Cologne: Böhlau, 1992), pp. 102–27; Robert Davidsohn, *Geschichte von Florenz* (Berlin: E. S. Mittler und Sohn, 1912), III: 545–7.

[91] Allen, *The Friar as Critic*, p. 62.

Nevertheless, in his attempts to accommodate a wide range of accusations, Gower continued to contradict himself, claiming that the orders' original ideals have been abandoned because of the friars' pride and that consequently the orders have lost their appeal, a notion which is at odds with his own earlier accusation that there were too many friars and that they appealed to people by granting easy absolution (MO: 21505; VC: IV.16.713; 22, 1021, 1055–6, 1101–2). In general, though, despite his antifraternal polemics, Gower did not conclude that the mendicants should be abolished but simply demanded their reform (VC: IV.16.701–4, 206; 17.807–8). Thus, whilst those friars who do not perform their duties should be punished, those who follow St Francis deserve to be treated honourably (VC: IV.20.979–80). However, the *Miroir de l'Omme* leaves little hope for such virtue on the part of the mendicants amongst whom corruption is rife: 'Du Jacobin, Carme et Menour, N'est qui se gart a son honour, Des toutez partz sont perverti' (21760–2).

Despite the parallels between the *Mirour de l'Omme* and *Vox Clamantis* and the repetition of material between them, the treatment of the friars in the two texts is not entirely identical. A key objection to the mendicants' way of life is the allegation that they only pretend to be poor and that they preach poverty while they make a living off the sins and the work of others. In *Mirour de l'Omme* Gower accuses them of 'covoitise' (21219), a sin which was introduced earlier in the poem as an offspring of avarice (6181). Deception and lies also characterise their language when they pass in pairs through the country. Friar Hypocrisy acts as confessor of a lady who is released from her sins by friar Flattery. The mendicant ministry and especially the confessional is lax: even though the confessor is prepared to hear the confession, he is not interested in instilling contrition because the whole exercise is none of his business: 'ce n'est pas de son affaire' (21259). The speaker implies that the mendicant confessor intrudes in ordinary parish business and – even worse – that this intrusion takes place only for profit. Absolution is available for a payment and the whole purpose of confession is thus subverted (21282–3). The accumulation of these negative characteristics in *Mirour de l'Omme* leaves hardly any hope for reform. Yet, by contrast, the section on the mendicants in *Vox Clamantis* begins with the statement that only a few friars are guilty: 'Non volo pro paucis diffundere crimen in omnes' (IV.16.689). This poem suggests that the majority of devout religious are not burdened by the crimes committed by a few.

Among the anti-mendicant polemicists, Gower produced the most comprehensive critique of the four orders. He collected an impressive array of arguments against the friars and must have searched numerous texts, including perhaps *Insurgent gentes*, a forged prophecy attributed to Hildegard of Bingen.[92] No other English poet of his time refers to the allegations of assassination made against the Dominicans after the death of Henry VII in

---

[92] Kerby-Fulton, 'Hildegard of Bingen', p. 396.

1313. However, this bookish diligence caused its own problems.[93] Gower seems to have been unaware of the fact that the material he collected had actually been created with different objectives in mind. The dispute at the University of Paris in the 1250s had firstly generated the image of the friar as 'hypocrite', 'Pharisee' and proud academic who wanted to be called 'master'.[94] It had also reminded the public involved in the debate that there already existed a model of the Church in which the mendicants had no place. Following the bull *Ad fructus uberes* (1281) there was more opposition to the friars' ministry and especially to their right to hear confession and to grant absolution. This episode was – again – largely restricted to France. Richard FitzRalph, archbishop of Armagh, resented the brusque treatment he had received from some Irish Franciscans and began to question the friars' privileges and their exemption from episcopal control.

It is impossible to say how much Gower knew about this and the controversies involving the mendicants. His attempt to accommodate all the material he had collected firstly led to an assembly of stereotypical allegations in which different forms of criticism were merged and no clear message was generated. Secondly, he paid no attention to the fact that different types of anti-mendicant criticism were designed to achieve different objectives and were part of a variety of dispute strategies in theological conflicts or disagreements about status or the allocation of resources. In addition, Gower showed no interest in the attempts of the mendicants to reform themselves, especially those in the Franciscan order which were being made during his lifetime, when observant friars began to be institutionally integrated into the order. It is also unlikely that he knew of the mendicant orders which had disappeared in the wake of the Second Council of Lyons or that he was aware of the fact that the Church had already taken action against the friars in the previous century. Thus, although earlier criticism had already led to consequences, Gower makes no reference to such precedents. He is unlikely to have known that the transition of the Carmelites into a mendicant institution had led to a debate in the order which was documented in the treatise *Ignea sagitta*. Nor did he show any interest in the theological debates about apostolic poverty or the accusations made against Jean de Pouilly, who had to defend himself before Pope John XXII for having condemned the friars' practice of confession, an affair in which, once again, the mendicants'

---

[93] Burrow, *Ricardian Poetry*, p. 61; Robert R. Raymo, 'The General Prologue', in *Sources and Analogues of the Canterbury Tales*, eds Robert M. Correale and Mary Hamel (Cambridge: D. S. Brewer, 2003–05), II: 1–86, at 24–5; Robert R. Raymo, 'Vox Clamantis, IV, 12', *Modern Language Notes*, 71.2 (1956), pp. 82–3; Szittya, *The Antifraternal Tradition*, p. 72.

[94] Sita Steckel, 'Narratives of Resistance: Arguments against the Mendicants in the Works of Matthew Paris and William of Saint-Amour', in Janet Burton, Philipp Schofield and Björn Weiler, eds, *Thirteenth-Century England XV. Authority and Resistance in the Age of Magna Carta* (Woodbridge: Boydell Press, 2015), pp. 157–77, at 158.

role in the Church was questioned.⁹⁵ Finally Gower ignored the fact that the material he was collecting had actually emanated in disputes and had provoked responses from the mendicants. Thus, Bonaventure, John Pecham and Thomas Aquinas had defended themselves against the allegations made by the Parisian secular masters and the affair begun by Richard FitzRalph in London led to the presentation of counter arguments. In his assembling of illustrative material Gower was remarkably diligent provided that it contributed to the image of the mendicants that he wanted to present, but he showed no interest in the context of its creation or in the arguments of the other side. Even then he only managed to organise his colourful collage of accusations into a rather simplistic message: the mendicant orders had originally been good; they have deteriorated and become dangerous; they should reform and become good again.

The Poet's Criticism and Historical Evidence

There can be no doubt that Gower was correct in observing that, by the late fourteenth century, the mendicant orders were different from the institutions that had originally been created between the pontificates of Innocent III (1198–1216) and Alexander IV (1254–1261). Gower's experience of them was restricted to their English provinces. Robert Swanson has been able to show that in England there was occasional friction between the secular clergy and the orders, even though prospective confessors were regularly presented to the diocesan bishops so that they could be licensed for the ministry.⁹⁶ Gower was right in saying that the mendicants were influential. A number of English queens and other female members of the royal family had been in close contact with the Franciscans, including Eleanor of Provence, the wife of Henry III, Margaret, the second wife of Edward I, and Isabella, the wife of Edward II.⁹⁷ However, this relationship changed over time. Members of the English Dominican province had acted as royal confessors since the thirteenth century and Richard II still had confessors from this order, men he rewarded with high posts in the Church. Dominicans had also been close to other leading families such as the Clares and the Bohuns. However, this did

---

[95] Josef Koch, 'Der Prozeß gegen den Magister Johannes de Polliaco und seine Vorgeschichte, 1312–21', *Recherches de théologie ancienne et médiévale*, 5 (1933), pp. 391–422, at 393: Sikes, 'Jean de Poulli and Peter de la Palu', pp. 225–6.

[96] Robert Swanson, 'The "Mendicant Problem" in the Later Middle Ages', in Peter Biller and Barrie Dobson, eds, *The Medieval Church: Universities, Heresy, and the Religious Life. Essays in Honour of Gordon Leff*, Studies in Church History, subsidia, 11 (Woodbridge: Boydell Press, 1999), pp. 217–39, at 220–6.

[97] *The Letters of Adam Marsh*, ed. Clifford Hugh Lawrence (Oxford: Clarendon Press, 2006–10), II: 368–91; Michael Robson, 'Queen Isabella (c. 1295/1358) and the Greyfriars: an Example of Royal Patronage Based on her Accounts for 1357/1358', *Franciscan Studies*, 65 (2007), pp. 325–48, at 327.

not mean that the Dominicans had a significant influence on English politics in the second half of the fourteenth century. Indeed, Richard II encountered political resistance when he tried to let his Dominican confessors, Thomas Rushok and Alexander Bache, benefit from royal patronage.[98] After 1399, the Black Friars' prominence at the royal court ended and Carmelite confessors obtained access to the monarch.[99] The English Carmelite province began to flourish in the late fourteenth century when a number of excellent academics, among them Stephen Patrington and Thomas Netter, came to prominence. Netter enjoyed the trust of King Henry V and was employed on at least one important diplomatic mission. However, these men did not seek to play an independent role in political life, perhaps having been warned by the fate of a fellow Carmelite who, in 1384, had tried to inform Richard II of an alleged plot against him, an attempt which resulted in a political scandal and the man's death.[100] The Austin Friars, an amalgamation of eremitical groups, had also established an English province, with some of their members being present in London even before Pope Alexander IV's *Magna Unio* of 1256.[101] In Gower's time there were public disputes among the English Austin Friars. He must have known of the scandal in 1387 when the former London Austin friar Peter Pateshull called for an abolition of the mendicant orders and led an attack on his old friary.[102] In his *Cronica Tripertita* he mentions the burial of the executed Richard Fitzalan, earl of Arundel, at the London Austin Friars, whose soul he places in heaven ('Corpus ad ima cadit ... Spiritus in celis' (II.150–8)), which may link Gower with those who began

---

[98] *The Westminster Chronicle, 1381–1394*, eds Leonard Hector and Barbara Harvey (Oxford: Clarendon Press, 1982), pp. 144, 434; Richard Davies, 'Richard II and the Church', in Anthony Goodman and James Gillespie, eds, *Richard II and the Art of Kingship* (Oxford: Clarendon Press, 1999), pp. 83–106, at 87–90.

[99] Henry IV adopted the pattern of payments which were developed in his grandfather's reign. Extra payments to friars are rare, an exception being the Franciscans of Walsingham (The National Archives, London, E403/538, m. 8).

[100] Jens Röhrkasten, 'Thomas Netter: Carmelite and Diplomat', in Johann Bergström-Allen and Richard Copsey, eds, *Thomas Netter of Walden: Carmelite, Diplomat and Theologian (c.1372–1430)*, Carmel in Britain, 4 (Faversham: Saint Albert's Press, 2009), pp. 113–35; *Westminster Chronicle*, eds Hector and Harvey, pp. 68–80; May McKisack, *The Fourteenth Century, 1307–1399* (Oxford: Clarendon Press, 1959), p. 434. Thomas Walsingham, *Historia Anglicana*, in *Chronica Monasterii S. Albani*, ed. Henry T. Riley (seven volumes: London: Rolls Series, 1864–76), II: 114–15.

[101] Kaspar Elm, 'Die Bulle "Ea quae iudicio" Clemens' IV, 30.VIII. 1266. Vorgeschichte, Überlieferung, Text, Bedeutung, *Augustiniana*, 14 (1964), pp. 500–22; 15 (1965), pp. 54–67, 493–530; 16 (1966), pp. 95–145, 501–2; Francis Roth, *The English Austin Friars 1249–1538*, Cassiciacum, 4, (New York: Augustinian Historical Institute, 1961–66), I: 16.

[102] Jens Röhrkasten, *The Mendicant Houses of Medieval London* (Münster: Lit. 2004), p. 529.

to worship the executed nobleman as a martyr and sought to establish a cult at the tomb.[103]

Gower may have been aware of the scandal at the city's Crutched Friars, who tried to recruit a young boy, an attempt which led to an official intervention by the London authorities.[104] Certainly, there had been criticism of the mendicant practice of accepting youngsters who were under age as early as the thirteenth century and a statutory minimum of twenty-one years for entry to the friars was set by parliament in 1402.[105] It is also plausible to assume that Gower was familiar with the topography of the six London mendicant convents, including also the Friars of the Cross and the Franciscan nuns, although in his works he made no reference to the latter two and he made no bequests to the friars in his testament (see above, p. 89). There were close links between the city's Grey Friars and the Minoresses near Aldgate, but this is ignored by Gower who prefers to argue at a general level rather than to refer to specific scandals of the time. It may be assumed too that he knew about the dispute between the archbishop of Armagh and the mendicants because an essential element of it had taken place in London. As a man of property with legal knowledge and an interest in public affairs he must also have known about the royal enquiry into the holding of real estate by the mendicants in England after the Black Death, although this measure predates FitzRalph's sermons and was most likely a government response to property transfers in the wake of plague mortality.[106]

Gower must have been aware of the fact that the splendour of the London mendicant churches was not typical of the English province because he is likely to have encountered the much more modest friaries in the English county towns, including those in Canterbury. However, it was not his intention to describe the complexities of this reality. The fact that Gower included the mendicants in his array of social groups is in itself significant. He needed them to complete his wide assembly of social and professional groups in order to present a comprehensive picture of moral decay and to draw attention to the dangers threatening the English kingdom. Drawing

---

[103] McKisack, *The Fourteenth Century*, p. 484; Davies, 'Richard II and the Church', p. 97; *Johannis de Trokelowe et Henrici de Blaneforde, monachorum S. Albani Chronica et Annales*, in *Chronica Monasterii S. Albani*, ed. Riley, III: 218–19; Sheila Delany, *Medieval Literary Politics. Shapes of Ideology* (Manchester: Manchester University Press, 1990), p. 133; Chris Given-Wilson, *Henry IV* (New Haven/London: Yale University Press, 2016), pp. 393, 401.

[104] *Calendar of Select Pleas and Memoranda of the City of London*, ed. Arthur H. Thomas (Cambridge: Cambridge University Press, 1926–61), IV: 182.

[105] *Fratris Thomae vulgo dicti de Eccleston Tractatus de Adventu Fratrum Minorum in Angliam*, ed. Andrew G. Little (Manchester: University of Manchester Press, 1951), pp. 12, 23–4; *Rotuli Parliamentorum ut et petitiones et placita in Parliamento* (London: Record Commission, 1783), III: 502a, no. 62.

[106] Andrew G. Little, 'A Royal Inquiry into Property Held by the Mendicant Friars in England in 1349 and 1350', in James Edwards, ed., *Historical Essays in Honour of James Tait* (Manchester: Printed for the Subscribers, 1933), pp. 179–88.

attention to the various threats to society was a first step to return to the good old days in which each member of society had performed the role assigned to them by God.[107]

---

[107] Winthrop Wetherbee, 'Latin Structure and Vernacular Space: Gower, Chaucer and the Boethian Tradition', in Robert F. Yeager, ed., *Chaucer and Gower: Difference, Mutuality, Exchange*, English Literary Studies, 51 (University of Victoria: English Department, 1991), pp. 7–35, 18; Rigby, *Chaucer in Context*, p. 21.

PART IV

GOWER AND GENDER

CHAPTER 10

WOMEN AND POWER

Katherine J. Lewis

Gower's works contain a great deal of comment on the nature and character of women, drawing on established medieval ideologies of gender to measure their conduct against ideals of femininity. However, the principal concern of both the *Vox Clamantis* and the *Mirour de l'Omme* is the sinfulness of men, delineated by their social status and occupation, including tactics for the wholesale reform of male immorality. Women barely feature in Gower's discussion of the estates of society in either work, although he does include three chapters on nuns in the *Vox Clamantis*.[1] While Gower acknowledges that there are virtuous nuns who do correctly carry out their duties, in common with his assertions about men in religious orders (and, indeed, in society as a whole), the emphasis is on those who do not. With respect to nuns this entails a rehearsal of conventional antifeminist invective:

> ...a woman's foot cannot stand as steady as a man's can, nor can it make its steps firm. Neither learning nor understanding, neither constancy nor virtue such as men have flourishes in woman. But you often see women's morals change because of their frail nature, rather than by conscious choice (IV.13.557–62).[2]

Similarly, while Chapter 6 of Book V of the *Vox Clamantis* sets out to speak about the good woman, the majority of the chapter confirms Gower's contention that:

> All evils have usually proceeded from an evil woman; indeed, she is a second plague to men. With her blandishments, a cunning woman

---

I am very grateful to Steve Rigby for his very helpful comments on draft versions of this essay. I would also like to thank Sarah Wilma Watson for providing me with a copy of her unpublished paper on Jacquetta of Luxembourg.

[1] Nuns are not included in Gower's diatribe on the religious orders in the *Mirour de l'Omme* (20833–21780).

[2] For the wider traditions of antifeminism upon which this passage rests, see *Woman Defamed and Woman Defended*, ed. Alcuin Blamires (Oxford: Clarendon Press, 1992).

gently touches upon a man's evil inclination and breaks down his manly honour. Through her various wiles she destroys his feelings, his riches, his virtues, his strength, his reputation, and his peace (Book V. 6.333–7).

Most of the chapter describes women in conventionally misogynistic terms as deceitful, conniving, shameless and fundamentally deleterious to men: 'Neither the strength of Samson nor the sword of David nor the wisdom of Solomon is of any worth against her' (V.6.459–60). Gower's discussion of marriage in the *Mirour de l'Omme* is more even-handed in its recognition of the benefits which a good woman can offer her husband, alongside the harm which an evil wife can do. But, in keeping with the contemporary assumption that men were inherently superior to women, the good wife is characterised as being entirely subservient: 'modest and gracious, in deed, word, and countenance, without doing anything displeasing to her husband' (17689–17700). Thus, when women do appear in either of Gower's first two major works, they are essentially one-dimensional illustrations of various aspects of patriarchal or misogynistic discourse. By contrast, depictions of women in the *Confessio Amantis* are far more complex and rounded. They are characters with an interior life, whose thought processes and emotions are described in some detail, and for whom Genius displays sympathy, compassion and admiration in response to their individual circumstances. As we shall see, many of them are also women who display initiative and autonomy.

This shift in Gower's portrayal of women has often been noted, but there has been relatively little comparative discussion of the implications of the favourable attitude to women displayed in the *Confessio Amantis* as opposed to the more misogynistic sentiments expressed in the *Vox Clamantis* and the *Mirour de l'Omme*.[3] One possibility is that in the *Confessio Amantis* Gower sought, in part, to appeal to a female readership by adopting a more nuanced assessment of women's moral conduct. Christopher Fletcher highlights the masculine perspective of the *Confessio Amantis*, pointing out that its female characters have often been interpreted in relation to the interests and experiences of male readers (below, pp. 351–2). Nevertheless, a number of women did own copies of the poem, so here we focus, instead, on the issue of how the *Confessio Amantis* spoke to female readers, not only in terms of its depiction of women but also in relation to the active role that such women could play in contemporary politics. The connections of a number of royal and noble women with some of the surviving copies of the *Confessio Amantis* have been well-established. Although much scholarship on medieval women's book ownership, and on their status as patrons and/ or dedicatees of literature, has focused on religious and devotional texts,

---

[3] For further discussion see María Bullón-Fernandez, 'Gower and Gender', in *RRC*, pp. 21–36, at 30–3. She notes that the lack of gendered scholarship on Gower's works other than the *Confessio Amantis* is gradually being redressed.

women, especially of royal or noble status, also owned a wide range of other forms of literature. These included mirrors for princes and other didactic works, often including historical narratives, and the *Confessio Amantis* itself belongs in this category. Given this context, we will consider what royal and noble female readers might have made of its female characters as women.[4] How might the wider literary interests and political roles of such women have affected their reception of Gower's text and, in turn, what light does Gower's text throw on women as readers and as political actors? This essay thus responds to Theresa Earenfight's call for more research 'on how queenship and a queen's role in society were expressed by male authors; for example, John Gower's *Confessio Amantis*'.[5]

Recent feminist scholarship on medieval women and power provides a rich conceptual and evidential ground against which to assess Gower's dramatisation of women's exercise of influence and agency in the *Confessio Amantis*. When considering these issues in relation to fifteenth-century England, it is vital to note that there has been an influential scholarly tradition which either plays down or criticises the roles played by women in English medieval politics. This is part of a wider historiographical perspective which holds that, by the later Middle Ages, women were positioned outside of formal political structures, and which tends to devalue women's political activities, seeing them as extraneous, if not detrimental to 'real' politics.[6] For instance, some scholarly treatments of Margaret of Anjou, the wife of Henry VI, exemplify the influence of misogynistic stereotype when they claim that politically-active medieval women such as Margaret were viewed by their contemporaries as abnormal and reprehensible and contrasts them with those such as Cecily Neville, wife of Richard, duke of York, and mother of Edward IV and Richard III, who is seen as a 'good' woman for having confined her interests and actions to devotional and domestic concerns.[7] However, this binary opposition

---

[4] My approach here has been influenced by Diane Watt, 'Gender and Sexuality in *Confessio Amantis*', in Siân Echard, ed., *A Companion to Gower* (Cambridge: D. S. Brewer, 2004), pp. 197–213, at 211. The Findern Manuscript, which includes excerpts from the *Confessio Amantis* and was annotated by five women of gentry or mercantile status has often been discussed as a compilation reflecting the interests of a female audience of middling social status, e.g. Ashby Kinch, '"To Thenke what was in his wille": A Female Reading Context for the Findern Anthology', *Neophilologus*, 91 (2007), pp. 729–44.

[5] Theresa Earenfight, *Queenship in Medieval Europe* (Basingstoke: Palgrave Macmillan, 2013), p. 245.

[6] 'Beyond Women and Power: Looking Backward and Moving Forward', *Medieval Feminist Forum*, 51/2 (2015), explores these issues in relation to a variety of geographical and chronological settings; see also Theresa Earenfight, 'Medieval Queenship', *History Compass*, 15 (2017), pp. 1–9.

[7] For discussion and rebuttal of the historiography surrounding Margaret of Anjou see Patricia Ann Lee, 'Reflections of Power: Margaret of Anjou and the Dark Side of Queenship', *Renaissance Quarterly*, 39 (1986), pp. 183–217; Helen E. Maurer, *Margaret*

between the 'unnatural' grasping Margaret and the 'normal' self-effacing Cecily misrepresents the actualities of their roles and how these were understood at the time.[8] Assertions of Margaret's ambitious and rapacious character derive much of their substance from hostile Yorkist sources which cannot be taken at face value as evidence for what she was 'really' like or to support the claim that the notion of a queen taking an active part in government could not be countenanced by contemporaries.[9] Firstly, rather than being a sign of her ambition, Margaret's attempt to be appointed as regent following Henry VI's breakdown in 1453 and her subsequent actions in rallying support to defend her husband and son's position were actually a response to events. Secondly, Margaret enjoyed substantial levels of support in these endeavours. Conversely, Joanna Laynesmith's important recent study has shown how Cecily Neville was the owner and manager of vast estates and the head of a powerful household and was also active in political affairs in support of her sons.[10] Moreover, in their exercise of various aspects of lordship, these women were by no means exceptions to the rule, or stepping outside their 'normal' (i.e. domestic) sphere. The varied ways in which they and other women managed to wield authority even within established patriarchal structures is an essential context for understanding the appeal and function of the *Confessio Amantis* for high status women in later medieval England. Yet these recent developments in the analysis and appreciation of women's engagement in politics and exercise of authority have not, to date, been brought to bear on the text. Reading the *Confessio Amantis* against this backdrop challenges characterisations of its depiction of women's experience of power as a compelling and constraining force, which has been the predominant emphasis in previous studies of women in the text.[11]

---

of Anjou: Queenship and Power in Late Medieval England* (Woodbridge: Boydell Press, 2003), pp. 1–4; for Cecily Neville see Joanna L. Laynesmith, *Cecily, Duchess of York* (London & New York: Bloomsbury, 2017).

[8] Discussions of later medieval English queenship have often focused on intercession as the primary means by which queens could engage in politics, but their political roles were rather more wide-ranging than this emphasis implies, and intercession seems not to have been such a conspicuous part of English queenship in the fifteenth century; see Joanna L. Laynesmith, *The Last Medieval Queens: English Queenship 1445–1503* (Oxford: Oxford University Press, 2004), for a detailed analysis of queens' responsibilities and activities, and pp. 95, 139 for the point about intercession.

[9] Katherine J. Lewis, *Kingship and Masculinity in Late Medieval England* (London: Routledge, 2013), pp. 229–46 for examples and further discussion of the gendered significance of Yorkist propaganda against Margaret.

[10] Laynesmith, *Cecily, Duchess of York*, pp. 89–114.

[11] E.g. Elliot Kendall construes both women in Gower and contemporary women as essentially conduits of power between men and argues that real women were able to exercise agency only as widows (*Lordship and Literature: John Gower and the Politics of the Great Household* (Clarendon Press: Oxford, 2008), pp. 132–49).

Approaches to Women in the *Confessio Amantis*

A. S. G. Edwards has argued that, in comparison to Chaucer, Gower had a fairly negligible interest in women as protagonists. According to Edwards, Gower marginalised women, saying very little about their desires or their suffering or, alternatively, presenting their suffering as the result of what they had done to men.[12] Certainly the *Confessio Amantis* has no characters comparable to Chaucer's Wife of Bath, either in terms of her personality or of her explicit discussion of antifeminist discourse and its implications for women's status and experiences. Nevertheless, Gower's depiction of women's use of writing to challenge men who have wronged them can be read against contemporary patterns of women's literacy and book ownership, and the concerns which this raised in some quarters, and allows us to explore the issues about women's virtue famously raised by the 'Wife of Bath's Prologue'.[13] Thus, if the *Confessio Amantis* provides a guide to contemporary ideals about, and prejudices against, women, it can also be read, in places, as an unveiling of these same ideals and prejudices.[14] Indeed, there is a growing scholarship interrogating Gower's engagement with medieval ideologies of gender and sexuality as they applied both to women and men.[15] Certainly, despite Gower's reputation as an upholder of the social status quo, his text should not be read as unequivocally antifeminist.[16] Thus, the *Confessio Amantis* does not simply assume that the good woman is silent and passive, as Gower's *Mirour* suggested, but rather, as we shall see, offers female characters who are intelligent, astute and active in their own and others' interests. Some have argued that the *Confessio* can therefore be read as evidence of Gower's own sympathetic attitude to women.[17] However, in what follows we are concerned instead with how these depictions of women may have been received by contemporary women themselves.

---

[12] Anthony S. G. Edwards, 'Gower's Women in the *Confessio*', *Mediaevalia*, 16 (1993, for 1990), pp. 223–37. This is part of a wider tendency to measure Gower against Chaucer and find him wanting. See Siân Echard, 'Gower's Reputation', in Echard, *Companion to Gower*, pp. 1–22, at 17–21.

[13] Amanda Leff, 'Writing, Gender, and Power in Gower's *Confessio Amantis*', *Exemplaria*, 20 (2008), pp. 28–47.

[14] This approach is fundamental to Isabelle Mast, 'The Representation of Women in John Gower's *Confessio Amantis* (Unpublished University of Oxford Ph.D. thesis, 1997); see pp. 9–10 for her critique of Edwards.

[15] Bullón-Fernandez, 'Gower and Gender' is an excellent guide to recent developments in scholarship in these areas.

[16] Watt, 'Gender and Sexuality', esp. p. 198; Blamires, *Woman Defamed, Woman Defended*, pp. 248–9.

[17] E.g. Isabelle Mast, 'Rape in John Gower's *Confessio Amantis* and Other Related Works', in Katherine J. Lewis, Noël James Menuge and Kim M. Phillips, eds, *Young Medieval Women* (Stroud: Sutton Publishing, 1999), pp. 103–32; Eve Salisbury, 'Promiscuous Context: Gower's Wife, Prostitution, and the *Confessio Amantis*', in Malte Urban, ed., *John Gower: Manuscripts, Readers, Contexts* (Turnhout: Brepols, 2009), pp. 219–40.

It has often been noted that female saints' lives are conspicuous among the few Middle English texts which are known to have been dedicated or commissioned by lay women.[18] As a result these lives have often been interpreted not only in relation to other evidence for women's devotional interests, but also to how they related to women's experiences at different life-cycle stages.[19] It is therefore revealing that Gower's portrayals of some of his female characters have strong resonances with aspects of the narrative persona of St Katherine of Alexandria, whose cult was extremely popular in late medieval England, with devotees drawn from across the social spectrum.[20] There are more surviving Middle English versions of her life than of any other saint.[21] Distinctive to St Katherine's life from its earliest iterations is an emphasis on her erudition, gained from a scholarly education.[22] The narrative describes St Katherine employing her learning and eloquence in public to defend the truth of Christianity in exchanges with male pagans who are unable to match her rhetorical brilliance. A crucial aspect of the life of St Katherine is her ability to confound the gendered preconceptions of the men of her day about her inherent female inferiority, and their own inevitable superiority. Thus, when Katherine first confronts the evil pagan Emperor Maxentius and encourages him to recognise the truth of Christianity, he denies the veracity of her words because '[T]hou arte but one frayle woman', thus ascribing to her the physical and moral weakness commonly attributed to women in medieval antifeminist thought, even though he is attracted by her beauty.[23] Similarly the fifty philosophers whom Maxentius subsequently summons to defeat Katherine in a public debate are disdainful of the idea that any one of them

---

[18] For examples see Anthony S. G. Edwards, 'Fifteenth-Century English Collections of Female Saints' Lives', *The Yearbook of English Studies*, 33 (2003), pp. 131–41.

[19] E.g. Jacqueline Jenkins, 'St Katherine and Laywomen's Piety: The Middle English Prose Life in London, British Library, Harley MS 4012', in Jacqueline Jenkins and Katherine J. Lewis, eds, *St Katherine of Alexandria: Texts and Context in Western Medieval Europe* (Turnhout: Brepols, 2003), pp. 153–70; Kim M. Phillips, *Medieval Maidens: Young Women and Gender in England, 1270–1540* (Manchester: Manchester University Press, 2003), pp. 46–51, 80–1.

[20] Katherine J. Lewis, *The Cult of St Katherine of Alexandria in Late Medieval England* (Woodbridge: Boydell Press, 2000).

[21] Jennifer Revyn Bray, 'The Legend of St Katherine in Later Middle English Literature' (Unpublished University of London Ph.D. thesis, (1984)). Bray's excellent survey also includes Latin and Anglo-Norman versions composed in medieval England.

[22] Christine Walsh, *The Cult of St Katherine of Alexandria in Early Medieval Europe*, (Aldershot: Ashgate, 2007), pp. 8–20. For a translation of the influential late thirteenth- century version of her life contained in the *Legenda Aurea*, see Jacobus de Voragine, *The Golden Legend: Readings on the Saints*, volume 2, trans. William Granger Ryan (Princeton: Princeton University Press, 1993), pp. 334–41.

[23] This quotation is from William Caxton's translation of the *Legenda Aurea*, the *Golden Legend*, originally published in 1483, accessed via http://historicaltexts.jisc.ac.uk/; This quotation is on fol. 387v which has not been properly scanned from the 1483 edition and so is quoted from the 1487 edition (Westminster), Short Title Catalogue 24874, accessed via Jisc Historical Texts, 22 February 2018.

would be incapable of out-arguing 'one mayde yonge and fraylle', let alone all fifty.[24] Yet, much to their shock, none of them are able to gainsay Katherine's defence of Christianity. The narrative makes it clear that she defeats them not solely through divine grace, but also because she is extremely clever and has studied hard so as to acquire knowledge. Many scholars have argued that this aspect of the life of St Katherine rendered it very attractive to female readers and that the saint provided validation for their own status as readers and household educators.[25]

Gower's 'Tale of the Three Questions' in Book I of the *Confessio Amantis* provides a similarly admirable example of a woman who publicly uses her eloquence to defeat an intellectual challenge set by a man who has power of life and death over her. Peronelle is described thus:

> ...of visage
> Sche was riht fair, and of stature
> Lich to an hevenely figure,
> And of manere and goodli spece,
> Thogh men wolde alle Londes seche,
> Thei scholden noght have founde hir like (I.3134–39).

Whilst Peronelle is not explicitly said to be educated, her learning is implicit in her response to the three questions which the king has set her father. In an echo of the rhetoric underpinning St Katherine's unexpected ability to defeat the philosophers (unexpected to them at any rate), Peronelle reassures her father '...ofte schal a woman have/ Thing which a man mai noght areche'. (I.3207–8). She intellectually trounces the king, who responds by saying that he would like to marry her, if only she were a peer's daughter. Instead he offers to grant her anything she requests, so she promptly asks for her father to be given an earldom. Once the king has made this grant, Peronelle points out that since she is now 'An Erles dowhter' (I.3374) the king can marry her,

---

[24] William Caxton, *Golden Legend* 1483 edition (Westminster), Short Title Catalogue 24873, fol. 388r.

[25] E.g. Lewis, *St Katherine of Alexandria*, pp. 175–226; Emily C. Francomano, '"Lady, You Are Quite a Chatterbox": The Legend of St Katherine of Alexandria, Wives' Words, and Woman's Wisdom in MS Escorial h-I-13', in Jenkins and Lewis, *St Katherine of Alexandria*, pp. 153–70; Christine Walsh points out that some authors were evidently uncomfortable with St Katherine's educated eloquence and thus emphasised its status as a gift from God ('"Erat Abigail Mulier Prudentissima": Gilbert of Tournai and Attitudes to Female Sanctity in the Thirteenth Century', *Studies in Church History*, 47 (2011), pp. 171–80). Similarly, Karen A. Winstead argues that the subversive potential of St Katherine and other virgin martyrs was downplayed in some fifteenth-century Middle English versions of their lives (*Virgin Martyrs: Legends of Sainthood in Late Medieval England* (Ithaca, New York & London: Cornell University Press, 1997), pp. 112–146).

which he does. The text makes it clear that the king loves Peronelle not only for 'Hire beaute' but also for 'hir wit' (I.3378).[26]

Another counterpart to St Katherine is found in Gower's depiction in Book VIII of the *Confessio Amantis* of Thais, the daughter of Apollonius of Tyre. When Apollonius leaves Thais with Strangulio and Dionise, he instructs that '...whan sche hath of age more,/ That sche be set to bokes lore'. (VIII.1299–1300). This is accomplished and when Thais is older:

> Sche was wel tawht, sche was wel boked,
> So wel sche spedde his in hire youthe
> That sche of every wisdom couthe,
> That forto seche in every lond
> So wys an other noman fond,
> Ne so wel tawht at mannes yhe (VIII. 13228–33).

However, Dionise becomes jealous of the fame which Thais wins by her intellectual accomplishments while her own daughter remains unknown. She thus arranges to have Thais abducted and murdered, but instead Thais is taken by pirates and sold to a brothel where the young men who come to her are moved by her sorrow and so do not rape her.[27] She manages to persuade Leonin, the brothel owner, that she can earn money more effectively for him by using her education and proposes to set up a school for the daughters of lords in which 'I schal hire teche of things newe,/ Which as non other woman can/ In al this lond'. (VIII.1463–6). The school is a great success:

> Sche can the wisdom of a clerk,
> Sche can of every lusti werk
> Which to a gentil woman longeth,
> And some of hem sche underfongeth
> To the Citole and to the Harpe,
> And whom it liketh forto carpe
> Proverbes and demandes slyhe,
> An other such their nevere syhe,
> Which that science so wel tawhte:
> Whereof sche grete yiftes cawhte,
> That sche to Leonin hath wonne;
> And thus hire name is so begonne
> Of sondri things that she techeth,

---

[26] For more on Peronelle and her qualification for queenship, see below.
[27] This is similar to an episode in the life of the virgin martyr St Agnes in which the saint is sent to a brothel for her refusal to recant Christianity, but the young men sent to rape her are terrified by a miraculous light shining around her and flee. For the full life of St Agnes, see Jacobus de Voragine, *The Golden Legend: Readings on the Saints*, volume 1, trans. William Granger Ryan (Princeton: Princeton University Press, 1993), pp. 101–4.

> That al the long unto hir secheth
> Of yonge women forto liere (VIII.14883–97).

Here Gower presents us with a woman who, like St Katherine, is highly educated but who also passes her education on to other young women. Given the widespread dissemination of lives of St Katherine and their popularity with female readers it seems reasonable to suggest that they would have spotted the similarities between her virtues and intelligence and those of women such as Peronelle and Thais.[28] The issue of women's intellect and education was certainly current in the later fourteenth century. Denouncements of women's intellectual abilities and objections to any suggestion that they should be educated formed part of attacks on Lollardy, in response to the active participation of lay women in the dissemination of Lollard texts and theology.[29] The question of whether women could learn and teach therefore formed part of the heresy trial of Walter Brut in 1391, at which it was stated, in defence of orthodoxy, that '...women in general have weak and unstable natures and thus they are incomplete in wisdom; therefore they are not allowed to teach in public'.[30] The depiction both of St Katherine and of educated women in the *Confessio Amantis* presents a challenge to such antifeminist pronouncements about women's lack of a capacity for learning and reason.[31]

Royal Women within and without the *Confessio Amantis*

It is also important to note that the lives of St Katherine depicted her as a sovereign queen. She is the only child of King Costus, and thus his heir, and her life describes her as an exemplary ruler.[32] As Christine de Pizan said of Katherine in *The Book of the City of Ladies*: 'Though this worthy maiden was only eighteen years old when she inherited her father's lands, she conducted

---

[28] Much scholarship on the Middle English lives of St Katherine has focused on female readers, but her life was also read by men. For further discussion, see Katherine J. Lewis, 'A King, Not a Servant: The Prose Life of St Katherine of Alexandria and Ideologies of Masculinity in Late Medieval England', in Samantha Kahn Herrick, ed., *Hagiography and the History of Latin Christendom, 500–1500* (Leiden: Brill, forthcoming 2019).

[29] Rita Copeland, 'Why Women Can't Read: Medieval Hermeneutics, Statutory Law, and the Lollard Heresy Trials', in Susan Sage Heinzelman and Zipporah Batshaw Wiseman, eds, *Representing Women: Law, Literature, and Feminism* (Durham, N.C.: Duke University Press, 1994), pp. 253–86.

[30] Quoted in Blamires, *Woman Defamed, Woman Defended*, p. 253.

[31] The number of women in the *Confessio Amantis* who can both read and write is also significant in this respect. See Leff, 'Writing, Gender and Power'.

[32] Early lives do not specify where Costus rules, but by the fifteenth century he was identified as the king of Cyprus. Lewis, 'A King, Not a Servant', further discusses St Katherine's depiction as an ideal ruler.

both her private life and her public affairs with great discernment.'[33] This partly explains the levels of devotion to St Katherine displayed by royal women.[34] The vast majority of the female characters in the *Confessio Amantis* share St Katherine's royal status. Thus, the old woman (actually an enchanted princess) in the 'Tale of Florent' is the daughter of a king, as are Canace, Procne, Philomena and Thais' mother. In addition, Thais' mother, Constance, the Sultan's daughter in the 'Tale of the False Bachelor', Iphis and Rosiphelee are all, like St Katherine, their royal father's heir, while Dido, Thameris, Phyllis and Penthesilea are sovereign queens.[35]

The prominence of queens and princesses within the *Confessio Amantis* is significant given that a number of royal and noble women owned copies of or are associated with the *Confessio Amantis*.[36] For instance, the Portuguese translation of the *Confessio Amantis* was very likely created at the behest of Philippa, daughter of John of Gaunt, and subsequently queen of Portugal.[37] Furthermore she may also have been behind the Castilian translation of the *Confessio*, based on the Portuguese version, which she perhaps had made for her half-sister, Catherine, queen of Castile.[38] The extant copy of this Castilian version may later have been in the hands of Isabel I of Castile.[39] Joan Beaufort, who was Philippa and Catherine's half-sister and

---

[33] Christine de Pizan, *The Book of the City of Ladies*, trans. Rosalind Brown-Grant (London: Penguin, 1999), p. 203.

[34] E.g. Lewis, *St Katherine*, pp. 63–79; Tracey R. Sands, *The Company She Keeps: The Medieval Swedish Cult of Saint Katherine of Alexandria and its Transformations* (Tempe: Arizona Center for Medieval and Renaissance Studies, in collaboration with Brepols, 2010), pp. 69–105. This is not to suggest that St Katherine's cult exclusively appealed to royal women, or to those of high status; but her own royal status does seem to have played a part in elite devotion to her.

[35] Araxarathen, in the 'Tale of Iphis and Araxarathen' in Book IV, is of low social status, but she is the exception to this rule (IV.3515–3684).

[36] In part this is a dimension of wider Lancastrian interest in the text (Kate Harris, 'Ownership and Readership: Studies in the Provenance of the Manuscripts of Gower's *Confessio Amantis*' (Unpublished University of York D.Phil. thesis (1993)), pp. 122–56.

[37] Robert F. Yeager, 'Gower's Lancastrian Affinity: The Iberian Connection', *Viator*, 35 (2004), pp. 483–515; Joyce Coleman, 'Philippa of Lancaster, Queen of Portugal – and Patron of the Gower Translations?', in María Bullón-Fernández, ed., *England and Iberia in the Middle Ages, 12th – 15th Century: Cultural, Literary, and Political Changes* (New York: Palgrave Macmillan, 2007), pp. 135–65. For Philippa's life see Anthony Goodman, 'Philippa [Philippa of Lancaster] (1360–1415), queen of Portugal, consort of João I', Oxford Dictionary of National Biography. Accessed 22 February 2018, from http://www.oxforddnb.com/view/10.1093/ref:odnb/9780198614128.001.0001/odnb-9780198614128-e-22111.

[38] This is posited by the works cited in the previous note. For Catherine's life, see Anthony Goodman, 'Katherine [Catalina, Katherine of Lancaster] (1372–1418), queen of Castile, consort of Enrique III', Oxford Dictionary of National Biography. Retrieved 22 February 2018, from http://www.oxforddnb.com/view/10.1093/ref:odnb/9780198614128.001.0001/odnb-9780198614128-e-48316.

[39] Harris, 'Ownership and Readership', p. 156.

the mother of Cecily Neville, also owned a copy of the *Confessio Amantis* in its original Middle English.[40] Focusing on the version of the 'Tale of Tereus' as it is recounted in the Iberian versions, María Bullón-Fernandez makes a persuasive case that both translations reflect the issues and potential concerns occasioned by royal and noble daughters marrying abroad.[41] Philippa married João I in 1387 and the couple were the patrons of a number of literary works all concerned with issues of education and morality appropriate for high status readers.[42] Similarly Pierpont Morgan MS M. 126, a lavishly illustrated copy of the *Confessio Amantis*, was probably made for Edward IV and Elizabeth Woodville.[43] Elizabeth's own knowledge of the *Confessio Amantis* may have come originally from her mother, Jacquetta of Luxembourg, who owned and annotated the copy contained in Cambridge, Pembroke College 307. Given the close relationship between the two women, Sarah Wilma Watson suggests that Jacquetta's copy may have been copied to produce Elizabeth and Edward's version, or at least provided the inspiration for its creation.[44] Another woman who played a decisive role in later medieval

---

[40] Joanna L. Laynesmith, '"To please... Dame Cecely that in latyn hath lityll intellect": Books and the Duchess of York', in Linda Clark, ed., *The Fifteenth Century XV: Writing, Records and Rhetoric* (Woodbridge: Boydell Press, 2017), pp. 37–57, at 38; in 1431 Sir John Morton of York left Joan 'unum librum de Anglico vocatum Gower' in his will which Laynesmith and others argue was most likely the *Confessio Amantis*. For Joan's life see Anthony Tuck, 'Beaufort [married names Ferrers, Neville], Joan, countess of Westmorland (1379?–1440), magnate', Oxford Dictionary of National Biography. Retrieved 22 February 2018, from http://www.oxforddnb.com/view/10.1093/ref:odnb/9780198614128.001.0001/odnb-9780198614128-e-53026.

[41] María Bullón-Fernandez, 'Translating Women, Translating Texts: Gower's "Tale of Tereus" and the Castilian and Portuguese Translations of the *Confessio Amantis*', in Urban, *John Gower*, pp. 109–32, at 127–8.

[42] Clara Pascual-Argente, 'Iberian Gower', in *RRC*, pp. 210–22, at 215.

[43] Sonja Drimmer, 'The Visual Language of Vernacular Manuscript Illumination: John Gower's *Confessio Amantis* (Pierpont Morgan MS M. 126)' (Unpublished Columbia University Ph.D. dissertation (2011), pp. 169–83. I agree with Drimmer's reading of joint patronage rather than with Martha W. Driver's exclusive focus on Elizabeth Woodville ('Women Readers and the Pierpont Morgan MS M. 126', in Urban, *John Gower*, pp. 71–109). The manuscript is available online, http://www.themorgan.org/manuscript/77039, accessed 22 February 2018. It may have been bequeathed by Elizabeth Woodville to Grace, an illegitimate daughter of Edward IV and one of the few people to attend Elizabeth's funeral. (Drimmer, 'Visual Language', p. 169, n. 16). Drimmer does not explicitly state this, but the evidence she presents tends towards this supposition, which further supports the sense of this as a work deemed of interest to women.

[44] Sarah Wilma Watson, 'Women Readers of John Gower's *Confessio Amantis* – Jacquetta of Luxembourg and Pembroke College MS 307', a paper delivered at the IVth International Congress of the John Gower Society, held at the University of Durham in July 2017; women readers of the *Confessio Amantis* and other works will be discussed further in her forthcoming Ph.D. thesis. For Jacquetta's life, see Lucia Diaz Pascual, 'Luxembourg, Jaquetta de, duchess of Bedford and Countess Rivers (c. 1416–1472), noblewoman', Oxford Dictionary of National Biography. Retrieved 22 February 2018,

English politics and who also probably owned a copy of the *Confessio Amantis* was Margaret Beaufort, mother of Henry VII who, in her will, left 'a book of velomm of Gowere in Englishe' to her great-niece Alice Parker, which was very probably the *Confessio Amantis*.[45]

Bullón-Fernandez argues that a crucial part of the appeal of the *Confessio Amantis* to such women was its inclusion of several strong, authoritative and intelligent high status female characters, who are, as noted above, themselves royal.[46] Similarly, speaking of the Pierpont manuscript Martha Driver observes that 'In such a book, a queen might see her own reflection'.[47] The influence of women within the political arena was often depicted as inevitably harmful. The chronicler Thomas Walsingham recounted that in 1376 Edward's knights in parliament became very concerned about the levels of power which the elderly king had allowed his mistress Alice Perrers to attain, and about the ramifications for the king and the realm. They attacked her in these terms:

> ...she had gone far beyond the limits set for women, and forgetting her femininity and her frailty, she had on some occasions sat besides the king's justices and on others placed herself next to the doctors in the ecclesiastical court, and had not been in the least afraid of urging her point of view in defence of the accused or even of making demands which were contrary to the laws. The result of these scandals was that the king was getting a very bad name not only in his own land but also abroad, and the knights demanded that she be sent right away from him.[48]

Gower's retelling of the 'Tale of Wine, Women and Truth' in the *Mirour de l'Omme* evinces the same attitude, stating that '...women are stronger than the king because women can tame the king; we see an example of this every day. Many a king has been brought to ruin by them, for hardly anyone knows how to protect himself' (22777–82). His remarks have been interpreted as an attack on Edward III's relationship with Alice Perrers, which was an issue at the time that Gower was writing this work.[49] The emphasis within this

---

from http://www.oxforddnb.com/view/10.1093/ref:odnb/9780198614128.001.0001/odnb-9780198614128-e-101258.

[45] Susan Powell, 'Lady Margaret Beaufort and Her Books', *The Library*, sixth series, 20/3 (1998), pp. 197–240, at 202.

[46] Bullón-Fernandez, 'Translating Women', pp. 130–1; see also Driver, 'Women Readers', pp. 71–2.

[47] Driver, 'Women Readers', p. 107.

[48] *The Chronica Maiora of Thomas Walsingham (1376–1422)*, trans. David Preest with introduction and notes by James G. Clark (Woodbridge: Boydell Press, 2005), p. 26. For Alice Perrers' career and significance, see W. Mark Ormrod, 'The Trials of Alice Perrers', *Speculum*, 83 (2008), pp. 366–96.

[49] Cathy Hume, 'Why did Gower Write the Traitié?', in Elisabeth Dutton, with John Hines and Robert F. Yeager, eds, *John Gower, Trilingual Poet: Language, Translation*

discourse on the dangers of involving women in politics was very often on the inimical effects of love on men; as Gower puts it in the Prologue to the *Confessio Amantis*, love 'doth many a wonder/ And many a wys man hath put under' (Pro.75–6). Men lose their reason to love, and thus their position and authority. Latin verses near the start of Book I cite the classic examples of Samson and Hercules who were conquered by love (Book I, Latin verse ii); as we saw above Samson was also mentioned in this capacity in the *Mirour de l'Omme*.

Yet, despite these critical remarks, there is a shift in tone between the *Mirour de l'Omme* and the *Confessio Amantis* with respect to the nature and implications of women's effect on the men (especially male rulers) who love them.[50] Book VII's discussion of chastity as an inherent aspect of statecraft specifies that should a king indulge himself sexually, his masculinity, and thus his very authority, would be compromised, as he would 'change for the wommanhede/ The worthinesse of his manhede' (VII.4255–6).[51] Medieval commentators often depicted men's sexual immorality and consequent damnation as the fault of women who had ensnared them. This point is developed at length in a number of surviving later medieval sermons which criticise women for lavish and immodest clothing: 'suche women that so attyreth hem... may be cleped the develis grenes or snares. Ffor many a man by such grennes beth take and broght to the develis hond.'[52] However, Gower takes a different tack, emphasising the responsibility of men to exercise self-mastery and surmount the temptation offered. When describing Alexander's exemplary conduct in this regard Gower judges that 'For in the woman is no guile/ Of that a man himself bewhapeth,/ When he his oghne wit bejapeth,/ I can the women wel excuse' (VII.4266–9).[53] The contention that men should take responsibility for their own sexual misconduct, rather than claiming that they had been deceived by women, was an established approach in texts which questioned some aspects of antifeminist invective. For example, there is substantial discussion of this issue in the early fifteenth-century pastoral treatise *Dives and Pauper*: 'Men lechourys gon & rydeyn fro town to town to getyn women at her lust... þei castyn many wylys to getyn womanys assent

---

    and Tradition (Cambridge: D. S. Brewer, 2010), pp. 263–75, at 272–3. As discussed below, the version of this tale in the *Confessio Amantis* is more positive about women's influence on men.

[50] Linda Barney Burke, 'Women in John Gower's *Confessio Amantis*', *Medievalia*, 3 (1977), pp. 239–59. Gower was not alone in writing both negatively and positively about women, which complicates the question of whether or not such writings reflect an author's personal opinion rather than constituting a rhetorical exercise in argument and counterargument (Blamires, *Woman Defamed, Woman Defended*, p. 223).

[51] See Lewis, *Kingship and Masculinity*, pp. 24–8 for the interrelationship between chastity, kingship and masculinity.

[52] Quoted by Gerald R. Owst, *Preaching in Medieval England* (Cambridge: Cambridge University Press, 1926), p. 400; for other examples see pp. 396–404.

[53] The same point is reiterated a number of times between lines VII.4257–4312.

in synne. Men comounly ben warkeris & begynnerys of lecherie, and þan weþer þe woman assente or nout assente ȝit þe man is gylty.'⁵⁴ Here women are the ones being trapped by men who ought to have the moral strength to behave better.

Significantly, the version of the 'Tale of Wine, Women and Truth' which Gower offers in the *Confessio Amantis* is markedly less antifeminist than that in the *Mirour de l'Omme*. The *Confessio Amantis* version does not describe women's influence in terms of taming and ruining the king, but instead highlights its beneficial potential: 'Thurgh hem men finden out the weie/ To knithode and to worldes fame; / Thei make a man to dred schame,/ And honour forto be desired' (VII.1905–8). Love for a woman can inspire men to courageous endeavour and thus be the means for them to display masculine accomplishments and achieve renown. Indeed, Misty Schieberle highlights that while male advisors in the *Confessio Amantis* are both good and bad, female advisors, such as Peronelle and the old woman in the 'Tale of Florent', are uniformly presented as a positive influence on men.⁵⁵

The notion that women's influence and agency can be valuable for men and can advance their fortunes also helps to explain the sympathetic attitude displayed towards Medea in the *Confessio Amantis*. The text emphasises that Medea, inspired by her great love for Jason, enabled all his success and rewards: 'Ferst sche made him the flees to winne,/ And after that fro kiththe and kinne/ With gret tresor with him sche stal' (V.4179–1). She also used her magic to restore Jason's father's youth 'Which thing non other woman couthe'. However, the text continues: 'Bot hou it was to hire aquit,/ The remembrance dulleth yit' (V.4184–6). Despite everything which Medea does for Jason, including bearing him two sons, he betrays her by marrying another king's daughter, Creusa. Having murdered Creusa, Medea berates Jason as 'The moste untrewe creature' (V.4213) and wreaks terrible vengeance by killing their sons in front of him. But before Jason can kill Medea she is taken up to the Court of Pallas. That the text presents Medea in a sympathetic light is underlined by her reappearance in Book VIII among a group of women abandoned by the men they love, where she declaims 'Fy on alle untrewe!' (VIII.2566). Thus, while a key theme of the *Confessio Amantis* is the advantageous influence which women could have on men, the text makes it clear that men, like Jason, are not always deserving of the efforts of these women. The majority of women in the text are wives and Isabelle Mast argues that this emphasis on marital love is a tactic by which Gower

---

[54] *Dives and Pauper*, volume 1, part 2, ed. Priscilla Heath Barnum (EETS, o.s. 280 (1980)), p. 87. Blamires explains that this attitude had its origins in some patristic writings and was also expressed in other late medieval responses to antifeminism (Blamires, *Woman Defamed, Woman Defended*, p. 260).

[55] Misty Schieberle, '"Things Which A Man Mai Noght Areche": Women and Counsel in Gower's *Confessio Amantis*', *The Chaucer Review*, 42/1 (2007), pp. 91–109, at 92.

'rehabilitates women and shows them with all their good capacities'.[56] Thus, the women given pride of place at Venus' court towards the end of the work are identified as wives who demonstrated exemplary loyalty and devotion to their husbands: Penelope, Lucrece, Alceste and Alcione (VIII.2605–60).

Whether or not Gower was actually setting out to dispute antifeminist stereotypes, his portrayal of women in this text certainly offers material for debating their nature and their capabilities. Indeed, the fact that claims about women's essential inferiority and their need for male rule were so repeatedly reasserted within medieval culture actually suggests that this contention was not straightforwardly accepted by all.[57] For instance, Anthony, Earl Rivers, the brother of Elizabeth Woodville (who, as we saw above, probably owned a copy of the *Confessio Amantis*), translated *The Dicts and Sayings of the Philosophers* into English, an edition of which was published by Caxton in 1477. In the epilogue, Caxton states that Rivers had given him permission to amend the text as he saw fit and that when he compared Rivers' translation with the French source he discovered that 'my saide lord hath left out certain and dyverce conclusions towchyng women'.[58] These 'conclusions' were various antifeminist aphorisms about women, purportedly written by Socrates, which include the observation that the ignorance of a man can be gleaned from three things: 'whan he hath no thought to use reason, whan he cannot refrayne his covetises, and whan he is governed by the conceyll of women in that he knoweth that they knowe not.' Furthermore Socrates opines: 'be wel waar that ye obeye not to women.'[59] Rivers' original version is preserved in Lambeth Palace MS 265 and, as its illuminated frontispiece records, was presented by him to Edward IV, although it was presumably intended to be used by Prince Edward (the future Edward V), whose governor Woodville was and who is depicted alongside his mother, Elizabeth Woodville, and Edward IV.[60] In this version of the text Rivers states: 'And

---

[56] Mast, 'Representation of Women', pp. 101, 294. See also Sharon Farmer, 'Persuasive Voices: Clerical Images of Medieval Wives', *Speculum* 61 (1986), 517–43, for positive assessments of wives' influence more generally.

[57] As noted, for example, by Emily Francomano, *Three Spanish Querelle Texts* (Toronto: Center for Reformation and Renaissance Studies, 2013), p. 22.

[58] Norman F. Blake, *Caxton's Own Prose* (London: Andre Deutsch, 1973), pp. 73–4. Blake questions Caxton's contention that he knew Woodville personally (*William Caxton and English Literary Culture* (London & Rio Grande: The Hambledon Press, 1991), pp. 99–100). Susan Schibanoff also discusses Rivers' omission of these passages ('"Taking the Gold out of Egypt": The Art of Reading as a Woman', in Ruth Evans and Lesley Johnson, eds, *Feminist Readings in Middle English Literature: The Wife of Bath and All Her Sect* (London: Routledge, 1994), pp. 221–45, at 221–3.

[59] Blake, *Caxton's Own Prose*, p. 75.

[60] Nicholas Orme, 'The Education of Edward V', *Bulletin of the Institute of Historical Research*, 57 (1984), pp. 119–30. The illumination is reproduced in Michael Hicks, 'Woodville [Wydeville], Anthony, second Earl Rivers (c. 1440–1483), magnate', Oxford Dictionary of National Biography. Retrieved 22 February 2018, from

the said Socrates had many seyinges ayenst women which is not translated.'[61] In explaining this omission Caxton speculates that perhaps the wind blew these pages over and Rivers missed them out by accident.[62] As an alternative he suggests that 'som fayr lady hath desired hym to leve it out of his booke', or that Rivers acted out of love for 'somme noble lady'. Finally, he raises the possibility that Rivers removed the passages 'for the very affeccyon, love and good wylle that he hath unto ladyes and gentylwomen he thought that Socrates spared the soothe and wrote of women more than trouthe'. Caxton himself refuses to believe that Socrates could speak anything other than truth and restores the critical passages in the epilogue whilst hedging them around with various caveats: they may apply to Greek women in the past, but not to English women in the present, if the reader does not like them they can be scribbled over or torn out.[63]

Caxton purports to be puzzled by Rivers' excision of antifeminist material but, significantly, Rivers had read Christine de Pizan. His mother Jacquetta owned a compilation of Christine's works, including the *Epistle of Othea* and the *Book of the City of Ladies*, which was inscribed both by Jacquetta and by Rivers.[64] Rivers also translated Christine's *Moral Proverbs*, which were published by Caxton in 1478.[65] In this context, Rivers' attitude to the misogynistic passages in *The Dicts and Sayings* appears rather less surprising than it apparently was to Caxton. *The Book of the City of Ladies* presents a detailed and reasoned dismantling of antifeminist invective and Rivers had presumably read Christine de Pizan's account of how she felt 'sick at heart', crushed, demoralised and utterly miserable, after reading exactly the same sort of misogynist claims as those which are included in *The Dicts and Sayings*.[66] Rivers encountered many instances of intelligence and initiative among his female relatives and other women with whom he interacted at court and he had witnessed his mother's and sister's capable and decisive interventions in both family and national politics. He *knew* 'that Socrates spared the soothe and wrote of women more than trouthe', that women's 'concyll' could be wise and productive and well worth obeying and so he removed those passages

---

http://www.oxforddnb.com/view/10.1093/ref:odnb/9780198614128.001.0001/odnb-9780198614128-e-29937.

[61] *The Dicts and Sayings of the Philosophers*, ed. Curt F. Bühler (EETS, o.s. 211 (1941)), p. 345.
[62] Blake, *Caxton's Own Prose*, p. 74 for this and what follows.
[63] Blake, *Caxton's Own Prose*, p. 76.
[64] This is now British Library Harley 4431 and is available online, http://www.bl.uk/catalogues/illuminatedmanuscripts/record.asp?MSID=8361, accessed 22 February 2018. Christine de Pizan had this manuscript created for presentation to Isabeau of Bavaria, queen of Charles VI.
[65] *Morale Prouerbes, Composed in French by Christyne de Pisan, translated by the Earl Rivers, and reprinted from the Original Edition of William Caxton, A.D. 1478*, ed. William Blades (London: Blades, East & Blades, 1859).
[66] Christine de Pizan, *Book of the City of Ladies*, pp. 5–7, at 7.

which claimed the contrary. Rivers was surely familiar with the *Confessio Amantis* via his mother's copy. Thus, we should consider that its depictions of women as educated, perspicacious and resourceful were attractive to some male, as well as female, readers.

Royal Love and Marriage

In the case of two other readers of the *Confessio Amantis*, Rivers' sister Elizabeth and brother-in-law Edward IV, Gower's positive depictions of women would not only have been appealing but also politically useful as a means of justifying their extraordinary marriage. Royal marriages were almost always, in the first instance, a matter of politics and diplomacy. But, having been contracted, love, or at least some level of affection, was a vital dimension of successful royal partnerships.[67] However, the extremely anomalous marriage between Edward IV and Elizabeth Woodville was depicted as having been contracted entirely for love. The precise circumstances in which the marriage happened are a matter for debate.[68] But by the late 1460s it was described, by the author of *Gregory's Chronicle*, as an example of 'what love may doo, for love wylle not nor may not caste no faute nor perelle in noo thyng'.[69] The chronicle explains that Edward and Elizabeth were secretly married on 1 May 1464, which is, as Laynesmith points out, 'a suspiciously apt day for a young king to marry for love.'[70] But presenting the marriage as an act of love would have helped explain Edward's choice to marry a widowed commoner with two sons, rather than the conventional candidate: a foreign virgin princess. This approach may also have been designed to counter two other contemporary explanations for the marriage, one describing it as having originated in Edward's thwarted attempt to rape Elizabeth, who threatened suicide rather than suffer assault, the other claiming that Elizabeth and/or her mother had literally enchanted Edward to bring about the marriage.[71] Neither of these accounts cast Edward in a favourable light, which gives credence to the contention that a lovematch narrative was the official 'spin' on the marriage.[72]

---

[67] Laynesmith, *Last Medieval Queens*, pp. 62–70.
[68] Laynesmith, *Last Medieval Queens*, pp. 65–6.
[69] *Gregory's Chronicle The Historical Collections of a Citizen of London in the Fifteenth Century*, ed. James Gairdner (London: Camden Society, 1876) available online http://www.british-history.ac.uk/camden-record-soc/vol17/pp210-239 accessed 22 February 2018, entry for 1469.
[70] Laynesmith, *Last Medieval Queens*, p. 66.
[71] Laynesmith, *Last Medieval Queens*, pp. 68–9.
[72] Laynesmith, *Last Medieval Queens*, p. 62 argues that love was the most likely motive, especially as Elizabeth does seem to have been very beautiful. An alternative explanation, given later claims that Edward IV had contracted marriage to another woman before he married Elizabeth, is the possibility that Edward may have promised

Significantly, the *Confessio Amantis* provides plenty of validation for a marriage contracted for love rather than for other more material reasons. The ideal that marriage should primarily be made for love was often expressed by contemporary moralists, William Langland's *Piers Plowman* putting it thus:

> Forthi I counseille alle Cristene coveite noght be wedded
> For coveitise of catel ne of kynrede riche;
> Ac maidens and maydenes macche yow togideres;
> Wideweres and wodewes, wercheth the same;
> For no londes, but for love, loke ye be wedded,
> And thane gete ye the grace of God, and good ynough to live with.[73]

Similarly, in Book V of the *Confessio Amantis*, Genius states that covetousness is an immoral motive for marriage, criticising men who marry 'Noght for the beaute of hire face,/ Ne yit for vertu ne for grace,/ Which sche hath ells riht ynowh,/ Bot for the Park and for the plowh,/ And other thing which therto longeth' (V.2521–6).[74] Amans reassures him that he loves his lady for all the right reasons, because she is graceful and beautiful, but also because 'sche is wys/ And sobre and simple of contenance,/ And al that to good governance/ belongeth of a worthi with/ Sche hath pleinli' (V.2588–92). Amans does concede: 'I seie noght sche is haveles' (V.2616) but affirms that monetary considerations play no part in his affection for her. As noted above, of all medieval people, those of royal status were those whose marriages were most determined by the financial and strategic motives which Amans forswears.[75]

---

marriage to Elizabeth in order to get her into bed, and was subsequently unable to extricate himself from the arrangement. This is suggested by Michael Hicks, 'Elizabeth [née Elizabeth Woodville] (c. 1437–1492), queen of England, consort of Edward IV', Oxford Dictionary of National Biography. Retrieved 22 February 2018, from http://www.oxforddnb.com/view/10.1093/ref:odnb/9780198614128.001.0001/odnb-9780198614128-e-8634.

[73] William Langland, *The Vision of Piers Plowman: A Complete Edition of the B-Text*, ed. Aubrey V. C. Schmidt (London: Dent, 1987), IX.173–8. For examples of the same sentiments in sermons see Owst, *Preaching in Medieval England*, pp. 381–2.

[74] In the *Mirour de l'Omme* Gower also stated that a man should make marriage for 'good, loyal, pure love, without covetousness or evil intent, either for riches or intrigue', but continued that these days land and money are the main motive (17245–56).

[75] Edward the Black Prince (the eldest son of Edward III) and Joan of Kent provide the only other example of an English royal marriage at the highest level made for love. Joan was a granddaughter of Edward I, and had been brought up by Edward III's queen, Philippa of Hainault. But her betrothal to Prince Edward was undertaken privately, and at a time when Edward III was negotiating an international marriage for his heir. Besides which Joan, like Elizabeth Woodville, had been married before and already borne five children, so she was certainly not a conventional candidate, and love therefore does seem to have been the cause of the marriage. Prince Edward predeceased his father, so Joan never became queen. See Richard Barber, 'Joan, *suo jure* countess of Kent, and princess of Wales and of Aquitaine [called the Fair Maid of Kent] (c.

This is what made Edward's marriage to Elizabeth Woodville so unusual and, in the eyes of many, so foolish and even potentially dangerous. Edward had deposed Henry VI, but Henry was still at large in the north of England at this time, and Margaret of Anjou was working tirelessly to raise armed support for her husband and their son. Marriage to a royal woman from an established dynasty would have lent prestige and legitimacy to Edward's rule, as well as crucial financial and military support.[76] Elizabeth could offer none of these advantages. However, the premium which the *Confessio Amantis* places on the value of love, and the exempla adduced in Book V to illustrate this, would have supported the unusual rationale of a royal marriage made for love. The figure of Peronelle who 'mad hirself a qweene' (I.3400) is also relevant here. In common with Peronelle, Elizabeth was the daughter of a knight, yet she attracted and married a king, not solely with her beauty but by her intelligence.[77] Neither women were of royal status by birth, but both were presented as possessing attributes and accomplishments which proved that they were qualified for such an elevation.

Another woman within the *Confessio Amantis* who provides a counterpart to Elizabeth Woodville is Penelope, the wife of Ulysses, who is named first among the four wives given pride of place at the court of Venus in Book VIII. She also appears as an exemplar in Book IV and Book VI. During the readeption of Henry VI from 1470–71, Edward IV was in exile in Flanders, while Elizabeth lived in sanctuary at Westminster Abbey with her children. The figure of patient Penelope, virtuously waiting for her husband Ulysses to return from the Trojan War would have been extremely relevant to Elizabeth's situation.[78] In Book VI Penelope is described as superior even among admirable wives, a wife of whom her husband may justifiably boast:

> A betre wif ther may non be,
> And yit ther ben ynowhe of goode.
> Bot who hir goodschipe understode
> Fro ferst that sche wifhode tok,
> Hou many loves sche forsok
> And ho sche bar hire al aboute,
> Ther whiles that hire lord was oute,

1328–1385)', *Oxford Dictionary of National Biography*. Retrieved 23 February 2018, from http://www.oxforddnb.com/view/10.1093/ref:odnb/9780198614128.001.0001/odnb-9780198614128-e-14823.

[76] Jacquetta of Luxembourg was the daughter of Pierre, count of St Pol, but her second husband, Richard Woodville, was from a modest gentry family. Her unusual 'marriage down' meant that her own aristocratic status was not deemed to pass to her children, as witnesses the occasion in 1460 when the future Edward IV and Richard Neville, earl of Warwick, insulted her son Anthony Woodville to his face as a socially inferior upstart. See Michael Hicks, 'Woodville [Wydeville], Anthony, second Earl Rivers (c. 1440–1483)'.

[77] Laynesmith, *Last Medieval Queens*, p. 56 also notes the similarities between the two.

[78] CA: IV.147–2303. This parallel is also noted by Drimmer, 'Visual Language', p. 240.

> He mihte make a gret avant
> Amonges al the remenant
> That sche was on of al the beste (VI.1472–81).

Penelope's exemplary excellence is reiterated a few lines later: 'His wif was such as sche be scholde' (VI.1506). Following Edward's triumphant return to England in 1471 the righteousness of his cause and the inevitability of his victory were celebrated in the propagandist chronicle the *Historie of the Arrivall of Edward IV*. Here Elizabeth is described as having waited at Westminster for Edward's return 'in right great trowble, sorow, and hevines, which she sustained with all manner patience that belonged to any creature'.[79] This image renders Elizabeth as exemplary as Penelope in her patience and endurance.

Sonja Drimmer posits that the Pierpont Morgan manuscript of the *Confessio Amantis* was commissioned as part of a literary programme designed as a propagandist response to Edward's deposition and his resumption of the throne in 1471.[80] This programme included a range of historical and didactic works which collectively contributed towards a reassertion both of Edward's right and his fitness to rule.[81] The useful parallels which could be drawn between Elizabeth and a number of the admirable women depicted in the *Confessio Amantis* may therefore have played a key role in choosing it to form part of this programme. The *Confessio Amantis* helped support the contention that, regardless of the circumstances of the marriage, and despite Elizabeth Woodville's apparent unsuitability for the role, she was an excellent queen in many respects. Not only did she bear the king many children, she also supported him in other ways, for example through her administration of lands in East Anglia where she helped to create a substantial royal affinity in the mid-1470s.[82]

Women, the *Confessio Amantis* and Works of Political Instruction

The value of the *Confessio Amantis* to elite women such as Elizabeth Woodville lay not only in its depiction of women, but also in the wider lessons about rulership which it offered. The *Confessio Amantis* sets out a

---

[79] Paul Strohm, *Politique: Languages of Statecraft between Chaucer and Shakespeare* (Notre Dame: University of Notre Dame Press, 2005), pp. 51–86 for the full text, quotation at 65. For further discussion of Elizabeth's presentation post 1471, see Laynesmith, *Last Medieval Queens*, pp. 173–4.
[80] Drimmer, 'Visual Language', pp. 206–46.
[81] See below for other didactic works associated with Elizabeth.
[82] Laynesmith, *Last Medieval Queens*, p. 238. She contends that Elizabeth and other queens were actively involved in such administration.

blueprint of exemplary kingship, one framed by ideals of masculinity.[83] In particular, Book VII expatiates on the precepts with which Aristotle was said to have instructed Alexander and which were to be found in the Pseudo-Aristotelian *Secretum Secretorum*. Gower's discussion of good kingship helps to account for the popularity of the *Confessio Amantis* amongst male members of the royal family, with all three of Henry V's brothers, the dukes of Clarence, Bedford and Gloucester, owning copies of it.[84] Mirrors for princes such as that provided by Gower played a central part in the education of princes and nobles, although the possession of these works also intimated that the owner was familiar with the properties of the ideal ruler which they set out.[85] Thus deluxe manuscripts such as the Pierpont *Confessio Amantis* were designed not only for individual reading, but also for display to courtiers and international visitors.[86]

In Book VII of the *Confessio Amantis*, Genius observes that 'To evey man behoveth lore,/ Bot to noman belongeth more/ Than to a king, which hath to lede/ The poeple' (VII.1711–14). However, it is crucial to note that the didactic function of the *Confessio Amantis*, with its emphasis on good government, made it useful not just to kings and princes, but also to queens and princesses.[87] As was noted above, medieval women's patronage and ownership of works of political instruction have not been much considered by scholars.[88] The consequent emphasis on interest in such works as a male trait further compounds the idea that, ordinarily, women were external to politics, and not habitually expected to concern themselves with the precepts of government as outlined in mirrors for princes. But in fact royal English women owned and commissioned a variety of politically didactic texts and it is vital to survey this evidence when considering their engagement with the *Confessio Amantis*. For example, the stunningly illuminated Talbot Shrewsbury Book, created as a gift for Margaret of Anjou to mark her marriage to Henry VI in 1445, compiles romances, chronicles,

---

[83] For gendered analysis of mirrors for princes, see Lewis, *Kingship and Masculinity*, pp. 17–44.

[84] Harris, 'Ownership and Readership', p. 129.

[85] Nicholas Orme, *From Childhood to Chivalry: The Education of the English Kings and Aristocracy, 1066–1530* (London: Methuen, 1984), pp. 86–106.

[86] Drimmer, 'Visual Language', pp. 245–6.

[87] This is also pointed out by Bullón-Fernandez, 'Translating Women', pp. 131–2. More broadly, mirrors for princes also contain moral and practical advice applicable to householders of non-royal status.

[88] A point made by both Jenni Nuttall, 'Margaret of Anjou as Patron of English Verse? The *Liber Proverbiorum* and the *Romans of Partenay*', *The Review of English Studies*, 67 (2016), pp. 636–59, at 651 and Catherine Nall, 'Margaret Beaufort's Books: A New Discovery', *Journal of the Early Book Society*, 16 (2013), pp. 213–20, at 213. But for an important exception which does examine women as readers of this type of literature see Anne Clark Bartlett, 'Translation, Self-Representation, and Statecraft: Lady Margaret Beaufort and Caxton's *Blanchardyn and Eglantine* (1489)', *Essays in Medieval Studies*, 22 (2005), pp. 53–66.

chivalric treatises and other instructional texts, all in French, including Giles of Rome's *De Regimine Principum*.[89] Jenni Nuttall shows that while the Talbot Shrewsbury manuscript was a gift, Margaret did take an active interest in the types of text it contained. She argues that Margaret commissioned the *Liber Proverbiorum*, a Middle English verse translation of a collection of ancient wisdom and moral advice, soon after her arrival in England in 1445.[90] Moreover, Margaret may have been the 'ryght hi' princesse' addressed by Stephen Scrope in the one surviving copy of his translation of Christine de Pizan's *Epistle of Othea*.[91] On the basis of Margaret's literary interests and book ownership Raluca Radulescu describes her as 'a politically engaged and savvy queen'.[92] There is no evidence for Margaret's ownership of the *Confessio Amantis*.[93] But it is certainly possible that she knew it; she and Jacquetta of Luxembourg were close friends, and would thus have been familiar with each other's interests and books.

As we have seen, in addition to owning a copy of the *Confessio Amantis*, Jacquetta possessed a compilation of the works of Christine de Pizan, which was also annotated by her son Earl Rivers.[94] This manuscript was perhaps passed to Elizabeth Woodville after Rivers' execution in 1483.[95] Another copy of the *Book of the City of Ladies* belonged to Cecily Neville and may have been given by her to Elizabeth Woodville when she married Edward IV.[96] Elizabeth may also have been the intended recipient of a manuscript containing the *Secretum Secretorum* alongside two other texts outlining ideal rulership, which was possibly created for her after the birth of Prince Edward (the future Edward V), in 1471.[97] Indeed, women's ownership of such texts was evidently, in part, a dimension of their role as mothers, with responsibility

---

[89] This is now British Library Royal MS 15 E VI and is available online, http://www.bl.uk/manuscripts/FullDisplay.aspx?ref=Royal_MS_15_e_vi, accessed 22 February 2018.
[90] Nuttall, 'Margaret of Anjou', passim.
[91] Nuttall, 'Margaret of Anjou', pp. 649–50.
[92] Raluca L. Radulescu, 'Preparing for Mature Years: The Case of Margaret of Anjou and her Books', in Sue Niebrzydowski, ed., *Middle-Aged Women in the Middle Ages* (Cambridge: D. S. Brewer, 2011), p. 117.
[93] I am grateful to Joanna L. Laynesmith for pointing out to me that the claim Margaret of Anjou owned a copy of the *Confessio Amantis* made in her *Last Medieval Queens*, p. 253, is an error.
[94] For further discussion see Sarah Wilma Watson's blog post 'Jacquetta of Luxembourg – A Female Reader of Christine de Pizan in England', on the 'Women's Literary Culture and the Medieval Canon' website: https://blogs.surrey.ac.uk/medievalwomen/2017/02/27/jacquetta-of-luxembourg-a-female-reader-of-christine-de-pizan-in-england/ accessed 22 February 2018.
[95] Driver, 'Women Readers', p. 98.
[96] Laynesmith, 'Books and the Duchess of York', pp. 46–7.
[97] Drimmer, 'Visual Language', pp. 196–7. For a description and edition of one of the texts contained in this manuscript, *The III Consideracions Right Necesserye to the Good Governaunce of a Prince*, see *Four English Political Tracts of the Later Middle Ages*, ed. Jean-Philippe Genet (London: Camden Society, fourth series, 18 (1977)),

for the upbringing of future kings, and of girls who may become queens.[98] It is often argued that Elizabeth was the unnamed 'noble lady which hath brought forth many noble and fayr daughters which ben virtuously nourished and lerned' to whom Caxton dedicated his 1484 edition of the *Book of the Knight of the Tower*, a conduct text aimed explicitly at young women.[99] The case for Elizabeth's ownership of didactic works is circumstantial. But given her status as queen and the firmer evidence relating to women to whom she was connected by birth and marriage, it seems valid to assume that she was an active participant in this culture.[100]

Certainly Margaret Beaufort who, like Cecily Neville, has more often been discussed in terms of her piety and devotional reading habits than her political activities, owned a number of works of political instruction.[101] Catherine Nall discovered Margaret's signature in a copy of William Caxton's 1489 translation of Christine de Pizan's *The Book of Fayttes of Armes and of Chyualrye*. She suggests that this may have been one of the copies given by Caxton to Henry VII (who commissioned the translation) and then passed on by Henry to his mother. Christine de Pizan's original French version was among the texts included in Margaret of Anjou's manuscript compilation, and a number of women also owned copies of Vegetius' *De Re Militari*, which was one of Christine's chief sources.[102] In addition Margaret Beaufort was bequeathed another of Christine's works, 'the pistilles of Othea', by her sister-in-law Anne Stafford.[103] Margaret's will lists a number of other advisory and historical texts, most of which she bequeathed, appropriately, to her son, Henry VII.[104] For example she makes reference to a book by Boccaccio,

---

pp. 174–209. This text is notable for its mention of the role of the queen in education of the prince (p. 205).

[98] See Laynesmith, *Last Medieval Queens*, pp. 150–6 for more on English queens' roles in raising heirs, including the use of didactic texts.

[99] Blake, *Caxton's Own Prose*, p. 111; Blake, *William Caxton and English Literary Culture*, pp. 30–2.

[100] See Driver, 'Women Readers', pp. 98–107, for further discussion of Elizabeth's literary interests.

[101] Michael K. Jones and Malcolm G. Underwood, *The King's Mother: Lady Margaret Beaufort* (Cambridge: Cambridge University Press, 1992), p. 5. Carol M. Meale, '"... alle the bokes that I haue of latyn, englisch, and frensch": Laywomen and their Books in Late Medieval England', in Carol M. Meale, ed., *Women and Literature in Britain, 1150–1500* (Cambridge: Cambridge University Press, 1993), pp. 128–58 notes further examples of female ownership of politically didactic works, e.g. Eleanor de Bohun, wife of Thomas of Woodstock, the youngest son of Edward III, owned a copy of Giles of Rome's *De Regimine Principum* among a number of other chivalric and didactic works, which she bequeathed to her son Humphrey (p. 136).

[102] Nall, 'Margaret Beaufort's Books', pp. 214–5.

[103] Meale, 'Laywomen and their Books', p. 143. It is unclear whether this was the French original of Christine's *Epistre Othéa* or Stephen Scrope's Middle English translation of it, but since the latter was originally dedicated to Anne's father, Humphrey Stafford, duke of Buckingham, it may have been the English version.

[104] Powell, 'Lady Margaret Beaufort', for full discussion of books in Margaret's will.

which may be the copy of *Des cleres et nobles femmes* now Royal MS 20 C V which contains the Beaufort badge.[105] A copy of Boccaccio's *Des cas des nobles homes et femmes* contains the name of 'Marie Rivieres', the second wife of Earl Rivers, and may originally have belonged to Jacquetta.[106]

Thus the *Confessio Amantis* formed just one part of a wider 'syllabus' of works of political and courtly instruction owned by high status women. The political and ethical advice contained in Book VII is gendered in its expectation that a ruler will be a man, as when 'Iconomique', the good rule of the household, is said to 'techeth thilke honestete/ Thurgh which a king in his degree/ His wif and child schal reule and guie' (VII.1671–3). Yet in presenting kingship as a syllabus of ideal attributes which need to be learned and practised, the text renders it a matter of performance rather than simply of gender. Thus, merely having been born to be king was not sufficient. Rather a man had to 'do' kingship correctly and productively, for the benefit of his subjects, as when Edward IV claimed the throne not simply by his dynastic descent but also because, in contrast to Henry VI, he could perform kingship properly.[107] But to present kingship as a set of properties to be mastered and enacted intimates that the practitioner does not necessarily have to be male. This is demonstrated by the frequency with which the status and authority of female rulers was rationalised in terms of their having demonstrated the acuity and prudence of a man. Thus, in *The Treasure of the City of Ladies*, Christine de Pizan advised high status women to take on 'the spirit of a man' and 'the heart of a man', especially when standing in for an absent husband.[108] Catherine of Lancaster, for whom the Castilian translation of the *Confessio Amantis* was likely created, married the future Enrique III in 1388 and when he became king two years later at the age of eleven she (then eighteen) ruled on his behalf until he came of age in 1393. When he died in 1406, she became regent again for their infant son, Juan II.[109] Notably, Catherine was described by her contemporary Fernán Pérez de Guzmán thus: 'In her figure and her movements she seemed as much like a man as a woman. She was very virtuous and reserved in her person and in her reputation.'[110] Such descriptions belonged to a wider discourse, one also

---

[105] This is available online, http://www.bl.uk/catalogues/illuminatedmanuscripts/record.asp?MSID=8355, accessed 22 February 2018.

[106] Scott McKendrick, John Lowden and Kathleen Doyle, eds, *Royal Manuscripts: The Genius of Illumination* (London: British Library, 2011), pp. 246–7.

[107] Lewis, *Kingship and Masculinity*, pp. 253–4.

[108] Christine de Pisan, *The Treasure of the City of Ladies*, trans. Sarah Lawson (Harmondsworth: Penguin, 1985), pp. 128–9.

[109] Theresa Earenfight, 'Royal Women in Late Medieval Spain: Catalina of Lancaster, Leonor of Albuquerque, and María of Castile', in Charlotte Newman Goldy and Amy Livingstone, eds, *Writing Medieval Women's Lives* (New York: Palgrave Macmillan, 2012), pp. 206–26 for further discussion of Catherine's political career and significance.

[110] Quoted by Goodman, 'Katherine [Catalina, Katherine of Lancaster] (1372–1418)'. Guzmán also noted that she was 'greatly ruled' by favourites, but identified this as 'a

found in religious texts and hagiography, whereby a woman could transcend her 'natural' inferiority by eschewing feminine qualities and pursuits and taking on masculine ones instead.[111]

Diane Watt finds this same rhetoric of performative masculinity in the account of Iphis' transformation from female to male in Book IV of the *Confessio Amantis*. Here King Kigdus, in the course of an argument with his pregnant wife, Thelacuse, tells her that if her baby should be female, he would have it slain. Thelacuse subsequently gives birth in secret to a girl who is named Iphis but who is brought up as a boy: 'And clothed and arrayed so/ Riht as a kings Sone scholde' (IV.472–3). Subsequently Iphis is married to Ianthe, a duke's daughter. Out of pity for the love that Iphis and Ianthe have for each other, which is expressed sexually, Cupid 'Transformeth Iphe into a man' (IV.501) so that Iphis' body matches his masculine gender identity. Watt argues that since the adoption of masculine traits was understood as enabling women to 'better' themselves, this transformation is not presented as unnatural and that it even presents the masculine woman as a 'positive exemplary role model'.[112] Implicitly Iphis has to be disguised as a boy because her father will not countenance a female heir. Yet Iphis successfully impersonates a 'kings Sone' through the means of dress and conduct which can be related both to the assumption that a ruler will be masculine, and also to the notion that a woman would become masculine in order to be a successful ruler.

That some women could exercise the qualities essential to both the self and the realm is also illustrated by the 'Tale of Spertachus and Thameris' which appears in Book VII of the *Confessio Amantis* as an illustration of one of the five key 'points' of ideal kingship: mercy. Spertachus, the cruel king of Persia, is described thus: 'For this condicion he hadde,/ That where him hapneth the victoire, His lust and al his moste gloire/ Was forto sle and noght to save' (VII.3422–5). He makes war on Thameris, the queen of Marsagete, 'What he was heihest in his Pride,/ In his rancour and in his hete' (VII.3442–3), and captures and kills Thameris' son. When Thameris hears this she resolves to defeat Spertachus, so she forges alliances in order to create a formidable army: 'A gret pouer til that sche ladde' (VII.3458). She then traps Spertachus by pretending to flee through a pass in which his troops are surrounded and two hundred thousand of them are killed or captured. When Spertachus is brought before her, Thameris pays him back in his own coin; rather than showing him mercy she drowns him in a vessel filled with the blood of his own chief advisors. Significantly, Thameris' status

vice common to royal personages' rather than attributing this to her gender.
[111] Anke Bernau, 'Gender and Sexuality', in Sarah Salih, ed., *A Companion to Middle English Hagiography* (Cambridge: D. S. Brewer, 2006), pp. 104–21.
[112] Watt, 'Gender and Sexuality', pp. 204–7 notes that Genius' attitude is sympathetic throughout, and that the threatening potential of female same-sex attraction is removed by Gower's handling of the tale.

as a woman is not an issue in the tale, which clearly establishes her as a brave, clever and capable ruler, in both political and military terms. The words with which Thameris addresses the vanquished Spertachus are revealing:

> O man, which out of mannes kinde
> Reson of man hast left behind
> And lived worse than a beste,
> Whom Pite myhte noght areste,
> The mannes blod to schede and spille
> Thou haddest nevere yit thi fille (VII.3489–94).

These lines draw on a common trope whereby a tyrant is rendered essentially unmanly ('out of mannes kinde') because his actions are not governed by reason but by pride, anger and insatiable bloodlust.[113] Thameris contrasts Spertachus with beasts, a distinction which is often found in definitions of medieval masculinity.[114] Yet the narrative also draws a telling contrast between Thameris, as a woman, and Spertachus, as a man. Implicitly Thameris plays into Spertachus' unwarranted sense of his own superiority by pretending to be a stereotypical woman too frightened to stand against him. Yet, it is actually Thameris who here is the embodiment of rational masculine leadership. She kills Spertachus, but it is his own failure to show mercy to others, which is fundamentally a failure of his kingship and masculinity, that condemns him. Thus Thameris' actions are presented as entirely justified and render her a kingly exemplar.

As we saw in relation to Christine de Pizan's advice to women, royal women were particularly likely to have to adopt the properties of ideal rulership because of the absence of an adult male. This applied to Catherine of Lancaster and Margaret of Anjou, as we have seen, although this situation is not directly reflected in any of the tales of the *Confessio Amantis*. The only intimation of it comes in the 'Tale of Constance' when Constance's father, the emperor of Rome, dies and 'the yer suiende' (II.1591), Constance herself dies; only then are we told that 'hir Sone was corouned' (II.1595) which may imply that she herself had ruled in the interim. However, it was not only in the absence of men that women could rule. In conceptualising medieval monarchy, it is essential to acknowledge that this did not just constitute 'the king' but rather involved the king and queen working as a partnership. As a result, queens and other high status women were not expected simply to be quiet, passive and decorative and to provide an heir for their husbands.[115]

---

[113] As discussed by Elizabeth A. Lehfeld, 'The Political Legitimacy of Isabel of Castile', *Renaissance Quarterly*, 53 (2000), pp. 31–56 and Cynthia Herrup, 'The King's Two Genders', *Journal of British Studies*, 45 (2006), 493–510.

[114] Ruth Mazo Karras, *From Boys to Men: Formations of Masculinity in Later Medieval Europe* (Philadelphia: University of Pennsylvania Press, 2003), pp. 67–108.

[115] Laynesmith, *Last Medieval Queens*, pp. 2–4 for the point that scant references to queens in mirrors for princes should not be taken as evidence that they were excluded from politics.

Rather, by her actions, the queen also helped to legitimate her husband's position.[116] In this capacity, and as controller of her own household and estates, she would need quotidian knowledge of politics and management. Watson thus argues that for Jacquetta of Luxembourg the *Confessio Amantis* served as 'a guide to political history and a manual of political strategy'.[117] Jacquetta's first husband was John, duke of Bedford, to whom she was married from 1433 until his death in 1435. Bedford was the eldest surviving brother of Henry V and the young Henry VI's heir presumptive. Thus, Jacquetta was a potential queen-in-waiting for two years. It is important to bear this in mind when considering Jacquetta as a mentor for Elizabeth Woodville, her daughter by her second marriage, who did become queen.

The idea of the queen as an intrinsic aspect of the monarchy is also observable in verses describing the pageants performed to welcome Margaret of Anjou into London on 28 May 1445 which were copied into one surviving manuscript of the *Confessio Amantis*.[118] When Margaret married Henry VI in 1445 there had not been a queen of England since the death of Henry V in August 1422. Even the latter's queen, Catherine de Valois, had occupied this position for only two years and had subsequently played no political role during her son's minority. Thus, Margaret's advent was extremely significant, and not just because she was expected to produce an heir. Indeed, Laynesmith observes that the pageant outlines a version of queenship which emphasises neither motherhood, nor intercession, but which presents it as 'a powerful, quasi-divine office'. The pageant renders the queen in relation to the king as, unusually, something like an assistant judge. Whoever copied the pageant verses into the manuscript of the *Confessio Amantis* may well have done so because of a perceived correspondence between the formula for ideal rulership which they outlined for Margaret, and the contents of Gower's work. The creation of an actively political queenship for Margaret in the pageant arguably reflects contemporary concerns about Henry VI's character and kingship and expresses the hope that she, as queen, would enable him to become a more effective and virile king.[119] As discussed above, this idea is

---

[116] Laynesmith, *Last Medieval Queens*, pp. 72–130; Benz St John, Lisa, *Three Medieval Queens: Queenship and the Crown in Fourteenth-Century England* (Houndmills: Palgrave Macmillan, 2012), pp. 17–20 and passim.

[117] Watson, 'Women Readers of John Gower's *Confessio Amantis*'; see also Nuttall, 'Margaret of Anjou', on the function of the Talbot Shrewsbury MS for Margaret, perhaps designed 'to suit and to help craft Margaret's image and self-image as a new queen', (p. 642).

[118] This is now British Library MS Harley 3869; for a description see the entry on the International John Gower Society website, https://www.wcu.edu/johngower/scholarship/PearsallMS/MSS/Harley3869.html, accessed 22 February 2018. For an edition of the verses, see *John Lydgate: Mummings and Entertainments*, ed. Claire Sponsler (Kalamazoo: Medieval Institute Publications, 2010), available online, http://d.lib.rochester.edu/teams/text/sponsler-lydgate-mummings-and-entertainments-appendix-margaret-of-anjous-entry-into-london-1445, accessed 22 February 2018.

[119] Laynesmith, *Last Medieval Queens*, pp. 83–4; Lewis, *Kingship and Masculinity*, pp. 195–7.

articulated by Gower in the 'Tale of Wine, Women and Truth' in Book VII, whilst Book IV examines at greater length the role of love as a spur to men's knightly prowess and achievement, including the examples of Hercules and Aeneas.

Thus, reading the *Confessio Amantis* in the light of recent and more nuanced assessments of the roles women played in later medieval English politics enhances our understanding of the text's attraction to high status female readers such as Jacquetta of Luxembourg, Elizabeth Woodville and Margaret Beaufort. As we have seen, this is partly because Gower included a number of female characters within it whose representation and experiences spoke to their own responsibilities as women expected to be active in furthering the political and dynastic interests of their parents, husbands and children. But it is also essential to acknowledge that the discourse of the book itself, as a work of political guidance, also helps to explain why so many copies belonged to, or are associated with, women who needed to be equipped to rule autonomously as the occasion demanded.

CHAPTER 11

MASCULINITY

Christopher Fletcher

Making Masculinity Visible

Whilst early work on gender history focused on representations of women and on their social experience, in recent years masculinity has gradually emerged, not without some difficulty, as a legitimate category of historical analysis.[1] Studying John Gower's works through the lens of masculinity poses many of the same methodological difficulties which have attended the historical study of masculinity as a whole.[2] Whilst women can seem to be a clearly identifiable object of study, masculinity is more difficult to define. This is partly because many of our sources take a male point of view for granted, dealing with women as an exception from an assumed male norm. Paradoxically, this can make it easy to forget when it is in fact adult males who are at issue.

In the case of John Gower, although his works often deal with women, and can be sympathetic to their plight, a number of scholars have argued that

---

Thanks to Isabel Davis, Siân Echard, Katherine Lewis, Steve Rigby and Robert F. Yeager for comments on earlier drafts of this chapter.

[1] The possibility of the history of masculinity was opened up by Joan W. Scott, 'Gender: A Useful Category of Historical Analysis', *American Historical Review*, 91 (1986), pp. 1053–75, and developed by John Tosh, 'What Should Historians Do with Masculinity? Reflections on Nineteenth-Century Britain', *History Workshop Journal*, 38 (1994), pp. 179–202.

[2] For reviews of the early work in the field see Karen Harvey and Alex Shepard, 'What have Historians Done with Masculinity? Reflections on Five Centuries of British History, circa 1500 to 1950', *Journal of British Studies*, 44 (2005), pp. 274–80. For a critical look back, see John Tosh, 'The History of Masculinity: An Outdated Concept?' in Sean Brady and John Arnold, eds, *What is Masculinity? Historical Arguments and Perspectives* (Basingstoke: Palgrave Macmillan, 2011), pp. 17–34. For the particular case of medieval studies see Christopher Fletcher, 'The Whig Interpretation of Masculinity? Honour and Sexuality in Late Medieval Manhood', in Brady and Arnold, *What is Masculinity?*, pp. 57–75; Christopher Fletcher, '"Sire, uns hom sui" : Transgression et inversion par rapport à quelle(s) norme(s) dans l'histoire des masculinités médiévales?', *Micrologus' Library*, 78 (2017), pp. 23–50.

his moral and literary project is focused on masculine experience.[3] Women are far from forgotten in Gower's works, but if his major poetic works are united by a common moral enterprise, as many scholars have argued, this project does seem to entail the formation of a certain kind of subject who is usually male. In the *Vox Clamantis* and the *Mirour de l'Omme*, for example, women figure less prominently than the male estates, the clergy, knights, lawyers and merchants, whose sins occupy the bulk of the estates satire parts of these poems. When Gower cites women as the occasion for the sexual sins of male priests (VC: III.20.1581–1622), monks (VC: IV.11.431–490; MO: 21048–21060), kings (MO: 22779–22824) and knights (VC: V.1.19–6.468), it is the correction of male morality which concerns him. He does deal with nuns on their own account, regarding them as more likely to fall into sin than men, and consequently as being more meritorious if they succeed in resisting it (VC: IV.13.547–676).[4] Women also figure amongst Gower's urban sinners (although not, interestingly, amongst noble miscreants) with female bourgeois being targeted for wearing finery which would be more appropriate for a countess (MO: 25681–25704). Although Triche is a male merchant in the *Mirour de l'Omme* (MO: 25177–26220), Fraud in the *Vox Clamantis* is a female tradesperson (VC: V.13.735–834), and Gower notes that both regrating and its attendant sins are normally a woman's business (MO: 26329–26340). This, though, is the limit of Gower's concern with women in two poems dominated by the extensive treatment of the sins of ecclesiastical and noble males.

Thus, given that Gower's avowed object is less to raise indignation at the sins of others than to inspire his audience to correct themselves (CA: Pro.514–528; VC: III.Pro.9–42), it has to be said that men are better served than women in the range of moral exempla offered in his major works. Even in the *Cinkante Balades*, where the female addressee of forty-five of the poems is given the opportunity to reply in the other five, most critics have

---

[3] Anthony S. G. Edwards, 'Gower's Women in the *Confessio*', *Mediaevalia*, 16 (1993), pp. 223–37; Diane Watt, 'Gender and Sexuality in *Confessio Amantis*' in Siân Echard, ed., *A Companion to Gower* (Cambridge: D. S. Brewer, 2004), pp. 197–213, esp. 197; Amanda M. Leff, 'Writing, Gender and Power in Gower's *Confessio Amantis*', *Exemplaria*, 20 (2008), pp. 28–47. For earlier views which stressed Gower's empathy for women's plight, see Derek Pearsall, 'Gower's Narrative Art', *PMLA*, 81 (1966), pp. 475–84, reprinted in Peter Nicholson, ed., *Gower's Confessio Amantis: A Critical Anthology* (Cambridge: D. S. Brewer, 1991), pp. 62–80; Linda Barney Burke, 'Women in John Gower's *Confessio Amantis*', *Mediaevalia*, 3 (1977), pp. 239–59. Later writers continue to find in Gower a critic of the sufferings imposed on women, notably in courtly romance, e.g. Carolyn Dinshaw, 'Rivalry, Rape and Manhood: Gower and Chaucer' in Anna Roberts, ed., *Violence against Women in Medieval Texts* (Gainesville: University Press of Florida, 1998), pp. 137–70, although such interpretations do not deny Gower's male-centredness.

[4] See Matthew Irvin, 'Genius and Sensual Reading in the *Vox Clamantis*', in Elisabeth Dutton, with John Hines and Robert F. Yeager, eds, *John Gower, Trilingual Poet: Language, Translation, and Tradition* (Cambridge: D. S. Brewer, 2010), pp. 196–205.

read the work as a whole as a process by which the male speaker approaches his moral fulfilment.[5] Likewise, in the *Confessio Amantis*, although women feature prominently both in the stories Gower tells and in the poem's framing narrative, many recent critics have remarked upon a tendency to return to a masculine perspective. Even when they are talking about women, Genius and Amans conspire to draw the moral for men.[6] Like the representation of the peasant rebels in Book I of the *Vox Clamantis*,[7] it has been argued that women in the *Confessio Amantis* serve as a stimulus to action and self-exploration on the part of the male, educated, gentry or noble public who formed both his imagined and much of his actual audience.[8]

The would-be analyst of the role of masculinity in Gower's work thus shares the first difficulty experienced by historians of masculinity: how to make visible what is simply assumed. Recent critics have responded to this challenge by reading Gower through modern theoretical categories, for example concentrating on male heterosexual sexuality or on fatherhood as themes which can be linked objectively to certain kinds of male experience, even if they are not experienced by all men.[9] Another possible approach would be to analyse Gower's writing in the context of models of manhood and youth which were available in contemporary scholastic writing and in

---

[5] Holly Barbaccia, 'The Woman's Response in John Gower's *Cinkante Balades*', in Dutton, Hines and Yeager, *John Gower, Trilingual Poet*, pp. 230–8; Robert F. Yeager, 'John Gower's French', in Echard, *A Companion to Gower*, pp. 137–51, at 147.

[6] See e.g. the story of Rosiphelee and Jophthah's daughter, which Amans interrupts to demand advice applicable to men (CA: IV.1596–1607), discussed in Isabel Davis, 'John Gower's Fear of Flying: Transitional Masculinities in the *Confessio Amantis*', in Nicola F. McDonald and W. M. Ormrod, eds, *Rites of Passage: Cultures of Transition in the Fourteenth Century* (York: York Medieval Press, 2004), pp. 131–152, at 136; and the use of the story of the Trojan horse (CA: I.1077–1225), discussed below. For further examples see Edwards, 'Gower's Women', and Leff, 'Writing, Gender and Power'.

[7] For a reading of Book I of the *Vox Clamantis* as Gower's inclusion of the rebellion of 1381 as part of his moral self, see Isabel Davis, 'Calling: Langland, Gower, and Chaucer on Saint Paul', *Studies in the Age of Chaucer*, 34 (2012), pp. 53–94, at 79–81, 85–9, 91–3. The sins of labourers also have an 'added on' feel in the *Mirour de l'Omme*, being dispatched in a mere 59 lines following 8100 dedicated to the sins of the other estates (MO: 26425–26484).

[8] For Gower's implied and actual audiences see Anthony I. Doyle and Malcolm B. Parkes, 'The Production of Copies of the *Canterbury Tales* and the *Confessio Amantis* in the Early Fifteenth Century', in Malcolm B. Parkes and Andrew G. Watson, eds, *Medieval Scribes, Manuscripts and Libraries* (London: Scolar Press, 1978), pp. 163–210; Derek Pearsall, 'The Gower Tradition', in Alastair J. Minnis, ed., *Gower's Confessio Amantis: Responses and Reassessments* (Cambridge: D. S. Brewer, 1983), pp. 179–97, at 184; Kate Harris, 'Ownership and Readership: Studies in the Provenance of the Manuscripts of Gower's *Confessio Amantis*' (Unpublished University of York D.Phil. thesis (1993)).

[9] Maria Bullón-Fernández, *Fathers and Daughters in Gower's Confessio Amantis: Authority, Family, State and Violence* (Cambridge: D. S. Brewer, 2000); Isabel Davis, *Writing Masculinity in the Later Middle Ages* (Cambridge: Cambridge University Press, 2007), pp. 76–107.

didactic works such as sermons, encyclopaedia and 'mirrors for princes'.[10] Yet these two methods both have drawbacks if they are employed exclusively. On the one hand, it can be difficult to navigate between modern theoretical models and medieval conceptual structures, and there is a high risk of unacknowledged slippage between the two.[11] On the other, a contextualising approach based on normative works necessarily privileges interpretations which a highly or even adequately read public would ideally impose on Gower's works, and discards as misreading their likely reception by the partially educated and the inattentive, who nonetheless make up a substantial proportion of any audience.

The present article thus pursues a different, complementary method, focusing on lexicon and the use of words. This approach, pioneered by the German *Begriffsgeschichte* and the French school of *textométrie*, has not often been employed by historians of late medieval England.[12] This methodology does not annul or supersede methods based either on other kinds of close-reading, on the identification of intertextuality, or on the analysis of Gower's literary project in terms of medieval literary theory.[13] Rather, by focusing on particular lexical items across a large corpus of works, or simply in a very large single text such as the *Confessio Amantis*, it foregrounds how less attentive audiences were likely to understand them, those who perhaps only half-remembered their Giles of Rome but who understood and practised the

---

[10] An approach taken in the analysis of fifteenth-century kingship and masculinity presented by Katherine Lewis, *Kingship and Masculinity in Late Medieval England* (London: Routledge, 2013).

[11] See Fletcher, 'The Whig Interpretation of Masculinity'.

[12] For *Begriffsgeschichte*, see Reinhart Kosselleck, *The Practice of Conceptual History*, trans. T. S. Presner (Stanford: Stanford University Press, 2002). For a late medieval case study inspired by this approach, see Richard F. Green, *A Crisis of Truth: Literature and Law in Ricardian England* (Philadelphia: University of Pennsylvania Press, 1998). For the application of this approach to early modern England, see Phil Withington, *Society in Early Modern England: The Vernacular Origins of Some Powerful Ideas* (Cambridge: Polity, 2010). For a different, lexically-based approach see Christopher Fletcher, *Richard II: Manhood, Youth and Politics, 1377–99* (Oxford: Oxford University Press). For *textométrie*, see Christopher Fletcher, 'What Makes a Political Language? Key Terms, Profit and Damage in the Common Petition of the English Parliament, 1343–1422' in Jan Dumolyn, Jelle Haemers, H. R. Oliva Herrer and Vincent Challet, eds, *The Voices of the People in Late Medieval Europe: Communication and Popular Politics* (Turnhout: Brepols, 2014), pp. 91–106, at 93–5.

[13] For approaches based on literary theory which emphasise the structural unity of Gower's works, see Alastair J. Minnis, 'John Gower, *Sapiens* in Ethics and Politics', *Medium Ævum*, 49 (1980), pp. 207–29, and Alastair J. Minnis, 'Moral Gower and Medieval Literary Theory' in Minnis, *Gower's Confessio Amantis*, pp. 50–78; James Simpson, *Sciences and the Self in Medieval Poetry: Alan of Lille's Anticlaudianus and John Gower's Confessio Amantis* (Cambridge: Cambridge University Press, 1995), esp. chapters 5 and 6.

Middle English language.[14] This study is focused on the *Confessio Amantis*, and the use within it of a number of key words, notably 'man' and 'manhood'. The use of the vocabulary of manhood in the *Confessio Amantis*, which was probably composed c.1386–90, cannot stand in for his works as a whole, and a full study would need to analyse his complete oeuvre in three languages. Yet there are a number of reasons for beginning with this work. First, the *Confessio Amantis* is of particular interest amongst his three major works as a poem which, being written in Middle English, was accessible to learned, unlearned and semi-learned audiences. Second, through the changing dedications attached to the various versions of the *Confessio Amantis*, Gower sought to attach this work to the politics of the late 1380s and 1390s, a period in which the nature of manhood was of crucial political importance.[15] By moving from lexical analysis, to a concentration on particular sections of the *Confessio Amantis*, and then back to their resonance with contemporary political events, and by keeping different meanings of manhood always in view, I hope to offer new perspectives both on the interpretation of Gower's works and on late fourteenth-century political culture.

Masculinity and Politics

Manhood was of particular importance throughout the reign of Richard II (1377–99) as a result of a complex and changing set of political circumstances.[16] As a result of the king's accession at the age of ten, and of the political and social instability caused by an expensive, losing war on the Continent, the 1380s were marked by a series of violent confrontations in which the question of whether the king should be treated as a man or a boy was central. From the age of thirteen onwards, the young king was formally held to be exercising his full powers as monarch, even though all parties were aware that a man of knightly class of this age would be a minor.[17] This difficult situation put the question of the king's manhood to the fore. One strategy pursued by the king and those about him to demonstrate his manhood, and hence his personal authority, was to push for a royal military campaign on the Continent, where he would win 'honour and manhood'.[18] This project was unimpeachable in ideological terms, but it was undermined

---

[14] On the use and reception of Giles of Rome, see Stephen H. Rigby, 'Aristotle for Aristocrats and Poets: Giles of Rome's *De Regimine Principum* as Theodicy of Privilege', *The Chaucer Review*, 46 (2012), pp. 259–313; Charles F. Briggs, *Giles of Rome's De Regimine Principum: Reading and Writing Politics at Court and University, c.1275–c.1525* (Cambridge: Cambridge University Press, 1999).

[15] For the dedications, see George B. Stow, 'Richard II in John Gower's *Confessio Amantis*: Some Historical Perspectives', *Mediaevalia*, 16 (1993), pp. 3–31.

[16] For a full discussion, see Fletcher, *Richard II*.

[17] *Ibid.*, pp. 74–96.

[18] *Ibid.*, pp. 97–150. For the king's honour and manhood, *Ibid.*, pp. 146–7.

by rival schemes, by the fear of another revolt, like that of 1381, which might be generated by war taxation, and by the belief that money granted for war would be siphoned off for other uses, a doubly frustrating experience for the king since the liberality of his household was another means to demonstrate manhood.[19] Instead, in 1386, just as he reached the age of eighteen, Richard II was forced to accept the re-imposition of compulsory counsel-taking mechanisms which had been removed when he was thirteen years old. The king's attempts to resist these mechanisms reached a climax in the defeat of his allies at the battle of Radcot Bridge in 1387 and the exile or execution of his friends and supporters in the Merciless Parliament of 1388.[20]

Thus, whilst the *Confessio Amantis* was being composed, the young king to whom it was initially dedicated was undergoing a series of humiliations in which he was denied the full status of a man. This state of affairs, and Richard II's reaction to it, resonated strongly with contemporary concepts of manhood as they are apparent in the broader use of the language of 'manhood' and 'manly' action. In the 1390s, that is to say after the composition of the *Confessio* but during the period of its first circulation, the king's manhood took on a different resonance. In contemporary language, one significant kind of 'manly' action was to take revenge.[21] After a period of uneasy peace, during which it was not clear whether Richard had forgotten his earlier humiliations and in which he gradually assumed the powers which would normally be wielded by an adult king, it finally became apparent that he had forgiven and forgotten nothing. In 1397–99, he took judicial revenge on those who had humiliated him a decade earlier, ultimately provoking his own deposition at the hands of the other dedicatee of the *Confessio Amantis*, Henry Bolingbroke, earl of Derby.[22] Although Gower did not react to these events by revising the presentation of manhood in later versions of the *Confessio*, it is possible to detect a change of emphasis, and the assumption of a narrower position within the full range of the possible meanings of manhood, after the deposition of Richard II, in his revisions to certain passages of the *Vox Clamantis* and in his *Cronica Tripertita*.

This chapter attempts to make a contribution to the study of masculinity in John Gower's works and in contemporary political culture in four interlinked ways. First, it examines how the word 'man' was used in the *Confessio Amantis* and what this suggests about the 'point of view' of this work. Second, it analyses the vocabulary of 'manhood' and 'manly' action in the *Confessio Amantis* in order to establish how Gower's use of these words was situated within the range of possibilities offered by the Middle English language.

---

[19] On household expenditure, which was actually very restrained in the 1380s, but which was rendered problematic by the ongoing debt occasioned by the royal wedding of 1382 and by the continuing desire to control royal finances, see *Ibid.*, pp. 194–204.
[20] *Ibid.*, pp. 151–91.
[21] *Ibid.*, pp. 33–5.
[22] *Ibid.*, pp. 249–74.

Third, it turns to a specific book within the *Confessio Amantis*, Book I on the sin of pride, to show how Gower sought to moderate and control certain of the contemporary associations of manhood. Finally, it contrasts the treatment of one theme closely linked to contemporary concepts of manhood – that of vengeance and justice – in one tale from Book III of the *Confessio Amantis*, which dates from the late 1380s, with the portrayal of the manhood of Richard II which Gower offered after the king's deposition in his revisions to the *Vox Clamantis*, and in his *Cronica Tripertita*. It will be argued that Gower's desire to moderate lay noble manhood ultimately provided little practical guidance as to where precisely the just measure of manhood might be found. In the end it was only hindsight that enabled Gower to select from contemporary commonplace ideas, and indeed from his own earlier works, and to rule which manifestations of manhood ought to be emulated and which ought to be shunned.

What Is a 'Man' in the *Confessio Amantis*?

What, then, does a 'textometric' approach tell us about the presentation of 'man', 'manhood' and 'manly' action in the *Confessio Amantis*?[23] First, it is possible to gain an impression of what a 'man' is, or normally is, in this poem by analysing the use of the words 'man' and 'wyht'. Focusing on these lexical items or 'lemma' provides support for those critics who argue for the male-centredness of this work. Putting together variant spellings, singulars and plurals, Gower uses the lemma 'man' 878 times in the course of the *Confessio Amantis*, and 'wyht' some 66 times, compared with 135 instances of 'woman' and 180 uses of 'wife'. Both 'man' and 'wyht' can be used to refer to human beings or people in general, for example at the end of the world when 'every man schal thanne arise / To Joie or elles to Juise [i.e. bitterness]...' (Pro.1041–2); or when Genius declares that 'natheles a man mai se' (IV.1227) how nowadays many do not know what love is, or when he asserts, as a universal truth, that 'schame hindreth every wyht' (VII.1967). The phrase 'this man' can be used to denote an individual who has been invoked earlier in the same passage, although this is only ever done for males: no woman is referred to as 'this man' (I.2138, 2578; III.1255; VI.1190, 1728;

---

[23] The following analysis was made using the text of the *Confessio Amantis* available online in the Middle English Corpus of Prose and Verse, University of Michigan: <https://quod.lib.umich.edu/c/cme/>. This text was prepared using the lemmatisation platform PALM <http://palm.huma-num.fr/PALM/>, developed as part of the European Research Council project 'Signs and States'. It was then analysed using TXM, a software package which permits the exploration (concordances, contexts...) and statistical analysis (cooccurrences; lexical progression; factorial analysis) of a digitised textual corpus, developed at the École Normale Supérieure, Lyon: <http://textometrie.ens-lyon.fr/>.

VII.2458; VIII.762, 802, 845, 917, 1441, 1448, 1466). 'Wyht', on the other hand, can be used of both men and women: the hag in the 'Tale of Florent', for example, is referred to as 'this olde wyht' (I.1548, 1672) or 'that foule wyht' (I.1785); but the same word is also used, for example, to denote the 'yonge clerc' who assists the future Boniface VIII in persuading Celestine V to abdicate by becoming his 'prive wyht' (II.2858).

In the case of 'man', further information can be garnered by focusing on the use of this lemma in opposition (antinomy), or in lists. 'Man' is thus sometimes placed in opposition to 'beste' in phrases such as 'Noght as a man bot as a beste' (I.1240); 'For he was half man and half beste' (V.5276); 'Which myhte grieve man or beste' (VII.929).[24] It is also placed in lists which suggest that 'man' and 'beste' are different things, such as: 'For every man and bridd and beste, / And flour and gras and rote and rinde...' (I.3260–1); 'Of man, of beste, of herbe, of ston / Of fissche, of foughl, of everychon / That ben of bodely substance...' (VII.139–141). 'Man' is sometimes distinguished from a god or an angel, for example: 'bothe angel and man ... obeien goddes myht' (VII.7117–9); 'An other god of Hercules / Thei made, which was natheles / A man...' (V.1083–1085).[25] These usages imply that a 'man' is a being which is not a god, an angel or an animal. On this evidence alone, we might think that a 'man' was simply a human being. Elsewhere, however, 'man' is used in opposition to 'woman' or 'wife', for example: 'Yit makth a man the ferste chace, / The womman fleth and he pourseith' (VII.4286–7); 'Which of the tuo more amorous is / Or man or wife...' (III.745–6).[26] It is thus often clear that 'man' refers not just to a human being but specifically to an adult male. When one female character changes sex, we are told that Cupid '[t]ransformeth Iphe into a man...' (IV.501): Iphe is already a human being, now she becomes a male human being. Similarly, we are told that Minerva 'was wyse, and of a man / The wit and reson which he can / Is in the celles of the brayn...' (V.1461–3), and are warned how 'a man ... leve that a man schal do' through effeminate stupidity (VII.4303–5). In these examples, 'a man' is clearly an adult male.[27]

On a number of occasions, when Gower talks in general about what 'a man' might do in a way which might at first seem to refer to all human beings, he then quickly uses a masculine pronoun, raising the suspicion that 'man' does not apply to females in these cases but only to males. This seems likely not only when the subject matter is boasting or military activity, for example when we are told that 'Good is therfore a man to hide / His oghne pris...' (I.2648–9), or 'In time of werre a man is fre / Himself, his hous and ek

---

[24] See also CA: III.383, 2596–8. 'Man' is on one occasion a privileged subset of 'beste': 'That ilke ymage bar liknesse / Of man and of non other beste.' (I.908–9).
[25] See also CA: VII.2462–7.
[26] See also CA: IV.1516; V.2569–70, 4175–7.
[27] Cf. the discussion of jealousy in Book V, in which the husband is referred to throughout simply as 'a man' (CA: V.452–69).

his lond / Defende with his oghne hond...' (III.2236–8), but also when moral self-improvement and rhetorical technique are in question, for example when the lesson is that 'Ther may a man the sothe wite, / If that he wolde ensample take...' (IV.3312–3), or 'Hou Tullius his Rethorique / Componeth, ther a man mai pike / Hou that he schal hise wordes sette' (VII.1589–91). On occasion, Gower also makes an opposition between 'god' and 'man' in a context which makes clear that women are not included with the latter. When Alexander's mother 'thoghte hou that sche was deceived, / That sche hath of a man conceived, / And wende a god it hadde be...' (VI.2331–3), 'a man' is not just a human being, but also specifically an adult male.

An analysis of the use of 'man' in the *Confessio* thus confirms what recent critics have argued on the basis of the analysis of particular passages or the structural characteristics of his works: that Gower, although superficially offering instruction for all humanity, is above all concerned with the male half of that population.[28] Even without understanding Gower's moral and literary project, anyone capable of understanding Middle English would have absorbed, without necessarily being able to say exactly why, that for Gower a 'man' was normally an adult male. This was a characteristic that he shared with many contemporary writers, and with contemporary culture in general, but it does suggest that Gower's moral project was not equally concerned with female and male experience.

However, when the connotations of words which superficially share the same referent ('man') are considered, such as 'manly' and 'manhood', a rather less mainstream Gower emerges.[29] In these cases, it can be shown that Gower mobilises many of the common uses of these words, but neglects others. This partiality, once revealed, makes it possible to demonstrate the selectivity of Gower's presentation of manhood. This has consequences not only for understanding how his moral project was situated within contemporary society and culture, but also sheds light on a different kind of selectivity, specifically in the way in which he deals with contemporary politics. Gower's works contain within them tools which can be used to attack his own later presentation of political events. This opens up the broader question of how Gower's works might legitimately be read, whether in terms of his general authorial project, or the possible counter-readings which persisted, despite his best efforts.

---

[28] That said, Gower does use the word 'mankinde' 11 times in the *Confessio*, always referring to mankind in opposition to God, a god or the gods (II.3108, 3387; IV.2443; V.1609, 4110; VI.7; VII.1033, 3336, 3820; VIII.67, 82).

[29] On the ambiguity of 'man' and its consequences for the semantics of 'manhood', 'manly', etc., see Fletcher, *Richard II*, pp. 25–8.

The Nature of 'Manhood' in the *Confessio Amantis*

How did Gower's works relate to commonplace associations of manhood as they circulated in the language and culture of late medieval England?[30] At its simplest, in Middle English 'manly' action denoted strength, energy and forceful activity, especially when an individual was hard pressed, particularly in battle.[31] This language was an inheritance of the Latin language, of classical philosophy and medical theory, but it was nonetheless still current not only in medieval Latin but also in late medieval vernacular languages and in everyday assumptions about the particular characteristics of an ideal adult male human being.[32] From the later Roman republic and into the early Middle Ages, the ideal qualities of a man were summed up in the concept of *virtus* which retained its etymological link to *vir*: the man.[33] It has been argued that, in the Roman republic, *virtus* was chiefly associated with courage, physical force and military efficiency.[34] Nevertheless, long before the arrival of Christianity, *virtus* had also begun to take on moral connotations, under the influence of the Stoic association between manly strength and moral resistance.[35] In the hands of Christian writers, this mobilisation of the strength and constancy of the *vir* in the face of moral as well as physical challenges was redeployed to permit converted Roman nobles to show *virtus* by suffering patiently.[36] The Latin Middle Ages inherited this double conception of *virtus*.[37] On the one hand, the nature of man was thought to derive from physical strength; on the other, virtue continued to be seen as a struggle, and virtuous living required manly vigour.[38]

---

[30] For a survey of the late medieval language and theory of manhood, see Fletcher, *Richard II*, pp. 25–73. For the early and central medieval background: Fletcher, '"Sire, uns hom sui"'.

[31] *MED*, 'manli (adj.)', 3; 'manli (adv.(1))', 2. Additional examples and commentary in Fletcher, *Richard II*, pp. 32–9.

[32] For earlier medieval examples, see Fletcher, '"Sire uns hom sui"', pp. 38–42. For a comparable language in late medieval Spanish, see Hipólito Rafael Oliva Herrer, 'Masculinity and Political Struggle in the Cities of the Crown of Castile at the End of the Middle Ages', in Christopher Fletcher, Sean Brady, Rachel Moss and Lucy Riall, eds, *The Palgrave Handbook of Masculinity and Political Culture in Europe* (London: Palgrave Macmillan, 2018), pp. 161–178.

[33] Mathew Kuefler, *The Manly Eunuch: Masculinity, Gender Ambiguity and Christian Ideology in Late Antiquity* (Chicago: University of Chicago Press, 2001), pp. 19–20, 31, 68–9; Myles McDonnell, *Roman Manliness: Virtus and the Roman Republic* (Cambridge: Cambridge University Press, 2006).

[34] Ibid., esp. pp. 12–71.

[35] Ibid., pp. 72–141.

[36] Kuefler, *Manly Eunuch*, pp. 105–17.

[37] Silke Schwandt, *Virtus: Zur Semantik eines politischen Konzepts im Mittelalter* (Frankfurt: Campus, 2014).

[38] Ibid., ch. 9, esp. pp. 187–91; Fletcher, '"Sire, uns hom sui"', pp. 38–42. For the use of *viriliter* in the metaphor of a combat against sin in central medieval monastic

Gower uses 'manhood' 21 times in the course of the *Confessio Amantis*. On at least eight of these occasions, this lemma is used to denote military effectiveness, courage and strength.[39] When a 'worthi povere kniht' pursues his case at the court of Julius Caesar, finally obtaining personal justice by confidently asserting his military ability and his suffering on an earlier campaign in Africa, we are told from the start that he 'lacketh nothing of manhede' (VII.2070). It is the 'mighty hond of his manhode / As he which hath ynowh knihthode' which permits Philip of Macedon sorely to grieve the Romans (II.1639–1640). The Trojans, too, hesitate to make war on the Greeks because, 'Stant nou in Grece the manhode / Of worthinesse and of knighthode...' which has enabled them to conquer all Europe (V.7337–8). Gower also uses 'manhood' not only to refer to military energy but also to invoke more general qualities of vigour and the avoidance of sloth. Thus, when Genius defines pusillanimity as the characteristic of 'He that hath litel corage / And dar no mannes werk beginne' (IV.316–7), he asserts that he who suffers from this vice is always fearful and 'woll no manhed understonde' (IV.325). In the same vein, when Amans asks Genius to provide examples of knightly deeds done for love, Genius advises that the lover should 'for no Slowthe lette / To do what longeth to manhede' (IV.2033), and concludes his examples with the assurance that 'wommen loven worthinesse / Of manhode and of gentilesse' (IV.2197–80). This kind of 'gentilesse' is not simply a matter of riches and good birth, however. Instead 'love honeste' makes the villain courteous and the coward hardy, 'so that verrai prouesse / Is caused upon loves reule / To him that can manhode reule' (IV.2302–4). Elsewhere in the *Confessio Amantis*, Genius mobilises manhood specifically to admonish those rulers who fear to slay in a just cause and so display not pity but pusillanimity: 'For if manhode be restreigned, / Or be it pes or be it werre, / Justice goth al out of here, / So that knyhthode is set behinde' (VII.3540–43).

However, the resonances of 'manhood' in late medieval England went considerably beyond these basic associations with energy, courage and military accomplishment. 'Manhood' was also a synonym for honour, both in the sense of renown and of worthiness of respect.[40] Gower uses this word seven times in this sense in the *Confessio Amantis*.[41] 'Manhood' in one sense

---

sources, see Katherine Allen Smith, *War and the Making of Medieval Monastic Culture* (Woodbridge: Boydell Press, 2011).

[39] 'At least' because it is not always possible to be sure of the connotations of a usage which also has a simpler referent, for example when knightly youths are brought up to manhood. See CA: II.794 and III.1964, discussed below.

[40] MED, 'manhede', 2c, 3e. Cf. MED, 'manli (adj.)', 4a; 'manli (adv.(1))', 4a, 4c. For discussion see Fletcher, *Richard II*, pp. 25–44. See also Derek G. Neal, *The Masculine Self in Late Medieval England* (Chicago: University of Chicago Press, 2008), pp. 13–55. For comparable resonances in medieval Spanish, see Oliva Herrer, 'Masculinity and Political Struggle'.

[41] In addition to the examples discussed in this section, see also CA: I.1212, 3044, considered in the next part of this chapter.

was the honour which was acquired by those who accomplished military deeds, much like the Greeks in the examples given above. Gower tells the story, for example, of an emperor's son, frustrated by the *pax romana*, 'Whos herte stod upon knyhthode: / Bot most of all of his manhode...' (II.2513–4). He takes service with the Sultan so that he can accumulate military renown and hence social status. The spectrum of uses of 'manhood' went beyond purely military renown to include honour in the sense of social status, and finally to mean honour in the sense of morally right action. The poor knight who petitioned Julius Caesar (VII.2070) wished to stress not only his military deeds but also the respect and good treatment which he deserved.

Whilst remaining closely tied to military deeds, 'manhood' could be undone by shameful or dishonourable behaviour. Thus when Ulysses feigns madness in order to avoid participating in the Trojan War, Nauplus berates him both for the use of subterfuge, which 'is gret schame to a king' (IV.1862), and for the neglect of his military reputation when he 'for Slouthe of eny love ... leve of armes the kyhthode, / Which is pris of thi manhode' (IV.1877, 1879–80). Ulysses' trickery thus threatens his manhood not only in the sense of his military renown but also in the sense of his personal reputation and social standing. In his discussion of chastity in Book VII of the *Confessio Amantis*, Gower explicitly plays on the link between 'manhood' as renown and 'manhood' as the worthiness of respect associated with honourable action. Having dealt with truth, largesse and pity with justice, Genius turns to chastity, which turns out to be a requirement, first of all, of manhood in the sense of honourable behaviour. Every good man knows that at marriage 'His trouthe pliht lith in morgage / Which if he breke, it is falshode, / And that descordeth to manhode' (VII.4228–30).

This need to maintain one's manhood is especially true of princes, who should avoid falling into 'such riote / And namely that he nassote / To change for the wommanhede / The worthinesse of his manhede' (VII.4253–6). The meaning of '[t]o change for the wommanhede' is at first ambiguous: it is not initially clear whether the king risks losing his manhood on account of womankind or in exchange for their characteristics. As the discussion continues, the latter reading comes to the fore at the same time as the political consequences of such behaviour. A man who loses his wits for love becomes effeminate and 'leve that a man schal do' (VII.4305). Genius then presents King Sardanapaulus as an example of a prince who 'for love himself mislede / Wherof manhode stode behind' (VII.4310–11). Sardanapaulus does not only become 'wommannyssh', he spends so much time with women that he starts to make lace, weave purses and sew on pearls (VII.4332–4). '[T]his king in wommanhede / Was falle fro chivalerie' (VII.4336–7), and is soon deposed by a more militarily-minded opponent. Thus whilst Gower often employs 'manhood' to refer to energy and vigour, especially in a military context, and to the renown which is acquired by deeds of military courage, he also uses it to refer to the honourable reputation which is lost by subterfuge and duplicity, and by effeminacy in the sense of assuming feminine occupations and feminine characteristics.

These were not the only ways that 'manhood' and its cognates could be used in Middle English, yet these other usages occur more rarely in the *Confessio Amantis* than those carrying connotations of military and moral courage, the honour of renown or the honour of right action. Gower sometimes uses 'manhede' in opposition to divinity, in the case of the manhood of Christ, apparently without any other connotations (V.1772); sometimes as a generic way of talking about all men, sometimes possibly including female human beings (Pro.260); and sometimes in explicit opposition to women (VII.1878). He also uses this word to refer to the adulthood of a male individual, perhaps with the connotation of strength, as when a youth, raised to be a knight, is 'updrawe into manhede' (II.794; cf. III.1964). Another use of 'manhood' in Middle English was as a synonym for largesse, a usage which linked together the qualities of *virtus*, of Christian *humanitas*, and the generosity which attached to the status of a noble or a knight.[42] Gower employs this link between manhood and largesse only once, and then it is embedded in a metaphor in which 'lack of manhode' is shown by men who ungenerously and jealously monitor their wives (V.455). On the one occasion in the *Confessio Amantis* in which Gower uses the adjective 'manlich', it is used in a context of vengeance. After the rape and suicide of Lucretia, Brutus 'with a manlich herte' drives her husband and father to leave their sorrow and avenge the deed (VII.5093–5105).[43] Yet nowhere else in this work does Gower make the link between 'manhood' and vengeance, even though this association was common, for example, in Middle English romance.[44]

A survey of Gower's use of 'manhood' and its cognates in the *Confessio Amantis* leaves the impression that he approves of the 'manhood' in the senses of energy and vigour, of the 'manhood' of social status and reputation, and of military renown. Reading this work through the lens of 'manhood', it is very difficult to accept the view that Gower was a pacifist, rather than simply a critic of certain kinds of war which he considered to be unjust.[45] Arguably, it was because the rightness of these associations of manhood were so widely assumed, and were shared by Gower, that they have been neglected at the expense of the criticisms of particular kinds of knightly violence made by Genius and Amans in Books III, IV and V. It is also clear that, in Gower's

---

[42] MED, 'manhede', 2d. Cf. MED, 'manli (adj.)', 4b; 'manli (adv.(1))', 4b; Fletcher, *Richard II*, pp. 45–56.
[43] Gower uses the expression '[w]ith manful herte' on another occasion, simply to imply courage (CA: VII.2881).
[44] For examples, see Fletcher, *Richard II*, pp. 34–5.
[45] For the suggestion of pacifism, see Robert F. Yeager, 'Pax Poetica: On the Pacifism of Chaucer and Gower', *Studies in the Age of Chaucer*, 9 (1987), pp. 97–121; Nigel Saul, 'A Farewell to Arms? Criticism of Warfare in Late Fourteenth-Century England' in Christopher Given-Wilson, ed., *Fourteenth Century England, II* (Woodbridge: Boydell Press, 2002), pp. 131–45.

view, neither the manhood of energy, of martial renown, or of social standing could be dissociated from the manhood accrued by faithfulness to one's word and the avoidance of double-dealing. Moreover, although Gower's use of 'manhood' in the *Confessio Amantis* suggests enthusiasm for the connotations of physical energy and moral rectitude which lay within the semantic range of 'manhood', he made only limited use of the associations of this term with largesse or vengeance, linking each to the 'manhood' of renown and social status only once, and then indirectly. To explore the significance of these findings, however, the 'view from above' provided by computer-aided discourse analysis is not enough, and we have to return to more traditional methods of close reading.

Pride and Social Status: Moderating Manhood

The theme of manhood and how it ought to be understood is considered most directly in Book I of the *Confessio Amantis*, which is concerned with the sin of pride. In this book, as in the discussion of chastity in Book VII, Gower does not simply deploy certain conventional uses of manhood and neglect others but rather actively seeks to impose a certain vision of manhood. Here he advocates a view of manhood which is opposed, quite conventionally, to duplicity and double-dealing, but he also seeks, more controversially, to impose limits on commonplace conceptions of manhood as a synonym for renown or social standing.

In the first tale illustrating the sin of pride, which is presented by Genius as an example of hypocrisy, the priests of Isis assist a duke in impersonating their god to allow him to have sex with Paulina, a virtuous and married noblewoman (I.761–1076). This tale is glossed as an illustration of the hypocrisy of the worldly priests (I.1023–1036). It is quickly followed with another tale of trickery: a variation on the tale of the Trojan Horse (I.1077–1189). This is portrayed as a lesson both not to trust 'such a peple' (I.1193) and for women to beware of men who feign their 'trowthe' (I.1199), a moral which resonates with the plight of Paulina. Nonetheless, Genius glosses these stories for the benefit of Amans as a lesson in the correct nature of manhood: 'Forthi, my Sone, as I thee mene, / It sit the wel to taken hiede / That thou eschuie of thi manhiede / Ipocrisie and his semblant' (I.1210–1213). 'Manhiede' here refers to honourable and trustworthy conduct and the avoidance of falseness. This vision of manhood is then developed as the discussion passes to the vice of disobedience which consists of not bowing to God, but instead following one's own will (I.1235–9). This is then developed, putting animality to the fore: 'Noght as a man bot as a beste, / Which goth upon his lustes wilde, / So goth this proude vice unmylde, / That he desdeigneth alle lawe' (I.1240–3). Being a 'man' as opposed to an animal means following 'the reule of conscience' and being sufficiently humble to obey God and, when appropriate, his fellow men (I.1244–1251).

The remainder of Book I of the *Confessio Amantis* deals with the more difficult issue of how to temper the need for honour and manhood in the sense of the need for the respect and recognition due to one's station. The tales which follow deal with this difficult balancing act for men of gentle, noble and, especially, kingly status: how to reconcile the necessary defence and display of one's own social status with the Christian requirement of humility. Gower next presents the 'Tale of Florent', his version of the story told by Chaucer as the 'Wife of Bath's Tale' (I.1407–1861).[46] Florent is a much more positive character than Chaucer's rapist knight, being a 'worthi knight' (I.1408) who seeks deeds of arms 'for the fame of worldes speche' (I.1415). He thus seeks the kind of 'manhood' pursued by the son of the emperor in Book II (II.2513–4), and which makes the Trojans think twice about making war on Greece in Book V (V.7337–8). Trapped by his enemies, Florent is tricked into trading his life against the solution to the question of '[w]hat alle wommen most desire' (I.1481), and finally agrees to marry a repulsive old woman in exchange for the answer. When the hag keeps her side of the bargain, Florent experiences the necessity of marrying her (which he must do to keep his word) primarily as a threat to his social status and honour. He smuggles her into his castle by night and marries her in the dark so that no one knows what she looks like (I.1727–1761). His honourable – in the sense of virtuous – conduct (keeping his word) forces him to run the gauntlet of dishonour in the sense of the disapprobation of the world. Yet the magical conclusion of this story defuses this contradiction. When Florent discovers that, by night, the hag is magically transformed into a beautiful eighteen-year-old, he is faced with a further conundrum: would he prefer her beautiful at night and ugly during the day, or vice versa? When Florent, in despair, submits to her will, he is delivered through his humility from the necessity of choosing between private and public fulfilment: his wife is transformed on a permanent basis into a beautiful woman, the daughter of a king (I.1821–61).

Book I follows a trajectory from pride to humility in a way which repeatedly touches on and seeks to moderate views of manhood as public honour and social status, specifically as a characteristic of knightly, noble men. The 'Tale of the Trump of Death', for example, begins as the 'wys and

---

[46] For a discussion of sources and different interpretations of this story, see Thomas Hahn, 'Old Wives' Tales and Masculine Intuition', in Thomas Hahn and Alan Lupack, eds, *Retelling Tales: Essays in Honor of Russell Peck* (Cambridge: D. S. Brewer, 1997), pp. 91–108. For a view which argues for Gower as the first person to put this tale into its present form, see Russell A. Peck, 'Folklore and Powerful Women in Gower's "Tale of Florent"', in S. Elizabeth Passmore and Susan Carter, eds, *The English 'Loathly Lady' Tales: Boundaries, Traditions and Motifs* (Kalamazoo: West Michigan University, 2007), pp. 100–45.

honeste' (I.2024) king of Hungary rides out of the city, surrounded by 'lordes and with gret nobleie / Of lusti folk that were yonge' (I.2032–3). As he does so, however, he sees two pilgrims 'of so gret age' that they look almost as if they were dead (I.2041–7). When they ask him for charity, the king gets down from his carriage, and takes them in his arms, kissing their hands and feet, in full view of the 'lordes of his lond', who do not look kindly on their monarch's humility. Murmur and disdain arise amongst them, and they say:

> 'Eche unto othre: 'What is this?
> Oure king hath do this thing amis,
> So to abesse his realte
> That every man it myhte se,
> And humbled him in such a wise
> To hem that were of non emprise' (I.2061–66).

Already in this opening passage it is clear that the king will triumph over the backbiters who think only of their 'oghne Pride' (I.2060). When the king's brother brings to his attention the muttering amongst his lords that 'he dede such a schame / In hindringe of his oghne name' (I.2095–6), he is humiliated by the king, who sounds before his door the trumpet that signals his death. Nonetheless, although I would not for a moment suggest that this is Gower's intended interpretation, it would have been possible to read this incident against its own explicit moral, since in terms of a number of contemporary conceptions of manhood, the murmuring courtiers certainly have a point. The story carries a clear moralistic interpretation from the outset – thinking on death ought to lead one to Christian humility – but at the same time it is acknowledged that abasing oneself to one's social inferiors could be perceived as humiliating. Kings who were not as politically secure as Hungarian kings of 'olde daies' (I.2023), and even more noblemen, knights or those less sure of their social status, had to be careful whose hands and feet they kissed, whatever the dictates of Christian morality.[47]

A slightly different approach to the need to reconcile forms of manhood related to personal status and honour with the virtue of humility occurs a little later in Book I in the 'Tale of Albinus and Rosamund'. This time, it is accepted that public honour is rightly associated with manly, military deeds. What goes wrong is that here the celebration of personal renown is

---

[47] This reading of the 'Tale of the Trump of Death' and the following readings of 'The Tale of Rosamund and Albinus' and the 'Tale of Nebuchadnezzar' differ from those recently proposed by T. Matthew N. McCabe, *Gower's Vulgar Tongue: Ovid, Lay Religion, and English Poetry in the Confessio Amantis* (Cambridge: D. S. Brewer, 2011), pp. 156–61. For reasons that will become clear, I think it would be incorrect to read 'manhood' as simply the nature of mankind in the sense of humankind. If, as McCabe argues, for theologians humility can be a 'natural' virtue for human beings, it is one which Gower has to recommend in the opposition to alternative interpretations of 'manhood'.

pushed to an exceptional extreme. At the beginning of this story, Albinus becomes king of Lombardy by defeating, amongst others, Gurmond, leader of the Geptes, whose skull he has made into a cup (I.2474–6). Then, once he has successfully conquered the entire country, Albinus marries Rosamund, Gurmond's daughter, since '[t]hei love ech other wonder wel' (I.1489). Now that he rules unchallenged, Albinus organises jousting and a feast, at which all the worthy knights speak of their deeds, inspiring the king to competitive boasting. Albinus calls for the cup, which is so covered in gold and jewels that it cannot be seen that it contains Gurmond's skull. He then bids his wife drink from it, saying 'Drink with thi fader, Dame' (I.2551). The king then tells her in front of all present that the cup was made from her father's skull. This leads Rosamund '[t]o vengen hire upon this man' for his 'despit / Of hire and of hire fader bothe' (I.2578, 2580–2581), and she duly conspires with her maid and the king's butler to have Albinus murdered. Yet, it has to be said that, until Albinus humiliated her by this public reminder of his killing of her father, Rosamund was quite prepared to accept him as her husband. This opens up the possibility of a more moderate attitude towards renown, in which social standing quite appropriately accrues through military victory – which, as we have seen, is implicitly accepted in the use of 'manhood' elsewhere in the *Confessio Amantis* – and that this well-merited reputation is only compromised by a very extreme form of boasting. Even as the manhood of renown is condemned for its excesses, the possibility of a more measured enjoyment of the social celebration of one's own military achievements remains an implicit possibility. Thus, in this tale, and in line with commonplace contemporary Aristotelianism, virtue can be found in moderation.[48] To that extent, Gower does acknowledge the legitimacy of manly honour, at least insofar as it is acquired by military deeds. The manhood of social status is not simply dismissed for its opposition to Christian humility, but is only condemned when it leads to the extreme, public humiliation of others, pushing them to violent revenge.

In the penultimate story against pride – the punishment of Nebuchadnezzar – an excessive attachment to the conventional associations of manhood is placed in more radical opposition to Christian humility.[49] Genius introduces the particular sub-sin which is to be targeted, in this case vainglory, by an attack on 'new', ever-changing fashions which an unambiguously male youth might adopt (I.2694–2702). Yet the tale which is used to condemn vainglory then takes the characterisation of this sin in a different direction. Nebuchadnezzar is so full of vainglory that he forgets that there is any god but him (I.2799–2801). He is warned in a dream of his imminent humiliation by God, who will take away his 'mannes herte' and replace it with a 'bestial' one.

---

[48] Stephen H. Rigby, 'Worthy but Wise? Virtuous and Non-Virtuous Forms of Courage in the Later Middle Ages', *Studies in the Age of Chaucer*, 35 (2013), 329–71; Fletcher, *Richard II*, pp. 68–71.

[49] Rigby, 'Worthy but Wise?', p. 358.

He will lose his 'mannes forme' and eat grass 'in the liknesse of a beste' for seven years (I.2921–5). His only hope is to give alms, do justice with mercy and pray for God's grace, but he does nothing of the sort, and his punishment duly falls. Nebuchadnezzar withdraws into the wild forest where he is transformed '[f]ro man into a bestes forme' (I.2961–72). The king grazes like an ox in a way which stresses not only his animality but his loss of superior status and its accoutrements. Where once he ate hot spices, now he eats cold grass; where once he drank wine, now he drinks from the well; where once he stayed in well-arrayed chambers, now he sleeps in a bush, having no pillow but the hard ground (I.2976–86). This continues until, after seven years, he eschews his vainglory, and, unable to speak, wails in a 'bestly' voice to heaven. Now that he is 'humble and tame' he receives God's mercy and is restored to '[h]is mannes forme' (I.3034). Like the fashionable young men who constantly transform their appearance, like so many chameleons (I.2698–2702), Nebuchadnezzar is transformed by his pride, but not into a man of honour and authority (as the young men hope) but into a beast.

A modern reader might be tempted to reduce the opposition between 'man' and 'beast' which runs through this story into 'human' and 'animal'.[50] Yet to do so would involve neglecting many of the late medieval resonances of 'manhood'. In this tale, the maleness of Gower's concerns is less evident than the socially situated nature of the issues he raises. It is possible that Gower might have argued that the moral he is presenting ought to apply to the whole human race, but in this story he draws lessons which are primarily adapted for an audience of men and, indeed, women of a certain rank: those who had the possibility of falling into the temptations of changing fashions, of consuming wine and spices, of sleeping on cushions, and of taking vainglorious pride in their authority and social status. All of this resonated strongly with contemporary commonplace assumptions about what 'manhood' was. The possibility of contradiction between some of these assumptions and the moral values espoused by Gower are brought out in a further paradox which Genius offers to Amans in the conclusion of this section: 'Forthi, my Sone, tak good hiede / So forto lede thi manhiede, / That thou ne be noght lich a beste' (I.3043–5). If 'manhood' simply meant 'humanity' this statement would be nonsensical since advising the lover to put a check on his humanity to stop him resembling an animal would be a contradiction in terms. But in the context of the full range of the associations of 'manhood' in late medieval culture, its links to personal status and its role as a synonym for honour, we can see how this moral works: true men needed to limit and control their 'manhood' as it was conventionally understood, lest they fall into animality.

Gower thus seeks to show that whilst men might start out by thinking that manhood lies in accruing the honour of deeds in war, as did Florent, they eventually learn that public approbation and private fulfilment are

---

[50] E.g. McCabe, *Gower's Vulgar Tongue*, p. 158.

won through submission to the will of another. Men might think that they lose manhood by humiliating themselves to their social inferiors, but in so doing they forget their mortality. Men might think that their manhood is promoted by boasting of their martial deeds and prowess, but such boasting leads to their downfall at the hands of those they humiliate. Men might think that manhood lies in their public authority, in the display of their station in life, in the clothes they wear and the food they eat, but if they do not acknowledge that all these come from God, then they are no better than animals. Although a contemporary Aristotelian moralist might argue that there is no contradiction here, simply the requirement to find a mean between two extremes, Gower does not seek to determine where such a mean might be found, but instead arranges his narrative to demonstrate the superiority of moral virtue over the social dictates of manhood. In Book I of the *Confessio*, after duplicity has been defined as a failure of manhood, the manhood of social status is portrayed either as something to be bridled by an insistence that all honour and virtue derives from God (a view which no late medieval person would have denied), or as something which is condemnable when taken to unimaginable extremes (making one's wife drink publicly from a cup made from the skull of her defeated father).

By such means, Gower seeks to impose his own interpretation of manhood, pushing aside genuine tensions between certain kinds of manhood and the dictates of Christian humility. Can a man really submit honourably to the will of a woman? Can a man really bow to his social inferiors without endangering his own status? Surely a man's military deeds do increase his honour, and he is quite right to celebrate them? Who is to judge when the clothing and lifestyle which pertains to nobility has been pushed to excess? Gower only comes close to providing a genuine accommodation in the case of military renown; for the rest the only guide to avoiding excessive display of one's social status is to acknowledge that this status comes from God. In the reality of social life, the moralised vision of manhood which Gower presents would have provided little help in reconciling the dictates of honour with those of Christian morality.

Vengeance, Justice and Politics

The delicate balancing act between the manhood of personal honour and the Christian requirement for humility was just one area in which Gower grappled directly with the question of how to create a moral manhood out of the raw material of its conventional associations. Another was his treatment of homicide, justice and vengeance in Book III of the *Confessio Amantis*, which discusses the sin of wrath. Analysis of this book has tended to focus on the tales which seem to criticise the excessive punishment of the crimes of lovers. Rather less commented upon has been the one story, the 'Tale of

Horestes', which stands out in the trajectory of this book in the sense that it argues for the necessity of extreme, exemplary violence and even a certain kind of vengeance in particular circumstances.[51] As we have seen, this tale had strong contemporary political resonances, yet it was composed before the consequences of the political crises of the 1380s had become fully apparent, and mobilised materials which could be used in different ways. The 'Tale of Horestes' suggests a very different reading of such events to the one which Gower would elaborate after the deposition of Richard II in 1399. As we shall see, in his *Cronica Tripertita* and in his revisions to certain passages in the *Vox Clamantis*, Gower portrayed Richard II, not as a man, but as a youth and even as an animal. This presentation was justified by Richard's duplicity, which, as we have seen, was set in opposition to 'manhood' both in contemporary language in general and in Gower's works in particular. Yet the 'Tale of Horestes' suggests how a different interpretation of the politics of the 1380s and 1390s could have been produced from within Gower's own works.

When Book III of the *Confessio Amantis* considered justice and mercy, it dealt with themes which were highly charged and which became even more so during the period of this poem's composition and immediate reception. At first, as one would expect given the way each book of the *Confessio Amantis* leads from a vice to its remedial virtue, Book III provides warning tales against excessive and uncontrolled indignation in response to the misdeeds of others. Many critics have commented on the 'Tale of Canace and Machaire', a story of incestuous love between two siblings brought up in close proximity, which is told in such a way as to condemn the excessive cruelty, induced by melancholy, of their father Eolus (III.143–360).[52] Similarly, in the story of Phoebus and Cornide, when the former learns of the sexual infidelity of the latter, it is his action in killing her which is presented as being at fault (III.783–817).[53] What has interested critics in Gower's telling of these tales has been the way they jar with Christian teaching on sexual morality, rather than with how they actually function within the structure of Book III.[54] For some this shows the potential openness of 'amoral Gower', for others it

---

[51] For earlier comments on this tale see Yoshiko Kobayashi, '*Principis Umbra*: Kingship, Justice and Pity in John Gower's Poetry', in Robert F. Yeager, ed., *On John Gower: Essays at the Millennium* (Kalamazoo: Medieval Institute Publications, 2007), pp. 71–103; Conrad van Dijk, 'Vengeance and the Legal Person: John Gower's *Tale of Orestes*', in Andreaa D. Boboc, ed., *Theorizing Legal Personhood in Late Medieval England* (Leiden: Brill, 2015), pp. 119–41.

[52] In an extensive bibliography, I have found useful Georgiana Donavin, '"When reson torneth into rage": Violence in Book III of the *Confessio Amantis*', in Yeager, *On John Gower*, pp. 216–34; Leff, 'Writing, Gender and Power', p. 35–8; Watt, 'Gender and Sexuality', pp. 198–9; Watt, *Amoral Gower*, pp. 82–3; Simpson, *Sciences and the Self*, pp. 176–7. See also the works cited by Watt, *Amoral Gower*, p. 164, n. 40.

[53] Donavin, '"When reson torneth"', pp. 220–1; Simpson, *Sciences and the Self*, pp. 177–8.

[54] Nicola F. McDonald, '"Lusti Tresor": Avarice and the Economics of the Erotic in Gower's *Confessio Amantis*', in Elizabeth M. Tyler, ed., *Treasure in the Medieval West* (York: York Medieval Press, 2000), pp. 135–56.

shows the unreliability and imperfection of the teachings of Genius.[55] Yet, in fact, these stories do accord with the general schema of Book III, notably in its unsympathetic attitude to Alexander, who is portrayed, in the 'Tale of Alexander and Diogenes' (III.1201–1330), as a man enslaved by his will and, in the 'Tale of Alexander and the Pirate', as a king who wages war purely out of a lust for worldly dominion (III.2363–2417). These themes are inherent in the structure of Book III and in Gower's larger moral project, and it would be wrong to suggest that they were introduced specifically in response to the political circumstances of the late 1380s. Nonetheless, certain tales did possess a particular contemporary relevance. The 'Tale of Demephon and Athemas', for example, in which two youthful kings swear vengeance on their rebellious people (III.1791–1860), must have seemed particularly pertinent during a period in which the king's allies had fought his noble opponents in the field. It was to be hoped that Richard II might, like them, be persuaded not to despoil his own realm, however just his cause.

The trajectory of Book III from wrath to mercy is disturbed by the 'Tale of Horestes', the only story to which Genius attaches a gloss advocating the necessity of just violence in response to a crime. What is more, although this tale precedes an explicit discussion of the legitimate homicide of criminals, it does not take place in a clearly judicial context. Horestes is a child when his father, Agamenon, returns from the Trojan wars and is slain '[b]e treson' in his bed by his wife Climestre and her lover Egistus (III.1919). Despite an opening Latin gloss which portrays this as being the tale of how 'Horestes then of minor estate counselled long afterwards with most cruel severity avenged himself',[56] in the actual body of the story Horestes' long-prepared vengeance is considered by all characters, except the guilty and their accomplices, to be fundamentally legitimate. Once Horestes, who has fled to the court of the king of Crete, has grown to be 'a man of brede and lengthe, / Of wit, of manhod and of strengthe' (III.1963–4), all parties rally round to provide him with the means to wage war against his mother and her lover and so '[t]o venge him at his oghne wille' (III.1957). The only hesitation concerns the specific punishment he exacts from his mother: killing her by ripping off her breasts. This is the act which turns vengeance into most cruel vengeance, but taking revenge in itself is not considered to be problematic by any of the tale's protagonists.

---

[55] Watt, 'Gender and Sexuality', pp. 198–9; Simpson, *Sciences and the Self*, p. 178.
[56] Latin gloss by l. 1885: 'cuius mortem filius eius Horestes tunc minoris etatis postea diis admonitus seueritate crudelissima vindicauit.' Kobayashi also finds hesitation in the suggestion at the beginning of the tale that Horestes 'wroghte mochel shame / In vengance of his fader deth.' (III.1960–1) and that, once he is a man, Horestes first sets out to pursue his cause 'As he that was in herte wroth' (III.1982). Both he and van Dijk, however, see this hesitation as overruled by the ensuing mission of exemplary vengeance conferred upon him by the gods, and which he regretfully accepts (Kobayashi, '*Principis Umbra*', pp. 93–4; van Dijk, 'Vengeance and the Legal Person', pp. 130–2).

The idea that the punishment visited upon Climestre might be excessive is first suggested by the fact that Horestes only agrees to it when he is told to exact it by the gods (III.2004–16). The gods do however justify their decision. The act's very cruelty is necessary to ensure its effectiveness:

> He was ansuerd, if that he wolde
> His astate recovere, thanne he scholde
> Upon his Moder do vengance
> So cruel, that the remembrance
> Therof mihte everemore abide,
> As sche that was an homicide
> And of hire oghne lord Moerdrice (III.1997–2003).

Faced with this logic of exemplary violence, Horestes reluctantly agrees to carry out the full and bloody vengeance he has been told to exact by the gods.

That such advice was provided by pagan gods could have provided Gower with a nice alibi, suggesting that such extreme vengeance, although acceptable before the coming of Christianity, could not be so thereafter. Yet, in the telling of the tale, this potential justification is not brought out, and instead it is implied that the logic of extreme violence reluctantly applied is also valid for Christians. Horestes' killing of his mother is preceded by a speech which resembles a judgement, in which she is condemned as a 'cruel beste unkinde' who slew 'thin oghne lord' and whose 'treson stant of such record, / Thou miht thi werkes noght forsake' (III.2055, 2059, 2060–1). Then, after Horestes kills her, the tale diverts into a discussion about how it is always so after some deed: every man has their own idea as to whether he acted rightly or wrongly (III.2112–30). Although this begins as opinion about whether it is right or wrong to kill one's own mother in this fashion, this is quickly diverted into uncertainty about the facts of the case. What matters in public opinion is not differing attitudes to the morality of Horestes' behaviour but rather each individual's precise or imprecise knowledge of events (III.2118–9). The way to resolve this is to call a 'parlement ... To nowe hou that the sothe was' (III.2130, 2133). Individual opinion about the morality of extreme judicial violence is less important than the reconstruction of a precise account of events. By this means, Horestes is unanimously let off. At the parliament, Horestes re-introduces his defence: the gods ordered him to do justice with his own hand (III.2139–42). In a moment, his act is justified since, as one lord, Menesteüs, argues, 'The wreeche which Horestes dede, / It was thing of goddes bede, / And nothing of his crualte' (III.2147–9). He offers combat to anyone who thinks otherwise, and nobody dares to contradict him. The subsequent suicide of 'false Egiona', daughter of Egistus and Climestre and party to the murder of Agamenon, is presented not as a consequence of the inadequacy of this judgement, but as her own fault for having been involved in her father's killing (III.2172–95).[57]

In glossing this story, in reply to Amans' question as to whether it is ever legitimate to kill a man, Genius declares that violence in an unjust cause is wrong (III.2241–2362). This is not such a ringing declaration as might be supposed, since Gower had already argued, in the *Vox Clamantis*, that the king ought to fight his enemies – following the example of his father, the Black Prince – if 'the faculty of necessity' demanded it (VC: VI.13.917–84). Indeed, Genius himself goes on to specify two general cases in which violence is always legitimate. The first of these, to defend one's home and country, is dealt with in a few lines (CA: III.2235–40). The second is treated in greater detail: violence to punish criminals is not only virtuous but compulsory (III.2201–34). Citing Seneca, Genius declares that the judge who spares one 'schrewe' grieves a thousand good men (III.2219–20). As we have seen, Gower would return to this theme in Book VII of the *Confessio Amantis*, declaring that to restrain violence in justice or in war is not pity but pusillanimity: 'For if manhode be restreigned, / Or be it pes or be it werre, / Justice goth al out of here' (VII.3540–42). Indeed, this was a theme which he had already elaborated in the *Mirour de l'Omme* in which the just judge Pité dispenses the sanction of death, all whilst regretting that the condemned '[a]d deservi d'estre tué' (MO: 13944).[58]

This insistence upon the necessity of judicial retribution marks a departure from the implications of many of the tales of justice and violence contained in Book III, and indeed from the overall structural trajectory of this book, which leads from wrath to the correcting power of mercy. At first sight it might also be thought to contradict that strand of late medieval thinking which recommended legal process over self-help as a response to crime. This tradition was represented, for example, by Albertanus of Brescia's *Liber consolationis et consilii* (1246), which was adapted into French in the mid-fourteenth century by Renaud de Louens as the *Livre de Melibée et Dame Prudence* and translated by Chaucer as the 'Tale of Melibee'.[59] In Chaucer's telling, Dame Prudence firmly advises her husband, a 'yong man ... myghty and riche', against taking vengeance himself on those who attacked his house, herself and his daughter.[60] He should instead follow due process of law, as a formidable range of authorities recommend. Nonetheless, this does not exclude the possibility of taking matters into one's own hands if formal

---

[57] Van Dijk, 'Vengeance and the Legal Person', concentrates on the case of Egiona, who is condemned by Genius in a way not found in Gower's sources. It seems reasonable to accept his view that Gower thus seeks to tie up loose ends, and ensure the exemplarity of Horestes' actions.

[58] Kobayashi, '*Principis Umbra*', pp. 71, 77.

[59] The tradition is discussed in *The Riverside Chaucer*, ed. Larry D. Benson (third edition; Oxford: Oxford University Press, 1987), p. 923.

[60] Geoffrey Chaucer, 'The Tale of Melibee', VII: 967.

mechanisms were wanting. Melibee's fault is to reach for his sword before seeking justice through the law. Similarly, when Genius remarked in his gloss on the 'Tale of Demephon and Athemas' that one should 'do nothing be myht, / Which mai be do be love and riht' (III.1859–60), this did not exclude the possibility that, love and right not being available, might and right would do just as well. The 'Tale of Horestes' is not, therefore, incompatible with formal justice as it was conceived of in the late fourteenth century. Horestes' act is finally made acceptable by the legitimate authority which stands behind it: that of the gods, whom he reluctantly obeys. Moreover, although critics have not drawn attention to this, probably because it is not explicitly stated by Gower, Horestes as his father's son is also the legitimate king of his country: he thus has every right to judge his mother. As Gower stressed in the *Vox Clamantis*, the king must execute justice in accordance with law, even though on earth he answers to no one, being subject only to the correction of God (VC: VI.8.581–642). Since he follows the orders of the gods, this is indeed what Horestes is doing. Even though there is a moment of public doubt following the execution of this judgement, which is also an act of vengeance, a parliament serves to clear matters up after the fact.

Whilst it would be wrong to read the 'Tale of Horestes' as either a commentary on contemporary events or as an attempt to intervene in them, it cannot be denied that the themes which it raises were of central political importance not only at the time it was written but also in the years that followed. The 'Tale of Horestes' taught a ruler such as Richard II, to whom the first recension of the *Confessio Amantis* was addressed, that whilst divine approval was the only guarantee of legitimate justice, he as king had every right to decide whether that approval was forthcoming or not and had a duty to act if he believed it was. He should justify his actions using legal mechanisms, but should not hesitate to execute justice in a way which anticipated legal process, especially in cases involving treason. This could include doing justice on those whose treason lay in their efforts to force the king to act against his own will, and thus to humiliate and dishonour him. In this way the requirements of the manhood of personal honour and the need for vengeance could be reconciled if the person avenging himself was the king. This was precisely what Richard II was to do in 1397–99, using pre-emptive violence mixed with parliamentary judicial process against those who had humiliated him and murdered his closest counsellors ten years previously.[61]

The moral of the 'Tale of Horestes' could thus have provided Gower with a means of defending Richard's actions in the last two years of his reign, presenting him as a king and a man who had avenged himself in accordance with divine justice. Indeed, this was precisely how Richard portrayed his own actions in a letter to Albert of Bavaria, count of Holland and Zeeland,

---

[61] Fletcher, *Richard II*, pp. 249–79.

after moving against his enemies in 1397.⁶² The king thanked God who had protected him from the cradle against those nobles, whom he himself had raised to honour, who had conspired treacherously whilst he was of tender age to disinherit the Crown and usurp royal rights. They had raised themselves in arms against the king's will. Taking royal authority upon themselves, they had condemned those faithful to the king to a public death. They had left him with hardly anything beyond his title, going so far as to threaten his person. Now, at last, he had brought them to justice.⁶³

Yet, in practice, when Gower composed his own version of the story of Richard II's rule, in the aftermath of his deposition in 1399, he let no suggestion emerge that the king's actions might be viewed in these terms. Instead, in his revisions to the *Vox Clamantis* and in its continuation, the *Cronica Tripertita*, Gower set the politics of the reign into an ethical schema which obscured the real origins of political instability in the 1380s.⁶⁴ In this schema, Richard's failure was first of all a failure to cultivate the right kind of manhood. In the revised Book VI of the *Vox Clamantis*, Gower declares that 'the king, an undisciplined boy, neglects the moral behaviour by which a man might grow up from a boy' (VC: VI.7.555–6). Here, the political instability of the 1380s was not presented as being the result of lack of consensus over military strategy, of unwillingness to grant taxation in the aftermath of the Peasants' Revolt, and of controversy over acceptable forms of governance, but was rather an expression of the king's desire to despoil, not even the

---

[62] British Library, Cotton MS Galba B.i, f. 22, printed in John H. Harvey, 'The Wilton Diptych – A Re-examination', *Archaeologia*, 98 (1961), pp. 1–28.
[63] *Ibid*.
[64] In three of the four earliest manuscripts which contain both the *Vox Clamantis* and the *Cronica Tripertita* (Oxford, All Souls MS 98; Glasgow, Hunterian Museum MS T.2, 17; British Library, Harleian MS 6291), the modifications to book VI.545–80 are written in, over erasures, in the same hand as the *Cronica Tripertita* but in a different hand from the rest of the *Vox Clamantis* (Macaulay, *Latin Works*, pp. lxi, lxiii, lxv). In the other manuscript which contains both the *Vox* and the *Cronica* (British Library, Cotton MS Tiberius A.iv) the corrections to Book I of the *Vox* have been added in a different hand from the text, and the text of the *Cronica* follows in yet another hand (Macaulay, *Latin Works*, pp. lxiii–lxiv). Of the three MSS which contain the *Vox Clamantis* and its revisions, but not the *Cronica Tripertita*, only one might support the hypothesis of a pre-deposition revision (the Ecton MS, described by Macaulay, p. lxvi), although Macaulay only ventures to suggest that it might possibly date before 1402. Both the Ecton MS, and the much later Digby MS 138 and Laud MS 719, could have been copied from MSS which once contained the *CT*. This, together with the way the themes of these revisions and those of the *CT* coalesce, seem to me to provide adequate grounds to propose a post-1399 date for both. On the close reliance of the *Cronica Tripertita* on the 'Record and Process' of Richard II's deposition for its telescoped and tendentious account of the reign, see David R. Carlson, 'The Parliamentary Sources of Gower's *Cronica Tripertita* and Incommensurable Styles' in Dutton, Hines and Yeager, *John Gower, Trilingual Poet*, pp. 98–111. For alternative views on these issues, see, Michael Bennett, below, p. 443.

common people, but the earls of Gloucester, Arundel and Warwick.[65] It was thus simply in self-defence that these lords 'arose manlily' (*viriliter insurrexerunt*).[66]

As the argument is developed in the *Cronica Tripertita*, the king, forsaking love, transgressed the law, and so the people rose up (I.4). The king, who always had a hard heart, followed vile, youthful counsel and so decided to make accusations against certain nobles, simply in order that he might despoil them (I.17–18). Luckily the king's partisans were defeated in battle by the duke of Gloucester, which sets the scene for 'the three men who were full of good sense (*pleni ... racione*)' (i.e. Gloucester, Arundel and Warwick) to seek for justice (I.121–2). Much as the nobles of Greece had done when murmuring arose about Horestes' actions, they called a parliament 'so that they might cleanse and repair the state of the realm' (I.128–30). This parliament executed and exiled the king's wicked counsellors: 'Gone was the flatterer, the villain, the plotter, the false counsellor, the schemer, the envious promoter' (I.202–3). The laudable aim of the three nobles was, like that of Gower himself, to reform the king's morality, and hence the kingdom: 'Thus they moulded a reformed, reinvigorated king' (*Sic emendatum Regem faciunt renouatum*) (I.210).

Yet it would soon become clear that better moral guidance was no solution, and for Gower this could only have been the result of the king's own recalcitrance. In particular, Gower's Richard II lacks one of the fundamental qualities of manhood insisted upon in the *Confessio Amantis*: he is false, untrustworthy and treacherous. Consequently, he lacks the 'manhood' of honourable conduct which was an essential bulwark to the 'manhood' of energy, vigour and military renown. Describing what is never portrayed as revenge, the *Cronica* instead describes how:

> 'The false, two-faced King feigned all things and hid his plottings with deceit (*dolos sub fraude tegebat*), although his ruin lay hiding in wait' (II.7–8).

Throughout the second part of the *Cronica Tripertita*, Gower insists on Richard's 'dolus', his double-dealing, fraud or deceit:

> 'O the deceit, and O the treachery, which the King had so long repressed, when the man unique in dissimulation poured forth wickedness' (II.23–4).

In the terms of the *Confessio Amantis*, Richard in the *Cronica Tripertita* is presented as the very model of 'Ypocrisie', which ought to be eschewed for

---

[65] See the Epilogue linking the *Vox Clamantis* to the *Cronica Tripertita* (Gower, *Complete Works*, IV, p. 313).
[66] *Ibid*. My translation.

manhood (CA: I.1210–13), and as the kind of man who, like an unfaithful husband, loses his manhood by failing to keep his word (VII.4228–30).

Richard's revenge is portrayed as long hidden and unexpected in its violence. First, 'like a whirlwind the violent young man made attack upon the rejected Swan [the duke of Gloucester], even while it thought itself at peace' (CT: II.27–8). '[F]iercer than the wolf' (II.36), the king apprehended the duke in his own home, before taking him away to be murdered in captivity in Calais. Then, 'with hidden guile in his spirit' (*conspirat fraude latente*) (II.54) Richard failed to honour charters of pardon granted to the earl of Arundel (II.126–30). The earl was condemned to death by 'other false men (*fallaces alii*), knights who came forth as followers of the king, who were neither honourable nor merciful' (II.139–40). Finally, the earl of Warwick, told that he will be forgiven if he admits all, was tricked into confessing and sent into exile on the Isle of Man: 'O! How clever this juvenile, violent piece of trickery (*fraus iuuenilis*) then appeared!' (II.165). The king is not only a youth, and therefore not fully a man, but also, like Nebuchadnezzar, both a tyrant and an animal:

> 'O woe for that year in which haughtiness abounded in the tyrant! That wild beast (*ferus*), so to speak, crushed those whom he wished (*voluit quos vincere, vicit*)' (II.282–3).

Gower concludes the second part of the *Cronica Tripertita* by praising the military accomplishments of Gloucester, Arundel and Warwick (II.326–9). He then seeks to underline, like the old soldier who petitioned Julius Caesar in Book VII of the *Confessio*, the wickedness of the ruler who fails to honour his own veterans:

> 'Alas, King, you who have betrayed such associates (*qui tales fraudasti collaterales*), may a ruinous destiny finally be your punishment!' (II.330–1).

For Gower in the *Cronica Tripertita*, Richard II cannot be a man because of his untrustworthy nature: he says one thing and secretly plots another. Nonetheless, what he secretly plots is not so removed from a different side of manhood. What he wants is revenge, which he would have perceived as justice, on those who had usurped the authority of the Crown, killed his friends and threatened the person of the king himself some ten years before. Thus, if Richard had been victorious, Gower could have written a work commending his actions in the same terms as he had sympathetically portrayed Horestes. For Gower, the just ruler should not take retribution in hot blood or in the sway of unreasonable passions. But then again, he must exact just retribution for crime, regretfully, in accordance with divine teaching, using judicial assemblies if necessary to confirm retrospectively the rectitude of his actions. For Gower, the wise man tempers his manhood so as not to be like a beast. But no man, in the real politics of the 1380s and 1390s, could safely turn the other cheek. John Gower's readers would have found no easy answers here simply because, in the highly disturbed political world of the late fourteenth century, such answers did not exist.

Manhood and Morality: Theory and Practice

In the *Confessio Amantis*, John Gower seeks to shape a certain kind of moral personality which is also a kind of manhood. The poet thus wholeheartedly embraces the broader associations of manhood with energy and vigour, with knightly courage and with military renown. He was keen, however, to stress how manly honour must be supported by honourable conduct, by the avoidance of falseness, duplicity and double-dealing. When he considers manhood explicitly, he tries to promote some of its associations and to palliate others, and he specifically attempts to limit the manhood of honour in the sense of personal status. Although he broadly seeks to temper wrath, he insists that retributive violence coolly exacted in a just cause is not only admissible but compulsory. Yet although Gower leaves a clear impression of the kind of manhood of which he approved in terms of personality and ethics, less clear is how his strictures might be applied to concrete social and political practice. The range of the themes he considered, the complexity of the framing structures of his works and the sheer variety of the narrative materials he used meant that he provided material which could be used to support and to condemn precisely the same line of action. Like many a public moralist, before and since, Gower could always have it both ways.

PART V

GOWER AND POLITICS

CHAPTER 12

POLITICAL THEORY

Stephen H. Rigby

'Absolutist' versus 'Constitutionalist' Gower

At one time, partly due to the influence of K. B. McFarlane's work on the English nobility, studies of late medieval English political life tended to focus on the private concerns, personal connections and individual interests of the king, magnates and gentry and, above all, on competition for patronage.[1] As a result, the role of ideas and values as causes of political action was often neglected, even though McFarlane himself warned against seeing medieval political choices as being entirely venal in their motivation.[2] More recently, however, historians have emphasised the significance of ideas and values within late medieval politics and have turned their attention to the political language of the period. Following Quentin Skinner's view of normative language as constituting one of the 'determinants' of political action, 'new constitutionalist' historians such as Christine Carpenter, Edward Powell and John Watts have presented the political principles which were available in late medieval England as being one of the determinants of the range of actions that was available to political agents, not least by constraining their

---

In writing this chapter, I have benefitted immensely from the comments and encouragement of Michael Bennett, Charles Briggs, Rosalind Brown-Grant, Gwilym Dodd, Siân Echard, Chris Fletcher, Chris Given-Wilson, Elliott Kendall, David Matthews, Sebastian Sobecki, Fiona Somerset and Robert Yeager. I am also grateful to Matthew Giancarlo and Nigel Saul, not only for their advice but also for allowing me to see forthcoming papers prior to publication. As always, particular thanks are owed to Robert C. Nash for the many stylistic and structural improvements which he suggested to my text.

[1] See, for instance, Kenneth B. McFarlane, *Lancastrian Kings and Lollard Knights* (Oxford: Clarendon Press, 1972), pp. 24–6, 226.
[2] Kenneth B. McFarlane, *The Nobility of Later Medieval England* (Oxford: Clarendon Press, 1973). pp. 287–95; Christine Carpenter, 'Introduction: Political Culture, Politics and Cultural History', in Linda Clark and Christine Carpenter, eds, *The Fifteenth Century, Volume IV: Political Culture in Late Medieval Britain* (Woodbridge: Boydell Press, 2014), pp. 1–19, at 1, 8.

freedom of manoeuvre in their attempts to justify themselves and to win the support of others.³ In the words of Laura Slater, political thought should be seen as 'a motivating force or explanatory principle for political action, and as a determining influence on its outcome'.⁴ As Michael Bennett said, despite the central part played by the Lancastrian and other magnate affinities in bringing about the deposition of Richard II, if we are to understand the 'revolution' of 1399, it is also 'necessary to take seriously the role of ideas'.⁵ Here both abstract theory, including the Aristotelian definition of tyranny, as well as more everyday assumptions about the relationship between the king and the political community, such as the belief that the monarch's will was limited by the common law and by his subjects' property rights, were key factors in generating opposition to Richard II.⁶ This renewed focus on the role of ideas in political life has led historians to study not only the language found in factional manifestos, parliamentary petitions and mirrors for princes but also that which was used in political songs and – of particular importance in our context – in public poetry and imaginative literature.⁷

The centrality of politics to Gower's poetry, his engagement with the ethical and political views which he found in works such as the Pseudo-Aristotelian *Secretum Secretorum*, Giles of Rome's *De Regimine Principum*

---

3   Quentin Skinner, 'Language and Social Change', in James Tully, ed., *Meaning and Context: Quentin Skinner and his Critics* (Princeton: Princeton University Press, 1988), pp. 119–32, at 132; John Watts, *Henry VI and the Politics of Kingship* (Cambridge: Cambridge University Press, 1996), p. 7; John Watts, *The Making of Polities; Europe, 1300–1500* (Cambridge: Cambridge University Press, 2009), pp. 130–1; Edward Powell, 'After "After McFarlane": The Poverty of Patronage and the Case for Constitutional History', in Dorothy J. Clayton, Richard G. Davies and Peter McNiven, eds, *Trade, Devotion and Governance: Papers in Later Medieval History* (Stroud: Alan Sutton, 1994), pp. 1–6, at 10–11. See also Christine Carpenter, 'Political and Constitutional History: Before and After McFarlane', in Richard H. Britnell and Anthony J. Pollard, eds, *The McFarlane Legacy: Studies in Late Medieval Politics and Society* (Stroud: Alan Sutton, 1995), pp. 175–206, at 191–6; Michael Hicks, *English Political Culture in the Fifteenth Century* (London: Routledge, 2002), pp. 5–6; W. Mark Ormrod, '"Common Profit" and "The Profit of the King and Kingdom": Parliament and the Development of Political Language in England, 1250–1450', *Viator*, 46 (2015), pp. 219–52, at 219–20; Gerald Harriss, *Shaping the Nation: England, 1360–1461* (Oxford: Clarendon Press, 2005), p. 13; Alison K. Gundy, *Richard II and the Rebel Earl* (Cambridge: Cambridge University Press, 2013), pp. 13–17.
4   Laura Slater, *Art and Political Thought in England, c.1150–1350* (Woodbridge: Boydell Press, 2018), pp. 8–10, 75 (quotation at p. 8).
5   Michael Bennett, 'Henry Bolingbroke and the Revolution of 1399', in Gwilym Dodd and Douglas Biggs, eds, *Henry IV: The Establishment of the Regime, 1399–1406* (York: York Medieval Press, 2003), pp. 9–33, at 25.
6   Caroline M. Barron, 'The Tyranny of Richard II', *Bulletin of the Institute of Historical Research*, 41 (1968), pp. 1–18, at 1–2, 17; Bennett, 'Henry Bolingbroke and the Revolution of 1399', pp. 10–17, 24–31.
7   Richard W. Kaeuper, 'Debating Law, Justice and Constitutionalism', in Richard W. Kaeuper, ed., *Law, Governance and Justice: New Views on Medieval Constitutionalism* (Leiden: Brill, 2013), pp. 1–14, at 3–6.

and Brunetto Latini's *Li Livres dou Tresor*,[8] and the support for the deposition of Richard II which he expressed in his later works means that his political outlook has attracted much attention from modern scholars.[9] Nevertheless, as yet, there is little consensus about the nature of Gower's political views. For some commentators, Gower was a proponent of strong, unqualified or even 'absolutist' kingship in which the ruler, exempt from any external restraint and limited only by his own conscience, was owed unconditional obedience by his subjects and was 'free towards all other than God'.[10] By contrast, others interpret Gower as having rejected absolutism in favour of 'constitutionalism' or of an 'Aristotelian limited monarchy' and as being closer in his outlook to the republican Brunetto Latini than to the 'absolutist' Giles of Rome. In this reading of Gower's work, he is seen as stressing the role of parliament and of counsel in mediating between the king and his subjects, as presenting the ruler as being subject to indictment by the political community, and as siding with those contemporaries who opposed the arbitrary use of royal power.[11]

---

[8] For editions of these sources, see *Secretum Secretorum cum Glossis et Notulis*, ed. Robert Steele (Oxford: Oxford University Press, 1920); *Egidio Colonna (Aegidius Romanus), De Regimine Principum Libri III* (Darmstadt: Scientia Verlag, 1967); Brunetto Latini, *The Book of the Treasure (Li Livres dou Tresor)*, eds Paul Barrette and Spurgeon Baldwin (New York: Garland Publishing, 1993). References to the *De Regimine Principum* below are, unless otherwise stated, from the Middle English translation by John Trevisa (*The Governance of Kings and Princes: John Trevisa's Middle English Translation of the De Regimine Principum of Aegidius Romanus*, eds David C. Fowler, Charles F. Briggs and Paul G. Remley (New York: Garland Publishing, 1997)) which, unlike the medieval French translation by Henri De Gauchi (*Li Livres du Gouvernement des Rois: A XIIIth Century French Version of Egidio Colonna's Treatise De Regimine Principum*, ed. S. P. Molenaer (New York: Macmillan, 1899)), retains the book, part and chapter divisions of the Latin original.

[9] For a useful survey, see Matthew Giancarlo, 'Gower's Courts', in *RRC*, pp. 150–7, at 152–4.

[10] Nigel Saul, 'John Gower: Prophet or Turncoat?', in Elizabeth Dutton, with John Hines and Robert F. Yeager, eds, *John Gower, Trilingual Poet: Language, Translation and Tradition* (Cambridge: D. S. Brewer, 2010), pp. 86–97, at 93; Elliott Kendall, *Lordship and Literature: John Gower and the Politics of the Great Household* (Oxford: Clarendon Press, 2008), pp. 243, 252–3, 261; Larry Scanlon, *Narrative, Authority and Power: The Medieval Exemplum and the Chaucerian Tradition* (Cambridge: Cambridge University Press, 1994), pp. 264–6, 283, 286, 289–90, 293–6; Patrica J. Eberle, 'The Question of Authority and the Man of Law's Tale', in Robert A. Taylor, *et al.*, eds, *The Centre and its Compass: Studies in Medieval Literature in Honor of Professor John Leyerle* (Kalamazoo: Western Michigan University, 1993), pp. 111–49, at 117–19; Harriss, *Shaping the Nation*, p. 7.

[11] George R. Coffman, 'John Gower in his Most Significant Role', in Edward Vasta, ed., *Middle English Survey: Critical Essays* (Notre Dame: University of Notre Dame Press, 1965 (first published 1945)), pp. 217–31, at 223, 225; James Simpson, *Sciences and the Self in Medieval Poetry: Alan of Lille's Anticlaudianus and John Gower's Confessio Amantis* (Cambridge: Cambridge University Press, 1995), pp. 224–6, 229, 270–1, 273–94; María Bullón-Fernández, *Fathers and Daughters in Gower's Confessio Amantis: Authority, Family, State and Writing* (Cambridge: D. S. Brewer, 2000), pp. 27–8, 61, 99–100, 153–4, 162–4; María Bullón-Fernández, 'Engendering Authority: Father and

In turn, the existence of such polarised interpretations of Gower's work relates to wider debates about the overall consistency of the poet's moral and philosophical outlook.[12] For some scholars, there is an underlying unity and coherence to Gower's world view as it appears within his individual works and even across his major poems. This was, after all, the view of his work which Gower himself set out in *Quia Unusquisque*, the colophon found in some of the manuscripts of the *Vox Clamantis* and the *Confessio Amantis* (ll. 1–4), and which his tomb effigy, with the poet's head resting on his three major works, also advertised.[13] For others, by contrast, Gower's works, particularly

---

Daughter, State and Church in Gower's Tale of Constance and Chaucer's Man of Law', in Robert F. Yeager, ed., *Re-Visioning Gower* (Asheville: Pegasus Press, 1998), pp. 129–46, at 131, 142–6; Judith Ferster, *Fictions of Advice: The Literature and Politics of Counsel in Late Medieval England* (Philadelphia: University of Pennsylvania Press, 1996), p. 132; Lynn Staley, *Languages of Power in the Age of Richard II* (University Park: The Pennsylvania State University Press, 2005), pp. 35–8; Anne W. Astell, *Political Allegory in Late Medieval England* (Ithaca: Cornell University Press, 1999), pp. 83–93; Robert F. Yeager, 'Gower's Lancastrian Affinity: The Iberian Connection', *Viator*, 35 (2004), pp. 483–516, at 511; Matthew Giancarlo, 'Gower's Governmentality: Revisiting John Gower as a Constitutional Thinker and Regiminal Writer', in Russell A. Peck and Robert F. Yeager, eds, *John Gower: Others and the Self* (Cambridge: D. S. Brewer, 2017), pp. 225–59, at 228, 234; Sebastian Sobecki, *Unwritten Verities: The Making of England's Vernacular Legal Culture* (Notre Dame: University of Notre Dame Press, 2015), pp. 84–7; Andrew Galloway, 'Gower's Quarrel with Chaucer, and the Origins of Bourgeois Didacticism', in Annette Harder, Alasdair A. Macdonald and Gerrit J. Reinink, eds, *Calliope's Classroom: Studies in Didactic Poetry from Antiquity to the Renaissance* (Paris: Peeters, 2007), pp. 245–67, at 260; Rosemarie McGerr, 'Gower's *Confessio Amantis* and the *Nova Statuta Angliae*: Royal Lessons in English Law', *Revista de Filología Inglesa*, 33 (2012), pp. 45–65, at 54–65; Conrad Van Dijk, '"Nede Hath No Lawe": The State of Exception in Langland and Gower', *Accessus*, 2/2 (2015), pp. 1–44, at 33.

[12] Roger A. Ladd, 'Review of Conrad van Dijk's *John Gower and the Limits of the Law*', *The Medieval Review*, 15.10.34. For guidance to these debates on the coherence of Gower's outlook, see Denise N. Baker, 'The Priesthood of Genius: A Study of the Medieval Tradition', in Peter Nicholson, ed., *Gower's Confessio Amantis: A Critical Anthology* (Cambridge: D. S. Brewer, 1991), pp. 143–57, at 143–5; Gregory M. Sadlek, *Idleness Working: The Discourse of Love's Labour from Ovid through Chaucer and Gower* (Washington: The Catholic University of America Press, 2004), pp. 170–1; Peter Nicholson, 'Irony v Paradox in the *Confessio Amantis*', in Dutton, Hines and F. Yeager, *John Gower, Trilingual Poet*, pp. 206–16, at 206; Conrad Van Dijk, *John Gower and the Limits of the Law* (Cambridge: D. S. Brewer, 2013), pp. 8–10; Simpson, *Sciences and the Self in Medieval Poetry*, pp. 135–8; Steele Nowlin, *Chaucer, Gower and the Affect of Invention* (Columbus: Ohio State University Press, 2016), pp. 95, 108.

[13] George R. Coffman, 'John Gower, Mentor for Royalty: Richard II', *Proceedings of the Modern Language Association*, 69 (1954), pp. 953–64, at 964; Thomas J. Hatton, 'The Role of Venus and Genius in John Gower's *Confessio Amantis*: A Reconsideration', *Greyfriars*, 16 (1975), pp. 29–40; Anne Middleton, 'The Idea of Public Poetry in the Reign of Richard II', *Speculum*, 52 (1978), pp. 94–114, at 98; Matthew W. Irvin, *The Poetic Voices of John Gower: Politics and Personae in the Confessio Amantis* (Cambridge: D. S. Brewer, 2014), pp. 4–5; *John Gower: Poems on Contemporary Events. The Visio Anglie (1381) and Cronica Tripertita (1400)*, eds David R. Carlson and Arthur G.

the *Confessio Amantis* with its multiple voices and the problematic figure of Genius, the priest of Venus, are inconsistent, incoherent, elusive or contradictory in their moral teachings. In turn, whilst some critics judge such inconsistencies to be a failure on Gower's part, others read them as an indication that, rather than providing easy answers to the questions which he raises, the poet was dialogically inviting his readers to engage with the range of competing discourses with which his text presented them.[14] How,

---

Rigg (Oxford: Bodleian Library, 2011), p. 5; Donald Schueler, 'The Age of the Lover in Gower's *Confessio Amantis*', *Medium Aevum*, 36 (1967), pp. 152–8, at 152, 158; Bruce Harbert, 'The Myth of Tereus in Ovid and Gower', *Medium Aevum*, 41 (1972), pp. 208–14, at 208; Robert S. Edwards, 'Gower's Second Cursus', in Ana Sáez-Hidalgo and Robert F. Yeager, eds, *John Gower in England and Iberia: Manuscripts, Influences, Reception* (Cambridge: D. S. Brewer, 2014), pp. 141–52, at 142–4; John H. Fisher, *John Gower: Moral Philosopher and Friend of Chaucer* (Methuen: London, 1965), p. 203; Dhira B. Mahoney, 'Gower's Two Prologues to the *Confessio Amantis*', in Yeager, *Re-Visioning Gower*, pp. 17–37, at 26–7; Nigel Saul, 'John Gower: Prophet or Turncoat?', in Dutton, with Hines and Yeager, *John Gower, Trilingual Poet*, pp. 86–97, at 91; Rita Copeland, *Rhetoric, Hermeneutics and Translation in the Middle Ages* (Cambridge: Cambridge University Press, 1991), pp. 203–20; Alastair Minnis, '"Moral Gower" and Medieval Literary Theory', in Alastair Minnis, ed., *Gower's Confessio Amantis: Responses and Reassessments* (Cambridge: Boydell and Brewer, 1983), pp. 79–105, at 91, 101; Elizabeth Porter, 'Gower's Ethical Microcosm and Political Macrocosm', *Ibid.*, pp. 135–62; Charles Runacres, 'Art and Ethics in the "Exempla" of "Confessio Amantis"', *Ibid.*, pp. 106–34, at 106, 114; Minnis, 'John Gower, *Sapiens* in Ethics and Politics', in Nicholson, *Gower's Confessio Amantis*, pp. 158–80, at 162, 165–8, 175; Katherine R. Chandler, 'Memory and Unity in Gower's *Confessio Amantis*', *Philological Quarterly*, 71 (1992), pp. 15–30; Paul Strohm, 'Form and Social Statement in the *Confessio Amantis* and the *Canterbury Tales*', *Studies in the Age of Chaucer*, 1 (1979), pp. 17–40, at 19–20, 27–30; Robert F. Yeager, *John Gower's Poetic: The Search for a New Arion* (Cambridge: D. S. Brewer, 1990), pp. 200–1; Carole Weinberg, 'Introduction', in *John Gower: Selected Poetry*, ed. Carole Weinberg (Manchester: Carcanet, 1983), pp. 7–23, at 12; Robert Edwards, *Invention and Authorship in Medieval England* (Columbus: Ohio State University Press, 2017), pp. 64–5, 77, 94, 99–101.

[14] Clive S. Lewis, *The Discarded Image: A Study in Medieval Tradition* (Oxford: Oxford University Press, 1936), pp. 219–21; David Aers, *Faith, Ethics and Church: Writing in England, 1360–1409* (Cambridge: D. S. Brewer, 2000), pp. 102–18; Theresa Tinkle, *Medieval Venuses and Cupids: Sexuality, Hermeneutics and English Poetry* (Stanford: Stanford University Press, 1996), pp. 181–5, 191–2, 197; Diane Watt, *Amoral Gower: Language, Sex and Politics*, pp. xii–xviii, 17, 21, 24, 28, 35, 64, 81, 151, 153, 156–9; Hugh White, 'Division and Failure in Gower's *Confessio Amantis*', *Neophilologus*, 72 (1988), pp. 600–16; James Simpson, 'Ironic Incongruence in the Prologue and Book I of Gower's *Confessio Amantis*', *Neophilologus*, 72 (1988), pp. 617–32; Winthrop Wetherbee, 'Latin Structure and Vernacular Space: Gower, Chaucer and the Boethian Tradition', in Robert F. Yeager, *Chaucer and Gower: Difference, Mutuality, Exchange* (Victoria: University of Victoria, 1991), pp. 7–35, at 29; Kurt Olsson, *John Gower and the Structures of Conversion: A Reading of the Confessio Amantis* (Cambridge: D. S. Brewer, 1992), pp. 13–14, 52, 62, 123, 139, 155, 247–8; J. Allan Mitchell, 'Gower for Example: *Confessio Amantis* and the Limits of Exemplarity', *Exemplaria*, 16 (2004), pp. 203–34; J. Allan Mitchell, *Ethics and Exemplary Narrative in Chaucer and Gower* (Cambridge: D. S. Brewer, 2004), pp. 37–78; John M. Ganim, 'Gower, Liminality and

then, did Gower conceive of the nature and functions of political power? How consistent were his political views? What was the relationship between the general political outlook which Gower set out in the *Mirour de l'Omme*, *Vox Clamantis* and *Confessio Amantis* and his support for the deposition of Richard II which he offered in his poetry after 1399? Why have his works been open to such conflicting interpretations? Here we are mainly concerned with Gower's explicit statements on politics and, in particular, on kingship which, naturally, was to be a central issue when he came to address the events of 1399.

The Legitimacy of the State and State Violence

When discussing the nature of political power, Gower was often extremely suspicious of the uses to which such power could be put, particularly when it was exercised for the ruler's own singular profit or to satisfy what St Augustine had deemed the 'lust for domination' which typified post-lapsarian humanity.[15] For instance, in Book III of the *Confessio Amantis*, as part of his denunciation of the evils of war and the sinfulness of those rulers who fought out of irrational wilfulness and a desire for 'lucre', Genius recounts

---

the Politics of Space', *Exemplaria*, 19 (2007), pp. 90–116, at 110–13; T. Matthew N. McCabe, *Gower's Vulgar Tongue: Ovid, Lay Religion and English Poetry in the Confessio Amantis* (Cambridge: D. S. Brewer, 2011), pp. 193, 197–8, 203–5, 227; Karma Lochrie, *Covert Operations: The Medieval Uses of Secrecy* (Philadelphia: University of Pennsylvania Press, 1999), pp. 205–25; María Bullón-Fernández, *Fathers and Daughters in Gower's Confessio Amantis*, pp. 4–5, 36–7; Patricia Batchelor, 'Feigned Truth and Exemplary Method in the *Confessio Amantis*', in Yeager, *Re-Visioning Gower*, pp. 1–15; Russell A. Peck, 'The Phenomenology of Make-Believe in Gower's *Confessio Amantis*', *Ibid.*, pp. 49–66; Kurt Olsson, 'Reading, Transgression and Judgement: Gower's Case of Paris and Helen', *Ibid.*, pp. 67–92; Hugh White, 'The Sympathetic Villain in the *Confessio Amantis*', *Ibid.*, pp. 221–36; Siân Echard, 'Glossing Gower: In Latin, in English, and *in absentia*: The Case of Bodleian Ashmole 35', *Ibid.*, pp. 237–56, at 238–9; Malte Urban, *Fragments: Past and Present in Chaucer and Gower* (Oxford: Peter Lang, 2008), pp. 55–6; Matthew W. Irvin, 'Voices and Narrative', in *RRC*, pp. 237–52; Elizabeth Allen, 'Newfangled Readers in Gower's "Apollonius of Tyre"', *Studies in the Age of Chaucer*, 29 (2007), pp. 419–64, at 423–4, 463; William Robins, 'Romance, Exemplum and the Subject of the *Confessio Amantis*', *Studies in the Age of Chaucer*, 19 (1997), pp. 157–81, at 159; Kim Zarins, 'Violence Without Warning: Sympathetic Villains and John Gower's Crafting of Ovidian Narrative', in Peck and Yeager, *John Gower: Others and the Self*, pp. 141–55, at 141; David W. Hiscoe, 'Heavenly Sign and Comic Design in Gower's *Confessio Amantis*', in Julian N. Wasserman and Lois Roney, eds, *Sign, Sentence, Discourse: Language in Medieval Thought and Literature* (Syracuse: Syracuse University Press, 1989), pp. 228–44, at 232, 336–41; Edwards, *Invention and Authorship in Medieval England*, pp. 65, 67, 92, 99.

[15] Augustine, *Concerning the City of God Against the Pagans*, trans. Henry Bettenson (Harmondsworth: Penguin Books, 1972), I: Preface (p. 5); Scanlon, *Narrative, Authority and Power*, pp. 268, 297.

the well-known story of the pirate who boldly told Alexander the Great that he differed from the emperor only in the extent of his crimes – with those of the emperor actually being much the greater (III.1280–92, 2251–2480, 2533–43; see also MO: 10000–01, 23257–68).[16] As Gower said in *In Praise of Peace*, whereas Solomon had asked God for wisdom (3 Kings 3:9), Alexander had asked to conquer the world, thereby showing himself to be a tyrant who grieved the world through 'infortune of sin' (ll. 29–49). Augustine's criticisms of the potential abuses of political power have often been seen as part of a 'negative', or at best 'neutral', view of politics and the state in which the function of government is not to promote right order and the good life but rather to minimise disorder and the effects of sin.[17] Yet, even Augustine regarded the institutions of the state as being just and reasonable not only in terms of holding the wicked in check but also in helping to secure the exercise of virtue.[18] This positive conception of political power was adopted by the early medieval thinkers for whom kingship within Christian societies was a form of ministry whose purpose was to help create justice and peace in this life. It was further developed in the twelfth and thirteenth centuries under the impact of Ciceronian and Aristotelian ideas in which government was seen as a means of securing the common good.[19] Thus, even those thinkers such as Vincent of Beauvais who argued that kingship had its origins in the evil usurpation of power by Nimrod (Genesis 10:8) could also allow that, since that time, royal authority had, by divine beneficence, been

---

[16] This story was familiar to medieval audiences from Augustine, *City of God*, IV: 4 (p. 139). Gower's account of this episode includes details which were not mentioned by Augustine but which were to be found in a version of the story which can be traced back to John of Salisbury's *Policraticus* (H. C. Mainzer, 'A Study of the Sources of the *Confessio Amantis* of John Gower' (Unpublished University of Oxford D.Phil. thesis, 1968), pp. 57–8, 335–6; *Ioannis Saresberiensis Episcopi Carnotensis Policratici*, ed. Clemens C. I. Webb (New York: Arno Press, 1979), III: XIV (508a–b). On Alexander and the pirate, see also G. Cary, *The Medieval Alexander* (Cambridge: Cambridge University Press, 1956), pp. 81–3, 95–8, 104, 156–8, 197, 252–4, 263, 281–2, 349, 302; Stephen H. Rigby, *Wisdom and Chivalry: Chaucer's Knight's Tale and Medieval Political Theory* (Leiden: Brill, 2009), pp. 174–5.

[17] Robert A. Markus, 'The Latin Fathers', in James H. Burns, ed., *The Cambridge History of Political Thought, c.350–c.1450* (Cambridge: Cambridge University Press, 1988), pp. 92–122, at 110–11. For a defence of the use of the term 'state' in relation to medieval government, see Kenneth Pennington, *The Prince and the Law, 1200–1600: Sovereignty and Rights in the Western Legal Tradition* (Berkeley: University of California Press, 1993), pp. 30–1.

[18] Augustine, *City of God*, I: 21 (p. 32), IV: 20 (p. 159), V: 24 (p. 220); Peter J. Burnell, 'The Status of Politics in St Augustine's *City of God*', *History of Political Thought*, 13 (1992), pp. 13–29.

[19] Space does not allow detailed references to the huge secondary literature on medieval political theory to be provided here. For an introduction, see Burns, *The Cambridge History of Political Thought, c.350–c.1450*. For primary and secondary sources on many of the themes addressed below, see also Rigby, *Wisdom and Chivalry*, chapter 4.

converted into a force for good.[20] Similarly, for Robert Holcot, although laws were introduced as a response to post-lapsarian sinfulness, the law also had an improving purpose, providing not just peace and security but also encouraging virtue.[21]

If, as is evident from his criticism of Alexander, Gower could be very distrustful of individual rulers and their motives, his poetry nonetheless adopts this positive attitude to the potential for political power to be used for the common good. Gower's views can clearly be perceived from the account of the origin of the state which is offered in Book VII of the *Confessio Amantis*. Here, in line with many medieval theologians and preachers, Genius explains that the world's goods had originally been held in common for the use of all (VII.1991–3; see also CA: V.1–5; MO: 24150–53; VC: VI.5.360).[22] Like Chaucer in *The Former Age*, Genius portrays the innocence of this original Golden Age of humanity, when wealth had been held in common, as having ended when money was invented and people came to worship gold, thereby turning themselves into the slaves of their own inanimate possessions.[23] As the wealth of the community became the private property of individuals, love was replaced by avarice, envy and discord, and the war of each against all broke out. Faced with such anarchy, 'the people fond/That it was good to make a king' who would rule over them as their superior and who, by means of the law, would maintain their property rights. Thus, whilst political authority was created as a result of sin, it could nonetheless be employed to promote social order, justice and harmony (VC: VI.1; VI.3; VI.7; CA: III.2308–9; V.1–21, 52–6, 328–48; VII.1991–2013, 2695–2714, 3052–3, 3062–83).[24]

---

[20] Charles L. Kingsford, 'Some Medieval Writers on Kingship', in *The Song of Lewes*, ed. Charles L. Kingsford (Oxford: Clarendon Press, 1890), pp. 123–46, at 130, 135.

[21] John T. Slotemaker and Jeffrey C. Witt, *Robert Holcot* (Oxford: Oxford University Press, 2016), pp. 194–7, 213–14.

[22] St Thomas Aquinas, *Summa Theologiae: A Concise Translation*, ed. Timothy McDermott (London: Eyre and Spottiswode, 1989), p. 288; *Wimbledon's Sermon Redde Rationem Villicationis Tue: A Middle English Sermon of the Fourteenth Century*, ed. Ione K. Knight (Pittsburgh: Duquesne University Press, 1967), ll. 520–1; Diana Wood, *Medieval Economic Thought* (Cambridge: Cambridge University Press, 2002), pp. 17–41.

[23] Geoffrey Chaucer, 'The Former Age'; Kurt Olsson, 'Natural Law and John Gower's *Confessio Amantis*', in Nicholson, *Gower's Confessio Amantis*, pp. 181–213, at 189–91; Robert Epstein, 'Dismal Science: Chaucer and Gower on Alchemy and Economy', *Studies in the Age of Chaucer*, 36 (2014), pp. 209–48, at 223–5. On the lost Golden Age, see Ovid, *Metamorphoses, Books I-VIII*, eds Frank J. Miller and G. P. Goold (third edition; Cambridge, Mass.: Harvard University Press, 1977), I: 76–215; Boethius, *The Consolation of Philosophy*, in *The Theological Tractates and The Consolation of Philosophy*, eds H. F. Stewart, E. K. Rand and S. J. Tester (Cambridge, Mass.: Harvard University Press, 1973), II, m. 5; Guillaume de Lorris and Jean de Meun, *Le roman de la rose*, volume II, ed. Félix Lecoy (Paris: Champion, 1973), ll. 9487–9510.

[24] A similar but rather more cynical version of the origin of the state appears in *Le roman de la rose*, volume II, ll. 9463–9606.

Given this explanation of the creation of the state as a response to human need, Gower, like most medieval thinkers, accepted that even non-Christian states were legitimate provided that they acted to defend the common good.[25] Naturally, Gower condemned the 'cursed' pagans for their 'insane' worship of false idols made of wood and stone (VC: II.10.1–534; see also CA: V.747–1802) and denounced the pagan tyrants who had persecuted the early Christians (VC.VI.1.53–4; MO: 12777–83). Nevertheless, whilst, as we have seen, he criticised Alexander as a ruler who was dominated by his passion for war and endless conquest, his works also include many other pagan rulers and lawgivers who are models of virtue, such as Darius, the wise sultan of Persia, Lycurgus, the Spartan lawgiver (whom Gower turned into an Athenian),[26] and Trajan, the Roman emperor who was famed for his goodness, justice and mercy (MO: 22165–71; VC: VI.20.1273; CA: VII.1783–95, 2917–3061, 3142–62; see also CA: II.2501–09; VC: V.16.1007–14). Thus, when Gower condemned non-Christian rulers, such as Leontius, Sardanapalus and Dionysius, for their immoral and tyrannical deeds, he did not criticise them because they were pagans but rather because they were corrupt individuals whose vices were recognised as such by their own pagan contemporaries (CA: VII.3267–87, 3341–54, 4313–43).[27]

Since the state's function was to help create justice, peace and order, Gower argued that rulers were entitled to employ violence as a necessary means to secure these virtuous ends. As a result, while he frequently reminded his readers that God loves peace and that His commandments forbade us to kill others (Exodus 20:13; MO: 24157–60; VC: III.9.647; CA: III.2251–4, 2288), Gower rejected the outright pacifism of the kind favoured by John Wyclif and some of his followers.[28] On the contrary, following Augustine, he argued that although pity was a virtue which was opposed to homicide, the death penalty should nonetheless be permitted as a regrettable necessity since, by destroying 'the iniquity of robbers and evil people', it defended the common good (MO: 13897–956; see also VC.V.16.943–48; VI.9.690–714;

---

[25] For detailed references to primary sources, see Rigby, *Wisdom and Chivalry*, pp. 222–6. See also J. Allan Mitchell, 'Gower's *Confessio Amantis*, Natural Morality and Vernacular Ethics', in Malte Urban, ed., *John Gower: Manuscripts, Readers, Contexts* (Turnhout: Brepols, 2009), pp. 135–53, at 135, 139; Linda Barney Burke, 'Genial Gower: Laughter in the *Confessio Amantis*', in Robert F. Yeager, ed., *John Gower: Recent Readings* (Kalamazoo: Medieval Institute Publications, 1989), pp. 39–63, at 46–7.

[26] On Lycurgus in the work of Gower and other medieval writers, see Ian Macgregor Morris, 'Lycurgus in Late Medieval Political Culture', in Stephen Hodkinson and Ian Macgregor Morris, eds, *Sparta in Modern Thought: Politics, History and Culture* (Swansea: The Classical Press of Wales, 2012), pp. 1–41.

[27] For Gower's range of attitudes to pagan antiquity, see Lynn Shutters, 'Confronting Venus: Classical Pagans and their Christian Readers in John Gower's *Confessio Amantis*', *Chaucer Review*, 48 (2013), pp. 38–65.

[28] Rory Cox, *John Wyclif on War and Peace* (Woodbridge: The Royal Historical Society/Boydell Press, 2014).

CA: III.2210–34; VII.3854–5; VIII.1936–62).[29] In such cases, although God's commandment forbade killing, this divine law could still be seen as being 'limited' in its application and as open to regulation or derogation by the prince.[30]

Gower applied the same logic to the permissibility of just war.[31] As a result, although he defined humanity's essential task as being the pursuit of peace and had Genius present killing and warfare as being against the laws of nature, of charity and of Christ, he did not reject the use of violence *per se* (CT: Preface; VC: VI.9.649–52; VI.15.1073; CA: III.2251–2362, 2533–43). Rather, he echoed the words of the wise Solomon in declaring that 'There is a time for war and there are likewise times for peace' (Ecclesiastes 3:8) since, although 'peace excels over every good', war sometimes has to be waged in defence of 'our tried and tested rights' and in defence of 'a demonstrably just cause' (MO: 22928–32, 23617–40, 23865–8, 23893–24000; VC: V.1.1–18; V.2–5; V.7.469–96; V.8.549; VI.13.971–3; VI.14; CA: III.2225–40; VII.3529–43, 3595–603).[32] From the time of Augustine onwards, medieval thinkers had frequently justified publicly-authorised warfare by the commonplace that the ultimate purpose of war was peace.[33] Similarly, in his *In Praise of Peace*, Gower argued that even though it was good to eschew violence, a king could still make war provided that 'of bataille the final ende is pees' (ll. 64–70; see also CA: Pro.129). In other words, Gower did not have to work very hard to 'reconcile' his criticisms of violence and of the motives from which men sometimes fight with his belief in the legitimacy of warfare provided that it was pursued for a just cause.[34] As he said in the *Vox Clamantis*, 'Let him who wishes to rule, protect justice with blood. Arms bring peace, arms curb the rapacious' (VI.9.712–13).

---

[29] Augustine, *City of God*, I: 21 (p. 32); Yoshiko Kobayashi, '*Principis Umbra*: Kingship, Justice and Pity in John Gower's Poetry', in Robert F. Yeager, ed., *On John Gower: Essays at the Millennium* (Kalamazoo: Medieval Institute Publications, 2007), pp. 71–103, at 76–8.

[30] Pennington, *The Prince and the Law*, pp. 130, 222.

[31] For detailed references, see Rigby, *Wisdom and Chivalry*, pp. 186–9, 213–9.

[32] Russell A. Peck, *Kingship and Common Profit in Gower's Confessio Amantis* (Carbondale: Southern Illinois University Press, 1978), p. 93; David R. Carlson, *John Gower, Poetry and Propaganda in Fourteenth-Century England* (Cambridge: D. S. Brewer, 2012), pp. 205–6; Porter, 'Gower's Ethical Microcosm and Political Macrocosm', p. 151.

[33] Augustine, *City of God*, XIX: 12 (p. 866); Giles of Rome, *The Governance of Kings and Princes*, p. 439. For detailed references, see Rigby, *Wisdom and Chivalry*, p. 197.

[34] Robert F. Yeager, '*Pax Poetica*: On the Pacifism of Chaucer and Gower', *Studies in the Age of Chaucer*, 9 (1987), pp. 97–121, at 98. For a recent study which emphasises the doubts about the utility of war expressed in Gower's *In Praise of Peace*, see Yoshiki Kobayashi, 'Letters of Old Age: The Advocacy of Peace in the Works of John Gower and Philippe de Mézières', in Peck and Yeager, *John Gower: Others and the Self*, pp. 204–22. See also David Green, above, pp. 154–60 and Chris Fletcher, above, p. 373.

Personal Virtue and Good Government

If political power had the potential to be used to promote justice within the community and to defend it against its enemies, how could this potential best be realised? As Skinner has shown, in answering this question, thirteenth- and fourteenth-century political theorists fell into two main schools of thought. The first of these, which had its roots in the teaching of rhetoric and which included writers such as John of Viterbo and Brunetto Latini, focused on the personal virtue of those who held political office as the key to good government since 'if the men who control the institutions of government are corrupt, the best possible institutions cannot be expected to shape or constrain them'. Within this tradition, the best defence against tyranny was the moral reform of the sovereign rather than his constraint by his subjects.[35] The second school of thought, which was grounded in Aristotelian scholastic thought and which included writers such as Bartolus of Sassoferrato and Marsiglio of Padua, was more interested in analysing the different forms of government and of political power. As a result, its emphasis was 'less on virtuous individuals than on efficient institutions' as the best means of promoting the common good and of preventing rulers from abusing their power.[36]

When Gower himself came to discuss how political power could be made to promote justice and virtue, he invariably adopted the 'rhetorical' approach, presenting political issues in terms of the personal morality of the ruler and his officials and paying scant attention to the actual machinery of government. Whilst late medieval political theory was increasingly concerned with concrete and practical issues and with the specifics of government policy, Gower's works remained within an older tradition of generic moralising.[37] His essential point, one with which it was perhaps difficult to disagree, was that the ruler should always hate vice and seek to be united with virtue (MO: 23032-4). Thus, if Gower presented individual repentance, moral reform and self-regulation as the general remedy for society's ills, with each person being, in a sense, a ruler who has to govern the kingdom of his own self, he saw such self-rule as being particularly necessary in the case of the king whose wisdom and conduct was the foundation of the moral health of the community as a whole (VC: VI.8; 7.20; MO: 22228-36, 22753-824, 22861-72, 22897-958, 22981-23028, 23041-88, 23173-84,

---

[35] Quentin Skinner, *The Foundations of Modern Political Thought, Volume One: The Renaissance* (Cambridge: Cambridge University Press, 1978), pp. 28-48; Luke Sunderland, *Rebel Barons: Resisting Royal Power in Medieval Culture* (Oxford: Oxford University Press, 2017), pp. 20, 39.

[36] Skinner, *The Foundations of Modern Political Thought, Volume One*, pp. 49-65. On Marsiglio, see, however, Sunderland, *Rebel Barons*, pp. 43-7.

[37] Chris Wickham, *Medieval Europe* (New Haven: Yale University Press, 2016), pp. 237-40.

27205–10, 27275–88; CA: VII.1711–13, 1745–8; VIII.2111–21).[38] As he said, invoking the metaphor of the prince as the head of the body politic which had been familiar from the time of John of Salisbury onwards, 'if the head is sick, there is no member that will not suffer pains' (MO: 22825–36, 23125–36; VC: VI.7.495–520).[39] Indeed, Gower was even more consistent in his stress on the need for rulers to be virtuous than were his sources.[40] For instance, although Giles of Rome had taught that rulers should be better than other men, he also acknowledged that the sinfulness of humanity meant that all rulers would be guilty of doing some wrong and had even allowed that a certain degree of tyranny might be less harmful than the evils that would come from disobedience to the ruler.[41] Gower, by contrast, made no such concessions towards expediency. As a result, the 'five points of policy' which Genius recommends to kings so that they can achieve 'worthi governance' – truthfulness, liberality, justice, mercy and chastity – are all concerned with individual morality rather than with pragmatic issues of governance or the particular courses of action which rulers should pursue (VII.1704–22,

---

[38] Arthur B. Ferguson, *The Articulate Citizen and the English Renaissance* (Durham, N.C.: Duke University Press, 1965), pp. 51, 57; T. Matthew N. McCabe, *Gower's Vulgar Tongue: Ovid, Lay Religion and English Poetry in the Confessio Amantis* (Cambridge: D. S. Brewer, 2011), pp. 46–7; Irvin, *The Poetic Voices of John Gower*, pp. 28–9; *John Gower's Poetic*, p. 267; Jonathan M. Newman, 'The Rhetoric of Logic in John Gower's *Confessio Amantis* Book 7', *Medievalia et Humanistica*, n.s. 38 (2013), pp. 37–57, at 39; Porter, 'Gower's Ethical Microcosm and Political Macrocosm', p. 144; Diane Watt, *Amoral Gower: Language, Sex and Politics* (Minneapolis: University of Minnesota Press, 2003), pp. 124–6; Helen Cooper, '"Peised Evene in the Balance": A Thematic and Rhetorical Topos in the *Confessio Amantis*', *Mediaevalia*, 16 (1990), pp. 113–39, at 122–3; Mahmoud A. Manzalaoui, '"Noght in the Registre of Venus": Gower's English Mirror for Princes', in Peter L. Heyworth, ed., *Medieval Studies for J. A. W. Bennett* (Oxford: Clarendon Press, 1981), pp. 159–83, at 162; Marie Collins, 'Love, Nature and Law in the Poetry of Gower and Chaucer', in Glyn S. Burgess, ed., *Court and Poet: Selected Proceedings of the Third Congress of the International Courtly Literature Society (Liverpool, 1980)* (Liverpool: Francis Cairns, 1981), pp. 113–28, at 122; Weinberg, 'Introduction', pp. 8–9; Russell A. Peck, 'The Politics and Psychology of Governance in Gower: Ideas of Kingship and Real Kings', in Siân Echard, ed., *A Companion to Gower* (Cambridge: D. S. Brewer, 2004), pp. 215–38, at 216; Sonja Drimmer, *The Art of Allusion: Illumination and the Making of English Literature* (Philadelphia: University of Pennsylvania Press, 2019), pp. 194, 197, 223.

[39] See also CA: Pro.151–6; VII.485–9 and John Gower, *O Deus Immense*, ll. 85–6. On Gower and John of Salisbury, see Robert F. Yeager, 'The Body Politic and the Politics of Bodies in the Poetry of John Gower', in Piero Boitani and Anna Torti, eds, *The Body and The Soul in Medieval Literature* (Cambridge: D. S. Brewer, 1999), pp. 145–65, at 149. For further reading on the metaphor of the body politic, see Stephen H. Rigby, 'The Body Politic in the Social and Political Thought of Christine de Pizan (Unabridged Version)', *Cahiers de Recherches Médiévales et Humanistes* [on-line], mis en ligne le 12 mars 2013. URL: http://crm.revues.org/12965.

[40] Porter, 'Gower's Ethical Microcosm and Political Macrocosm', pp. 152, 155.

[41] Giles of Rome, *The Governance of Kings and Princes*, pp. 7–8, 17, 31, 50, 97, 106–10, 132, 136–8, 141, 149, 211–12, 220, 225, 265–73, 332–3, 336–7, 343, 380, 382, 385, 388–9.

1718–82, 1950–2025, 2695–764, 3062–66, 3084–94, 3103–36, 4208–44).[42] Thus, although he has Genius praise the laws introduced by Lycurgus for bringing peace and prosperity to Athens, Gower showed 'little interest in the detail of the laws themselves'.[43] Occasionally, the poet did suggest some specific remedy for an abuse, as when he advised the king to take away the 'ill-gotten gains' of lawyers and to use them to help pay for the war with France (MO: 24337–48). At other times, the policy which he preferred is implicit as being the opposite of the situation about which he complained, as when he accuses the Lombard merchants of seeking to 'dwell in our country just as free and welcome as if they were born and brought up with us' (MO: 25561–72). Usually, however, Gower was more concerned to denounce the sins of his age than he was to suggest the kinds of policies that might actually remedy them.[44]

Even when Gower did discuss the functioning of royal government, he still assumed that its proper operation depended upon the personal virtue of the ruler. For instance, for Gower, as for most medieval political theorists, a wise ruler was one who would be willing to take counsel and to learn from the wisdom and experience of others: 'Althogh a man be wys himselve,/Yit is the wisdom more of tuelve' (CA: Pro.157–8).[45] Indeed, Genius claims that counsel is more necessary than anything else to a ruler (CA: VIII.2019–10). Nevertheless, this view still presupposed that the king himself would have the prudence that would lead him to listen to good counsel and to reject the advice of those who were flatterers, self-seekers or traitors (MO: 22801–03, 22869, 22978–80, 23168–70, 23185–208; VC: VI.7.531–2; VI.9.643–88).[46] This point is clearly illustrated in the *Confessio Amantis* by the story of Lucius, the king of Rome: when his chamberlain reassuringly tells him that his subjects chiefly blamed his 'conseil', rather than the king himself, for any lack of worthiness in his rule, the king's fool shrewdly replies that if the king was actually so wise and good then surely his council would not be so bad (VII.3945–4016).

Similarly, Gower's examination of the ruler's officials focused on their personal morality, rather than on the machinery of government or on institutional checks, as the key to good government. For example, although the *Mirour de l'Omme* saw the administration of justice in England as having been

---

[42] Peck, 'The Politics and Psychology of Governance in Gower', p. 220; Samantha J. Rayner, *Images of Kingship in Chaucer and his Ricardian Contemporaries* (Cambridge: D. S. Brewer, 2008), pp. 12–31.

[43] Macgregor Morris, 'Lycurgus in Late Medieval Political Culture', p. 13.

[44] Ferguson, *The Articulate Citizen and the English Renaissance*, pp. 22–3, 43, 51, 55–6, 68–70, 95–6.

[45] Irvin, *The Poetic Voices of John Gower*, pp. 65–6. On the ruler's need for counsel, see Rigby, *Wisdom and Chivalry*, pp. 35–6, 58, 183–4, 193–5.

[46] Ferguson, *The Articulate Citizen and the English Renaissance*, p. 70; Edwin D. Craun, *Lies, Slander and Obscenity in Medieval English Literature: Pastoral Rhetoric and the Deviant Speaker* (Cambridge: Cambridge University Press, 1997), pp. 126–32.

corrupted by the malfeasance of the king's sheriffs, Gower considered such abuses solely in terms of the sheriffs' personal avarice and lack of conscience (24853–836 ; see also VC:VI.6). Although he stressed that sheriffs should fulfil their oaths to serve the king and his people faithfully and should make a truthful account at the royal exchequer (MO: 24817–64), Gower showed no interest in contemporary debates about how sheriffs should be appointed, for how long they should serve, or from which ranks of society they should be drawn.[47] The same is true of Gower's critique of the legal system, the shortcomings of which he presented exclusively in terms of the moral failings of the lawyers and judges whose greed and favouritism prevented justice from being done (MO: 24181–816; VC: VI.1–7). Thus, although Gower taught that people needed good laws to govern them, he also emphasised that an effective legal system required judges whose personal integrity would lead them to render every man his due with impartial authority (CA: II.1678–1701; VII.2695–700, 2748–60, 2765–82, 2827–32, 2889–2902, 3062–66).[48] As he put it in the Vox Clamantis, 'What is a people without law, or what is law without a judge, or what is a judge without justice?' (VC: VI.7.481–2).

'Regal' and 'Political' Forms of Royal Authority

Since he conceived of political life mainly in terms of the individual virtue and vices of rulers and their officials, Gower showed little interest in the Aristotelian typology of the six possible forms of government (i.e. rule by the one, by the few or by the many, each of which could either be exercised either for the rulers' own benefit or for the common good) or in contemporary debates about which of these forms was best.[49] Instead, he simply assumed that government would take a monarchical form. This was perhaps inevitable when, as in his epistle to the young Richard II in the Vox Clamantis, the poet was engaging with a polity in which no constitutional alternative to kingship was on offer. Nevertheless, even when speaking in more general terms, Gower took it for granted that government would be monarchical, as in the Mirour de l'Omme where the estate of emperors and kings is said to have been 'ordained to govern the people of the world' (22225–27) and in the Vox Clamantis where he claimed that 'all men whatsoever of earthly

---

[47] W. Mark Ormrod, *The Reign of Edward III: Crown and Political Society, 1327–1377* (London: Guild Publishing, 1991), pp. 80, 155, 163–4; Richard Gorski, *The Fourteenth-Century Sheriff: English Local Administration in the Late Middle Ages* (Woodbridge: Boydell Press, 2007), pp. 37–42, 69–82, 111–14.

[48] Robert J. Meindl, 'Gower's *Speculum Judicis*: Judicial Corruption in Book VI of the *Vox Clamantis*', in Peck and Yeager, *John Gower: Others and the Self*, pp. 260–82, at 281.

[49] Aristotle, 'The Politics', in *The Politics and the Constitution of Athens*, ed. Stephen Everson (Cambridge: Cambridge University Press, 1996), III: 7; Giles of Rome, *The Governance of Kings and Princes*, pp. 28, 117–20, 211, 266, 280, 325–6, 344–5. For other references, see Rigby, *Wisdom and Chivalry*, pp. 176–7.

estate are governed under the justice of royal authority'. As he says, 'Of what use is the earth by itself, unless people are on it? Or of what use are the people to it, unless a king governs?' (VC: VI.7.529–30; VI.8; see also CA: VII.2695–97). Similarly, as we saw above, in explaining the emergence of the state as a response to the anarchy which followed the end of the Golden Age, Genius simply assumed that people's recognition of the need for some form of political authority had led them to conclude 'That it was good to make a king' (CA: VII.1998–2013).

Nonetheless, if Gower favoured monarchical government, this still left open the question of what specific form the relationship between the king and his subjects should take. Many medieval writers adopted a conception of political authority in which power flowed downwards from God to the king (John 19:11; Romans 13:1). Here, although the king had an obligation to take counsel, he could, in effect, make laws according to his own desire.[50] Such rulers possessed what Giles of Rome called a 'regal' mode of power, with their relationship to their subjects being like that of a father to his children, with his will being paramount.[51] Those who claimed that rulers could legislate without constraint could appeal to the familiar maxims of Roman law that 'what pleases the prince has force of law' and that 'the prince is not bound by the law' and so might even allow that the prince could enact laws that were unjust, unreasonable and arbitrary.[52] As a result of his emphasis on the royal prerogative, Richard II himself has often been interpreted by modern historians as, in effect, holding a regal conception of kingship.[53] Here they echo

---

[50] Walter Ullmann, *Principles of Government and Politics in the Middle Ages* (London: Methuen, 1961), pp. 117–37.

[51] *Egidio Colonna (Aegidius Romanus), De Regimine Principum Libri III*, p. 260; Giles of Rome, *The Governance of Kings and Princes*, pp. 190–2; Sir John Fortescue, *De Laudibus Legum Anglie*, ed. Stanley B. Chrimes (Cambridge: Cambridge University Press, 1942), chapter IX (pp. 24–5); Sir John Fortescue, *The Governance of England*, ed. Charles Plummer (London: Oxford University Press, 1926), chapter I, pp. 109–10; Roberto Lambertini, 'Political Thought', in Charles F. Briggs and Peter S. Eardley, eds, *A Companion to Giles of Rome* (Leiden: Brill), pp. 255–74, at 264–5.

[52] 'Institutiones', I.ii.6 (p. 3); 'Digesta', I.iii.31 (p. 6); I.iv.1 (p. 7), in *Corpus Iuris Civilis, Volume I: Institutiones and Digesta*, eds Theodor Momsen and Paul Krueger (Cambridge: Cambridge University Press, 2014); Gratian, *The Treatise on the Laws (Decretum DD 1-20) with the Ordinary Gloss*, eds Augustine Thompson and James Gordley (Washington: Catholic University of America Press, 1993), p. 8; Kingsford, 'Some Medieval Writers on Kingship', p. 98; Ewart Lewis, 'King Above Law? "Quod Principi Placuit" in Bracton', *Speculum*, 39 (1964), pp. 240–69, at 263; Kenneth Pennington, 'Law, Legislative Authority and Theories of Government, 1150–1300', in Burns, *The Cambridge History of Medieval Political Thought*, pp. 424–53, at 426; Pennington, *The Prince and the Law*, p. 206; Craig Taylor, '"Weep Thou For Me in France": French Views of the Deposition of Richard II', in W. Mark Ormrod, ed., *Fourteenth-Century England, Volume III* (Woodbridge: Boydell Press, 2004), pp. 207–22, at 210; Sunderland, *Rebel Barons*, p. 28.

[53] Nigel Saul, *Richard II* (New Haven: Yale University Press, 1997), pp. 173–5, 438–9; Simon Walker, 'Richard II's Views on Kingship', in Rowena E. Archer and Simon

the views of the king's opponents who, in the 'Record and Process' which justified Richard II's deposition, alleged that the king had frequently expressed the view that the 'laws were in his mouth' and that 'he alone could change or make the laws of his kingdom' and had claimed, in opposition to the laws and customs of the kingdom, that the lives and property of his subjects 'were his and subject to his will.'[54] Certainly, Richard Maidstone's *Concordia*, which describes the lavish reception given by the city of London in 1392 to mark its reconciliation with the king following his suspension of its liberties, depicts Sir Baldwyn Radyngton, whom the king had appointed as warden of the city, offering the citizens' surrender of themselves and all they have to the king's will so that their life and death are in his hands and has him conclude with the words 'May your royal rod guide subjects at its will'.[55]

Alternatively, other theorists favoured a conception of authority in which the ruler was not regarded as standing above the community but was rather seen as part of it and so as being constrained by the laws which the community made. For Giles of Rome, such a ruler possessed a 'political' form of power, with his relationship to his people being like that of a husband to his wife, so that his will was restrained by law and by the agreements which he has made with his subjects.[56] For Sir John Fortescue, writing in the mid-fifteenth century, royal authority in England was 'not only regal but also political' which meant that the king could not change the law or levy taxation 'without the assent of his subjects'.[57] Given the dangers of anachronism, it may be best to recast the debate about Gower's views into the issue of whether it was closer to 'regal' or to 'political' kingship rather

---

Walker, eds, *Rulers and Ruled in Late Medieval England: Essays Presented to Gerald Harriss* (London: The Hambledon Press, 1995), pp. 49–63; Michael Bennett, *Richard II and the Revolution of 1399* (Stroud: Sutton Publishing, 1999), pp. 25–9, 36, 43, 53, 55, 66, 110, 139–40, 194–6; Christopher Fletcher, *Richard II: Manhood, Youth and Politics, 1377–99* (Oxford: Oxford University Press, 2009); Andrew M. Spencer, 'The Coronation Oath in English Politics, 1272–1399', in Benjamin Thompson and John Watts, eds, *Political Society in Later Medieval England: A Festschrift for Christine Carpenter* (Woodbridge: Boydell Press, 2015), pp. 38–54, at 38–9. See also *Knighton's Chronicle, 1337–1396*, ed. Geoffrey H. Martin (Oxford: Clarendon Press, 1995), pp. 352–55.

[54] 'The Record and Process', in *Chronicles of the Revolution: The Reign of Richard II, 1397–1400*, ed. Chris Given-Wilson (Manchester: Manchester University Press, 1993), pp. 168–89, at 177–8, 180. For the original text, see *The Deposition of Richard II*, ed. David R. Carlson (Toronto: The Pontifical Institute of Medieval Studies, 2007), pp. 23–65.

[55] Richard Maidstone, *Concordia (The Reconciliation of Richard II with London)*, ed. David R. Carlson (Kalamazoo: Medieval Institute Publications, 2003), ll. 135–41, 210–14. See Caroline M. Barron, 'The Quarrel of Richard II with London', in F. Robin H. Du Boulay and Caroline M. Barron, eds, *The Reign of Richard II: Essays in Honour of May McKisack* (London: The Athlone Press, 1971), pp. 173–201.

[56] *Egidio Colonna (Aegidius Romanus), De Regimine Principum Libri III*, p. 260; Giles of Rome, *The Governance of Kings and Princes*, pp. 190–2.

[57] Fortescue, *De Laudibus Legum Anglie*, chapter IX (pp. 24–5); Fortescue, *The Governance of England*, chapter I (pp. 109–10).

than to 'absolutism' or 'constitutionalism'. The 'political' view of kingship certainly had a long tradition behind it. For instance, *The Song of Lewes* (1264), in defending the baronial opposition to Henry III, had rejected the claim supposedly made by the king and his son (the future Edward I) that the command of the prince has the force of law. Instead, its author argued that the law was superior to the king's will and that obedience was not due to a ruler who would not obey the law of God; men would be 'mad' (*insensati*) to obey such a king.[58] Similarly, William of Pagula's *Mirror of King Edward III* (A-version, 1330) taught that when a king acted 'against the precept of God', as he did when he exercised his prerogative claim to seize his subjects' property or to compel them to sell their produce at a lower price than they wished, then 'one must not obey, but rather resist, the king, and he who does this obtains reward for himself'.[59] Those who supported this 'political' outlook could appeal, as did William of Pagula himself, to Magna Carta in order to claim that the king was bound by the law and could only tax his subjects with their consent.[60] Certainly, Magna Carta remained central to conceptions of the relationship between kings and subjects in the period before the mid-fifteenth century. It influenced the actions of the Appellants in their opposition to Richard II in 1387–88 and was explicitly invoked in the 1399 'Articles of Deposition' which charged the king with having 'willfully contravened' the charter's famous provision that no man should be arrested or punished 'unless it be by the lawful judgement of his peers or by the law of the land'.[61] More generally, the Great Charter was associated with the view that kings were subject to the law of the land, thereby providing a defence of their subjects' life, liberty and property, a conception of royal authority that was also evident in the accusation that Richard had failed to observe his coronation oath to maintain the laws and customs of former

---

[58] *The Song of Lewes*, ll. 443–60, 501–4, 706–7, 871–90, 966–80. See also *The Mirror of Justices*, ed. William J. Whittaker (Selden Society, 7 (1895 for 1893)), pp. xxxviii–ix, 6, 7, 11, 155.

[59] William of Pagula, 'Admonition to King Edward III... First Version', in *Political Thought in Early Fourteenth-Century England*, ed. Cary J. Nederman (Tempe: Arizona Center for Medieval and Renaissance Studies, 2002), pp. 73–104, at 94.

[60] William of Pagula, 'Admonition to King Edward III', p. 78; David Carpenter, *Magna Carta* (London: Penguin Books, 2015), pp. 450, 458–60; Scott Waugh, 'Success and Failure of the Medieval Constitution in 1341', in Kaeuper, *Law, Governance and Justice*, pp. 121–60, at 121, 158–9.

[61] Nigel Saul, 'Feature of the Month: March 1215: Magna Carta and the Politics of the Reign of Richard II', *The Magna Carta Project*, (magnacarta.cmp.uea.acuk); Nigel Saul, 'Magna Carta in the Late Middle Ages', in Sophie Ambler and Nicholas Vincent, eds, *Magna Carta: New Interpretations* (forthcoming); 'The Record and Process', pp. 174–5; Anthony Musson, 'The Legacy of Magna Carta: Law and Justice in the Fourteenth Century', *William and Mary Bill of Rights Journal*, 25 (2016), pp. 629–63.

kings along with those which the community of the realm would determine in the future.[62]

As we have seen, Gower has sometimes been characterised as a critic of royal 'absolutism and as being an exponent of a 'limited monarchy' and so, in effect, as being closer to the 'political' than to the 'regal' conception of royal power.[63] Certainly, in works such as *In Praise of Peace* and the *Cronica Tripertita*, which were written after 1399, Gower was to show himself as an ardent supporter of those who had deposed Richard II (see below, pp. 414–21). Yet when Gower explicitly addressed the relationship between the ruler and the political community in the three major works which he wrote before 1399, he generally adopted the 'regal' viewpoint. For Gower, as for all medieval thinkers, it was the king's duty to maintain the law as he was sworn to do (CA: VII.2905–16, 3079; VIII.3067). Nevertheless, political theorists and legists had often argued that this duty was a matter of moral obligation rather than of legal necessity and that the king should observe the laws from his own will, love of justice and fear of divine punishment rather than from any legal compulsion. In this sense the king was like Christ and the Virgin Mary who were both above human law but had freely chosen to submit themselves to it.[64] Similarly, in the *Mirour de l'Omme*, Gower asserted that when the ruler failed to uphold the law and did wrong, 'there is no one who can punish his royalty' or limit his will (23101–48). Naturally, Gower preferred it when the king did observe the law: 'However much the royal power may be exalted above the laws', it is only proper that the king should 'govern himself under the laws of justice' and 'obey good laws at all times' (VC: VI.6.522; VI.8). Nevertheless, if he fails to do so, earthly law cannot punish him since the king is 'above the laws' and so 'all things are permissible to him'. The ruler can therefore do what is not allowed, even though he should not allow himself all things, since not everything is honourable, but should rather choose to govern himself according to the law (VC: VI.7.505–6; VI.8.611–20). Genius makes the same point in Book VII of the *Confessio Amantis* when he says that the king is 'above the lawe', his estate being 'fre/Toward alle othre in his persone', even though he should not choose to do things which are 'excessif/Ayein the lawe' (CA:

---

[62] 'Maria Wickert, *Studies in John Gower* (Washington: University Press of America, 1981), p. 139; John Baker, *The Reinvention of Magna Carta, 1216–1616* (Cambridge: Cambridge University Press, 2017), pp. 63–5; 'The Record and Process', pp. 175–6, 178–81; Gaillard Lapsley, 'The Parliamentary Title of Henry IV', EHR, 49 (1934), pp. 423–49, 577–606, at 577–80.

[63] See note 11, above.

[64] Gaines Post, 'Bracton as Jurist and Theologian on Kingship', in Stephan Kuttner, ed., *Proceedings of the Third International Congress of Medieval Canon Law* (Vatican City: Biblioteca Apostolica Vaticana, 1971), pp. 113–30, at 113–27; *Ioannis Saresberiensis Episcopi Carnotensis Policratici*, IV: 6 (523b–524b); *Bracton on the Laws and Customs of England*, ed. Samuel E. Thorne (four volumes; Cambridge, Mass.: Harvard University Press, 1968–77), II: 33.

VII.2718–36; see also VII.1825–48).⁶⁵ That the king was above the law was also illustrated by Genius' story of the worthy knight whom Alexander had wrongfully condemned in a fit of wrath. When the knight appealed against this judgement, the emperor replied that there was no one above him to whom appeal could be made, to which the knight answered that he did not seek to challenge Alexander's lordship but rather addressed himself to the emperor's pity, with this humility winning him mercy (CA: VII.3168–79*).⁶⁶ Just as the view of kingship in the C-text of Langland's *Piers Plowman* has been seen as closer to absolutist theories developed by some civil lawyers and theologians than to the traditions and practices of the poet's own country, so Gower in these passages showed himself to be much closer to the 'regal' conception of kingship than to the 'political' view enshrined in Magna Carta and the royal coronation oath in which the king of England was subject to the laws of the land.⁶⁷

Within the 'regal' conception of kingship, the emphasis was naturally on the obedience which the subject owed to his superior. In the *Mirour de l'Omme*, Gower presents Disobedience as one of the daughters of Pride who, in refusing 'to be subject to anyone because of rank or knowledge', causes 'great evil in the world' (2005–8), whereas Obedience, the daughter of Humility, is a virtue which leads us to submit to our superiors including parents, priests, judges and princes (12145–92). God therefore hated the pride and disobedience which had led the French to avoid 'doing homage and obedience' to Edward III, who was their rightful ruler (2137–48). Gower's ideal was one in which lords and their subjects both do 'good deeds to each other – the lord in his power and the people in their obedience' (MO: 22909–20). Accordingly, as he argued in the *Vox Clamantis*, although the king should show mercy towards his people, it was also right that he should 'curb the rebellious' (VI.10.733) and that he should be venerated by his subjects (I.15.1180).

The Fate of the Tyrant

In stressing that rulers were above the law and in emphasising the subject's duty of obedience to his superiors, Gower seems to be far from offering a defence of limited monarchy or providing a critique of absolutism.⁶⁸ Nevertheless,

---

⁶⁵ Irvin, *The Poetic Voices of John Gower*, pp. 59–60; Kathryn McKinley, 'Kingship and the Body Politic: Echphrasis and *Confessio Amantis* VII', *Mediaevalia*, 21 (1996), pp. 161–87, at 172.
⁶⁶ Kobayashi, '*Principis Umbra*', pp. 90–1. On Gower's reworking of his sources for this exemplum, see Porter, 'Gower's Ethical Microcosm and Political Macrocosm', p. 158.
⁶⁷ Anna P. Baldwin, *The Theme of Government in Piers Plowman* (Cambridge: D. S. Brewer, 1981), p. 18.
⁶⁸ Saul, 'John Gower', pp. 93–4.

even though Gower advocated a 'regal' conception of royal authority, he also criticised those princes who governed in a tyrannical fashion.[69] Accordingly, if modern commentators have sometimes equated absolutist rule with tyranny and with the suppression of all opposition,[70] Gower himself made a distinction between those rightful rulers who exercised a 'regal' power and those who were illegitimate tyrants. Gower accepted the Aristotelian definition of a tyrant as someone who pursued his own individual interests at the expense of the common good (VC: VI.18.1185–98; MO: 23233–49). Accordingly, he did not distinguish rightful kingship from tyranny in legal or institutional terms but rather in terms of the ruler's morality and, in particular, of the tyrant's wilful refusal to observe the 'five points of policy' which Aristotle had supposedly recommended to Alexander. Instead of displaying truthfulness and constancy, exercising liberality, ruling justly, showing mercy and following the way of chastity, a tyrant would deal 'treacherously' towards his subjects, pillage those beneath him, corrupt the law with bribery and fear, take a sadistic delight in cruelty and be guilty of lechery, rape and incest (CA: VII.1723–82, 1950–2035, 2695–3094, 3103–36, 3195–3333, 4208–44, 4593–4607, 4889, 4959–93; CT: I.27–32; II.1–30). For Olsson, Apollonius, the ideal king of Book VIII of the *Confessio Amantis*, embodies all five of the virtues which Aristotle had set out whereas the tyrannical Arrons, whose rape of Lucrece is recounted in Book VII, is deficient in each of them.[71]

What if a ruler abused his position and, rather than pursuing the common good, sought his own pleasure, profit and glory? Did his subjects have any right of redress against him? Given that all medieval political thinkers were agreed that a king should act virtuously, it was the consequences of a ruler's failure to do so that was, in practice, the main point at issue between the 'regal' and the 'political' conceptions of royal power. For those who advocated the 'regal' conception of power, in which the king was answerable only to God, there was little that the community (or those who claimed to speak on its behalf) could do to control the ruler if he failed in his duties. His subjects could only hope that their prince would listen to the wise advice of those who sought to guide him towards virtue. Indeed, as John of Gaunt told Richard II in 1385, it was the very fact that the king could not be

---

[69] Jeremy Griffiths, '*Confessio Amantis*: The Poem and its Pictures', in Minnis, *Gower's Confessio Amantis*, pp. 163–78, at 163.

[70] Bullón-Fernández, *Fathers and Daughters in Gower's Confessio Amantis*, pp. 22–3; María Bullón-Fernández, 'Engendering Authority', pp. 142–3; Simpson, *Sciences and the Self in Medieval Poetry*, pp. 227–8, 281–2.

[71] Kurt Olsson, *John Gower and the Structures of Conversion: A Reading of the Confessio Amantis* (Cambridge: D. S. Brewer, 1992), pp. 206–13. See also Porter, 'Gower's Ethical Microcosm and Political Macrocosm', p. 160; Katherine R. Chandler, 'Memory and Unity in Gower's *Confessio Amantis*', *Philological Quarterly*, 71 (1992), pp. 15–30, at 23–5. For a more critical assessment of Apollonius, see Diane Watt, 'Oedipus, Apollonius, and Richard II: Sex and Politics in Book VIII of John Gower's *Confessio Amantis*', *Studies in the Age of Chaucer*, 24 (2002), pp. 181–208, at 204, 207.

controlled by the law which made it all the more important that he should take heed of the wise counsel of others.[72] But if the ruler chose to ignore such counsel, he had to be endured as an instrument of God sent to punish the sinful. As Giles of Rome said in his *De ecclesiastica potestate*, the tyrant would eventually receive his just deserts but only when he came to be judged by God.[73] Even a jurist such as Accursius (d. 1263), for whom the prince was, in theory, subject to the law could also argue that, in practice, the political community had no coercive sanction available to it with which to compel the ruler to obey it.[74] By contrast, other thinkers, including John of Salisbury, Thomas Aquinas, Engelbert of Admont, John of Paris, Giovanni Boccaccio and Nicholas Oresme, followed Cicero in allowing – with various degrees of qualification – that resistance to a tyrant, and perhaps even his overthrow, was legitimate or even positively virtuous.[75] As was shown by the deposition of Richard II in 1399, whilst the 'regal' conception of kingship offered a defence of a monarch's right to govern according to his own will, it was actually the 'political' view of kingly power, in which the ruler was subject to constraint by the political community, that was more in line with the realities of contemporary English politics.[76] Where, then, did Gower stand in relation to these debates?

---

[72] *The Westminster Chronicle 1381–1394*, eds Leonard C. Hector and Barbara F. Harvey (Oxford: Clarendon Press, 1982), pp. 112–15; Olsson, 'Composing the King, 1390–1391', p. 148.

[73] Pennington, *The Prince and the Law*, p. 216; *Giles of Rome's On Ecclesiastical Power: A Medieval Theory of World Government*, ed. Robert W. Dyson (New York: Columbia University Press, 2004), II: IX (p. 161). See also Augustine, *City of God*, V: 24–6 (pp. 219–23); VII: 31 (p. 292); Anthony Black, *Political Thought in Europe, 1250–1450* (Cambridge: Cambridge University Press, 1992), pp. 150–1; Fritz Schulz, 'Bracton on Kingship', *EHR*, 60 (1945), pp. 136–76, at 153; Kingsford, 'Some Medieval Writers on Kingship', pp. 128–9, 131, 135; Van Dijk, *John Gower and the Limits of the Law*, p. 81; Spencer, 'The Coronation Oath in English Politics, 1272–1399', p. 44.

[74] Brian Tierney, '"The Prince is Not Bound by the Law": Accursius and the Origins of the Modern State', *Comparative Studies in Society and History*, 5 (1963), pp. 378–400 at 391–2, 395. See also Lewis, 'King Above Law', pp. 263–8.

[75] Cicero, *On Duties*, eds Miriam T. Griffin and E. Margaret Atkins (Cambridge: Cambridge University Press, 1991), III: 19, 32 (pp. 107, 111); *Aquinas: Selected Political Writings*, ed. Alexander P. D'Entrèves (Oxford: Basil Blackwell, 1959), I: VI (pp. 31–5); Giovanni Boccaccio, *De Casibus Virorum Illustrium* (*Tutte le Opere di Giovanni Boccaccio, IX)*, eds Pier G. Ricci and Vittorio Zaccaria (Milan: Arnoldo Mondadori, 1983), II, v: 7; Rigby, *Wisdom and Chivalry*, p. 183; Spencer, 'The Coronation Oath in English Politics, 1272–1399', pp. 44–5. Sunderland, *Rebel Barons*, pp. 28–34, 38–41. For the debate about John of Salisbury's seeming advocacy of tyrannicide, see Cary J. Nederman, 'John of Salisbury's Political Theory', in Christophe Grellard and Frédérique Lachaud, eds, *A Companion to John of Salisbury* (Leiden: Brill, 2015), pp. 258–88, at 278–88.

[76] Barron, 'The Tyranny of Richard II', pp. 17–18; Saul, *Richard II*, p. 442; Alastair Dunn, *The Politics of Magnate Power: England and Wales, 1389–1413* (Oxford: Oxford University Press, 2003), pp. 178–80.

Since, as was shown above, Gower could present the king as being above the law, he too could deny that the ruler's subjects had the right to restrain him. As he puts it in the *Mirour de l'Omme*, while those of lower degree can be punished for their misdeeds in this life, when a king does wrong, 'there is no one who can punish his royalty' or limit his will. Only in the next world would the ruler suffer for his sins (23101–48).[77] Similarly, in the *Vox Clamantis*, Gower argues that 'if a king is wicked, God, Who has power over everything, wills to punish him since the law cannot'. It is God who decides whether a king should reign or fall and who, when a king dies, will judge him according to his deeds (VI.16.1101–06; 7.505–6). Genius put forward the same claim in Book VII of the *Confessio Amantis*: if a king errs, he will have to 'justefie' himself to God who is the only one who can 'chastise' him (VII.2718–36; see also VIII.209–10).[78] Within the 'regal' view of royal power, the ideal form of government was, as Jean Dunbabin puts it, autocracy tempered by the autocrat's own conscience so that the personal virtue of the ruler, rather than efficient institutions, was seen as the basis of good government. Similarly, in these passages, Gower, like many earlier thinkers, relied on the fear of damnation to keep the king on the path of virtue.[79]

The *Confessio Amantis* does present us with examples where the punishment, or even the deposition, of tyrannical rulers by their subjects seems to be justified, but in these cases the ruler who is removed is actually a usurper who possesses the throne '*ex defectu tituli*'. For instance when Perseus, the younger son of Philip, king of Macedon, acquires the throne after he has had his older brother, Demetrius, unjustly condemned to death for treason, the 'comune' of the land imprison him and send his son into exile and poverty (II.1613–861). Similarly, in the 'Tale of the False Bachelor', when it is revealed that the squire of the son of the emperor of Rome has taken the place of his master as ruler of Persia by means of treachery, his subjects arrest him and hand him over to the Roman emperor for punishment (CA: II.2501–785). In such cases, the ruler who was deposed had not acquired power by rightful means and so, as Aquinas argued, he could lawfully be repudiated by his subjects.[80]

---

[77] Kurt Olsson, 'The Cardinal Virtues and the Structure of John Gower's *Speculum Meditantis*', *Journal of Medieval and Renaissance Studies*, 7 (1977), pp. 113–48, at 134.

[78] Peter Nicholson, *Love and Ethics in Gower's Confessio Amantis* (Ann Arbor: The University of Michigan Press, 2005), pp. 350–7.

[79] Jean Dunbabin, 'Aristotle in the Schools', in Beryl Smalley, ed., *Trends in Medieval Political Thought* (Oxford: Basil Blackwell, 1965), pp. 65–85, at 73; Fisher, *John Gower*, pp. 182–3; Kingsford, 'Some Medieval Writers on Kingship', p. 131; Post, 'Bracton as Jurist and Theologian on Kingship', pp. 114–18, 121–2; Baldwin, *The Theme of Government in Piers Plowman*, p. 21; Bernard Guenée, *States and Rulers In Later Medieval Europe* (Oxford: Basil Blackwell, 1985), p. 87.

[80] Van Dijk, *John Gower and the Limits of the Law*, pp. 72–3, 77–8, 81, 85; Robert W. Carlyle and Alexander J. Carlyle, *A History of Medieval Political Thought in the West, Volume V* (Edinburgh: William Blackwood and Sons, 1928), p. 91.

More problematic were those instances where the ruler was a tyrant '*ex parte exercitus*', i.e. where he had acquired power rightfully but then proceeded to exercise it in a wrongful manner. Could such a ruler be restrained or even removed by his subjects? A common way for medieval authors to deal with this awkward question was to avoid it so that although they did not explicitly advocate the removal of a tyrant, they nonetheless warned rulers that tyranny was an illegitimate and unnatural abuse of power which their subjects were unlikely to tolerate for long.[81] Giles of Rome, for instance, followed Aristotle and Cicero in arguing that tyranny will eventually always destroy itself since it inevitably generates resistance from its victims: the more tyrannical a ruler is, the shorter his reign will be.[82] It was this approach that Gower himself adopted when, following a long line of classical and medieval thinkers, he argued that virtue on the part of the ruler was not only admirable in itself but also had the pragmatic benefit of helping him to maintain his position.[83] If a king should be feared by his subjects, it is the exercise of pity which will win him their love and so secure his own rule (VC.V.16.949–56; VI.14.999–1001; VI.19.1191–92; CA: III.1757–1860; VII.2759–64, 3085–3159, 3162*, 3913–17, 4027–4133, 3913–17, 4173–80).

In cautioning rulers against the consequences of tyranny, Giles of Rome had warned them that being lustful towards their subjects' wives and daughters would particularly provoke their people to rise against them.[84] For Gower too, the hallmark of the tyrant was an uncontrolled indulgence in lechery, rape, incest and other illicit desires (CA: VII.4208–44, 4593–4607, 4889, 4959–93).[85] Genius illustrated this point in Book VII of the *Confessio Amantis* with the help of the tales of Virginia and Lucrece. When Apius, the 'governour' or 'king' of Rome, sought to ravish the virtuous Virginia at a time

---

[81] Jean Dunbabin, 'Government', in Burns, *The Cambridge History of Medieval Political Thought*, pp. 477–1519, at 494.

[82] Aristotle, *The Nicomachean Ethics*, ed. Harris Rackham (Ware: Wordsworth Editions, 1996), IV, v: 7; Aristotle, 'The Politics', III, 17; V, 10; Cicero, *On Duties*, II: 23 (p. 71); Giles of Rome, *The Governance of Kings and Princes*, pp. 25, 117–20, 328–9, 332–8, 340–9. For other medieval writers who adopted this view, see Rigby, *Wisdom and Chivalry*, p. 183.

[83] Cicero, *On Duties*, II: 23–6 (pp. 70–2); Seneca, 'On Clemency', 1, 8–12, 20, 25–6 (pp. 138, 146–52, 160, 163–4), in *The Stoic Philosophy of Seneca*, trans. Moses Hadas (New York: W. W. Norton, 1968); Giles of Rome, *The Governance of Kings and Princes*, pp. 95–7, 118–19, 128–9, 141–2, 340–1, 345, 348, 351, 378, 390–2; Arthur W. Bahr, 'Reading Codicological Form in John Gower's Trentham Manuscript', *Studies in the Age of Chaucer*, 33 (2011), pp. 219–62, at 234; Craun, *Lies, Slander and Obscenity in Medieval English Literature*, pp. 198–9. For detailed references, see Rigby, *Wisdom and Chivalry*, pp. 206–7.

[84] Giles of Rome, *The Governance of Kings and Princes*, pp. 68–74. For detailed references, see Rigby, *Wisdom and Chivalry*, pp. 44–5. King John had earlier been accused of this fault (Carpenter, *Magna Carta*, pp. 92, 276, 282).

[85] Michael Hanrahan, '"Speaking of Sodomy": Gower's Advice to Princes in the *Confessio Amantis*', *Exemplaria*, 14 (2002), pp. 423–46, at 441–3.

when her father, Livius Virginius, was away fighting on behalf of Rome, he was deposed by the 'comun conseil' of all the men of the city (CA: VII.5131–5306). Likewise, when the rape of Lucrece by Arrons, the tyrannical son of the equally tyrannical Tarquin, the king of Rome, was revealed, 'al the toun', both the great and the small, demanded an end to such misrule, with the result that the two men were exiled and 'betre governance' was introduced (VII.4593–4609, 4889, 4899, 4959–89, 5058–5123). Yet, even though these stories show that Gower recognised that a tyrant's victims would eventually rise against him, he did not use them to offer a theoretical defence of the subject's right of resistance.[86] Indeed, although Gower noted how the rape of Lucrece had led to the banishment of Arrons and his father, he omitted to specify how it had also resulted in the transition from monarchical to republican rule at Rome, even though this monumental constitutional change was noted in the versions of this story told by Ovid, Livy, and Chaucer.[87] Thus, rather than recounting the stories of Virginia and Lucrece in order to encourage the subjects of tyrants to revolt, Genius addressed these *exempla* to those rulers who would 'afterward govern' so that they might learn 'Hou it is good a king eschuie/The lust of vice and vertu suie' (VII.5301–6).[88] Here Gower does not seek to argue that a ruler can in principle be deposed by his subjects but rather warns the king that, in practice, he will meet this fate if he rules tyrannically. Rather than focusing on what the ruler's subjects can do in terms of their constitutional rights, Gower's 'rhetorical' approach to good government emphasises what the ruler should do in terms of his personal morality.[89]

---

[86] For a different interpretation, see Bullón-Fernández, *Fathers and Daughters in Gower's Confessio Amantis*, pp. 153–4.

[87] *Ovid in Six Volumes, V: Fasti*, eds James G. Frazer and G. P. Goold (second edition; Cambridge, Mass.: Harvard University Press, 1989), II: 685–852; Livy, *The History of Rome, Books I-II*, trans. B. O. Foster (Cambridge, Mass.: Harvard University Press, 1988), I: 53–60; II: 1; Geoffrey Chaucer, 'The Legend of Good Women', ll. 1869–70; Scanlon, *Narrative, Authority and Power*, pp. 293–6. See also John Gower, *Traitié selonc les auctors pour essampler les amantz marietz*, X: 8–14; Ellen S. Barkalian, *Aspects of Love in John Gower's Confessio Amantis* (New York: Routledge, 2000), p. 69. The constitutional consequences of the rape of Lucrece are also emphasised in Christine de Pizan, *The Book of the City of Ladies*, trans. Rosalind Brown-Grant (London: Penguin Books, 1999), II: 44 (p. 148) but are ignored in the version of the story in the *Gesta Romanorum* (*Gesta Romanorum: A New Translation*, trans. Christopher Stace (Manchester: Manchester University Press, 2016), no. 135).

[88] Peck, *Kingship and Common Profit in Gower's Confessio Amantis*, p. xxii. For a different interpretation of the story of Virginia, see Ferster, *Fictions of Advice*, pp. 119–23.

[89] Van Dijk, *John Gower and the Limits of the Law*, pp. 135–7.

Gower as an Exponent of 'Political' Kingship?

If the political outlook contained in Gower's three major poems was in line with the 'regal' view of royal power, why have these works been understood by some scholars as favouring a 'political' conception of authority? One reason is that a 'constitutionalist' or 'political' view of royal power might seem to be implicit in Gower's use of the maxim '*Vox populi, vox dei*' ('the voice of the people is the voice of God').[90] This pseudo-Biblical proverb had been in circulation since at least the late eighth century and had famously been used in 1327 by Walter Reynolds, the archbishop of Canterbury, in his sermon justifying the deposition of Edward II.[91] Gower himself employed it on a number of occasions. For instance, in the context of his discussion of the common complaints made about the corruption of the Church in Book III of the *Vox Clamantis*, Gower asserts that 'the voice of the people agrees with the voice of God' ('*Vox populi cum voce dei concordat*') (III.15.1267; see also MO: 12721–26; VC: IV.17.710; VI.1.15; VII.25.1447–8, 1469–70).[92] For Judith Ferster, Gower's invocation of the maxim '*Vox populi, vox dei*' suggests that he saw the king's key relationship as being with 'the people', who were his 'true counsellors' and 'best advisers', rather than with his 'aristocratic advisers'.[93] Gower's faith in the voice of the people could also seem to be indicated by his frequent claim that his complaints about the evils of the times were not just his own personal opinion but rather represented the views of 'all Christian folk' or expressed 'The comun vois, which mai not lie' (MO: 18445–8, 22248, 24938, 26126, 26180; CA: Pro.124).

Yet, it may be misleading to take Gower's use of the proverb *Vox populi, voix dei* as an indication of how he thought contemporary government should actually be organised. After all, though Gower allowed that the people could perceive the social, religious and political abuses of the day, he was much less positive about their ability to identify the causes of such abuses or to arrive

---

[90] Gower may have been familiar with this proverb from the *Speculum Stultorum* (*The Anglo-Latin Satirical Poets and Epigrammatists of the Twelfth Century, Volume I*, ed. Thomas Wright (London: Rolls Series, 1872), p. 100), a text to which he often turned (Robert R. Raymo, 'Gower's *Vox Clamantis* and the *Speculum Stultorum*', *Modern Language Notes*, 70 (1955), pp. 315–20).

[91] George Boas, *Vox Populi: The History of an Idea* (Baltimore: the John Hopkins Press, 1969), pp. 8–26; Edward Peters, '*Vox Populi, Vox Dei*', in Edward B. King and Susan J. Ridyard, eds, *Law in Medieval Life and Thought* (Sewanee: The Press of the University of the South, 1990), pp. 91–120. For Reynolds, see *Chronicon de Lanercost, MCCI-MCCCXLVI*, ed. Joseph Stevenson (Edinburgh: Impressum Edinburgi, 1839), p. 258.

[92] Roberts, *Invention and Authorship in Medieval England*, p. 72. For other references, see Wickert, *Studies in John Gower*, pp. 75–83; Paul Miller, 'John Gower, Satiric Poet', in Minnis, *Gower's Confessio Amantis*, pp. 79–105, at 102–4; Matthew Giancarlo, *Parliament and Literature in Late Medieval England* (Cambridge: Cambridge University Press, 2007), pp. 115–17.

[93] Ferster, *Fictions of Advice*, pp. 126–32.

at a remedy for them.⁹⁴ For instance, at the end of his estates satire in the *Mirour de l'Omme*, Gower says that each estate blames the others for the evils of the times and that 'No one confesses his own error'. It seemed that the prophecy of Hosea was now coming true 'for he prophesised that among the people of the earth there was no wisdom whatever that was pleasing to God', a failing for which God would take vengeance on the people and the beasts, birds and fishes of the earth (Osee 4: 1–3; MO: 26569–616).⁹⁵ Moreover, Gower certainly did not object to the king having aristocratic advisers. On the contrary, in the *Cronica Tripertita* Richard II's main fault is said to have been to listen to the 'poisonous counsel of brash youths' who urged him to 'prey upon the goods of his nobles', with Gower's emphasis being on how the king unjustly vowed to despoil and kill the duke of Gloucester and the earls of Arundel and Warwick (I.15–24).

In particular, although Gower was sometimes willing to express a positive view of the voice of the 'people' in the abstract, he was much more hostile when this voice was specified as being that of the lower orders of society in particular.⁹⁶ As he says in the *Mirour de l'Omme*, just as it would be unnatural and dishonourable for the foot of the body to rise up against the head which should rule it, so 'when the people rise up like savage beasts in a multitude and a tempest against the lords, it is a great error'. In such cases, the 'common clamour' of the lesser people does not express the voice of God but is 'only folly' (26473–508, 27229–40). Similarly, in the *Vox Clamantis*, even before he had written the vitriolic denunciation of the rebels of 1381 which appears in the *Visio*, Gower had explicitly stated that it was not acceptable that 'anyone from the class of serfs should try to set things right' (V.9.627–8), had dismissed the wage-labourers as 'a race without power of reason' (V.10.651) and had attacked those amongst the common people who would not stick to their proper station and sought mastery as an 'ungovernable rabble' (V.16.987–92). Likewise in the *Confessio Amantis*, in the very passage where Gower agrees with the 'comun clamour' when it complains that 'the world is al miswent', he also compares the 'comune' of 'sondri londes', which will

---

⁹⁴ Irvin, *The Poetic Voices of John Gower*, p. 34.
⁹⁵ For another instance where Gower did not accept the voice of the *plebs*, see CT: III.388–99; Robert F. Yeager, 'John Gower's Poetry and the "Lawyerly Habit of Mind"', in Andreea D. Boboc, ed., *Theorizing Legal Personhood in Late Medieval England* (Leiden: Brill, 2015), pp. 71–93, at 85.
⁹⁶ Pamela L. Longo, 'Gower's Public Outcry', *Philological Quarterly*, 92 (2013), pp. 357–87; Siân Echard, 'The Long and the Short of It', in Ana Sáez-Hidalgo and Robert F. Yeager, eds, *John Gower in England and Iberia: Manuscripts, Influences, Reception* (Cambridge: D. S. Brewer, 2014), pp. 245–60, at 252–6; Siân Echard, 'Gower's "bokes of Latin": Language, Politics and Poetry', *Studies in the Age of Chaucer*, 25 (2003), pp. 123–56, at 132–5, 139–40; Andrew Galloway, 'The Common Voice in Theory and Practice in Late Fourteenth Century England', in Kaeuper, *Law, Governance and Justice*, pp. 243–86, at 265–6; Edwards, *Invention and Authorship in Medieval England*, pp. 82–3.

not be ruled by law, to fermenting liquor which bursts out of a barrel which lacks the hoops needed to contain it (Pro.499–517). Thus, whilst Gower was prepared to accept that the voice of the people was the voice of God when it accorded with his own views, he was equally happy to dismiss it as idle chatter when it clashed with his own opinions about the causes of the world's ills (MO: 27217–28).

An alternative reason for regarding Gower as an exponent of the 'political' rather than the 'regal' view of royal power is set out by James Simpson in his important study of the *Confessio Amantis*. For Simpson, the *Confessio* can be interpreted as a psychomachia, i.e. as an allegory of the relationship between different faculties within the soul. Here Genius is seen as representing the imagination and Amans as personifying the concupiscent will which desires to please the body, with the interaction between them leading to the education, integration and perfection of the soul. In turn, this psychomachia should be read as a political allegory in which the soul is understood to represent a *res publica* which 'can only be ruled by consensus and mediation, not by diktat and suppression', meaning that absolutism is rejected in favour of a constitutionalist conception of power. Just as reason governs the body but can only do so by 'recognizing the rights of the body' and the 'proper place' of sensual desire, so that a '"constitutional" compromise between sensual desire and reason' is arrived at, so the good king can only rule his polity when he recognises 'the energies and rightful scope of the whole body politic'.[97]

Yet, even if we accepted that Amans represents the will, that Genius symbolises the imagination and that their relationship provides a model of how the body politic should be ordered, the emphasis in the *Confessio Amantis* is still on how both of these faculties of the soul should be firmly subordinated to reason. As Simpson himself puts it, for Gower, 'one part of the soul, the will, desires to please the body, while supremacy over the body is desired by reason', so that reason must triumph over will if we are to be turned towards virtue. Likewise, as he points out, for Gower the imagination can mislead us, whether in love or in politics, and, like the will, must be guided by reason, if it is to be a force leading us to virtue.[98] As Genius says in his discussion of Alexander's rapaciousness in Book III of the *Confessio Amantis*, the emperor's desire for endless conquest shows what happens 'whan reson is put aside/And will governeth the corage' (III.2420–60). As Genius later puts it, just as the heart is the 'chief lord' over the other organs of the body, being like 'a king in his Empire', so, in turn, the heart should be ruled by the 'governance' of reason (VII.463–89). The same point is made by Amans when he confesses that there is a battle within him between, on the one side, wit and reason, and, on the other, will and hope, with wit

---

[97] Simpson, *Sciences and the Self in Medieval Poetry*, pp. 229, 270, 274, 281–4.
[98] Simpson, *Sciences and the Self in Medieval Poetry*, pp. 264–5, 279.

and reason counselling him that, in order for reason to rule his heart, he 'scholde will remue/And put him out of retenue, or elles holde him under fotte' (III.1156–70). Amans himself accepts the division within himself can only be overcome if his will is 'governed/Of reson more than of kinde'.[99] His problem here, as so often, is that even though he acknowledges the course of action which he should pursue, he is still unable to govern himself so that he will act as he knows he should (III.1190–91, 1197–99).

In these passages, Gower's emphasis is on the need for hierarchy and obedience within the soul and the body, a perspective which was perfectly compatible with the 'regal' outlook which the poet explicitly advocated: just as reason should govern the body and the other faculties of the soul, so should the king reign supreme within the body politic and every subject should 'drede/His king and to his heste obeie' (CA: VII.490–520, 3122–29). For Simpson, the *Confessio* should not be read as championing the absolute sovereignty of reason even though explicit affirmations to this effect are made 'at the end of the poem'.[100] Yet, in medieval rhetorical theory, the ending of a text was often presented as the most appropriate place for the expression of those views which an author especially wanted to emphasise.[101] Accordingly, when Genius teaches Amans that he should resist love, which blinds its servants, and should instead set his heart 'under that lawe,/The which of reason is governed/And noght of will' (VIII.2130–36), his words, in being placed at the end of the *Confessio Amantis*, would seem to have a particular authority.

Another reason for seeing Gower as an advocate of the 'political' view of kingship is put forward by Rosemarie McGerr, who argues that we should read the views on kingship and law expressed in the *Confessio Amantis* in the context of the preface to the *Nova Statuta Angliae*, a copy of which was presented to Richard II around 1390. This collection of English statutes has a preamble which gives an account of Edward II's downfall in terms of the king's failure to observe his coronation oath and his refusal to be bound by the law of the land. For McGerr, Book VII of the *Confessio Amantis* echoes the *Nova Statuta Angliae* in stressing the 'central importance of law to good kingship' and in arguing that a king who does not uphold the law has 'lost his right to rule'.[102] Yet, in many of the passages which she cites to support this

---

[99] Chandler, 'Memory and Unity in Gower's *Confessio Amantis*', pp. 17, 26; Hugh White, 'Division and Failure in Gower's *Confessio Amantis*', *Neophilologus*, 72 (1988), pp. 600–16, at 606; Hilary E. Fox, 'Min Herte is Growen into Ston: Ethics and Activity in Gower's *Confessio Amantis*', *Comitatus*, 36 (2005), pp. 15–40, at 16, 27, 31, 38–9; Kurt O. Olsson, 'Rhetoric, John Gower and the Late Medieval Exemplum', *Mediaevalia et Humanistica*, n.s. 8 (1977), pp. 185–200, at 197.

[100] Simpson, *Sciences and the Self in Medieval Poetry*, p. 271.

[101] For references, see Rigby, *Wisdom and Chivalry*, p. 231.

[102] McGerr, 'Gower's *Confessio Amantis* and the *Nova Statuta Angliae*', pp. 48–55. If the fate of Edward II should have provided Richard with a warning about the dangers of setting himself above the law, it was a warning which he seems to have ignored, as is

interpretation of Gower's outlook, the poet does not actually advocate the right of subjects to overthrow a tyrannical ruler. On the contrary, although Genius teaches that a king *should* uphold the law when he has sworn to do so (CA: VII.2910–16, 3079), he also allows that, in certain respects, the king's power 'stant above the law' (CA: VII.2718–24) and that he is only answerable to God, who punishes rulers who break the law, rather than to his subjects since he is 'fre/toward alle othre in his person' (CA: VII.2728–36).[103]

Where, however, Gower *does* seem to favour a 'political' rather than a 'regal' conception of royal power is the passage in Book VII of the *Confessio Amantis* in which he has Genius explicitly claim that 'What king of lawe taketh no kepe,/Be lawe he mai no regne kepe' (CA: VII.3073–74).[104] Unfortunately, Genius does not specify which law (divine, natural or positive) allowed a ruler who overrode the law to be removed. Since Genius here is speaking in general terms about the fate of all kings who fail to obey the law, this would not seem to be a reference to English law in particular. In 1386, when Thomas, duke of Gloucester, and Thomas Arundel, bishop of Ely, reminded Richard II of the downfall of Edward II, they did claim that an 'ancient statute' allowed a king who would not be governed by the laws of the land or guided by the counsel of his lords and nobles to be deposed 'with the common assent and agreement of the people'. Even here, however, there was room for doubt since although Edward II had, in reality, been removed from the throne by force, he had, in theory, abdicated, making it 'very doubtful whether there had been an actual sentence of deposition in the legal sense of the term'.[105] Such doubts may explain why the account of Edward's downfall offered in the *Nova Statuta Angliae* does not specify the process whereby the king had been removed from the throne.[106] Similarly, although the language which had been used to explain Pope Innocent IV's deposition of the Emperor Frederick II in 1245 was invoked to justify the overthrow of Richard II in 1399, this deposition of a secular ruler by a pope did not constitute a precedent which would allow a king to

---

suggested by his attempts to have Edward canonised by the pope in 1390 and 1397 (Saul, *Richard II*, p. 323). For the coronation oath, see above, note 113, below.

[103] McGerr, 'Gower's *Confessio Amantis* and the *Nova Statuta Angliae*', pp. 55–8; Robert J. Meindl, 'The Failure of Counsel: Curial Corruption in Book VI of the *Vox Clamantis*', *Accessus*, 3/2 (2016), pp. 1–51, at 23–4.

[104] Nicholson, *Love and Ethics in Gower's Confessio Amantis*, p. 352.

[105] *Knighton's Chronicle, 1337–1396*, pp. 360–1; Gerard E. Caspary, 'The Deposition of Richard II and the Canon Law', in Stephan Kuttner and J. Joseph Ryan, eds, *Proceedings of the Second International Congress of Medieval Canon Law* (Vatican City: S. Congregatio de Seminariis et Studiorum Universitatibus, 1965), pp. 189–201, at 198; Lapsley, 'The Parliamentary Title of Henry IV', pp. 581–2, 586, 588; Spencer, 'The Coronation Oath in English Politics, 1272–1399', p. 51.

[106] McGerr, 'Gower's *Confessio Amantis* and the *Nova Statuta Angliae*', p. 52; Rosemarie McGerr, *A Lancastrian Mirror for Princes: The Yale Law School New Statutes of England* (Bloomington: Indiana University Press, 2011), pp. 6, 18–19, 76–80.

be overthrown by his own subjects.[107] Indeed, even though 'The Record and Process' listed the reasons why the estates of the realm had decided to 'depose' Richard II, it adopted a belt and braces approach by claiming that the king had also willingly renounced his throne.[108]

It may be that Genius' claim that 'What king of lawe taketh no kepe,/ Be lawe he mai no regne kepe' was a reference to the civil law teaching that although the emperor is the source of all law, he should also conduct his actions according to the law which was the source of his authority and that he should acknowledge himself as bound by the laws.[109] This teaching was potentially at odds with the civil law dictum that 'what pleases the prince has force of law', which was cited above.[110] However, jurists and political theorists had long been able to interpret this seemingly absolutist dictum to mean that the prince's will only had the force of law when it was in agreement with divine or natural law or when it accorded with reason, equity and the common interest or, as *The Song of Lewes* put it, with truth, justice and mercy.[111] Even Giles of Rome, who is often characterised as a defender of a monarchy 'in which the sovereign is not bound by the law', allowed that positive law (i.e. the law of a particular community) could take precedence over the ruler's will when it embodied the natural law which is valid everywhere, since no one was a rightful king unless he obeyed the law of nature.[112] Inevitably, such qualifications raised the thorny issues of precisely who was to

---

[107] Caspary, 'The Deposition of Richard II and the Canon Law', p. 201; Laura Ashe, *Richard II: A Brittle Glory* (London: Allen Lane, 2016), p. 4.

[108] 'The Record and Process', pp. 169–72, 185. See also *The Chronicle of Adam Usk, 1377–1421*, ed. Chris Given-Wilson (Oxford: Clarendon Press), p. 62.

[109] *Corpus Iuris Civilis, Volume II: Codex Iustinianus*, ed. Paul Krueger (Cambridge: Cambridge University Press, 2014), I.xiv.14 (p. 68); *Ioannis Saresberiensis Episcopi Carnotensis Policratici*, IV: 1 (514b-c).

[110] See note 52, above.

[111] *Aquinas: Selected Political Writings*, pp. 110–11; James of Viterbo, 'Is It Better to Be Ruled by the Best Man Than by the Best Laws?', in Arthur S. McGrade, John Kilcullen and Matthew Kempshall, eds, *The Cambridge Translations of Medieval Philosophical Texts, Volume II* (Cambridge: Cambridge University Press, 2001), pp. 321–5, at 322–5; *Ioannis Saresberiensis Episcopi Carnotensis Policratici*, IV: II (515a); Nicole Oresme, *Le Livre de Politiques d'Aristote. Published from the Text of the Avranches Manuscript, 223*, ed. Albert D. Menut (*Transactions of the American Philosophical Society*, n.s. 60/6 (1970), p. 243; Schulz, 'Bracton on Kingship', pp. 154–5; Giancarlo, 'Gower's Governmentality', pp. 253–4; Pennington, *The Prince and the Law*, pp. 76, 84, 90, 117–20, 182, 188–92, 208, 222, 231, 231–2; Tierney, '"The Prince is Not Bound by the Law"', *passim*; Fiona Somerset, '"Al Þe Comonys With O Voys Atonys": Multilingual Voice and Vernacular Verse in Piers Plowman', *The Yearbook of Langland Studies*, 19 (2005), pp. 107–36, pp. 131–2; *The Song of Lewes*, ll. 454–5, 608–26, 819–20 and notes on pp. 98, 113–18.

[112] Giles of Rome, *The Governance of Kings and Princes*, pp. 377–9; Lambertini, 'Political Thought', pp. 258–65, 274; Kurt Olsson, 'Composing the King, 1390–91: Gower's Ricardian Rhetoric', *Studies in the Age of Chaucer*, 31 (2009), pp. 141–73, at 147–9; Rigby, *Wisdom and Chivalry*, pp. 182–3.

decide whether or not the prince's will was in agreement with reason or the law of nature and what was to be done when this was not the case. There was a similar ambiguity in the oath which Richard II had sworn at his coronation in 1377. At this date, the final clause of the oath, which had been introduced at Edward II's coronation in 1308, by which the king promised to maintain the laws that were chosen by the community of the realm, had been qualified by the requirement that the king should uphold such laws as were 'justly and reasonably' chosen by the people – which once more raised the question of who was to determine what was just and reasonable and what remedy was available if the king should fail to keep this promise.[113]

In practice, then, the same texts could be interpreted by jurists and political theorists in either 'regal' or 'political' ways depending on whether their purpose was to emphasise the power of the ruler's will or to stress the restraints which should be imposed upon it.[114] For instance, certain passages of the thirteenth-century *De Legibus et Consuetudinibus Angliae*, ('Bracton'),[115] which was a standard work on English common law, argue that the king has no equal within the realm and that his only superior is God, whose vicar he is. The king should willingly place himself under the law, since it is the law which has made him king and there is no king (*rex*) where will rules rather than the law (*lex*). However, if the king does not obey the law, as he expects others to do, his subjects can only petition for a remedy against his injustice and may not presume to question, contravene or nullify his actions. The only 'bridle' on the king's actions is his own temperance and moderation but if the king will not amend himself, he must await punishment from God since he has no peer, let alone a superior.[116] Doubtless, if the king had the correct *habitus mentis*, he would have a disposition to follow the law and do justice firmly ingrained in his mind but, as Nederman points out, 'Bracton' showed 'little concern' for how this *habitus* was actually to be acquired. In its absence, the text seems to present the king as remaining 'insusceptible to correction by his earthly inferiors'.[117]

---

[113] *English Historical Documents, 1327–1485*, ed. Alec R. Myers (London: Eyre and Spottiswode, 1969), pp. 404–5; Saul, *Richard II*, p. 25. Richard renewed his coronation oath in 1388 (*The Westminster Chronicle 1381–1394*, p. 342).

[114] Pennington, 'Law, Legislative Authority and Theories of Government, 1150–1300', pp. 426–32, 436–8, 442, 446, 453; Pennington, *The Prince and the Law*, pp. 79, 92–3, 197, 213, 217–21, 231; Joseph P. Canning, 'Law, Sovereignty and Corporation Theory, 1300–1450', in Burns, *The Cambridge History of Medieval Political Thought*, pp. 454–76, at 454–63; Tierney, '"The Prince is Not Bound by the Law"', pp. 385–400; Lapsley, 'The Parliamentary Title of Henry IV', pp. 577–80.

[115] On the authorship of this text, see Carpenter, *Magna Carta*, p. 321, n. 16.

[116] *Bracton on the Laws and Customs of England*, II: 21–2, 33, 109–10, 305; III: 42–3; IV: 159, 217. For discussion of these issues, see also Lewis, 'King Above Law?', pp. 240–9; Carpenter, *Magna Carta*, p. 330; Spencer, 'The Coronation Oath in English Politics, 1272–1399', p. 46.

[117] Cary J. Nederman, 'Bracton on Kingship Revisited', *History of Political Thought*, 5 91984), pp. 61–77, at 63, 74.

Yet, elsewhere in the same work it is asserted that 'whatever has been rightly decided and approved with the counsel and consent of the magnates and the general agreement of the *res publica*, the authority of the king or prince having been added thereto, has the force of law' and so 'cannot be changed without the common consent of all those by whose counsel and consent they were promulgated'. As a famous *addicio* to the text puts it, even if 'private persons cannot question the acts of kings', the king is subject to God, to the law and to his *curia*, i.e. his earls and barons, who, if the king is without the bridle of the law, 'ought to put the bridle on him'. Far from the king having no peer, the text here claims that his earls are his partners and that, in effect, 'he who has a partner has a master'. Similarly, although 'Bracton' maintains that only God can punish the king it also qualifies this claim with the words 'unless one says that the *universitas regni* and his baronage may and ought to do this', which left it open whether or not the text itself was actually maintaining this.[118] Accordingly, although 'Bracton', like the *Tractatus de Legibus et Consuetudinibus Regni Anglie*, attributed to Glanvill (c.1188), quotes the legal maxim that 'What pleases the prince has the force of law', it also follows the *Tractatus* in arguing that whilst the law needs to be backed by royal authority, it should also be 'promulgated about problems settled in council on the advice of the magnates'.[119] We can see similar contradictions and equivocations in the views of political theorists such as John of Salisbury and Thomas Aquinas, who struggled to reconcile an ideal of strong monarchical sovereignty with some notion of the subject's right of resistance to tyranny.[120]

Given such conflicting traditions and authorities – conflicts which were also evident in the tensions and instabilities which characterised the actual practice of late medieval English government and politics – it is perhaps not surprising that, as Matthew Irvin puts it, Gower did not succeed in clarifying what centuries of legal theorists had 'left unresolved'.[121] Certainly, in arguing that the king was above the law whilst also insisting that the ruler had a moral duty to obey the law and that it was in his own interest to do so, Gower's views had the potential to lead to very different conclusions (VC: V.18.1159–1200; CA: VII.4019–26). We can see these divergent tendencies at work in the 'Tale of Apollonius', which is the final moral *exemplum* offered by Genius in the *Confessio Amantis*. On one reading of the story,

---

[118] *Bracton on the Laws and Customs of England*, II: 19–22, 109–10, 166–7, 305–6; III: 43; Spencer, 'The Coronation Oath in English Politics, 1272–1399', p. 47.

[119] *Bracton on the Laws and Customs of England*, II: 305; *The Treatise on the Laws and Customs of the Realm of England Commonly Called Glanvill*, ed. George D. G. Hall (London: Nelson, 1965), p. 2. See also *Fleta, Volume II: Prologue, Book I, Book II*, eds Henry G. Richardson and George O. Sayles (Selden Society, 72 (1953)), p. 2; *Britton: An English Translation and Notes*, ed. Francis M. Nichols (Washington: John Byrne, 1901), p. 1.

[120] Sunderland, *Rebel Barons*, pp. 22–3, 32–4, 36–41, 43–7.

[121] Harriss, *Shaping the Nation*, pp. 3–6; Irvin, *The Poetic Voices of John Gower*, pp. 60–1.

Gower would seem to have tended towards a 'political' rather than a 'regal' conception of kingship and to have favoured a form of royal power which, as Sebastian Sobecki has argued, was based on 'consensual rule and institutionalized counsel'.[122] Certainly, Apollonius is portrayed in the tale as ruling his own land with the advice of his lords in 'parlement' (VIII.1551–60). When he abruptly flees his country to avoid the murderous intentions of the king of Antioch, his subjects bewail his departure not simply because it means that they have been separated from their 'head' and governor but also because the king's decision to leave was made 'Withoute the commun assent' (VIII.466–94). Similarly, at the end of the tale, Apollonius becomes king of Pentapolis only after having taken counsel and then summoned a 'Parlement' at which 'al the lond of on assent/Forth with his wif hath him corouned' (VIII. 1988–91). Yet, even here Gower managed to have things both ways. For instance, although Apollonius rules Tyre with the help of his parliament, it is the king's 'ordinance' which is decisive in arranging the affairs which are discussed there (VIII.1915–20). Similarly, when, at the end of the tale, the 'commune' and the 'grete lordes' of Pentapolis beseech Apollonius to take the throne, they do so because the death of his father-in-law means that he is now their 'liege lord' and so should rightfully ascend to the position which God and 'fortune' have granted him (VIII.1963–91).

If, then, Gower's political outlook was characterised by vacillation and unresolved tensions, this was not simply because, as has been suggested, he chose to express his views in the form of imaginative literature but also because he was engaging with legal and political sources and traditions which were themselves inconsistent and contradictory.[123] Given the ambivalence of Gower's political outlook, it is understandable why his views have been open to such conflicting interpretation. Nevertheless, even though Gower's works display, as Matthew Giancarlo puts it, a 'cagy ambiguity about where legitimate foundational authority lies', in general, the explicit claims which Gower made about the nature of royal power in the *Mirour de l'Omme*, the *Vox Clamantis* and the *Confessio Amantis* set out a 'regal' rather than a 'political' view of royal power and so emphasised the ruler's answerability to God, rather than to his subjects.[124]

---

[122] Sobecki, *Unwritten Verities*, pp. 84–7; Sebastian I. Sobecki, 'Educating Richard: Incest, Marriage and (Political) Consent in Gower's "Tale of Apollonius"', *Anglia: Zeitschrift für Englische Philologie*, 125 (2007), pp. 205–16.

[123] Conrad van Dijk, 'Giving Each His Due: Langland, Gower and the Question of Equity', *Journal of English and Germanic Philology*, 108 (2009), pp. 310–35, at 335. For imaginative literature as inherently problematic as a vehicle for ideology, see Pierre Macherey, *A Theory of Literary Production* (London: Routledge and Kegan Paul, 1978), pp. 124–33.

[124] Giancarlo, 'Gower's Governmentality', pp. 236–7, 245–6, 252–4.

The Deposition of Richard II

Since both the *Vox Clamantis* and the *Confessio Amantis* (at least in its earliest version) are addressed to Richard II, it is not surprising that these works focus on the question of what a ruler should do in order to govern virtuously rather than on the constitutional consequences of his failure to do so.[125] Yet, in 1399, when Richard's opponents claimed that the king's rule had led to the realm being 'on the point of being undone by default of governance and the undoing of good laws', it was exactly this latter issue that Gower, along with the rest of England's political community, was obliged to address.[126] As we have seen, in advising princes on how to rule justly in his works written before 1399, Gower was mainly reliant upon the ruler's self-restraint, his prudential self-interest, and the influence of his counsellors' moral exhortation. The problem was that, as Gower himself acknowledged, many people lack self-restraint, do not recognise their own long-term interests, and will not be moved by moral exhortation. As he said in the *Vox Clamantis*, 'the man who is good listens to what is good, but the perverse man disregards it' (VC: VII.25.1471–74; see also VI.5.413–14; VII.2.91–2). By 1399, Gower had come to see Richard II as a perverse ruler, one who obdurately disregarded the wise counsel of 'older men' (VC: prose link to CT; CT: Preface; I.1–26, 188–89, 204–13; II.1–212; III.283), presumably including that which the poet himself had offered him in his epistle to the king in the *Vox Clamantis* and in Book VII of the *Confessio Amantis*, and who had wilfully persisted in his malice and lack of righteousness. What, then, was Gower's response to this situation?

According to the 'Record and Process', which gives the Lancastrian version of the downfall of Richard II, on 30 September 1399 all the estates of the realm which had gathered in Westminster Hall 'for the holding of parliament' were unanimously agreed that the 'many wrongs' committed by the king had rendered him 'worthy of deposition'.[127] Yet, if the pro-Ricardian *Chronicque de la Traison et Mort de Richard Deux, Roy Dengleterre* is to be believed, there was at least one voice of protest against Richard's deposition, that of the king's ally Thomas Merks, the bishop of Carlisle, who supposedly told the assembly that there was 'not one present' who was 'competent and fit' to judge the king who was their liege lord.[128] Whether or not the bishop did actually make this protest is questionable.[129] It would, however, have been logical for a defender of the 'regal' conception of royal power to deny the right of the king's subjects to judge or remove their superior. Thus,

---

[125] Yeager, *John Gower's Poetic*, pp. 268–9, 275–6.
[126] 'The Record and Process', p. 186.
[127] 'The Record and Process', pp. 171–2, 184–5.
[128] *Chronicque de la Traison et Mort de Richard Deux Roy Dengleterre*, ed. Benjamin Williams (London: English Historical Society, 1846), p. 221.
[129] 'The Protest of the Bishop of Carlisle', in *Chronicles of the Revolution*, pp. 190–1, at 190; Saul, *Richard II*, p. 422.

looking back on Richard II's deposition from 1444, Jean Juvénal des Ursins argued that even if the king had acted badly, his subjects did not have the right to judge him, something which would be monstrous and unnatural. The king's will was law and so only God had the right to judge him.[130] Certainly, as noted above, Gower himself had previously expressed very similar views, claiming that when a king did wrong, neither his subjects nor the law could punish him (MO: 23101–48; VC: VI.7.505–6; VI.16.1101–06; CA: VII.2718–36; VIII.209–10). Yet, in the *Cronica Tripertita*, which was probably written shortly after Richard's death in February 1400, Gower now adopted the Lancastrian view, one set out in the 'Record and Process', that the king's crimes and abuses justified his deposition and had led the people of the realm to renounce him and to replace him with Henry Bolingbroke (VC: VII, *Explicit*, pr. 7; CT: III, prose heading), Gower's 'oghne lord' to whom he had re-dedicated the *Confessio Amantis* (Pro.81–9) and whose livery collar he had received in 1393 (see Martha Carlin above, pp. 55–6).[131] Indeed, unlike the 'Articles of Deposition' which never actually use the word 'tyrant' in justifying the removal of the king, Gower himself was quite explicit in repeatedly describing Richard as a 'tyrannical' ruler (VC: *Explicit*, pr. 6; CT: II.282; III.288).[132]

This shift of allegiance on the part of Gower has sometimes led to the poet being attacked as a turncoat or an opportunist.[133] Yet, in itself, the criticism of Richard's conduct in the *Cronica Tripertita* did not represent a departure from the outlook which Gower had expressed in his earlier works since, even when he had advocated the exercise of 'regal' power by the king, Gower had always criticised those rulers who tyrannically abused their power and had warned the king about the likely consequences of such misrule.[134] What *was* new in the *Cronica Tripertita* was the remedy which Gower now offered to those who suffered from the tyrant's rod. Whereas the poet had previously claimed that the king was above the law and so was free from control by his

---

[130] Taylor '"Weep Thou For Me in France"', p. 210.
[131] Whilst Gower's views were in line with those set out in the 'Record and Process', it is not clear if the 'Record and Process' was a direct source for the *Cronica Tripertita*. Carlson has argued that it was (see David R. Carlson, 'The Parliamentary Source of Gower's *Cronica Tripertita* and Incommensurable Styles', in Dutton, Hines and Yeager, *John Gower, Trilingual Poet*, pp. 98–111; and Carlson, *John Gower, Poetry and Propaganda in Fourteenth-Century England*, pp. 154–95) but Michael Bennett has criticised this approach (below, p. 443).
[132] Gower, *Complete Works*, IV: 322, 326, 328, 330, 342; Stephen H. Rigby, 'Society and Politics', in Steve Ellis, ed., *Chaucer: An Oxford Guide* (Oxford: Oxford University Press, 2005), pp. 26–49, at 44–5. The chronicler Thomas Walsingham also referred to Richard as 'tyrannising' his subjects (*The St Albans Chronicle: The Chronica Maiora of Thomas Walsingham, Volume II, 1394–1422*, eds John Taylor, Wendy R. Childs and Leslie Watkins (Oxford: Clarendon Press, 2011), p. 60; II: pp. 322, 326, 328; III: pp. 330, 342).
[133] Fisher, *John Gower*, pp. 21–36.
[134] Saul, 'John Gower', pp. 93–4.

subjects, he now supported the deposition of Richard II and his replacement by a king who had been 'elected' (*electus*) by 'parliament' and who had been 'chosen by the people' (*eligitur a plebe*) to rule over them (CT: III, marginalia at pp. 337, 338; III.299–300, 335). How, given his earlier views on royal authority, was Gower able to justify his support for Richard's deposition by England's political community?

Gower certainly did not attempt to defend Richard's deposition *ex defectu tituli* which, as noted above, was the easiest way to defend the removal of a king. Thus, even though Bolingbroke may have briefly toyed with the idea of claiming the throne by right of descent from Henry III's second son Edmund 'Crouchback', on the basis that he was supposedly the elder brother of Edward I, the *Cronica Tripertita* only states that, following Richard's abdication, Henry 'succeeded as heir to the kingdom' (III.334).[135] Similarly, in *In Praise of Peace*, Gower refers only in vague terms to Henry's claim as being based on his 'ancestrie' (l. 12).[136] So how did Gower defend the overthrow of a king who had rightfully succeeded to the throne?

Although Gower's works from before 1399 presented kings as being above the law and so beyond correction by their subjects, the poet had also insisted that rulers could be punished by God. As he says in the *Mirour de l'Omme*, 'the higher the pride of the prince seated in his chair, and the more he vaunts himself and rejoices, the more does God hold him in contempt and cast him down to his misery' (2480–4). At times, Gower warned the tyrant of the chastisement which awaited him in the next life when God would decide whether his soul deserved the pleasantness of heaven or the harshness of the 'infernal prison', with his freedom from punishment by men in this world only leading to greater chastisement by God in the next (MO: 23101–48). Yet, elsewhere, Gower also allowed that God might punish tyrants in *this* world. As Genius says in the *Confessio Amantis*, God always shows himself to be a 'champion' of those who suffer from tyranny so that, even if cruelty may reign for a short while, God will ensure that those who inflict cruelty on their subjects will eventually endure it themselves (VII.3249–64, 3370–86). Even though rulers, including even tyrants, were beyond the control of human law, God himself could still punish them, as in the case of the Egyptian pharaoh, who had enslaved the Jews, on whom God took vengeance by having him drown beneath the Red Sea (CA: V.1654–65; VC: VI.8.625–6).

However, far more problematic for Gower's 'regal' claim that kings were above the law were those many instances that he cites in which the supposed divine punishment of the tyrant was not accomplished directly, by God's own

---

[135] *Chronicles of the Revolution*, pp. 43, 161, 166, 186, 195–6; Paul Strohm, *Hochon's Arrow: The Social Imagination of Fourteenth-Century Texts* (Princeton: Princeton University Press, 1992), pp. 77–8, 84–8; Paul Strohm, *England's Empty Throne: Usurpation and the Language of Legitimation, 1399–1422* (New Haven: Yale University Press, 1998), pp. 3–5; Bennett, 'Henry Bolingbroke and the Revolution of 1399', pp. 22–3.

[136] See also John Gower, *O Deus Immense*, l. 61.

hand, as it was in the case of the pharaoh, but was rather carried out by means of human agency. For instance, although in the *Confessio Amantis* it is God who has decided that the treacherous Perseus should reign 'bot a litel while', it is actually the 'comune' of his land who imprison him and exile his heir (II.1752–59, 1843–56; for other examples, see CA: VI.537–95; VII.3267–94, 3267–94, 3341–54, 3418–3513; MO: 2425–36). For Gower, the deposition of Richard II was just such a case in which the tyrant's subjects had functioned as the instruments of the divine will. Thus, although Gower described the deposition as having been brought about by the actions of Henry Bolingbroke who, in seeking the throne for himself, had freed the people of England from the 'melancholy prison' of Richard's rule, (CT: III.7–10), he also, like a number of pro-Lancastrian writers, presented the deposition of Richard as an instance of, as he put it in the prose ending which he added to the *Vox Clamantis*, how tyrants would undergo the 'scourge of divine vengeance'.[137] It was the 'Highest Judge' who had ordered Bolingbroke to return to England to recover his inheritance, who had 'cast the hateful Richard from his throne' and who had 'decided upon the glorious elevation' of the pious Henry Bolingbroke whom He had 'predestined' to reign as king (CT: Preface; III, prose heading, p. 329; III.128–9, 266–7, 314–20, 450–1, 485–6).[138] As Gower said in his *In Praise of Peace*, if God had declared Henry IV's right to be king of England, the 'folk' had also 'affermed' it, meaning that the new king's reign was both 'of god and man confermed' (ll. 8–14).[139]

If the human agency by which Richard II had been deposed was legitimate because it was in accord with the divine will, this inevitably raised the question of how the people of England could be sure that it was actually God's wish that Richard II should be overthrown. After all, Richard himself believed that God was on *his* side in his battle against the wicked enemies who had sought to usurp his power and to upset the peace of the kingdom.[140] Certainly, as medieval authors were fond of pointing out, the workings of God's will are often rather inscrutable.[141] As Gower himself put it, when God permits evildoers to flourish, rather than seeking to fathom the mysteries

---

[137] Gower, *Complete Works*, IV: 313.
[138] John Gower, *Rex Celi Deus*, ll. 15–25; Giancarlo, *Parliament and Literature in Late Medieval England*, p. 123; Michael Bennett, 'Prophecy, Providence and the Revolution of 1399', in Nigel Morgan, ed., *Prophecy, Apocalypse and the Day of Doom: Proceedings of the 2000 Harlaxton Symposium* (Donington: Shaun Tyas, 2004), pp. 1–18, at 14–18.
[139] Strohm, *Hochon's Arrow*, pp. 77–90; Frank Grady, 'The Lancastrian Gower and the Limits of Exemplarity', *Speculum*, 70 (1995), pp. 552–75, at 560.
[140] *English Historical Documents, 1327–1485*, pp. 174–5; John H. Harvey, 'The Wilton Diptych: A Re-Examination', *Archaeologia*, 98 (1961), pp. 27–8; Phillip Lindley, 'Absolutism and the Regal Image in Ricardian Sculpture', in Dillian Gordon, Lisa Monnas and Caroline Elam, eds, *The Regal Image of Richard II and the Wilton Diptych* (London: Harvey Miller, 1997), pp. 61–84, at 72–3.
[141] See, for instance, *The Tree of Battles of Honoré Bonet*, ed. George W. Coopland (Liverpool: Liverpool University Press, 1949), III: 3 (p. 120); IV: 54 (p. 158). For other references, see Stephen H. Rigby, 'Worthy but Wise? Virtuous and Non-Virtuous

of His judgement, all that the righteous can do is to have faith that sinners will eventually be punished by divine justice (VC: I.14.1151–2; II.9.427–72; VI.5.361–6, VII.22.1203213; MO: 11197–208, 14617–41, 28321–24).[142] That God allows both 'moral' and 'vicious' kings to wield the sword of power and sometimes permits 'just men' to be oppressed is certainly the case in the *Cronica Tripertita*.[143] Here Gower depicts Richard II successfully committing injustices such as the murder of Thomas, duke of Gloucester, the execution of Richard, earl of Arundel, the exiling of Thomas, earl of Warwick, Sir John Cobham and Henry Bolingbroke, and the expulsion of Thomas Arundel, the archbishop of Canterbury, from his see. As the poet lamented in response to these events: 'O how much God allows' (CT: III.122). If, in the long run, divine providence plays a beneficial role in human affairs, in the short term, its workings can often seem rather arcane.[144]

How then was God's will to be determined? One possible answer to this question was that God's design would eventually be revealed when the tyrant, in accordance with the divine will, was cast down by the Wheel of Fortune (CT: III.228–31, 460–1). As Gower put it, since Bolingbroke had conquered the realm, 'right is clearly on his side' (CT: III.333) which, in effect, meant that might was right.[145] One problem with this view was that Gower himself was aware that conquerors such as Alexander could often triumph even though their actions did not enjoy divine approval. Another was that this outlook did not really help the people of England to make moral or political choices since even if Bolingbroke's cause did enjoy the backing of divine providence, this would only be apparent with the benefit of hindsight – once Richard II had been successfully removed from the throne – rather than before the event.

Gower's response to such difficulties was to sidestep them by presenting Richard II's actions as being so obviously unjust that they were self-evidently counter to God's will and so were deserving of divine punishment (VC: VII, *Explicit*, pr. 7–8). The king was wicked, had lost all piety, and had gone 'from bad to worse, not fearing the rod of God' whereas his opponents, the virtuous Lords Appellant, had God on their side (CT: I.1–26, 109–10, 204–19). Richard's evil reign had 'put aside the law of both God and men' and so was abominated by God. His tyranny had turned his land into a prison over which he ruled like Herod or the Pharaoh, with Bolingbroke's overthrow of the jailer-king being an 'infinitely noteworthy deed for the glory of Christ'

Forms of Courage in the Later Middle Ages', *Studies in the Age of Chaucer*, 35 (2013), pp. 329–71, at 366–7.

[142] Gower, *Carmen Super Multiplici Viciorum Pestilencia*, ll. 50–83; CA: VI.1789–94.

[143] CT: Preface; Gower, *O Deus Immense*, ll. 1–3.

[144] McCabe, *Gower's Vulgar Tongue*, pp. 212–15, 224–5.

[145] For the difficulties raised by Henry's right to rule 'by conquest', see *The St Albans Chronicle, Volume II*, p. 208; Saul, *Richard II*, pp. 419–20; Grady, 'The Lancastrian Gower and the Limits of Exemplarity', p. 557.

(CT: III, prose heading, pr. 1–2; III.7–10). In disturbing the peace and killing just men, the king had carried out the 'profane work of hell', putting aside divine and human law, raging against Christ and forgetting 'those religious services he had once observed as his own'. He had shown himself to hate 'the actions of all honourable men' and had sought to ruin and destroy his own kingdom (CT: Preface; II.2, 91, 112, 237; III: prose heading; III.29, 43–4, 205, 2130).[146] In the *Vox Clamantis*, Gower could only understand the rebels of 1381 as having acted from a mad desire to commit crime (I.9.715–18, 729–30), even though the rebels had seen themselves as being 'lovers of truth and justice, not robbers and thieves'.[147] Similarly, in the *Cronica Tripertita*, Gower presented Richard II as having been consciously evil in opposing God's will even though, as we have seen, Richard believed that it was his actions and policies which enjoyed divine approval.

Just as, in the *Confessio Amantis*, Genius teaches that 'What king of lawe taketh no kepe,/Be lawe he mai no regne kepe' (CA: VII.3073–4) so Gower concludes the *Cronica Tripertita* by presenting Richard's downfall as demonstrating that 'He who is a sinner cannot be a ruler' (*'Est qui peccator, non esse potest dominator'*) (CT: III.485–6). His words here echo his epistle to Richard II in the *Vox Clamantis* where Gower had said that if he wished to be a king, Richard should rule himself and he would 'be one', but that if he failed to do so he would have no right to 'say he was a king'. It is when a king wields his power well that he is a king (*rex est*) whereas when he rules unjustly he becomes a tyrant (*tirannus erit*) and so arouses the anger of his subjects and the wrath of God (VI.8.607–9; VI.14.1003–09). A long critical tradition has seen these claims as being 'perilously near' to the Wycliffite doctrine of dominion by which *dominium*, including the right to own property, to govern or to confer the sacraments, 'pertains only to those who are in a state of grace', i.e. to the elect who are predestined to salvation.[148] If this was actually the case, Gower's use of the idea to justify Richard's deposition would have been particularly radical since Wyclif himself had tended to use this theory to attack clerical privilege whilst minimising its potentially revolutionary implications for the practice of secular political life.[149]

---

[146] See also Gower's, *O Recolende*.
[147] *The Peasants' Revolt of 1381*, ed. R. Barrie Dobson (second edition; London: Macmillan, 1983), pp. 127–9, 132, 134, 159, 161, 169–71, 184.
[148] Gower, *Complete Works*, IV: 416; Gower, *Major Latin Works*, p. 484; Anne Hudson, *The Premature Reformation: Wycliffite Texts and Lollard History* (Oxford: Clarendon Press, 1988), p. 410; Helen Barr, *Socioliterary Practice in Late Medieval England* (Oxford: Oxford University Press, 2001), pp. 76–8; Michael Wilks, 'Predestination, Property and Power: Wyclif's Theory of Dominion and Grace', *Studies in Church History*, 2 (1965), pp. 220–36, at 222.
[149] Gordon Leff, 'Wyclif and Hus: A Doctrinal Comparison', in Anthony Kenny, ed., *Wyclif in his Times* (Oxford: Clarendon Press, 1986), pp. 105–25, at 116–17; Wilks, 'Predestination, Property and Power', pp. 223–5, 228.

In fact, Gower's claim that 'He who is a sinner cannot be a ruler' may have had other, more traditional origins. After all, medieval political theorists often followed Isidore of Seville, with whose *Etymologies* Gower himself was familiar, in defining the office of a king in moral terms. As Isidore said, in a much-quoted passage: 'You will be king if you behave rightly; if you do not, you will not be' (*'Rex eris, si recte facias: si non facias, non eris'*).[150] Gower would also have come across this claim in the *De Regimine Principum* where Giles of Rome argued that a ruler who lacked prudence and who did not rule for the common profit was, as Trevisa's Middle English translation put it, 'not a verrey kyng' or a king 'in dede' but was only a king 'by name' or merely the 'signe of a kyng' and so was 'not worthi' to be a prince.[151] The idea was also to be found in legal texts. For instance, when 'Bracton' maintains that a ruler bears the name of king not simply from reigning but because he 'rules well', the corollary being that he loses that name and becomes 'a tyrant when he oppresses, by violent domination, the people entrusted to his care'.[152] It was this ancient tradition of thought, rather than Wyclif's more recent theory of dominion, that Gower invoked when he concluded that 'He who is a sinner cannot be a ruler'. And it was this ethical definition of kingship, in which kings who ruled badly necessarily ceased to be true kings, that enabled Gower to justify the deposition of Richard II, the possibility of which seemed to be

---

[150] *Isidori Hispalensis Episcopi, Etymologiarum sive Originum Libri XX*, ed., W. M. Lindsay (Oxford: Clarendon Press, 1911; two volumes), IX.iii.4; *The Etymologies of Isidore of Seville*, eds Stephen A. Barney, W. J. Lewis, J. A. Beach and Oliver Berghof (Cambridge: Cambridge University Press, 2006), IX.iii.4; 'On the Times', in *Political Poems and Songs Relating to English History Composed During the Period from the Accession of Edw. III to that of Ric. III, volume I* (London: Rolls Series, 1859), pp. 270–8, at 278; *Bracton on the Laws and Customs of England*, II: 305; Mainzer, 'A Study of the Sources of the *Confessio Amantis* of John Gower', pp. 279, 335; Somerset, '"Al Þe Comonys With O Voys Atonys"', pp. 120–2; Schulz, 'Bracton on Kingship', p. 151; Wickert, *Studies in John Gower*, pp. 141–3; Baldwin, *The Theme of Government in Piers Plowman*, pp. 14–15; Rigby, *Wisdom and Chivalry*, pp. 181–2. For other references, see John A. Alford, *Piers Plowman: A Guide to the Quotations* (Binghamton: Medieval and Renaissance Texts and Studies, 17, 1992), pp. 33–4 and Otto Gierke, *Political Theories of the Middle Ages* (Cambridge: Cambridge University Press, 1927), pp. 141–2.

[151] Giles of Rome, *The Governance of Kings and Princes*, pp. 50, 154, 329, 348–9, 377; Rigby, *Wisdom and Chivalry*, pp. 181–2.

[152] *Bracton on the Laws and Customs of England*, II: 305. 'Bracton' here was drawing on the so-called 'Laws of Edward the Confessor' which had claimed that Pope Zacharius had justified the replacement of the Merovingian kings by the Carolingians on the grounds that 'those ought to be called kings who vigilantly defend and rule the church of God and his people' (Bruce R. O'Brien, *God's Peace and King's Peace: The Laws of Edward the Confessor* (Philadelphia: University of Pennsylvania Press, 1999), pp. 174–5, 272; *Die Gesetze der Angelsachsen: Herausgegeben in Auftrage der Savigny-Stiftung, Volume I: Texte und 'bersetzung* (Cambridge: Cambridge University Press, 2015; first edition 1903), p. 637). In fact, the key Carolingian source for this episode focuses on the issue of whether those who bore the title of king actually possessed power in reality, rather than on whether they wielded this power virtuously (*Annales Regni Francorum*, ed. Friedrich Kurze (Hanover: Impensis Bibliopolii Hahniani, 1895), p. 8).

precluded by the view of the king as being above the law which the poet himself had expressed in his own earlier works.

Gower's Political Theory: Consistency and Flexibility

As we saw above, scholars have disagreed about the unity of Gower's outlook with some stressing the consistency of the poet's views and others focusing upon the seeming contradictions within his work.[153] As critics such as Porter and Minnis have emphasised, Gower certainly had an overarching philosophical and ethical outlook, an outlook which is to be found across his three major works.[154] For instance, throughout his work, Gower appealed to the concept of man as the microcosm of the macrocosm in order to teach that humans, who have free will, are responsible for their own fate, not Fortune or the stars, and so should employ their higher faculty, the reason which they share with the angels, to control their lower animal natures and to bring themselves into harmony with God and the cosmos (MO: 5065–70, 26785–27204; VC: II.5–6; VII.7–8; VII.24.1399–1402; CA: Pro.908–66). Nevertheless, despite the centrality of this cosmographical concept in Gower's work, it did not, in practice, provide any specific guidance as to whether, for instance, warfare in general – let alone any specific war – was justified or whether a tyrant could be deposed by his subjects.[155]

Similarly, whilst Gower repeatedly invoked the Aristotelian idea of virtue as a mean between two opposing vices, for instance to counsel rulers that they should be neither too cruel nor too merciful and should avoid being either too generous or too miserly (MO: 10981–92, 15937–84, 16213–60, 16381–92, 16417–41, 16501–12, 16537–72, 17557–68, 23041–52; VC: VII.2.111–20; VII.21.1141–52; CA: I.17–20, 541–2; V.7641–718; VII.2014–57, 2149–63, 3387–3415, 3520–31, 3604–7, 3846–8, 3918–21, 4170–2, 4235–7, 4297–99, 4559–73), this conception of virtue offered little direction about what moral choice should be made in any particular situation.[156] As Aristotle himself had pointed out, even when one knows that virtue in general is a mean, it can still be very difficult to identify what constitutes this mean in any specific instance.[157] For example, Gower taught that although kings should 'rule magnificently in the eyes of his people' they also needed to avoid the excessive haughtiness which would torment their people (VC: VI.18;

---

[153] See notes 11–13, above.
[154] Minnis, '"Moral Gower" and Medieval Literary Theory'; Minnis, 'John Gower, *Sapiens* in Ethics and Politics'; Porter, 'Gower's Ethical Microcosm and Political Macrocosm'.
[155] For detailed references to the idea of the macrocosm and the microcosm, see Rigby, *Wisdom and Chivalry*, pp. 238–9.
[156] Aristotle, *Nicomachean Ethics*, II, ii–ix. For detailed references to virtue as a mean, see Rigby, 'Worthy but Wise?', pp. 337–47.
[157] Aristotle, *Nicomachean Ethics*, II, ix: 1–8.

VI.18*). The problem for Richard II was that whilst the king seems to have regarded his courtly pomp as exemplifying the magnificence which medieval poets, moralists and political theorists saw as a virtue, Richard's opponents judged his particular degree of splendour to mean that he was guilty of the vice of vainglorious and ostentatious excess.[158] The two sides did not differ at the level of political ethics, since both accepted the need for royal magnificence, but rather disagreed about what this ethic meant in actual practice. Certainly, as Aristotle and his followers emphasised, ethics and politics, in dealing with what is changeable and individual, 'involve much difference of opinion and uncertainty' even in terms of general theory, let alone in relation to individual situations in which 'the agents have to consider what is suited to the circumstances on each occasion'.[159] Gower himself recognised how ethical choices had to be related to the situation at hand. He taught, for instance, that in making moral and political choices, the king should act with moderation 'unless the affair should require otherwise' (VC: VI.8.621). Similarly, he advised churchmen that, in correcting sin, they should adjust themselves to the character of the sinner since kind counsel sometimes achieves more than harsh words, whereas at other times righteous indignation is called for: 'There is nothing helpful which cannot also harm' (VC: III.13.1151–68).

This recognition of the flexibility of ethical and philosophical schemes when it comes to their actual application and of the disagreements that they can generate even amongst those who share them has important implications for how we assess the role of political ideas and language in actual political events. As we have seen, recent scholarship has emphasised the importance of ideas in late medieval politics and has stressed the centrality of principles and language in determining what was possible in the political sphere (above, pp. 381–2). Nevertheless, even if values and ideas play an important role in political life and even if, as Skinner claimed, political principles cannot be stretched 'indefinitely',[160] political language still seems to be very elastic in nature. In practice, such language often functions as a malleable rhetoric which may be used to justify an extremely wide range of actions and which can be readily used to buttress a variety of differing, conflicting or even contradictory viewpoints as the current situation requires.[161] For instance,

---

[158] *The Chronicle of Adam Usk, 1377–1421*, pp. 36–8. For detailed references, see Rigby, *Wisdom and Chivalry*, pp. 47–58, 198–204.

[159] Aristotle, *Nicomachean Ethics*, I, iii: 1–8; II, ii: 3–5; II, ix: 1–8; VI, i: 1–2; VI, viii: 1–9. See also Giles of Rome, *The Governance of Kings and Princes*, pp. 48–9, 194).

[160] Quentin Skinner, 'Some Problems in the Analysis of Political Thought and Action', in Tully, *Meaning and Context*, pp. 97–118, at 117.

[161] Thomas J. Renna, 'Aristotle and the French Monarchy, 1260–1303', *Viator*, 9 (1978), pp. 309–24, at 324; Rigby, *Wisdom and Chivalry*, pp. 52–3; Stephen H. Rigby, 'Review of K. Lewis, *Kingship and Masculinity in Late Medieval England*', in *EHR*, 130 (2015), pp. 725–7. For examples, see Slater, *Art and Political Thought in Medieval England*, pp. 15–16, 74–5, 162.

although the defence of strong kingship offered in Giles of Rome's *De Regimine Principum*, a copy of which was owned by Richard II's tutor, Simon Burley, has often been seen as the direct inspiration for Richard's own 'regal' view of royal power, Giles' treatise was also familiar to Richard's opponents, including Thomas, duke of Gloucester and Thomas, Lord Berkeley. Such men may well have looked sympathetically upon Giles' claim that a king who did not rule for the common good was not a 'true king' and that such tyrants were likely to face the resistance of the 'excellent men and noble' whom they had sought to destroy.[162]

That the principles and values which appear in political texts do not constitute premises from which particular conclusions or actions can automatically be deduced is certainly evident in the way in which Gower was able to tailor his ethical and political arguments to suit his own immediate purposes. Thus, when his priority was to denounce those clergy who engaged in wars, Gower invoked the commandment 'Thou shalt not kill' (Exodus 20:13) and reminded them that Christ had said, in absolute terms, that 'Whosoever (*Quicumque*) of men taketh the sword shall finally perish by the sword' (Matthew 26:52; Revelation 13:10; VC: III.6.337–8; III.9.647). Yet, when urging Richard II to follow the example of his father, the Black Prince, Gower's outlook was far from being pacifist. On the contrary, in praising the prince for being 'sober in his actions' he noted that he achieved such self-restraint even though his sword was 'often drunk with the blood of his enemy' and 'refused to go back into the sheath dry', its thirst only being slaked by a torrent of his foes' gore and blood (VC.VI.13.941–50). In the same way, although Gower criticised those knights who entered battle simply for the 'sake of gain' (VC: V.8.535–40), he was also able to commend the Black Prince for having penetrated deep amongst his enemies 'in order to seize booty' (VC: VI.13.957).[163] In such cases, Gower was more concerned to emphasise the point at hand than to ensure the overall coherence of his arguments. Similarly, when stressing the need for rulers to exercise self-control, Gower was happy to state that the king could not be punished by earthly law (VC: VI.7.505–6; VI.8.611–20) but in issuing a warning about the consequences of tyranny, he was prepared to claim that when a ruler did not obey the law, 'Be lawe he mai no regne kepe' (CA: VII.3073–4). Whilst such arguments may have been contradictory, they nonetheless suited Gower's broader rhetorical purpose, which was to urge rulers to embrace virtue and to eschew vice, rather than to arrive at a consistent constitutional theory.

---

[162] Giles of Rome, *The Governance of Kings and Princes*, pp. 50, 154, 329, 340, 348–9, 377; Rigby, *Wisdom and Chivalry*, pp. 179, 181; Fletcher, *Richard II*, p. 12; Charles F. Briggs, *Giles of Rome's De Regimine Principum: Reading and Writings Politics at Court and University, c.1275–c.1525* (Cambridge: Cambridge University Press, 1999), pp. 60–2.

[163] David Aers, *Faith, Ethics and Church: Writing in England, 1360–1409* (Cambridge: D. S. Brewer, 2000), p. 108.

The tractability of Gower's political principles and language is particularly evident in his response to the dramatic events of 1399. Previously, Gower had taught that only God could punish the king, not the law or the king's subjects (MO: 23101–48; VC: VI.16.1101–06; 7.505–6; CA: VII.2718–36; VIII.209–10), and had denounced the sin of 'supplantation' by which men sought to obtain the offices and dignities of others (MO: 3289–300, 3373–96; CA: II.2328–56). Yet now, far from adhering to such views 'to the end of his life', he welcomed the fact that Henry Bolingbroke had replaced Richard II on the throne and justified the king's deposition by presenting it as part of the workings of divine providence.[164] It would seem, then, that just as the voice of the people was the voice of God, except when it wasn't, so, for Gower, killing, fighting for gain and 'supplantation' were all wrong – except in those cases when they weren't. Gower's political language was thus extremely flexible and so could easily be adapted to changing rhetorical needs and shifting political circumstances. To interpret Gower in this way is not to condemn him as a political opportunist, as critics once did.[165] On the contrary, as Green puts it, Gower's belief in the justice of the deposition of Richard II seems to have been 'genuine and fervent'.[166] Indeed, in 1399, most of England's political community had readily accepted the accession of the man whom Chaucer hailed as the 'conquerour of Brutes Albyon' and as the 'verray kyng' by 'lyne and free eleccion'.[167] Whilst it is true that Gower's works in the years before 1399 had generally tended towards a 'regal' theory of kingship, in which the king was presented as being above the law and as subject only to God, the poet's view that divine providence could employ human agency to strike down evil tyrants had always possessed the potential to be used in support of a 'political' conception of the king's relationship with his subjects. It was this potential that Gower was to draw upon in the works which he wrote in the aftermath of the unprecedented crisis of 1399 and which allowed him, despite many of the opinions which he himself had previously expressed, to welcome the deposition of an anointed king.

---

[164] Meindl, 'Gower's *Speculum Judicis*', p. 263.
[165] See note 133, above.
[166] Richard F. Green, *Poets and Princepleasers: Literature and the English Court in the Late Middle Ages* (Toronto: University of Toronto Press, 1980), p. 182.
[167] Geoffrey Chaucer, 'The Complaint of Chaucer to his Purse', ll. 22–4; Nigel Saul, 'The Kingship of Richard II', in Anthony Goodman and James Gillespie, eds, *Richard II: The Art of Kingship* (Oxford: Clarendon Press, 1999), pp. 37–57, at 54–7.

Chapter 13

GOWER, RICHARD II AND HENRY IV

Michael Bennett

John Gower spent much of his life writing for and about Richard II and his nemesis Henry of Lancaster.[1] This chapter reassesses Gower's views on Richard's reign by examining the poet's writings in the context of his background in Kent, his social circle and political connections, the politics of Richard's reign, and contemporary perceptions of his rule. Key issues here are Gower's role as mentor to royalty in his letter to Richard in the *Vox Clamantis*; the dating of the critical comments about the king which Gower added to this text; Gower's stance in relation to the cause of the Appellants in 1387–88; the dating and significance of the changes which Gower made to the *Confessio Amantis*, particularly the change of dedication from Richard to Henry; the date of the composition of the three parts of the *Cronica Tripertita*, in which Gower wrote an account of Richard's misrule, his tyranny and overthrow; and the misleading nature of modern representations of Gower as a 'Lancastrian propagandist'.

Gower's Circle

A kinsman of Sir Robert Gower, John Gower evidently had the benefits of a good education and may have studied law. From the 1360s, he used his connections, legal knowledge and business acumen to acquire landed estate in Kent and East Anglia. He bought a moiety of the manor of Aldington near Maidstone from William Septvans at Christmas 1365 and, after William's grant was annulled in 1366 on account of his minority, he secured a re-grant

---

I should like to acknowledge the assistance of Stephen Rigby and Siân Echard, and the encouragement of Derek Pearsall and Robert Yeager. I am grateful for advice and leads to Adrian Ailes, Martha Carlin, Simon Payling and Matthew Ward.

[1] For the consistency with which the name Henry of Lancaster was used, see Ian Mortimer, *The Fears of Henry IV: The Life of England's Self-Made King* (London: Jonathan Cape, 2008), p. xi.

of the manor when William came of age in 1368.² His property dealings in the 1360s and the 1370s reveal his association with leading Kent knights and squires, including Sir John Cobham, Lord Cobham, who was appointed by the crown in 1366 to enquire into Septvans business, and Sir Nicholas Loveyne of Penshurst, with whom Gower was associated in managing or mismanaging the young man's affairs.³ In 1373, with his title firmly established, Gower granted his manor of Aldington to Lord Cobham and others to hold in trust for his use. He rebuilt the manor-house there shortly after the Peasants' Revolt in 1381 and probably retained it as his principal seat through the 1380s.⁴ Among his friends and neighbours were Thomas Brockhill, a trustee and eventually purchaser of Aldington, James Peckham of Wrotham, principal witness to the quitclaim of Aldington to Gower, and Arnold Savage of Bobbing, who later served as his chief executor.⁵ Over his career, Gower would have had dealings with men in the service of the archbishops of Canterbury and the bishops of Rochester and Winchester, if not with the prelates themselves.⁶ This network of friends and connections points to a social milieu that embraced the court and the capital as well as the county. Lord Cobham had a fine house in Tower ward in London, and Arnold Savage had a house in Southwark.⁷ Gower likewise presumably had lodgings in or around London prior to the move of his domicile to Southwark.

---

2   *Rotuli Parliamentorum*, II: 271–3; *CPR 1367–70*, pp. 83, 96; John H. Fisher, *John Gower: Moral Philosopher and Friend of Chaucer* (London: Methuen, 1965), pp. 51–3, 313–18, 334–5; Martha Carlin above, pp. 26–30.

3   The enquiry reported that after William Septvans entered his inheritance following the fraudulent proof of age he lived with Gower and an associate mainly in Canterbury until Michaelmas 1365 and then with Loveyne mainly at Penshurst, and during this time he was 'led and advised' by them to make various grants of land (*Rotuli Parliamentorum*, II: 271–3), presumably to acquit debts and meet other expenses. There is diversity of opinion as to Gower's honesty and fairness in his dealings with the young man, not least between G. C. Macaulay and J. H. Fisher (*Complete Works*, IV: xv and Fisher, *John Gower*, pp. 53–4. See Carlin above, pp. 26–30).

4   BL, Harl Ch 50 I 14; *CPR 1370–74*, p. 425; TNA, CP 40/483, m. 144v; Michael Bennett, 'John Gower, Squire of Kent, the Peasants' Revolt, and the *Visio Anglie*', *Chaucer Review*, 51 (2018), pp. 258–82.

5   L. S. Woodger, 'Brockhill, Thomas (d.c.1411), of Calehill in Little Chart and Aldington, Kent,' in *HPHC*, II: 364–5; L. S. Woodger, 'Peckham, James (d.1400), of Yaldham in Wrotham and Hadlow, Kent', in *HPHC*, IV: 37–9; *CCR 1364–8*, p. 184–5; J. S. Roskell and L. S. Woodger, 'Savage, Sir Arnold I (1358–1410), of Bobbing, Kent,' in *HPHC*, IV: 306–10.

6   A close neighbour was William Topcliffe, steward of the archbishop of Canterbury, whose house at the Le Mote, near Maidstone, was torched by the rebels in 1381 (Bennett, 'Gower, Squire of Kent', p. 270). Archbishop Arundel was a dedicatee of a manuscript of *Vox Clamantis* and the *Cronica Tripertita*. For a connection between Gower and Bishop Wykeham, also through Cobham, see Sebastian Sobecki, 'A Southwark Tale: Gower, the 1381 Poll Tax, and Chaucer's *The Canterbury Tales*', *Speculum*, 92 (2017), pp. 630–60, at 640–4.

7   Charles L. Kingsford, 'Historical Notes on Medieval London Houses', *London Topographical Record*, 10 (1916), pp. 44–144, at 93; Fisher, *John Gower*, p. 341. On

In considering the milieu for his literary work, Gower's circle of friends and connections in Kent has been rather overlooked.[8] The older generation of knights were Francophone, and may have provided encouragement for his early literary endeavours, beginning with the *Mirour de l'Omme*.[9] With long careers in war, diplomacy and government, Lord Cobham and Sir Nicholas Loveyne were proficient in French.[10] James Peckham of Wrotham, Gower's neighbour, owned a number of French books.[11] In his Latin works, Gower probably had a more clerical audience in mind. In his *Vox Clamantis*, as in the *Mirour de l'Omme*, he addresses the vices of his age in a manner reminiscent of the contemporary homilies of Bishop Brinton of Rochester, a close friend and associate of Cobham.[12] Like Brinton, Gower wrote a eulogy of Edward, the Black Prince, denounced the revolt of 1381 and the rebels' murder of Archbishop Sudbury, and wrote advice about the education of the prince's son, Richard II.[13] In his exploration of ethics and politics in *Confessio Amantis* and *Cronica Tripertita*, he may have found Lord Cobham and Sir Arnold Savage valuable sources of information and insights as well as members of his imagined audience. In his chronicle, Gower describes Cobham as 'conscientious and kind, far-sighted and just ... a true friend of the kingdom' and counts himself among his friends in lamenting his banishment (II.213–15, 231–2, trans. Bennett). Both Cobham and Savage, who served as Cobham's

---

Gower and Southwark, see Martha Carlin, above pp. 54–61.

[8] For an exception, see Elliot Kendall, *Lordship and Literature: John Gower and the Politics of the Great Household* (Oxford: Clarendon Press, 2008), pp. 35–41.

[9] Robert F. Yeager, 'Politics and the French Language during the Hundred Years War: The Case of John Gower', in Denise N. Baker, ed., *Inscribing the Hundred Years' War in French and English Culture* (Albany: State University Press, 2000), pp. 127–57, at 137–8.

[10] Rosamund Allen, 'Cobham, John, Third Baron Cobham of Cobham (c.1320–1408)', *Oxford Dictionary of National Biography* (www.oxforddnb.com). Cited below as ODNB. Cobham wrote his epitaph in French (Nigel Saul, *Death, Art and Memory in Medieval England: The Cobham Family and their Monuments 1300–1550* (Oxford: Oxford University Press, 2001), pp. 98–101). Loveyne undertook diplomatic missions to Avignon and made his long will in French (W. Mark Ormrod, *Edward III* (New Haven, CT: Yale University Press, 2011), pp. 419 n. 16, 433; Lambeth Palace Library, Register Sudbury, f. 86r).

[11] Lambeth Palace Library, Register Arundel I, f. 177v.

[12] *The Sermons of Thomas Brinton, Bishop of Rochester (1373–1389)*, ed. Mary A. Devlin (two volumes; Camden Society, third series, 85, 86 (1954)).

[13] Bennett, 'John Gower, Squire of Kent', pp. 280–1. For the case that Gower's encomium of the prince in the *Vox* was originally a separate poem, see David R. Carlson, 'Gower's Early Latin Poetry: Text-Genetic Hypotheses of an *Epistola ad regem* (ca. 1377–1380) from the Evidence of John Bale', *Mediaeval Studies*, 65 (2003), pp. 293–317, at 310–14. For Brinton's sermons on the prince's death, the revolt of 1381, and Richard's education, see *Sermons of Thomas Brinton*, II: 354–7, 455–62; I: 70.

executor, were thoughtful men, capable of making speeches in council and parliament that were eloquent, effective and carried moral authority.[14]

Gower's political outlook presumably took shape in Kent. It was a milieu in which the Black Prince was held in high esteem: Sir Nicholas Loveyne was the prince's comrade-in-arms and close friend,[15] whilst Arnold Savage's father and mother both served in the prince's household.[16] In the troubled last years of Edward III, many people placed their hopes in the prince who had a reputation for martial prowess and soldierly austerity. In spring 1376, he reportedly encouraged the party in parliament that was calling the government to account.[17] His death in June was widely lamented, not least in Canterbury, which he had chosen as his final resting place. In a Latin eulogy of the prince, Gower not only praised his prowess in arms but also observed that the land was quiet and people felt safe under his protection (VC: VI.13.961–4).[18] Members of Gower's circle felt some special loyalty and affection for the prince's widow, Joan of Kent, and his son, Richard II. Lord Cobham, a trusted counsellor and later executor of Joan of Kent, served on the initial council of regency in 1377, probably representing the king's mother, and was appointed in 1379 to a parliamentary committee to 'examine the estate of the king' and then to remain in his household for 'the safeguard of the king's person' into 1380.[19] Since his mother was Richard's nurse, Arnold Savage was an early beneficiary of Richard's patronage in 1380, was knighted by him in 1385, and was designated a king's knight.[20] In considering Gower's attitude to Richard II, his connections with Cobham and Savage should be borne in mind. Both men knew Richard intimately, and evidently came to have reservations about his character and kingship. Soldier, diplomat and statesman, Cobham has been described as 'one of the

---

[14] Allen, 'Cobham, John', *ODNB*. For Lord Cobham's speech in council in 1399 and a commendation of Arnold Savage's eloquence as Speaker of the House of Commons in 1401 see *The St Albans Chronicle. The Chronica Maiora of Thomas Walsingham*, eds John Taylor, Wendy Childs and Leslie Watkiss (two volumes; Oxford: Clarendon Press, 2003 and 2011), II: 250–53, 308–9.

[15] Loveyne was one of the five witnesses to the prince's marriage to Joan of Kent at Lambeth on 6 Oct 1361 (George F. Beltz, *Memorials of the Order of the Garter from Its Foundation to the Present* (London: Pickering, 1841), p. 18n.).

[16] Roskell and Woodger, 'Savage, Sir Arnold I (1358–1410)'.

[17] *St Albans Chronicle*, I: 12–13; *Polychronicon Ranulphi Higden monachi Cestrensis*, eds Churchill Babington and Joseph R. Lumby (nine volumes; London: Rolls Series, 1865–86), VIII: 386.

[18] Carlson, 'Gower's Early Latin Poetry', pp. 310–14.

[19] *A Collection of all the Wills, now known to be Extant, of the Kings and Queens of England … every Branch of the Blood Royal from the Reign of William the Conqueror, to that of Henry the Seventh*, ed. John Nichols (London: Society of Antiquaries, 1780), p. 79; Thomas F. Tout, *Chapters in the Administrative History of Medieval England* (six volumes; Manchester: Manchester University Press, 1920–38), III: 327–9, 347–9.

[20] *CPR 1377–81*, p. 450.

wisest heads in England' in the reign of Richard II.[21] Elected to a parliamentary committee to draft reforms for his government in 1385, he was appointed to the continuous council that took over the power of the crown in 1386. He was closely associated with three of the king's strongest critics. The brother-in-law of Archbishop Courtenay of Canterbury, he was a friend and political ally of Thomas of Woodstock, duke of Gloucester, the king's uncle, and Richard Fitzalan, earl of Arundel, two of the magnates, the so-called Lords Appellant, who defeated an army raised in the king's name in 1387. He played a prominent role in the Appellant regime that destroyed the king's party in parliament in 1388.[22] Sir Arnold Savage, who was in the service of the earl of Arundel, may even have taken the field with the Lords Appellant. After the settlement with the king, both Cobham and Savage continued in the royal service, but seem to have increasingly distanced themselves from court from the early 1390s, with Cobham banished in 1397, and Savage was working for the government established by Henry of Lancaster and his allies some weeks even before the formal deposition of Richard II.[23] If Gower was not increasingly concerned about and critical of Richard's character and government from the late 1380s, he would have been unusual among his friends and acquaintances.[24] In the late 1390s Richard II was firmly of the belief that the men of Kent were most hostile to him.[25]

Addressing the King: Gower's *Epistola ad regem* in *Vox Clamantis*

Though there was general celebration of Richard II's accession in 1377, there was naturally also concern about a ten-year-old coming to the throne.[26] Gower himself shows a shrewd understanding of the problems of a royal minority (VC: VI.7.545–572*). A suspicion of the ambitions of John of Gaunt, duke of Lancaster, the eldest surviving son of Edward III, carried over into the new reign. Though it may not have been widely known, Edward III had made a settlement of the crown in the male line in 1376 that laid down that, in the event of Richard's death without issue, the crown would pass

---

[21] Chris Given-Wilson, 'Richard II and the Higher Nobility', in Anthony Goodman and James L. Gillespie, eds, *Richard II: The Art of Kingship* (Oxford: Clarendon Press, 1999), pp. 107–28, at 112–13.
[22] Allen, 'Cobham, John', *ODNB*.
[23] Roskell and Woodger, 'Savage, Sir Arnold I'.
[24] James Peckham represented Kent in the two parliaments 'dominated by the Lords Appellant' in 1388 and was then appointed sheriff of Kent (Woodger, 'Peckham, James'). Sir Thomas Brockhill represented Kent in the parliament of 1399 (Woodger, 'Brockhill, Thomas').
[25] See above, p. 474.
[26] In the *Mirour de l'Omme*, Gower shows himself despondent about the state of England in Edward III's last years (G. Stillwell, 'John Gower and the Last Years of Edward III', *Studies in Philology*, 45 (1948), pp. 454–71).

to the king's surviving sons and their male issue in turn, which meant that until Richard II had a son, Gaunt was next-in-line to the throne.[27] There was some relief in London and doubtless elsewhere that Gaunt was not appointed as regent. Members of Gower's circle would have been reassured by the appointment of Lord Cobham and several of the prince's former servants to the ruling council in October 1377.[28]

Gower gave early thought to writing for the guidance and edification of the young king. In the late 1370s, he was at work on the *Vox Clamantis*, a Latin poem that discusses the duties and failings of the various orders and classes of English society, and the idea of including a mirror of kingship in Book VI, in which he addresses issues of law and government, may have emerged naturally from this enterprise. As David Carlson has argued, however, it is likely that the *Epistola ad regem* ('Epistle to the King'), extant as Chapter 8, was composed as a stand-alone piece, probably earlier, but possibly later, than the rest of the book. In either scenario, the section preceding the *Epistola*, in which the order and harmony under a righteous and well-counselled king is contrasted with the division and disorder under a child king (VC: VI.7.469–544, 545–580*), was presumably reworked to accommodate it. There is a distinct change of voice and stance after Chapter 7 that suggests that it was an insertion into the text. After presenting himself as expressing the 'common voice' in the earlier chapters, Gower here adopts the first person and, in the heading to Chapter 8, describes himself as writing 'an epistle, set forth for the sake of instruction, to our king now reigning at present' so that the king, 'now in his youthful time of life' may, by God's grace, 'be more plainly instructed by this letter in his royal functions when he has afterwards reached more mature years' (VI.8.Pro., trans. Stockton). Over the next ten chapters (VI.8.581–18.1200), he writes in the first person and addresses the king in the second person. He ends with the statement: 'I, a servant of your realm and eager for your honour, have written these verses to you for the glory of your rule. Receive these writings, which I have composed with humble heart for you, good king, as gifts of God for your praise' (VI.18.1191–4, trans. Stockton). There is then another obvious break. The heading to Chapter 19 signals the return of the 'common voice' and the final chapters offer reflection, learned but somewhat distant, on the decay of civilisations and decline of virtue over the ages (VI.19–21).

It may seem surprising that Gower felt himself equipped for the role of mentor of royalty but, although he was not a graduate, he was well-schooled and well-read: his poems in three languages amply attest his literary skills, his knowledge of the Bible and classical literature, and his ethical concerns.[29]

---

[27] Michael Bennett, 'Edward III's Entail and the Succession to the Crown, 1376–1471', *EHR*, 113 (1998), pp. 580–609.

[28] Tout, *Chapters in the Administrative History of Medieval England*, III: 327–9.

[29] George R. Coffman, 'John Gower, Mentor for Royalty: Richard II', *Proceedings of the Modern Language Association*, 69 (1954), pp. 953–64.

Given that he was not a priest, his claim that the instruction he was offering was less his own than God's (VC: VI.18.1195–6*) seems overly bold rather than modest. Although Gower knew some version of the *Secretum Secretorum*, the pseudo-Aristotelian work of advice to Alexander the Great, he would not have needed any special expertise on the business of kingship to offer wholesome advice to the king about the need to take good counsel, avoid vice and vicious company, acquire self-control, pursue justice, seek wisdom, and avoid unjust war.[30] Still, Gower has some distinctive emphases, most notably a focus on the needs of a young king, which strongly indicate that he was not simply writing a generic mirror of kingship but, as he himself states, was addressing 'the present king' (heading to VI.8), i.e. Richard II. In addition to the section in which he presents Richard's father, the Black Prince, as an exemplar of rulership, Gower appears to make his advice directly pertinent to the king. From the outset of his reign, Richard's handsome appearance was widely noted.[31] Addressing him as 'the flower of youths' (VI.19.1199*), Gower refers to his fine appearance (VI.8.629, 11.849), and stresses that such good looks need to be matched by inner beauty (VI.16.1081–92). More than in other texts of the *Secretum* tradition, Gower's address is specifically to a young king whom, interestingly, he urges to be circumspect about the advice of some older counsellors as well as the influence of 'silly' young companions (VI.10.761–70). Gower may have had some interest in pedagogy.[32] 'To boys', he writes with rare empathy, 'evils are not wrongdoing but joking, not dishonour but glorious sport' (VI.7.571–2*, trans. Stockton). Still, Gower's direct and highly personalised address to Richard is rather bold. It can best be explained by his association with men who were close to the king and the expectation that the letter, as a stand-alone piece, would at least be read by someone who could commend it to the king or his tutors. He presumably had some hope that, in time, the young king would read and heed his words but also that, as part of the *Vox Clamantis*, it would reach a broader audience of people who might read the letter as a more general guide for members of the governing class. Among the men in his circle of friends and acquaintances who may have encouraged and assisted in his enterprise were, of course, Lord Cobham and probably Bishop Brinton. In a sermon in 1377, Brinton stressed the need for prudent men to direct the king's education, guard him against sin and avarice, encourage him by example and by sound counsel to fear God and to love the people so as to win the good will of the nobles and the favour of the populace, and to attend to God's law and words.[33] For his part, Cobham

---

[30] Allan H. Gilbert, 'Notes on the Influence of the *Secretum Secretorum*', *Speculum*, 3 (1928), pp. 84–98.

[31] *Chronicle of Adam Usk 1377–1421*, ed. Chris Given-Wilson (Oxford: Clarendon Press, 1997), pp. 2–3.

[32] He presumably had some responsibility for the education of William Septvans in Canterbury (Fisher, *John Gower*, p. 315).

[33] *Sermons of Thomas Brinton*, I: 70.

was appointed by parliament to 'examine the state of the king' in May 1379, to remain in the king's household 'for the safeguard of the king's person' until early 1380, and again to oversee the affairs of the king's household at the end of 1380.[34]

The *Epistola ad regem* has been variously dated. Carlson suggests that it was written as an independent piece soon after 1377.[35] However, whilst its expressions of hope for the future indicate that it was composed relatively early in the reign, the poet does not appear to be addressing a ten-year-old but an adolescent who is already a known quantity. For this reason, it is easier to suppose a date in or after 1380, when Richard turned thirteen. One possible obstacle to a date after 1381 is the lack of any explicit reference in the *Epistola* to the Peasants' Revolt but, in fact, there is no obvious place within it for this sort of topical reference. In any case, Gower evidently had no wish to make any association between the young king and the rebellion. His long poem on the events of 1381, the *Visio Anglie*, later inserted as Book I of the *Vox Clamantis*, makes no reference to Richard. In this poem, many of Gower's allegorical figures are identifiable as historical characters, but the king of Troy (England) who fails to provide leadership and to prevent the death of the high priest (Archbishop Sudbury) is not Richard but an old man (I.995–1002, 1155–60). In the section of the *Vox Clamantis* that sets the scene for the *Epistola* (VI.7.545–80), Gower does seem to be avoiding mentioning the revolt. He refers generally to the problems of misgovernment, corruption, heavy taxation, all of which suggest the malaise of the late 1370s and early 1380s, 'for which the land grieves as if with a general murmur' (VI.7.558*, trans. Stockton). Gower's main point, though, is that the king himself, as a boy, was not to blame for these problems (VI.7.555*). The likelihood that he had the revolt in mind here is suggested by the fact that he later describes the *Vox Clamantis* as treating of the Peasants' Revolt and as 'pronouncing the innocence' of the king by reason of his youth.[36] Another reason to believe that the *Epistola* was completed after 1381 is its discussion of chastity and marriage.[37] Apart from its greater pertinence for a boy who is fifteen years or older, it also appears to be addressed to a king who is married, though perhaps showing signs of not living up to his married state (VI.12.853–916). 'You as a husband should enjoy your own wife according to law', Gower declares, 'and not deprive your holy marriage of honourable

---

[34] Tout, *Chapters in the Administrative History of Medieval England*, III: 347–9; Allen, 'Cobham, John', *ODNB*. In November 1380, parliament appointed another committee and Cobham was again chosen to 'oversee' its operations (Gwilym Dodd, 'Richard II and the Fiction of Majority Rule', in Charles Beem, ed., *The Royal Minorities of Medieval and Early Modern England* (New York: Palgrave, 2008), p. 144).

[35] Carlson, 'Gower's Early Latin Poetry', p. 317; David R. Carlson, *John Gower: Poetry and Propaganda in Fourteenth-Century England* (Cambridge: D. S. Brewer, 2012), p. 214.

[36] Fisher, *John Gower*, p. 312.

[37] See also Fisher, *John Gower*, pp. 107–8.

praise' (VI.12.855–6). In January 1382, Richard married Anne of Bohemia and, though he seems to have been pleased with his wife, there was early criticism of the unruliness of the king's entourage and there were soon hints of concerns about sexual improprieties at court.[38]

If Gower had access to information about the young king and his entourage in the late 1370s, when Cobham was engaged to enquire into the state of the king and his household, or in the early 1380s, it would help to explain the fact that his advice to Richard seems so perceptive in anticipating the concerns that were only documented in the chronicles from around 1386. For Fisher, the facts and opinions in Gower's *Epistola* could 'line for line' be 'paralleled in the chronicles and histories of the period between 1382 and 1386'.[39] In fact, the chronicle reports of the king's behaviour are even more disturbing than anything that Gower hints at and present a picture of the king as undisciplined, extravagant and violent. In 1382, Richard shocked the political nation by his peremptory dismissal of Sir Richard Scrope as chancellor after his refusal to approve some of the king's gifts to his favourites.[40] In autumn 1383, the lords in parliament alleged that the king followed 'unsound counsel' and 'did not admit good regimen around himself' and proposed to 'take the full burden of government on themselves'.[41] When in the next parliament, at Salisbury in 1384, Richard, earl of Arundel, declared that misgovernment was bringing the country to ruin, the infuriated king replied that if the earl was alleging that the king himself was responsible, he was lying through his teeth.[42] On retiring to his lodgings, Richard was approached by a friar who alleged that Gaunt was plotting to assassinate him. In response, Richard ordered his uncle's immediate execution and only changed his mind when Thomas of Woodstock, the king's youngest uncle, threatened to defend his brother against anyone accusing him of treason.[43] Though Richard accepted Gaunt's assurances of loyalty, ill will and suspicion continued to fester. Early in 1385, Gaunt was warned of a credible plot, with the king's connivance, against his life. He promptly led a retinue to Sheen, confronted Richard, and delivered a stern rebuke for his choice of counsellors and misgovernment.[44] William Courtenay, archbishop of Canterbury, who was no friend of Gaunt, was so concerned about Richard's behaviour that he told him that if he did not reform himself, the kingdom would come to grief. Fuming over the rebuke, Richard subsequently invited the archbishop

---

[38] *St Albans Chronicle*, I: 690–1, 798–9, 814–15, 822–3, 852–3.
[39] Fisher, *John Gower*, p. 108.
[40] *St Albans Chronicle*, I: 620–3. Scrope was a close colleague of Lord Cobham on council and in parliament (Given-Wilson, 'Richard II and the Higher Nobility', pp. 112–13).
[41] *The Westminster Chronicle, 1381–1394*, eds Leonard C. Hector and Barbara F. Harvey (Oxford: Clarendon Press, 1982), pp. 54–5; Christopher Fletcher, *Richard II: Manhood, Youth and Politics, 1377–99* (Oxford: Oxford University Press), pp. 114–15.
[42] *Westminster Chronicle*, pp. 68–9.
[43] *Westminster Chronicle*, pp. 68–81.
[44] *Westminster Chronicle*, pp. 110–15.

on board his barge on the Thames, perhaps expecting an apology. When the archbishop continued his reprimand, he drew his sword and, if not restrained, 'would have run him through'.[45] In February 1386, in a heated argument with the earl of Arundel in London, the king punched him and knocked him to the ground.[46]

There was mounting exasperation with Richard. Sir Richard Scrope, Cobham's colleague and, like him, well-respected as a soldier and statesman, declared that he would no longer serve the king.[47] Cobham was a friend of the earl of Arundel and brother-in-law of Archbishop Courtenay. Even if Gower was not privy to all that Cobham knew, he may have heard reports of the incidents and broader concerns about the king and his entourage from men in the service of the earl and the archbishop.[48] At some stage, he began to revise parts of the *Vox Clamantis* relating to the king, namely the section introducing the *Epistola* and its two final chapters. In the revision, he refers to Richard as '*indoctus puer*' (an untaught boy) (VI.7.555) and, though he still makes allowances for the king's youth, he expresses with some force concern about the company he is keeping and how his wilfulness and indulgence might cost him the love of the people (VI.7.545–80; VI.18.1159–1200). Though the revisions are not documented in manuscripts of the text from before the 1390s, the assumption in recent scholarship that the revisions cannot have been written in the 1380s seems unwarranted.[49] After all, Gower was more restrained in his criticisms than was the monk of Westminster and it is most unlikely that he did any more than share his revisions with likeminded friends.[50] Several passages are more obviously relevant to the 1380s than the 1390s. The description of the king as an '*indoctus puer*' makes more sense at a time when the king was still in his

---

[45] Joseph Dahmus, *William Courtenay, Archbishop of Canterbury, 1381–1396* (University Park: State University of Pennsylvania Press, 1966), pp. 173–4.

[46] Chris Given-Wilson, 'The Earl of Arundel, the War with France, and the Anger of King Richard II' in Robert F. Yeager and Toshiyuki Takamiya, eds, *The Medieval Python: The Purposive and Provocative Work of Terry Jones* (New York: Palgrave, 2012), pp. 27–38, at 27–9.

[47] *St Albans Chronicle*, I: 622–3.

[48] Arnold Savage was in the service of the earl of Arundel in 1387–88 (Roskell and Woodger, 'Savage, Sir Arnold I').

[49] In manuscripts that include copies of both the *Vox* and the *Confessio*, the revised version of the *Vox* is always paired with the Henrician version of the *Confessio*. Wickert's conclusion that the revisions to the *Vox* must postdate the Henrician version of the *Confessio*, however, does not follow if Gower did not circulate them until 1399 (Maria Wickert, *Studies in John Gower* (second edition; Tempe: Arizona Center for Medieval and Renaissance Studies, 2016), pp. 3–6). For fuller discussion, see Siân Echard, 'Last Words: Latin at the End of the *Confessio Amantis*', in Richard F. Green and Linne Mooney, eds, *Interstices: Studies in Late Medieval English and Anglo-Norman in Honour of A. G. Rigg* (Toronto: University of Toronto Press, 2004), pp. 99–121.

[50] In parts of his chronicle written before 1388, for example, the monk states that Richard was involved in plots to murder Gaunt in 1384 and the duke of Gloucester in 1387 (*Westminster Chronicle*, pp. xxi, 110–17, 184–5).

teens and when his failures were attributed to evil counsel. The criticism of 'older men of greed who in pursuing their gains tolerate many scandals for the boy's pleasure' (VI.7.565–6, trans. Stockton) is most certainly apposite to this period. Gower is presumably referring here to Sir Michael de la Pole and Sir Simon Burley, Richard's former tutor and sub-chamberlain of the household, who was greatly resented in Kent where he secured advancement through royal patronage.[51] In another passage in the revised version, after making further allowance for the king's youth, Gower adds: 'A mother, to be sure, does not know what fate is designed for her child, but in the end every secret is revealed' (VI.7.575–6, trans. Stockton). This cryptic statement can be set alongside the early tradition that, after Richard's attempt on Gaunt's life, Joan of Kent had said that, although she had rejoiced to be the mother of the crowned king, she now grieved as she foresaw his downfall because of the accursed flatterers.[52] In so far as Gower writes with a sense of foreboding, it should not be assumed that he was anticipating the events of 1399. After all, as will be seen, Richard's ruin was not a remote contingency in 1386–87.

In the mid-1380s, it was still possible, however, to see signs of great promise in Richard. He was a handsome young man and showed some qualities befitting a king. His marriage to Anne of Bohemia was affectionate, and it could be expected that a wife and then children would bring maturity. Richard and his queen presided over a lively court, young and fashionable. In his chronicle, Thomas Walsingham criticised the courtiers as 'knights of Venus rather than Mars, showing more prowess in the bedroom than in the field of battle, being alert with their tongues, but asleep when martial deeds were required'.[53] Yet, in fact, the king was ready to lead the nation in arms. In summer 1385, he led one of the largest armies assembled in England across the Scottish border and advanced as far as Edinburgh, providing the opportunity to create new peerages and dub new knights, including Arnold Savage.[54] Above all, Richard was taking a serious interest in monarchy, especially the royal heritage and sacral kingship. He was keenly aware of what he regarded as a malign strand in English political history that had led to rebellion and regicide and despatched a mission to Rome to seek the canonisation of Edward II, who had been deposed in 1327.[55]

It was around this time that Gower had his chance encounter with Richard on the Thames, when he was invited onto the royal barge and the king encouraged him to write something new for him (CA: Pro.34–60*).

---

[51] For their careers and influence on the king, see Nigel Saul, *Richard II* (New Haven: Yale University Press, 1997), pp. 112–20.
[52] *Chronicle of Adam Usk*, pp. 10–11. Usk was writing after the deposition and evidently misdates the context in which Joan of Kent may have made the remarks. For the likely context see *Westminster Chronicle*, pp. 114–15.
[53] *St Albans Chronicle*, I: 814–15.
[54] *St Albans Chronicle*, I: 756–7; Roskell and Woodger, 'Savage, Sir Arnold I'.
[55] Michael Bennett, *Richard II and the Revolution of 1399* (Stroud: Sutton, 1999), p. 41.

Some scholars have rejected the historical reality of the meeting described in the Prologue to the *Confessio Amantis*.[56] It is hard to credit, however, that Gower invented an occurrence that his readers would have found improbable and that the king and Gower's own friends would have known to be a fabrication.[57] The episode offers some interesting insights. Richard evidently knew Gower at least by name and reputation (Pro.53*). In taking up the royal request to write something new, Gower inferred that the king would welcome a poem in English about love, one that was both diverting and didactic. The scale and ambition of the *Confessio* suggests that he spent several years working on it. In the Prologue, he also attributes some delay in writing the work to his illness (Pro.79–80*). Given the consensus that he completed the first version of the *Confessio* around 1390, it makes sense to assume that he began work in the mid-1380s, and to date the encounter on the Thames no later than 1385 or spring 1386.[58] From May 1386, Richard was away from London, and on his return in September found himself locked in conflict with parliament. He spent most of 1387 in the Midlands, returning to the capital in November. It is hard to imagine that the *Confessio* was commissioned during the political crisis, resort to arms and brutal reprisals of 1387–88.

Rebuking the King:
Revising the *Vox Clamantis* and Part I of the *Cronica Tripertita*

Whether in Kent or the capital, Gower would have been aware of the escalating conflict between the king and his noble and parliamentary critics. It was probably during this time that he revised passages in *Vox Clamantis* (VI.7.545–80, VI.18.1159–1200; above pp. 434–5) to express concern about Richard's behaviour and the consequences of misrule. After showing contempt for reforms imposed in late 1385, the king and his ministers faced determined opposition in parliament in autumn 1386. The Commons called for the dismissal of his ministers and set about the impeachment of the chancellor, De la Pole. Declaring that he would not, at their bidding, remove even the lowest of his servants, Richard withdrew to Windsor. When Gloucester and Bishop Arundel of Ely went to treat with him and pointed out parliament's role in doing justice and providing for the good of the realm, Richard reportedly declared that the proceedings were tantamount

---

[56] Frank Grady, 'Gower's Boat, Richard's Barge, and the True Story of the *Confessio Amantis*: Text and Gloss', *Texas Studies in Literature and Language*, 44 (2002), pp. 1–15.

[57] The fact that this story was not reassigned to Henry of Lancaster after 1399 suggests its authenticity (Robert F. Yeager, *John Gower's Poetic: The Search for a New Arion* (Cambridge: D. S. Brewer, 1990), pp. 267–8).

[58] Richard spent time at Sheen and Eltham, his palaces near the Thames, in April–June and September 1385 and in April–May 1386 (Saul, *Richard II*, p. 470).

to rebellion and threatened to seek aid, if necessary, from the French king. Appalled, the lords warned Richard that 'if the king, upon some evil counsel, or from wilfulness and contempt' should 'estrange himself from his people, and will not be governed or guided by the laws of the land [and] wholesome counsel', it would then 'be lawful with the common assent and agreement of the people of the realm to put down the king from his royal seat, and raise another of the royal lineage in his place'.[59] Seemingly backing down, the king agreed to govern on the advice of a council nominated in parliament for the term of a year.

Richard soon made it evident, however, that he did not intend cooperating in conciliar rule. He and his inner circle, including his favourite, Robert de Vere, earl of Oxford and duke of Ireland, spent most of 1387 in the western and midland counties. Over Easter, he and his supporters discussed a plot to murder Gloucester.[60] In August, he held a council at Nottingham, to which he summoned a panel of judges, delegates from the city of London, and sheriffs from the neighbouring counties. The judges advised that the continual council in Westminster was illegal and its members merited punishment as traitors.[61] The king received assurances of support from the Londoners, but was less successful in brow-beating the sheriffs. In September, Richard's counsellors drew up an indictment of treason against Gloucester and two other magnates, the earls of Arundel and Warwick.[62] In October, Richard made a ceremonial entry into London, accompanied by a large retinue. Forewarned of the king's intentions, the three magnates mobilised to defend themselves and England teetered on the brink of civil war.[63]

Gower cannot have remained aloof from developments. He knew people on both sides of the political divide. Geoffrey Chaucer, for example, was well connected at court and a beneficiary of royal patronage. His appearance as knight of the shire for Kent in 1386 is best explained as a somewhat desperate attempt by the court party to strengthen its position in parliament. The poet proved to have sound political instincts, giving up his controllership of the customs and withdrawing from London.[64] Another poet, Thomas Usk, was more dangerously exposed. An associate of Nicholas Brembre, a former mayor of London and closely aligned with the court, he sought to

---

[59] *Knighton's Chronicle, 1337–1396*, ed. Geoffrey H. Martin (Oxford: Clarendon Press, 1995), pp. 358–61.
[60] *Westminster Chronicle*, pp. 184–5; *St Albans Chronicle*, I: 824–5.
[61] Bennett, *Richard II and the Revolution of 1399*, pp. 28–9.
[62] *Westminster Chronicle*, pp. 206–7; *St Albans Chronicle*, I: 826–7; *Knighton's Chronicle*, pp. 394–5; Thomas Favent, 'Historia sive narracio de modo et forma Mirabilis Parliamenti apud Westmonasterium anno Domini millesimo CCCLXXXVI per Thomam Favent clericum indicatum', ed. May McKisack, *Camden Miscellany XV* (Camden Society, third series, 37 (1926)), pp. i–viii, 1–27 (separate pagination), at 7.
[63] *Knighton's Chronicle*, pp. 402–3.
[64] Paul Strohm, *The Poet's Tale: Chaucer and the Year that Made* The Canterbury Tales (London: Profile, 2015), pp. 141–4, 172–83.

raise troops for the king and was subsequently convicted and executed for treason in 1388.[65] Given his association with Lord Cobham, Gower would probably have looked to him for guidance. A member of the continual council, Cobham was close to the heart of the opposition to the court. A friend and ally of Gloucester and Arundel, he had close connections with other council members, notably Archbishop Courtenay, Bishop Wykeham of Winchester, and Sir Richard Scrope. There can be little doubt that the larger part of the kingdom was solid in support of the continual council and held De Vere and other courtiers in great contempt. When the king asked the sheriffs in August to organise the election of members of parliament favourable to his cause and to raise forces on his behalf, they reportedly told him that they wished to uphold the custom of free election and that since 'all the commons supported the lords' it 'was not in their power to muster an army for this cause'. Professing loyalty to the king later in the year, Lord Basset told the king, 'I must tell you that if I have to go into battle, I wish unmistakably to be with the party that is true and seeks the truth, and that I am not going to offer to have my head broken for the duke of Ireland.'[66] Sir Arnold Savage, who attached himself to the earl of Arundel in 1387–88, and James Peckham, who was elected to represent Kent in 1388, were likewise aligned with the 'party of truth'.[67]

Over the winter of 1387–88, Richard came to grief. The king found that the promises of military support in London were worthless. Wearing armour under their gowns, Gloucester, Arundel and Warwick came to negotiate with the king, who gave them leave to present an 'appeal' of treason in parliament against five of the king's 'evil counsellors'. Richard, however, secretly sent letters and a royal standard to De Vere to raise an army in Cheshire and advance on London. Apprised of this development, the three magnates mobilised, secured support from two young nobles, Thomas Mowbray, Earl Marshal, and Gaunt's son, Henry of Lancaster, earl of Derby, and found themselves at the head of a popular cause. Furious at the king's perfidy, Gloucester and Arundel proposed securing his person and dethroning him, but the other lords saw the defeat of De Vere's army as the priority.[68] On the news of the rout of De Vere at Radcot Bridge near Oxford, Richard retreated to the Tower of London. After Christmas, the Lords Appellant arrived in force in the capital and confronted the king, accusing him of breaking his oaths and conspiring to murder them.[69] To bring home to the king his dire

---

[65] Paul Strohm, 'Politics and Poetics: Usk and Chaucer in the 1380s', in Lee Patterson, ed., *Literary Practice and Social Change in Britain, 1380–1530* (Berkeley: University of California Press, 1990), pp. 83–112, at 85–90.
[66] *Knighton's Chronicle*, pp. 406–7.
[67] Roskell and Woodger, 'Savage, Sir Arnold I'; Woodger, 'Peckham, James'.
[68] *Westminster Chronicle*, pp. 218–19.
[69] *Knighton's Chronicle*, pp. 426–7. The Appellants showed Richard the letter he had sent to De Vere and some intercepted correspondence from France (*St Albans Chronicle*, I: 846–7).

straits, they took him to a high window to look out on the large host arrayed against him.[70] According to one chronicle, he was threatened with deposition and, according to another, he was actually deposed for three days and only reinstated because Gloucester's bid for the crown was opposed by Henry, who claimed to be the next heir.[71] Richard had no choice but to acquiesce in the purge of the royal household and the trial of his counsellors in parliament. In his precarious position, Richard asked Henry to stay behind to dine with him, probably seeing him as potentially the most helpful to his cause.[72]

In the new year, Richard was confronted by a parliament determined to punish the 'evil counsellors' who were held responsible for Richard's attempted coup against the lords of the council. De Vere and others who had already fled the realm were attainted and banished, while Sir Robert Tresilian, the chief judge, Nicholas Brembre, former mayor of London, and several others were put on trial and executed. In May 1388, the execution of Sir Simon Burley, notwithstanding pleas on his behalf by Queen Anne, Henry of Lancaster and others, marked the end of the bloodletting. By this stage, Richard was becoming more directly involved in government, though his acts were subject to the approval of a small council that included Lord Cobham. In June, the king acceded to a petition to issue a general pardon to all except some of his own supporters, and to swear not to do harm to the Lords Appellant and the men who supported them at Radcot Bridge and in parliament. There was some determination to draw a line under the recent past and prevent further conflict. It was laid down that anyone who sought to annul or reverse the decisions of parliament 'should be adjudged and executed as traitor and enemy of the king and kingdom'. The Lords and Commons then repeated the oaths sworn at the beginning of the parliament to maintain its statutes and judgements, and writs were sent to the sheriffs to administer the same oath to all freeholders in the kingdom.[73] On 3 June, in Westminster Abbey, the king repeated his coronation oath and the magnates performed homage to him.[74]

---

[70] *St Albans Chronicle*, I: 426–7.
[71] *Westminster Chronicle*, pp. 218–19, 228–9; Maude V. Clarke and Vivian H. Galbraith, 'The Deposition of Richard II', *Bulletin of the John Rylands Library*, 14 (1930), pp. 125–81, at 157–61.
[72] *St Albans Chronicle*, I: 846–7; *Knighton's Chronicle*, pp. 426–7.
[73] Bennett, *Richard II and the Revolution of 1399*, p. 33. Five hundred and eighty-three Londoners took the oath (Caroline M. Barron, 'Richard II and London', in Goodman and Gillespie, *Richard II: The Art of Kingship*, pp. 129–54, at 149n.). There are also extant lists of oathtakers in Lincolnshire and Sussex (*Rotuli Parliamentorum*, volume III, p. 401; Nigel Saul, 'The Sussex Gentry and the Oath to uphold the Acts of the Merciless Parliament', *Sussex Archaeological Collections*, 135 (1997), pp. 221–39).
[74] At the end of the ceremony, thirteen bishops declared they would excommunicate anyone who violated the oaths and sought to arouse the king's anger against the magnates (Bennett, *Richard II and the Revolution of 1399*, p. 33).

In the *Cronica Tripertita*, Gower provides an account of the events of 1387–88. After a reference to the Revolt of 1381, he presents the recent troubles as a consequence of Richard's bad behaviour and misrule, his spurning of good advice and his harkening to evil counsellors, and his attempt to destroy the duke of Gloucester and the earls of Arundel and Warwick by compelling the judges to frame charges of treason against them (I.1–25). His main concern is to celebrate the achievement of these three magnates, identified from their livery badges as the Swan, the Horse and the Bear respectively, who in defending themselves also saved the kingdom from ruin. He reports that they were supported by the two younger lords, Mowbray and Henry of Lancaster, who are identified by their heraldic badges as 'Crowned Feather' and the 'Esses', adding that the earl of Northumberland ('Northern Moon') was with them in spirit (I.51–6). In the rest of the narrative, however, he restricts his praise to the triumvirate. He describes their arrival in London with a large army to demand justice, the king seeing the size of the host from the battlements and recognising the game was up, the three lords according the king royal honours, and the decision to call a parliament to do justice and reform the kingdom (I.121–30). He accords considerable space, though, to a description of the humiliation and destruction of the king's 'evil counsellors' and agents. He relates with distasteful relish the flight and banishment of De Vere, Archbishop Neville of York, the earl of Suffolk and Bishop Rushook, the king's confessor (I.83–120), the trial and execution of Burley, Sir John Beauchamp, Brembre and Tresilian (I.139–69), the exile of other royal judges and clerks, and the purging from the court of more than a hundred servants and hangers-on (I.170–204). Finally, he returns to praise his three heroes. He declares that while they were in charge the kingdom was reinforced, the laws were strengthened, and faulty rulings were set aside, and in this manner 'they amend the king and make him anew' (I.208–10).

Although Gower's account of the conflict between the king and the Appellant lords is generally assumed to have been written after 1399, it merits being taken seriously as a source for the events of 1387–88. After all, Gower lived through the crisis and knew people who were closely involved in it. If his account in Latin rhyming hexameters is too compressed to provide an entirely satisfactory narrative, it bears comparison with other contemporary sources in its general accuracy. He is aware, for example, that the king's judges were required to set their seals to indictments of the magnates that were then distributed through the realm (CT: I.32–4, 172–3).[75] Unlike the other chroniclers, who refer to the chief protagonists by names and titles, Gower, writing in verse and needing to meet the demands of his metre, identifies them, accurately, by their livery badges (I.37–54).[76]

---

[75] Favent, '*Historia Mirabilis Parliamenti*', p. 7.
[76] Mowbray's badge of the 'Crowned Feather' was initially hard to document. A charter of Thomas Mowbray, Earl Marshal, dated 1391, however, with an illuminated initial featuring a shield of the Mowbray arms framed by two feathers rising from a crown, is

He states, uniquely but insightfully, that Richard's ruin began in London (I.57–62) when the Londoners declined to provide the military support they had promised. Though some chronicles are hazy about the date and site of the battle of Radcot Bridge, Gower states, correctly, that it took place on a Friday on the banks of the Thames (I.79–81).[77] He writes derisively of the Boar's humiliation near Oxford, the town associated with his comital title, and his flight across the river and then overseas (I.83–6, 91–4). He notes that, in leading the rout, Gloucester bore a fox's tail on his lance (I.87).[78] Gower's account, of course, is decidedly partisan, presenting solely the perspective of the Lords Appellants and their supporters. Though more intemperate, his political stance is little different from most of the other chronicles, which almost all present a positive account of the Appellant cause. If it was composed after 1399, Gower certainly showed a remarkable capacity to imagine himself as a partisan of the Lords Appellant.

When Was Part I of the *Cronica Tripertita* Written?

There has been little discussion of the chronology of the writing of the *Cronica Tripertita*. Since the three parts of the verse chronicle survive only as a single work, were written sequentially in the same metre, and have a thematic unity independent of the linkages subsequently added to give the trilogy greater coherence, it has been assumed that the entire text must have been composed after the revolution of 1399 described in Part III. Although Gower generally writes as if he did not know what came after the events he is describing, and at the end of Parts I and II appears to express anxieties about future contingencies, it is generally assumed that this is a literary device to heighten the drama or which allows him to present himself as a shrewd analyst or prophet. It needs to be borne in mind, though, that at the beginning of Part I, in lines written over earlier text, he informs his readers that what they are reading was written at an earlier time: 'As this book attests, this chronicle was written before this time, it was recited in other places, nor has it been lost to aural recollection' (CT: I.9–10, trans. Bennett).[79] Furthermore, Gower

---

to be found in McPherson Library/Special Collections, University of Victoria, British Columbia, Document Brown 4.

[77] Cf. *Knighton's Chronicle*, pp. 420–5; *St Albans Chronicle*, I: 836–9; and *Westminster Chronicle*, pp. 220–5.

[78] For a prophecy, reportedly circulating in 1387–88, in which Gloucester is identified as the Fox's Tail, see *St Albans Chronicle*, II: 72–3.

[79] '*Libro testante, stat cronica scripta perante. / Est alibi dicta, transit nec ab aure relicta*' (CT: I 9–10). Rigg renders it, more loosely in verse as 'This book attests, this chronicle was told before; / It's said elsewhere, but ears retain it evermore' (John Gower, *Poems on Contemporary Events: The Visio Anglie (1381) and Cronica Tripertita (1400)*, ed. David R. Carlson, trans. A. George Rigg (Toronto: Pontifical Institute of Medieval Studies, 2011), p. 250).

expressly tells his readers in Part II that he is reporting observations as they occurred in September 1397. It would be unwise to dismiss such statements as simply a literary fiction. Gower presents himself as a chronicler and, as is shown later, is accurate on almost all points of detail. In any case, he wrote for an audience of men like Henry IV, Archbishop Arundel, Lord Cobham and Sir Arnold Savage, who had known him, his work and his politics for a decade or more.

Although the *Cronica Tripertita* appears to be a single poem, and its three parts, relating to the events of 1387–88, 1397–98 and 1399–1400 respectively, hold together tolerably well as a three-act drama, there are features of the work that suggest that it was actually written in three stages. Part I is the shortest and can stand as an independent poem. Parts II and III are progressively longer, and struggle to find clear end points. Furthermore, as David Carlson observed, Part I appears to anticipate recitation (CT: I.47–8), while Part II seems to envisage readership (II.2–4).[80] A critical instance is the revised lines in Part I in which Gower appears to suggest that some people may recall hearing some of the matter that is in the book (I.9–10). Gower was parsimonious with his Latin verse, writing groups of lines slowly, adding to them, reordering them and sometimes recycling them in later compositions.[81] He would have been hard pressed to find time for all the new work that is generally attributed to him in the last quarter of 1399. It is instructive that, even in a poem that he would have given some priority, *Rex Celi Deus*, which was written in praise of Henry IV at the time of his coronation, he recycles lines from a stanza from *Vox Clamantis*, written for Richard II around two decades earlier.[82]

A poem about the crisis of 1387–88, of course, was still highly pertinent to the crisis that began in 1397 and concluded with the revolution of 1399. After ordering the arrest of Gloucester, Arundel and Warwick in July 1397, the king himself felt the need to assure his subjects, disingenuously as it soon proved, that the lords were not being arrested for their actions a decade earlier. It soon became apparent that the king was deliberately intent on reversing the political outcomes of 1387–88. It is not surprising then that in the 'Record and Process' of the deposition of Richard II, the first three Articles of Deposition relate to the problems with his rule in the 1380s, the

---

[80] According to Carlson, the opening lines of Part II seem more indicative of 'the literary (as opposed to oral-performative) nature of Gower's undertaking' (Gower, *Poems on Contemporary Events*, ed. Carlson, p. 343).

[81] Carlson, 'Gower's Early Latin Poetry', pp. 293–317; Siân Echard, 'Gower's "bokes of Latin": Language, politics and poetry', *Studies in the Age of Chaucer*, 25 (2003), pp. 123–56, at 153–4.

[82] Seventeen lines are taken word for word from *Vox Clamantis*, and less than half of the lines are wholly new (Carlson, 'Gower's Early Latin Poetry', pp. 302–3). See also the discussion of *Rex Celi Deus* in Arthur Bahr, *Fragments and Assemblages. Forming Compilations of Medieval London* (Chicago: University of Chicago Press, 2013), pp. 209–54, at 223–5.

establishment of the continual council, the attempted resort to arms, the king's acceptance of the proceedings of 1388, his solemn oath to accept the judgements of parliaments, and his pardons to the men who had opposed him. The general interest of Gower's account of the crisis of 1387–88 in Part I of the *Cronica* to the men involved in the revolution of 1399 needs little explanation. It does not mean, though, that Gower wrote it after 1399 or, as David Carlson has argued, that it was a 'versification' of the Articles of Deposition.[83]

In arguing the case for dependence of Part I on the Articles, and thus for a date of composition of 1399 or later, Carlson points to Gower's reference to De Vere's use of the royal standard, describing it as a 'literary-topical' invention based on the second deposition article. He later acknowledges, though, that it is 'an unsettling phenomenon' that Gower's 'single use of *vexillum*, such as it is' is the best verbal parallel 'between the *Cronica* and its source' in the Articles.[84] However, De Vere's raising of the royal standard was inherently plausible given that he was raising an army on the king's behalf against the lords and, anyway, was widely observed and reported in 1387, being noted in contemporary chronicles, all of which use the word *vexillum*.[85] Superficially more plausible is Carlson's argument that Gower's reference to the earl of Northumberland (the 'Northern Moon') as being present at Radcot Bridge in spirit, if not in person, (I.55–6) can only be explained by Northumberland's prominence in the events of 1399.[86] Apart from the oddity that Northumberland is not mentioned at all in Part III, where his role could have been roundly applauded, it can be quite plausibly claimed that the reference in fact attests Gower's specific knowledge of events in 1387–88. Along with some other members of the continual council, notably Lord Cobham, Northumberland was in the capital when the crisis broke in November 1387. Though he was at the king's company, he showed his support for the Appellants by failing to execute the king's order to arrest the earl of Arundel, by telling the king that the lords were loyal and had the support of the country, and by supporting the regime in 1388.[87]

When examined closely, Part I of the *Cronica Tripertita* reveals other elements that suggest composition in the late 1380s, immediately after the

---

[83] Carlson, *John Gower: Poetry and Propaganda*, p. 197.
[84] David R. Carlson, 'The Parliamentary Source of Gower's *Cronica Tripertita* and Incommensurable Styles', in Elisabeth Dutton, with John Hines and Robert F. Yeager, eds, *John Gower, Trilingual Poet. Language, Translation and Tradition* (Cambridge: D. S. Brewer, 2010), pp. 98–111, at 108–9; Carlson, *Gower*, pp. 190–2.
[85] Favent, '*Historia Mirabilis Parliamenti*', p. 11; *Knighton's Chronicle*, p. 420; and *Westminster Chronicle*, p. 222.
[86] Carlson, *John Gower: Poetry and Propaganda*, p. 220.
[87] *St Albans Chronicle*, I: 830–1; *Knighton's Chronicle*, pp. 406–9; Anthony Goodman, *The Loyal Conspiracy: The Lords Appellant under Richard II* (London: Routledge and Kegan Paul, 1971), pp. 48–9.

events which it narrates. After the reference back to the troubles of 1381, it begins with a diatribe against the king for his obduracy and for setting himself on a course that would lead to the destruction of the kingdom. Gower's poem on the events of 1387–88, as it perhaps can be conveniently termed, is less about Richard's misdeeds than about the achievement of magnates who stood against him and the punishment of his 'evil counsellors'. Indeed, there are many lines in the poem that only obliquely fit the agenda in 1399. For instance, it makes only brief reference to the future Henry IV. Thus, whilst Gower's presentation of Henry as the 'young and valiant' noble and particularly his description of his intervention on the side of Gloucester, Arundel and Warwick as being 'heaven sent' (CT: I.51–4) would not have gone amiss in 1399, they probably do no more than register Henry's growing reputation in 1387–88 and his critical intervention in 1387, when it could not have been assumed that he would commit the Lancastrian affinity to the Appellant cause. Interestingly, and somewhat surprisingly if he were writing in 1399, Gower does not follow the lead of some contemporary chroniclers in assigning Henry a leading role in securing the victory at Radcot Bridge, in opposing moves to depose Richard, and in presenting himself as Richard's next heir.[88] More generally, Gower's relish for detailing the humiliation and savage punishment of Richard's 'evil counsellors' is oddly aligned with Henry and Arundel's concern to present themselves as measured and merciful in contrast to Richard's alleged ferocity.[89] Gower cannot have been writing to please Henry IV when he wrote about Burley's death and the queen's appeals on his behalf. He would surely have known that Henry, along with his uncle, the duke of York, another pillar of the new regime, had stoutly opposed Burley's execution.[90]

There are many other details in the text that not only point to composition in 1387–88 but also suggest the milieu in which Gower was writing. His view that Richard's ruin began in London, his observation that Northumberland supported the Lords Appellant, and his evocation of Richard's alarm in the Tower of London at the arrival of their vast army all suggest that Gower was relying on reports circulating in the capital or on insights derived from sources close to the action such as Lord Cobham or Sir Arnold Savage. His reference to the leading magnates in 1387–88 by their heraldic emblems would seem quite obvious – though perhaps less so in Latin – in the context of the recent military mobilisation, in which liveries and badges were distributed

---

[88] *Knighton's Chronicle*, pp. 420–3; *Westminster Chronicle*, pp. 218–19; Clarke and Galbraith, 'Deposition of Richard II', pp. 157–61.

[89] Some of the nobles who supported Henry IV's accession, most notably Ralph Neville, earl of Westmorland, nephew of Archbishop Neville, were the heirs of men exiled or executed in 1388. A poet writing in 1399, especially writing on Henry's terms, would surely have avoided opening old sores.

[90] *St Albans Chronicle*, I: 852–3; *Westminster Chronicle*, pp. 328–9.

on some scale.⁹¹ The callousness of Gower's account of Burley's execution is only explicable in the context of the escalation in tension and hatred at the time.⁹² In the poem, Gower names him *vestis stragulata* (CT: I.140), the Latin translation of 'burel', the cheap and cheerful woollen cloth worn by servants. The interlingual pun, brilliantly deciphered by Carlson, would be less opaque if Gower was addressing an audience that was already in the habit of referring to Burley as 'burel cloth', a play on his name the more delicious in its application to a courtier who took notorious pride in fine apparel.⁹³ Gower's description of Sir John Beauchamp, steward of Richard's household and another victim of the Appellants in 1388, whom he names 'Bridge of the North', is likewise instructive. In saying that Richard gave him this title when making him a baron (I.152–3), Gower makes a slight but revealing error. In October 1387, Richard controversially raised Beauchamp to the peerage as baron of Kidderminster. Gower's reference is to his longstanding position as constable of Bridgnorth Castle. Since he was dismissed from this post in May 1387, Gower was making an allusion that presumably had some currency among Beauchamp's detractors in 1387, but which would have been very obscure in 1399.⁹⁴ Gower's mockery of him and his slighting allusion to his barony again suggests an audience for whom Beauchamp's elevation was a recent memory. One of the leading members of the baronage, Lord Cobham would have especially deplored the unprecedented creation of a barony by letters patent.⁹⁵ As the grandson of the first Baron Beauchamp of Somerset, and the cousin of the last of the line, Cobham had reason to feel personally affronted.

It is thus possible to argue that Gower's account of 1387–88 was written shortly after the events that it describes, rather than after Richard II's deposition, and that it was originally a self-standing work rather than the first part of the *Cronica Tripertita*. It is likely that it was written in at least two stints, with the first instalment perhaps coming as early as winter of 1387–88. Since Gower does not report the proceedings against the king's advisers and agents in chronological order, he must have at least reordered the stanzas

---

⁹¹ In the parliament of autumn 1388, the Commons demanded the abolition of badges (Nigel Saul, 'The Commons and the Abolition of Badges', *Parliamentary History*, 9 (1990), pp. 302–15).

⁹² There was popular agitation in Kent and neighbouring counties against the moves in parliament to be lenient with Burley (Favent, '*Historia Mirabilis Parliamenti*', p. 21). For Burley's unpopularity in Kent, see Saul, *Richard II*, pp. 163–4.

⁹³ Gower, *Poems on Contemporary Events*, ed. Carlson, p. 340. Walsingham states that, 'wherever he went', Burley did not present himself 'as a knight appropriate to his station in life, but as duke or prince by all the apparel he wore' (*St Albans Chronicle*, I: 852–3).

⁹⁴ CPR 1385–89, p. 363; CPR 1385–89, pp. 292, 301.

⁹⁵ For the controversial nature of this creation, not dependent on tenure of lands by barony, see Chris Given-Wilson, *The English Nobility in the Late Middle Ages: The Fourteenth Century Political Community* (London: Routledge and Kegan Paul, 1987), p. 63.

after the conclusion of parliament in June 1388.[96] It is striking that Gower's attitude to Richard appears to change over the course of the poem from an initial anger against a would-be tyrant to an eventual acceptance of an apparently chastened king at the end, a change in stance that all the king's critics and opponents had to adopt in 1388. The poem was not written to promote the Lancastrian cause, but to celebrate the achievement of Gloucester, Arundel and Warwick in defending themselves against the king's evil counsellors, working to reform the king and kingdom, and then, to the acclaim of the populace, withdrawing from the public stage:

> Thus they amend the king and make him new once more,
> As they believe for sure, and thus, acclaimed withdraw
> (CT: I.208–11, trans. Rigg).

Although Gower applauds the solidarity of the triumvirate, presenting them as 'models of good Englishmen' (CT: I.217, trans. Bennett), he appears to have been a special admirer of Gloucester and, as is suggested below, may have looked to him as a patron. Since the poem was written for recitation, it is possible that it was originally read to an audience of supporters of the Appellant cause.[97] The climate in which the poem was composed, however, changed dramatically in the summer of 1388. The new compact between king and kingdom involved an act of forgetting. Now, Gower would have needed to put away his poem on the events of 1387–88 and indeed his revisions to the *Vox Clamantis*.[98] The poem itself ends on a sombre note, with prayers for the three magnates (I.214–20). If Gower had forebodings about

---

[96] Gower reports the moves against Richard's counsellors and servants in order of their significance. He begins with Sir Simon Burley, describing him as the '*capitalis*' [the chief] (I.139) of the men punished in parliament. Rigg's translation as the 'first to go' (Gower, *Poems on Contemporary Events*, ed. Carlson, p. 261) is misleading in that it suggests that Gower was in error. In any case, although Burley was not executed until May, he was first put on trial in March.

[97] Possible venues would be the inn of Lord Cobham in Tower Ward or the palace of Bishop Arundel of Ely in Holborn, where Arundel was in residence until a week after the end of parliament (Margaret Aston, *Thomas Arundel: A Study of Church Life in the Reign of Richard II* (Oxford: Clarendon Press, 1967), p. 387). When Gower came to write a sequel on the events of 1387–88, Part II of the *Cronica Tripertita*, he had Cobham and Bishop Arundel very much in mind (CT: II.1p).

[98] It should not be assumed that Gower would have been in great danger if he kept the poem on 1387–88 and his revisions to *Vox Clamantis* under lock and key. After all, the monk of Westminster's hostile account of Richard in the 1380s was kept at Westminster Abbey, where Richard II was a regular visitor. For the career of a royal clerk who supported the Appellants, remained in government service until 1397, re-emerged as Henry IV's chancellor, and was perhaps the source of the pro-Appellant narrative in the *Westminster Chronicle*, see Alison McHardy, 'John Scarle: Ambition and Politics in the Late Medieval Church', in Linda Clark, Maureen Jurkowski and Colin Richmond, eds, *Image, Text and Church, 1380–1600: Essays for Margaret Aston* (Toronto: Pontifical Institute of Mediaeval Studies, 2009), pp. 68–93, at 90–3.

their future, he was by no means alone since a prophecy then in circulation warned the three nobles to be on their guard.[99] According to the continuator of the *Eulogium*, the king was by no means reconciled to the proceedings and only reluctantly pardoned his antagonists, while Gloucester, Arundel and Warwick, believing that Richard would seek revenge, agreed among themselves that they would avoid being together in the king's presence.[100] Like them, Gower had no choice other than to accept Richard as king, trust that he had learned his lesson, and hope that he would govern advisedly and well in the future.

Conciliating the King: the Ricardian Version of the *Confessio Amantis*

In May 1389, Richard II asserted his authority as king in a *coup de théâtre* by declaring his majority and appointing new ministers. Affirming again his readiness to rule wisely and advisedly, Richard issued proclamations affirming his intention to honour the pardons and accept the decisions of 1388 and promising good government and the just implementation of the law.[101] In July 1389, a three-year truce with France was proclaimed and the cessation of hostilities held the promise of relieving the tax burden and easing political tensions. Later in the year, John of Gaunt returned to England from Castile, where he had spent several years prosecuting his claim to the crown. Since he had not been involved in the recent domestic conflicts, Gaunt was well placed to play a mediating role between the king and his former antagonists, and his prestige, power and wealth could be used to add ballast to the ship of state. The king recognised the value of his uncle's support for his regime and loaded him with honours, including a grant of the duchy of Guyenne in tail male. Gaunt probably had some expectation that Richard would at some stage acknowledge the precedence of the Lancastrian line in the succession.[102] After seven years of marriage, Richard lacked issue, while Henry presented Gaunt with a third grandson in 1389 and a fourth in 1390. During his father's absence, Henry had greatly enhanced his reputation, and many people, including Gower, probably saw Henry's relationship with the king as a sign of hope.

Around this time, Gower completed the *Confessio Amantis*. If he began his English masterpiece around 1385, he may have set it aside for a time during

---

[99] In the prophecy, Gloucester, Arundel and Warwick were figured as the Fox's Tail, the Horse and the Ravening Beast (Bear) (*St Albans Chronicle*, II: 72–3).
[100] *Eulogium Historiarum sive Temporis*, ed. Frank S. Haydon (three volumes; London: Rolls Series, 1858–63), III: 367.
[101] *Rotuli Parliamentorum*, volume III, p. 404; CCR 1385–89, p. 671; Saul, *Richard II*, pp. 203–4.
[102] Bennett, *Richard II and Revolution of 1399*, pp. 38–9.

the crisis of 1387–88 and returned to complete it in 1389–90. Lynn Staley has written compellingly of a change in the courtly milieu between the mid-1380s, when poets like Chaucer could write poems 'to be read as focused by the terms of festive courtly address', and the 1390s, when the monarch became more powerful and forms of address became more elevated.[103] In this perspective, the *Confessio Amantis*, especially the Ricardian version, provides a bridge between these two different milieux. It is likely, for example, that the part of the Prologue in which he presents his poem as a 'bok for king Richardes sake' and describes his meeting the king on the Thames (Pro.24, 40–53*) was written before the crisis of 1387–88 but that most of the text, especially its later books, was composed after Richard's rehabilitation. If so, they were written in the period in which the political imperative was to draw a line under the trauma of the recent past and to promote concord in the kingdom. Peace in England depended on the acceptance of the propositions that the young king had been led astray, that the realm had been purged by his true subjects, and that the king was committed to wise and just rule. Gower had little choice other than to accept Richard's self-representation and to seek to reinforce this image. His inclusion of the story of the meeting on the Thames, at least in the first version of the poem, perhaps served to remind the king of the royal commission and invoked more innocent times. He expressed hope for a new Arion, the singer and harpist of ancient myth whose music tamed wild beasts, who would be able to put warring parties 'in good accord; So that the comun with the lord, / And the lord with the commun also, / He sette in love in bothe tuo / And putte away melancolie' (Pro.1062–69).[104] For Gower, the *Confessio* was a peace-offering, providing instruction for the king and the governing class and contributing to a spirit of concord in the realm.

In 1389–90, Gower was not alone in professing loyalty to the king and seeking to contribute to the reconstruction of his monarchy. Leading churchmen were especially to the fore in seeking to rebuild royal authority. Bishop Wykeham of Winchester, the veteran royal clerk, was drafted into office as chancellor of England. From 1389, a series of writers presented Richard with books aligned to the king's new image of regal magnificence and wise rule.[105] Some of the laudatory addresses were doubtless intended to

---

[103] Lynn Staley, 'Richard II, Henry of Derby, and the Business of Making Culture', *Speculum*, 75 (2000), pp. 68–96, at 70; Nigel Saul, 'Richard II and the Vocabulary of Kingship', *EHR*, 110 (1995), pp. 854–77.

[104] Yeager, *John Gower's Poetic*, pp. 237–42.

[105] James Sherborne, 'Aspects of English Culture in the Late Fourteenth Century', in V. J. Scattergood and James W. Sherborne, eds, *English Court Culture in the Later Middle Ages* (London: Duckworth, 1983), 1–27; Michael Bennett, 'The Court of Richard II and the Promotion of Literature', in Barbara Hanawalt, ed., *Chaucer's England: Literature in Historical Context* (Minneapolis: University of Minnesota Press, 1992), pp. 3–20; Patricia J. Eberle, 'Richard II and the Literary Arts', in Goodman and Gillespie, *Richard II: The Art of Kingship*, pp. 187–204; Lynn Staley, *Languages of Power*

confirm the king in his professedly good intentions.[106] Even Gloucester wrote in praise of Richard at this time: in a treatise written before 1390, addressed to 'his most excellent and powerful prince, Richard king of England', he outlined the procedures of the court of chivalry, 'as it should be governed by justice and equity to your honourable renown, in which all justice should remain and be'.[107] Even more to Richard's taste was a manuscript miscellany presented to him in 1391, which included a treatise on geomancy, purportedly compiled at the request of the king who 'through long and arduous acquaintance with astronomy has not declined to taste the sweetness of the fruit of the subtle sciences for the prudent government of himself and his people', and a short version of the *Secretum Secretorum*, dedicated to him as 'the most powerful of princes' who 'by a kind of marvel of intellect and insight, not maintained for show but genuine, is seen to excel the subjects of his own realm and his contemporaries'.[108]

In *Confessio Amantis*, Gower addresses the king, although he may also have had an intimate group of friends in mind, one which would appreciate his efforts responding to the king's request for something new by offering a work 'somwhat of lust, somewhat of loore', which offered 'wisdom to the wise, and pley to hem that lust to pleye' (Pro. 18–19, 84–5*).[109] Above all, though, he appears to have in mind a broader reading public. As Anne Middleton observes, his mode of addressing Richard in the Prologue was not just 'a matter of deferential politeness to a ruler', but a means of 'rising to sufficient largeness of mind and of reference for a public occasion, and a broad common appeal.'[110] Adopting the confession of Amans to Genius as a framework, Gower presents a series of engaging stories about love that seem designed to lead the auditor and the work's readers from the self-centredness of romantic love to larger conceptions of charity and concord. Since most of the stories

---

in the Age of Richard II (University Park: Pennsylvania State University Press, 2005), pp. 122–3.

[106] Judith Ferster, *Fictions of Advice: The Literature and Politics of Counsel in Late Medieval England* (University Park: University of Pennsylvania Press, 1996), pp. 670–8. Note especially the collection of statutes and texts, including Magna Carta and the Ordinances of 1311, all of which point to constraints on arbitrary royal rule (Rosemarie McGerr, 'Gower's *Confessio* and the Nova Statuta Angliae: Royal Lessons in English Law', in Laura Filardo-Llamas, Brian Gastle and Marta Gutiérrez Rodríguez, eds, *Gower in Context(s): Scribal, Linguistic, Literary and Socio-Historical Readings* (Special Issue of ES: Revista de Filogia Inglesa, 33) (Valladolid, 2012), pp. 45–65, at 49–54.

[107] *The Black Book of Admiralty*, ed. Sir Travers Twiss (four volumes; London: Rolls Series, 1871), I: 300.

[108] *Four English Political Tracts of the Later Middle Ages*, ed. Jean-Philippe Genet (Camden Society, fourth series, 18 (1977)), pp. 22–3, 31–9; Hilary M. Carey, *Courting Disaster. Astrology at the English Court and University in the Later Middle Ages* (London: Palgrave Macmillan, 1992), pp. 102–3; Bennett, *Richard II and the Revolution of 1399*, p. 43.

[109] Yeager, *John Gower's Poetic*, esp. pp. 267–9.

[110] Anne Middleton, 'The Idea of Public Poetry in the Reign of Richard II', *Speculum*, 53 (1978), pp. 94–114, at 107.

raise issues of self-discipline and sound government, it is possible to see the whole poem as about 'good and bad rule'. It is in Book VII, however, that Gower is most explicitly concerned with kingship.[111] Although he draws heavily on earlier works on kingship, including the *Secretum Secretorum*, it is hard not to see the pertinence of some of his emphases to Richard. For instance, in presenting five points of policy that are essential for good kingship, namely truth, liberality, justice, pity and chastity, Genius presents truth as the 'chief' point which the king should particularly embrace: 'So that his word be trewe and plein, / Toward the world and so certain / That in him be no double speche; / For if men scholde trouthe seche / And found it noght withinne a king, / it were an unsittende thing' (VII.1731–36).[112] In the late 1380s, of course, there was great concern about the lack of 'truth', both in terms of truth-telling and good faith, at Richard's court.[113] As has been observed above, the opponents of the court party in 1387–88 saw themselves as the 'party of truth'.[114] The king's obligation to keep faith with his subjects began, of course, with his coronation oath and was implicit in the symbolism of the crown. The reference to the crown and to truth in speech (VII.1723–82) seems especially pointed when it is borne in mind that Richard had recently renewed his coronation oath at his re-enthronement in June 1388.

It is generally accepted that Gower had the king in mind throughout the *Confessio Amantis*. For Andrew Galloway, the *Confessio* 'offers a deep meditation on the ethical and legal problems' arising from 1387–88.[115] In the original version of the Prologue, Gower presents himself as Richard's loyal servant, although given that Richard had recently been threatened with deposition his prayer to God 'Which causeth every king to regne, / That his crowne longe stonde' (Pro.32–3*) appears a little pointed. In the Epilogue, too, there is some hint of reservation about Richard as, although Gower generously declares that in the king 'hath evere yit be founde /

---

[111] Russell Peck, 'The Politics and Psychology of Governance in Gower: Ideas of Kingship and Real Kings', in Siân Echard, ed., *A Companion to Gower* (Cambridge: D. S. Brewer, 2004), pp. 215–38, at 219.

[112] In outlining the five points of policy, Gower refers to Aristotle, but none of the better-known versions of the pseudo-Aristotelian *Secretum Secretorum*, his likely source, includes this precise formulation (Gilbert, 'Influence of *Secretum Secretorum*', pp. 85–6).

[113] Richard F. Green, *A Crisis of Truth: Literature and the Law in Ricardian England* (Philadelphia: University of Pennsylvania Press, 1999), especially pp. 221–7, 233–5.

[114] In December 1387, the Londoners reportedly refused to fight for the king against the lords whom they held to be 'defenders of truth' (*ueritatis defensores*), and Lord Basset likewise professes his support for 'the party that is true and seeks the truth' (*partem ueracem et ueritatis sectatricem*) (*Knighton's Chronicle*, pp. 406–7).

[115] Andrew Galloway, 'The Literature of 1388 and the Politics of Pity in Gower's *Confessio Amantis*', in Emily Steiner and Candace Barrington, eds, *The Letter of the Law. Legal Practice and Literary Production in Medieval England* (Ithaca: Cornell University Press, 2002), pp. 67–104, especially 90–2, 102–4.

Justice medled with pite, / Largesce forth with charite' (VIII.2988–90*), his endorsement, as Olsson suggests, appears rather provisional: the king has 'yit nevere' sought cruel vengeance on his lieges for the faults he had found in them (VIII.2994–97*).[116] In any case, as Galloway points out, the king's mercy has a hard edge: it throws into relief his capacity to exercise retribution.[117] Although Gower presents the king as having come through a period of troubles, like the sun 'bischadewed' by clouds, unscathed 'evere briht and feir, / Within himself and noght empeired' (VIII.3010–11*), Olsson wonders whether the poet is not showing some unease here at the king's insouciance and self-absorption.[118] As James Simpson observes, if the *Confessio* begins in a mood of cautious optimism, it ends on a rather pessimistic note: Amans fails to fully apprehend the teaching offered to him by Genius. Needless to say, in the revised version of the poem, dedicated to Henry in 1393, Gower is even more explicit about the need to pray that God will establish good government and peace in England, 'That he this lond in siker weie / Wol sette upon good governance / For if men taykn remembrance / What it is to live in unite, / Ther ys no staat in his degree / That noghte to desire pes, / With outen which, it is no les, / To seche and loke in to the laste, / Ther may no worldes joye laste' (VIII.2986–94).[119]

In offering the first version of *Confessio Amantis* to Richard II, Gower reminds the king of the work's royal commission and makes some effort to compose a piece suited to a prince who was aspiring to rule well and wisely. In praising Geoffrey Chaucer (VIII.2941–57*), he may have hoped that his fellow-poet, recently appointed as clerk of the king's works, would help to promote it at court. He was also interested in signalling his literary standing and it was around this time that he penned the first version of a Latin colophon in which he advertises his three major poems. The first version of the colophon appears only in manuscripts containing the original version of the *Confessio*. It is distinguished by its association of the *Vox Clamantis* with the Revolt of 1381 and in presenting 'the king as excusable in this matter because of his minor age'.[120] It can be inferred that the version of the *Vox* in general circulation at this time lacked the passages that were more critical of Richard. For the present, too, he had no wish to publicise the poem of the events of 1387–88 that, it has been argued above, he had probably already

---

[116] Kurt Olsson, 'Composing the King, 1390–1: Gower's Ricardian Rhetoric', *Studies in the Age of Chaucer*, 31 (2009), pp. 141–73, at 167–8.
[117] Galloway, 'The Literature of 1388 and the Politics of Pity in Gower's *Confessio Amantis*', pp. 90–2, 102–4.
[118] Olsson, 'Composing the King, 1390–1', pp. 167–8.
[119] James Simpson, *Sciences and the Self in Medieval Poetry. Alan of Lille's Anticlaudianus and John Gower's* Confessio Amantis (Cambridge: Cambridge University Press, 1995), p. 225.
[120] Wickert, *Studies in John Gower*, pp. 3–6.

written and that he presumably hoped could now be forgotten as a relic of a troubled time.

Gower and Henry of Lancaster: The Henrician Version of *Confessio Amantis*

There is no evidence about Richard II's reception of the *Confessio Amantis*. No presentation copy is extant nor is there any evidence that the king ever acknowledged the poet's work. In the earliest extant version of the *Confessio*, there may already have been a nod towards Henry of Lancaster. In calling for a new Arion, who would make the king and commons love one another (Pro.1062–69), Gower may have had in mind Henry who, in addition to his moderating and mediating role in 1387–88, was known for his musical proficiency and included the harp among his instruments.[121] In May 1389, he was the only one of the former Lords Appellant to witness Richard's declaration on his majority.[122] There may have been some hope that Richard would keep Henry close to his side and, if he had no children, designate him his heir. In some eight copies of the 'Ricardian' version of the *Confessio*, the Latin *explicit* contains two additional lines: 'Go unvarnished book to the earl of Derby, whom well-informed men look on with praise, in future rest in his care.'[123] Although it is unlikely that the lines would have appeared in any presentation copy to Richard II, constituting a true double dedication, they appear to have been an early addition.[124]

Soon after completing the *Confessio Amantis*, Gower apparently began to make changes to its Prologue and the Epilogue. Although G. C. Macaulay thought in terms of three main recensions, and six distinct versions of the poem, modern scholars find it more useful to think of two basic versions of the text, one Ricardian and the other Lancastrian, or more accurately Henrician (see Chapter 2 above, p. 133).[125] In relation to Gower's addresses to Richard and Henry, there was nonetheless a staged process, arguably beginning with the commendation of the earl of Derby in the Latin *explicit*.

---

[121] Chris Given-Wilson, *Henry IV* (New Haven: Yale University Press, 2016), pp. 78, 385–7.

[122] Mortimer, *Fears of Henry IV*, p. 83.

[123] 'Derbeie comiti, recolunt quem laude periti, / Vade liber purus sub eo requiesce futurus' (Gower, *Complete Works*, II: xxiv). For the number of copies see Peter Nicholson, 'The Dedications of Gower's *Confessio Amantis*', *Medievalia*, 10 (1984), pp. 159–80, at 159, where the lines are translated as 'To the Earl of Derby, whom the experienced honour with praise, / Go, fair book; rest beneath him in future'.

[124] Cf. Nicholson, 'Dedications of Gower's *Confessio Amantis*', pp. 159–60.

[125] Peter Nicholson, 'Gower's Revisions of *Confessio Amantis*', *Chaucer Review*, 19 (1984), pp. 123–43; Derek Pearsall, 'The Manuscripts and Illustrations of Gower's Works', in Echard, *Companion to Gower*, pp. 73–97, at 93–4; Joel Fredell, 'The Gower Manuscripts: Some Inconvenient Truths', *Viator* 41 (2010), pp. 231–50, at 232.

The first revision to the English text (Macaulay's 'second recension') saw the excision of the praise of Richard and the kindly reference to Chaucer in the Epilogue (164 lines) and their replacement by a generalised conclusion and a prayer for the state of England (232 lines).[126] The revised lines have traditionally been dated, though not entirely convincingly, by reference to a date in the margin, to the fourteenth year of Richard's reign, i.e. the year beginning 22 June 1390. The revised Epilogue seems to anticipate a significant revision of the Prologue that involves the removal of all reference to Richard, including the celebrated account of the meeting on the Thames. In this version, the poem is presented as a book 'for Engelondes sake' (Pro.24) and its laudatory address to Richard is replaced by reflections on the uncertainties of the time. Finally, the poem is commended to Henry, 'With whom myn herte is of accord' (Pro.85). According to Peter Nicholson, the sentiment of the lines relating to Henry is not so different from that in the two-line commendation of the book to him in some copies of the Ricardian version.[127] Still, the excision of his laudatory address to Richard II does seem significant. Furthermore, Gower is explicit in identifying his main patron as 'my oghne lord / Which of Lancastre is Henry named' and in adding the highly complimentary lines: 'The hyhe god him hath proclaimed / Ful of knythode and alle grace' (Pro.86–9).

The date and import of the Henrician version of the *Confessio* have been the focus of a great deal of discussion. Gower himself dates the revision in the Prologue to the 'yer sextenthe of kyng Richard' (Pro.25), that is the year beginning 22 June 1392. Given Henry's absence from England, first on the Baltic crusade in 1390–91 and then in Europe and the Holy Land between June 1392 and July 1393, it is probable that Gower regarded Henry as a patron before the latter's departure from England in summer 1392 and that he was in a position to present Henry with a copy of the revision soon after his return.[128] This chronology, of course, is in line with the older scholarship that accepted Gower's dating of the revision as 1392–93 and is at odds with the recent tendency to argue, on the basis of the dating of the manuscripts of the Henrician version, that after 1399 Gower deceitfully sought to backdate his conversion to the cause of Henry of Lancaster.[129] This chapter has argued that, in fact, Gower was already highly critical of Richard in the late 1380s,

---

[126] Fisher, *John Gower*, p. 117.
[127] Nicholson, 'Dedications of Gower's *Confessio Amantis*', pp. 164–5.
[128] For Henry's overseas adventures and their role in enhancing his reputation, see F. Robin H. Du Boulay, 'Henry of Derby's Expeditions to Prussia 1390–1 and 1392', in F. Robin H. Du Boulay and Caroline M. Barron, eds, *The Reign of Richard II: Essays in Honour of May McKisack* (London: Athlone, 1971), pp. 153–72 and Given-Wilson, *Henry IV*, chapter 5.
[129] Terry Jones, 'Did John Gower Rededicate his *Confessio Amantis* before Henry IV's Usurpation?' in Simon Horobin and Linne R. Mooney, eds, *Middle English Texts in Transition: A Festschrift Dedicated to Toshiyuki Takamiya on his 70th Birthday* (York: York Medieval Press, 2014), pp. 40–74.

and that it is his praise of the king in the first version of the *Confessio* that is the aberration, albeit one which is explicable in terms of the accord that followed the crisis of 1387–88. In the following section, it is argued that, notwithstanding the re-establishment of political stability after 1389, there were many unresolved tensions and, especially perhaps for people who knew Richard, many causes for alarm. Given so much that is uncertain, it is fortunate at least that there is incontrovertible evidence of a close association between Gower and Henry in 1393. The chance survival of Henry's wardrobe accounts reveal that he granted Gower a livery collar, presumably a Lancastrian collar of 'esses', in summer or early autumn 1393.[130] As is well known, in his tomb effigy, Gower is depicted as wearing a collar of 'esses' with a pendant swan. One possibility is that Henry, who like Gloucester was a son-in-law of the last of the Bohuns, adopted the pendant swan as a mark of difference from his father's livery collar.[131] If Gower's admiration of Gloucester can be dated back to 1387–88, however, it seems very probable that, as the herald John Anstis suggested three centuries ago, Gower received the swan badge from Gloucester, and combined the insignia of the two magnates.[132]

Scholars who maintain the old view that Gower began the process of revision and re-dedication of the *Confessio Amantis* in the early 1390s have taken different views of its significance. Peter Nicholson, for example, has pointed to the possibility of an original double dedication and that the subsequent changes may have been literary in motivation. Assuming that Richard was presented with the *Confessio*, there is no telling how he received it. He knew Gower – perhaps too well – and in so far as he was apprised of its contents may not have appreciated its provisional praise and patronising tone. The poem may well have been more to Henry's taste.[133] Nicholson is certainly right in arguing that the change of the poem's dedication should not be interpreted as a sign that Gower had renounced his allegiance to Richard or that he was already indicating his support for a Henrician bid

---

[130] The record is the reimbursement of another squire, seemingly in October or November, for the cost of the livery collar assigned to him that had been granted to Gower (TNA, DL 41/424, m. 15; Matthew Ward, *The Livery Collar in Late Medieval England and Wales: Politics, Identity and Affinity* (Woodbridge: Boydell Press, 2016), p. 45). See also above, pp. 55–6.

[131] In 1401, Henry IV authorised Henry, Prince of Wales, his son by Mary Bohun, to use a swan pendant on his collars of *esses* (Ward, *Livery Collar*, p. 57).

[132] John Anstis, *The Register of the Most Noble Order of the Garter* (two volumes; London: Barber, 1724), II: 117–18. The duke of Gloucester owned a salt in the form of a swan with a collar of *esses*, perhaps a gift from Gaunt or Henry (Jenny Stratford, *Richard II and the English Royal Treasure* (Woodbridge: Boydell Press, 2012), p. 266).

[133] Henry would have been interested in the philosophical and ethical issues raised in the *Confessio*. According to John Capgrave, he liked to discuss the finer points of ethics with learned clerks (*Johannis de Capgrave Liber de Illustribus Henrici*, ed. Francis C. Hingeston (London: Rolls Series, 1858), pp. 108–9). For Henry's intellectual interests, see Given-Wilson, *Henry IV*, pp. 387–90.

for the crown. Still, he may overstate his case when he says nothing in the new dedication indicates that Gower 'was already looking to [Henry] as the country's saviour'.[134] Like Chaucer, Gower would naturally have seen Richard as the 'lord of this langage'.[135] His commendation of the *Confessio*, his English masterpiece, to Henry's protection thus implies some lack of trust in the king. Furthermore, Henry was no mere noble. After Richard, he was the eldest grandson of Edward III and, on his mother's side, the only grandson of Henry of Grosmont, duke of Lancaster, the last of an important cadet line of the Plantagenets. Henry's marriage to Mary Bohun added to his credit and connections in elite circles.[136] His emergence on the national stage in 1387 and role in brokering a compact with the king in 1388 would have encouraged the expectation that he would hold an important place in the new order. After his return to England in 1389, John of Gaunt committed his wealth and influence to rebuild the king's authority, probably with the expectation that, if he remained childless, Richard would, like his grandfather, settle the crown in the male line, which meant that Henry would be his heir. The complicating factor, which must have soon become evident, was that whilst Richard was seeking to manipulate his uncle by indulging him, he had little liking for his cousin.[137]

If Gower, like Gloucester, Lord Cobham and other men he admired, felt bound to accept Richard's promises that he would rule advisedly and would not seek revenge against the Appellant lords, he and other former supporters of the Appellants can have had few illusions to shed in the early 1390s. Even in 1388, there were strong expressions of concern that Richard held a grudge against his former antagonists.[138] On his return to England, Gaunt provided some protection for his brother Gloucester, but Arundel and Warwick were left exposed. In his desire to exalt the crown, restore his prerogatives, and enforce obedience, Richard showed himself politically astute and resourceful. He appointed a council that appeared broad-based but proved highly amenable.[139] He drew into his service able and ambitious

---

[134] Nicholson, 'Dedications of Gower's *Confessio Amantis*', p. 164.
[135] Geoffrey Chaucer, *A Treatise on the Astrolabe*, ll. 56–7.
[136] The Bohuns, the earls of Hereford, hereditary constables of England, were at the heart of baronial opposition to royal misrule in the late thirteenth and early fourteenth centuries.
[137] *Westminster Chronicle*, pp. 440–1; Mortimer, *Fears of Henry IV*, pp. 74–6, 123–5. According to a later chronicle, Richard was warned by an astrologer to beware of a toad and, after Henry arrived at a Christmas 'disguising' in a gown decorated with toads, came to see him as his nemesis (*The Brut, or the Chronicles of England*, ed. Friedrich W. D. Brie (two parts; EETS, o.s., 131 (1906), 136 (1908)), II: 589–90).
[138] For mistrust between Richard and Gloucester in 1388 and the threat of conflict between the king and some magnates in 1389, see *St Albans Chronicle*, I: 866–7, 894–5.
[139] Richard accepted an ordinance by which no grant at the crown's expense could be made without the assent of his three uncles, Lancaster, York and Gloucester, and the chancellor, *or any two of them*, which gave him ample room for manoeuvre (Tout, *Chapters in the Administrative History of Medieval England*, III: 465–6).

knights who supported him in parliament and increased royal influence in the provinces.[140] He acceded to parliamentary petitions in 1390–91 that 'the king be and remain as free in his regality, liberty and royal dignity in his time, as any of his royal progenitors', notwithstanding statutes and ordinances from the reign of Edward II to the contrary.[141] Gloucester's slow political demise was a source of anguish to his friends and admirers. His decision to go on crusade in 1391 caused popular consternation. According to Walsingham, the people were 'afraid that some new catastrophe would take place in his absence [as] the hopes and comfort of the whole country seemed to repose in him'.[142]

In 1392, Richard demonstrated his capacity to threaten and oppress his subjects in a contrived quarrel with the city of London.[143] In an ominous sign at the end of 1391, William Mildenhall, a Londoner, sought and probably bought the king's pardon for not having revealed that his father, Peter, had declared, seemingly in late 1387, that Richard 'was not able to govern any realm', that he should stay 'in his *latrina*', and that he could be readily taken captive on the road between Sheen and London.[144] In May 1392, the king's summons to the mayor and aldermen to come to Nottingham to answer certain matters to be put before them must have been a chilling reminder of the failure of the Londoners to offer the king the military support that they had agreed to provide at a similar council at Nottingham in 1387.[145] In July, the city-fathers learned that they had been found guilty on several counts of misgovernment for which the city's liberties were withdrawn and that a crippling fine of £100,000 was being imposed. With the appointment of a new warden of the city of London, the tough-minded Sir Baldwin Raddington, Sir Simon Burley's nephew and husband of Nicholas Brembre's widow, the city-fathers moved rapidly to make a submission to the king and managed to

---

[140] The king backed his household knights in challenging the power of the earl of Warwick in the West Midlands and the earl of Devon in the West Country (Alison K. Gundy, *Richard II and the Rebel Earl* (Cambridge: Cambridge University Press, 2013), chapter 4; Martin Cherry, 'The Courtenay Earls of Devon: The Formation and Disintegration of a Late-Medieval Aristocratic Affinity', *Southern History* 1 (1979), pp. 71–97).

[141] *Rotuli Parliamentorum*, volume III, pp. 279, 286; Saul, *Richard II*, p. 255; Gwilym Dodd, 'Richard II and the Transformation of Parliament', in Gwilym Dodd, ed., *The Reign of Richard II* (Stroud: Tempus, 2000), pp. 71–84, at 72–3. For the likely relevance of this episode to Gower, see George B. Stow, 'Richard II in John Gower's *Confessio Amantis*: Some Historical Perspectives', *Medievalia*, 16 (1993 for 1990), pp. 3–31, at 15–17.

[142] *St Albans Chronicle*, I: 912–13.

[143] Caroline M. Barron, 'The Quarrel of Richard II with London, 1392–7', in Du Boulay and Barron, *The Reign of Richard II*, pp. 177–201.

[144] *CCR 1389–92*, p. 527. The king was at Sheen in November 1387 (Saul, *Richard II*, p. 471). Mildenhall was in prison in Nottingham on treason charges as early as January 1389 (*Calendar of Select Pleas and Memoranda of the City of London, 1381–1422*, ed. Arthur H. Thomas (Cambridge: Cambridge University Press, 1932), p. 151.)

[145] *Westminster Chronicle*, pp. 492–5.

secure a royal pardon at the cost of only £10,000.[146] The triumphal entry of the king and queen into the city with a large entourage, celebrated in Richard Maidstone's *Concordia*, added to the humiliation and cost for the citizens. Significantly, Richard did not restore all the city's liberties, and those he did restore were to be held only at the king's pleasure.[147] It is possible that this demonstration of royal might and spite against the city was a factor in Gower's decision to excise from the *Confessio* his flattering address to Richard.[148]

In considering the date of Gower's rededication of the *Confessio*, much attention has focused on the early manuscripts. Since the new version would probably not have been in wide circulation in the reign of Richard II, it would not be entirely surprising if there were no surviving copy from before 1399. After all, there are no copies of the Ricardian version that can be dated before 1400. Most surprising perhaps is the scholarly consensus that one of the earliest witnesses to the *Confessio* is an Henrician text. San Marino, Huntington Library, MS Ellesmere 26.A.17, is dated on palaeographical grounds to around 1400. A well-executed manuscript, with an illuminated first folio, it contains nothing other than the Henrician *Confessio*. According to Derek Pearsall, it was probably prepared under Gower's own direction. Other scholars have used it to demonstrate Gower's orthographic preferences.[149] The heraldry on the first folio has been the focus of most attention. As part of the original arrangement of the text on the first folio, three shields are depicted, one showing the royal arms, incompletely rendered, a second showing three ostrich feathers and a third showing a swan (see Fig. 13.1).

From the outset, scholars recognised the Lancastrian associations of some of the heraldry and assumed that the incomplete coat-of-arms, showing the royal quarterings but lacking the label of difference, belonged either to John of Gaunt or to Henry before he became king. It was observed, too, that the house of Lancaster, especially after 1399, made use of the feathers and the swan as emblems.[150] In all the discussion of the heraldry, however, it has

---

[146] Barron, 'The Quarrel of Richard II with London', pp. 187–9, 193–5; Norman B. Lewis, 'Sir Simon Burley and Baldwin of Raddington', *EHR*, 52 (1937), pp. 662–9.

[147] Barron, 'The Quarrel of Richard II with London', pp. 190–201; Richard Maidstone, *Concordia (The Reconciliation of Richard II with London)*, trans. A. George Rigg, ed. David R. Carlson (Kalamazoo: Medieval Institute Publications, 2003).

[148] Fisher, *John Gower*, pp. 118–19. Cf. Nicholson, 'Dedications of Gower's *Confessio Amantis*', pp. 166–7.

[149] Gower, *Complete Works*, II: clii–cliii; C. W. Dutschke, *Guide to the Medieval and Renaissance Manuscripts in the Huntington Library* (two volumes; San Marino: Huntington Library, 1989), I: 40–1; Derek Pearsall, 'The Manuscripts and Illustrations of Gower's Works', in Echard, *Companion to Gower*, pp. 73–97, at 80; Michael L. Samuels and Jeremy J. Smith, 'The Language of Gower', *Neuphilologische Mitteilungen* 82 (1981), pp. 295–304.

[150] For arguments against dating this manuscript before 1399, Wim Lindeboom, 'Re-thinking the Recensions of *Confessio Amantis*', *Viator*, 40 (2009), pp. 319–48, at 342–4; Fredell, 'The Gower Manuscripts', p. 233; and Jones, 'Did Gower Rededicate *Confessio* before Henry's Usurpation?', pp. 45–54.

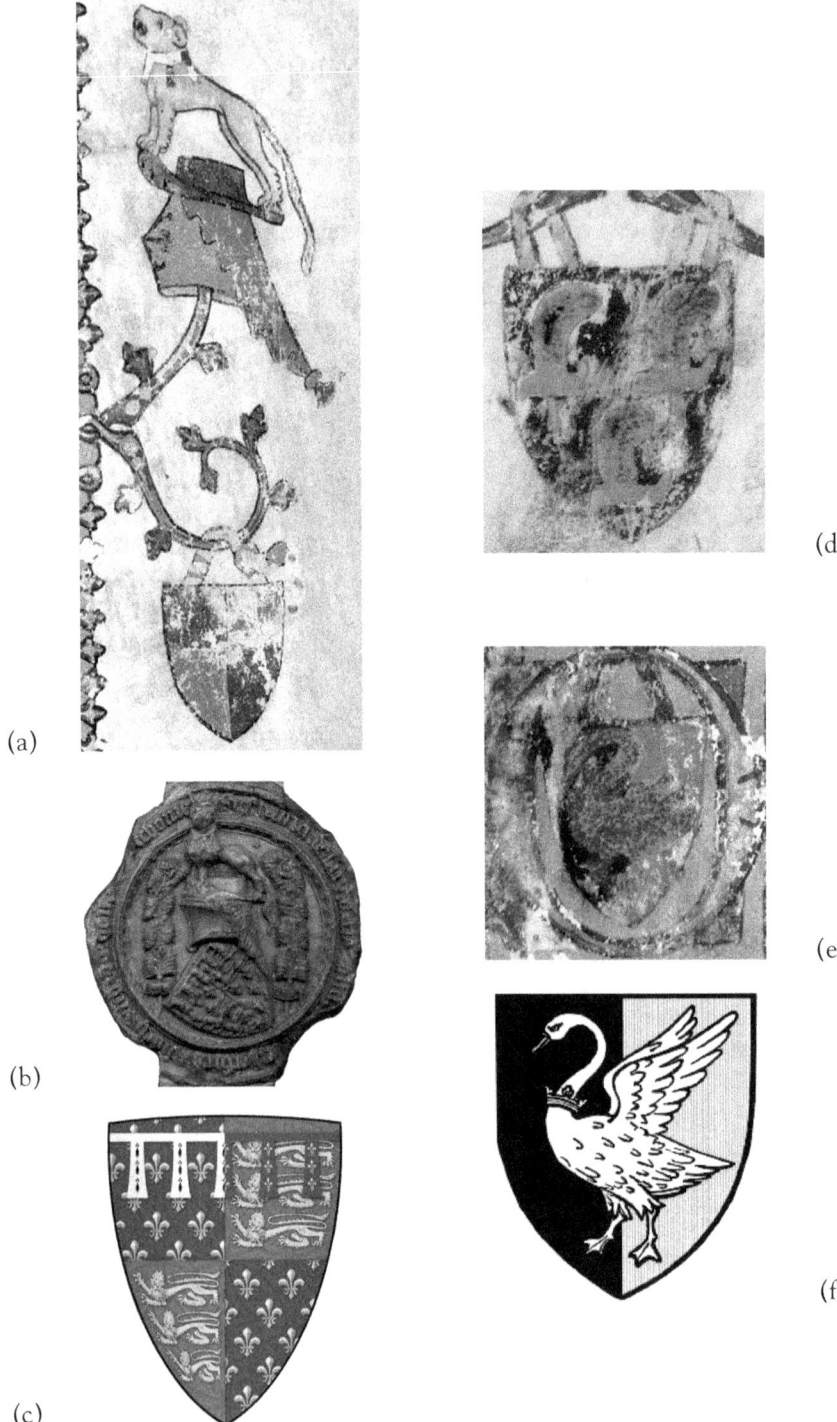

Figure 13.1 (left): Heraldry depicted on the first folio of the 'Stafford MS' of Gower's *Confessio Amantis* (EL 26 A 17, Huntington Library, San Marino, CA).

(a) Shield on Huntington MS EL 26 A 17, f. 1r. Incomplete shield with royal quarterings as base. The lion lacks a crown but has collar of cadency with colours corresponding to the label of cadency of Henry of Lancaster, earl of Derby, to whom the poem is dedicated.

(b) Seal of Henry of Lancaster, earl of Derby, 1394. The lion has a crown and a collar of cadency. The label of cadency is five-pointed and appears parti-coloured with fleurs de lis (John of Gaunt's label was three-pointed and wholly ermine).

(c) Visualisation of arms of Henry of Lancaster, earl of Derby, c. 1395, from *A Roll of Arms of the Reign of Richard II*, ed. Thomas Willement (London, 1834), pp. 4–5, where the label is described as 'a label of five points, per pale, ermine, and azure charged with nine fleurs de lis, or'.

(d) Shield on Huntington MS EL 26 A 17, f. 1r. The 'Shield of Peace' of Edward, Prince of Wales (d. 1376), displayed at his funeral and around his effigy in Canterbury Cathedral.

(e) Shield on Huntington MS EL 26 A 17, f. 1r. Shield with swan badge on black and red field, the badge and livery colours of Thomas of Woodstock, duke of Gloucester and earl of Buckingham (d. 1397).

(f) Depiction of livery of Thomas of Woodstock, duke of Gloucester, inherited by his grandson Humphrey, duke of Buckingham (d. 1460), and later adopted as the arms of the town of Buckingham ('Party per pale, sable and gules, a swan, with expanded wings, argent, ducally engorged').

been assumed that the three shields, set apart on the folio, denote a single person. Yet, in fact, it seems more likely that they designate three separate individuals. Firstly, the shield with three feathers on a sable background can readily be identified as the Black Prince's 'shield of peace', probably used in tournaments rather than in battle, that he asked to be displayed at his funeral in Canterbury.[151] Although Richard II and other members of the royal family made use of such feathers, they did so in the prince's honour and as part of their own distinctive heraldic assemblages. Secondly, the swan appears in a shield on a field of red and black, the livery colours of Thomas of Woodstock, duke of Gloucester.[152] Although Henry and his sons took pride in the Bohun connection and used the swan as a secondary emblem,

---

[151] *Collection of all the Wills*, ed. Nichols, p. 68.
[152] Michael P. Siddons, *Heraldic Badges in England and Wales* (four volumes; Woodbridge: Boydell Press, 2009), volume II, part 1, p. 13.

an association between them and this livery can be categorically ruled out. Finally, the royal shield points directly to Henry rather than his father or sons. Given that it adorns the text of a poem dedicated to Henry, and that the lines identifying the poet's own lord as Henry 'of Lancastre' appear almost exactly on the obverse of the image, its association with Henry of Lancaster should never have been seriously in doubt. A close study of the arms and crest resolves the matter. The arms in the manuscript are consistent with his arms in an armorial of c. 1395 and on his seal of 1394. More specifically, the collar of the lion in his crest in the manuscript is blue and white, Henry's livery colours and the tinctures of the label that distinguished his arms from the labels of his father and other royal kinsmen, namely five points, two of ermine and three of *azure flory*.[153] The three shields thus denote the three members of the royal family, namely the Black Prince, Thomas of Woodstock and Henry of Lancaster, whom Gower most evidently admired. Furthermore, they provide a good indication of the date of the manuscript, presumably sometime after 1392–93, the date that appears on the first folio. The shield of the Black Prince, who died in 1376, is obviously commemorative. The author of a eulogy of the prince, Gower would have often seen the prince's shield of peace on display near his tomb in Canterbury Cathedral. The prince was still greatly revered in the 1390s: John of Gaunt, for example, included his brother's shield on his tomb. The shield denoting Gloucester by reference to his badge and livery colours is less obviously commemorative and perhaps suggests that he was still active at the time the manuscript was prepared. Fortunately, Henry's coat-of-arms goes a long way to putting this issue beyond doubt. It certainly dates from before Henry became king in 1399 and probably dates from before 1397, when he was authorised to impale his arms with those of St Edward the Confessor.[154] The dating of the heraldry, the shields of Gower's three heroes, and the incompleteness of the shield of his chief patron, suggest that the manuscript belonged to Gower or someone close to him and that it should be dated to the period 1396–97, i.e. prior to Richard's deposition.

---

[153] John H. Pinches and R. V. Pinches, *The Royal Heraldry of England* (London: Tuttle, 1974), p. 86. John of Gaunt's label was three points ermine (*Ibid.*, p. 77).

[154] The incomplete shield may reflect uncertainty regarding Henry's arms after Richard II's impalement of the arms of St Edward the Confessor around 1394–96 and his authorisation of his cousin Edward, earl of Rutland, to follow suit in 1396. Henry was permitted to do likewise, probably in 1397 (John H. Harvey, 'The Wilton Diptych – A Re-examination', *Archaeologia*, 98 (1961), pp. 1–39, at 6; Adrian Ailes, 'Heraldry in Medieval England: Symbols of Politics and Propaganda', in Peter R. Coss and Maurice Keen, eds, *Heraldry, Pageantry and Social Display in Medieval England* (Woodbridge: Boydell Press, 2002), pp. 83–104, at 98).

The Tyranny of the King: Part II of the *Cronica Tripertita*

The period between the quarrel with London in 1392 and the beginnings of his so-called 'tyranny' in 1397 appears to have been, at least on the surface, one of political stability. Beneath the veneer of calm, however, the old apprehensions remained and events served to raise the stakes. Early in 1394, Gaunt petitioned in parliament that Henry be recognised as heir to the throne. His move provoked a firm response from a rival claimant, Roger Mortimer, earl of March, but Richard called the debate to an end without declaring his position.[155] Queen Anne's sudden death in June devastated Richard, broke up the court, and raised new issues. On setting out for Ireland in 1394, Richard appointed York as regent in England, a role often assigned to the heir to the throne, overlooking Henry who, with Gaunt overseas in Aquitaine, represented the senior cadet line.[156] Furthermore, his expedition to Ireland in 1394–95 served to consolidate a new group of courtiers and ministers in his service and encouraged an imperial conception of his kingship. Richard's status as a widower raised new possibilities, including a match with a French princess offering the prospect of peace with France and Anglo-French collaboration in healing the papal schism and uniting Latin Christendom on crusade. Though plans for a second marriage raised the possibility of children, Richard's betrothal in June 1395 to Isabella, a five-year-old princess, made it appear a remote contingency. Behind the scenes, there were signs that, in looking to his kinsmen in the male line, Richard was inclined to settle the crown not on Gaunt and Henry but on York's line. He regarded York's son, Edward, earl of Rutland and later duke of Aumerle, as a special favourite and began to refer to him as his 'brother'.[157]

Gower would not have been alone if he found the politics of this period difficult to read. The older generation of statesmen to whom he had looked for leadership were passing from the stage. Richard had succeeded in dividing the old triumvirate. Gloucester was compromised by his dependence on royal patronage and by Richard's association of him with policies that he

---

[155] John of Gaunt emphasised Henry's descent from Edmund 'Crouchback', earl of Lancaster, the son of Henry III, reportedly claiming that Edmund was the eldest of Henry's sons and displaced in the succession because of his alleged disability (*Eulogium Historiarum sive Temporis*, III: 369–70). For this episode, see Ian Mortimer, 'Richard II and the Succession to the Crown', *History*, 91 (2006), pp. 320–36 at 329–31; Given-Wilson, *Henry IV*, pp. 96–7.

[156] Mortimer, 'Richard II and the Succession to the Crown', pp. 329, 333–4. On his return from Aquitaine late in 1395, the king received Gaunt formally but without affection (*St Albans Chronicle*, II: 38–9).

[157] Mortimer, 'Richard II and the Succession to the Crown', pp. 333–4. Richard's describing Edward as his brother may have originated in a proposal around 1395 for his marriage to a sister of Richard's proposed new bride (Rosemary Horrox, 'Edward [Edward of Langley, Edward of York], Second Duke of York (c. 1373–1415), *ODNB*.

might otherwise oppose.¹⁵⁸ Arundel had the means to withdraw from public life but, as the richest of the magnates, was very much a marked man. In an ugly incident at the queen's funeral, Richard struck the earl of Arundel for a perceived insult, causing blood to be shed in Westminster Abbey. Appointed Arundel's executor in March 1393,¹⁵⁹ Lord Cobham was himself looking to retire. Although he remained on the king's council after 1389, his attendance became less frequent over the course of 1391 and came completely to an end in 1394. In the following years, he spent increasing time in semi-monastic retreats, including the Charterhouse in London and Maiden Bradley, a cell of Nutley Abbey.¹⁶⁰ Living at Southwark by this stage, Gower was well placed to pick up news and gossip. He knew men in the service of Henry of Lancaster, notably William Loveney, clerk of the wardrobe, and in the household of Gloucester, like Thomas Feriby, Gloucester's chancellor.¹⁶¹ He would have been close to the events surrounding Queen Anne's death. One of the four stations, at which her funeral cortège briefly halted and *herces* of candles were set up, was at Southwark.¹⁶²

In literary terms, it was evidently a quiet time for Gower. He presumably spent time in the mid-1390s arranging his work. In *Quia Vnusquisque*, he named the three poems in three languages on which he would rest his claims to literary fame. The earliest of three distinct versions describes the *Vox* as being about the Peasants' Revolt, and the statement that the king was held to be excused from blame on account of his minority reflects the spirit of the unrevised *Vox*.¹⁶³ Since it was written after 1387–88, however, it rather begs the question of his culpability in the crisis that almost cost him his throne. After 1393, Gower presumably drafted the more non-committal version to link with the Henrician *Confessio*, whilst the version including the

---

¹⁵⁸ After appointing Gloucester lieutenant of Ireland in April 1392, the king cancelled the appointment in July (Anthony Tuck, 'Thomas (Thomas of Woodstock), Duke of Gloucester (1355–97), Prince', ODNB). In 1393, Richard appointed Gaunt and Gloucester to lead the English delegation at a peace conference in Calais at which, in conformity with Richard's wishes, major concessions were made to France. A rising in Cheshire that called for the deaths of Gloucester, along with Gaunt and Henry, as potential traitors was seemingly fomented by Richard's agents (John G. Bellamy, 'Northern Rebellions in the Later Years of the Reign of Richard II', *Bulletin of the John Rylands University Library*, 47 (1964–65), pp. 254–74).

¹⁵⁹ *Collection of all the Wills*, ed. Nichols, p. 143.

¹⁶⁰ Goodman, *Loyal Conspiracy*, pp. 82–4; Allen, 'Cobham, John', ODNB. Cobham died at Maiden Bradley in 1408. (H. C. Maxwell-Lyte, 'An Account Relating to Sir John Cobham, AD 1408', *Antiquaries Journal*, 2 (1922), pp. 339–43).

¹⁶¹ For Loveney, identified as one of Gower's executors, and Feriby, who took Gower to court over a house in Southwark, see Carlin above, pp. 75–6.

¹⁶² Seven hundred pounds of wax were purchased for the *herce* at Southwark (TNA, E 403/549, m.2).

¹⁶³ Wickert, *Studies in John Gower*, pp. 3–13; Fisher, *John Gower*, pp. 311–12; Echard, 'Last Words', pp. 113–15; Echard, 'Gower's "bokes of Latin"', pp. 149–53.

denunciation of the 'most cruel king' presumably appeared only after 1399.[164] In 1394, Gower may have been persuaded to write one of the three recently discovered Latin eulogies posted near Queen Anne's tomb in Westminster Abbey.[165] Written in Leonine hexameters with disyllabic rhyme, Gower's style in the *Cronica, Anglica Regina* is the only one of the three eulogies that does not praise Richard or mention him by name.[166] Although the poet praises the queen, he may have the king's demerits, rather than the queen's merits, in mind when he states that 'while the lady held sway, there was no downfall for the English' (2) and that 'she did everything in conformity with the law' (4).[167] In his *Carmen super multiplici viciorum pestilencia* ('A poem on the manifold plague of vices'), a poem dated to the twentieth year of Richard's reign, i.e. the year beginning June 1396 (pr.8), Gower showed himself to be despondent of the state of the realm and lamented the sins which had 'infected' England. Though he does not expressly criticise Richard, he certainly communicates a sense of malaise that he associated with his rule.[168] More ominously, in *O Deus immense*, a poem on the rule of princes composed at some stage late in Richard's reign, and perhaps complementing the *Carmen*, Gower wrote: 'Therefore let the king see how he travels in his chariot, / And take care lest he lose a wheel and suffer a fall' (ll. 101–2, trans. Yeager).

Early in 1397, Richard II signalled a new determination to bend the kingdom to his will. A parliamentary petition which included complaints about the size and the cost of the king's household provided him with

---

[164] Echard, 'Gower's "bokes of Latin"', pp. 149–50.
[165] The three poems are anonymous, but Van Dussen tentatively assigned the longest poem, '*Nobis Natura Florem*', to Richard of Maidstone (Michael Van Dussen, *From England to Bohemia: Heresy and Communication in the Later Middle Ages* (Cambridge: Cambridge University Press, 2014), pp. 26–30).
[166] For the texts of *Anglica Regina, Femina Famosa* and *Nobis Natura Florem*, see Van Dussen, *England to Bohemia*, pp. 130–41; Carlson, 'Rhyme Distribution Chronology of John Gower's Latin Poetry', pp. 15–55.
[167] *Angelica Regina*, ll. 2, 4, in Van Dussen, *England to Bohemia*, p. 130. After praising her role in settling disputes and smoothing discord, the author reports that Londoners had testified to him how she favoured the meek, pleaded on behalf of the distressed, and ministered to all of them in their troubles (ll. 5–8).
[168] Gower's emphasis on lechery probably reflected concern about sexual irregularity in court circles. Given Richard's childlessness, his marriage to a child seemed incomprehensible to many people (*Chronicle of Adam Usk*, pp. 18–21). John of Gaunt's marriage to Katherine Swynford, his long-time mistress, early in 1396 was regarded as scandalous (*St Albans Chronicle*, II: 38–9). Edward of York, Richard's 'brother', married the recently widowed Lady Mohun around 1398. Expelled from court as a bad influence in 1388, she was twenty years his senior (Horrox, 'Edward, Second Duke of York'). Isabel, duchess of York (d. 1394), Edward's mother, was described as 'worldly and lustful' (*St Albans Chronicle*, I: 962–3) and the paternity of her second son, Richard's godson, was a matter of speculation (W. Mark Ormrod, 'The DNA of Richard III: False Paternity and the Royal Succession in Late Medieval England', *Nottingham Medieval Studies*, 60 (2016), pp. 187–226, at 200–6).

the opportunity to display righteous anger and to reaffirm his mastery of parliament, with the Commons being obliged to accept that they had no business raising questions about the king's household and being required to beg forgiveness.[169] In spring, a rumour circulated that the king sought to entrap the earl of Arundel, and on 13 July, Richard announced the arrest of Gloucester, Arundel and Warwick, and declared assemblies of men on their behalf as treasonable.[170] Two days later, he ordered the sheriffs of southern and midland counties, including Kent, to arrest all the supporters of the three magnates found to be in arms and, in a move to allay unrest, had it proclaimed that the lords were not arrested for old offences but for new crimes to be declared in parliament.[171] At a council in Nottingham in August, Richard arranged for the eight nobles – the earls of Rutland, Nottingham, Kent, Huntingdon, Dorset, and Salisbury, Lord Thomas Despenser and Sir William Scrope – who had been earlier named as giving their assent to the arrests of Gloucester, Arundel and Warwick – to carry an appeal of treason against them.[172] Soon afterwards, Lord Cobham, too, was taken into custody.[173]

On the eve of the opening of parliament, the king and select magnates brought large retinues into London.[174] Parliament opened with a sermon by the chancellor, Bishop Stafford of Exeter, on the text of 'There shall be one king over them all' (Ezechiel 37:22). After a flattering address by the speaker, Sir John Bushy, the statute which had set up the council of 1386 was repealed and the pardons issued to Gloucester, Arundel and Warwick in 1388 were annulled. When Archbishop Arundel rose to protest, he was dismissed and subsequently impeached and convicted of treason.[175] On 21 September, the earl of Arundel was then condemned as a traitor and executed. When Gloucester was summoned to stand trial, it was announced that he had already died at Calais and, after a doctored version of his confession was read out, he was condemned posthumously. On 28 September, the earl of Warwick was tried and banished for life to

---

[169] Richard H. Jones, *The Royal Policy of Richard II: Absolutism in the Later Middle Ages* (Oxford: Blackwell, 1968), p. 73; Alison K. McHardy, 'Haxey's Case, 1397: The Petition and Presenter Reconsidered' in James L. Gillespie, ed., *The Age of Richard II* (Stroud: Sutton, 1997), pp. 93–114, at 104–5.

[170] *Eulogium Historiarum sive Temporis*, III: 371; CCR 1396–9, p. 197; Bennett, *Richard II and Revolution of 1399*, pp. 90–105.

[171] CCR 1396–99, pp. 137–8, 208. Meanwhile he ordered the sheriff of Cheshire to raise 2,000 archers as soon as possible (TNA, CHES 2/70, m. 7r.).

[172] The dukes of Lancaster and York and Henry, earl of Derby, also reportedly gave their consent to the arrests 'after they came to the king's person' (CCR 1396–99, p. 197).

[173] CCR 1396–99, p. 157.

[174] CCR 1396–99, p. 192; *The London Chronicles of the Fifteenth Century: A Revolution in English Writing. With an Edition of Bradford, West Yorkshire Archives MS 32D6/42*, ed. Mary-Rose McLaren (Cambridge: D. S. Brewer, 2002), p. 178.

[175] Saul, *Richard II*, pp. 376–7.

the Isle of Man.[176] Now triumphant, Richard lavished honours and lands on his supporters, promoting five earls to dukedoms, including Henry of Lancaster, Edward of York and Thomas Mowbray, who became dukes of Hereford, Aumerle and Norfolk respectively.[177] On 30 September, the king prorogued parliament, presided over a ceremony in which the lords and the members of parliament swore to uphold its judgements, held a celebratory feast, and withdrew from the capital. When the parliament reassembled at Shrewsbury in late January 1398, the acts of the parliament of 1388 were formally annulled, Lord Cobham was convicted of treason and banished to Jersey, and a standing committee was established to handle outstanding business, not least dealing with all who might feel it necessary to compound with the king for pardons for their actions a decade earlier.[178]

Given what we have argued above about his circle and political leanings, Gower must have been greatly aggrieved by the destruction of the heroes of 1387–88. Based at Southwark, with his connections in Kent, he was well-placed to hear reports of Gloucester's arrest and incarceration in Calais.[179] Since the earl of Arundel himself was led through the streets of London to be beheaded at Tower Hill, Gower would have had access to first-hand accounts of the circumstances of his death and burial.[180] The earl of Warwick was arrested at his inn in London in July and his abject confession in parliament was widely publicised. The king's dealings with Archbishop Arundel were presumably followed across England, but nowhere more closely than in London and Kent. After his condemnation, the archbishop was allowed six weeks to settle his affairs in Canterbury. Gower may have known him

---

[176] For the trials, verdicts and punishments, see Bennett, *Richard II and Revolution of 1399*, pp. 101–6.

[177] The other new 'duketti' were Thomas Holland, duke of Surrey, and John Holland, duke of Exeter. Apart from the earl of Salisbury, all the men who prosecuted the appeal of treason were raised in rank, with John Beaufort becoming marquis of Dorset and Thomas Despenser and William Scrope becoming respectively earls of Gloucester and Wiltshire (Bennett, *Richard II and Revolution of 1399*, p. 106).

[178] *Rotuli Parliamentorum*, volume III: p. 382; *St Albans Chronicle*, II: 104–7; John Goronwy Edwards, 'The Parliamentary Committee of 1398', *EHR*, 40 (1925), pp. 321–33.

[179] In setting out to arrest Gloucester, the king and his noble allies summoned Londoners, unaware of the business at hand, to accompany them to Pleshey, Gloucester's residence, thirty or so miles to the north-east of the capital. On route to detention in Calais, Gloucester and his escort spent the night at Tillingbourne, half-way between Southwark and Gower's former house at Aldington (Chris Given-Wilson, *Chronicles of the Revolution, 1397–1400* (Manchester: Manchester University Press, 1993), p. 54). In early September, the king sent a message late at night to the home of Justice William Rickhill at Islingham near Rochester in Kent to go to Calais to obtain Gloucester's confession (James Tait, 'Did Richard II Murder the Duke of Gloucester?' in *Historical Essays by Members of Owen's College, Manchester published in Commemoration of its Jubilee (1851–1901)*, ed. Thomas F. Tout and James Tait (London: Longmans, 1902), pp. 193–216, esp. at 199–200).

[180] For a detailed account of Arundel being led through London and executed, see *St Albans Chronicle*, II: 90–7.

quite well and subsequently dedicated a manuscript containing the *Vox* and the *Cronica* to him. He was well-placed to hear about the change of regime upriver at Lambeth, with Roger Walden's promotion to the vacant see and the removal of Arundel's arms from the palace.[181] If Gower saw less of Cobham after his retirement from public life, he would have been able to keep up with news of him through other members of his connection, notably Sir Arnold Savage.

In Part II of the *Cronica Tripertita*, Gower provides a politically engaged but generally accurate account of the events of 1397–98. He begins by expressing sorrow at what he had to write, namely the destruction of the Swan (Gloucester), the Horse (Arundel) and the Bear (Warwick), who had accepted Richard's pardons and been seduced into believing his good faith (CT: II.1–28). Denouncing Richard for his treachery and wickedness, the lack of the 'trouthe' that men seek in a king, as he had stressed in the *Confessio* (VII.1731–6), he reports the king's role in the seizure of Gloucester at Pleshey, his ploys to persuade Arundel to surrender, and Warwick's arrest in London (II.31–42, 53–70). In regard to Gloucester, he refers to the tears of the people at his departure, the premature report of his death, his murder at the king's command, the return of his body and his burial-place, astonishment and outrage at a king's son being put to death by a king, and England's sorrow when it learned what had happened (II.43–6, 85–118). In describing the proceedings against the two earls, Gower reports that Arundel took his stand on the pardons accorded him, faced death with dignity and was buried in a secret place (II.125–8, 143–58),[182] and that Warwick was tricked into making a confession that vindicated the king's proceedings only to be further deceived by the king (II.165–96). Showing himself aware of some of the detail, he deprecates Richard's resolve to punish not only the magnates but also their heirs and criticises the greed of some of the nobles who gained their lands (II.202–4, 294–9). He relates, with some bitterness at the fickleness of the mob in London, a mocking refrain that was doing the rounds: 'The Swan is feather-free, the Horse has lost its mane, / The Swan's been plucked, the Horse is flayed (O what a shame), / The Bear can't bite, he's tethered by a biting chain!' (II.314–17, trans. Rigg).[183] Gower shows himself aware of the news that reached England late in 1397 that the pope had translated Arundel from his see at Canterbury

---

[181] Adam Usk reports the reinstatement of Archbishop Arundel's coats-of-arms and the recovery of his furnishings in 1399 (*Chronicle of Adam Usk*, pp. 78–83).

[182] Gower's account, compressed and a little cryptic, suggests that he knew (CT: II.102) that Arundel was purposely beheaded on the site of Sir Simon Burley's execution (*Eulogium Historiarum sive Temporis*, III: 375) and that his body was exhumed and reburied when the burial site threatened to become the centre of a cult (*St Albans Chronicle*, II: 94–7).

[183] According to Carlson, Gower's report of a celebration is 'manifestly absurd' because 'no celebration is otherwise in evidence' in London (Carlson, *John Gower: Poetry and Propaganda*, p. 134). However, the king and his allies did hold celebratory banquets,

(II.239–41, 265–71). He has much to say about Lord Cobham, observing that though he had withdrawn to religious life he was dragged back by the 'fisc' (II.220–4), perhaps indicating pressure on him to pay heavily for pardon. Cobham was under arrest and interrogation through September. He reports his final trial and condemnation, presumably from hearsay, as it was only delivered after parliament reconvened in Shrewsbury in January 1398 (II.228–30). His main concern is to attest to Cobham's character as honest and prudent, a truth-teller, loyal to 'the Three' (II.213–16, 225–8). In wishing to see Cobham home from exile, he appears to speak on behalf of his friends (II.231–2).

When Was Part II of the *Cronica Tripertita* Written?

It was argued above that Part I of the *Cronica Tripertita* was written as an independent poem celebrating the events of 1387–88, was perhaps recited at a gathering of supporters of the Lords Appellant, and was then set aside as the political nation bound itself to draw a line under the recent discord and bloodletting. Like Thomas Favent, who wrote a history of the late 1380s expressly for the benefit of posterity,[184] Gower may have anticipated a future readership, especially when hopes for Richard's reform rapidly evaporated. He would not then have seen his poem as the first part of a larger work but instead probably regarded it as a coda to the *Vox Clamantis*. After all, the first stanza sets the scene for the crisis of 1387–88 by describing the popular rising earlier in the decade. In manuscripts containing both the *Vox* and *Cronica Tripertita* they are linked by a colophon that presents them both as chronicling the troubles of Richard's reign.[185] There are two versions of this colophon, one referring generally to the misfortunes of the times and one referring specifically to the deposition, suggesting a staged process of composition.[186] The common core of the two extant versions is a summary of Part I, although neither includes summaries of Parts II and III. It is possible, then, that Gower began with a colophon linking the *Vox* with the poem on 1387–88 and slightly revised it to form a link between the *Vox* and the entire trilogy. In a final gloss to the colophon, Gower made a retrospective attempt to describe the three parts. Offering a new conceptualisation of the trilogy,

---

and there were large numbers of the king's supporters in London, not least his Cheshire guardsmen.
[184] Favent, '*Historia Mirabilis Parliamenti*', p. 1.
[185] Echard, 'Gower's "bokes of Latin"', pp. 149–50.
[186] Gower, *Poems on Contemporary Events*, ed. Carlson, p. 249; Gower, *Complete Works*, IV: 313–14.

he presents the three parts as chronicling respectively the work of man, the work of hell and the work of God.[187]

It is natural to see Gower's account of events in 1397–98 as being, first and foremost, a sequel to his poem on 1387–88. If in the earlier work he celebrates the achievement of Gloucester, Arundel and Warwick, his concern in the sequel is to deprecate and lament Richard's destruction of the triumvirate and their supporters, Archbishop Arundel and Lord Cobham. If Gower appears to temper his hostility to Richard over the course of Part I, he maintains his rage throughout Part II. In his exasperation, he even wishes that, rather than him harming others, the king would himself withdraw and die (II.205–6). It can be safely assumed that if Part II of the *Cronica* was written before Richard's deposition, Gower would not have shared it with any but his closest friends. Still, Richard's destruction of the five magnates alienated and alarmed so many people (II.150) that there were some grounds for hope that Richard's 'tyrannous pomp' (II.282) would prove transient.[188] Even though Gower is describing events in Part II which led, in less than two years, to the deposition of Richard II, nothing indicates that he was writing from a Lancastrian perspective. His narrative is more concerned with Richard's revenge on his former antagonists than with building a larger indictment of a royal tyrant. Interestingly, he makes no mention of Henry of Lancaster, or indeed Thomas Mowbray, both of whom had won Gower's praise in his earlier poem for supporting the Appellant cause, but who secured special pardons from the king. Indeed, Gower himself states that he took up his pen in September 1397 (II.340–1) and the statement deserves to be taken seriously. The argument here is that rather than being composed from the perspective of 1399, the verse chronicle that eventually became the second part of his trilogy was written close to events, probably between September 1397 and February 1398.

Previously, critics have always assumed that all three parts of the *Cronica* were written after the overthrow of Richard II. More recently, David Carlson has sought to give substance and precision to this assumption by looking in some detail at Gower's account in relationship to other sources.[189] His thesis is that not only was the *Cronica* written after the revolution of 1399 but that it owed its conception, in terms of its beginning with the events of 1387–88 and then proceeding to the events of 1397, and much of its content to the 'Articles of Deposition' in the 'Record and Process' of Richard's deposition in 1399. Yet, as was argued above, it seems likely that Gower wrote Part I

---

[187] *Complete Works of Gower*, IV: 313–14.
[188] In concluding his narrative of Richard's triumph in parliament in October 1397, Adam Usk pauses to remark that 'as will become apparent, like the image of Nebuchadnezzar in all its vainglory this parliament and its supporters came crashing to the ground' (*Chronicle of Adam Usk*, pp. 26–7).
[189] Carlson, 'Parliamentary Source of Gower's *Cronica Tripertita*'; Carlson, *John Gower: Poetry and Propaganda*; Gower, *Poems on Contemporary Events*, ed. Carlson.

as an independent poem which was composed long before the Articles of Deposition. Certainly, the view that Richard's determination to destroy opposition in 1397–98 was a direct, if delayed, response to his humiliation in 1387–88 was commonplace long before its encapsulation in the Articles. After all, Richard himself made a point of systematically reversing the outcomes of 1388 and doing so with a high degree of theatricality.[190]

In regard to Part II of the *Cronica*, Carlson regards it as significant that, in relating the king's dealings with Gloucester, Arundel and Warwick (II.9–212) before his treatment of Archbishop Arundel (II.239–81), Gower is following the order in which the king's dealings with the archbishop are made in Articles 30 and 33.[191] It may be countered, however, that this order not only makes sense thematically, given his focus on the three magnates in Part I, but also chronologically given that Richard began proceedings against the three magnates two months before his confrontation with Archbishop Arundel at the beginning of parliament. Furthermore, the archbishop was not convicted of treason until after the execution of his brother and Gloucester's death and his predicament and the depth of the king's deceit only became evident in stages. Even when he left England in late October, he was given to understand that he would soon be recalled, and it was not until a month or so later that it was known that he was deprived of the see of Canterbury.[192]

Other details in Part II of the *Cronica* that have been regarded as anomalous or as evidence of his use of hindsight can also be shown to reflect what he might have heard or believed in late 1397. His account of the arrest, imprisonment and murder of Gloucester, especially as compressed in his Latin verse, has been the subject of quizzical attention. The puzzling lines – 'When Richard knew for sure the Swan was not yet dead, / He feigned that he had died, the normal way, in bed' (II.85–6, trans. Rigg) – almost certainly reflect a premature report of Gloucester's death that was in circulation in August 1397. From later evidence, it appears that the king had ordered Thomas Mowbray, captain of Calais, to do away with Gloucester. When he realised that Gloucester was still alive, he ordered Chief Justice Rickhill to go to Calais to secure a confession and subsequently dispatched more dependable servants to murder him. The confession, dated 8 September, was presented in parliament on 24 September.[193] Carlson's point that Gower could not have known in 1397 that Gloucester was smothered with a feather mattress

---

[190] Bennett, *Richard II and Revolution of 1399*, pp. 101–8, 110.
[191] *Deposition of Richard II*, ed. Carlson, pp. 32–3, 49–50, 52–4; Carlson, *John Gower: Poetry and Propaganda*, pp. 157–62.
[192] Bennett, *Richard II and Revolution of 1399*, pp. 90–105; Aston, *Thomas Arundel*, pp. 371–2.
[193] Tait, 'Did Richard II Murder the Duke of Gloucester?', pp. 193–216; Mathew Giancarlo, 'Murder, Lies, and Story-Telling: The Manipulation of Justice(s) in the Parliaments of 1397 and 1399', *Speculum*, 77 (2002), pp. 76–112, at 79–92. For a crisp overview, see Ian Mortimer, *Medieval Intrigue: Decoding Royal Conspiracies* (London: Continuum, 2010), pp. 322–4.

(II.113–15) because this information, 'possibly fabricated, was only made known', when John Hall's confession was read in parliament in October 1399 is less compelling than it seems at first sight. The return of Gloucester's corpse to England in October 1397 must have occasioned much discussion of the manner of his death and probably elicited some information. It is unsafe to assume that there was no credible story of how he had met his end in circulation among his family and friends in late 1397. Foul play was certainly assumed and, as will be seen, proved highly destabilising politically. Walsingham reports Gloucester's strangulation and suffocation under the year 1397, twenty-five folios before his account of the interrogation of John Hall, the focus of which was establishing culpability for the murder.[194]

Gower took some interest in the fate of Gloucester's corpse. Carlson presents as idiosyncratic Gower's dedication of a dozen lines (II.99–108, 117–18) to lamenting the king's refusal to allow Gloucester to be buried at Westminster and praying that he would receive his rightful resting place, and seeks to explain it as a means of attributing virtue to Henry for honouring Gloucester's wishes in 1399, which Gower does not mention at all.[195] If Gower was writing in late 1397, as an admirer of Gloucester and with connections in his household, and indeed when his hero's body lay in Bermondsey Abbey, two miles downriver from Southwark, his interest and concern in the matter appear entirely natural.[196] It is notable, too, that Gower laments Richard's failure to keep his promise to Warwick that he would make honourable provision for him and his wife. If he completed this part of the chronicle by spring 1398, he would not have been aware of the king's grant of an annuity to Warwick's wife in May.[197]

Other aspects of Part II of the *Cronica* also make more sense if they were written in late 1397 or early 1398 rather than after the revolution. For instance, in contrast with Part I, in which he spends time denouncing Richard's evil counsellors and agents, Gower is reticent about the men who supported the king in 1397–98. He mentions Richard's noble favourites riding with him to arrest Gloucester, mounting the appeal of treason against Gloucester, Arundel and Warwick, joining in the condemnation of Arundel, and eagerly grabbing the forfeited estates of the three magnates. He obviously knows them – there were eight of them (II.77), he correctly notes, in relation to the Counter-Appellants – but he does not name them. His reticence is more explicable in a text written in the winter of 1397–98

---

[194] *St Albans Chronicle*, II: 98–101, 258–61. Carlson's case for Gower's dependence on Hall's confession is not supported by quotation from the record. If Gower took the detail that Gloucester had been suffocated by a feather bed, he seems not to have taken anything else (*Rotuli Parliamentorum*, III: 452–3). Carlson's analysis assumes that he could not otherwise have known or believed that Gloucester was killed at Calais, at night, by men of the lower rank (Carlson, *John Gower: Poetry and Propaganda*, p. 181).
[195] Carlson, *John Gower: Poetry and Propaganda*, pp. 182–3.
[196] *CCR 1396–99*, pp. 149–50, 157.
[197] Goodman, *Loyal Conspiracy*, p. 69.

than after the revolution of 1399. After all, by the time Gower had finished the *Cronica*, one of the eight had been executed, one had died in exile, and four had been killed by angry mobs. In not naming names, however, Gower makes an exception of three men – the 'black-hearted' Scrope, Bushy and Green – who, he states, 'sought all evil means to do [his heroes] greater harm' (II.320–1, trans. Bennett). According to Carlson, Gower names them only because they were killed at Bristol during Henry's 'conquest' of England in July 1399 and the Lancastrian regime wished to present their extra-judicial deaths by reference to popular hatred of them. He asserts that Gower's 'characterisation' of them 'as widely much hated is implausible'.[198] It is wrong to assume, however, that they had no prior notoriety as agents of Richard's oppressive rule. From August 1397, the three men were active on the king's council and were playing a key role in the regime.[199] As speaker of the Commons, Bushy orchestrated the proceedings against Archbishop Arundel.[200] In late September, Bushy and Green were appointed to a small committee to summon and interrogate persons exempted from the general pardon, determine what they should pay to merit royal mercy, and keep the proceeds in a special bag.[201] At the end of his narrative of 1397, Walsingham names them as three of the chief men in the king's council who were 'particularly hated by the country's common people'.[202] Their flight to Bristol Castle from the army assembled on Richard's behalf in July 1399 was explained at the time by reference to their fear of the populace.[203] Long before this time, Bushy and Green had a special notoriety among the friends of Lord Cobham. In September 1397, Cobham was among the first to be brought before their committee. On 3 October, Bushy and Green were granted Cobham's inn in London for their lives in survivorship.[204]

---

[198] Carlson, *John Gower: Poetry and Propaganda*, pp. 135–44.

[199] After examining the records, Anthony Tuck concluded that Scrope, Bushy and Green were largely 'responsible for the day-to-day business of government' in Richard's last years (Anthony Tuck, *Richard II and the English Nobility* (London: Arnold, 1973), p. 199).

[200] *St Albans Chronicle*, II: 78–85.

[201] *Proceedings and Ordinances of the Privy Council of England. Volume 1: 10 Richard II to 11 Henry IV*, ed. Sir Nicholas Harris Nicolas (London: Commissioners of Public Records, 1834), pp. 75–6; Caroline M. Barron, 'The Tyranny of Richard II', *Bulletin of the Institute of Historical Research*, 41 (1968), pp 1–18, at 8, n. 1, correctly dates the ordinance as the last week of September. Cf. Helen Lacey, '"Mercy and Truth Preserve the King": Richard's Use of the Royal Pardon in 1397 and 1398', in Jeffrey S. Hamilton, ed., *Fourteenth-Century England IV*, (Woodbridge: Boydell Press, 2006), pp. 124–35, at 128.

[202] *St Albans Chronicle*, II:104–5. They were appointed to the committee authorised in January 1398 to conclude outstanding parliamentary business (*Rotuli Parliamentorum*, volume III, pp. 368–9; Tout, *Chapters in the Administrative History of Medieval England*, IV: 31; Edwards, 'Parliamentary Committee of 1398', pp. 322–5, 329).

[203] *St Albans Chronicle*, II: 104–5, 146–7.

[204] CPR 1396–99, p. 253.

All in all, Gower's account of events in Part II of the *Cronica* appears to reflect the uncertainties of 1397–98 rather than their outcomes in 1399–1400. Though anti-Ricardian, it is categorically not pro-Lancastrian. Indeed, if in Part I of the *Cronica*, Gower gives Henry of Lancaster a brief honourable mention, he makes no reference to him at all in Part II. The major problem for Gower, as someone who had vested some hopes in Henry, is that Richard had thoroughly implicated the house of Lancaster in his coup. In his proclamation in July 1397, the king announced that Gaunt, York and Henry, after coming to court, had approved the arrests of Gloucester, Arundel and Warwick. In August, he authorised Gaunt and Henry to bring retinues totalling over 1,500 men to Westminster.[205] On the eve of the parliament, Henry himself hosted a feast at his inn in Fleet Street.[206] For Gower, it must have been a time of great anguish. As steward of England, Gaunt himself presided over the trials of the lords in parliament. According to Adam Usk, Henry joined in the attack on Arundel, accusing him of having proposed to seize the king in November 1387, and so eliciting the response: 'You, earl of Derby, lie through your teeth!'[207] Though he does not report this specific exchange, Gower presents the shameful scene of Richard's supporters, raised in rank, sitting at his side, hurling abuse against the earl and backing up the king's claims (II.121–2, 131–2). Henry, promoted by Richard as duke of Hereford, was implicitly among their number. At the end of his account of 1397–98, Gower gives priority to the memorialisation of Gloucester and Arundel (II.327–9). His second verse chronicle, which begins and ends as a sequel to his earlier poem, makes no sense at all as a work written in Henry's honour or according to his specifications.

Over winter 1397–98, as political tensions continued to rise, Gower may well have had some sense of a forthcoming resolution. The suspicious circumstances of Gloucester's death in Calais may have prompted Gaunt, Henry and York to consider confronting Richard to seek justice.[208] Among the king's closest associates, Mowbray became a loose cannon. As the captain of Calais, he was a focus of suspicion in Gloucester's death and yet was also concerned that the king still bore him a grudge for his role in the events of 1387–88. Meeting up with Henry of Lancaster, he confided in him his doubts about the value of the king's pardons and divulged the existence of plots at court against the house of Lancaster.[209] Fearing entrapment, Henry reported the conversation to his father and, on the king's orders, put the

[205] CPR 1396–99, p. 241, 192.
[206] *London Chronicles of the Fifteenth Century*, ed. McLaren, p. 178.
[207] *Chronicle of Adam of Usk*, pp. 27–31.
[208] Jean Froissart, *Oeuvres*, ed. Kervyn de Lettenhove (twenty-five volumes; Brussels: Académie Royale de Belgique, 1867–77), XVI: 79–83.
[209] Mowbray allegedly reported a conspiracy to kill Gaunt, Henry and some other lords at Windsor, if they had come there after the parliament at Windsor, and a plan to annul the judgement of 1327 by which Henry's grandfather had been allowed to inherit the lands forfeited by Thomas of Lancaster. There is some evidence to suggest that both

potentially treasonous conversation in writing. In response, Mowbray alleged treason against Henry. For Gower, who makes no report on these matters, it must have seemed that England was in the final stage of a crisis that would either destroy the king or kingdom. In the penultimate stanza of his second historical chronicle, he wrote that many people wept in private but dared not speak out (II.324–5). He himself prays that things will end badly for the king (II.331). In reflecting on the 'blood-filled' year (II.340), that is the regnal year beginning in June 1397, his mood is one of lamentation. He ends, though, in the hope of a turn in fortune and that man's destiny lies in God's hands (II.344–7).

Deposing Richard: Part III of the *Cronica Tripertita*

It is hard to know exactly when Gower began the verse chronicle which became the third part of the *Cronica Tripertita*. He certainly could not have written the opening stanza until after the accession of Henry IV since he makes specific reference to the new king's coronation which took place on 13 October 1399 (III.1–26). Even if, as has been traditionally assumed, Gower wrote his account of Richard's tyranny in Part III after the revolution of 1399, it would be reasonable to assume that Gower would have drawn on what he saw, heard and felt before the overthrow of Richard II rather than simply following a script written by the new regime.[210] It is possible, however, that Gower was working on what was to become the first half of Part III of the *Cronica Tripertita* some time before Henry's return and seizure of power. Indeed, for sixty lines (III.11–72), Gower focuses on Richard's tyrannous rule, and is silent about Henry, and for a further fifty lines (III.73–121) his attention is arguably more on Richard's malice towards Henry than on Henry's virtue. Gower may thus have composed what is now Part III of the *Cronica* in various stints, perhaps beginning in autumn 1398. It is possible, of course, that he simply sought to create the illusion that he was writing without any knowledge of Henry's future triumph. It is argued, nonetheless, that his account of events leading to the return of Henry of Lancaster is entirely credible in terms of what Gower could have seen, heard and believed before the revolution.

The second stanza begins by recalling Richard's destruction of the triumvirate and then presents the king as being 'like a prince of hell performing wildly on a stage', raging and oppressing his people (CT: III.27–72). Its passionate tone is suggestive of the bitter hatred and impotent anger that preceded rather than followed Richard's overthrow. Over the following

---

schemes were considered and partly pursued (Chris Given-Wilson, 'Richard II, Edward II, and the Lancastrian Inheritance', *EHR*, 109 (1994), pp. 553–71).

[210] Nigel Saul, 'John Gower: Prophet or Turncoat?', in Dutton, with Hines and Yeager, *John Gower, Trilingual Poet*, pp. 85–97, at 90–1.

stanzas the chronicle becomes more specific in relating Richard's oppressions. While there is common ground between Gower's allegations and those included in the 'Articles of Deposition', there is nothing to show that his account of Richard's demands on his subjects to seek pardons, pay fines and set their seals to admissions of guilt uses the Articles as a direct source. After all, Gower was all too aware of what was going on. He knew two of the men who were among the first to be summoned before the council committee established in September to harass prominent supporters of Gloucester, Arundel and Warwick: Lord Cobham, who refused to be bullied, but was stripped of his property, and Thomas Feriby, Gloucester's former chancellor, who paid £100 for his pardon.[211] In April 1398, Sir Arnold Savage, Gower's friend and future executor, was ordered to appear before the council 'to declare what shall there be laid before them' and returned to Southwark £100 the poorer.[212] All in all, over 4,000 people from across England felt compelled to seek out and pay for a royal pardon in 1398–99.[213] Interestingly, London and Kent, where surprisingly few men chose to seek a pardon, were regarded by king as the heartland of opposition to him. As he 'placed no trust in the city of London or the county of Kent', according to a contemporary chronicle, he went on pilgrimage to Canterbury at Easter 1399 'surrounded by a great crowd of Cheshire men, who watched over him night and day'.[214] The leading men of London and the surrounding sixteen counties were also required to make collective admissions of treason or misprision of treason and compound for the king's mercy, with each county paying £1,000 or 1,000 marks for the king's good will.[215] The process also involved rituals of submission with proctors petitioning and performing obeisance to the king on behalf of their respective communities. Bishops and other churchmen often acted as intermediaries between the king and the communities. Gower uniquely expresses dismay at reports of churchmen collaborating with the king in this fashion, though he admits he does not know the truth of the matter (III.51–2).

In his denunciation of Richard's regime, Gower makes other telling points in a manner that suggests how events were perceived at the time rather than how they were presented in the Articles of Deposition. Thus, whilst his terse statement that the king kept parliament in existence so that he could use its power to authorise his evil deeds, describing it as 'an abomination of the law' (CT: III.27–30, 33), goes to the heart of the matter of Article 8,

---

[211] Lacey, '"Mercy and Truth Preserve the King"', p. 127.
[212] CCR 1396–99, p. 277.
[213] Lacey, '"Mercy and Truth Preserve the King"', p. 131.
[214] Goodman, *Loyal Conspiracy*, pp. 37–8; *Eulogium Historiarum sive Temporis*, III: 380.
[215] *Anglo-Norman Letters and Petitions*, ed. Mary Dominica Legge (Oxford: Anglo-Norman Text Society, 1941), pp. 11–13; *Deposition of Richard II*, ed. Carlson, p. 44; *St Albans Chronicle*, II: 126–7; *A Chronicle of London, from 1089 to 1483*, ed. Nicholas Harris Nicolas (London: Longman, 1827), p. 83.

it is expressed in entirely different terms.²¹⁶ Likewise, his condemnation of Richard (III.35–8) for having sought 'papal bulls' to bolster his regime did not require a knowledge of Article 10, which explains how the king had sought papal confirmation of the decisions in parliament and the excommunication of anyone seeking to contravene them, since the king himself wished his subjects to know that the acts of his parliament had spiritual sanction. At the end of the session of September 1397, the papal legate, on the pope's behalf, endorsed the acts and pronounced sanctions on anyone who sought to contravene them; in January 1398, Richard announced his intention to seek papal bulls to confirm the decisions taken at Shrewsbury; in summer 1398, the papal legate extended the threats of excommunication to include challenges to decisions of the parliamentary committee; on 13 October, he repeated his fulminations in London and sent to Rome for further bulls to confirm his actions, which were duly issued in January 1399.²¹⁷

Gower may thus have begun his third verse chronicle, which became Part III of the *Cronica Tripertita*, before autumn 1398. Though he came to see Henry as the hero of the final part of his trilogy, he evidently struggled for some time to find a coherent story-line. A major factor was that the political situation was hard to read. Though the tendency of Richard's rule towards tyranny was all too apparent, it was hard to discern how the drama would all end. The relations between the king and the powerful house of Lancaster were probably the subject of most speculation. In 1397–98, Gaunt and Henry acted with studied loyalty, although they were presumably uncomfortable and anxious about the king's actions and intentions. The royal succession was a matter of some moment. According to Sir William Bagot's report of a conversation with the king, probably around June 1398, Richard had spoken of resigning the crown once he had restored the kingdom to obedience. Although he identified his two cousins in the male line, Henry of Lancaster and Edward of York, as the men whom he might choose to succeed him, he expressed a definite preference for Edward.²¹⁸ The quarrel between Henry and Mowbray added to the confusion. It festered for over six months, with the king relishing the predicament of the two magnates. Eventually, he resolved that the matter would be determined by judicial duel, raising the prospect of ruining both men. Although Gower makes no explicit reference to the quarrel, he evidently had it in mind in referring to new troubles in 1398 (CT: III.73–4). It was presumably only after the resolution of the conflict

---

[216] *Deposition of Richard II*, ed. Carlson, p. 37; Edwards, 'Parliamentary Committee of 1398', pp. 322–5, 329. Cf. Carlson, *John Gower: Poetry and Propaganda*, pp. 169–70.
[217] *Deposition of Richard II*, ed. Carlson, p. 38; *Chronicle of Adam Usk*, pp. 76–7, *Calendar of Papal Letters*, V, pp. 259–60; Richard G. Davies, 'Richard II and the Church in the Years of Tyranny', *Journal of Medieval History*, 1 (1975), pp. 329–62, at 348; Cf. Carlson, *John Gower: Poetry and Propaganda*, pp. 170–1.
[218] *Chronicles of London*, ed. Charles L. Kingsford (Oxford: Clarendon Press, 1905), p. 52; Given-Wilson, *Chronicles of the Revolution*, p. 211.

between Henry and Mowbray, with Richard's intervention to stop the duel and banish both parties, that Gower could discern a larger meaning in the affair: it made it possible for Henry to build up his standing in England and, indeed, break the nexus with Richard.

Gower's observation that 'all England' followed the contest between the two magnates and generally favoured Henry's cause (CT: III.75–80) appears accurate.[219] Richard's intervention in the duel and banishment of both parties allowed Henry, generally held to be the innocent party, to emerge unscathed, with his honour intact and his popularity increased. While the Articles of Deposition stress the injustice of Richard's sentence, Gower presents a subjective sense of Henry's not having merited such treatment: 'I haven't written all the favours that he showed; / If merit's work is paid, no harm to him was owed' (III.93–4). In the next stanza, he moves from describing Henry in honourable exile in France to relating Richard's further malice towards him after his father's death in January 1399. Gower's reference to Gaunt is brief and barely respectful: 'The death of his father, whom God absolve, changed everything' (III.102, trans. Bennett). He would not have known the details relating to Richard's letters patent allowing Henry to sue for his inheritance, his cancellation of the letters after Gaunt's death, his use of the parliamentary committee to make petitioning on Henry's behalf treasonable, and his capacity, through the parliamentary committee, to disinherit Henry entirely. Instructively, he does not rely on the wording of the Articles of Deposition in presenting Richard's abrupt declaration that Henry was outlawed and disinherited (II.110). The likelihood is that he is reflecting the manner in which Richard's action was presented among Henry's well-wishers in spring 1399.

Gower was not well informed about Henry's movements in exile or his plan to return to England.[220] In his account of Henry's departure from France and arrival in England in Part III of the *Cronica Tripertita*, he is reporting rumours as they came to hand in July 1399 rather than facts that he would have learned after Henry's arrival in London in August. He implies that Henry set out from Calais (III.134), when it was probably from Boulogne, and says that he landed 'near Grimsby' (III.122m) when, in fact, he arrived across the Humber at Ravenspur. Gower reports that, on landing in England, Henry kissed the ground and performed many devotions and pious vows. Though not mentioned in other sources, the action is plausible – there is an early record of a cross being erected and a hermitage established on the site – and would have soon been known about in London.[221] He presents Henry as returning to assert defend his hereditary rights but hints at a larger

---

[219] Mortimer, *Fears of Henry IV*, p. 156. The bishop of Lincoln ordered prayers for Henry's success in the duel (Bennett, *Richard II and Revolution of 1399*, p. 132).

[220] Gower refers to Henry's seeking his kin on the continent (CT: III.101), perhaps aware that Gaunt had advised his son to do so (Froissart, *Oeuvres*, XVI: 110–11).

[221] *CPR 1399–1401*, p. 209; Bennett, *Richard II and Revolution of 1399*, p. 230, n. 132.

providential role by describing him as 'inspirited' to take up arms against Richard's misrule. Walsingham's use of similar language probably reflects the way in which Henry's supporters rapidly came to see Henry's return and rapid success in providential terms.[222]

Gower was no better informed about Richard's expedition to Ireland, his return through Wales or his surrender to Henry at Chester. He presents the king as a malicious and boastful tyrant but also as a wretched figure consumed by fear and given to tears. In two very obscure lines (CT: III.162–3) he states that Richard went to Ireland because he was alarmed because 'he foreknew the duke's advent from the mouth of men who knew' (III.162, trans. Bennett).[223] Gower is probably referring here to the rumours that Richard was troubled by prophecies and seeking advice from astrologers, and that he intended to use his military power in Ireland to maintain his tyrannous rule in England.[224] Needless to say, Gower takes delight in reporting Richard's change of fortune on his return from Ireland and the crumbling of the edifice of his power with some of his followers laughing 'and others grief-stricken and weeping (III.200–1). He offers no detail about Richard's movements in North Wales and the negotiations at Conwy and Flint with the earl of Northumberland and Archbishop Arundel, both of whom had served as intermediaries between the king and magnates in 1387. In presenting the king as being not truly contrite and as planning stratagems to recover his position (III.210–17), Gower was making assumptions.[225] Still, he knew Richard of old, and may have soon heard first-hand accounts from men in the king's company. Even Jean Creton, a French knight in Richard's entourage, reports the king's scheme to take a different route than Henry to London, raise men in Wales to support his cause, and ultimately flay some of his adversaries alive.[226] It is likely enough that Gower penned his final admonishment – 'No man can save himself whom Christ does not keep safe: / This lesson, Richard, now to you I say, though too late' (III.224–5, trans. Rigg) – while Richard was still alive.

Gower glosses over the stages by which Henry's initial declaration that he was only seeking to recover his inheritance as duke of Lancaster mutated

---

[222] *St Albans Chronicle*, II: 136–7; Michael Bennett, 'Prophecy, Providence and the Revolution of 1399', in Nigel J. Morgan, ed., *Prophecy, Apocalypse and the Day of Doom: Proceedings of the 2000 Harlaxton Symposium* (Harlaxton Medieval Studies, XII, Donington: Paul Watkins, 2004), pp. 1–18, at 14–18. Cf. Carlson, *John Gower*, p. 188.

[223] '... presciuit ab ore scientum.' Cf. '... he knew in advance by word of mouth' (trans. Stockton) and, more freely, 'From shrewd reports he'd known ... before' (trans. Rigg).

[224] For some of the prophecies and apprehensions, see *St Albans Chronicle*, II: 130–7; Bennett, 'Prophecy, Providence and the Revolution of 1399', pp. 3–5, 7–11.

[225] [Jean Creton,] 'A French Metrical History of the Deposition of Richard II', trans. John Webb, *Archaeologia* 20 (1824), pp. 1–423, at 137–40.

[226] Creton, 'French Metrical History', pp. 137–40.

into a claim to the crown.[227] Henry's inheritance, it needs to be borne in mind, included his status as Richard's heir in the male line and his claim to the stewardship of England, with its ill-defined leadership role in times of crisis. After a slow start, Henry and his allies began to gather broad support, not least from the common people. As Gower wrote, Henry enjoyed a strong groundswell of popular support: 'When England knew that the duke had arrived safely, / Everyone ran, jubilant, to him from all parts' (CT: III.157–9, trans. Rigg). Even the pro-Ricardian French chroniclers had no doubts about the popular hostility to Richard's regime.[228] After his meeting with the duke of York, and the dispersal of the army that he had raised in Richard's name, Henry was effectively master of the kingdom. As the movement broadened, the only outcome could be the overthrow of the regime.[229] After all, Henry, Archbishop Arundel and other allies, not least the earl of Warwick whose former retinue joined Henry's host,[230] knew from personal experience how little faith could be put in the king's promises. Henry's arrival in London with the captive king was the occasion of great celebration. Despite his loyalty to Richard, Creton reported that the crowds were overjoyed at Henry's miraculous success in securing the kingdom.[231] Gower presumably witnessed the hero's homecoming: like the 'sands of the sea', he wrote, people gathered to sing Henry's praises, 'blessing the deeds of the great and powerful victor' (III.244–7, trans. Stockton). Conversely, the captive king was ill-received. According to Creton, the Londoners pressed for his immediate execution. The author of the *Chronicque de la Traïson et Mort* reports that Richard knew the game was up when he was told that he would not be attended by his own servants but 'by men of Kent'.[232]

---

[227] For an attempt to reconstruct Henry's view of events, see Mortimer, *Fears of Henry IV*, pp. 171–88. More generally, see Bennett, *Richard II and Revolution of 1399*, and Michael Bennett, 'Henry of Bolingbroke and the Revolution of 1399', in Gwilym Dodd and Douglas Biggs, eds, *The Reign of Henry IV: The Establishment of the Regime, 1399–1406* (Woodbridge: Boydell Press, 2003), pp. 9–33. For a more positive reading of Richard II's military position, see Douglas Biggs, *Three Armies in Britain: The Irish Campaign of Richard II and the Usurpation of Henry IV, 1397–1399* (Leiden: Brill, 2006).

[228] Jean Froissart evidently believed that Richard was very unpopular, especially in London (Jean Froissart, *Chronicles of England, France, Spain and the Adjoining Countries*, ed. Thomas Johnes (two volumes; London, 1848–49), II: 687–96). For the observations of Jean Creton and the author of the *Chronicque de la Traïson et Mort*, who were in London in September 1399, see below.

[229] According to Walsingham, 'the common people' were ready to assist Henry 'to recover their former liberty and to remove this insupportable yoke' but were 'hesitant to take up arms for fear of the king and anxious that if it happened that the duke was outwardly reconciled with the king, the king would want to go back on his word, as was his custom, and after that to crush the duke along with all his supporters' (*St Albans Chronicle*, II: 140–1).

[230] Gundy, *Richard II and Rebel Earl*, p. 224.

[231] Creton, 'French Metrical History', pp. 175, 178–9, *Chronicle of Adam Usk*, pp. 136–9.

[232] Creton, 'French Metrical History', pp. 176–7, 178–9; *Chronicque de la Traïson et Mort de Richart Deux Roy Dengleterre*, ed. Benjamin Williams (London: English Historical

For Gower, there is a sense of a larger homecoming of the banished and disaffected. He praises Henry for reinstating Archbishop Arundel, for recalling the exiles and hostages, and for other acts of grace (III.250–65). He likewise commends his good offices towards Thomas, son and heir of the late earl of Arundel, and Humphrey, son and heir of the duke of Gloucester, whom Richard had taken to Ireland along with Henry's own son (III.256–9). He celebrates Henry's recall of the earl of Warwick and the return of 'that just man', Lord Cobham, 'redeemed not by pleading or bribery but by the mediation of Christ his patron' (III.262–4). Since Gower reports the recall of the exiles as taking place before Richard's deposition, Carlson presents it as 'a fabrication' designed 'to establish that Henry was possessed of *bonitas*, already producing *bona tam grata*' before he became king.[233] There can be little doubt, however, that the exiles were all back in London, and that their former positions and properties were in the process of being restored before Henry's accession.[234] Sir Arnold Savage was working for the regime at least three weeks before Richard's deposition, when he was instructed to inquire into the chattels of Archbishop Walden, now ejected, prior to the return of Archbishop Arundel to Lambeth Palace.[235] Another arrival in the capital in September was Sir Thomas Brockhill, one of Gower's trustees in 1373 and the purchaser of the manor of Aldington in the early 1390s. Elected knight of the shire for Kent in September, he would have been able to keep Gower informed of the proceedings in parliament.[236]

Celebrating Henry's Accession

After securing the kingdom and the king's person, Henry and his advisers had to address the problem of establishing the new political order. The central problem was that there was no legal way to depose a king and there was no real interest in creating a legal mechanism to do so. Eventually, Henry and his allies proceeded on the legal fiction that Richard had both abdicated and had been deposed and that these processes were intertwined.[237] In presenting the change of regime, Gower gives priority to Richard's renunciation of his office. In describing the meeting of parliament on 30 September, he begins

---

Society, 1846), p. 227.
[233] Carlson, *John Gower: Poetry and Propaganda*, pp. 178–9.
[234] Archbishop Arundel and Thomas, son of the earl of Arundel, arrived in England with Henry, while Humphrey, Gloucester's son and heir, joined them at Chester (Creton, 'A French Metrical History', pp. 173–4). Warwick was released and reinstated two weeks before Henry's accession (Gundy, *Richard II and Rebel Earl*, p. 224). Cobham evidently took ship at the first opportunity and was present for the opening of parliament (*Rotuli Parliamentorum*, volume III, p. 427).
[235] Roskell and Woodger, 'Savage, Sir Arnold I'.
[236] Woodger, 'Brockhill, Thomas'.
[237] See Rigby, above, p. 410.

dramatically with the words 'Non sedet in sede' [he is not sitting on his throne]. If he were not himself present, Gower would have soon heard the news.[238] After reporting that Richard had surrendered his sceptre to Henry, he describes the election of Henry as king, the formal deposition of Richard, the decision to call a new parliament in Henry's name, and the provision for his coronation. Gower expresses some anxiety among the people about the slowness of proceedings, especially when the new parliament, convened on 6 October, dealt only in formalities (CT: III.308–11). This passage suggests that Gower was writing while recollection of the anxious mood was still fresh. In between the stanza in which he describes the recall of the exiles, which reflects on events over a month or so before the meeting of parliament on 30 September, and the stanza in which he relates the dramatic developments in the parliament, Gower has another stanza (III.272–84) referring to the unfortunate death of Humphrey, Gloucester's son, early in September, and the death on 3 October of Humphrey's grief-stricken mother, Eleanor Bohun, duchess of Gloucester, Henry's sister-in-law.[239]

By this time, Gower would presumably have paid his respects to Henry. Adapting a poem, *Rex Celi Deus*, that he had first composed for Richard, he rededicated it to King Henry, 'singled out by God and men with every blessing'. In thanking God for sending Henry to deliver them from oppression, blessing the day that Henry sought the kingship for himself and that God granted it to him, and praying that he would rule advisedly and enjoy all prosperity, it was probably designed for presentation to him to mark his accession or coronation (ll. 1–56). Though it honoured the new monarch, this Latin poem does not appear to be designed for broad propagandist purposes. A major new poem in English, *In Praise of Peace*, is likewise more concerned to counsel the king and influence his policy than being an unconditional endorsement of his rule. In its opening stanzas, Gower praised Henry as the elect of God, chosen 'in comfort of ous alle' (l. 4), but such high praise also underlined the need for humility on the part of the new king and the obligation to rule to show 'pité and grace' and, above all, ensure that 'The Law of riht schal noght be leid aside' (ll. 50–6). He stressed the need for the king to obey God and seek good counsel to protect the land and look after the common people, the main victims of conflict (ll. 106–47). Gower then broadens his canvas to talk about the duties of knights to protect the Church and, finally, addresses his message to other princes in Christendom. It is instructive that, in his only major vernacular poem other than the *Confessio Amantis*, Gower is very far from being a Lancastrian propagandist. Though *In Praise of Peace* celebrates Henry's providential triumph, it also reminds him

---

[238] The words would presumably have been on the lips of all who witnessed the opening of parliament and widely reported by the end of the day. Cf. Gower 'even uses the patently stage-managed symbolic portents built into the 'Record and Process' that the other sources sensibly avoid' (Carlson, *John Gower: Poetry and Propaganda*, p. 175).

[239] Creton, 'French Metrical History', p. 174n.

of his high obligations. In terms of topical reference, Gower was probably concerned about the implications of Henry's military triumph. Already hailed as a new Alexander, Henry might be tempted to pursue larger dreams of empire.[240] There must have been some anxiety in and around the capital at the arrival of large companies of soldiers, many of them northerners, who after risking their lives for Henry's cause were inclined to regard Henry as king by right of conquest and to expect some share in the spoils of war.[241] He was presumably concerned, too, by the larger danger of war with France, prior to the confirmation of the truce in May 1400.[242]

During this period, Gower was also at work on the poem that was to become the third part of the *Cronica Tripertita*. In his stanza on Henry's coronation on 13 October he felt able to be fulsome in his praise of God's providence in choosing the time and the man who would rule the kingdom with justice; to record the people's songs of jubilation and gratitude to Christ for their new king, 'just and merciful, fierce and strong'; and to declare Henry's threefold right to the crown: conquest, inheritance and popular election (III.316–37).[243] He describes, two days later, the creation of Henry's eldest son, the future Henry V, as Prince of Wales and his acceptance as heir to the throne (III.350–9). Gower's four-line poem, *H[enricus] Aquile Pullus*, likewise relates to Henry's coronation, though it has some pertinence too to the elevation of his son. In addressing Henry as the 'Son of the Eagle', who has 'crushed his enemies and broken the tyrannical yokes' (ll. 1–2), the poem alludes to a prophecy of Merlin that was in wide circulation in 1399. The prophecy spoke of the 'Son of the Eagle' who would return and defeat the 'White King' and free England from injustice and tyranny. It presents Henry as having received the oil of the Eagle (l. 3), a reference to the holy oil of Canterbury with which he had been recently anointed at his coronation, reputedly discovered by his maternal grandfather, Henry of Grosmont, duke of Lancaster. The final line (l. 4) – 'thus a new branch has returned, anointed, and joined to the old stem' – alludes to the prophecy of St Edward the Confessor about a green tree, split asunder, whose branches would grow together again.[244] It seeks to present Henry as restoring unity, presumably by

---

[240] Creton, 'French Metrical History', pp. 178–9; Frank Grady, 'The Lancastrian Gower and the Limits of Exemplarity', *Speculum*, 70 (1995), pp. 552–75, at 563–4.
[241] Bennett, 'Henry of Bolingbroke and 1399', pp. 21–3.
[242] Sebastian Sobecki, '*Ecce patet tensis*: The Trentham Manuscript, *In Praise of Peace*, and John Gower's Trembling Hand', *Speculum*, 90 (2015), pp. 925–59, at 946–51.
[243] Gower's formulation had no official status but probably reflected how Henry's title was presented by the supporters of the new regime. For discussion, see Mary Dominica Legge, 'The Gracious Conqueror', *Modern Language Notes*, 68 (1953), pp. 18–21; Paul Strohm, *Hochon's Arrow. The Social Imagination of Fourteenth-Century Texts* (Princeton: Princeton University Press, 1992), pp. 75–94; Gower, *Poems on Contemporary Events*, ed. Carlson, p. 372n.
[244] *Vita Ædwardi Regis*, ed. Frank Barlow (Oxford University Press, 1992), pp. 116–19; Lesley A. Coote, *Prophecy and Public Affairs in Later Medieval England* (York: York

representing the union of the two main branches of the house of Plantagenet that had been a source of division and discord in the reign of Edward II.

In between the coronation and the investiture of the Prince of Wales, the king and parliament addressed themselves to setting the kingdom to order, including annulling the statutes of the parliament of 1397–98. A major issue was the fate of Richard and of the lords, six of whom were now under arrest, who had aided and abetted his misrule, especially the appeals of treason in 1397 and Gloucester's murder in Calais. Gower, who had a close interest in the three lords who had been his heroes in 1387–88, described the members of parliament as 'recalling the deeds of the barons', united in their regard for 'the gentle Swan', and calling for 'the vindication of true justice' for his death (CT: III.368–71). His account of the turbulent proceedings is very terse. He notes the opprobrium heaped on the former king, who was condemned to imprisonment, and how the Ricardian lords were indicted, made their responses, and submitted themselves to the new king's grace (CT: III.374–81). He relates with some relish that the king's favourites lost the titles awarded them in 1398, but does not report the specific allegations made against them. The most serious charge, over which Gower casts a veil, was that Edward of York and several other lords were complicit in Gloucester's death and that the absent Mowbray was instrumental in his murder. From other accounts, Edward and the other lords insisted that they had not dared to do other than to obey Richard and (rightly) pointed out that many of their accusers were also complicit in the king's schemes.[245] After the first round of accusations and challenges in parliament, Henry convened a special meeting of his council to provide advice. Lord Cobham, Gower's former trustee friend, was the first to speak. According to Walsingham, he spoke at some length about the wrongs of recent times, observed that Richard had been deservedly deposed, and noted with contempt the Ricardian lords, who 'glorying in the evils of that present time', had called themselves Richard's 'foster-children'. He lamented that under such a king and his favourites 'the behaviour of the English had become worse than that of all other heathen nations' who at least 'spoke the truth, did what was true and accepted what was true', while the English, for fear of the loss of their worldly goods, or of being ruined through exile or death, had not 'dared to do what was true, or spoken the truth while such men were their rulers'. His view that the lords should be tried and punished won general support.[246]

Gower evidently followed events in parliament in late October and early November 1399 with keen interest. His verse chronicles on the events of 1387–88 and 1397–98, now reworked as the first two parts of a trilogy, would have had new relevance. Henry, however, was more inclined to look forward rather than back, not least as he, too, was complicit in some of the late king's

---

Medieval Press, 2000), pp. 167–8.
[245] *Chronicque de la Traïson et Mort*, pp. 223–4; *St Albans Chronicle*, II: 246–51.
[246] *St Albans Chronicle*, II: 250–3.

actions. Although John Hall, one of Mowbray's servants, who confessed to a part in Gloucester's murder, was condemned to a traitor's death, there were no other reprisals. In his account of the proceedings in the *Cronica Tripertita*, Gower stresses Henry's clemency, describing him as the 'enemy of no enemy' (III.390). In stating that he sought a '*tempus amenum*' ('a pleasant time') as 'he thought in that way to please Christ' (III.392–3), however, he appears a little ambivalent. He goes on to report that Henry's leniency towards the Ricardian lords prompted criticism and claims that key parties had been bribed (III.390–5).[247] Like Cobham, Gower may have felt that they should be imprisoned and notes that Henry's stance was informed by 'some secret matter of state' (III.395–99).[248]

After the end of his first parliament, Henry IV showed his gratitude to Gower. On 21 November, he granted him two pipes of wine annually, a highly acceptable, though by no means munificent, gift. In his poem, *O recolende*, Gower addresses the new king as his 'patron' and appeals to him to be mindful of 'his responsibility for what you have wrested from Pharaoh' and to uphold the law and seek virtue (ll. 2, 5–9). He also appears to playfully allude to the gift of wine: 'While one drinks dutiful toasts, your fame cannot thirst' (ll. 21–2, trans. Bennett).[249] Several scholars have discerned in the last lines – 'If you will pursue virtue, your chronicle will show an equal perfection' (ll. 26–8, trans. Fisher) – a specific link between Henry's gift and Gower's writing, suggesting that Henry knew about it and was encouraging Gower to complete it.[250] In this case, the reference to 'your' chronicle may refer specifically to Part III which celebrates Henry's triumph. The argument here, of course, is that Gower had written Parts I and II by this stage and may already have been well advanced in his account of Henry's first parliament, concluding with his account of the mercy shown to the Ricardian lords (CT: III.374–99).

Around this time, too, Gower may have begun work on assembling and linking the three verse chronicles as the *Cronica Tripertita*. He probably made an early start on preparing the stanza that he would use to end Part III, in which he contrasts 'R.' (Richard) with 'H.' (Henry) point by point, culminating in the lines 'R. laid waste the realm, vengeful in all things; / Merciful H. assuaged fear and brought back love' (III.472–3). As Gower may have

---

[247] Thomas Walsingham reports grumbling among the people, criticism of the king, Archbishop Arundel and the earl of Northumberland, and even the threat of rebellion over the lenient treatment of the lords (*St Albans Chronicle*, II: 276–7).

[248] The 'matter of state' may have been a deal between Henry of Lancaster and Edmund, duke of York, that Edward of York would be given immunity from prosecution (Given-Wilson, *Henry IV*, pp. 130–1).

[249] '*Dum pia vota bibit, tua fama satire nequibit*'. Cf. translation in Fisher, *John Gower*, pp. 68–9.

[250] Fisher, *John Gower*, pp. 68–9; Carlson, *John Gower: Poetry and Propaganda*, pp. 201–2. Cf. Yeager's translation of '*cronica*' as 'record' (John Gower, *The Minor Latin Works, with In Praise of Peace*, eds Robert F. Yeager and Michael Livingston (Kalamazoo: Medieval Institute Publications, 2005), p. 76).

anticipated, however, he had some further events to report. Over Christmas 1399, four of the Ricardian lords were involved in a conspiracy against the new regime. The plan involved the assassination of Henry and his sons and a series of risings across the kingdom. In his account of the episode, Gower takes delight in reporting how the common people moved against the rebels and did summary justice on the rebel leaders and in commending the exemplary loyalty of the Londoners in protecting Henry's family (III.400–31). He then records Richard's response to the failure of the rebellion, his refusal to take food, and his death (III.432–51). His statement that Henry gave Richard a decent burial at King's Langley (III.452–9) brings his narrative to a close at the beginning of spring 1400.

Lancastrian Gower?

For a quarter of a century, Gower took a close interest in Richard II, one that was originally well-informed and supportive but became increasingly critical and hostile. Earlier in this chapter it was suggested that Gower's connections in Kent, notably Lord Cobham, prompted and informed his letter of advice to Richard in the *Vox Clamantis*, and subsequently the revisions censuring his behaviour. Gower's perception of Richard correlates well with the career of Lord Cobham, his principal trustee through the 1380s. A close friend and ally of the duke of Gloucester, Cobham was called to reform the king's household, served on the continual council and was a key figure in the Appellant regime. It has been argued here, of course, that Gower wrote the poem celebrating the triumph of the Lords Appellants and the humiliation of Richard's supporters in 1388. Although a supporter of the Appellant cause, Gower had to accept, as Gloucester and Cobham did, the settlement of 1388, in which Richard was put back on his throne, with the fiction that as a minor he had been misled by 'evil counsellors'. It was in the context of this spirit of accord that Gower completed the *Confessio Amantis*, a work commissioned by the king and partly written before the troubles of 1387–88. As is well recognised, Gower's laudatory address to Richard is somewhat at odds with the general tone of the rest of the work in which he presents lessons of good and bad rule, often pointed in terms of their application to Richard, and seems pessimistic about their being taken to heart.

By this stage, of course, Gower had become acquainted with Henry of Lancaster. His intervention, in his father's absence, on the side of Gloucester, Arundel and Warwick delivered the Lancastrian affinity to the cause of the 'party of the truth'.[251] He likewise probably had some sense of the important role Henry played in appeasing Richard and brokering a settlement in 1388. He may have entertained some hope that Richard would keep Henry at his

---

[251] *Knighton's Chronicle*, pp. 406–7.

side as a counsellor and acknowledge his status, after Gaunt, as his heir in the male line. More crucially, perhaps, he found some meeting of minds with Henry, releasing copies of the *Confessio* with an *explicit* commending it to him.[252] In 1393, he excised all reference to Richard from the *Confessio*, rededicated the poem to Henry, and re-presented his masterpiece as a work for 'England's sake'. In this revision, Gower was not repudiating his allegiance to Richard, still less anticipating a Lancastrian coup. Although it is unlikely that he circulated it beyond his own circle, it does clearly register his alienation from the king.

If it is accepted that Gower lost his illusions about Richard in the late 1380s, there is no need to assume any sudden change of heart in the early 1390s. Still, the king's harsh dealing with London in 1392, and the signs of other grudges dating back to 1387, may have settled the matter for Gower. During this period, Richard was playing his hand carefully, building up the edifice of royal majesty, winning new supporters and dividing his former antagonists, acting in conformity with the letter though not the spirit of the settlement of 1388. If Richard's aims and ambitions were hard to read in the mid-1390s, they became manifest in July 1397. As Richard himself told European princes, he intended to punish his antagonists of a decade earlier, to reduce England to obedience, and indeed to reverse the political outcomes of earlier struggles. It was Gloucester, Arundel and Warwick and the men who supported them who bore the brunt of the king's anger and avarice. In his second verse chronicle, Gower showed himself confirmed about their fate and its implications for the people of England living under a tyrant. In his last general pardon in February 1399, Richard still excepted men who had served the Appellants and, as Maude Clarke observed, it is 'startling to discover, the exception was interpreted to cover London and the sixteen counties' which together made up 'more than half the population of England'.[253]

Nevertheless, hostility to Richard and his regime in the late 1390s cannot be equated with Lancastrian sentiment. For a time, Gaunt and even Henry himself appeared to be complicit in Richard's tyranny. It was Richard's denial of justice to Henry and Gaunt's death that allowed Gower to present Henry, in seeking his inheritance and all that entailed, as a righteous righter of the kingdom's wrongs. After Henry's success in making himself master of the kingdom, he had few doubts that he was God's elect and the people's choice to succeed Richard as king. He seems not to have been troubled by the legal fiction of Richard's abdication.[254] Even the pro-Ricardian chronicles suggest

---

[252] In addressing Henry soon after his accession, Gower refers to books on government of which 'Y wot wel thow art lerned' (*In Praise of Peace*, l. 25).

[253] Clarke, *Fourteenth Century Studies*, p. 105.

[254] Interestingly the men involved in the negotiations with Richard in 1399, notably Archbishop Arundel and the earl of Northumberland as well as Henry himself, had been involved in negotiating with him in 1387, and had experience of his slipperiness and dissimulation.

that Richard, at various times, expressed a willingness to concede the rule of the kingdom to Henry.[255] In celebrating Richard's downfall and Henry's accession, Gower was expressing the immense relief and joy at the almost miraculous turn of events that was evidently widely shared in south-east England. Although his writing was extremely acceptable to the new regime, it would still be somewhat misleading to present him as a Lancastrian propagandist. After all, the movement that overthrew Richard II was broad-based and the men who organised the change of regime in Westminster did not follow a Lancastrian script. Since the king's injustice and oppressive policies were widely experienced and presumably widely noted and discussed, it is to be expected that Gower's account of them would have some correspondence with the Articles of Deposition, which themselves would have been constructed by sifting through lists of grievances.

Above all, there is little evidence that Gower wrote at anyone's bidding.[256] Even when celebrating England's providential deliverance, he was not writing to the specifications of the new king. In presenting Henry's accession as providential he sets terms to his approval and most of his laureate poems express a conditionality that is far from adulatory.[257] Gower's *In Praise of Peace* makes it clear that Henry needs to be humble in what he has achieved, and that he has a special responsibility to bring peace to the land. In his account of Henry's leniency in dealing with the Ricardian lords in Part III of the *Cronica*, Gower reserves his judgement. In reporting the conspiracy of four of the pardoned nobles in January 1400, Gower may have been inclined to see the folly of the king's leniency. It was the common people who took it into their own hands to suppress the rising and execute the ringleaders. Several scholars have suggested that Gower may have moderated his enthusiasm for Henry over the following years.[258] It was entirely in his form to do so. Sir Arnold Savage, his old friend and executor, might serve as proxy for his views. A close friend and counsellor of Henry, Savage was nonetheless willing, as speaker of the House of Commons, to go head to head with Henry in defending parliamentary liberties and the interests of the kingdom.[259] Henry found himself facing challenges to his legitimacy and a major rebellion in 1403 that led to bloodshed on a larger scale than in Richard II's

---

[255] Giancarlo, 'Murder, Lies, and Story-Telling', pp. 100–1.
[256] Saul, 'Gower: Prophet or Turncoat?', pp. 90–1.
[257] Grady, 'Lancastrian Gower and Limits of Exemplarity', pp. 552–75; Carlson, *John Gower: Poetry and Propaganda*, pp. 209–14.
[258] Grady, 'Lancastrian Gower and Limits of Exemplarity', pp. 559–75; Carlson, *John Gower: Poetry and Propaganda*, pp. 221–6; Robert F. Yeager, 'Gower in Winter: Last Poems', in Yeager and Takamiya, eds, *Medieval Python*, pp. 87–103, at 96–7.
[259] John S. Roskell, *The Commons and their Speakers in English Parliaments 1376–1523* (Manchester: Manchester University Press, 1965), pp. 142–4; Given-Wilson, *Henry IV*, pp. 230–1, 282.

last years. The execution of Archbishop Scrope in 1405 was a particularly shocking act.[260]

The revolution of 1399 provided Gower with a new platform for his writing. Over the autumn and winter of 1399–1400, he was evidently very busy. In standard accounts of his career, he wrote at this time three Latin poems celebrating Henry's accession, the entirety of the *Cronica Tripertita*, and *In Praise of Peace*.[261] For scholars who insist on Gower's opportunist reinvention of himself as a Lancastrian, he also wrote *O Deus Immense*, revised his letter to Richard in the *Vox Clamantis*, reworked the Prologue and Epilogue of the *Confessio Amantis* to give the impression that he had long identified Henry as England's great hope, and presumably wrote the additional stories that appear only in some Henrician versions. The change of regime doubtless increased the demand for the texts stripped of Ricardian associations: the extant copies of the Henrician version of the *Confessio* antedate the surviving copies of the Ricardian version which, after the initial wave of hostility towards Richard subsided, reasserted itself as the favoured version. Although he was less active in correcting and supervising copies of his revisions than has previously been assumed, he was still centrally involved in revising and rearranging for posterity the entire corpus of his work in three languages. Since Gower claims that he was going blind in the first year of Henry's reign, that is before September 1400, and that he was finally putting down his pen in the following year, it is hard to imagine how he could have had the time for all the work. In some recognition of this workload, scholars have sought to date the completion of the *Cronica* and the composition of *In Praise of Peace* to later in Gower's life.[262] There is a strong counter-trend, however, recognising the topicality of the works, to argue that all his major pieces were substantially written by early 1400.[263]

By looking again at his writings on Richard II and Henry IV, and setting them alongside what he would have observed and heard in the circles in which he moved, it has been argued here that Gower had already made the revisions to *Vox Clamantis* and *Confessio Amantis* that some scholars have argued were made after 1399. The larger claim that Gower wrote his first two verse chronicles around 1388 and 1398 respectively leaves his workload in his last active years more feasible. It has been argued that he wrote what came to be the final part of the *Cronica Tripertita* in increasingly short stints as events unfolded between summer 1399 and spring 1400. There is no evidence that he undertook any major new literary work after this time. He doubtless used whatever capacity he still had to seek to establish his literary legacy. He prided himself on his trilingual *oeuvre* and, in respect of his Latin works, he linked the *Vox* and the *Cronica* as an account of the troubles of

---

[260] Given-Wilson, *Henry IV*, pp. 268–70.
[261] Carlson, 'Gower's Early Latin Poetry', pp. 302–3.
[262] Yeager, 'Gower in Winter', p. 96.
[263] E.g. Sobecki, '*Ecce patet tensis*', esp. pp. 89–91.

Richard's reign and presented a fine manuscript containing the two works to Archbishop Arundel.[264] He presumably dictated some short pieces, including his epitaph, in the last years of his life. He gave some attention to his tomb and memorial in St Mary Overy in Southwark. Even if he had given up some of the high hopes he entertained for Henry IV, he remained proud of the association and chose to have himself depicted wearing the collar of *esses* in his tomb effigy. It is worth noting, though, that the collar had a pendant swan pointing not to Henry's ancestors but to the Bohuns. It may be, as was supposed in the seventeenth century, that Gower was at some stage in the service of Gloucester, and added the swan to the collar. The depiction of Gloucester's badge and livery colours on the folio of the Ellesmere MS greatly strengthens that supposition. If so, it would better reflect and commemorate Gower's political background.

---

[264] Fisher, *John Gower*, p. 100.

PART VI

GOWER AND COSMOGRAPHY

CHAPTER 14

NATURAL SCIENCES

Seb Falk

The natural sciences play a fundamental role in John Gower's work. Education, whether for personal or political improvement, is an explicit theme of his writing, and he makes clear that 'the wyse man' should seek understanding of 'The world which neweth every dai' (CA: Pro.59–65). To this end, he furnishes his readers with a multi-layered cosmology. Scholars have confidently traced the encyclopaedic sources on which Gower drew, painting a portrait of a writer whose scientific interests reliably reflected late medieval scientific orthodoxy. However, some of his lesser known sources have remained unidentified or unappreciated. Gower's use of these sources in some pivotal passages of his writing reveals subtle but significant features of his scientific interest that have not previously been recognised, and offers new insights into the debated issue of his scientific expertise. Medieval natural philosophy was an enormously wide-ranging field, so the main focus of this chapter will be 'the science of Astronomie / ... Withoute which, to telle plein, / Alle othre science is in vein' (CA: VII.625–32). A close examination of Gower's descriptions of stars in Book VII of his *Confessio Amantis* – whose details, sources and scientific significance have previously been poorly understood – will allow us to draw wider conclusions about Gower's overall scientific knowledge and beliefs. An updated understanding of the significance of sciences, from mathematics to magic, provides a more nuanced picture of the scientific interests that not only inform Genius's education of the king within the *Confessio*, but also feed into the wider worldview present throughout Gower's work.

First, a caveat: for the purposes of this chapter, 'scientific' refers to the description and exploration of nature: ideas and practices that bear a 'family

---

I am grateful, for advice received in the course of preparing this paper, to Siân Echard, Clare Fletcher, Brian Gastle, Rob van Gent, Matthew Giancarlo, David Juste, Sophie Page, Russell Peck, Jennifer Rampling, Stephen Rigby, Robert F. Yeager, and the other contributors to this volume.

resemblance' to modern science.¹ This definition does not encompass the full breadth of science as defined by Gower himself. For Gower in Book VII of *Confessio Amantis*, the 'sciences' are the branches of philosophy in its entirety, divided first into theory, rhetoric and practice (VII.27–41), and, in turn, subdivided into sciences ranging from theology, via arithmetic, to ethics.² Some justification may therefore be required for an approach that discusses knowledge about nature separately from other subjects. After all, one of the themes of Book VII is the interrelationship of the different points of philosophy.³ However, Gower himself does demarcate the different 'intelligences' [categories] (VII.28) of sciences, so it is reasonable to concentrate on some of them, notwithstanding the accepted 'unitary character of late medieval learning'.⁴ In addition, even for Gower, knowledge about nature was to be found in different texts from other subjects; these texts are the principal subject of this chapter.

Surprisingly, there has been little research on Gower's scientific reading since the subject was first treated systematically, by George G. Fox in 1931.⁵ Fox identified the sources of many of Gower's ideas about nature which Macaulay had not noted in his edition of Gower's poetry, and his work remains a vital starting-point. More recent scholars have eschewed Fox's approach, preferring to integrate Gower's treatment of the natural sciences into discussion of other subjects, showing, for instance, how Gower's scientific interests relate to his political or moral concerns, or how he exploited scientific concepts for poetic gain. This perspective, exemplified in studies by James Simpson and, more recently, by Kellie Robertson, has been very fruitful, but it tends to push questions about Gower's sources and about the normality (or otherwise) of his knowledge to the margins and to examine the scientific content of his work only in passing.⁶ Where scholars have

---

[1] Michael H. Shank and David C. Lindberg, 'Introduction', in David C. Lindberg and Michael H. Shank, eds, *The Cambridge History of Science, Volume 2: Medieval Science* (Cambridge: Cambridge University Press, 2013), pp. 1–26, at 6.

[2] Gower's concept of science, and use of that word (and 'conscience') to describe different forms of knowledge, has recently been discussed by Russell A. Peck, 'Gower and Science', in *RRC*, pp. 172–196.

[3] See, for example, Genius's remark that 'theorique' is 'the conserve and kepere of the remnant' (CA: VII.54–5).

[4] See, for example, John E. Murdoch, 'From Social into Intellectual Factors: An Aspect of the Unitary Character of Late Medieval Learning', in John E. Murdoch and Edith Dudley Sylla, eds, *The Cultural Context of Medieval Learning* (Dordrecht: Reidel, 1975), pp. 271–348.

[5] George G. Fox, *The Mediaeval Sciences in the Works of John Gower* (Princeton: Princeton University Press, 1931). An important exception is H. C. Mainzer, 'A Study of the Sources of the *Confessio Amantis* of John Gower' (Unpublished University of Oxford D.Phil. thesis, 1967).

[6] James Simpson, *Sciences and the Self in Medieval Poetry: Alan of Lille's* Anticlaudianus *and John Gower's* Confessio Amantis (Cambridge: Cambridge University Press, 1995), which includes a critique of Fox on p. 211, n. 15; Kellie Robertson, *Nature Speaks:*

addressed Gower's scientific knowledge directly, it has largely been with the intention of challenging Fox's dismissive assessment of his understanding, a quest closely allied to the rehabilitation of Gower's reputation as poet; in both cases the (often explicit) comparison is with Chaucer, whose scientific awareness is often assumed to have been greater than Gower's.[7] There is thus scope for a fresh look at the technical content of Gower's poetry, using recent research into the history of medieval science to shed new light on his scientific sources, inspirations and abilities.

Scientific language and concepts appear throughout Gower's work as part of a frame of reference common to most medieval literature.[8] It is, however, no accident that the greatest concentration of scientific content occurs in Book VII of *Confessio Amantis*. Some scholars, striving to place Gower's scientific writing in its learned context, have removed his ideas from their immediate functions within his works. For instance, Fox's assessment of Gower's astronomy as 'puerile' is coloured by his unwillingness to give serious consideration to the complex ways in which the poet used such scientific material.[9] Fox's study is valuable in paying close and expert attention to the content of Gower's scientific writing, but some of his analysis needs to be updated to reflect not only recent scholarship in history of science but also readings of Gower that have suggested possible poetic or moral purposes of the inclusion (or omission) of scientific material. As we have seen, within the sciences, Gower emphasises the importance of astronomy (CA: VII.625–32), and the subject seems also to have been of special interest to at least some of his readers, to judge by the way they excerpted or illustrated astronomical material.[10] Furthermore, Gower's astronomical writing reveals sources quite distinct from the encyclopaedic genres on which scholars have previously focused. Where Gower strays from his main sources to explore the esoteric doctrine of lunar mansions and lore of fifteen stars, stones and herbs in Book VII of *Confessio Amantis*, he shows his readers the boundaries of sciences such as alchemy and astronomy, mathematics and magic. Passages on these subjects, which have long fed into the reputation of Gower's work for a lack

---

Medieval Literature and Aristotelian Philosophy (Philadelphia: University of Pennsylvania Press, 2017). See also Ann W. Astell, *Chaucer and the Universe of Learning* (Ithaca, NY: Cornell University Press, 1996).

[7] See, for example, Kimberly Zarins, 'Writing The Literary Zodiac: Division, Unity, And Power In John Gower's Poetics' (Unpublished Cornell University Ph.D. thesis, 2009). On Chaucer's science, see J. D. North, *Chaucer's Universe* (Oxford: Clarendon Press, 1988).

[8] C. S. Lewis, *The Discarded Image; An Introduction to Medieval and Renaissance Literature* (Cambridge: Cambridge University Press, 1964), p. 14. Cf. Robertson, *Nature Speaks*, p. 7.

[9] Fox, *The Mediaeval Sciences*, p. 83.

[10] See the extracts from Book VII copied in Longleat House MS 174 and British Library, Sloane MS 3847, as well as the abundance of astronomical miniatures painted in Morgan Library MS M.126.

of 'descriptive grace' or 'real feeling', nonetheless make an important contribution to the articulation of a coherent and inspiring worldview.[11]

Cosmology, Astronomy and Astrology: Theory and Practice

Gower's worldview is decisively shaped by the astral sciences. In its general outline Gower's universe resembles the common medieval conception, but his is perhaps remarkable for its emphasis on change and division at all levels of creation: from eclipses of the Sun and Moon, and corrupt air, to strife among men, to discordant elements within the human body (MO: 26605–940; CA: Pro.915–78; VC: VII.8.637–60). The blame for such disorder is unequivocally ascribed to man, the microcosm of the world.[12] Study of a universe ordained from top to bottom by God is inextricable from, and invariably brings our attention back to, Gower's human concerns, whether those concerns be politics or love. Gower's use of the concepts of the microcosm and macrocosm, in which man and the universe mirror and influence each other, has been extensively studied, and his core principle is clear: despite the great distance of the stars, they are never remote from humanity.[13] It should be noted that Gower shows little practical interest in the medical implications of this cosmic interconnectedness: although he discusses the four complexions (CA: VII.393–462), he does not name the humours and makes little reference to diseases or medical authorities; his concern is rather to emphasise that 'man ... is mad upon divisioun' (Pro.974–6), and perhaps secondarily that the needs of the body should be subordinate to reason (VII.485–9).[14]

The intimacy of the stars and humanity means that astronomy is no detached science, despite the first impression created by Gower's distinction between astronomy and astrology. Astronomy, he tells us, is the science:

> Which makth a man have knowlechinge
> Of sterres in the firmament,
> Figure, cercle, and moevement
> Of ech of hem in sondri place,

---

[11] Adolphus W. Ward, *Chaucer* (London: Macmillan, 1880), p. 82.
[12] Gower cites Gregory the Great's *Moralia* (CA: Pro.945; MO: 26869) as well as Aristotle (MO: 26929); Winthrop Wetherbee has noted the Boethian themes in Gower's presentation of this universal instability ('Classical and Boethian Tradition in the *Confessio Amantis*', in Siân Echard, ed., *A Companion to Gower* (Cambridge: D. S. Brewer, 2004), pp. 181–96.
[13] See, for example, Elizabeth Porter, 'Gower's Ethical Microcosm and Political Macrocosm', in Alastair J. Minnis, ed., *Gower's Confessio Amantis: Responses and Reassessments* (Cambridge: D. S. Brewer, 1983), pp. 135–62.
[14] For details of the scattered references to disease (and assaults on apothecaries and physicians) in Gower's work, see Fox, *The Mediaeval Sciences*, pp. 23–36.

> And what betwen hem is of space,
> Hou so thei moeve or stonde faste (CA: VII.672–7).

Astrology, by contrast, is:

> The which in juggementz acompteth
> Theffect, what every sterre amonteth,
> And hou thei causen many a wonder
> To tho climatz that stonde hem under (VII.681–4).

It was common to make a distinction between astronomy and astrology, and here Gower may be drawing on the definition in one of his sources, the pseudo-Aristotelian *Secretum secretorum*, and perhaps also the distinction made between 'the two wisdoms' (*duae sapientiae*) both named 'astronomy' in the *Speculum astronomiae* (sometimes attributed to Albertus Magnus).[15] Yet, despite these separate definitions, Gower did not consistently distinguish between these two forms of knowledge.[16] He later describes 'Astronomie' as the 'science' which 'dieme betwen wo and wel' (VII.1439–41) and, like many writers of the period, he seems to treat the terms 'astronomy' and 'astrology' as interchangeable.

Gower's attitude to both the validity and the permissibility of astrology seems to vary across his writings. In the *Mirour de l'Omme* he states that, whatever the malicious nature of the planets, 'A single worthy man, praying to God, can instantly shatter all the worst of their influence' (26743–5). This hard-line denial of determinism was matched by few medieval thinkers; more popular was the carefully reasoned view of Thomas Aquinas (1225–74). Aquinas warns that divination of human actions would be a denial of free will:

---

[15] 'The Governance of Lordschipes', in *Three Prose Versions of the Secreta Secretorum*, ed. Robert Steele (London: Kegan Paul, 1898), pp. 41–118, at 65–66; cf. the four divisions in 'The Secrete of Secretes', *ibid.*, pp. 1–39, at 21. See also *Opera Hactenus Inedita Rogeri Baconi. vol. 5, Secretum secretorum* (Oxford: Clarendon Press, 1920), p. 3; *Speculum astronomiae*, chapters 1–3, in Paola Zambelli, *The Speculum Astronomiae and Its Enigma: Astrology, Theology, and Science in Albertus Magnus and his Contemporaries* (Dordrecht: Kluwer, 1992), pp. 208–20 (on its attribution, see Agostino Paravicini Bagliani, Le Speculum Astronomiae, *une énigme? Enquête sur les manuscrits* (Florence: Galluzzo, 2001); George L. Hamilton, 'Some Sources of the Seventh Book of Gower's "Confessio Amantis"', *Modern Philology*, 9 (1912), pp. 323–46, at 341; Fox, *The Mediaeval Sciences*, p. 58. Brunetto Latini's *Tresor*, perhaps Gower's most significant scientific source, does not make such a distinction. Cf. the division of 'astronodia' into astronomy and astrology in the (possibly) twelfth-century *Ut testatur Ergaphalau* (Charles Burnett, 'Adelard, Ergaphalau and the Science of the Stars', in Charles Burnett, ed., *Adelard of Bath: An English Scientist and Arabist of the Early Twelfth Century* (London: Warburg Institute, 1987), pp. 133–45).

[16] Fox, *The Mediaeval Sciences*, pp. 52–3.

if anyone were to use observation of the stars to foreknow fortuitous or chance future events, or to know future human actions with certainty, his actions are based on a false and empty belief; and so the work of the demon creeps in, whence it will be a superstitious and unlawful divination.

Nevertheless, he also notes that celestial influence on terrestrial bodies is observable:

On the other hand, if anyone were to use observation of the stars to foreknow future things that are caused by heavenly bodies, such as drought or rain or others of this sort, it will be neither an unlawful nor a superstitious divination.[17]

Aquinas further admits that, since human will is affected by bodily appetites, 'celestial bodies have an effect on bodies ... [and] on powers of the soul that are acts of bodily organs'.[18] This balanced position is, in effect, a middle way between the extreme stances held, in Gower's summary, by 'the naturien / Which is an Astronomien', who believes that 'Al is thurgh constellacion'; and that of 'the divin', who 'seith otherwise, / That if men weren goode and wise ... Thei scholden noght the sterres drede' (CA: VII.642–54).[19] A similar balance is struck by the Latin heading to this section of Book VII on astronomy, which states that:

> Lege planetarum magis inferiora reguntur,
> Ista set interdum regula fallit opus.
> Vir mediante deo sapiens dominabitur astris,
> Fata nec immerito quid nouitatis agunt (VII.iv).[20]

This balance informs Gower's account of the struggle between the will and reason, most poignantly expressed by Amans at the end of Book VII when, having heard Genius's instructive tales, he nonetheless admits 'Bot yit myn herte is elleswhere' (5412). But we should also read Gower's consideration

---

[17] Thomas Aquinas, *Summa Theologiae*, 2.2.95.5, ed. Fundación Tomás de Aquino, http://www.corpusthomisticum.org (accessed 30 November 2016); Aquinas was drawing on St Augustine, *De civitate Dei*, V.6. For background on the status of astrology in medieval theology, see Theodore Otto Wedel, *The Mediaeval Attitude toward Astrology, Particularly in England* (New Haven: Yale University Press, 1920), pp. 63–89.
[18] Aquinas, *Summa Theologiae*, 1.115.4.
[19] Cf. Troilus's discussion of destiny and free will, in Geoffrey Chaucer, 'Troilus and Criseyde', IV: 953–1078.
[20] 'Things lower down are ruled by the law of the planets, and this rule sometimes foils our ventures. The wise man, through God, will dominate the stars, and the fates will not do anything unexpected without cause.' The third line closely resembles a maxim often attributed to Ptolemy, but not found in his extant writings and probably apocryphal. See Hamilton, 'Some Sources', pp. 343–4.

of these issues in light of the rising popularity of astrology at the English court. The subject began to flourish during the reign of Edward III and his successor, Richard II, expanded courtly support for its practitioners.[21] Although the extent of Richard's personal interest in astrology is a matter for debate, the book of divination made for him in 1391 is testament to the rising respectability of the subject in courtly circles.[22] By the time Gower was writing, deterministic prediction was acceptable to an extent Aquinas could not have countenanced; one historian has written that 'the theology of astrology was in disarray'.[23] In this confused context, it is not surprising that Gower's explicit rejection of astrology in the *Mirour* is followed by a more neutral perspective – and the lengthy and apparently uncritical reporting of astrological theories – in the *Confessio*. Yet, as we shall see, the portrayal of the evil magician Nectanabus as an astrologer indicates that Gower retained strong doubts about the acceptability of astrological practice.[24]

What was not in doubt was the power of unexpected events, 'the chances of the world also, / that we fortune clepen so' (CA: VII.639–40). 'Fortune's wheel is forever turning lightly', irrespective of the abilities of astrologers to predict its outcomes, and kings and peasants are both equally subject to her power (VC: II.4.175–83). In this context it is unsurprising that Gower should emphasise, within the king's education, his subjection to a higher (divine) power. But Gower is also making a wider point about the relationship between nature and human order, physics and ethics, about all of which a wise king needed to be informed.[25] Such a rounded royal education was a conventional scholarly objective; in order to be recognisable as such, Gower's explanation of the sciences is necessarily loyal in structure and core content to his sources.[26] The most important of these – with some

---

[21] Hilary M. Carey, 'Astrology at the English Court in the Later Middle Ages', in Patrick Curry, ed., *Astrology, Science and Society* (Woodbridge: Boydell Press, 1987), pp. 41–56, at 44. It is debatable whether Edward III himself took any interest in astrology; Carey thinks he probably ignored it (Hilary Carey, *Courting Disaster: Astrology at the English Court and University in the Later Middle Ages* (Basingstoke: Macmillan, 1992), pp. 79–91).

[22] Oxford, Bodleian Library MS Bodley 581, which also contains excerpts from the *Secretum secretorum* while implicitly critiquing that work. The compiler bound his reader to explicit rules in using and communicating the book's geomantic contents (Katharine Breen, 'A Different Kind of Book for Richard's Sake: MS Bodley 581 as Ethical Handbook', *The Chaucer Review*, 45 (2010), pp. 119–68, at 120, 143–4). See also Carey, *Courting Disaster*, pp. 98–9; John North, 'Astronomy and Astrology', in Lindberg and Shank, *The Cambridge History of Science, Volume 2*, pp. 456–84, at 474.

[23] Carey, *Courting Disaster*, p. 15.

[24] See also Gower's attack on physicians in *Mirour de l'Omme*, 25623–80. See also Fox, *The Mediaeval Sciences*, pp. 91–4.

[25] Robertson, *Nature Speaks*, p. 29; Wetherbee, 'Classical and Boethian Tradition', p. 184.

[26] For analysis of how Gower's poetry blends study of the natural world with classical narratives within an encyclopaedic education, see Amanda Gerber, 'The Mythological

significant additions, which will be discussed below – was Brunetto Latini's *Li Livres dou Tresor*, a vernacular encyclopaedia with a clear thread of moral and political education, probably written for Charles of Anjou in the early 1260s.[27] Gower follows Latini's Aristotelian division of philosophy, with the theoretical branch divided into theology, physics and mathematics, of which the last is subdivided into arithmetic, music, geometry and astronomy.[28] The ostensible intention is that scientific instruction will aid the development of the king – specifically the imperfect Alexander, whom we see, for example, failing to understand the philosophy of Diogenes (CA: III.1201–1313) – into the *vir sapiens* who, while still physically subject to the laws of the planets, need not fear the whims of the fates. Alexander's education comes mainly from Aristotle, identified by the ubiquitous medieval epithet 'the Philosophre' (e.g. VII.717), but Gower hints too at knowledge imparted by the magician Nectanabus (VII.1295–1300), about whom Genius remarks:

> I not what helpeth that clergie
> Which makth a man to do folie (VI.2363–4).

For Gower, then, theoretical sciences form a necessary – but certainly not sufficient – component of a king's education. Knowledge is useless to a ruler who lacks the moral education to use it appropriately.[29]

Gower's own interests in the uses of the sciences were narrow, being restricted to their theory. Just as when he discusses the microcosm he shows no interest in medical methods, so even when he explores his most fully detailed science, astronomy, he gives no sense of its practices: observation, computation, nor instruments. Yet these were the common concerns of most astronomical writing in the later middle ages, in which writers often blurred the boundaries of theory and practice: texts called *Theorica planetarum* describe instruments; instrument treatises include lengthy introductions to geometrical and planetary theory; Ptolemaic primers contain pages of tables for calculating movable feasts or eclipses.[30] Chaucer had promised to reveal this variety to his son, through 'diverse tables of longitudes and latitudes of

---

Sciences of John Gower, Medieval Classicists, and Morgan MS M. 126', *Studies in the Age of Chaucer*, 40 (2018), pp. 257–88.

[27] David Napolitano, 'Brunetto Latini's *Tesoro* in Print', *Ex Historia*, 5 (2013), pp. 19–47, at 27; Brunetto Latini, *Li Livres dou Tresor*, eds Spurgeon Baldwin and Paul Barrette (Tempe: Arizona Center for Medieval and Renaissance Studies, 2003), p. x. Fox gives an extended comparison of the sections of Book VII of the *Confessio* and the *Tresor* which discuss the elements, showing similarities between both their content and language (*The Mediaeval Sciences*, pp. 37–42.

[28] Simpson, *Sciences and the Self*, pp. 32–3, 211–12; Latini, *Li Livres dou Tresor*, I.3.

[29] Simpson, *Sciences and the Self*, p. 211.

[30] See, for example, Francis S. Benjamin and G. J. Toomer, eds, *Campanus of Novara and Medieval Planetary Theory: Theorica Planetarum* (Madison: University of Wisconsin Press, 1971); 'Tractatus Albionis', in *Richard of Wallingford: An Edition of His Writings*, ed. J. D. North (Oxford: Clarendon Press, 1976), volume 1, pp. 248–401. For a general

sterres fixe for the Astrelabie ... and tables as well for the governaunce of a clokke', and 'a gret part of the general rewles of theorik in astrologie', in parts of his *Treatise on the Astrolabe* that have not come down to us.[31] Astronomical practices also abound in Chaucer's poetry, which thus provides a marked contrast with Gower's works. Whilst Chaucer may not have attempted Gower's impressive feat of explaining astronomical theory in octosyllables, the practical culture of the science infuses his writing. When he has the lecherous monk in the 'Shipman's Tale' exclaim that 'by my chilyndre it is pryme of day', Chaucer is not only employing his familiarity with the cylindrical sundial to make a smutty joke, but also setting the scene explicitly at a particular moment. He is thereby often able to add the symbolism of a computed celestial configuration to an astrological allegory.[32] Gower, by comparison, is much less specific. *Confessio Amantis* is set in 'the monthe of Maii, / Whan every brid hath chose his make' (I.100–1), and this lovers' month is mentioned on many occasions in the poem (e.g. I.2089; IV.1283; VII.2276), but Gower never specifies a date.[33] He does work some astronomical details into the prayer of Cephalus for a long night (IV.3197–3252), with the Sun in the midwinter sign of Capricorn and the Moon full in Cancer; Capricorn is, he tells us here as in Book VII, the house of Saturn. Cephalus's request that the Moon also 'Behold Venus with a glad yhe' (IV.3245) would, according to agreed astrological theory (such as Albumasar, whom Gower cites elsewhere), place the two planets in trine aspect (120°). Venus's restricted elongation from the Sun (and the requirement for the Moon and Sun to be in opposition) would limit the years in which such a configuration could occur, but not so much as to make it likely that Gower had computed the planetary positions for a particular day, as was Chaucer's habit.[34] Here, as also with his allusion to the practices of arithmetic (VII.153–62), Gower is content to communicate some theoretical detail without involving himself in the practices of the science.

The most notable absence from Gower's presentation of scientific practice is instrumentation. Where Chaucer's poetry is replete with references to clocks, dials and astrolabes, such details are largely absent from Gower's writing. This is despite his frequent citation of Ptolemy (e.g. CA: VI.1403, VII.983, VII.1201, VII.1459–60) who had described the construction and

---

survey of the field, see John North, *Cosmos: An Illustrated History of Astronomy and Cosmology* (Chicago: University of Chicago Press, 2008), pp. 251–65.

[31] Geoffrey Chaucer, 'A Treatise on the Astrolabe', Pro.78–103.
[32] North, *Chaucer's Universe*, pp. 456–68.
[33] Cf. 'Whan Phebus [the Sun] doth his brighte bemes sprede / Right in the whyte Bole [Taurus], it so bitidde / As I shal singe, on Mayes day the thridde' (Chaucer, 'Troilus and Criseyde', II: 54–6).
[34] If opposition and trine are defined simply as being in the seventh and fifth (or ninth) signs distant from a planet, it is possible. Gower cites Albumasar in VII.1239. See Abū Maʿšar, *The Abbreviation of The Introduction to Astrology*, eds Charles Burnett, Keiji Yamamoto, and Michio Yano (Leiden: E. J. Brill, 1994), II.10, IV.2.

use of an *astrolabon* (armillary sphere) in Book V of the *Almagest* and had laid out the mathematical foundations of the planispheric astrolabe in his *Planisphaerium*.³⁵ Gower's omission of such material is, however, consistent with the approach taken by Latini, as well as by most versions of the *Secretum secretorum*.³⁶ It bears repeating that this was not the view apparent in most scientific writing of the period; the prevailing opinion is made clear in the opening line of a treatise written a few decades before the *Confessio*: 'the very noble science of astronomy cannot be well understood without the appropriate instruments.'³⁷ But Gower's editorial choice accords well with the human focus of his account of the sciences.³⁸

Apart from the axletree which Gower apparently added as an equatorial mount for Diogenes's barrel (III.1209), making the philosopher's observation post an instrument, the one unquestionable instrument in the text of the *Confessio Amantis* is the astrolabe carried by Nectanabus in Book VI (VI.1890). It is perhaps telling that it is the nefarious necromancer whom Gower depicts with an astrolabe, though equally it may simply be because the instrument also appears in Gower's source for the story, Thomas of Kent's *Le Roman d'Alexandre*.³⁹ Either way, for Gower, Nectanabus's more interesting possession was his book of stars (VI.1894). One manuscript of the *Confessio* may seem to indicate the importance of instruments for the mathematical sciences, with a brass instrument illustrated at the opening to the mathematical section of Book VII (VII.145) in Morgan Library MS M.126, f. 150v. This enormous circular device, with sixteen divisions and a rotating pointer, stands on the floor of a library where it is indicated by the pointing figure of a richly dressed scholar. However, although it bears some similarities to compass roses and early-modern sixteen-point tidal calculators, it does not really resemble any extant contemporary instrument and was most likely

---

35 *Ptolemy's Almagest*, trans. G. J. Toomer (London: Duckworth, 1984), V.1, p. 217–19; Ptolemy, *Ptolemaei Planisphaerium*, ed. Federico Commandino (Venice: Manuzio, 1558). An Arabic version of the *Planisphaerium* has recently been edited and translated by Nathan Sidoli and J. L. Berggren: 'The Arabic Version of Ptolemy's Planisphere or Flattening the Surface of the Sphere: Text, Translation, Commentary', SCIAMVS, 8 (2007), pp. 37–139.
36 Latini, *Li Livres dou Tresor*, I.110. Instruments are absent from all of the *Three Prose Versions of the Secreta Secretorum*, as well as Roger Bacon's edition (*Opera Hactenus Inedita Rogeri Baconi. vol. 5, Secretum secretorum*), but an astrolabe does appear in the Arabic version translated by A. S. Fulton in the same volume (p. 256).
37 'Quia nobilissima scientia astronomie non potest bene sciri sine instrumentis debitis' (Seb Falk, 'A Merton College Equatorium: Text, Translation, Commentary', SCIAMVS, 17 (2016), pp. 121–59, at 136).
38 Simpson, *Sciences and the Self*, p. 224.
39 Paris, Bibliothèque nationale de France, Ms. français 24364, f. 1v; Thomas de Kent, *Le Roman d'Alexandre ou le Roman de Toute Chevalerie*, eds Brian Foster and Ian Short (Paris: Champion, 2003), para. 4a; translation online at http://www.kcl.ac.uk/artshums/ahri/centres/clams/evarch/reading1112/ToKtranslations.pdf (accessed 13 April 2017).

inspired by the illustrator's imagination, suggesting perhaps that readers of the *Confessio* were not particularly interested in scientific precision.[40]

The Twelve Signs of the Zodiac

The longest section in Gower's treatment of the theoretical sciences deals with the twelve signs of the zodiac. Its purpose, and particularly its sources, have long troubled scholars. It comes after a passage on the seven planets and before another on the fifteen stars, stones and herbs (which will also be discussed below), and Gower alerts the reader to its importance:

> Bot overthis touchende his lore,
> Of thing that thei him tawhte more
> Upon the scoles of clergie
> Now herkne the philosophie (VII.951–4).

The following 316 lines on the signs of the zodiac have long been celebrated for their dullness. In what the editor of a popular version of the *Confessio* calls 'laborious verse', Gower details the constellations one by one.[41] The following example is characteristic. Gower explains that the eighth sign is Scorpio, whose violence is symbolised by its depiction as a scorpion. It has nineteen stars, eight of which are shared with Libra. He states that Scorpio's elemental quality [*kinde*] is wet and cold (which links it with the element water), and that it is a house of Mars and detriment of Venus (a planet's detriment was diametrically opposite its house, and Gower indeed tells us that Taurus, 180° around the zodiac, is the house of Venus). Finally, he states that Scorpio's month is October, the gateway to winter.

> Among the signes upon heighte
> The signe which is nombred eighte
> Is Scorpio, which as feloun
> Figured is a scorpioun.
> Bot for al that yit natheles
> Is Scorpio noght sterreles;
> For Libra granteth him his ende
> Of eighte sterres, wher he wende,
> The whiche upon his heved assised
> He berth, and ek ther ben divised

---

[40] Cf. the volvelles in Jean-Baptiste Denoville's *Traité de navigation* (Rouen, Bibliothèque municipale Ms GG8, 1760), facsimile edition: Éditions point de vues, 2008, p. 13. See online discussion on *Rete* mailing list: https://web.maillist.ox.ac.uk/ox/arc/rete/2017-04/thrd1.html and thrd2.html (accessed 2 May 2017).

[41] John Gower, *Confessio Amantis (The Lover's Shrift)*, ed. and trans. Terence Tiller (Harmondsworth: Penguin, 1963), p. 234n.

> Upon his wombe sterres thre,
> And eighte upon his tail hath he.
> Which of his kinde is moiste and cold
> And unbehovely manyfold;
> He harmeth Venus and empeireth,
> Bot Mars unto his hous repeireth,
> Bot war whan thei togedre duellen.
> His propre monthe is, as men tellen,
> Octobre, which bringth the kalende
> Of wynter, that comth next suiende (VII.1121–40).

With some minor omissions, Gower follows this pattern for each sign: he gives its name and iconic image, the number of stars in each of three sub-divisions of the constellation, its elemental quality (hot or cold; wet or dry), its astrological status as the house or (less often) detriment of a planet, and its associated month, together with a description of that season (which is sometimes much more detailed and evocative than in the above example). After each sign has been laid out in this way (each with a two-part Latin gloss, whose latter sentences collectively form regular verse), the whole passage ends with a description of the Earth as being divided into four 'climat[es]' (1243), each of which is governed, 'as I am lerned' (1251), by a group of three signs.[42]

Most of the information contained in this passage is commonplace and could have been gleaned from any number of sources. However, Gower's groupings of stars within each sign are highly unusual. Whilst it was normal to describe the beginning and end of each astronomic sign starting from Aries as its 'head' and 'tail' ('caput' and 'cauda' in Latin texts), to allocate numbers of stars to these parts of constellations was much less common.[43] Such allocations do not appear in any of the encyclopaedic works which Gower could have drawn upon, such as the *Tresor* or the *Speculum Naturale* of Vincent of Beauvais.[44] It is also striking that the groups overlap: the eight stars in the head of Scorpio are shared with the eight which Libra has 'doun benethe'; the eight on Scorpio's tail, we later learn, are also shared, with the following sign, Sagittarius.[45] Taking this overlap into account, across the twelve signs there

---

[42] On the Latin glosses, see Peck, 'Explanatory Notes to Book 7', in John Gower, *Confessio Amantis*, volume III, ed. Russell A. Peck (Kalamazoo: Medieval Institute Publications, 2004), p. 449.

[43] Gower does not stick rigidly to these terms, referring to 'ende' as often as tail and describing the 'hornes' of Taurus or the 'feet' of Virgo in ways that highlight the imagery of the constellations.

[44] Gower certainly used the *Tresor*, as mentioned above. His use of the *Speculum Naturale* is less certain but seems likely given the many coincidences of detail. See Mainzer, 'A Study of the Sources of the *Confessio Amantis*', p. 213; Fox, *The Mediaeval Sciences*, p. 43.

[45] Kimberly Zarins argues that the overlap of stars between signs is Gower's way of emphasising harmony and continuity between the constellations: what she calls

are twenty-eight groups, each containing between one and twenty stars: 152 in total. George Fox identified these twenty-eight groups as mansions of the Moon (an astrological concept which will be explained below).[46] He found quite similar groupings of stars in a book of astrological prediction compiled by a Lyon physician, Richard Roussat, in the mid-sixteenth century.[47] The title of that book attributes the doctrines to an '*Arcandam doctor peritissimus ac non vulgaris Astrologus*', and Fox dedicated some pages to reconstructing scraps of evidence about the 'shadowy figure' whose name he also found rendered 'Alchandrus' or 'Alchandrinus'.[48] Drawing on Lynn Thorndike's monumental *History of Magic and Experimental Science* (1923), Fox identified references to Alchandrus in the work of better-known astronomers such as Michael Scot.[49] Most significant, for Fox, was the most similar star grouping he could find, in a Hebrew manuscript described in an article by Moritz Steinschneider.[50] Noting the similarities and discrepancies between Gower's stars and those of Roussat and the Hebrew manuscript, Fox argued that 'it is reasonable to postulate [Gower's use of] a Latin manuscript of the Alchandrine line, not now known, which combines these two versions'.[51]

There the matter has rested for eighty-five years; readers of Gower have, perhaps reasonably, seen no need to find out more about Alchandrus or the scattered writings attributed to him. However, recent studies in the history of astronomy allow us to add significantly to the picture adduced by Fox, in a way which provides new insight into Gower's reading.[52] These studies have shed little light on the person of Alchandrus (now more commonly known as Alchandreus), and it remains unclear whether an astronomer of that name ever existed, or if it is a corruption of another name, such as the Arab philosopher al-Kindi, or, as Gower may have supposed and will be discussed

---

'celestial *rime riche*' ('Writing The Literary Zodiac', pp. 216–17). Gower may certainly have appreciated these poetic possibilities, but I would argue that his main reason for using these groupings was straightforward fidelity to his astrological sources.

[46] Fox, *The Mediaeval Sciences*, pp. 65–80.
[47] Richard Roussat, *Arcandam doctor peritissimus ac non vulgaris Astrologus, de veritatibus, et praedictionibus Astrologiae* (Paris, 1542), ff. A1r-K6r.
[48] Fox, *The Mediaeval Sciences*, p. 69.
[49] Lynn Thorndike, *A History of Magic and Experimental Science* (New York: Macmillan, 1923), volume 1, pp. 710–18; Fox, *The Mediaeval Sciences*, p. 69.
[50] M. Steinschneider, 'Über die Mondstationen (Naxatra), und das Buch Arcandam', *Zeitschrift der Deutschen Morgenländischen Gesellschaft*, 18 (1864), pp. 118–201.
[51] Fox, *The Mediaeval Sciences*, p. 74.
[52] See above all David Juste, *Les Alchandreana primitifs: étude sur les plus anciens traites astrologiques latins d'origine Arabe (Xe siècle)* (Leiden: Brill, 2007). Also, Charles Burnett, 'Michael Scot and the Transmission of Scientific Culture from Toledo to Bologna via the Court of Frederick II Hohenstaufen', *Micrologus*, 2 (1994), pp. 101–26; Charles Burnett, 'King Ptolemy and Alchandreus the Philosopher: The Earliest Texts on the Astrolabe and Arabic Astrology at Fleury, Micy and Chartres', *Annals of Science*, 55 (1998), pp. 329–68; Burnett, 'Adelard, Ergaphalau and the Science of the Stars'.

below, Alexander.⁵³ However, a great deal is now known about a broad corpus of Latin writings which may be called Alchandreana, which like many other medieval scientific writings had their origins in Arabic sciences. They spread north from Catalonia in the late tenth century, reaching England by the early twelfth century.⁵⁴ Their composition thus predates the introduction of the astrolabe to Europe, which helps explain the striking absence, from the corpus, of texts about instruments.⁵⁵ David Juste compiled a magisterial edition of this corpus from a variety of complete and partial texts in seventy-two manuscripts; since its publication in 2007, many more have come to light.⁵⁶ The corpus of seven main texts is united thematically and linguistically, yet covers a wide range of general astrological material on the powers of the planets and zodiacal signs, as well as providing instructions for answering specific questions such as the location of a thief, the culpability of a woman suspected of adultery, or the diagnosis of disease, and supplying solutions to a host of astrological problems, many concerned with birth, such as the number and sex of children that will be born to a marriage.

Of the seven Alchandrean texts, the groups of stars used by Gower feature in one, whose title is taken from its incipit *Benedictum sit nomen Domini*.⁵⁷ The *Benedictum* is divided into two parts, concerning the planets and signs, and each is subdivided to provide first theory and then prognostic instructions; the prognostic questions to be answered are the same as those elsewhere in the corpus.⁵⁸ Far from the impression Fox gives of this theory appearing in only one Hebrew source, the treatise is extant in twenty-eight Latin manuscripts. Although only a small minority of those have the complete work, the chapter that appears most often (sixteen times) is the final and longest one, chapter 18, which describes the twenty-eight groups of stars.⁵⁹ Each group is given a name – Alnat, Albotam, Aldoraia and so on – and the situation of the group as 'caput', 'venter' or 'finis' of a constellation, and the number of stars in the group, are given. There then follows a paragraph describing a person born under that mansion: his skin colour, body shape and some features of his character, two or three possible ages at which he may die, and the way that will occur. All copies of this text are in Latin, except for one Anglo-Norman translation in an early fourteenth-century manuscript, and an English summary preceding the full Latin version in a sixteenth-century copy.⁶⁰ In almost all manuscripts

---

53 Juste, *Les Alchandreana primitifs*, pp. 52–4.
54 Juste, *Les Alchandreana primitifs*, pp. 234–40, 264.
55 Juste, *Les Alchandreana primitifs*, p. 247.
56 Juste, *Les Alchandreana primitifs*, pp. 297–390; David Juste, personal correspondence, 18 March 2017. As an example, ten new manuscripts of the *Benedictum*, the text from which Gower's stars are drawn, have been identified.
57 Edited in Juste, *Les Alchandreana primitifs*, pp. 609–38.
58 Juste, *Les Alchandreana primitifs*, pp. 77–9.
59 *Benedictum* ch. 18, in Juste, *Les Alchandreana primitifs*, pp. 628–38.
60 Cambridge, Corpus Christi College MS 37, ff. 52r-61r; London, British Library Sloane MS 1437, ff. 90v-91r. The former uses 'chief', 'ventre' or 'queor', and 'fyn' for the three

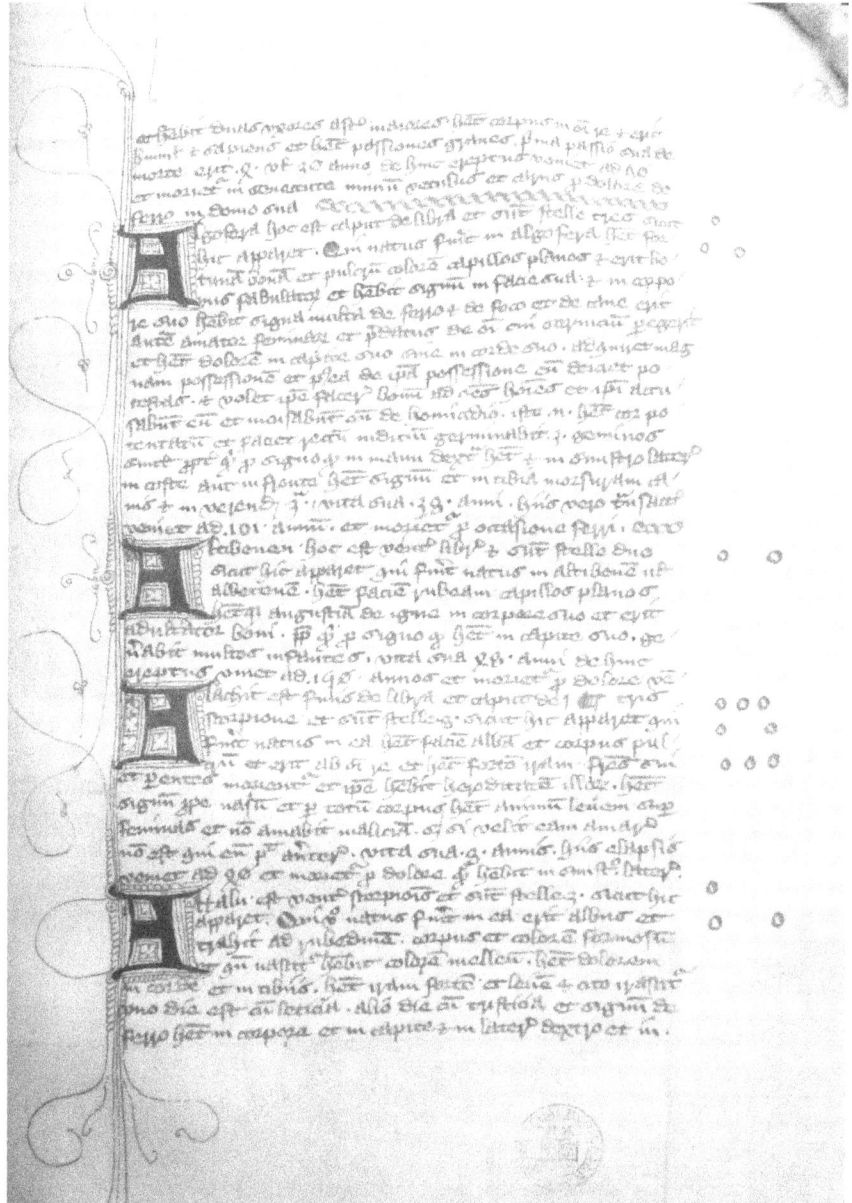

Figure 14.1: Alchandreus', *Benedictum*, 18:15–18. Oxford, Bodleian Library MS Digby 147, f. 123r. By permission of The Bodleian Libraries, The University of Oxford.

there is a diagram of the layout of stars in each group (see Fig. 14.1), which calls the reader's eye to this treatise among the many detailed texts in each manuscript. Thus, although Alchandreus himself remains a shadowy figure, the astrological corpus Gower drew on was well established.

Chapter 18 of the *Benedictum* has been edited twice, both times from the same twelfth-century French copy, but its editors have not called attention to the fact that not every manuscript of it lists the same stars.[61] The limited but significant variety that occurs between the fifteen copies is shown in Table 1 (below), and points to a small subgroup of manuscripts containing the version most likely to have been used by Gower. The table lists the copies by approximate year of production; the final two columns give the two slightly different versions used by Fox, for comparison. Highlighted cells in the table indicate where the numbers of stars differ from those given by Gower (G), or are omitted from that manuscript. The table serves to highlight how much variety can occur even within otherwise very similar copies of the same text; the final two columns, which Fox found sufficiently close to postulate a link to Gower, show how quickly differences arise as the tradition of a text develops. Consequently, the table suggests that the fact that Gower's pattern of stars is similar or identical to that in some copies of the *Benedictum* is unlikely to be coincidence. One copy (Bodleian Library MS Digby 147) has stars completely identical to Gower's, and two others differ from Gower's stars in only one group (the tail of Scorpio/head of Sagittarius): the copies in Erfurt MS Amplon Q.351 and Cambridge University Library MS Gg.6.3. All three copies were made in England in the fourteenth century.[62]

These manuscripts which are closest to Gower's work are worth examining, as they suggest a picture of the poet's reading that is quite different from his known dependence on courtly encyclopaedias like that of Brunetto Latini. All three manuscripts are varied compilations of scientific texts that were popular in university and other learned settings. Each has its own distinctive contents, but they also have a number of texts and interests in common.[63] Chief among these are astronomy, astrology and the instruments

---

subdivisions; the latter uses 'hed', 'wombe' and 'end'.

[61] London, British Library Egerton MS 821 ff. 17v-23v. Before Juste, chapter 18 alone was edited by Emanuel Svenberg, *Lunaria et Zodiologia Latina*, Studia graeca et latina Gothoburgensia XVI (Gothenburg: Elanders, 1963), pp. 45–59.

[62] It is perhaps also worth noting that two other copies (O1 and O2) differ only in one more group, and that in that further group (#17), three of the four manuscripts have only a picture rather than a stated number of stars. One might therefore suggest links between the manuscripts that explain how the difference arose in stages in the processes of copying, with omission of the number followed by miscounting of the stars pictured.

[63] Noteworthy among the distinctive texts is Q.351's glossary of plant names in English, French and Latin (for which see Max Förster, 'Kleinere Mittelenglische Texte', *Anglia*, 42 (1918), pp. 145–224, at 158–62. For a brief description of Gg.6.3, which the cataloguer M. R. James called 'a labyrinthine book', see Falk, 'A Merton College Equatorium', pp. 130–1.

Table 14.1: Stars enumerated in all known manuscripts of *Benedictum* ch. 18

		G	L1	F	E2	C1	O2	P	V^b	O1	E3	C2	O4	E1^e	O3	M2	M3	L2	R^g	M1
1	♈1	3	3	3	3	3	3	3	2	3	3	3	3	3	3	3	3	3	3	3
2	♈2	2	2	2	3	2	2	2	-	2	2	2	2	2	3	2	3	2	3	2
3	♈3, ♉1	7	7	7	7	7	7	7	-	7	7	7	7	7	7	7	7	7	1,7	7
4	♉2	18	17	17	17	18	18	17	7	18	18	18	18	16	18	18	18	18	17	18
5	♉3, ♊1	2	2	2	2	2	2	2	2	2	2	2	2	2	2	2	2	2	2,5	2
6	♊2	5	5	5	5	5	5	5	2	5	5	5	5	5	5^f	5	5	5	4	6
7	♊3	2	2	2	2	2	2	2	-	2	2	2	2	2	2	2	2	2	2	3
8	♋1	10	10	10	10	10	10	10	10	10	10	10	10	8	10	10	10	10	10	9
9	♋2	2	2	2	2	2	2	2	2	2	2	2	2	2	2	2	2	2	-	2
10	♋3, ♌1	4	4	4	4	4	4	4	2	4	4	4	4	4	4	3	4	4	2,4	4
11	♌2	4	4	4	4	4	4	4	4	4	4	4	4	4	4	4	4	4	4	4
12	♌3, ♍1	1	1	1	1	1	1	1	4	1	1	1	1	1	1	1	1	1	1,5	1
13	♍2	5	5	5	5	5	5	5	5	5	5	5	5	5	5	5	5	5	-	5
14	♍3	5	5	5	5	5	5	5	5	5	5	5	5	5	5	5	5	5	5	5
15	♎1	3	3	3	3	3	3	3	2	3	3	3	3	3	3	3	3	3	4	3
16	♎2	2	2	2	2	2	2	2	2	2	2	2	2	2	2	2	2	2	-	2
17	♎3, ♏1	8	7	7	7	7	7^a	7	7	7	8^c	8^d	8	7	7	7	7	7	2,7	9
18	♏2	3	3	3	3	3	3	3	3	3	3	3	3	3	3	3	3	3	3	3
19	♏3, ♐1	8	6	6	6	6	6	6	-	6	6	6	8	6	6	6	6	6	6,8	5
20	♐2	8	8	8	8	8	8	8	8	8	8	8	8	9	8	8	8	8	-	7
21	♐3	7	7	7	7	7	7	7	-	7	7	7	7	7	7	7	7	4	7	12

Table 14.1: *Continues*[64]

	G	L1	F	E2	C1	O2	P	V[b]	O1	E3	C2	O4	E1[e]	O3	M2	M3	L2	R[g]	M1
22 ♑1	3	3	3	3	2	3	3	3	3	3	3	3	3	3	3	3	3	3	3
23 ♑2	2	2	2	2	2	2	2	2	2	2	2	2	2	2	2	2	2	-	-
24 ♑3, ♒1	2	2	3	2	2	2	2	2	2	2	2	2	3	2	2	2	2	2,2	2
25 ♒2	12	12	12	12	12	12	12	13	12	12	12	12	11	12	12	12	12	12	12
26 ♒3, ♓1	2	2	2	2	2	2	2	-	2	2	2	2	2	2	2	2	2	2,2	3
27 ♓2	2	2	2	2	2	2	2	-	2	2	2	2	2	2	2	2	2	-	20
28 ♓3	20	20	20	-	20	20	10	-	20	20	20	20	20	20	20	-	20	20	2

a: number not given but 7 stars pictured; b: several numbers in this manuscript have been amended in a later hand; c, d: number not given but 8 stars pictured; e: numbers not stated until house #14, but stars are pictured; f: text states 5 stars; 4 stars pictured; g: Roussat's groupings differ significantly from other sources; he does not use overlapping signs and has 30 groups in total.

[64] **G**: John Gower, *Confessio Amantis*, VII.979-1236; **L1**: London, British Library Egerton MS 821, ff. 17v-23v (s. xii); **F**: Florence, BML Plut 30.29, ff. 26v-28r (c. 1280); **E2**: Erfurt, UFB, Amplon. Q.316, ff. 24v-26v (s. xiii-xiv); **C1**: Cambridge, Corpus Christi College MS 37, ff. 52r-61r (s. xivin); **O2**: Oxford, Bodleian Library MS Digby 228, ff. 14v-15v (s. xiv); **P**: Paris, BNF lat.7408A ff. 132r-134r (s. xiv); **V**: Venice, BNM, lat. XIV.271 (4577), ff. 17r-29v (s. xiv); **O1**: Oxford, Bodleian Library MS Ashmole 360, ff. 76r-79r (s. xiv); **E3**: Erfurt, UFB, Amplon. Q.351, ff. 86r-88v (s. xiv); **C2**: Cambridge University Library MS Gg.6.3 ff. 119v-121v (s. xiv); **O4**: Oxford, Bodleian Library MS Digby 147, ff. 121r-124v (s. xiv); **E1**: Erfurt, UFB, Amplon. Q.223, ff. 172r-173r (s. xivex); **O3**: Oxford, Bodleian Library MS Laud Misc 594, ff. 156r-v (s. xiv-xv); **M2**: Munich, BSB, Clm 27001, f. 11r-21r (s. xv); **M3**: Munich, BSB, Clm 458, ff. 28r-35v (s. xv); **L2**: London, British Library Sloane MS 1437, ff. 91r- (s. xvi); **R**: Richard Roussat, *Arcandam doctor peritissimus* (1542), ff. A1r-K6r; **M1**: Munich, BSB hebr. 73, ff. 150-160 (s. xvii-xviii), printed in M. Steinschneider, 'Über die Mondstationen', p. 145. The text also appears without numbers in Burgo de Osma, Archivo de la Catedral MS 7 (107r-110v). Partial copies are found in Avranches, BM, 226, ff. 60v-66v, Florence, BML, S. Marco 194, f. 124r, and Florence, BR, 917, ff. 29v-30v. A slightly different version survives in two fifteenth-century copies, London, BL Add. 18752, ff. 60r-65v and Oxford, All Souls MS 81, ff. 118v-137v; the latter is entitled 'liber qui dicitur alkandrinus'. I am grateful to David Juste for sharing images of several of these manuscripts with me.

of those sciences, communicated via Muslim and Jewish cultures down the centuries. All three manuscripts have copies of the popular textbook *On the Sphere* written by the Oxford scholar and later bishop of Lincoln Robert Grosseteste; they all have texts on practical geometry and surveying.[65] Among several texts that appear in two of the three manuscripts are: the anonymous *Theorica planetarum* treatise sometimes attributed to Gerard of Cremona; John of Seville's translation of the ninth-century Baghdad astrologer Abū Ma'shar's *Kitāb taḥāwīl sinī al-'ālam* (*Book of Revolutions of the World-Years*), known in its Latin as *Flores Albumasaris*; the *New Quadrant* treatise of Jacob ben Machir ibn Tibbon, known to Christian astronomers as 'Profatius the Jew of Montpellier'; and the empirical treatise on the magnet by the French master Pierre de Maricourt.[66] The same or similar texts are in other manuscripts containing the Alchandrean stars. These manuscripts, cheaply made using relatively low-quality parchment and with minimal decoration, lead us into a world of learned astrology, inhabited by physicians and university scholars.

How would Gower have had access to such texts? One possible answer is via the Augustinian Priory of St Mary Overy in Southwark. Although the dates of his residence there and the extent of his involvement with the priory are a matter of some debate (see Martha Carlin, above, p. 54), if he did indeed have access to the priory's library at the time he was writing *Confessio Amantis*, it is quite possible that a copy of the *Benedictum* was located there. Works of astrology were often held in monastic libraries: one surviving St Mary Overy manuscript from Gower's time is an impressively broad scientific and theological compendium that includes works of arithmetic, computus, medicine and the popular astronomical primer *On the Sphere* by John of Sacrobosco.[67] Several of the extant copies of the *Benedictum* are associated with religious houses, including the identical copy, MS Digby 147, which was owned by another Augustinian priory, that of Merton. Others include MS Gg.6.3, which was donated by the Oxford-educated Benedictine cardinal, Adam Easton, to Norwich cathedral priory, and the Anglo-Norman Corpus Christi College Cambridge MS 37, which belonged to the Cistercian monks of Boxley in Kent.[68] The reader of an introductory

---

[65] Lynn Thorndike and Pearl Kibre, *A Catalogue of Incipits of Mediaeval Scientific Writings in Latin* (Cambridge, MA, 1963), col. 763c (hereafter TK).

[66] TK223j; TK1013k; TK18i; TK91a. A Middle English translation of the *Flores* survives in a late fourteenth-century manuscript, Cambridge, Trinity College MS O.5.26.

[67] Oxford, Bodleian Library MS Ashmole 1285. See Jean-Pascal Pouzet, 'Southwark Gower: Augustinian Agencies in Gower's Manuscripts and Texts – Some Prolegomena', in Elisabeth M. Dutton, with John Hines, and Robert F. Yeager, eds, *John Gower, Trilingual Poet: Language, Translation, and Tradition* (Cambridge: D. S. Brewer, 2010), pp. 11–25, at 15.

[68] Patrick Zutshi, 'An Urbanist Cardinal and His Books: The Library and Writings of Adam Easton', in *Der Papst Und Das Buch Im Spätmittelalter (1350–1500)*, ed. Rainer Berndt, *Erudiri Sapientia*, 13 (Münster: Aschendorff Verlag, 2018), pp. 24–46.

text like *On the Sphere* (whether in the Grosseteste or Sacrobosco version, which both appear in MS Digby 147) could easily progress from that to a more esoteric work like the *Benedictum*.

If it is easy to see how Gower might have become acquainted with the Alchandrean lunar mansions, a more difficult question is why he chose to incorporate them into the *Confessio Amantis*. A few features of the *Benedictum* might have appealed to Gower, beyond supporting his apparent desire to illustrate the eternally changing, yet continuous circularity of the cosmos. First, it has already been noted that manuscripts of *Benedictum* chapter 18 are, unusually among astronomical manuscripts, invariably decorated by diagrams of the groups of stars. Such images seem to have appealed to Gower: one detail he added to his story of Nectanabus, which does not appear in his source, Thomas of Kent, is that the astrologer carries something similar: 'the hevenely figures / Wroght in a bok ful of peintures' (VI.1893–4).[69] This may refer to the whole-constellation figures which often accompanied lists of stars and other astronomical material, and which Gower mentions in his description of the twelve signs. It is likely that Gower had read Michael Scot's *Liber introductorius* (*Introduction to Astrology*), whose proemium closes with a genealogy of astronomers similar to the list Gower gives (CA: VII.1449–80);[70] many copies of the *Liber introductorius* contain figures of the constellations and other astrological images such as the zodiac man.[71] One of the few details in Gower's section on the seven planets which he could not have drawn from Latini's *Tresor* is the Sun's crown and chariot; he could have found them pictured in the *Liber introductorius*.[72] This work often has imaginative figures of the constellations, some similar to those in

---

[69] Cf. Paris, Bibliothèque nationale de France, Ms. français 24364, f. 1v; Thomas de Kent, *Le Roman d'Alexandre*, para. 4a. This may reflect the metal astrological tablet carried by Nectanabus in some versions of the story. See, for example, Julius Valerius (s. iv), *Res gestae Alexandri Macedonis* I.4, ed. Michaela Rosellini; digital eds Raffaella Tabacco and David Paniagua (Vercelli, DigilibLT Project, 2011), p. 2, http://www.digiliblt.unipmn.it; Juste, *Les Alchandreana primitifs*, p. 119.

[70] Gower's main source for that section may have been the *Speculum astronomiae* ch. 2 (see Zambelli, *The Speculum Astronomiae and Its Enigma*, pp. 212–18); Macaulay in Gower, *Complete Works*, III: 527. However, parts of Gower's list are more similar to Michael Scot's (Fox, *The Mediaeval Sciences*, pp. 81–2; Glenn Edwards, 'The Liber Introductorius of Michael Scot' (Unpublished University of Southern California Ph.D. thesis, 1978), pp. 223–33). On the *Liber introductorius*, see Glenn M. Edwards, 'The Two Redactions of Michael Scot's "Liber Introductorius"', *Traditio*, 41 (1985), pp. 329–40. Cf. Mainzer, 'A Study of the Sources of the *Confessio Amantis*', pp. 319–24.

[71] Dieter Blume, Mechthild Haffner, and Wolfgang Metzger, *Sternbilder des Mittelalters und der Renaissance: Der gemalte Himmel zwischen Wissenschaft und Phantasie* (Berlin: De Gruyter, 2016), volume 2, pp. 185–330.

[72] Fox, *The Mediaeval Sciences*, pp. 62–5; Latini, *Li Livres dou Tresor*, I.108–17. See, for example, Oxford, Bodleian Library MS Bodley 266, ff. 49r, 116r. Cf. Hamilton, 'Some Sources', pp. 345–6.

NATURAL SCIENCES

Figure 14.2: Pisces, in John Gower, *Confessio Amantis*. The Morgan Library & Museum. MS M.126, f. 157v. Purchased by J. Pierpont Morgan (1837–1913), 1903. Photograph: The Morgan Library & Museum, New York.

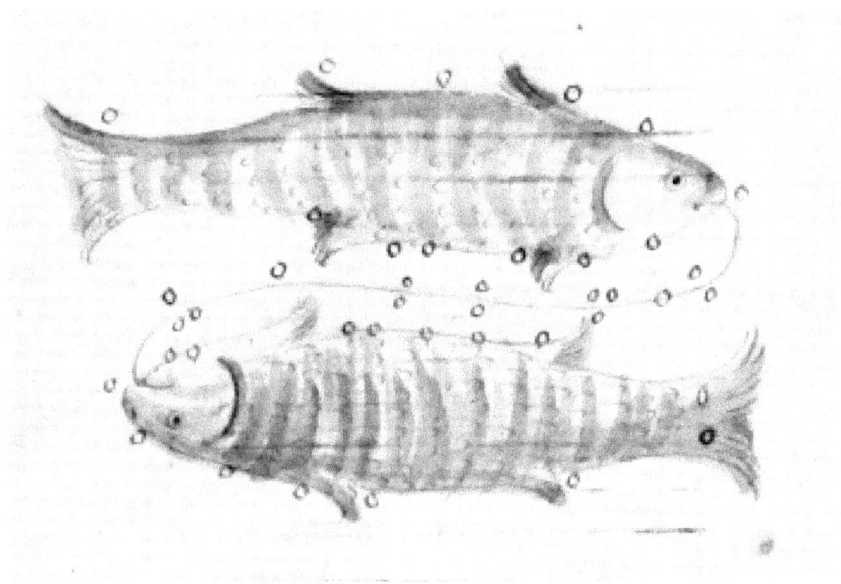

Figure 14.3: Pisces, in Michael Scot, *Liber introductorius*. Oxford, Bodleian Library MS Bodley 266, f. 109v. By permission of The Bodleian Libraries, The University of Oxford.

Morgan Library MS M.126 (see Figs 14.2 and 14.3).[73] Although these images include individual stars, they are not portrayed in groups; but they may have inspired Gower to search for other images of the constellations, where he did find such groups.

Michael Scot's *Liber introductorius* cites 'Archandrinus' and draws on Alchandrean materials, and Gower may also have been inspired to explore these materials by the intuitive link which some medieval authors drew between Alchandreus and Alexander.[74] If, as Porter and others have argued, the unity of macrocosm and microcosm in the *Confessio Amantis* makes Alexander's quest for 'ethical self-governance' relevant even to the foolish lover, it would be natural for Gower to mine texts associated with Alexander for his account of the king's education.[75] This starts, of course, with the *Secretum secretorum*, the manual for kingship supposedly written by Aristotle for his great pupil, a pedagogical relationship Gower flags up in the opening lines of Book VII (VII.4–5).[76] Yet as Gower repeatedly has Genius remind us here, he is working from not one but many 'olde bokes' (VII.1042, 1075, 1424, etc.). Apart from the similarity of name, the Alchandrean corpus includes more than enough direct references to Alexander to have tempted Gower. The *Liber Alchandrei*, perhaps the most important work in the corpus, names Alexander as an astrologer on three occasions; it also lays out the twenty-eight lunar mansions, albeit without the star groupings Gower found in the *Benedictum*.[77] The corpus also contains an *Epistola Argafalau ad Alexandrum*, which addresses 'Regi Macedonum, Alexandro, astrologo et universa philosophia perfectissimo', before laying out some prognostic techniques.[78] Furthermore, in two manuscripts that contain both the *Book of Alchandreus* and the *Letter from Argafalau*, the final chapter of the former is entitled 'Excerpts from the books of Alexander, the astrologer king'.[79] That

---

[73] One is also reminded of the carefully configured astrological ceiling decorations in some Renaissance villas. See, for example, Kristen Lippincott, 'Two Astrological Ceilings Reconsidered: The Sala Di Galatea in the Villa Farnesina and the Sala Del Mappamondo at Caprarola', *Journal of the Warburg and Courtauld Institutes*, 53 (1990), pp. 185–207.

[74] The citation of Archandrinus is in a part of the *Liber introductorius* that has never been edited. But see, for example, Bodleian MS Bodley 266, f. 179v, where a later (perhaps sixteenth-century) reader has re-emphasised the citation. See also Juste, *Les Alchandreana primitifs*, p. 282.

[75] Porter, 'Gower's Ethical Microcosm', p. 144.

[76] Hamilton, 'Some Sources'.

[77] Juste, *Les Alchandreana primitifs*, pp. 38–9. *Liber Alchandrei*, chs. 19 and 22, edited in Juste, *Les Alchandreana primitifs*, pp. 433–72. The text is also known as *Mathematica Alhandrei summi astrologi*.

[78] Edited in Juste, *Les Alchandreana primitifs*, pp. 473–86. For discussion of the identity of Argafalau, see *ibid.*, pp. 37–8, and Burnett, 'Adelard, Ergaphalau and the Science of the Stars', pp. 140–1.

[79] Juste, *Les Alchandreana primitifs*, p. 39, n26. See also Thorndike, *A History of Magic and Experimental Science*, I.713.

chapter includes advice on using astrology to learn the physical and temperamental characteristics of a thief (a subject also covered in *Benedictum* chapter 10); and in the 'Tale of Lucius and the Statue', which appears in some manuscripts of the *Confessio*, when a thief despoils the temple of Apollo:

> forto knowe in special
> What maner man hath do the dede,
> Thei soghten help upon the need
> And maden calculacioun,
> Wherof be demonstracioun
> The man was founde with the good (V.7160–5*).

Even if we accept David Juste's reluctance (in contrast to earlier scholars such as Charles Burnett) to accept a simple identification of Alchandreus as Alexander, there was surely enough relevant material in the Alchandrean corpus for Gower to be tempted to pursue it.[80]

A more general reason for Gower to have included the Alchandrean stars in his description of the constellations is that they allowed him to emphasise the numerical precision of astronomy, which he saw as the most important mathematical science (VII.621–32). He specifies that numerous authorities 'recorden' 1022 stars (VII.1486–9), rather than the round 1200 mentioned by Latini; 1022 is the number in Ptolemy's star catalogue, but the absence of the Alexandrian astronomer's name here suggests that Gower had found the number elsewhere; it appears in many texts, including Michael Scot's *Liber introductorius*.[81] Cataloguing the constellations (and, as we shall shortly see, the fifteen stars, stones and herbs) with such precision provided two benefits for Gower: it emphasised the order and predictability of the cosmos, and it demonstrated his detailed knowledge, as a prerequisite for a moral judgement about the use of such knowledge. This desire for numerical precision may be highlighted in at least one copy of the *Confessio*, where the number of stars in some mansions is given in numerals rather than words.[82] These manuscripts were made in a period when methods of representing numbers were changing: Hindu-Arabic numerals were well established for calculation, appearing in tables in many of the manuscripts

---

[80] Juste, *Les Alchandreana primitifs*, pp. 52–4; Burnett, 'Adelard, Ergaphalau and the Science of the Stars', p. 140.

[81] Ptolemy does not supply a total number of stars, and since he includes duplicates, counting them is not as straightforward as one might expect; 1022 is the number usually given. See Michael Scot, *Liber introductorius*, in MS Bodley 266, f. 64v (this part of the *Liber introductorius* has not been edited). Latini (I.100) attributes his 1200 stars to 'the book of Almagestes which good King Ptolemy made'. (The confusion between the Ptolemaic dynasty of Egypt and the Alexandrian astronomer was common in this period, though it was not a mistake made by Gower himself).

[82] See, for example, the 'v' stars in Virgo's womb, and the 'viii' in the head of Scorpio, in Cambridge, Pembroke College MS 307, f. 152v.

containing the *Benedictum*; but their place-value notation, meaning that a single digit can represent different numbers (such as hundreds, tens or units) depending on where it appears among other digits, was not intuitively clear. Roman numerals, which always represent the same number regardless of context, persisted, especially within prose texts where numbers were also often written out as words. The manuscripts often contain more than one style of presentation: all three of Hindu-Arabic numerals, Roman numerals and (Latin) words are used in the copy in MS Gg.6.3, suggesting that the *Benedictum* had a scientific status somewhere between rhetorical and mathematical.[83] The presentation of numbers did not affect how they were read – any more than we would pronounce 'Book VII' differently from 'Book 7' – but they may have reflected how their scribes and readers perceived the texts. Just as the addition of a high frequency of Latin glosses in this part of the *Confessio* adds an aura of scholarly complexity, so the specification of numerals underlines Gower's demonstration of scientific expertise.

The true level of Gower's scientific expertise has been contested. Fox took the view that Gower's astronomical knowledge was 'extremely limited', but this has recently been contested by Kimberly Zarins, who concludes that his writing is 'up to snuff scientifically and poetically'.[84] We have already seen that Gower read more widely in scientific manuscripts than has hitherto been known, but how much of what he read did he really understand? One important strand of Fox's criticism of Gower was that he showed no understanding of an astrological principle implicit in the *Benedictum*'s twenty-eight groups of stars, and present throughout the Alchandrean corpus: the doctrine of lunar mansions.[85] These are divisions of the sky representing the twenty-eight days of the lunar month: not the synodic month between successive new moons, which was known to be twenty-nine and a half days, but the sidereal month, the twenty-seven days and eight hours it took for the Moon to return to a similar position among the fixed stars. The zodiac could thus be divided into arcs of about thirteen degrees, each representing the position of the Moon on a given day. Only when we understand this does it make sense to describe 'he who was born in Alnat' or another mansion; but despite Gower's use of the twenty-eight groups, he gives the reader no sense of the underlying doctrine.[86] However, the basic principles are not explicitly stated in the *Benedictum* and even the word 'mansions' does not always appear: although one copy bears the colophon 'explicit tractatus de 28 mansionibus lune', most do not formally mark the ending or use vaguer

---

[83] John N. Crossley, 'Old-Fashioned versus Newfangled: Reading and Writing Numbers, 1200–1500', *Studies in Medieval and Renaissance History*, 3rd series, 10 (2013), pp. 79–109.
[84] Fox, *The Mediaeval Sciences*, p. 94; Zarins, 'Writing The Literary Zodiac', p. 223.
[85] Fox, *The Mediaeval Sciences*, pp. 78–80.
[86] *Benedictum* 18.1. Gower ignored the names of the mansions, which are Arabic in origin, though the doctrine has older, Indian, roots. See Juste, *Les Alchandreana primitifs*, pp. 123–6.

phrasing, such as the 'explicit liber iste de 28 constellationibus' of MS Digby 147, or the 'explicit tractatus de constellationibus' found in MSS Gg.6.3 and Amplon Q.351.[87] So although knowledge of the theory of lunar mansions was essential for a full understanding of the *Benedictum* text Gower used, we cannot judge Gower's theoretical understanding based on his omission of information that is also absent from his source.

However, an indication that he did misunderstand this material is his conflation of signs and constellations. The signs were the divisions of the zodiac (the band surrounding the ecliptic line of the Sun's annual path) into regular 30° segments counted from the head of Aries, where the ecliptic intersects the celestial equator; the constellations were the irregular shapes into which ancient stargazers had grouped the stars. Although the constellations and signs shared the same names, the precession of the equinoxes had caused them to diverge, so that the Sun's crossing of the equator into the sign Aries no longer coincided with its arrival in front of the stars of that constellation. Medieval astronomers were well aware of this phenomenon (which they tended to call simply 'the motion of the apogees and fixed stars'), and Chaucer too shows his understanding of 'the eighte and twenty mansiouns / That longen to the moone' when he writes in the 'Franklin's Tale' of the clerk of Orleans who 'knew ful wel how fer Alnath was shove / Fro the heed of thilke fixe Aries above'; in other words, how far precession had taken the stars of the 'eighte speere' from the zero mark on the circle of signs, the 'ninthe speere'.[88] By contrast, Gower makes no such distinction, introducing what 'mai be seie' (VII.1106) in the night sky as 'signes'. He was not alone in this: the eighth and ninth spheres are often left undistinguished in texts about the lunar mansions. The explanation in one highly decorative astronomical compilation, that 'the first mansion starts in the tenth degree of Aries, on account of the motion of the eighth sphere', is rare, but it is not surprising that the scribe saw the need to clarify matters, and not surprising, too, if Gower's reading of the Alchandrean corpus left him with a somewhat shaky grasp of the doctrine of lunar mansions.[89]

Gower closes his section on the zodiac with a final statement of astrological doctrine concerning how 'the londes ben diversed' according to signs. It begins as follows:

---

[87] MS Digby 228, f. 15v; MS Digby 147, f. 124v; MS Gg.6.3, f. 121v; MS Amplon Q.351, f. 88v.

[88] Geoffrey Chaucer, 'The Franklin's Tale', V: 1130–1, 1280–3; North, *Chaucer's Universe*, pp. 153–6. The Franklin dismisses the lunar mansions as 'swich folye / As in oure dayes is nat worth a flye' (V: 1131–2), but we can see throughout his work that Chaucer took such astrological theories quite seriously. Chaucer has the Franklin protest that 'I ne kan no termes of astrologye' (V: 1266), and immediately follows this with a litany of technical language, all correctly used.

[89] 'incipit prima mansio in decimo gradu arietis propter motum octave spere' (British Library Sloane MS 702, f. 27r).

> Nou hast thou herd the propreté
> Of signes, bot in his degré
> Albumazar yit over this
> Seith, so as th'erthe parted is
> In foure, riht so ben divised
> The signes tuelve and stonde assised,
> That ech of hem for his partie
> Hath his climat to justefie.
> Wherof the ferst regiment
> Toward the part of Orient
> From Antioche and that contré
> Governed is of signes thre,
> That is Cancer, Virgo, Leo (VII.1237–49).

The specification of regions governed by signs had been common in astrological treatises since Ptolemy's *Tetrabiblos*.[90] Most writers allocated a country to each sign; some use groups of three, as Gower has here.[91] But the precise assignment Gower uses, with regions corresponding to cardinal points each assigned to three consecutive signs, is not known in contemporary astrological writings.[92] It certainly did not come from 'Albumazar' (Abū Maʿshar), despite Gower's claim: his *Introduction to Astrology* lists countries for individual signs in turn, so Cancer, for example, governs Lesser Armenia and a few other regions.[93] Nor did Gower find it in the Alchandreana. In the *Benedictum* (chapter 14) we do find groups of three signs, but these are the conventional triplicities of non-consecutive signs (e.g. Cancer, Scorpio, Pisces) grouped according to their elemental qualities; and they are not associated with regions. One Alchandrean work, the *In principio*, does contain what has been termed 'astrological chorography' but, like Abū Maʿshar, does so according to individual signs.[94] The particular regions, it should be noted, differ somewhat between texts: it seems translators felt a degree of freedom to adapt unfamiliar names inherited from ancient sources, even perhaps to change

---

[90] Auguste Bouché-Leclercq, *L'astrologie grecque* (Paris: E. Leroux, 1899), pp. 328–47.

[91] Al-Qabīṣī (Alcabitius) assigns triplicities to cardinal points, but also assigns individual signs to regions. See al-Qabīṣī (Alcabitius), *The Introduction to Astrology*, eds Charles Burnett, Keiji Yamamoto, and Michio Yano (London: Warburg Institute, 2004), I.16, 25–36.

[92] Hamilton ('Some Sources', p. 342) suggested that this, along with the rest of the passage on the twelve signs, was suggested to Gower by a short section in the *Secretum secretorum* (implying that Gower made up the precise details). We have seen that Gower had a source for the other details he gives of the twelve signs, and the passage Hamilton cites is very general on stellar influences, so there is no reason to suppose the *Secretum secretorum* was Gower's source here.

[93] Abū Maʿšar, *The Abbreviation of The Introduction to Astrology*, I.32.

[94] *In principio*, ch. 24, edited in Juste, *Les Alchandreana primitifs*, pp. 597–8. See Bouché-Leclercq, *L'astrologie grecque*, pp. 328–47.

them to places more relevant to their readers.[95] So it would not be surprising if, both in this section and in the previous one where he assigns regions to planets, Gower devised his own basic system, simplifying those he had seen in his sources.[96] Although it was an unconventional choice to depart from the ubiquitous triplicities, the zodiacal quadrants Gower uses do appear in texts he could have seen, such as Alcabitius, where they are associated with elemental qualities and seasons.[97] Moreover, Gower's allocations – placing Cancer, Leo and Virgo in the east, for example – are similar to systems shown in medieval microcosmic diagrams.[98]

Whatever the source of Gower's ideas here, his explicit – but misleading – citation of Albumasar should give us pause. Despite long-held suspicions that such citations by Gower were more rhetorical than bibliographical, some scholars are still tempted to take them literally.[99] Even if Gower really believed that the information he relayed was from the authors he names, it seems likely that their distribution throughout Book VII of the *Confessio* is illustrative rather than exact; we cannot read the insertion of 'wise Tholomeus' (VII.1043) as a parenthetical citation. Either way, they are certainly not reliable indicators of Gower's scientific sources. Rather, when Gower cites 'Almageste' as the source of his information about the twelve signs, we should take heed of the legendary connotations of that work's English title, traceable back through Latin and Arabic to the Greek word *megiste*, 'greatest'.[100] Citation was an essential feature of medieval astronomical writing, but even in purely astronomical works, where citations were often given for particular parameters or mathematical methods and were certainly intended to be believed, Ptolemy was probably more cited than read.[101] Even if (as we have seen in the case of the 1022 stars), some

---

[95] Note, for example, the addition of France possibly made by Adelard of Bath in his translation of Abū Ma'shar's *Ysagoga minor* (Abū Ma'šar, *The Abbreviation of The Introduction to Astrology*, I.81, p. 101, n14). See also Juste, *Les Alchandreana primitifs*, pp. 122–3.

[96] See the discussion in Peck, 'Explanatory Notes to Book 7', pp. 446–7. Al-Qabīṣī also assigns regions to planets in part II of his *Introduction to Astrology*. This had been translated into English by Gower's time: see Cambridge, Trinity College MS O.5.26, ff. 1r-27v. The great variety of treatments of this subject in medieval manuscripts means it is still possible that Gower was working from an as-yet-unidentified source.

[97] Al-Qabīṣī (Alcabitius), *The Introduction to Astrology*, I.11; for Middle English translation, see Trinity College MS O.5.26, f. 1v.

[98] See, for example, Oxford, St John's College MS 17, f. 7v (Thorney Abbey, s. xii).

[99] Scepticism is implicit in Macaulay's notes (Gower, *Complete Works*, III: 526–7) and explicit in Fox, *The Mediaeval Sciences*, p. 82. Cf. Peck, 'Introduction' to John Gower, *Confessio Amantis*, volume III, p. 27, who writes 'Chaucer claims to have had sixty books at his bed's head; Gower cites them, sometimes word for word!' – though elsewhere (p. 445) he does note that Gower is not following the source he cites.

[100] Toomer, 'Introduction' to *Ptolemy's Almagest*, p. 2. Its earlier title translates as *Mathematical Systematic Treatise*.

[101] Seb Falk, 'Improving Instruments: Equatoria, Astrolabes, and the Practices of Monastic Astronomy in Late Medieval England' (Unpublished University of Cambridge Ph.D.

of Gower's information ultimately came from Ptolemy, his citation – three times just within the passage on the twelve signs – tell us more about his reputation among the 'scoles of clergie' than about Gower's reading.

Astrology and Magic

The influence of Ptolemy has also been identified within the section of Book VII of the *Confessio Amantis* following the Twelve Signs: on the fifteen stars, stones and herbs. However, it is buried more deeply than some readers have supposed. This section contains a different kind of astronomy from that in the passage on the twelve signs, and it seems Gower was well aware of such subtle differences. He writes:

> Nectanabus in special,
> Which was an astronomien
> And ek a gret magicien,
> And undertake hath thilke emprise
> To Alisandre in his aprise
> As of magique naturel
> To knowe, enformeth him somdel
> Of certein sterres what thei mene;
> Of whiche, he seith, ther ben fiftene,
> And sondrily to everich on
> A gras belongeth and a ston (VII.1296–1306).

These fifteen stars were well known in the later middle ages, appearing in Dante's *Divine Comedy*, and are probably ultimately influenced by the fifteen first-magnitude stars Ptolemy mentions in Books VII and VIII of the *Almagest*.[102] However, it would be a mistake to see this section as part of a Ptolemaic astronomical tradition, as Ptolemy never highlighted this group among his 1022 stars.[103] He did not compile a separate list of first-magnitude

---

thesis, 2016), p. 1; see examples given on pp. 150–2.

[102] Dante Alighieri, *La Divina Commedia: Paradiso*, ed. Natalino Sapegno (Florence: La Nuova Italia, 1985), XIII.4; M. A. Orr, *Dante and the Early Astronomers* (London: Gall and Inglis, 1913), p. 155.

[103] In his explanatory notes to the section on the twelve stars, Peck notes that 'Gower is not actually following Ptolemy's *Almagest*, although that work certainly underlay the sources he was working with, namely Alchandrus' ('Explanatory Notes' to VII.739–946, p. 445). That may be literally true, but in both sections Gower's sources were so far removed from Ptolemy as to make it misleading. Likewise, Tamara O'Callaghan claims a link between Gower's fifteen stars and Ptolemy, arguing that 'when viewed within the context of astronomical tradition, his entire discussion begins to take on a logical form' (Tamara F. O'Callaghan, 'The Fifteen Stars, Stones and Herbs: Book VII of the *Confessio Amantis* and its Afterlife', in Dutton, Hines and Yeager, *John Gower, Trilingual Poet*, pp. 139–56, at 144).

stars, nor even state that there were fifteen of them. The separate subgroup he does list in *Almagest* VII.3, which he describes as 'a few easily recognisable stars', contains eighteen stars (omitting some of first magnitude and adding others of lesser magnitude).[104] More importantly, he makes clear that his purpose in listing stars in this very mathematical work is to record their positions, and explain the method by which he observed those positions using an armillary sphere. At no point does he attribute any importance, let alone powers, to particular stars.[105] Of the fifteen stars Gower lists (VII.1310–1439), some appear in Ptolemy's table of eighteen recognisable stars; some are among his first-magnitude stars; some are both, others neither.

This may seem a fine distinction, but separating the tradition of the fifteen stars from Ptolemaic astronomy not only points us to important information about Gower's real sources, but also allows us to make sense of Gower's citation of Nectanabus at the beginning of the passage, and of Hermes at the end of it. The source, as Macaulay first pointed out, is a treatise that brings fifteen stars together with an equal number of stones and plants.[106] The manuscripts cited by Macaulay, which carry the title *Liber Hermetis de 15 stellis et de 15 lapidibus et de 15 herbis*, are close in content to Gower's presentation but list the stars, stones and herbs separately, whereas Gower integrates them:

> Sterre Ala Corvi upon heihte
> Hath take his place in nombre of eighte,
> Which of his kinde mot parforne
> The will of Marte and of Satorne:
> To whom lapacia the grete
> Is herbe, bot of no beyete;
> His ston is honochinus hote,
> Thurgh which men worchen gret riote (VII.1371–8).

Gower's layout, as Mainzer has noted, is employed in a version of the material known as the *Tractatus Enoch*, extant in at least thirteen manuscripts.[107] Similarly to the *Benedictum*, paragraphs in this version are punctuated by quasi-geomantic diagrams which may have caught Gower's eye.[108] The names in this version are also closer to those given by Gower than the *Liber*

---

[104] *Ptolemy's Almagest*, pp. 330–2, 339–40. O'Callaghan ('The Fifteen Stars', p. 144) claims incorrectly that these are the same stars described by Gower.
[105] Cf. O'Callaghan, 'The Fifteen Stars', p. 144.
[106] Macaulay, notes to Gower, *Complete Works*, III: 526.
[107] Mainzer, 'A Study of the Sources of the *Confessio Amantis*', pp. 287–93. This text has been edited in *Textes latins et vieux français relatifs aux Cyranides*, ed. Louis Delatte (Paris: Les Belles Lettres, 1942), pp. 276–89. The *Liber Hermetis* is extant in at least thirty-two manuscripts. See Paolo Lucentini and Vittoria Perrone Compagni, *I testi e i codici di Ermete nel Medioevo* (Florence: Polistampa, 2001), nos. 13–14, pp. 44–8.
[108] Where these appear in manuscripts of the *Liber Hermetis*, they are collected at the end of the treatise. See, for example, Bodleian Library MS Ashmole 341, ff. 127r-v.

Hermetis, which allows us to identify some of the unfamiliar star names that Gower uses, such as 'The sefnthe sterre in special / Of this science is Arial' (VII.1363–4). Here the *Tractatus Enoch* states 'Septima stella est Cor Leonis, et vocant aliqui Arexal', thus confirming the suggestion Macaulay made for this star.[109] But more important than such identifications is the scientific status of this text. Enoch and Hermes were seen as the same person by some writers, and their names at the start of the two versions of the text – and Gower's citation of the latter (VII.1437) – signal what becomes apparent as we read it: that this is not a work of astronomy, but of magic.[110]

Gower himself signals that this material is 'magique naturel' (1301), and scholars have discussed the significance of this magic within the poem as a whole.[111] However, more may be said about the subtle and often hazy distinction between magic and the astronomy discussed above. Magic was, as its pioneering historian put it, 'studied with some interest and some horror' in late medieval Europe.[112] Although magic in general was theologically suspect, increasingly investigated alongside heresy and legally proscribed, there was also increasing acknowledgement that some forms of natural magic could be licit.[113] Gower succinctly explains that magic is acceptable if it uses the natural properties of objects, and is carried out for good motives:

> these craftes, as I finde,
> A man mai do be weie of kinde,
> Be so it be to good entente (VI.1303–5).

These two criteria were widely agreed on. We see them broken, for example, in the following description of the sin of avarice from the *Ayenbite of Inwyt*, translated from French into the Kentish dialect earlier in the fourteenth century:

> To þise zenne / belongeþ / þe zenne: of ham / þet uor pans / makeþ to clepie / þane dyeuel. and makeþ þe enchauntemens. and makeþ to loky ine þe .zuord. oþer ine þe nayle / of þe þoume. uor to of-take / þe þyeues. oþer uor oþre þinges. And of ham alsuo / þet makeþ / oþer porchaceþ

---

[109] *Tractatus Enoch*, in Delatte, *Textes latins*, p. 282. One manuscript, Erfurt Amplon. Q. 381, has 'areyal'; Macaulay, notes to Gower, *Complete Works*, III: 526. Presumably Macaulay suggested Cor Leonis because it was listed as the seventh star in the *Liber Hermetis* (edited in Delatte, *Textes latins*, pp. 237–75, at 252). For other examples, see Mainzer, 'A Study of the Sources of the *Confessio Amantis*', pp. 288–90.
[110] Thorndike, *A History of Magic and Experimental Science*, I.310.
[111] O'Callaghan, 'The Fifteen Stars', pp. 140–7.
[112] David Pingree, 'The Diffusion of Arabic Magical Texts in Western Europe', in *La Diffusione Delle Scienze Islamiche Nel Medio Evo Europeo* (Roma: Accademia nazionale dei Lincei, 1987), pp. 57–102, at 57.
[113] Sophie Page, *Magic in the Cloister: Pious Motives, Illicit Interests, and Occult Approaches to the Medieval Universe* (University Park: Pennsylvania State University Press, 2013), p. 2.

> / be charmes / oþer be wychecreft. oþer be kueadnesse / huet þet hit by. þet uolk / þet byeþ ine spoushod / togydere / ham hatieþ. oþer ne moȝe habbe uelaȝrede / þe on wyþ þe oþre / be spoushod. Oþer þet uolk / þet ne byeþ naȝt ine spoushod: louieþ ham togidere / folliche: and be zenne.[114]

The sin here consists in using illicit techniques (invoking the devil, using a sword or thumbnail for divination, and so on) for unworthy motives; not only avarice, but also to prevent marital intercourse or facilitate adultery. A distinction is being made between learned magic and popular – perhaps commercial – techniques.[115] The author of this translation, Michael of Northgate, was a monk of St Augustine's, Canterbury, where a large number of magical texts were collected, including two of the surviving copies of the *Liber Hermetis*.[116] That and the *Tractatus Enoch* are works of image magic: a fashionable genre of learned magic, in which practitioners performed rituals in order to harness or enhance the magical powers of objects or images.[117] The presence of such works in a Benedictine monastery does not seem to have attracted condemnation, and image magic was also popular among medical practitioners.[118] Within this genre, the *Liber Hermetis* and *Tractatus Enoch* are close to the boundary with astrology: they discuss the general effects of the stars but also how to make use of them. So, while Gower's description of the eighth group quoted above is sparse, his source is more explicit:

> The eighth star is *Ala Corvi*, and it is in the 3rd degree of Libra and is of the nature of Saturn and Mars.[119] And it has many bad meanings and is full of all ill … The stone accompanying this star is *onichius* [onyx] …

---

[114] Michael of Northgate, *Ayenbite of Inwyt*, ed. Pamela Gradon (London: Oxford University Press, 1866), p. 43. 'To this sin belongs the sin of them that for pence have the devil summoned, and make enchantments, and cause to look into a sword or into the nail of the thumb, in order to overtake thieves or for other things. And of them also that cause or obtain by charms or by witchcraft or by evil, whatever it be, that folk that are in wedlock together hate one another, or cannot have fellowship the one with the other in wedlock; or that folk, that are not in wedlock, love one another foolishly and in sin.' Translation from *The Ayenbite of Inwyt (Remorse of Conscience): A Translation of Parts into Modern English*, trans. A. J. Wyatt (London: W. B. Clive, 1889), p. 35.

[115] Page, *Magic in the Cloister*, pp. 24–5.

[116] Oxford, Corpus Christi College MS 125, ff. 69r-74v; Oxford, Bodleian Library MS Ashmole 341, ff. 120v-127v.

[117] Page, *Magic in the Cloister*, p. 73.

[118] One surviving copy of the *Tractatus Enoch* comes from the renowned medical school at Montpellier (Montpellier, Bibliothèque de la Faculté de Médecine MS 490, ff. 143r-201r).

[119] Ala Corvi is probably the third-magnitude star described by Ptolemy as 'the star in the advance, right wing' (VIII.1, Constellation XLIII), now known as Corvi. It was widely known as Algorab; see, for example Oxford, Bodleian Library MS Rawlinson C.117, f. 156r.

Its power is to make men angry, rash and wicked, thinking and speaking evil; and it makes demons flee, and gathers them at will. Its herb is *lapatia maior*; and if you put some of its seed or leaves or root with the tongue of a frog under onyx when the Moon is within one degree of Ala Corvi, the ring will be of great power against enemies and demons and ill winds.[120]

Thus, although there is significant overlap in subject matter between the sections on the twelve signs and fifteen stars – and Gower's sources for both could quite possibly have been held in a respectable setting like a monastic library – they have undeniably different connotations.[121] Gower makes it clear that he understands this, bookending his description with references to Hermes and the reprobate 'magicien' Nectanabus. It seems his readers too understood this: the section on fifteen stars was excerpted and paraphrased away from the rest of the *Confessio* by later readers interested in medical magic. A collection of charms and magical and medical recipes in British Library MS Sloane 3847 includes a seventeenth-century list headed 'What stones and hearbes are appropiated unto the 15 starres according to John Gower in his booke intituled, de Confessione Amantis'. The following numbered list draws on Gower's Latin marginalia, with entries such as '8. Alacorui, Lapis honochinus, herba, Lappacia'.[122] Similarly, almost the entire section on the fifteen stars (VII.1281–1438, with Latin notes) was copied in the late fifteenth century into a medical compilation in Longleat House MS 174.[123] These texts, along with Book IV's distilled account of alchemy that draws heavily on authoritative sources, must surely have contributed to Gower's later reputation as a notable 'Hermetique Philosopher'.[124] In her

---

[120] *Tractatus Enoch*, in Delatte, *Textes latins*, pp. 282–3; my translation from 'Octava stella est Ala Corvi, et est in 3o gradu Librae et est de natura Saturni et Martis. Et habet multas malas significationes et est plena omni malo ... Lapis conveniens stellae est onichius ... Virtus eius est facere hominem iratum et audacem et pravum cogitantem et loquentem malum; et facit fugere daemones et eos congregat quando vult. Herba eius est lapatia maior; et si ponas de semine eius vel foliis vel radice cum lingua ranae sub onichio quando Luna erit cum Ala Corvi in uno grado, multum valet anulus contra inimicos et daemones et ventos malos.'

[121] The *Benedictum* and *Tractatus Enoch* do not appear together in any surviving manuscripts, but manuscripts where they do appear have texts in common (e.g. Robert Grosseteste's *De impressionibus aeris* in MS Gg.6.3 and Harley MS 1612).

[122] London, British Library MS Sloane 3847, f. 83r (as numbered).

[123] Longleat House MS 174, ff. 159r-160r. See Kate Harris, 'The Longleat House Extracted Manuscript of Gower's *Confessio Amantis*', in Alastair J. Minnis, ed., *Middle English Poetry: Texts and Traditions. Essays in Honour of Derek Pearsall* (Woodbridge: Boydell Press, 2001), pp. 77–90.

[124] Elias Ashmole, *Theatrum Chemicum Britannicum: Containing Severall Poeticall Pieces of Our Famous English Philosophers, Who Have Written the Hermetique Mysteries in Their Owne Ancient Language* (London: Grismond, 1652), p. 484. On the alchemy underlying *Confessio Amantis* IV.2457–2632 and especially the three stones, see Jennifer M. Rampling, *The Experimental Fire: Inventing English Alchemy, 1300–1700* (forthcoming).

study of Longleat House MS 174, Kate Harris argues that this 'mantle of scientific authority ... fits the poet ill', and that the inclusion of Gower's fifteen stars in a medical manuscript 'implies a gulf between the manuscript compiler and the learned scientific circles of his day'.[125] But in this case the compiler was putting Gower's extract of natural magic right back into the arcane medical context from which it had come.

Nevertheless, readers may have made connections from Gower's writing to medical material that did not appear in his sources. This is suggested by the Portuguese translation of *Confessio Amantis* in Madrid, Real Biblioteca MS II-3088, produced in 1430. Ten years later a reader added a contents page in Spanish, together with two versions of a table showing lunar positions in the zodiac throughout the year.[126] Such tables are common in medical almanacs, but to find one sandwiched between the contents and the text of the *Confessio* makes it unavoidable to suppose that the copyist had seen the connection between the practical table of lunar positions and the closely related, but more arcane, lunar mansions.[127]

Science, Magic and Morality

Magic and medicine, alchemy and astrology; all were popular parts of late medieval learning. As historians of science have increasingly turned their attention towards more occult or esoteric sciences, more manuscripts are being identified and studied, and the place of such sciences in society is being reassessed. This chapter has focused on sciences that in modern terms may seem marginal, partly in order to bring this new historical understanding to bear on our reading of Gower, and partly because it is precisely in these areas that Gower departs from the familiar encyclopaedic sources.[128] Sciences concerning the cosmos and elements are, of course, present throughout

---

Many alchemical treatises were written and collected by monks; Michael of Northgate left several alchemical books to his monastic library. On Gower's reputation and Ashmole's citation, see Siân Echard, 'Introduction: Gower's Reputation', in Echard, *A Companion to Gower*, pp. 1–22, at 20.

[125] Harris, 'The Longleat House Extracted Manuscript', p. 90.
[126] Madrid, Real Biblioteca MS II-3088, ff. 7v-8r (accessible online at http://fotos.patrimonionacional.es/biblioteca/ibis/pmi/II_03088/index.html). The production of this manuscript and inclusion of the zodiac are discussed in Mauricio Herrero Jiménez, Tamara Pérez-Fernández, and Marta María Gutiérrez Rodríguez, 'Castilian Script in the Iberian Manuscripts of the Confessio Amantis', in *John Gower in England and Iberia: Manuscripts, Influences, Reception*, eds Ana Sáez-Hidalgo and R. F. Yeager (Cambridge: D. S. Brewer, 2014), pp. 17–32.
[127] For other examples of this table, see, for example, London, Wellcome Library MS 8004, p. 57, and London, British Library MS Harley 3812, f. 5v (both freely available online).
[128] Mainzer, 'A Study of the Sources of the *Confessio Amantis*', pp. 335–7, provides a list of these.

Gower's works. But what this chapter has shown is that the poet incorporated some ideas further from the mainstream of modern science and that although scholars have previously thought them, as Fox put it, 'not quite respectable', they were in fact widely accepted and copied.[129] Fox made that criticism of the respectability of the lunar mansions because of their association with illicit image magic, but it should now be clear that the two ideas could be treated separately.[130] Gower understood such distinctions, writing clearly of the powerful but problematic sorcery of Ulysses and Nectanabus:

> Ful many a wonder thing he doth,
> That were betre to be laft (VI.1286–7).

and, in the marginal case of the fifteen stars, associating that doctrine explicitly with a mage who we know was punished for his presumption:

> Nectanabus his craft miswente,
> So it misfell him er he wente (VI.2361–2).

The boundaries between learned and occult sciences, licit and illicit arts, were hard to navigate in fourteenth-century England. By including elements of both astrology and image magic in his account of astronomy, while drawing a distinction between the people who practise them, Gower trod a reasonably straight and careful path.

Still, despite his broad reading of scientific texts, we should be careful not to mistake the depth or purpose of Gower's technical writing. Scientific content, taken out of its original context, does not, as O'Callaghan suggests, transform 'moral' Gower into 'scientific' Gower; rather, Gower's science is part of an education in morality.[131] The flow of precise numbers through his poetry did more than underline his expertise; it captured the carefully ordered structure of the cosmos. Whether the poet fully understood the mathematical implications of the science he described is moot; his aim was to educate and entertain more than to inform. His readers surely understood this: Chaucer acknowledged the moral value of his colleague's earlier writings in his sincere tribute at the end of *Troilus and Criseyde*, and such a judgement could equally be made of the *Confessio Amantis*; as we have seen, Chaucer would undoubtedly have understood Gower's account of astrology.[132] Thus,

---

[129] Fox, *The Mediaeval Sciences*, p. 78.
[130] One image magic text, the *Liber imaginum lunae*, draws on the doctrine of lunar mansions; see Page, *Magic in the Cloister*, pp. 75–80. The *Speculum Astronomiae* (ch. 11) condemns image magic that co-opted the lunar mansions 'in order to render itself credible to some extent' (Zambelli, *The Speculum Astronomiae and Its Enigma*, trans. Burnett, Lippincott, Pingree and Zambelli, p. 241).
[131] O'Callaghan, 'The Fifteen Stars', p. 156.
[132] Chaucer, 'Troilus and Criseyde', V: 1856. On sincerity, see Derek Pearsall, 'The Gower Tradition', in Minnis, *Gower's Confessio Amantis*, pp. 179–97, at 179.

whilst narrow focus on a selection of scientific details has revealed something of Gower's sources and place among contemporary learning, this is perhaps not how Gower's readers experienced his poetry; he bathed his readers in sciences, and they surely let the learning wash over them.

Nevertheless, just as science was part of medieval culture, so Gower's art becomes part of science. The astrological doctrines he transmitted through the *Confessio Amantis* proved highly durable, and indeed the numbers of stars in the lunar mansions are more consistent in manuscripts of Gower's work than in copies of his source, demonstrating the scientific stability as well as mnemonic power of poetry. In this sense, Gower's scientific writing should be seen not only alongside works of moral and political education ranging from the *Secretum secretorum* to the *Livres dou Tresor*, but also alongside popular calendrical and computistical verses like the 'Cisio-Janus'.[133] And in conjuring lyrical images of scorpions and lions, constellations 'beset in sondri wise' (VII.1221) with stars, Gower's poetry – whether in manuscripts decorated with miniatures or simply punctuated with Latin apothegms – aptly conveyed and perpetuated the legacy of the diagrammatic illustrations that may have drawn the poet's eye down to such texts. Gower evocatively demonstrates mankind's intimate, unbreakable connection to the cosmos, lifting scientific ideas from the manuscript page, and lifting his readers' eyes to the divinely-ordered universe.

---

[133] Laurel Means, '"Ffor as Moche as Yche Man May Not Haue þe Astrolabe": Popular Middle English Variations on the Computus', *Speculum*, 67 (1992), pp. 595–623, at 615.

SELECT BIBLIOGRAPHY

Full publication details of all the works referred to in the notes to the chapters above are given the first time that they are cited within each chapter. This select bibliography is intended simply to suggest some introductory works on Gower along with some key studies relating to each chapter. There is a comprehensive, searchable, on-line bibliography of scholarship relating to Gower on the website of the International John Gower Society.

Modern editions of Gower's works begin with the four volumes of his *Complete Works*, edited by George C. Macaulay: John Gower, *The Complete Works Volume I: The French Works* (Oxford: Clarendon Press, 1899); *The Complete Works, Volumes II and III: The English Works* (Oxford: Clarendon Press, 1901); and *The Complete Works, Volume IV: The Latin Works* (Oxford: Clarendon Press, 1902) and these remain indispensable. A more recent edition of the *Confessio Amantis*, with detailed notes, is provided by the three volumes of John Gower, *Confessio Amantis*, ed. Russell A. Peck (Kalamazoo: Medieval Institute Publications; Volume 1, revised edition, 2006; Volume 2, revised edition, 2005; Volume 3, 2005). For a translation of the *Mirour de l'Omme*, see *The Mirror of Mankind*, trans. William B. Wilson; revised by Nancy W. Van Baak (East Lansing: Colleagues Press, 1992). For translations of the *Vox Clamantis* and *Cronica Tripertita*, see *The Major Latin Works of John Gower: The Voice of One Crying and the Tripartite Chronicle*, trans. Eric W. Stockton (Seattle: University of Washington Press, 1962). More recent translations of Book I of the *Vox* and of the *Cronica Tripertita* appear in John Gower, *Poems on Contemporary Events: The Visio Anglie (1381) and Cronica Tripertita (1400)*, ed. David R. Carlson, trans. A George Rigg (Toronto: Pontrifical Institute of Medieval Studies, 2011). More recent editions and translations of the *Traitié selonc les auctors pour essampler les amantz marietz* and *Cinkante Balades* are provided in John Gower, *The French Balades*, ed. Robert F. Yeager (Kalamazoo: Medieval Institute Publications, 2011), whilst modern editions and translations of his shorter Latin works and of *In Praise of Peace* are given in John Gower, *The Minor Latin Works with In Praise of Peace*, eds Robert F. Yeager and Michael Livingston (Kalamazoo: Medieval Institute Publications, 2005).

Modern work on Gower owes much to the inspiration of John H. Fisher's *John Gower: Moral Philosopher and Friend of Chaucer* (first published by New York University Press, 1965) although, as the chapters in this volume show, some of his claims have to be treated with caution. Another important early study was Maria Wickert, *Studies in John Gower* (Washington: University Press of America, 1981; first published in German in 1953). Two recent indispensable introductions to Gower's work are provided by *Companion to Gower*, edited by Siân Echard (Cambridge: D. S. Brewer, 2004) and Ana Sáez-Hidalgo, Brian Gastle, and Robert F. Yeager, eds, *The Routledge Research Companion to John Gower* (London: Routledge, 2017).

Key monographs on Gower include: Russell A. Peck, *Kingship and Common Profit in Gower's Confessio Amantis* (Carbondale: Southern Illinois University Press, 1978); Robert F. Yeager, *John Gower's Poetic: The Search for a New Arion* (Cambridge: D. S. Brewer, 1990); Kurt Olsson, *John Gower and the Structures of Conversion: A Reading of the Confessio Amantis* (Cambridge: D. S. Brewer, 1992); James Simpson, *Sciences and the Self in Medieval Poetry: Alan of Lille's Anticlaudianus and John Gower's Confessio Amantis* (Cambridge: Cambridge University Press, 1995); Peter Nicholson, *Love and Ethics in Gower's Confessio Amantis* (Ann Arbor: The University of Michigan Press, 2005); Elliott Kendall, *Lordship and Literature: John Gower and the Politics of the Great Household* (Oxford: Clarendon Press, 2008); Matthew N. McCabe, *Gower's Vulgar Tongue: Ovid, Lay Religion and English Poetry in the Confessio Amantis* (Cambridge: D. S. Brewer, 2011); David R. Carlson, *John Gower, Poetry and Propaganda in Fourteenth-Century England* (Cambridge: D. S. Brewer, 2012); Conrad Van Dijk, *John Gower and the Limits of the Law* (Cambridge: D. S. Brewer, 2013); Matthew W. Irvin, *The Poetic Voices of John Gower: Politics and Personae in the Confessio Amantis* (Cambridge: D. S. Brewer, 2014); Ana Sáez-Hidalgo and Robert F. Yeager, eds, *John Gower in England and Iberia: Manuscripts, Influences, Reception* (Cambridge: D. S. Brewer, 2014).

Many studies of Gower have appeared or been reprinted in edited collections of essays including: Alastair Minnis, ed., *Gower's Confessio Amantis: Responses and Reassessments* (Cambridge: D. S. Brewer, 1983); Robert F. Yeager, ed., *John Gower: Recent Readings* (Kalamazoo: Medieval Institute Publications, 1989); Peter Nicholson, ed., *Gower's Confessio Amantis: A Critical Anthology* (Cambridge: D. S. Brewer, 1991); Robert F. Yeager, ed., *Revisioning Gower* (Asheville: Pegasus Press, 1998); Robert F. Yeager, ed., *On John Gower: Essays at the Millennium* (Kalamazoo: Medieval Institute Publications, 2007); Malte Urban, ed., *John Gower: Manuscripts, Readers, Contexts* (Turnhout: Brepols, 2009); Elizabeth Dutton, with John Hines and Robert F. Yeager, eds, *John Gower, Trilingual Poet: Language, Translation and Tradition* (Cambridge: D. S. Brewer, 2010); and Russell A. Peck and Robert F. Yeager, eds, *John Gower: Others and the Self* (Cambridge: D. S. Brewer, 2017).

Recent general monographs with significant treatments of Gower include Arthur Bahr, *Fragments and Assemblages: Forming Compilations and Medieval London* (Chicago: University of Chicago Press, 2013), Jonathan Hsy, *Trading Tongues: Merchants, Multilingualism, and Medieval Literature* (Columbus: Ohio State UP, 2013) and Sonja Drimmer, *The Art of Illusion: Illuminators and the Making of English Literature, 1403–1476* (Philadelphia: University of Pennsylvania Press, 2019).

BIBLIOGRAPHY

Chapter 1. Gower's Life

Carlin, Martha, *Medieval Southwark* (London: Hambledon, 1996). A detailed study of Southwark, where Gower spent his later years.

Echard, Siân, ed., *A Companion to Gower* (Cambridge: D. S. Brewer, 2004). The chapters by John Hines, Nathalie Cohen, and Simon Roffey, by Robert Epstein, and by Derek Pearsall are especially relevant to the discussions in 'Gower's Life'.

Fisher, John H., *John Gower: Moral Philosopher and Friend of Chaucer* (London: Methuen, 1965). Fisher's biographical study of Gower is flawed but has been extremely influential.

Roskell, John S., Linda Clark, and Carole Rawcliffe, eds, *The History of Parliament: The House of Commons, 1386–1421* (Stroud: Alan Sutton, for the History of Parliament Trust, 1993). Available online at http://www.historyofparliamentonline.org/research/members/members-1386-1421. An outstanding resource, providing brief biographies of individual members of parliament.

Sáez-Hidalgo, Ana, Brian Gastle, and Robert F. Yeager, eds, *The Routledge Research Companion to John Gower* (London: Taylor and Francis, 2017). The chapters by Joyce Coleman, Martha Carlin and Roger A. Ladd discuss images of Gower, Southwark in Gower's day, and Gower's possible background in commerce.

Sobecki, Sebastian, '*Ecce patet tensus*: The Trentham Manuscript, *In Praise of Peace*, and Gower's Autograph Hand', *Speculum*, 90 (2015), pp. 925–59; and idem, 'A Southwark Tale: Gower, the 1381 Poll Tax, and Chaucer's *The Canterbury Tales*', *Speculum*, 92 (2017), pp. 630–60. Two major recent articles that reach different conclusions from those offered here about Gower and Southwark.

Chapter 2. Gower's Works

Coleman, Joyce, 'Philippa of Lancaster, Queen of Portugal and Patron of the Gower Translations', in Bullón-Fernandez, Maria, ed., *England Iberia in the Middle Ages: Cultural, Literary and Political Exchanges* (New York: Palgrave Macmillan, 2007), pp. 135–65. An interesting study of the Iberian translations of the *Confessio Amantis*.

Macaulay, George C., 'Introduction' to John Gower, *The Complete Works, Volume II: The English Works*, ed. George C. Macaulay (Oxford: Clarendon Press, 1901), pp. cxxvii–clxvii. Sets out Macaulay's view that the manuscripts of the *Confessio Amantis* fall into three main recensions (comprised of six sub-variants) which has been the beginning for much modern discussion of the text.

Mooney, Linne R., and Estelle Stubbs, *Scribes and the City: London Guildhall Clerks and the Dissemination of Middle English Literature, 1375–1425* (York: York Medieval Press, 2013). Argues that many of the manuscripts of Gower's poems were copied out by clerks associated with the London Guildhall.

Nicholson, Peter, 'The Dedication of Gower's *Confessio Amantis*', *Mediaevalia*, 10 (1984), pp. 159–80. A useful introduction to the political implications of

Gower's change of dedication to the *Confessio Amantis*. See also the chapter by Michael Bennett, above.

Pearsall, Derek, 'The Manuscripts and Illustrations of Gower's Works', in Siân Echard, ed., *A Companion to Gower* (Cambridge: D. S. Brewer, 2004), pp. 72–97. A key work of reference on the manuscripts of Gower's works.

Sáez-Hidalgo, Ana, Brian Gastle, and Robert F. Yeager, eds, *The Routledge Research Companion to John Gower* (London: Routledge, 2017). Includes useful chapters on the French, Latin, Middle English and Iberian manuscripts of Gower's poetry and discussions of the dating of Gower's works.

Chapter 3. Nobility and Chivalry

Bellis, Joanna, and Laura Slater, eds, *Representing War and Violence, 1250–1600* (Woodbridge: Boydell Press, 2016). Among various essays which discuss representations of medieval warfare, Sara V. Torres considers Gower's 'In Praise of Peace'.

Goodman, Anthony and James L. Gillespie, eds, *Richard II: The Art of Kingship* (Oxford: Clarendon Press, 1999). In addition to many useful essays, those by Chris Given-Wilson and John Taylor help place Gower's view on chivalry and nobility in context.

Green, David, *The Hundred Years War: A People's History* (New Haven: Yale University Press, 2014). Offers an overview of the Anglo-French war and its impact on different social groups.

Peck, Russell A., and Robert F. Yeager, eds, *John Gower: Others and the Self* (Cambridge: D. S. Brewer, 2017). As well as considerations of many aspects of Gower's works, including his attitudes to social dysfunction, Yoshiko Kobayashi's contribution to this volume considers Gower's advocacy of peace.

Saul, Nigel, *For Honour and Fame: Chivalry in England, 1066–1500* (London: Bodley Head, 2011). A fine survey of chivalric culture in medieval England.

Chapter 4. The Peasants and the Great Revolt

Barker, Juliet, *1381. The Year of the Peasants' Revolt* (Cambridge, Mass.: Harvard University Press). Accessible, informed and lucid general account of events.

Bennett, Michael, 'John Gower, Squire of Kent, the Peasants' Revolt and The Visio Anglie', *The Chaucer Review*, 53 (2018), pp. 258–82. A useful reconstruction of Gower's background and whereabouts in 1381.

Dobson, R. Barrie, ed., *The Peasants' Revolt of 1381* (second edition; London: Macmillan, 1983). Still the best compilation on the revolt, it provides a scholarly introduction along with sources in translation and a commentary on them.

Galloway, Andrew, 'Gower in his Most Learned Role and the Peasants' Revolt of 1381', *Mediaevalia*, 6 (1993), pp. 329–47. Still the best single article on Gower and 1381.

Rigby, Stephen H., and Alastair J. Minnis, eds, *Historians on Chaucer: The General Prologue to the Canterbury Tales* (Oxford: Oxford University Press, 2014). Individual essays examine the historical context for various categories of late fourteenth-century peasants.

Robertson, Kellie, *The Laborer's Two Bodies. Literacy and Legal Productions in Britain 1350–1500* (Basingstoke: Palgrave Macmillan, 2006). A thoughtful exploration of literary perspectives on labour.

Chapter 5. Towns and Trade

Barron, Caroline M., *London in the Later Middle Ages: Government and People 1200–1500* (Cambridge: Cambridge University Press, 2004). An important work on the civic politics and governance of late medieval London.

Bertolet, Craig E., *Chaucer, Gower, Hoccleve and the Commercial Practices of Late Fourteenth-Century London* (Farnham: Ashgate, 2013). A literary study that examines Gower's attitude to trade within its London context.

Carrel, Helen, 'Food, Drink and Public Order in the London *Liber Albus*', *Urban History*, 33 (2006), pp. 176–94. A contextual study of London's food trade and its regulation.

Ladd, Roger, *Antimercantilism in Late Medieval English Literature* (New York: Palgrave Macmillan, 2010). Includes a chapter devoted to the *Mirour de l'Omme* and Gower's depiction of merchants.

Nightingale, Pamela, 'Capitalists, Crafts and Constitutional Change in Late Fourteenth-Century London', *Past and Present*, 124 (1989), pp. 3–35. Analyses the constitutional upheaval taking place in London during Gower's lifetime.

Rexroth, Frank, *Deviance and Power in Late Medieval London* (Cambridge: Cambridge University Press, 2007). Includes a discussion of John of Northampton's mayoral reforms.

Chapter 6. Men of Law

Barrington, Candice, 'John Gower's Legal Advocacy and *In Praise of Peace*' in Elizabeth Dutton, with John Hines and R. F. Yeager, eds, *John Gower, Trilingual Poet: Language, Translation and Tradition* (Cambridge: D. S. Brewer, 2010), pp. 112–25. A useful study emphasising the sophistication of Gower's legal vocabulary.

Musson, Anthony, *Medieval Law in Context: the Growth of Legal Consciousness from Magna Carta to the Peasants' Revolt* (Manchester: Manchester University Press, 2001). A survey which brings together the legal, political and social history of medieval England.

Musson, Anthony, 'Men of Law and Professional Identity in Late Medieval England', in Travis R. Baker, ed., *Law and Society in Later Medieval England and Ireland* (Abingdon: Routledge, 2017), pp. 225–53. Examines the shared ethos of a broadly-defined legal profession.

Sobecki, Sebastian, 'A Southwark Tale: Gower, the 1381 Poll Tax and Chaucer's *Canterbury Tales*', *Speculum*, 92 (2017), pp. 630–60. Attempts to revive the claim that Gower had a legal training.

Steiner, Emily, and Candace Barrington, eds, *The Letter of the Law: Legal Practice and Literary Production in Medieval England* (Ithaca: Cornell U. P., 2002). Includes a number of studies of the intersection of law and literature in medieval England; the chapter by Andrew Galloway is particularly relevant.

Van Dijk, Conrad, *John Gower and the Limits of the Law* (Cambridge: D. S. Brewer, 2013). An important work which stresses the legal and political context of Gower's poetry even though it does not see Gower as himself being a lawyer.

Chapter 7. The Papacy, Secular Clergy and Lollardy

Brown, Andrew, *Church and Society in England, 1000–1500* (Basingstoke: Palgrave Macmillan, 2003). A comprehensive exploration of religious practice in medieval England.

Heath, Peter, *Church and Realm 1272–1461* (London: Fontana Press, 1988). Surveys relations between the Church and the state.

Holmes, George, *The Good Parliament* (Oxford: Clarendon Press, 1975). Gives a detailed account of the events of the 1370s.

Swanson, Robert N., *Church and Society in Late Medieval England* (Oxford: Basil Blackwell, 1989). Reliable and wide-ranging, still the best overview of the institutions of the medieval English Church.

Whalen, Brett E., *The Medieval Papacy* (Basingstoke: Palgrave Macmillan, 2014). An up-to-date discussion of the development of the papacy.

Chapter 8. Monastic Life

Harvey, Barbara F., *Living and Dying in Medieval England, 1100–1540: The Monastic Experience* (Oxford: Clarendon Press, 1993). An in-depth analysis of the evidence for everyday monastic life in Westminster Abbey.

Hines, John, Nathalie Cohen and Simon Roffey, '*Iohannes Gower, Armiger, Poeta*: Records and Memorials of his Life and Death', in Siân Echard, ed., *A Companion to Gower* (Cambridge: D. S. Brewer, 2004), pp. 23–41. A valuable survey of the records for Gower's life and his preparations for death, on which see also Martha Carlin's chapter above.

Irvin, Matthew, 'Genius and Sensual Reading in the *Vox Clamantis*', in Elizabeth Dutton, with John Hines and Robert F. Yeager, eds, *John Gower, Trilingual Poet. Language, Translation and Tradition* (Cambridge: D. S. Brewer, 2010), pp. 196–205. Analyses the role of Genius in the *Vox Clamantis*, in which he appears as a confessor, visitor and teacher for nuns.

Knowles, Dom David, *The Religious Orders in England* (three volumes; Cambridge: Cambridge University Press, 1950–59). A classic treatment of English medieval monasticism.

Pearsall, Derek, '"If Heaven be on this Earth, it is in Cloister or in School": The Monastic Ideal in Later Medieval English Literature', in Rosemary Horrox and

Sarah Rees Jones, eds, *Pragmatic Utopias: Ideals and Communities, 1200–1630* (Cambridge: Cambridge University Press, 2001), pp. 11–25. Furnishes a useful literary context for Gower's depiction of the monastic life.

Yeager, Robert F., 'Gower's French Audience: the *Mirour de l'Omme*', *Chaucer Review*, 41/2 (2006), pp. 111–37. A thought-provoking discussion of the possible circumstances surrounding the composition of Gower's *Mirour*.

Chapter 9. The Friars

Burr, David, *The Spiritual Franciscans. From Protest to Persecution in the Century After St Francis* (University Park: Pennsylvania State University Press, 2001). Traces the arguments of the purists in the Franciscan Order up to the time of their suppression.

Dufeil, Michel-Marie, *Guillaume de Saint-Amour et la polémique universitaire parisienne, 1250–1259* (Paris: Éditions A. et J. Picard, 1972). Examines the emergence of fundamental criticism against the mendicant orders in the thirteenth century.

Erickson, Carolly, 'The Fourteenth-Century Franciscans and Their Critics', *Franciscan Studies* 35 (1975), pp. 107–35, 36 (1976), pp 108–47. Investigates the reception of thirteenth-century criticism of the mendicants in the time of the Avignon papacy.

Glorieux, Palémon, 'Prélats français contre religieux mendiants. Autour de la bulle "Ad fructus uberes" (1281–1290)', *Revue d'histoire de l'église de France* 11 (1925), pp. 309–31, 471–95. A study of some French prelates' responses to new papal privileges for the mendicant orders.

Roth, Francis, *The English Austin Friars 1249–1538* (two volumes) (Cassiciacum 4) (New York: Augustinian Historical Institute, 1961–66). The standard history of the order's medieval English province.

Szittya, Penn, *The Antifraternal Tradition in Medieval Literature* (Princeton: Princeton University Press, 1986). Distinguishes between criticism of the mendicants coming from circles within the Church and from secular authors.

Chapter 10. Women and Power

'Beyond Women and Power: Looking Backward and Moving Forward', *Medieval Feminist Forum*, 51/2 (2015). An important special edition of the journal which explores women's political activities and discusses the historiography of this topic.

Bullón-Fernandez, Maria, 'Gower and Gender', in Ana Sáez-Hidalgo, Brian Gastle, and Robert F. Yeager, eds, *The Routledge Research Companion to John Gower* (London: Routledge, 2017), pp. 21–36. The most recent survey of scholarship examining gender in Gower's works.

Coleman, Joyce, 'Philippa of Lancaster, Queen of Portugal – and Patron of the Gower Translations?', in María Bullón-Fernández, ed., *England and Iberia in the Middle Ages, 12th–15th Century: Cultural, Literary, and Political Changes* (New York: Palgrave Macmillan, 2007), pp. 135–65. Discusses the possibility that

Philippa commissioned translations of *Confessio Amantis* into Portuguese and Castilian.

Laynesmith, Joanna L., *The Last Medieval Queens: English Queenship 1445–1503* (Oxford: Oxford University Press, 2004). A detailed discussion of the roles and responsibilities of English queens.

Meale, Carol M., '"...alle the bokes that I haue of latyn, englisch, and frensch": Laywomen and their Books in Late Medieval England', in Carol M. Meale, ed., *Women and Literature in Britain, 1150–1500* (Cambridge: Cambridge University Press, 1993), pp. 128–58. A very useful survey of the range of texts owned by medieval English women.

Watt, Diane, 'Gender and Sexuality in *Confessio Amantis*', in Siân Echard, ed., *A Companion to Gower* (Cambridge: D. S. Brewer, 2004), pp. 197–213. A nuanced discussion of the representation and function of gender and sexuality as it pertains both to female and male characters.

Chapter 11. Masculinity

Davis, Isabel, *Writing Masculinity in the Later Middle Ages* (Cambridge: Cambridge University Press, 2007). A revealing set of studies of masculinity in a number of Ricardian writers, including Gower.

Davis, Isabel, 'Calling: Langland, Gower, and Chaucer on Saint Paul', *Studies in the Age of Chaucer*, 34 (2012), pp. 53–94. Useful for the question of voice, especially in the *Vox Clamantis*.

Fletcher, Christopher, *Richard II: Manhood, Youth and Politics, 1377–99* (Oxford: Oxford University Press, 2008). Uses an analysis of contemporary language and theory of manhood to propose a new interpretation of the reign of Richard II.

Fletcher, Christopher, '"Sire, uns hom sui": Transgression et inversion par rapport à quelle(s) norme(s) dans l'histoire des masculinités médiévales?', *Micrologus' Library*, 78 (2017), pp. 23–50. Places late medieval ideas of manhood in the context of their Latinate roots, their long-term development and their transfer into the French vernacular in the twelfth and early thirteenth centuries.

Lewis, Katherine, *Kingship and Masculinity in Late Medieval England* (London: Routledge, 2013). A pioneering study of the role of masculinity in fifteenth-century kingship.

Chapter 12. Political Theory

Burns, James H., ed., *The Cambridge History of Political Thought, c.350–c.1450* (Cambridge: Cambridge University Press, 1988). Still a very useful survey of medieval political thought.

Giancarlo, Matthew, *Parliament and Literature in Late Medieval England* (Cambridge: Cambridge University Press, 2007). Stresses the ambivalence of Gower's political outlook.

Irvin, Matthew W., *The Poetic Voices of John Gower: Politics and Personae in the Confessio Amantis* (Cambridge: D. S. Brewer, 2014). An important recent study.

Minnis, Alastair, ed., *Gower's Confessio Amantis: Responses and Reassessments* (Cambridge: D. S. Brewer, 1983). The chapters by Minnis and Porter place Gower's political views in the wider context of his ethical and cosmographical outlook.

Rigby, Stephen H., *Wisdom and Chivalry: Chaucer's Knight's Tale and Medieval Political Theory* (Leiden: Brill, 2009). Discusses the ethical and political theory of Giles of Rome, one of the key sources for Gower's views.

Simpson, James, *Sciences and the Self in Medieval Poetry: Alan of Lille's Anticlaudianus and John Gower's Confessio Amantis* (Cambridge: Cambridge University Press, 1995). Provides an alternative interpretation of Gower's views of kingship to that offered here.

Chapter 13. Gower, Richard II and Henry IV

Bennett, Michael, *Richard II and the Revolution of 1399* (Stroud: Sutton, 1999). A closely contextualised account of Richard II, the vicissitudes of his reign, and the revolution of 1399.

Carlson, David, *John Gower: Power and Propaganda in Fourteenth-Century England* (Cambridge: D. S. Brewer, 2012). Claims that Gower's *Tripartite Chronicle* is based on the official record of the deposition of Richard II.

Fisher, John H., *John Gower: Moral Philosopher and Friend of Chaucer* (London: Methuen, 1965). Full of insight, dated but still indispensable.

Given-Wilson, Chris, *Henry IV* (New Haven: Yale University Press, 2016). A thorough and engaging account of Henry IV and his reign.

Harriss, Gerald, *Shaping the Nation. England 1360–1461* (Oxford: Clarendon, 2005), ch. 12. A crisp and authoritative account of politics c. 1360–1413.

Saul, Nigel, *Richard II* (New Haven: Yale University Press, 1997). A comprehensive history of Richard II and his reign.

Chapter 14. Natural Sciences

Carey, Hilary M., *Courting Disaster: Astrology at the English Court and University in the Later Middle Ages* (Basingstoke: Macmillan, 1992). A nuanced survey of the cultural importance of the astral sciences.

Fox, George G., *The Mediaeval Sciences in the Works of John Gower*, Princeton Studies in English 6 (Princeton: Princeton University Press, 1931). A thorough survey of Gower's scientific sources. May be usefully supplemented with later treatments by Mainzer and Hamilton cited in the notes to this chapter.

Juste, David, *Les Alchandreana primitifs: étude sur les plus anciens traites astrologiques latins d'origine Arabe (Xe siècle)* (Leiden: Brill, 2007). Scholarly edition of an important source of Gower's scientific knowledge, tracing its roots back into tenth-century astrology.

North, J. D., *Chaucer's Universe* (Oxford: Clarendon, 1988). Not only an exhaustive survey of astronomical references and influences in Chaucer's work, it is also an outstanding introduction to medieval sciences and instruments.

Page, Sophie, *Magic in the Cloister: Pious Motives, Illicit Interests, and Occult Approaches to the Medieval Universe* (University Park: Pennsylvania State University Press, 2013). Traces the contested boundaries and practices of astrology, astronomy and magic.

Porter, Elizabeth, 'Gower's Ethical Microcosm and Political Macrocosm', in Alastair J. Minnis, ed., *Gower's Confessio Amantis: Responses and Reassessments* (Cambridge: D. S. Brewer, 1983), pp. 135–62. Shows the importance of the natural sciences to an education for ethical kingship.

INDEX

Abbot, John 6
Abū Ma'shar 509, 516, 517 n.95
Adelard of Bath 517 n.95
Ad fructus uberes 300
admiralty, court of 229
Agincourt, battle of 76, 149, 150
Agnes, Saint 330 n.27
Albert of Bavaria, count of Holland and Zeeland 374
Albertanus of Brescia 373
Albertus Magnus 495
Albinus, in *Confessio Amantis* 366–7
Albornoz, Cardinal 263
'Albumazar' *see* Abū Ma'shar
Alcabitius 516 n.91, 517
Alceste, in *Confessio Amantis* 337
Alchandreus (Alchandrus) 503–6, 509–10, 512–16, 518 n.103
Alchandrinus *see* Alchandreus
Alcione, in *Confessio Amantis* 337
Aldington, Kent 4, 8, 9, 15, 27–9, 32, 33, 35–6, 37 n.41, 40–1, 44, 46, 52, 54, 57, 59, 62–3, 67–71, 425–6, 465 n.179, 479
Aldington Cobham (East Court), Kent 27
Aldington Septvans (West Court), Kent 27
Alexander IV, Pope 298, 317, 318
Alexander of Hales 295
Alexander the Great 130, 153, 335, 343, 359, 371, 387–9, 399–400, 407, 418, 431, 481, 498, 504, 512–13
Al-Kindi 503
Alliterative Morte Arthure 148 n.24
Amans, in *Confessio Amantis* 99 n.272, 130, 160, 161, 340, 353, 361, 363, 364, 368, 373, 407–8, 449, 451, 496
Anne of Bohemia, first wife of Richard II 128, 433, 435, 439, 461–3
Anstis, John 99, 454
Anthony, Saint 283
Antichrist 258, 262, 299, 310
antichristi 298–9
anticlericalism 244, 258, 264, 266, 268
  see also friars, new anticlericalism, nuns, papacy, regular clergy, secular clergy

antifeminism 323, 327, 328, 331, 335–8
antifraternalism *see* friars
Apollonius of Tyre, in *Confessio Amantis* *see* Gower, John, works of, 'Tale of Apollonius'
Apostle Friars 300
apprentices of law 215, 217–8, 220, 221, 223 n.54
Aquinas, Thomas 158, 401 402, 412, 495–7
Aquitaine 461
Arion, in *Confessio Amantis* 448, 452
Aristotle (and Aristotelianism) 130, 228, 343, 367, 369, 382, 383, 387, 391, 394, 400, 403, 421–2, 450 n.112, 494 n.12, 498, 512
'Articles of Deposition', of Richard II 397, 415, 442, 443 468–9, 474, 476, 486
  see also Record and Process
artisans 62, 126, 171–2, 194, 195, 198, 201, 206
Arundel, earls of *see* Fitzalan
Arundel, Thomas, bishop of Ely, archbishop of York, archbishop of Canterbury 20, 23–4, 90, 109, 115, 117, 119, 137, 243, 245, 248, 250–1, 265, 409, 418, 426 n.6, 436, 442, 446 n.97, 464–7, 468, 471, 477, 478, 479, 483 n.247, 485 n.254, 488
  see also Gower, John, works of, *Epistola*, to Archbishop Arundel
Ashburnham, Sussex 70
Ashburnham, John 70
Ashburnham (Asshebournham), Roger de 8, 10, 11, 35
Ashebourne, Roger de *see* Asshebournham, Roger de
Ashford, Kent 51, 61
Askewythe, John 77
Asshebournhame (Assheborhnam) Roger de *see* Ashburnham, Roger de
Aston, Herefordshire 254
astrology 494–7, 506, 509, 513, 518, 521, 523, 524
astronomy 449, 491–525

INDEX

see also astrology; scientific instruments; stars; zodiac
Athens xx, 393
Aubrey, John 92, 105, 107, 108
Augustine of Hippo 158, 293, 309, 386, 387, 387 n.16, 389, 390, 496 n.17
Augustinian canons 125, 271–4
see also Southwark, St Mary Overy
Aumerle, duke of see Edward of York
Austin (Augustinian) friars 274, 292, 300, 307, 309, 318
Avignon 156, 259, 262–3, 304–6, 427 n.10
see also Great Schism, papacy
Ayenbite of Inwyt 520–1
Ayscough, William 224

Bache, Alexander 318
Bagot, Sir William 475
Bale, John 84, 91, 95, 97, 98
Balsham, Cambridgeshire 72
Barbour, John 11, 12, 43
Barking Abbey 278 n.28, 279
Bartolus of Sassoferrato 391
Basset, Ralph, Lord 438, 450 n.114
Bearsted, Kent 5
Beauchamp, Sir John, Lord Kidderminster 440, 445
Beauchamp, Thomas, earl of Warwick 137, 376, 377, 406, 418, 437, 438, 440, 442, 444, 446, 447, 455, 456 n.140, 464–6, 468–70, 472, 474, 478, 479, 484, 485
Beauchamp, William de 13, 37 n.44
Beaufort family 99 n.274, 346
Beaufort, Joan 332, 333 n.40
Beaufort, John, marquis of Dorset 465 n.177
Beaufort, Margaret 334, 345, 350
Bedfordshire 11
Bel, Jean le 147
Belknap, Robert 235
bellicose clergy, see warlike clergy
Benedictine order and rule 272, 273 n.15, 285, 288, 509, 521
Benedictum 504–7, 509–10, 512–16, 519, 522 n.121
beneficed clergy 248, 251–3, 257, 266
Benyngton, Simon de 6, 32, 45, 111
Berkeley see Thomas, Lord Berkeley
Bermondsey, Surrey
abbey 38, 470
church of St Mary Magdalen by 86, 87 n.230

Bernard of Clairvaux 152
Berthelette, Thomas 20, 88, 91, 92, 96, 98, 103 n.281, 108
Beverley, Yorkshire 185
Bexley, Kent 71
Bilsington, Kent 14, 53
Bilsington Priory 235
Bisham Priory 272
bishops 82, 248–51, 253, 257, 258, 263–4, 266, 268, 287, 301, 305, 317, 439 n.74, 474
Black Death, effects of 44, 143–7, 172, 173–6, 189, 198–200, 203, 237
Blackfriars Council (1382) 266
Blake, Peter 18
Blakelake, Thomas 13, 38
Blanche, daughter of Henry IV 19
Blosme, William 72
Bobbing, Kent 30, 74, 426
Boccaccio, Giovanni 259, 294 n.11, 345–6, 401
Bochier, Roger 11, 12, 43
Bockyng, Robert de 11
Boethius 388 n.23
Bohun, de, family 99, 317, 454, 455 n.136, 459, 488
Bohun, Eleanor de 345 n.101, 480
Bohun, Humphrey de, earl of Hereford and Essex 37
Bohun, Mary de 75, 99, 454 n.131, 455
Bolingbroke, Henry see Henry of Lancaster
Bologna 26
Bonaventure of Bagnoregio 298, 302–3, 317
Bonet, Honoré 156
Boniface VIII, Pope 257, 258–60, 262, 300–1, 358
Book of the Knight of the Tower 345
Bouland (de Boulande, Bowland, Bowlond), John 11, 33, 37, 64–5
Boulogne 476
Bourbon, duke of 76
Bouvet, Honoré see Bonet, Honoré
Boxley Abbey 509
Bozon, Nicholas 145 n.15
Brabourne, Kent 4, 25–6, 32, 45, 78 n.197, 96, 100
'Bracton' (*De Legibus et Consuetudinibus Angliae*) 233, 411–12, 420
Braose, Thomas de, fourth baron Braose 100 n.280

INDEX

Brembre, Nicholas 206–7, 437, 439, 440, 456
Brenchesle (Brynchele), John 66
Brétigny, treaty of 125, 154
Bridgnorth, Shropshire 72
   castle of 445
Brinton, Thomas, bishop of Rochester 156, 251, 427, 431
Bristol 471
   castle of 471
Brokhell, Joan *see* Pympe, Joan
Brokhell, Thomas de (Brockhill, Brockhull, Brokhill, Brokhull) 7, 8, 9, 10, 15, 35, 36–7, 62, 67, 68, 70, 71, 109, 426, 429 n.24, 479
Bromesford, Isabel 11
Bromesford (Brounesford?), William 11, 15
Bromyard, John 145 n.15, 156
Brounesford, William *see* Bromesford
Bruges, Treaty of 260
Bruni, Leonardo 147
Brut, Walter 331
Brynchele, John *see* Brenchesle, John
Buckingham, earl of, *see* Thomas of Woodstock; Humphrey
Buckingham, John, bishop of Lincoln 249
Burbache, Thomas *see* Burbage, Thomas
Burbage (Burbache), Thomas 14, 15, 48, 53, 54
Burford, Oxfordshire 72
   hospital of St John 77, 253
Burgh, John 10
Burley, Simon 423, 435, 439, 440, 444, 445, 446 n.96, 456, 466 n.182
Burniston, Yorkshire 18
Burton, John (de), various men of this name 14, 20, 21, 74, 77–9, 90, 117, 119, 223
Burton, William 10
Bury, Adam de 57, 112–13
Bury St Edmunds, Suffolk 185
   abbey of 273 n.15
Buttes, John atte 16, 17, 43, 49, 55
Buxhull, Thomas *see* Godyn

Caesar, Julius 232, 261, 362, 377
Calais 206, 377, 462 n.158, 464–5, 469, 470 n.194, 472, 476, 482
Cambridge 185
Cambridgeshire 184, 186
Canace *see* Gower, John, works of, 'Tale of Canace'
Canterbury, Kent 4, 5, 14, 27, 29, 45, 49, 51, 53, 56, 61, 62, 63, 64, 66, 71, 185, 225, 237, 426 n.3, 428, 431 n.32, 465, 474, 481
   Cathedral 459, 460
   Christ Church Priory 70
   friaries in 319
   St Augustine's Abbey 521
Canynges, William 19, 61
Capgrave, John 454 n.133
Carlisle, diocese of 64
Carmelite friars 292, 300, 303, 309, 316, 318
Carthusian order 266, 288
Castile 260, 332, 447
   see also Catherine; Enrique III; Gower, John, works of, *Confessio Amantis*, Castilian version; Isabel I; Juan II
Cataline Revolt 232
Catherine, daughter of John of Gaunt, queen of Castile 136, 332, 346, 348
Catherine de Valois, wife of Henry V 349
Catherton, Thomas de 12, 38
Caudre, Thomas 18, 60, 82, 83
Cauntelo, John 11
Caxton, William 99, 328 n.23, 337–8, 345
Celestine V, Pope 256, 260, 358
Cephalus, in *Confessio Amantis* 499
Chancery, royal, 14, 35, 54, 72, 77–8, 222–3, 225, 228–30, 248
Charles V, king of France 153
Charles VI, king of France 338 n.64
Charles of Anjou 498
Charles of Blois 69
Charny, Geoffroi de 154, 159, 165 n.92
Chaucer, Geoffrey xx–xxi, 10–11, 14, 23, 46, 54, 61–2, 64, 66, 109, 134, 135, 142, 145 n.15, 156, 161, 164, 180, 181, 186, 194, 214, 215, 219, 221, 222, 224, 225, 226, 229, 245, 256, 273, 274, 281, 288, 292–4, 302 n.41, 310, 327, 365, 373, 388, 404, 424, 437, 448, 451, 453, 455, 493, 496 n.19, 498, 499, 515, 517 n.99, 524
Chaumbre, Reginald atte 210
Chelsea, Middlesex 71
Cheshire 438, 462 n.158, 464 n.171, 467 n.183, 474
Chester 477, 479 n.234
Chevereston (Chyuereston), Sir John 37 n.45
Chichester, Sussex 253
chivalry 141–65

539

see also Court of Chivalry; knights and knighthood
Chronicque de la Traison et Mort de Richard Deux, Roy Dengleterre 414, 478
Chyuereston, Hugh de 37 n.45
Chyuereston, Sir John *see* Chevereston
Cicero 232, 387, 401, 403
Clare family 317
Clay, Edward de 11
Clement V, Pope 263, 303, 304
Clement VI, Pope 259 n.59, 305
Clement VII, Pope 124, 127, 262, 263
Clerc, Robert 11
clergy *see* regular clergy; secular clergy
Clericis Laicos 259
Clerk (Clerkes), Walter 19, 39, 44, 51
Clerkenwell Priory 183
Clider, Walter 12
Clopton, Katharine de 11, 36, 67 n.138, 69, 70, 71
Clopton, Thomas de 11, 36, 67 n.138, 69, 70, 71
Cobham family, of Sterborough 27, 30 *see also* Cobham, Reginald, second Lord Cobham of Sterborough
Cobham, Agnes 29, 30
Cobham, John, second Lord Cobham 29
Cobham (Cobeham; Kobham), John, third Lord Cobham 7, 8, 9, 10, 11, 12, 30, 35, 36 n.36, 38, 43, 44, 62, 66–8, 80, 105, 109, 229, 418, 426–9, 430, 431–4, 438, 439, 442–5, 446 n.97, 455, 462, 464, 465–8, 471, 474, 479, 482, 483, 484
Cobham (*née* Luttrell), Margaret 38, 67
Cobham, Ralph de 10
Cobham, Reginald, first Lord Cobham 30
Cobham, Reginald, second Lord Cobham of Sterborough 10, 100
Cobham College, Kent 289
Cobeham, Sir John *see* Cobham, John, third Lord Cobham
Coggeshall, Essex 73
Collingbourne, Henry, prior of St Mary Overy 57, 112 n.299
common clamour *see* common voice
common good and common profit 160, 168, 170, 182, 188, 190, 193, 196–8, 204–6, 209, 229, 236, 297, 313, 387–91, 394, 400, 420, 423
common voice 163 n.85, 195, 230, 406–7, 430
see also vox populi

Company of the Star 154
Concanen, Matthew 92–4
Concordia see Maidstone, Richard
Constance, in *Confessio Amantis see* Gower, John, works of, 'Tale of Constance'
Constantine, Emperor *see* Donation of Constantine; Gower, John, works of, 'Tale of Constantine and Sylvester'
Conwy 477
Cook, John 18, 39, 44
Cook (Cookes), Walter 12, 36, 46, 71
Cook, William 18, 39, 44
Cookes, Walter, *see* Cook, Walter
Cornewaille, William 7
Cornwall, duchy of 235
Courtenay, Elizabeth *see* Luttrell, Dame Elizabeth
Courtenay, Hugh, tenth earl of Devon 37
Courtenay, Margaret *see* Cobham, Margaret
Courtenay, William, bishop of Hereford, bishop of London, and archbishop of Canterbury 38, 250, 252, 429, 433, 434, 438
Court of Chivalry 67, 151, 223, 229, 449
Coventry Charterhouse 288
Cranewelle, John 19, 61
Crécy, battle of 150, 153
Creton, Jean 477, 478
Creusa, in *Confessio Amantis* 336
Crundale, Kent 19, 51, 59, 61
crusades 55, 161–2, 164, 453, 456, 461
see also Despenser's Crusade
Crutched Friars *see* London, places in
Cueta 136
Cupid, in *Confessio Amantis* 130, 347, 358

Dancastre, Richard 16, 55–6
Dane, William 6
Dante Alighieri 259, 518
Dartford, Kent 30 n.19, 49, 56, 225 n.63, 226
David (in Old Testament) 324
Debenham, Norfolk 38 n.45
Despenser, Henry, bishop of Norwich 263
see also Despenser's Crusade
Despenser, Lord Thomas, earl of Glocuester 464, 465 n.177
Despenser's Crusade 156, 161, 263
De Vita Monachorum 273, 280, 286–7
Devon, earl of 221, 456 n.140
see also Courtenay, Hugh

INDEX

The Dicts and Sayings of the Philosophers 337–8
Dido, in *Confessio Amantis* 332
Dinham, Sir John 100 n.280
Diogenes 498, 500
 see also Gower, John, works of, *Confessio Amantis*, 'Tale of Alexander and Diogenes'
Dionysius, in *Confessio Amantis* 389
Dives and Pauper 335–6
Dominic, Saint 295, 298, 314
Dominican friars 292, 293, 295–6, 298, 299–301, 303, 308 n.75, 309, 314, 315, 317–8
dominion, Wyclif's theory of 257, 419–20
Donation of Constantine 261, 265 284
Donne, William *see* Doune, William
Dorset, earl of 464
Dorset, marquis of, *see* Beaufort, John
Doune (Doun, de Doune, Donne), William 21, 74, 77, 90, 117, 119, 223, 253
Dover, Kent 49, 56
 castle of 14, 15, 48, 54, 59, 62, 109
Drake, John 18, 39 n.52, 73
Dugdale, Sir William 10, 26 n.8

Eardisley, Herefordshire 254
Easebourne Priory 278 n.28
East Anglia 54, 55, 59, 184, 252, 342, 425
East Court, Kent *see* Aldington Cobham
Easton, Adam 509
Edington, William, bishop of Winchester 249
Edmund 'Crouchback', son of Henry III 416, 461 n.155
Edmund of Langley, duke of York 444, 445 n.139, 461, 464 n.172, 472, 478, 483 n.248
Edward I 317, 340 n.75, 397, 416
Edward II 227, 317, 405, 408, 409, 411, 435, 456, 482
Edward III 29, 66, 69, 106, 107, 108, 122, 124, 125, 142, 145, 153, 154, 219 n.31, 248–9, 334, 340 n.75, 345 n.101, 399, 428, 429, 497
Edward IV 325, 333, 337, 339, 341–2, 344, 346
Edward V 337, 344
Edward of Langley/York, earl of Rutland, duke of Aumerle, duke of York 461, 463 n.168, 465, 475, 482, 483 n.248
Edward, the Black Prince, 340 n.75, 428

Edward the Confessor 460, 481
 see also 'Laws of Edward the Confessor'
Eleanor of Provence, wife of Henry III 317
Eltham, Kent 52, 53, 67, 436 n.58
Elyngton, William, various men of this name 17, 56, 72–3, 112, 115
Emery, William 12, 36, 71, 226, 237
Engelbert of Admont 401
Enrique III, of Castile 136, 346
episcopacy *see* bishops
Erik IX, of Denmark 75
Essex 5, 7, 8, 10, 28, 33, 41, 73, 75, 76, 184
Essex, William de 7
estates satire 126, 194, 196, 211, 244, 245, 246, 247–58, 262, 264, 266–7, 268, 275, 279, 280, 286, 287, 294, 301, 314, 352, 406
Etsi animarum 197–8
Eulogium Historiarum, continuator of 447
Everdon, Northamptonshire 77, 253
Exning, Suffolk 18

false apostles (and pseudo-apostles) 299, 309, 310
Favent, Thomas 467
Feltwell (South Hall), Norfolk 12–13, 14, 17, 18, 19, 21, 34, 37–40, 41, 42, 43, 44, 47, 52, 54, 55, 59, 65, 67, 73, 77 n.192, 84, 85, 89, 117, 119, 223
Feriby, Thomas de 16–17, 50, 56–7, 66, 68, 72, 111–15, 225 n.66, 462, 474
Ferrara 263
Fisshere, Denise 19, 39, 44, 51
Fisshere, William 19, 39, 44, 51
Fitzalan, Richard, earl of Arundel 137, 318, 376, 377, 406, 418, 429, 433, 434, 437–8, 440, 442–4, 446–7, 455, 462, 464–6, 468–70, 472, 474, 484, 485
Fitzalan, Thomas, earl of Arundel 19, 40, 479
FitzRalph, Richard, archbishop of Armagh 156, 293, 304–8, 312, 316, 317, 319
Flanders 156, 161, 263, 341
Flemings, in London 83, 183, 185–6
Flint 477
Flixton, prebend of 65
Florence 260, 263
Florent, in *Confessio Amantis see* Gower, John, works of, 'Tale of Florent'
Forester, Richard 10, 46, 64, 225
Forester, Thomas 17, 18, 39, 50, 73, 134
Fortescue, Sir John 224 n.57, 396

541

Fountains Abbey 273 n.15
Foxe, John 271
France 64, 67, 124, 137, 142, 147, 148, 153 n.44, 154–6, 158, 186, 260, 263, 293, 296, 300, 316, 393, 438 n.69, 447, 461, 462 n.158, 476, 481, 517 n.95
see also Hundred Years War
Francis, Saint 295, 298, 299, 300, 301, 302, 304, 312, 314, 315
Franciscan friars 292, 293, 295, 296, 297, 298, 301–3, 307, 308, 309, 312, 314, 315, 316, 317, 319
see also Franciscan Spirituals
Franciscan nuns 319
Franciscan Spirituals 301–3, 304, 307
Fratres de Poenitentia Jhesu Christi 300
Frederick II 409
Frederick of Aragon 259
French language 82–3, 85, 100, 103, 123–5, 189, 195, 222, 246
Frenche, John 18
Frenyngham, John 15
friars 89, 244, 267, 279, 291–320
see also individual orders
Friars of the Cross 319
Friars of the Sack *see* Fratres de Poenitentia Jhesu Christi
Froissart, Jean 159, 478 n.228

Galoun, William 7
game laws 146
Gandre, Thomas 18
Garnieri, Arnaud 260
Gay, John 17–18, 39, 50, 73
Genius, in *Confessio Amantis* 130, 142, 152, 157, 159–61, 279 n.31, 324, 340, 343, 347 n.112, 353, 357, 361–4, 367, 368, 371, 373, 374, 385, 386, 388, 390, 392–3, 395, 398, 399, 402, 403, 404, 407–10, 412, 416, 419, 449–51, 491, 492 n.3, 496, 498, 512
Genius, in *Vox Clamantis* 279 n.31
gentry 10, 26, 30, 42 n.60, 62, 109, 143–4, 146, 149, 178, 184, 189, 237, 289, 325 n.4, 341 n.76, 353, 381
Gerard of Borgo San Donnino 297
Gerard of Cremona 509
Gesta Henrici Quinti 148–9
Gesta Romanorum 404 n.87
Gest of Robyn Hode see Robin Hood
Ghent 263
Giles, Saint 283

Giles of Rome 250, 344, 345 n.101, 354, 355 n.14, 382–3, 392, 395, 396, 401, 403, 410, 420, 423
'Glanvill' (*Tractatus de Legibus et Consuetudinibus Regni Anglie*) 412
Glastonbury Abbey 235
Gloucester, Thomas, duke of *see* Thomas of Woodstock
Godfrey of Viterbo 280
Godyn, Thomas (*alias* Buxhull) 72
Good Parliament *see* parliament, of 1376
Gornay, Sir Matthew 38
Gough, Richard 23, 97, 98–9, 100 n.278, 103, 107
Gour, John, 219–20
Gour, Nicholas 219
Gower, Agnes *see* Groundolf, Agnes
Gower, Earl 90
Gower, Joan 7, 8, 11, 32, 34, 35, 36, 45, 46, 78 n.157
see also Neve; Spenythorn; Syward
Gower, John, life of:
associates of 61–79, 109, 425–9
see also entries for individual names
date of birth of 4, 29, 45
death of 20, 88, 108
Henry of Lancaster (Henry IV) and xxii–xxiii, 16, 19, 49, 55, 61, 96, 99, 107–8, 109, 123, 131–3, 136–8, 153, 163, 415–8, 424, 440, 444, 451, 452–60, 462, 468, 472, 473, 475–88
illness and blindness of 23–4, 121, 131, 436, 487
income of 40–4
Lancastrian poet? 96, 132–3, 136,415, 417, 446, 457, 468, 472, 480–1, 484–8
legal career? 23, 218–26
legal knowledge and terminology xxii, 29, 62, 218, 226–9
livery collar of 16, 49, 55–6, 61, 75, 91, 96–101, 108, 132, 163, 415, 454, 488
marriage of 19, 50, 60, 79–85, 109, 122
see also Groundolf, Agnes
moneylending by 42–4
places of residence 44–61
property dealings 26–9, 31–40, 56–9
see also Gower, John, life of, income
Richard II, meeting of Gower with 14, 48, 52–3, 130–1, 133, 435–6, 448, 453

testament of 20–1, 25, 40, 42, 51, 59, 60, 75, 78–9, 84, 85–90, 91, 95, 108, 109, 115–20, 122, 223, 226, 256, 265–6, 271 n.3, 319
tomb of 16, 22, 25, 26 n.8, 29, 30, 42, 84 n.223, 87, 90–109, 123 n.10, 132, 163, 271, 384, 454, 488
Gower, John, works of:
  Anglica Regina 463
  Carmen Super Multiplici Viciorum Pestilencia 121, 243, 265, 279 n.30, 285 n.56, 463
  Cinkante Balades 123, 132 n.40, 137, 159, 352–3
  Confessio Amantis, dating and versions of xxii–iii, 81, 108, 130–4, 136, 182, 374, 414, 434 n.49, 447–60, 462, 485, 487
    summary of 129–30
    see also Gower, John, themes in works of; names of individual characters; psychomachia
  Confessio Amantis, individual tales in:
    'Tale of Actaeon' 152
    'Tale of Albinus and Rosamund' 366–7
    'Tale of Alexander and Diogenes' 371
    'Tale of Alexander and the Pirate' 371
    'Tale of Apollonius' 134, 330, 400, 412–3
    'Tale of Boniface' 244, 245, 256, 260–1, 262, 268, 358
    'Tale of Canace and Machaire' 134, 332
    'Tale of Constance' 134, 332, 348
    'Tale of Constantine and Sylvester', 244, 245, 261
    'Tale of the False Bachelor' 152, 332, 402
    'Tale of Florent' 134, 159, 332, 336, 358, 365, 368
    'Tale of Horestes' 369–74, 376, 377
    'Tale of Iphis and Araxarathen' 332, 347
    'Tale of Lucius and the Statue' 513
    'Tale of Nebuchadnezzar' 366 n.47, 367–8, 377
    'Tale of Spertachus and Thameris' 347–8
    'Tale of Tereus' 333
    'Tale of the Three Questions' 329
    'Tale of the Trump of Death' 365–6
    'Tale of Wine, Women and Truth' 334, 336, 350
    see also names of individual characters
  Confessio Amantis
    Castilian version of 136, 332–3, 346
    Portuguese version of 136, 332–3, 523
  Cronica Tripertita 137–8, 162, 163, 248, 250, 318, 356, 357, 370, 375–8, 398, 406, 415–6, 418, 419, 426 n.6, 427, 440–7, 466–79, 481, 483, 486–7
  Cultor in Ecclesia 122
  De Lucis Scrutino 122, 243, 262
  Dicunt Scripture 89–90, 122
  Ecce Patet Tenus 123
  Epistola, to Archbishop Arundel 23, 137, 243, 248, 265, 426 n.6, 466
  Epistola ad regem 127–8, 137, 394, 414, 419, 430–6
  Est Amor 19, 23, 80, 85, 109, 122, 123
  H[enricus] Aquile Pullus 136–7, 481
  In Praise of Peace 137, 153, 155, 157–8, 387, 390, 398, 416, 417, 480–1, 486, 487
  Mirour de l'Omme
    date and context of 124–5, 127, 134, 182, 192, 193, 194, 201, 203, 207, 211, 235–6, 259–60, 262, 265–8, 272–3, 275, 284–5, 288, 289, 429 n.26
    summary of 123–4
    see also Gower, John, themes in works of; *Speculum Hominis*; *Speculum Meditantis*
  O Deus Immense 122, 463, 487
  O Recolende 136–7, 419 n.146, 483
  Presul Ouile Regis 20, 24, 121
  Quam conxere freta xxi
  Quia Unusquisque (Quia Vnusquisque) 97, 384, 462
  Quicquid Homo Scribat (In Fine) 23–4, 121
  Rex Celi Deus 136–7, 442, 480
  Speculum Hominis 97, 123 n.10
    see also Mirour de l'Omme
  Speculum Meditantis 97, 123 n.10
    see also Mirour de l'Omme
  Traitié selonc les auctors pour essampler les amantz marietz (Traitié pour essampler les amantz marietz) 80 n.207, 82–3, 122, 273
  Unanimes Esse Qui Secula 137

Visio Anglie 125, 126–7, 169, 171, 183–88, 406, 432
  see also Great Revolt of 1381
Vox Clamantis
  date, context and stages of composition of 126–9, 134, 137, 182, 187, 206, 207, 236, 262, 265–9, 273, 275, 284–5, 289, 356, 357, 375, 376 n.65, 417, 427, 429–36, 446, 484, 487
  summary of 125–6
  see also Gower, John, works of, *Epistola*, to Archbishop Arundel; *Epistola ad regem*; *Visio Anglie*; Gower, John, themes in works of
Gower, John, themes in works of: *see* anticlericalism; artisans; astronomy; Augustinian order; chivalry; common profit; common voice; crusades; estates satire; friars; gentry; Great Revolt of 1381; Great Schism; Henry of Lancaster; heresy; judges; just war; knights; kingship; law and lawyers; Lollardy; love; magic; masculinity; merchants; new anticlericalism; nobility; nuns; paganism; papacy; peasants and labourers; political theory; regular clergy; Richard II; retailers; royal officials; salvation; secular clergy; social mobility; three orders; trade; vices; virtues; warfare; women
Gower, John, other men of this name 6, 54, 219–20
Gower, Katherine 32
Gower, Nicholas *see* Gour, Nicholas
Gower, Sir Robert 4, 7, 8, 25–6, 30, 32, 34, 35, 45, 78 n.197, 96, 100, 425
Grace, illegitimate daughter of Edward IV 333 n.43
Gratwicke, John 27 n.11
Gratwicke, Richard 27 n.11
Gravesende (Grauesende), John 6–7, 10, 32, 33, 45
Gray, John *see* Gay
Gray, Sir Thomas 149, 159
Great Revolt of 1381 xx–xxi, 63, 121, 125–6, 129, 146, 147–8, 152, 162, 164, 167, 169, 171, 175, 182–90, 207, 208, 230, 234, 236, 274, 353, 356, 375, 406, 419, 426, 427, 432, 440, 451, 462
Great Schism, of papacy 121, 122, 124, 127, 129, 247, 262, 265, 461

Green, Sir Henry 471
Greene, Ralph 100 n.280
Gregory XI, Pope 260, 263
Gregory's Chronicle 339
Grimsby, Lincolnshire 476
Grosseteste, Robert, bishop of Lincoln 509, 510, 522 n.121
Groundolf, as a surname 83–4
  see also Grundolf
Groundolf, Agnes 19, 23, 25, 50, 60, 79–85, 87–9, 95, 108, 109, 110, 111–14, 116–17, 119, 122
Grundolf, as a surname 83–4
Grundolf, John 84
Guesclin, Bertrand du 153
Guildford, Surrey 16, 56
Guyenne, duchy of 447
Guzmán, Fernán Pérez de 346

Hall, John 470, 483
Harfleur 76
Harrietshaw, Kent 237
Harvard, John 94
Hastings, prebendary of 72
Hatfield, Thomas, bishop of Durham 263
Hautwysel (Hautwysell), Thomas 17, 57, 112–15
Hawkedon, Suffolk 11
  Thomas, parson of 11
Henry IV *see* Henry of Lancaster
Henry V 74, 76, 137, 149, 318, 343, 349, 481
Henry VI 325–6, 341, 343, 346, 349
Henry VII, king of England 334, 345
Henry VII, Holy Roman Emperor 314, 315–6
Henry of Grosmont, duke of Lancaster 455, 481
Henry of Lancaster (Henry Bolingbroke), earl of Derby, duke of Hereford, Henry IV
  pre-1386 75, 99
  1386–88 137, 438, 439, 440, 468, 472
  1388–97 xxiii, 16, 49, 55–6, 75, 96, 97, 108; 109, 131, 132–3, 161, 163, 415, 452–5, 457, 459, 460, 462
  see also Gower, John, life of, livery collar
  1397–99 68, 75, 133, 356, 417, 418, 429, 464 n.172, 465, 471, 472–3, 475, 477–9
  1399–1413 16, 19, 61, 68, 72, 74 75–6, 78, 91, 107–9, 123, 131, 136–7,

153, 162, 265, 318 n.99, 415, 416, 417, 424, 436, 442, 444, 446 n.98, 454 n.131, 473, 479–88
Henry, Prince of Wales *see* Henry V
Henry, John 11, 12, 43
Hercules, in *Confessio Amantis* 335, 350, 358
Here, Robert 64
Hereford, diocese of 254
Herefordshire 220, 223 n.54
heresy 121, 127 n.21, 207, 264–6, 331, 520
  see also Lollardy; Wyclif, John
Hertfordshire 75, 76, 184, 235
Hertilpole, John 73
Heylesdon, John 12, 43, 47
Higden, Ralph 251
Highclere, Hampshire 19, 50, 79
Hildegard of Bingen 315
Hilton, Walter 218
Historie of the Arrivall of Edward IV 342
Hoccleve, Thomas 77, 135, 159 n.66, 253
Hockwold–cum–Wilton, Norfolk *see* Wylton
Holcot, Robert 388
Holland, John, duke of Huntingdon 465 n.177
Holland, Thomas, duke of Surrey 465 n.177
Horestes, in *Confessio Amantis see* Gower, John, *Confessio Amantis*, 'Tale of Horestes'
Horsham, Sussex 100 n.280
Hosyer, John 66
Hull *see* Kingston-upon-Hull
Humbert of Romans 300
Humphrey, earl of Buckingham 343, 345 n.101, 479, 480
Hundred Years War 76, 153, 154–5, 156, 263, 278, 343–4, 427
  see also Agincourt, Crécy, Despenser's Crusade, France, Poitiers
Hungerford, Walter 148–9
Huntingdon, earl of 265
Huntyngdon, William de 11
Huntyngfeld, Agnes 11
Huntyngfeld, Henry 11
Huntyngfeld(e), Isabel de 11, 12, 14, 33, 37, 47, 48, 53
Huntyngfeld(e), Walter de, 11, 12, 14, 33, 37, 47, 48, 53
Hurst, Richard de 4, 27–9, 45, 51, 62, 63
Hurworth, County Durham 252–3

Ianthe, in *Confessio Amantis* 347
Ignea sagitta 303, 316
Inner Temple 222, 225
  see also inns of court
Innocent III, Pope 317
Innocent IV, Pope 296–8, 409
Innocent V, Pope 263
Innocent VI, Pope 263
inns of court 135, 224–5, 226
  see also Inner Temple; Middle Temple
In principio 516
Insurgent gentes 315
Iphis, in *Confessio Amantis see* Gower, John, works of, *Confessio Amantis*, 'Tale of Iphis and Araxarathen'
Ireland 151, 219, 220 n.34, 304–5, 306, 316, 461, 462 n.158, 477, 479
Isabeau of Bavaria, wife of Charles VI of France 338 n.64
Isabel, duchess of York 463 n.168
Isabel I, of Castile 332
Isabella, wife of Edward II 124, 154, 317
Isabella of France, second wife of Richard II 461
Isidore of Seville 420
Isle of Man 377, 464–5
Islingham, Kent 465 n.179
Italy 134, 304
Iwade, Kent 4, 6, 27, 29, 30, 33, 40, 41, 42, 45, 63, 64, 67, 70

Jacob ben Machir ibn Tibbon 509
Jacquetta of Luxembourg 333, 338, 341 n.76, 344, 346, 349, 350
Jason, in *Confessio Amantis* 336
Jean II, king of France 154
Jersey 68, 465
Joan of Kent, wife of Edward, the Black Prince 340 n.75, 428, 435
João I, king of Portugal 136, 333
John XXII, Pope 259 n.59, 264, 299 n.31, 303, 304, 307, 316
John, duke of Bedford 343, 349
John, king of Bohemia 314
John of Cuenca 136
John of Gaunt, duke of Lancaster 55, 131, 136, 147, 183, 235, 260, 332, 400–1, 429–30, 433, 435, 438, 447, 454 n.132, 455, 457, 459, 460, 461, 462 n.158, 463 n.168, 464 n.172, 472, 475, 476, 485
John of Paris 401
John of St Giles 295

INDEX

John of Sacrobosco 509
John of Salisbury 387 n.16, 392, 401, 412
John of Seville 509
Juan II, king of Castile 346
Justices, Statute of (1384) 234
just war 155–8, 390, 431
   see also violence
Juvénal, Jean (des Ursins) 415

Katherine, Saint 328–32
Kempe, Thomas 19, 61
Kent 4, 7, 8, 9, 10, 12, 13, 14, 15, 19, 25–6, 28, 29 n.18, 30, 32, 33, 35, 36, 37, 38, 39, 41, 43, 45, 47, 48, 51, 52, 54, 56, 59, 61, 63, 64, 67, 70, 71, 74, 77, 109, 183, 184, 226, 235, 237, 289, 425–9, 435, 436, 437, 438, 445 n.92, 464, 465, 474, 478, 479, 484, 520
Kent, earl of 464
Kentwell, Suffolk 7, 8, 9, 10, 11, 25, 32, 34, 35, 36, 41, 42, 57, 62, 67, 68, 69, 70, 71, 78 n.197
Kigdus, in *Confessio Amantis* 347
Kingskerswell, Devon 100 n.280
Kingsland, near Hackney, leper house 86 n.229
King's Langley, Hertfordshire 484
Kingston-upon-Hull, Yorkshire 16, 49, 54, 55
   Charterthouse 288
Kirkeby, John de 11
Kirton, William 20, 60
knighthood *see* knights
Knighton, Henry 147, 178
knights and knighthood 126, 237, 251, 283 n.50, 352, 363, 365, 366, 423, 435, 445 n.93, 480
Knightsbridge, leper house at? 86 n.229
Knolles, Sir Robert 149
Kobham, John *see* Cobham, John

labour legislation (and justices of) 146, 177–82, 186, 189–90, 199, 213, 220
Labourers, Ordinance and Statutes of *see* labour legislation
Lakyngheth (Lakynghethe), Edmund 13, 38, 84
Lambeth Palace 20, 38, 51, 90, 117, 119, 120, 466, 479
Langland, William 135, 142, 180–1, 194, 197 n.21, 209 n.88, 216 n.11, 231, 256, 273, 274, 280, 281, 282, 283–4, 288, 293, 302 n.41, 340, 399

Latini, Brunetto 232, 383, 391, 495 n.15, 498, 500, 506, 510, 513
law and lawyers 127, 195, 213–39, 352, 393, 394, 399
   see also inns of court; serjeants of law
'Laws of Edward the Confessor' 420 n.152
Legge, Joan 69
Legge, John 69
Leicester, prebend of 72
Leicester Abbey 272
Leland, John 84, 87, 91, 98, 107 n.289, 108
Leontius, in *Confessio Amantis* 389
Liber Hermetis de 15 stellis et de 15 lapidibus et de 15 herbis 519, 520 n.109, 521
Liber Proverbiorum 344
Lichfield, cathedral and diocese of 65, 250
Lincoln, bishop, cathedral and diocese of 252, 257, 264, 476
   see also Buckingham, John; Grosseteste, Robert
Lincolnshire 439 n.73
Little Chart, Kent 70
Livy 404
Llanthony Priory 75
Lollardy and Wycliffism 156, 181 n.77, 207, 244–5, 261, 262, 264–6, 278, 279 n.30, 282 n.47 285, 331
   see also heresy; Wyclif, John
Lombardy and Lombard merchants 10, 64, 263, 268, 367, 393
London, city of xxii, 6, 7, 8, 11, 12, 14, 16, 17, 18, 19, 23, 28, 30, 32, 33, 34, 35, 38, 39, 41, 43, 44, 45, 46 48, 49, 50, 51, 52, 53, 54, 55, 56, 57, 58, 59, 60, 61, 65, 66, 68 n.147, 70, 71, 72, 73, 75, 77, 78, 82, 84, 91, 111, 115, 135, 136, 147, 162, 180, 183, 184, 185, 192–212, 221, 225 n.63, 235, 256, 265, 272, 282, 288, 289, 304, 306–7, 317, 318, 319, 349, 430, 434, 436, 437, 438, 439, 440, 441, 444, 450 n.114, 463 n.167, 464, 465, 466–71, 474–9, 484, 485
   quarrel with Richard II 54–5, 133, 396, 456–7, 461, 485
London, places in:
   Aldgate 319
   Austin friary 307, 318
   Charterhouse 288, 462
   Cheap 203
   Cornhill 210
   Crutched friars 319

546

INDEX

Domus Conversorum 78
Elsing Spital, priory and hospital of 86, 116, 118
Fleet prison 54, 147
Fleet Street 472
Franciscan friary 319
Franciscan nunnery 319
Friars of the Cross 319
Guildhall 135, 221
Guildhall College 289
Holborn 446
Holborn, leper hospital 86 n.229
Lombard Street 203
London Bridge 30, 58, 59, 60 n.98, 74, 75 n.182
Mile End 185
Mile End, leper hospital 86 n.229
Queenhithe 235
St Anthony, hospital of 86, 116, 118
St Bartholomew's hospital, Smithfield 87
St Giles, leper hospital, Holborn 86 n.229
St Martin Ludgate, parish of 77
St Mary 'Bedlem' (Bethlehem), hospital of 86, 116, 118
St Mary Colechurch, parish of 5, 30, 32, 34, 45, 64
St Mary Somerset, parish of 78
St Mary Spital (St Mary Rounceval), hospital of 86, 87, 118
St Michael's College, Crooked Lane 289
St Paul's cathedral 38, 221, 306
St Thomas the Martyr of Acon, parish of 5, 6, 110, 111
Savoy Palace 147, 183, 185
Smithfield 87, 185
Tower Hill, 465
Tower of London 183, 438, 444
Tower ward 426, 446 n.97
Walbrook 203
see also Southwark; Westminster
Longchamps, Nigel de 257, 258, 280, 312, 405 n.90
Long Melford, Suffolk 7, 9, 32
see also Kentwell
Louens, Renaud de 373
Louis IX, king of France 295
Louis of Bavaria 263
love, romantic 80, 122–3, 130, 142, 152, 159, 160, 330, 335–6, 338, 339–42, 347, 350, 357, 361–2, 367–8, 369, 370, 371, 407, 408, 436, 449, 494, 499, 512, 521 n.114
Loveney (Loveneye), William 16, 21, 73, 90, 117, 119
Loveyne, Sir Nicholas 426, 427, 428
Lucius, king of Rome, in *Confessio Amantis* 393
Lucrece (Lucretia), in *Confessio Amantis* 337, 363, 400, 403–4
Luttrell, Sir Andrew 37
Luttrell (Luterell), Dame Elizabeth (*née* Courtenay) 13, 34, 37, 38, 40, 67, 77 n.192, 85
Luttrell, Sir Hugh 34, 40, 73, 85, 90
Lycurgus, in *Confessio Amantis* 389, 393
Lydgate, John 272, 274, 349 n.118
Lynn, Norfolk 16, 49, 54, 55, 228
Lyons, Council of (1274) 299, 316
Lyons, Richard 201–4

Macarius, Saint, in *Mirour de l'Omme* 283
Macaulay, George 23 n.2, 24, 29, 56 n.88, 57, 97 n.264, 99, 100, 103 n.281, 130, 131, 219 n.31, 228, 375 n.64, 426 n.3, 452, 453, 492, 517 n.99, 519, 520
macrocosm and microcosm, theory of 141, 421, 494, 512
Maghfeld, Gilbert 16, 17, 42, 49, 50, 54, 55
magic and magicians 336, 365, 491, 493, 497, 498, 518–24
Magna Carta 233, 397, 399, 449 n.106
Magna Unio 318
magnificence 141, 250, 422, 448
Maiden Bradley, Wiltshire, priory of 68, 462
Maidstone, Kent 4, 27 n.11, 425, 426 n.6
College 289
Maidstone, Richard 396, 457, 463 n.165
maintenance 227, 230
Makenade, William 15
Malvern Hills 231
'man', Gower's use of 356–9 364–5, 368
'manhood', Gower's use of 355–7, 359, 360–9, 376–8
Manny, Sir Walter 288
Mannyng, Robert 145 n.15
Maplescombe, Kent 5, 7, 28, 33, 41, 63
March, earl of *see* Mortimer, Edmund
Marck Castle, Picardy 70
Margaret of Anjou, wife of Henry VI 325–6, 341, 343–4, 348, 349
Margaret of France, wife of Edward I 317

～ de 509
33
₀
, John 100 n.280
of Padua 391
...am, Norfolk 83 n.219
..ry, Blessed Virgin 124, 125, 159 n.68, 266, 272, 398
masculinity xxii, 335, 343, 347, 348, 351–78
  see also 'man'; 'manhood'
Maxentius, Emperor 328
mean, virtuous 369, 421–2
Medea, in *Confessio Amantis* 336
Melcombe, Dorset 6
mendicant orders see friars
men of law see law and lawyers
merchants 62, 126, 170, 178, 191, 212, 222, 238, 254, 276, 352, 393
Merciless Parliament see parliament, of 1388
Merks, Thomas, bishop of Carlisle 414
Merlin 481
Merton Priory 509
Mézières, Philippe de 142, 161
Michael of Northgate 521, 523 n.124
Middlesex 75, 76
  archdeacon of 78–9
Middle Temple 225
  see also inns of court
Milan 260, 263
Mildenhall, Peter 456
Mildenhall, William 456
Milton, Kent 29, 45, 51, 62
misogyny see antifeminism
Modena 263
Mohun, Lady Philippa de 463 n.168
Mokkynge, John 20
monasticism see friars; nuns, regular clergy
money and prices 143, 193, 197–201, 203–4, 208–9, 211, 397
Montagu, John, earl of Salisbury 464, 465 n.177
Morgan, Aaron 92, 94
Morice, Thomas 224
Mortimer, Edmund, earl of March 78
Mortimer, Roger, earl of March (d. 1330) 220 n.34
Mortimer, Roger, earl of March (d. 1360) 220
Mortimer, Roger, earl of March (d. 1398) 461
Morton, Sir John 333 n.40

Moss, William 94
Moulton, Suffolk 12, 13, 14, 18, 21, 34, 37, 38, 39, 40, 41, 44, 47, 52, 54, 55, 59, 65, 67, 77 n.192, 84, 89, 117, 119, 223
Mowbray, Thomas, Earl Marshal, earl of Nottingham, duke of Norfolk 438, 440, 464, 465 468, 469, 472–3, 475–6, 482, 483
Mult est diableis curteis 257
Multon, see Moulton
Munday, Anthony 91, 92, 106, 108

Nebuchadnezzar, dream of 126, 468 n.188
  see also Gower, John, works of, *Confessio Amantis*, 'Tale of Nebuchadnezzar'
Neckham, Alexander 272, 273
Nectanabus, in *Confessio Amantis* 497, 498, 500, 510, 518, 519, 522, 524
Nene see Neve
Netter, Thomas 318
Neve, Joan (née Gower) 32
Neve, William 32
Neville, Alexander, archbishop of York 250, 251, 440
Neville, Cecily, duchess of York 325–6, 333, 344, 345
Neville, Ralph, Lord Neville of Raby, earl of Westmorland 251, 444 n.89
Neville, Richard, earl of Warwick 341
Neville's Cross, battle of 263
new anticlericalism 244–6, 266–8
Newcastle-on-Tyne, Northumberland 72
Neweton, Geoffrey de 10
Newington, Kent 7, 11, 12, 42, 43, 45, 46, 49, 56, 74
New Romney, Kent 228
Nicopolis, battle of 161
Nightingale, Joseph 94
Nimrod 387
Nine Worthies 153
nobility 10, 26 n.8, 62, 141–65, 171, 174, 184, 185, 187, 196 n.19, 234, 324–5 332, 333, 343, 352, 353, 357, 363, 365–6, 369, 371, 375, 376, 381, 406, 409, 423, 431, 465
Noreys, Thomas 12
Norfolk 17, 18, 34, 39 n.52, 40, 43, 83
Northampton, John 193, 206–12
Northamptonshire 17, 43, 115
North Crawley, Buckinghamshire 78
Northfolk, John 12

548

INDEX

Northumberland, earl of *see* Percy, Henry
Northwode, family 25, 26, 30, 60 n.101, 69
   Agnes de 5, 6, 29, 30, 32, 69, 110, 111
   see also Cobham, Agnes
   Eleanor de 75
   James 20, 60
   John de 5, 6, 7, 12, 30, 32, 34, 60 n.101, 63, 64 n.112, 75, 109, 110, 111
   Juliana de (*née* de Say) 63
   Robert de 69
   Roger de 4, 5, 6, 29, 30, 32, 45, 60 n.101, 63, 64 n.112, 71, 75, 110, 111
Northwode Schepeye, Kent 63
Norwich Castle 9, 11, 36
Norwich Cathedral Priory 509
Norwode, James *see* Northwode
Nostell Priory 273
Nottingham 437, 456, 464
   castle of 69
Nottingham, earl of *see* Mowbray, Thomas
Nova Statuta Angliae 408–9, 449 n.106
nuns 274, 276 n.24, 278–80, 285, 287, 289, 304, 319, 323, 352
   see also Franciscan nuns
Nutley Abbey 462

obedientiaries 276, 281, 286
Olivi, Peter 196, 303 n.46
Olyuer, William, *see* Olyver, William
Olyver, Agnes, *see* Wacche, Agnes
Olyver (Olyuer), William 10, 57, 113–4
Order of the Garter 151
Oresme, Nicholas 401
Orleans, duke of 76
Ospringe, Kent 49, 56
Over, Cambridgeshire 78
Overton, John 12
Ovid 130, 279, 388 n.23, 404
Oxford 225 n.63, 438, 441
Oxford, University of 304, 509

paganism 328, 372, 389
Page, John 7
papacy 156, 244, 258–64, 265, 266, 267, 268, 295–302, 305, 308, 313, 475
   see also Avignon; *Clericis laicos*; Great Schism; individual popes; papal courts; papal taxation; papal provisions; Rome; *Unam sanctam*
papal courts 259, 260, 261, 265
papal provisions 251–3, 259, 260, 261, 265, 268
   see also Provisors, Statute of
Papal States 260, 263
papal taxation 245, 259, 260, 261, 265, 267
Paris, University of 293, 295, 297, 298, 302, 303, 304, 312, 316
Parker, Alice 334
parliament 64, 67, 68–9, 128, 144, 172, 174, 178, 213, 215, 222, 223, 230, 235, 236, 238, 259, 267, 374, 382, 383, 413, 438, 456; of 1363: 64; of 1366: 6, 28–9, 62; of 1373: 260; of 1376: 64, 124, 193, 201–6, 207, 235, 260, 267, 334, 428; of 1379: 428, 432; of 1380: 63, 432 n.34; of 1382: 236; of 1383: 179, 186, 433; of 1384: 236, 433; of 1385: 429, 436; of 1386: 436, 437; of 1388 (Merciless Parliament): 179, 251, 356, 429, 439–40, 442, 446 n.96; of autumn 1388: 445; of 1393: 61; of 1394: 461; of 1395: 61; of January 1397: 463–4; of 1397–8: 65, 464–5, 467, 468 n.188, 469, 471 n.202, 475, 482; of 1399: 68, 162, 414, 416, 428, 429 n.24, 467, 470, 479–80, 482–3; of 1401: 75; of 1402: 319; of 1406: 68, 78; of 1407: 75; of 1413: 75; of 1414: 61; of 1416: 61
Pateshull, Peter 318
Pathorn, Thomas 12, 52, 66, 71, 72
Patrington, Stephen 318
Payn, Robert 136
Payne, John 56
peasants and labourers 125–6, 143–6, 163, 167–90, 194, 237, 497
Peasants' Revolt *see* Great Revolt of 1381
Pecche, John 201–4
Pecham, John 317
Peckham, James 5, 426, 427, 429 n.24, 438
Pembridge, Herefordshire 219–20
Penelope, wife of Ulysses, in *Confessio Amantis* 337, 341–2
Penthesilea, in *Confessio Amantis* 332
Percy, Henry, earl of Northumberland 78, 440, 443, 444, 477, 483 n.247, 485 n.254
Peronelle, in *Confessio Amantis* 337, 341–2
Perrers, Alice 122, 124, 334
Perseus, in *Confessio Amantis* 402, 417
Pharisees 299, 309

549

f France 124, 259, 260
...nerset Herald 25 n.8

...ter of Henry IV 75
Hainault, wife of Edward III
, 340 n.75
...ippa of Lancaster, daughter of John of Gaunt, queen of Portugal 136, 332–3
Philomena, in *Confessio Amantis* 332
Phyllis, in *Confessio Amantis* 332
Picardy 70, 75
Pierre, count of St Pol 341 n.76
Pizan, Christine de 157, 159, 331, 338, 344, 345, 346, 348, 404 n.87
Plays, John de 13
Pleshey, Essex 465 n.179, 466
Poitiers, battle of 150, 153
Poitiers, count of 296
Pole, Sir John de la 10
Pole, Sir Michael de la, earl of Suffolk 14, 435, 436, 440
'political' conception of kingship 396–401, 405–13, 424
political theory 342–50, 381–424 *see also* common profit; common voice; dominion; just war; magnificence; mean; paganism; 'regal' conception; 'political' conception; state; tyranny; warfare, violence; *vox populi*
poll taxes 147, 172, 186, 217, 255
Pontefract, Yorkshire 76
Portugal 136, 332–3
see also Gower, John, works of, *Confessio Amantis*, Portuguese version; João I; Philippa of Lancaster
Potyn, Nicholas 10
Pouilly, Jean de 316
Praemunire, Statute of (1353) 260
Premonstratensian order 296
Preston, Thomas de 8, 9, 10, 11, 35, 36 n.36, 52, 62, 66, 67, 68, 70–1, 72
prices *see* money and prices
prostitution 83, 196, 220, 330
see also Southwark, places in, Stews
Provisors, Statutes of (1351, 1380) 230, 260
see also papal provisions
pseudo-apostles *see* false apostles
psychomachia, *Confessio Amantis* as 407–8
Ptolemy 496 n.20, 499, 513, 516, 517–9, 521 n.119
Pyel, John 5, 43

Pympe, Joan (*née* Brokhell) 15 37 n.41
Pympe, William 15 37 n.41

queens and queenship 317, 325–6, 331–2, 334, 342 n.82, 343–9
see also individual queens
Quixley, Robert de 273

Radcot Bridge, battle of 356, 438, 439, 441, 443, 444
Radyngton (Raddington), Sir Baldwin 396, 456
Ravensere, Richard 8, 35, 42, 46
Ravenspur, Yorkshire 68, 476
Record and Process 375, 396, 410, 414, 415, 442, 443 n.84, 468, 480 n.238
see also 'Articles of Deposition'
rectors and vicars 251, 253–4, 256
Reed, Richard 7
'regal' conception of kingship 395–402, 405, 407–9, 411, 413–16, 423–4
regular clergy 126, 271–320
see also friars; individual orders; nuns; obedientiaries
Repyndon, William 12, 43
retail trade 170, 191–3, 195–8, 199, 201–3, 206, 208, 211–12
Reynolds, Walter, archbishop of Canterbury 405
Richard II, reign of:
1377–86 14, 52–3, 67, 74, 127–8, 131, 153, 158, 185, 208, 263, 318, 356, 394, 400–1, 411, 419, 427, 428, 429–36
marriage to Anne of Bohemia (1382) 128, 433, 435, 439, 461–3, 484
1386–88 14, 48 52–3, 67, 137, 251, 356, 397, 408, 411 n.113, 429, 436–47, 448, 450, 452, 484
1388–97 xxiii, 54, 55, 97, 132–3, 151, 318, 356, 371, 396, 429, 447–57, 460 n.154, 461–3, 485, 497
marriage to Isabella of France (1396) 461
1397–99 67, 76, 80, 97, 122, 137, 145, 162–3, 251, 356, 370, 374–77, 395–6, 406, 409 n.102, 417–9, 422, 429, 463–77, 485
deposition of (1399) 68, 121, 129, 131, 136, 137–8, 162, 356, 357, 370, 375, 382, 383, 386, 397–8, 401, 409–10, 414–21, 422, 424, 429, 442–3, 473, 477–80, 482, 486

550

INDEX

death of (1400) 20, 76, 138, 415
  see also entries for individual people; Gower, John, life of, meeting with Richard II; London, city of, quarrel with Richard II
Richard, duke of York 325
Rickhill, Sir William 465 n.179, 469
Riga, Peter 272, 280
Rivieres, Marie, wife of Earl Rivers 346
Robert III, king of Scotland 78
Robertsbrigge, Sussex 72
Robin Hood 149–50
Rochester, Kent 9, 36 n.33, 49, 56, 226, 465 n.179
  castle of 4 10, 15, 37 n.41
  diocese of 250, 426
Roiston, John 7
Roland of Cremona 295
Roman de la Rose 279, 293, 311, 388 nn23–4
Rome 124, 127 n.21, 215 n.5, 259–63, 265, 348, 393, 402, 403–4, 435, 475
  see also Great Schism; papacy
Rosamund, in *Confessio Amantis*, see Gower, John, works of, *Confessio Amantis*, 'Tale of Albinus and Rosamund'
Rosiphelee, in *Confessio Amantis* 332, 353 n.6
Rouclif, Guy de (Rouclyf, Rouclyff) 12, 13, 34, 38, 47, 77, 223, 252–3
Rouheved, John 7
Roussat, Richard 503, 508
rural society see peasants and labourers; Great Revolt of 1381
Rushok (Rushook), Thomas, bishop of Chichester 318, 440
Rutebeuf 293, 298, 304
Rutland, earl of see Edward of York

St Albans, Hertfordshire 185
  abbey of 185
  see also Walsingham, Thomas
St Amour, William of 294 295, 297, 298–9, 305, 307, 309, 310, 312, 313
Saintliger, Sir Arnald de 10
Salimbene di Adam 300
Salisbury, 433
  cathedral, 253
Salisbury, earl of see Montagu, John
Saltwood, Kent
salvation 80, 124, 126, 128, 136 n.55, 168, 243, 259, 260, 276, 278, 288, 416, 419

Samson 324, 335
Sandwich, Kent 6
Sandyforde (Sandeforde), John 19, 20, 60, 61
Sardanapalus (Sardanapaulus), in *Confessio Amantis* 362, 398
Saundres, Thomas 17, 57, 112, 114, 115
Savage
  Sir Arnald (d. 1375) 74
  Sir Arnald (d. 1410) 20, 21, 30, 63, 67, 73–5, 90, 109, 117, 119, 426–9, 434 n.48, 435, 438, 443, 444, 466, 474, 479, 486
  Eleanor de 74 see also Northwode, Eleanor de
  Joan de 74–5
Say, Sir Geoffrey de 63
Say, Juliana de, see Northwode, Juliana
Scarborough, Yorkshire 185
scholars, Gower's critique of 253–7
science 491–525
  see also astronomy
scientific instruments 498–501, 504, 506
Scot, Michael 503, 510, 511, 512, 513
Scot, William 11
Scotland, 53, 7, 78, 148, 251, 263, 435
Scrope, Richard, archbishop of York 487
Scrope, Sir Richard 433, 434, 438, 464
Scrope, Stephen 344, 345 n.103
Scrope, Sir William, earl of Wiltshire 465 n.177, 471
Scrope-Grosvenor controversy 151
Secretum secretorum 343, 344, 382, 383 n.8, 431, 449, 450, 495, 497 n.22, 500, 512, 516 n.92, 525
secular clergy 243–69
  see also beneficed clergy; bishops; rectors and vicars; scholars; unbeneficed clergy; warlike clergy
Seneca 373, 403 n.83
Septvans, Elizabeth de 62
  Joan 67
  William de (junior) 4, 5–6, 7, 27, 28, 29, 32, 33, 41, 43, 44, 45, 51, 52, 62–3, 64, 66, 67, 229, 425–6, 431 n.32
  William de (senior) de 4, 5–6, 7, 27, 43, 62
serjeants of law 215, 216, 217, 219, 221, 222, 224, 228, 231, 233, 234 n.109
Settle, William atte 210
Shareshull, William 235
Sheen, Surry 433, 436 n.58, 456

551

'ssex 27 n.11
shire 67, 79, 467, 475
., bishop of Bath and

, Norfolk 19, 39, 42, 44, 51
..ire 220
..y 259
Simco, John 103
Simonie, The 209 n.88, 253, 257, 258, 282 n.47
Sittingbourne, Kent 11, 12, 43, 46, 49, 56, 71, 74
social mobility 143–4, 146, 148, 169, 214, 229, 236–8, 281–2, 309
Socrates 337–8
Solas, John 20, 60–1, 68
Solomon 153, 163, 324, 387, 390
Song of Lewes 397, 410
soul, faculties of 407–8, 496
South Hall, Norfolk *see* Feltwell
Southwark, Surrey 16, 17, 19, 20, 23, 25, 26 n.8, 30, 38, 48–54, 56–61, 63, 64, 65, 66, 68, 74, 79–83, 85–88, 90–108, 115, 116–18, 125, 135, 163, 183, 186, 196, 218–19, 220, 225 n.66, 226, 229, 266, 271, 272–4, 288, 426, 462, 465, 470, 474, 488, 509
  places in:
  Cathedral 90, 93, 94
  see also Gower, John, life of, tomb; Southwark, priory of St Mary Overy; Southwark, St Saviour
  Chain Gate 58
  Chequer Alley 58
  Kent Street 86
  The Lock, leper house 86
  palace of bishop of Winchester 58, 59 n.96, 65, 229
  Pepper Alley 58
  St George, parish of 86, 116, 118
  St John the Baptist, chapel of, in priory of St Mary Overy/St Saviour's church/Southwark Cathedral 16, 25, 84, 86, 87, 88, 91–6, 116, 118, 266
  St Margaret, parish of 86, 90, 116, 118
  St Mary Magdalen, parish of 19, 50, 59, 60, 79, 80, 82, 86, 90, 116, 118
  St Mary Overy, priory of 16, 17, 18, 19, 20, 23, 26 n.8, 42, 47, 50, 51, 52, 56, 58, 59, 60, 65, 79, 81–2, 85–90, 90–3, 107, 112, 117, 118, 119, 125, 135, 219, 271, 272–4, 287, 289, 488, 509
  see also Collingbourne, Henry; Gower, John, life of, tomb; Southwark, Cathedral; Southwark, St John the Baptist; Southwark, St Mary Magdalene; Southwark, St Saviour
  St Olave, parish of 64, 74, 75, 83, 116, 118
  St Saviour, parish of 90, 92, 93–6
  St Thomas the Martyr, hospital of 86, 116, 118
  Stews, 83, 220
  Tooley Street 64, 74
  Winchester House, *see* Southwark, places in, palace of bishop
'Southwell' in 'Northamptonshire' *see* Feltwell
Sparta 389
Speculum astronomiae 495, 510 n.70
Speculum Stultorum see Longchamps, Nigel de
Spencer, Thomas 66
Spenythorn, Joan (*née* Gower) 8, 11, 35, 36, 46, 78 n.197
Spenythorn (Spynythorn), John 8, 11, 14, 35, 36, 46, 48, 77, 78 n.197
Spertachus, in *Confessio Amantis see* Gower, John, works of, *Confessio Amantis*, 'Tale of Spertachus and Thameris'
Spigurnell, Ralph 6
Spilsby, Lincolnshire 100 n.280
Sporle, Katherine 73
Spynythorn, John *see* Spenythorn, John
Stafford, Anne 345
Stafford, Edmund, bishop of Exeter 464
Stafford, Humphrey, duke of Buckingham 345 n.103, 459
Stalisfield, Kent 11, 33, 37, 41, 61, 64
Stapulgate (Staplegate), Edmund 14, 48, 53–4
stars, in astronomy 491, 493, 494, 496, 500, 501–25
state, origins and purpose of 386–90
Stodeye, John de 7
Stoffolde, John 19, 51, 61
Stone, Richard 30 n.19
Stow, John 26 n.8, 91, 92, 96, 98, 103 n.281, 105, 106 n.285, 107, 108
Strode, Ralph 134
Strype, John 91 n.243, 92, 106 n.286, 107
Sudbury, Suffolk 78

552

INDEX

Sudbury, Simon, bishop of London, archbishop of Canterbury 71, 250, 268, 427, 432
Suffolk, earl of *see* Pole, Michael de la
sumptuary legislation 145, 146 176, 199
Super cathedram 301, 305
Surrey 19, 20, 21, 50, 60, 61, 63, 66, 69, 72, 85, 112
Sussex 60, 63, 69, 70, 235, 439 n.73
Swine Priory 278 n.28, 279
Swynford, Katherine 463 n.168
Sybile, John 13, 38
Symme, William 7
Syward, Joan (*née* Gower) 7, 8, 32, 34, 35, 45, 46
Syward, Thomas 7, 8, 32, 34, 35 n.29, 45, 46

Taillour, John 6
Tanner, Simon 15, 48, 54
Thairyoor, John 7
Thais, in *Confessio Amantis* 330, 331, 332
Thameris, in *Confessio Amantis see* Gower, John, works of, *Confessio Amantis*, 'Tale of Spertachus and Thameris'
Thelacuse, in *Confessio Amantis* 347
Theorica planetarum 498, 509
Thetford Priory 278 n.28
The III Consideracions Right Necesserye to the Good Governaunce of a Prince 344 n.97
Thirning, William 233
Thomas, duke of Clarence 343
Thomas, earl of Lancaster 472
Thomas, Lord Berkeley 423
Thomas of Kent 500, 510
Thomas of Woodstock, earl of Buckingham, duke of Gloucester 56, 137, 376, 377, 406, 409, 418, 423, 429, 436–41, 442, 444, 446, 447, 449, 454–6, 458–62, 464–66, 468–70, 472, 474, 479, 480, 482–5, 488
Thompson, William 94–5, 101
Thoresby, John, archbishop of York 249
Thorpe, John 218
three orders, theory of 123, 126, 155, 168–9, 182, 283, 352, 353 n.7, 394–5
see also estates satire
Throwley, Kent 11, 33, 37, 41, 61, 64
Thurgarton, Lincolnshire 218
Thurnham, Kent 27, 29, 30, 37, 63
Tiler, Arthur 94
Tillingbourne, Kent 465 n.179

Topcliffe, William 426 n.6
Tornegold, John 7
Totum regit saeculum 257
Trace, John 12
Tracies, manor of, in Newington, Kent 74
Tractatus Enoch 519, 520, 521–2
trade 41 n.59, 171, 191–212
  see also merchants; retailers
Treasons, Statute of (1352) 226
Tresilian, Sir Robert 439, 440
Trevisa, John 284, 308, 383 n.8, 420
Tunstall, Kent 8, 35, 71
Tydde, John 12
Tye, John de 4
Tyler, Wat 162, 183
tyranny 348, 377, 382, 387, 389, 391, 392, 399–404, 409, 412, 415–21, 423–4
  see also Richard II, 1397–99

Ulysses, in *Confessio Amantis* 341, 362, 524
Unam Sanctam 259
unbeneficed clergy 245, 254–5, 257, 266–7, 268
Upton, Nicholas 149
Urban V, Pope 263
Urban VI, Pope 124, 127
urban society *see* artisans; Great Revolt, London, merchants; retailers; trade
Ursins, Jean Juvénal des *see* Juvénal
Usk, Thomas 207, 437
Ut testatur Ergaphalau 495 n.15

Vegetius 345
Venice 263
Venus, goddess 153, 160 n.73, 435
  in *Confessio Amantis* 130, 134, 279 n.31, 337, 341, 385
  in *Vox Clamantis* 152, 279 n.31
Venus, planet 499, 501–2
Vere, Robert de, earl of Oxford, duke of Ireland 437, 438, 439, 440, 443
Vertue, George 99, 102, 106, 107
victuallers *see* retailers
Vincent of Beauvais 387–8, 502
violence, morality of 142, 155–60, 162, 164, 171, 363, 367, 370–4, 377–8, 389–90, 420, 433
  see also just war, tyranny
Virginia, in *Confessio Amantis*, 134, 403–4
Voragine, Jacobus de 328 n.22, 330 n.27
Vynch, Joan 57, 58, 59, 112–14
Vynch, Thomas 57, 58, 59, 112–14

'7, 52, 54, 57, 58, 59, 65,

_ne), John 47, 52, 54, 57,
ȷ5–6, 70, 71, 72, 112–14
.+3, 145, 171, 173–4, 176, 177–80,
.89, 198, 199, 268
see also labour legislation
Wakefield, Henry, bishop of Worcester 249
Waldeby, John 274
Walden, Roger, archbishop of Canterbury 466, 479
Wales 477
Walsingham, Franciscan friars of 318 n.99
Walsingham, Thomas 153, 185, 207, 334, 415 n.132, 435, 445 n.93, 456, 470, 471, 477, 478 n.229, 482, 483 n.247
warlike clergy 262–4, 266–9
War of Eight Saints 260
Warwick, Thomas, earl of see Beauchamp, Thomas
Waterton, Hugh 16, 55–6
Waterton, Robert 56 n.88
Wecche, John, see Wacche, John
Wenlock, Giles 253
Wermyngton, John 13, 14, 39
West Clandon, Surrey 69
West Court, Kent see Aldington Septvans
Westminster 5, 23, 39, 43, 45–8, 50–1, 52–3, 54, 59, 65, 86, 87, 147, 216, 223 n.54, 253, 437, 472
    royal chapel in 21, 74, 90
    see also Westminster, St Stephen
    St James, leper house 86 n.229
    St Mary Spital (St Mary Rounceval), hospital of 86, 87, 116, 118
    St Stephen, chapel of, 77, 253
    Westminster Abbey 13, 39, 47, 52, 76, 77 n.193, 235, 341–2, 439, 446 n.98, 462, 463, 470
    Westminster Hall 224, 228, 414
Westminster Chronicle 434, 446 n.98
Westminster, Statute of (1275) 218
Weston, William de, various men of this name 7, 8, 9, 10, 11, 17, 20, 35, 36 n.36, 56–7, 60, 62, 68–9, 73, 109, 112, 114, 115
West Tanfield, Yorkshire 100 n.280
Wethersfield, Essex 84
Wexham, Cristina 66
Wexham, William 66, 115
Wigborough, Essex 5, 28, 33, 63

William of Pagula 397
William of St Amour see St Amour, William of
Willoughby, John, third baron 100 n.280
Willoughby, Richard 230
Willougby, William, fifth baron 100 n.280
Willson (Wilson), Henry 96
Wimbledon, Thomas of 145 n.15, 169, 388 n.22
Winchester, Hampshire 199 n.25
    bishop of, palace in Southwark, see Southwark, places in, palace of bishop
    diocese of 250, 426
    St Mary's nunnery (Nunnaminster) 279
Windsor Castle 76, 436, 472 n.209
    royal chapel of 65
Windsor, John de 225 n.63
wine and wine trade 19, 61, 136, 195, 199, 201–4, 209, 277, 368, 483
    see also Gower, John, works of, *Confessio Amantis*, 'Tale of Wine, Women and Truth'
Wireker, Nigel see Longchamps, Nigel de
Wisborough, prebend of (Chichester) 253
women 58, 86, 118, 176, 198, 287, 299, 323–50, 351–3, 358, 359, 362, 363, 364, 368
    see also antifeminism; Gower, John, works of, *Confessio Amantis*, 'Tale of Wine, Women and Truth'; love; nuns; prostitution; queens and queenship
Woodville, Anthony, Earl Rivers 337–8, 341 n.76, 344
Woodville, Elizabeth 333, 337, 339–41, 342, 344, 349, 350
Woodville, Richard 341 n.76
Wyclif (Wycliffe), John 156, 160, 232, 244–5, 246, 249, 264–6, 267, 268, 284, 308, 389, 419–20
    see also dominion; heresy, Lollardy
Wycliffites see Lollardy
Wykeham, William, bishop of Winchester 19, 50, 58, 60, 65, 79, 80, 122, 228, 229, 249, 250, 426 n.6, 438, 448
Wylton (Hockwold–cum–Wilton), Norfolk 16, 17, 43, 49, 55
Wynnere and Wastoure 235
Wyntere, John 6

York 16, 24, 49, 54–5, 185, 333 n.40

INDEX

York, dukes of *see* Edmund of Langley;
　　Edward of Langley; Richard
Yorkshire 11, 16, 54, 59, 72, 83–4, 273

zodiac 501–18 523
Zouche, William, archbishop of York 263

VOLUMES ALREADY PUBLISHED

I   *Concordance to John Gower's* Confessio Amantis, edited by J. A. Pickles and J. L. Dawson, 1987
II   *John Gower's Poetic: The Search for a New Arion*, R. F. Yeager, 1990
III   *Gower's Confessio Amantis: A Critical Anthology*, Peter Nicholson, 1991
IV   *John Gower and the Structures of Conversion: A Reading of the* Confessio Amantis, Kurt Olsson, 1992
V   *Fathers and Daughters in Gower's* Confessio Amantis: *Authority, Family, State, and Writing*, María Bullón-Fernández, 2000
VI   *Gower's Vulgar Tongue: Ovid, Lay Religion, and English Poetry in the* Confessio Amantis, T. Matthew N. McCabe, 2011
VII   *John Gower, Poetry and Propaganda in Fourteenth-Century England*, David R. Carlson, 2012
VIII   *John Gower and the Limits of the Law*, Conrad van Dijk, 2013
IX   *The Poetic Voices of John Gower: Politics and Personae in the* Confessio Amantis, Matthew W. Irvin, 2014
X   *John Gower in England and Iberia: Manuscripts, Influences, Reception*, edited by Ana Sáez-Hidalgo and R. F. Yeager, 2014
XI   *John Gower: Others and the Self*, edited by Russell A. Peck and R. F. Yeager, 2017

www.ingramcontent.com/pod-product-compliance
Lightning Source LLC
Chambersburg PA
CBHW070754300426
44111CB00014B/2400